40,00

HAMLIN GARLAND

HAMLIN GARLAND

A Life

Keith Newlin

University of Nebraska Press

Lincoln and London

Publication of this book was
assisted by grants from the
Andrew W. Mellon Foundation
and the University of North
Carolina Wilmington.

Acknowledgments for previously
published material appear on
pages xi–xii, which constitutes an
extension of the copyright page.

Library of Congress
Cataloging-in-Publication Data

Newlin, Keith.
Hamlin Garland: a life / Keith
Newlin.
    p. cm.
Includes bibliographical references and index.
ISBN 978-0-8032-3347-8 (cloth:
alk. paper)
1. Garland, Hamlin, 1860—1940.
2. Authors, American—19th
century—Biography.
3. Authors, American—20th
century—Biography. I. Title.
PS1733.N48 2008
813'.52—dc22
[B]   2007047681

Set in New Baskerville.
Designed by A. Shahan.

TO JOHN AHOUSE

CONTENTS

ILLUSTRATIONS

Following page 216

ACKNOWLEDGMENTS

All biographies are written with the help of others, and I am pleased to acknowledge the aid of two people who were instrumental in the composition of this book. Garland's granddaughter Victoria Doyle-Jones (daughter of Constance) granted permission to quote from his papers and from her aunt Mary Isabel's unpublished memoir of her father, which revealed many heretofore unknown details of Garland's life. I am grateful for her hospitality in opening to me not only her home but also her aunt's trunk, which contains a number of family papers and photographs that proved instrumental in my reconstruction of Garland's life. My dedication expresses my debt to John Ahouse, who until his retirement in 2005 was the curator of the Hamlin Garland Papers at the Edward L. Doheny Memorial Library of the University of Southern California. Over the course of nearly ten years, John graciously shared his considerable knowledge of Garland while also being unfailingly courteous and prompt in responding to queries and requests for photocopies. Just as important were his occasional proddings to reconsider the effect of some detail in the larger context of Garland's life, and his careful reading of the manuscript, which saved me from some embarrassing errors.

I am especially grateful to six other scholars who wrested time from their own projects to read and astutely comment on drafts of this book: Gary Culbert, Philip Furia, Jerome Loving, Kurtis Meyer, Joseph B. McCullough, and Donald Pizer. For responses to queries and other assistance, I wish to thank William "Gene" Aisenbrey, Suzanne Bloomfield, Donna Campbell, Bill Ferraro, Robert Fleming, Keith Gumery, Charles Johanningsmeier, Errol Kindschy, Monte Kloberdanz, James Nagel, Constance Harper Nelson, Jennifer

Raspet, Roger W. Smith, Paul Sorrentino, and Stanley Wertheim. For help in acquiring the photographs for this volume, I am grateful to Gary Culbert, Victoria Doyle-Jones, Matthew S. S. Johnson, Jon Morris, Michael Ward, the West Salem Historical Society, and Claude Zachary. For her remarkable patience and able assistance, I thank Sophie Williams, interlibrary loan librarian extraordinaire of Randall Library, University of North Carolina Wilmington (UNCW). I also thank my department chair, Christopher Gould, who has enthusiastically supported this project from the beginning.

Every writer of biography builds on the work of others, and my notes will indicate how frequently I have drawn on Donald Pizer's *Hamlin Garland's Early Work and Career* (1960), still the benchmark for studies of the writer's formative influences. Jean Holloway's *Hamlin Garland: A Biography* (1960) and Joseph B. McCullough's *Hamlin Garland* (1978) provide useful surveys of the writer's life, and the essays collected in *Critical Essays on Hamlin Garland* (1982, ed. James Nagel) and *The Critical Reception of Hamlin Garland* (1985, ed. Charles L. P. Silet, Robert E. Welch, and Richard Boudreau) gather the most important studies of Garland's writings. My many debts to other scholars are acknowledged in the notes.

Garland's voluminous letters, manuscripts, and especially his diaries are the chief sources for details of his personal life. After the success of *A Son of the Middle Border* (1917), Garland realized that his daily diary, which he had begun keeping on January 1, 1898, could provide the source material for later installments of his family history, and so be began transcribing it for use in his memoirs. With rare honesty, he resisted the opportunity to rewrite his personal history, believing that any autobiography should recall his defeats as well as his triumphs, and his transcriptions are typically accurate in substance though revised to polish style. But since memoirs are inevitably selective, I have tended to quote from them only to register the emotional truth of a moment and have instead relied upon the diaries themselves for first impressions and the details of his remarkably varied life. I am grateful to the Huntington Library for permission to quote from them and from other correspondence held in its collection.

This biography had its genesis in the *Selected Letters of Hamlin Garland* (1998), which I coedited with Joseph B. McCullough, and I am grateful to the many archives that opened their collections in the preparation of that volume. For their assistance during a second round of visits for the preparation of this book, I again take pleasure in thanking the archivists at the American Academy of Arts and Letters, New York City; Archives of the Pulitzer Prizes, Columbia University; Rare Book and Manuscript Library, Columbia University; Miami University Library, Oxford, Ohio; the Newberry Library, Chicago; Manuscripts and Archives Division, New York Public Library; Osage Public Library, Osage, Iowa; Rare Books and Manuscripts Library, The Ohio State University; Rare Book and Manuscript Library, University of Illinois at Urbana-Champaign; Folger Library, University of Maine; Wilson Library, University of North Carolina at Chapel Hill; Edward L. Doheny Memorial Library, University of Southern California; Clifton Waller Barrett Library of American Literature, University of Virginia Library; West Salem Historical Society; and the Beinecke Rare Book and Manuscript Library, Yale University.

This book could not have been written without the generous financial support of a number of institutions. A fellowship from the National Endowment for the Humanities and a Faculty Research Reassignment award from UNCW provided the precious gift of time to write a draft of this book. A UNCW Charles L. Cahill Research Grant provided funds to travel to archives. I am also grateful for a University of Southern California Wallis Annenberg Research Grant, which enabled me to spend a month at the major Garland archive.

Finally, I am especially grateful to Robin Briggs Newlin, who encouraged me when I conceived this book and who never complained about the many hours I stole from her for its completion.

Portions of this book have been revised from the following:

"'I am as ever your disciple': The Friendship of Hamlin Garland and W. D. Howells," *Papers on Language and Literature* 42, no. 3 (2006): 264–90. Copyright © 2006 by the Board of Trustees, Southern Illinois University Edwardsville. Reprinted with permission.

Introduction to Hamlin Garland, *Rose of Dutcher's Coolly* (Lincoln: University of Nebraska Press, 2005). Reprinted with permission.

Introduction to Hamlin Garland, *The Book of the American Indian* (Lincoln: University of Nebraska Press, 2005). Reprinted with permission.

"Melodramatist of the Middle Border: Hamlin Garland's Early Work Reconsidered," *Studies in American Fiction* 21 (1993): 153–69. Reprinted with permission.

"Prospecting for Health: Hamlin Garland's Klondike Adventures," *American Literary Realism* 35, no. 1 (2002): 72–92. Copyright © 2002 by the Board of Trustees of the University of Illinois. Reprinted with permission of the University of Illinois Press.

"Uplifting the Stage: Hamlin Garland and the Chicago Theater Society," *Journal of American Drama and Theatre* 8, no. 1 (1996): 1–17. Reprinted with permission.

"Why Hamlin Garland Left the Main-Travelled Road," *Studies in American Naturalism* 1, nos. 1–2 (2006): 70–89. Reprinted with permission.

HAMLIN GARLAND

PROLOGUE
March 14, 1940

A bitter March wind streamed through the coulees and buffeted the gathering of thirty-five mourners who stood before the rough grave at Neshonoc Cemetery, near the small village of West Salem, Wisconsin. Snow fell lightly upon their shoulders, the ground hard-frozen beneath their feet, as the sexton stood nearby, sweating from his labor. A few stamped the cold from their feet; others clutched the arms of their companions. Few tears were shed, for these mourners were mostly remote acquaintances, a few friends from decades ago, and a couple of distant relatives who were balefully staring at the grave, mindful that all too soon they too would be interred. A flashbulb went off, startling these country folk, reminding those assembled that this was no common burial. Hamlin Garland, the Dean of American Letters, was dead.

"We are assembled here to inter the remains of Hamlin Garland," intoned the Reverend John B. Fitz, who then went on to praise Garland for celebrating the Midwest's natural beauty while also delineating its occasional human misery. He concluded by reading one of Garland's poems, "The Cry of the Age," first published more than forty years earlier, its opening lines summarizing the guiding purpose of the author's life:

> What shall I do to be just?
> What shall I do for the gain
> Of the world—

The mourners shivered as the urn containing his ashes was lowered into the frozen ground, beside the graves of his parents, Richard and Isabelle, who in 1859 had settled nearby. Clods of frozen earth, mixed with snow, fell on the urn, and then a few of his former neighbors laid a wreath upon the mound of dirt before shuffling off to their cars.[1]

A week before, on March 7, a more elaborate memorial had taken place at Forest Lawn Cemetery's Wee Kirk o' the Heather in Glendale, California, a mere four miles from Garland's Hollywood home on DeMille Drive overlooking Griffith Park. Among the crowd of mourners in the flower-lined chapel were Hermann Hagedorn, biographer of Theodore Roosevelt; Rufus B. von KleinSmid, president of the University of Southern California; Harry Chandler, publisher of the *Los Angeles Times*; and many others, but not his closest friends—William Dean Howells, Augustus Thomas, John Burroughs, James Whitcomb Riley, Henry B. Fuller, James A. Herne—for Garland had outlived them all.

The seventy-nine-year-old author had been at work on the final volume of his memoirs, "The Fortunate Exiles," when he was stricken with a cerebral hemorrhage. As word of his death on March 4 reached the world, newspapers across the country printed obituaries and tributes that would have gratified him, for he was certain that his fifty years of literary life, recorded in forty-seven books and hundreds of magazine articles, had been forgotten. Only two weeks before his death he had made an address to the Mission Inn and was mortified by the sparse attendance. As he recorded dourly in his diary, honest to the end, "There is no value in keeping up a pose. I am no longer 'a personage' to any considerable part of the public. It was a humiliating experience."[2] He may have contemplated his former triumphs, the days when he was in demand as a speaker at the nation's universities. "The people mobbed me in the college in K.C.," he had written to his wife after one lecture engagement in Missouri. "I could hardly escape them. They all wanted autographs." He might have remembered his glory days when he was an international celebrity, feted by such authors as Arthur Conan Doyle, George Bernard Shaw, James M. Barrie, Rudyard Kipling, and Joseph Conrad. Or he may have recalled his final trip to New York City when he stopped in Chicago for three days to visit with friends, only to encounter fans who still remembered his work—all celebrated in a *Chicago Daily News* article headlined, "Hamlin Garland Returns; Admirers Besiege Author."[3]

Garland had not been forgotten; he had simply outlived his vogue.

When Hamlin Garland left his prairie homestead in Dakota Territory and journeyed to Boston in 1884 to make his fortune, he was an uncouth, ill-educated youth of twenty-four with a half-formed ambition to become a writer. When he died fifty-six years later, he knew virtually every significant writer of his day, both in the United States and England, had won a Pulitzer Prize, and had dined with presidents. He traveled among the Indians, learned sign language to communicate with them, and wrote some of the most sympathetic stories of his time about Native Americans. His wanderlust and productivity were such that during one two-year period he published four books, lectured throughout the United States, made repeated trips to the West to study conditions on the reservations, embarked on a five-month, thousand-mile trek through the Canadian wilderness to prospect for gold in the Klondike, sailed to Europe to arrange for the British publication of his books—and got married. He achieved considerable acclaim for his realistic stories of pioneer life, and he campaigned assiduously against romanticism and sensationalism in literature. As Walt Whitman noted, "Garland looks like a man who is bound to last—to go on from very good to very much better."[4]

Garland's first book, *Main-Travelled Roads*, occasioned controversy upon publication in 1891 because of its unabashed look at the hardships of farm life. Four years (and eight books) later, the controversy escalated with his frank depiction of sexuality in his novel of the "New Woman," *Rose of Dutcher's Coolly*. Garland published two volumes of poetry, a respected biography of Ulysses S. Grant, eleven novels about the mountain West, and eight volumes of autobiographical reminiscences. He wrote a number of plays and saw three of them produced; four of his novels were made into films; and for more than fifty years he lectured extensively throughout the United States. At the height of his critical acclaim he was the nation's most outspoken advocate of realism, vigorously promoting a literature that accurately represented the conditions of American life. In his later years, after William Dean Howells died, he assumed Howells's role as elder literary statesman and inherited his title, "The Dean of American Letters."

In recognition of his achievement in literature, Garland received four honorary doctorates, election to the American Academy of Arts and Letters, and frequent invitations to lecture at the nation's universities. He was a founder of many influential literary organizations that still exist, among them the American Academy of Arts and Letters, the Authors' League of America, the Society of Midland Authors, the Cliff Dwellers' Club, and the MacDowell Colony. As he aged, literary historians such as Arthur Hobson Quinn, Fred Lewis Pattee, and Van Wyck Brooks probed his memories to write their books, and graduate students wrote theses about him. And today Garland is still celebrated, along with Laura Ingalls Wilder and Willa Cather, for the clarity with which his work illustrates prairie life, with its blend of the realistic delineation of its landscape and his social activism.

His accomplishments reveal his devotion to belles lettres, a genius for friendship, and a rare talent for organization, yet his temperament occasioned both admiration and ridicule. Although Garland was kind and generous (especially to young writers), his passionate commitment to his causes also elicited, at times, a patronizing dismissal—both from his contemporaries and from later critics. Booth Tarkington wrote, "It is impossible to think of Garland without thinking of his kindness, the greatness of heart that was in all of his work and in all of his life; and I believe that one next thinks of his integrity, his almost incorrigible intellectual probity." The critic Robert Morss Lovett praised his "strong humanitarian feeling" and his generosity "to those who need help, particularly younger authors." Henry James thought Garland's ability to saturate his stories with the detail of time and place "to have almost the value of genius." And William Dean Howells counseled, "Watch Garland, he is the most worthwhile of his generation." Yet to the Chicago journalist Robert Peattie, "Garland become so inflated with the praise of Howells . . . that he assumed the appearance of Jove and the finality of judgment of Dr. Johnson"; and even Garland's friend Theodore Roosevelt once noted that Garland "is a man with some power and with half an idea, but he is such a hopeless crank that nothing can be done with him." His contentious personality sometimes provoked derision even amid recognition of his talent. "If Hamlin Garland sometimes makes one itch to pick up the first thing that comes handy to be thrown," his friend Charles Lummis once remarked, "he has also a redeeming way of impelling one to choose a bouquet for a missile."[5]

His life was, by anyone's standards, successful, yet Garland was plagued with a lifelong sense of having failed to measure up to his own ambition. Even in 1899, one of his most productive years, he mourned to his diary, "I dont feel that the last five years has brought me very much. There is no feeling of having widened my reputation or made any considerable impression on the art and literature of my country."[6] In his later years he became bitter and cranky, obsessed with the rise of the modernism that had supplanted his own work, unable to set aside his Victorian sense of propriety when the intellectual currents shifted inward to probe the psychological and sexual motives for action. As other writers ascended to claim the public's attention, he suffered a keen fear that he might not have achieved a lasting place in American letters. As his friend and Macmillan editor Harold Latham noted, Garland was "sensitive to a high degree, easily hurt, overgenerous toward others, firm in his convictions, he was a man deeply admired and respected by the editors who worked with him . . . [but] he was easily discouraged, and his publishing friends tried ever to stress the recognition which his work had aroused throughout the world."[7]

The life I have tried to sketch in this biography is of an extraordinarily ambitious and energetic man with a modest talent who, through sheer determination and strength of will, skyrocketed into international fame before he was forty. Ironically, even at the height of his fame and influence, doubts about the permanency of his achievement and the responsibilities of a growing family led Garland to putter away with a number of reform movements through which he hoped to attain more lasting recognition. His tunnel vision of what American literature should be caused him to miss the significance of modernism, the century's most noteworthy literary movement. At the time of his death he had been eclipsed by writers more responsive to the times, thereby failing to live up to Whitman's and Howells's prophecy of his eventual greatness. Garland's life is a story of ironic contradictions: the radical whose early achievement thrust him to the forefront of literary innovation but whose evolutionary aesthetic principles could not themselves adapt to changing conditions; the self-styled "veritist" whose credo demanded that every "individual impression [be] corrected by reference to the fact" but whose credulity led him to spend a lifetime seeking to verify the existence of spirits. His need for recognition caused him to cultivate rewarding friendships with the leaders of literary culture, yet even when he attained it, for Garland the recognition was never enough, and his self-doubt subjected him to fits of black despair.

Hamlin Garland is an important figure in American literature, one whose achievements as an advocate of realism were matched, and perhaps surpassed, by his accomplishments in professionalizing the craft of writing. But he is also significant as a representative man of letters of his age. A nineteenth-century sensibility shaped his advocacy of and achievement in literature, but at the same time it determined his resistance to the advance of modernism. What follows is the story of his personal and professional struggle with that historic divide.

1

RETURN OF THE PRIVATE, 1860–68

The central fact of life for Hamlin Garland was a constant awareness that he was the son of a pioneer with a bad case of land fever
who drifted ever westward in search of better opportunities, each
time seeking to augment his landholdings but finding betrayal in
the land or its crops. Before he was sixteen years old, Hamlin would
move five times, often living under conditions of extreme hardship
as his family faced the unknown. His pioneer background affected
everything he did later in life, from the selection of subjects for his
writing, to the organizations with which he became involved, to the
shape he gave his own life when he wrote a series of memoirs. He
would call the land of his family's emigration the "middle border,"
a phrase he coined to refer to the moving line between frontier
and settlement from the 1860s to the 1890s, extending roughly
along the upper Mississippi valley from eastern Iowa, Wisconsin, and
Minnesota, and then from western Iowa along the upper Missouri
River into Dakota Territory as the frontier expanded in the 1880s.
When George Bernard Shaw once asked Garland what he meant
by "the middle border," Garland explained, "In a sense it does not
exist and never did. It was but a vaguely defined region even in my
boyhood. It was the line drawn by the plow and, broadly speaking,
ran parallel to the upper Mississippi when I was a lad. It lay between
the land of the hunter and the harvester."[1]

Hamlin Garland was born on the eve of the Civil War, on
September 14, 1860, in a squatter's cabin on the outskirts of West
Salem, Wisconsin. Hamlin's father, Richard Hayes Garland, with
his wife, the former Isabelle McClintock, and two-and-a-half-year-
old daughter, Harriet, was then in the midst of building a cabin on

a parcel of land he had recently bought in the middle of Green's Coulee, near the village of Onalaska, just north of La Crosse and less than ten miles from present-day West Salem. *Coulee* is the French name for the wide, usually wooded valleys separating the high ridges of southwestern Wisconsin. When the glaciers scoured the land at the end of the last ice age, they missed a narrow section of about fifty miles east to west, abutting the Mississippi River and extending half the length of the state and down into northeastern Iowa and northwestern Illinois. In this "driftless" area, so called because of the absence of glacial debris, rivers and streams scored narrow valleys from the existing strata of the Minnesota plateau to the west and the Wisconsin uplands to the east. While the topography is rough, the land is fertile and, once cleared of trees, attractive to farmers, and it was the prospect of productive farmland that brought Garland's father to Wisconsin.

Hamlin's father was born in 1830 in the small town of Norway, Oxford County, Maine, on the border of New Hampshire, the son of Harriet and Richard Garland, a sometime carpenter and shop-keeper struggling to make ends meet in the town of Greenwood, ten miles from where Dick had been born. The young Dick Garland's life was marked by considerable hardship and continual westward movement as his family sought to wrest a living from the land. At age ten, Dick went to work for a neighboring farmer for five dollars per month and attended school for a few weeks during the winter months, where he picked up a smattering of an education. Working the steep and rocky Maine farmland soon led to dreams of flat, rock-less lands of the Midwest which promised both opportunity and riches. By the time he was sixteen, he was working for a railroad, and at age eighteen Dick had drifted to Boston, where he worked as a driver of a dray team hauling stone from a quarry and, later, as the driver of an express wagon. For a time he clerked in a dry goods store, and later he was promoted to shipping agent.[2]

Back in Maine, Dick's father showed considerable interest in the booming of the new state of Wisconsin, which had entered the Union in May 1848. As Garland would later write of his grand-father, "The word 'prairie' held out to him, as it did to thousands of his kind, a release from the stone walls and a promise of harvests such as the best acres of his home county could never produce. To be free of hills, to plough an unbroken furrow in a level field, had become an obsession with him."[3] Harriet Garland's brother, John Bridges, immigrated in 1849 to the township of Spring Grove, in Green County, on the southern border of the state. On May 21, 1850, Richard, Harriet, and their fourteen-year-old daughter, Susan, left for Wisconsin to join her brother, settling in Monticello, Green County, where they bought a forty-acre farm for one hundred dollars. They left twenty-year-old Dick and his twenty-two-year-old brother, Addison, behind in Boston, working to save money to buy their own parcels of land. Dick left for Wisconsin the next year in time to help out with the harvest, but he seems not to have been ready to settle down, for he soon departed for the northern part of the state to seek employment as a lumberman. A new state with hordes of immigrants pouring in needed lumber, and Dick soon found work in a camp at Big Bull Falls, near Wausau. Hamlin later recalled that his father "bossed a crew of choppers" during the winter, "and in summer, he ran rafts of lumber down the river to Dubuque." Known as "Yankee Dick, the Pilot," Dick was curiously unlike most of his companions, for he did not smoke, did not particularly like to drink, and was not known to consort with the women who followed the camps. But he was a fearsome brawler. He gained a reputation as a daredevil who would undertake any challenge. "The thing which made him dangerous," Garland remembered about his father, "was the spirit which flamed out of his big gray eyes. He literally knew nothing of fear. He loved to ride the whirlpools, and shoot the rapids, and he spent weeks in water up to his knees, and slept at night in wet clothing."[4]

When the Garlands arrived in Monticello in 1850 they met the McClintock clan, who had settled there in 1846 after migrating from Virginia by way of Ohio, where several of the thirteen McClintock children were born. Headed by fierce Hugh, an Adventist who thundered about the coming end of the world, the McClintocks soon befriended the Garlands. A photograph reveals Hugh to be the incarnation of an Old Testament prophet, with piercing, deep-set eyes, tangled white locks, and fringe beard. To the young Hamlin he was a distant, visionary presence: "He was both a mystic and poet. . . . He loved the Bible, especially that part of it which contained prophecies and lamentations. The poetry of Job's curses, the whirling visions of the Apocalypse, formed his emotional outlet, his world of imagination. Absent-minded, careless of dress, he was forever drumming on his chair (keeping time to some inaudible tune), or with faintly moving lips repeating for the hundredth time the impassioned lines of Hezekiah or John or Job."[5] In 1875, Hugh McClintock would be one of the organizers of a local branch of the Sons of Temperance. His wife, Edith, was a warmer presence, but she was overshadowed by the dominance of her husband. Her photograph shows a stern-faced, ascetic woman in bonnet, her dour, unsmiling face lined from toil. Despite the grimness of her photograph, Hamlin remembered her as "cheerful in the midst of her discomfort. . . . I do not suppose she ever knew what it was to have a comfortable, well-aired bedroom even in childbirth, which came to her fourteen times. Her dresses were faded and poor. Her home was small, poorly furnished, without pictures, without art, save music."[6] What he most remembered about the McClintocks was their innate sensitivity, all of them "bards and dreamers, inarticulate and moody," who "could be thrown into sudden melancholy by a melody, a line of poetry or a beautiful landscape." Their receptive sensitivity led naturally to music, and all of the sons and daughters played instruments, with his uncle David being especially proficient with the violin. His visits were always cheerful affairs, for Hamlin was spoiled by his aunts and uncles. He would always attribute his own artistic sensibilities to them: "They furnished much of the charm and poetic suggestion of my childhood," he later wrote. "Most of what I have in way of feeling for music, for rhythm, I derive from my mother's side of the house, for it was almost entirely Celt in every characteristic."[7] From his father he would inherit a restless desire to seek new opportunities and a relentless drive to succeed.

When Dick Garland rejoined his parents in 1851, he was particularly attracted to thirteen-year-old Isabelle McClintock, christened Charlotte Isabelle but often called Belle, and visits to his parents during her adolescence only confirmed the attraction. Family tradition has it that he was singularly captivated by her melancholy voice, shy smile, and large brown eyes, in marked contrast to the vivacity of her siblings. In 1854 the McClintock clan relocated to La Crosse County, where Dick continued his visits to Isabelle.

After six years of lumbering and piloting, Dick Garland had risen to supervise some twenty-five men under the employ of one Ben Cooper, but his long hours in frigid water began to affect his health. Advised by a doctor to mind his health and dry out, in 1856 he piloted his last lumber raft to Dubuque, where he boarded a steamer up the Mississippi River bound for Trempealeau, Wisconsin, just across the river and a dozen miles southeast of Winona, Minnesota. There he debarked and began traipsing across country looking for affordable land, with the intention of settling down and marrying Isabelle. In the spring of 1856 he rented a farm near the tiny village of Neshonoc, established the year before on the La Crosse River about a mile north of West Salem. Platted in November 1856, West Salem soon engaged in a bidding war with Neshonoc over right-of-way for the Milwaukee–La Crosse Railroad, then under construction. Neshonoc's citizens offered the rights for forty thousand dollars; West Salem countered by offering a gift of ten acres and no charge for right-of-way—and the railroad, no fool, established its tracks in West Salem, and the village of Neshonoc soon died, with most of its inhabitants moving to West Salem.[8]

In March 1856, with the intention of joining their son, the elder Garlands sold their farm in Monticello and moved to Burns, a few miles northeast of West Salem. On August 3, 1856, Dick and Isabelle were married in Neshonoc, with Dick not yet twenty-six and his bride eighteen. Having found that desirable farms cost more than he had saved, to increase his savings during the winters Dick returned to the lumber camps with Isabelle, who cooked for the lumberjacks, and in the summers worked his rented farm. To them a daughter, Harriet Edith, named for both of their mothers, was born on April 15, 1858.

But a new family and especially a rented farm did not quell Dick's restlessness and hunger for a farm of his own. In May 1858,

Minnesota was granted statehood, and Dick, leaving his infant daughter and wife behind, set out in the company of eleven others to establish homesteads in the new state. As Hamlin later wrote, "He drove a yoke of oxen, and in his wagons was a year's provisions. They got far away from civilization, a long distance north west of St. Paul, where Fergus Falls now stands [twenty-six miles from the North Dakota border]."[9] Hamlin was never able to extract from his father a clear reason why he had journeyed so far: after all, he had crossed much farmable land—what was the attraction of this particular spot, where the nearest neighbor was fifty miles away and the soil not as good as that of a dozen other valleys that they had crossed? "The grass was no sweeter," Hamlin concluded, "the river no brighter, the woodlands no more attractive than in many other localities they had surveyed, and yet they halted, satiated, I suspect, with surveying."[10]

But they weren't there long. The invading settlers had encroached upon Sioux land, and soon a troop of cavalry appeared, "rounded them up, and headed them eastward, saying that the Sioux were on the warpath, and the sooner they got back to Wisconsin, the better."[11] When Dick returned to West Salem in July, he again rented a farm, collected Isabelle and Harriet from her parents, and set to work to buy land, rather than homestead. In 1859 he bought a parcel from his old employer, Ben Cooper, in Green's Coulee. To clear the mortgage, Dick worked for a sawmill during the day and, "having secured permission of the boss to run the mill nights, sawed the lumber for his own house and afterwards, freighted it to his farm."[12]

It was in the midst of building this house while living in the cabin on the outskirts of West Salem that one September evening in 1860 Dick Garland rushed out into the night in search of Dr. William H. Stanley. "Late one night," Stanley's son recalled, "there was a heavy knocking on our West Salem door and an excited young man urged my father to hurry—his wife was about to have a baby. His name was Garland. Father dressed and was driven several miles into the country, where he ushered into the world a baby boy."[13] Named for Maine senator Hannibal Hamlin, who was then campaigning for the vice-president slot under Lincoln, young Hannibal Hamlin Garland possessed as his earliest memory his father's return from the Civil War, a memory he would later use as the basis of one of his best-known stories, "The Return of the Private," and which provided the opening scene of his autobiography, *A Son of the Middle Border.*

When war broke out, Dick Garland, like many others of his generation, was eager to volunteer, but he could not do so until he had paid off the mortgage on his farm and ensured the provision of his wife and three small children, for another son, Franklin McClintock, had been born on March 11, 1863. On December 23 of that year Dick made his last payment, and on Christmas Eve he promptly enlisted in La Crosse, joining Company D, Fourteenth Regiment of the Wisconsin Volunteer Infantry.[14] He was thirty-three years old. Hamlin (who early on dropped the unwieldy "Hannibal") later reflected, "Consider what this means. He now had three children. Harriet five, Hamlin three, and Franklin, nine months of age. His farm was only partly under cultivation, his house was a rude shanty, and yet, responding to the call of his country, he left his young wife and three children, to go into military service, from which he was almost sure never to return."[15] But Dick was not to join the fighting until April 1864, for illness intervened, sufficiently serious to prevent his immediate transportation, and instead he was put in charge of the barracks.[16] With a son's natural pride in his father's accomplishments, Hamlin noted that his father could have remained in that position until the end of the war. "But I couldn't do that," Dick told him. "I couldn't stand to have all my friends sneering at me and saying 'He'll never smell powder!'"[17] He left to rejoin his regiment in April in Tennessee, serving in May and June on detached service (likely as a teamster) at Kennesaw Mountain, Georgia, and then in July and August at the battle of Atlanta, which led to Sherman's siege of the city. By January 1865 Dick was driving wagons for the Quartermaster Department, Third Division, in New Orleans, Mobile, and Montgomery. Somehow, in the midst of his service in the war, he found the means to increase his landholdings in Green's Coulee, adding 118 acres in December 1864 and another 20 in May 1865.[18]

Back home in Wisconsin, things weren't going well with the farm.

Prior to leaving for service, Dick had sent his family to live with the McClintocks, leased his acreage, and arranged for his tenant to manage the farm and bring in the harvest. Upon learning that his tenant had planted the fields but then robbed his house and absconded with the goods, Dick arranged for a furlough, on July 25, 1865, so that he could return home and arrange for the immediate needs of his family. The long journey home led to an extended illness, referred to variously as "southern fever," intermittent fever," and "ague," and on August 11 his physician requested a one-month extension of the furlough, which was due to expire on August 24. Dick received a certificate of disability, which his physician forwarded to his regiment in Mobile, and on October 9 his regiment was mustered out.[19] Hamlin would later alter the sequence and some of the events of his father's service for dramatic effect in "The Return of the Private," where the father returns after the end of the war. In *Trail-Makers of the Middle Border* he would depict his father as Richard Graham, who serves undercover as a spy for General Grant before contracting typhoid and returning home to reenact the scene of "The Return of the Private."

Dick Garland soon put his farm in order, and that fall he supplemented the income from crops by running a threshing machine, a huge horse-powered device that separated the grain from the stalks. His two years' service greatly influenced his disposition, forever shaping his attitude toward child rearing. Hamlin's earliest memories of his father involved work and discipline: "He was always at work, and always in command of things around him. He was a soldier in his manner of speech, his walk, and in his insistence upon instant obedience."[20] At five feet, eight and a half inches tall, Dick did not have a looming presence, but most memorable to the young Hamlin was his "keen eagle-gray terrifying eyes," eyes that never missed a boyish prank or lapse of household duty.[21] Later, when he came to write his autobiography, Hamlin would characterize his father as a stern disciplinarian who engendered fear in his sons at the slightest infraction. Upon his return from the war, "his scheme of discipline impressed itself almost at once upon his children." When the Garland boys misbehaved, "we soon learned . . . that the soldier's promise of punishment was swift and precise in its fulfillment. We seldom presumed a second time on his forgetfulness or tolerance." While Dick loved his children and was fond of regaling them with stories of his own boyhood and war service, "the moments of his tenderness were few and his fondling did not prevent him from almost instant use of the rod if he thought either of us needed it."[22]

Because he had known only work and sacrifice in his own life, Dick expected the same for his children. "My father believed in service," Hamlin noted. "At seven years of age, I had regular duties."[23] As the eldest boy at a time when much physical labor was necessary for daily living, the young Hamlin did as much for his family as his size and maturity would allow. He stacked firewood, fed corn to the cows and chickens, and, later, drove cattle to the fields. Among his earliest memories were "the little tasks we had in winter," he recorded in a notebook. "To break nubbins for the yearlings—and to shell corn for the chickens. It seemed like a dreadful task on those cold days. We were so cold the wind whistled through the corn-crib and the snow lay on the corn."[24] At seven, too, he began to go to public school in Onalaska after receiving a rudimentary education in neighboring farmhouse kitchens. What he remembered most about his early schooling were visits to the town, where he observed a faster-paced life of shops and storekeepers and welcome relief from chores, rather than the schooling itself.

But counterpoised to these memories of work and discipline was the remembrance of the protective arms of his mother, who shielded him from his father's wrath and comforted him with soothing lullabies. Isabelle Garland was a "large, handsome, smiling woman—deft and powerful of movement, sweet and cheery of smile and voice," the son remembered. "She loved games, practical jokes and jesting of all kinds. Her natural gayety was almost unquenchable; not even unending work and poverty could entirely subdue her or embitter her." Isabelle was an accomplished singer—with "a compass of three octaves and one note"—and her singing provided a calming reprieve from the harsh commands of his father. But she was not a demonstrative mother. Hamlin remembered that "she never expressed her deeper feelings. She seldom kissed her children," and after they reached their teenage years "she never embraced us."[25]

The combination of a stern father and an undemonstrative mother forever colored Hamlin's own attitude toward the outward expression of love. As an adult he was painfully shy about interacting with women directly: not until he was thirty-nine would he marry. In his fiction he would find it difficult to depict romantic feeling convincingly. And still later, when other novelists wrote frankly and explicitly about sex, he was so appalled at this assault upon his notions of propriety that he would dismiss their work as "pornography." But throughout his boyhood, when Isabelle still comforted him with an embrace, young Hamlin would turn first to her whenever he faced the calamities of youth, forever establishing an enduring bond that would sustain him in times of sorrow and, much later, prompt a nagging remorse that he had not done more to ease her burden.

2

BOY LIFE ON THE PRAIRIE, 1868–81

When Hamlin was eight years old, his father decided, once again, to push on to better opportunities, his dream of flat, clear land revived by news that affordable land was available in Winneshiek County, Iowa. His Green's Coulee farm, while conveniently located near his parents (who in 1861 had moved to Onalaska to start a grocery store) and close enough to his in-laws for visits, had the singular disadvantage of being rife with hills and trees, for when he had settled in the area in 1859, the coulee land was all he was able to afford. By 1868 much of his 160 acres was still uncleared and so unplowed, and the unremitting toil revived his dreams of prairie lands to the west. As Hamlin later remembered, "It irked him beyond measure to force his reaper along a steep slope, and he loathed the irregular little patches running up the ravines behind the timbered knolls, and so at last like many another of his neighbors he began to look away to the west as a fairer field for his conquest."[1] On March 24, 1868, Dick Garland sold his farm for $3,500, but apparently he arranged to remain through the harvest, for the Garlands didn't leave their home until February 1869.[2]

In his autobiography, Hamlin recalls a long-held tradition in the Garland family, dating back to his grandparents: at times of moving, they would sing a song he calls "O'er the Hills in Legions Boys!" for the song expresses the optimism of the pioneer for the possibilities inherent in westward expansion.[3] "Cheer up brothers, as we go," the song begins, "O'er the mountains, westward ho —" Then the chorus:

> Then o'er the hills in legions, boys,
> Fair freedom's star
> Points to the sunset regions, boys.
> Ha, ha, ha-ha!

While his father's face "shone with the light of the explorer," the effect on his mother was less cheering, for the move meant leaving behind her parents and most of her siblings. "To her this song meant not so much the acquisition of a new home as the loss of all her friends and relatives," Garland remembered. And then he went on to sound a theme that resonates throughout his autobiography: "To all of the pioneer wives of the past that song had meant deprivation, suffering, loneliness, heart-ache."[4]

The harvest over and good-byes said, in February the Garlands loaded their belongings onto a sled and began the two-day journey to the farm Dick had bought in Winneshiek County, Iowa, two miles west of the small village of Hesper in Hesper Township, which had been settled in 1856 largely by members of the Society of Friends. Although they were only about forty miles away from their old home in Wisconsin and less than two miles from the Minnesota-Iowa border, the steep hills of the Wisconsin Drift had subsided into rolling and wooded hills, which must have appeared flat to the eyes of Dick Garland, so tired of struggling on his coulee farm. Hamlin, eight years of age at the time, would later remember comparatively little of the thirteen months he would spend in the log house on their farmstead, and his dominant memory is of a smallpox scare. His father had hired some Norwegian laborers to help in clearing the land, and they passed on to a housemaid a case of the contagion. At the time, Isabelle was pregnant with Jessie Viola, who would be born on June 6, 1869, and the maid was there to assist with the housework. "It was a fearsome plague in those days," Hamlin recalled, "and my mother with three unvaccinated children, a helpless handmaid to be nursed, was in despair when father developed the disease." Fortunately, a neighbor, a bare acquaintance, volunteered to come to their aid; Hamlin and Harriet were vaccinated (no mention of Franklin), baby Jessie was born, and Dick escaped the characteristic pitting of the disease.[5] With a novelist's eye for the telling anecdote, Hamlin would later transform this event into a pivotal scene in *Trail-Makers of the Middle Border* (1926), where the young Susan Garland comes down with the disease during the family's migration to Wisconsin, and only a fearless and heroic Hugh

McClintock is willing to provide shelter for Garlands, thus bringing the two families together.

Hamlin was too young to remember why, but in March 1870 his father once again uprooted his family and moved from his Hesper farm to a rented farm six miles due west. What he did remember was the effect on his mother: "I see now that she must have suffered each time the bitter pangs of doubt and unrest which strike through the woman's heart when called upon to leave her snug, safe fire for a ruder cabin in strange lands."[6] But his father's restless spirit was unsatisfied; as soon as he had seeded his land, Dick again set out "O'er the Hills" in search of his dream of flat land. He wandered over southern Minnesota and northern Iowa, eventually settling on the tall-grass prairie of Mitchell County, Iowa, some sixty miles west-southwest. He could hardly have chosen flatter land, for the quarter section he purchased on July 14, 1870, in Burr Oak Township, seven miles northeast of Osage, is as flat as the proverbial pancake in an otherwise generally undulating prairie.[7] After the harvest in August, the family moved to their new home. "I felt for the first time the poetry of the unplowed spaces," Hamlin remembered of their journey.[8] But their house, a rude box of unpainted pine boards about sixteen feet square, with two rooms below and a garret for the children above, must have dismayed Isabelle. "The cabin faced a level plain with no tree in sight," Hamlin wrote. "A mile away to the west stood a low stone house and immediately in front of us opened a half section of unfenced sod. To the north, as far as I could see, the land billowed like a russet ocean."[9]

Dick likely moved his family for a number of reasons. His farms in Winneshiek County were wooded and hilly—less hilly than Green's Coulee, to be sure, but hilly nonetheless. In contrast, only two sections of Burr Oak Township were wooded, with the remainder being open prairie. In 1870 the land in Winneshiek County was relatively crowded, boasting 23,570 citizens, while Mitchell County counted a mere 9,582, the difference in settlement reflecting the counties' proximity to the Mississippi River. There were twice as many farms and four times the number of improved areas as there were in Mitchell County, all of which affected Dick's desire to expand the number of acres he would put under cultivation, for his intention was to grow wheat, and wheat demanded room.[10] Mitchell County therefore afforded better opportunities for an ambitious and hardworking farmer. Just as important were the probable social motives for moving, in particular the desire for the comfort of the familiar in a new land. Hesper Township had been largely settled by Norwegians, and two out of three residents of Burr Oak Township, Winneshiek County, had been born outside of the United States. In contrast, the vast majority of Dick's Mitchell County neighbors had been born in New York, Vermont, and Wisconsin, so their customs and especially their language were his own. Finally, David McClintock, Isabelle's brother, had settled on a farm a mere ten miles away, and the comforts of family were added to the mix.[11]

Hamlin's dominant memory of his tenth year is of hard physical labor. Because his father needed to expand the house to make room for the family, to Hamlin fell the labor of plowing unbroken sod. The tough, thick roots of prairie sod required a heftier plow, and so a heavy-duty breaking plow had evolved. Unlike its conventional cousin, a breaking plow "boasted a ponderous beam six to twelve feet long, the fore end resting on small sturdy wheels, the rear end firmly attached to a massive share—ultimately of steel—and mould board as well as to the handles of the plowman."[12] Hamlin's plow likely turned a furrow of sixteen inches and was drawn by four horses. "I plowed seventy acres of land when I was 10 years old and more each year after that," he told an interviewer in 1897. "I was so small that I had to reach up to catch the handles of the plow."[13] His arms aching, at times tormented by flies or blasted by a bitter north wind, his small legs slowed by the accumulation of mud, for two months, during October and November, he plowed two acres a day, ten hours at a stretch. Small wonder that his "heart was sometimes bitter and rebellious," even though he well understood that child labor was a necessity on a frontier farm.[14] Knowing so didn't make the labor any more pleasant.

That winter he attended Burr Oak School No. 1, a one-room schoolhouse about a mile and a half southeast of their farm. At that time, county schools were typically "a log house or shanty probably 10 x 12 feet in size. . . . Often these huts had but one window, a small doorway cut through the logs or boards at the most convenient place, while the furniture consisted of slab seats for the scholars and a three-legged stool and a hazel or hickory rod for the teacher. As for books, but few were needed; the less the better, as the teacher could get along the more readily." In 1870 Mitchell County boasted sixty-nine schools, with 394 pupils, but only a scant forty-five books in the school libraries to serve them all.[15] Lessons were primarily oral, with students reciting in unison. As one historian explains, "Reading out loud by individuals enabled the teacher to assess progress and gave the children practice in declamation. It also functioned as a form of social control; joint activities enabled a single, inexperienced young woman or man to keep large numbers of potentially unruly children in order, as deviant behavior was easily spotted when everyone was supposed to be engaged in the same task."[16] Burr Oak Township may have been more prosperous than neighboring townships, for Garland's school seems to have been better appointed. Though it was a "square pine box painted a glaring white on the outside," it boasted "two doors on the eastern end and three windows on each side." Because the county schools' libraries were ill-equipped, Garland's school required that he outfit himself with a McGuffey *Reader*, as well as geography and arithmetic books, and a slate, which remains preserved among Garland's papers.[17]

At school Hamlin formed a friendship with Burton Babcock, a fellow student two years his senior, that would last until Babcock's death in 1911. When spring came, Hamlin again went to the fields, this time running a harrow to break up the furrows of sod that had rotted over the winter. What he most remembered about the job was the unrelenting tediousness of the task, for "your heels sinking deep into the soft loam bring such unwonted strain upon the tendons of your legs that you can scarcely limp home to supper, and it seems that you cannot possibly go on another day,—but you do—at least I did."[18] When school resumed, Harriet and Franklin returned—but the eldest son remained in the field, since Dick could not then afford to hire a hand.

But all was not unrelieved hardship. The young Hamlin was also extraordinarily sensitive to the natural beauty of the landscape. "How shall the careworn man tell the glory, the majesty of those nights and days as they filled the boy's heart with a pleasure so deep as almost to be pain," he mused when he was not yet twenty-eight. "O, to bury my feet again in that moist, warm earth; to lie on the mellow ground in the sun; to walk across the fields and hear the steady click of the hoe at my heel, and the laugh of the girls working beside!"[19] While Hamlin remembered those first years on the prairie with a mixture of bitterness and pleasure, his brother, Franklin, recalled the majestic open spaces and the boyish pleasures of horseback riding. "We both rode Horses like wild Indians," he reminisced in 1940, "bareback mostly. . . . We indulged in some wonderful races over the Prairies. We did a lot of the Cowboy stuff, swinging down to pick wild flowers with our mounts on a dead run, throwing our hats ahead to be picked up also with the horses on the dead run, then lean down, unbuckle the saddle, throw it to the ground, unbuckle the bridle, throw that aside then ride without anything to guide the Pony but the swaying of the Body or the touch of the hands on the side of the neck."[20] Hamlin's experience of the physical hardship and squalid conditions of a frontier farm would forever color his memories and shape his fiction and poetry, but he simultaneously developed an attachment to the land itself that he would later incorporate in every story, poem, and reminiscence that came from his pen.

In September 1872 Dick Garland once again uprooted his family to move them to a new 160-acre farm that he had purchased to increase his landholdings, this time a mile and a half south, and there they would remain for the next nine years.[21] Above all else, Dick was an ambitious farmer, determined to make his fortune in wheat and corn, and his farming methods not only shaped his son's perception of farm life and determined his view of agriculture as an economical and political force but also planted in him the awareness that hard work was necessary for success—an attitude that would later shape Hamlin's own literary ambitions. With the end of the Civil War and the mustering out of armies, the United States had a surplus of labor, for with war industries ended and the laborers out of work, the country had about four million unemployed citizens,[22] many of whom immigrated to newly opened western lands, made accessible by the growth of the railroads and the Homestead Act of 1862, which granted 160 acres of unassigned public land to anyone over twenty-one who was willing to work it for five years. The rapid spread of the railroads to these new homesteads made it easier to get crops to market, and the development of labor-saving machinery such as mechanical threshers and seeders meant that fewer laborers were needed. The combination of free land, workers to occupy it, labor-saving machinery, and an effective means to move goods to market meant a corresponding drop in crop prices—which further meant that a farmer, to be successful, needed to expand his acreage. When Dick Garland began farming in Iowa in 1869, the average price of corn in the United States was $0.60 per bushel. By 1872, when he moved to his second Burr Oak farm, it had dropped to $0.35 per bushel. Clearly, corn farming wasn't going to pay. But wheat fared better. In 1869 the average U.S. price was $0.77 per bushel, and by 1872 it had climbed to $1.11 per bushel.[23]

By the time the Garlands migrated to Iowa in 1869, available land at an affordable price was not always prime. Dick's first tract of 132 acres, on the upper reaches of Burr Oak Creek (which Hamlin refers to as "Dry Run"), did not satisfy: it may not have been as productive as he wished, or he may simply have had an opportunity to increase his acreage at a price he could afford.[24] During the spring of 1872, eleven-year-old Hamlin and his uncle David plowed the unbroken sod of the new quarter section while Dick built a house, completing it in July. It was quite similar to their existing house, with three rooms below and a garret for the children above, accessible not by means of a staircase but by an outside ladder, but it was better built, for Dick lined the house with bricks to stabilize it against the prairie wind. Soon they would plant trees to establish a windbreak and shade. During the summer Dick fashioned outbuildings, and in September the family moved in time for Hamlin to attend school, which was conveniently located on the northeast corner of their farm, at the intersection of the branch road that connected their farm to the neighboring Babcock farm.

Hamlin was an ambitious student and a voracious reader. He devoured books—when he could get them—but the usual fare were farm journals and newspapers. He consumed a steady diet of Beadle's Dime Novels, thrilling to the escapades of Old Sleuth and Jack Harkaway, as yesterday's readers similarly thrilled to the Hardy Boys and Nancy Drew and young people today devour Harry Potter. The serial version of Edward Eggleston's *The Hoosier Schoolmaster* made an impression, as he later remembered: "This book is a milestone in my literary progress as it is in the development of distinctive western fiction, and years afterward I was glad to say so to the aged author."[25] At school, in the pages of the McGuffey *Eclectic Readers*, Hamlin encountered "the poems of Scott, Byron, Southey, Wordsworth and a long line of the English masters."[26] With little else to read, he pored over the *Readers* until he had much of the contents memorized—later in life, he and Henry Ford once had a contest to see "who could remember most of the poems and name the titles of the prose pieces."[27] Ford won the contest, but Hamlin's taste in literature was profoundly shaped by the McGuffey *Readers*, which combined moral lessons with exemplary stories and poems.

After school, Hamlin roamed the neighboring fields with his brother, Franklin, and best friend, Burton Babcock, snaring gophers and learning to shoot—chiefly ducks and gophers—in part as boyish sport but also to protect the new crops from ravenous appetites. He excelled at baseball—Franklin later recalled that "Hamlin was our star pitcher and was a good one. He threw the curves, and had one particularly effective sinker that had the big boys swinging wildly and missing. He was so effective that we beat the County seat team more often than they did us."[28] And, in the winter, he was fond of skating and other winter sports, playing "Pom, Pom, Pull-Away," which he celebrated in an early poem:

> Out on the snow the boys are springing,
> Shouting blithely at their play;
> Through the night air their voices ringing,
> Sound the cry "*Pom, pull-away!*"[29]

He and his friends also indulged in a rather dangerous activity using a "whirligig," a long pole "hung on the top of a short upright post, set in the midst of ice. To the longer end of the pole was attached a sled with ropes as long as the size of the pond admitted." A couple of boys, pushing against the short end, would walk in a circle; the sled would soon attain magnificent speed—"the sled was like a stone in a sling, and there was a point where it rose in the air . . . to touch the ice only at intervals."[30]

But always the chores: plowing in the fall, harrowing in the spring, followed by planting, then reaping, then threshing. His experiences as a teenage farmhand marked him forever. "This farm life it will be seen was attractive," Hamlin would write in 1888, "not because of the home-life so much, as because of the superb setting of color and light in the atmosphere and landscape." But not even the beauty of the landscape could compensate for the endless grind of hard, physical labor, especially for the farm wife, who toiled without cessation. "Slaves on the treadmill or in the Roman galleys could not have endured greater hardships than many of these women," he remarked. "Sallow, weazened, old before their time, with a dull, patient, hopeless look on their faces; condemned to a life of littleness and vacuity, occupied in running from stove to pantry, from cradle to frying-pan," life "was a prison for the patient women who had long since abandoned hope."[31] And for a teenage boy who did the work of a hired hand instead of playing, the daily routine at times prompted rebellion. One September, impatient with the task of plowing after the harvest of wheat, Hamlin decided to clear out a thicket of vines and weeds by setting fire to the field, youthfully confident that he could keep the fire from advancing to the four stacks of wheat awaiting threshing. He miscalculated, and the fire soon made a beeline to the stacks. "I trampled the fire with my bare feet," he recalled. "I beat at it with my hat. I screamed for help.—Too late I thought of my team and the plow with which I might have drawn a furrow around the stacks." The flame reached the stacks, and "in less than twenty minutes the towering piles had melted into four glowing heaps of ashes. Four hundred dollars had gone up in that blaze."

His feet were badly burned—but worse was his fear of his father's reaction to the news that such a large portion of the farm's profits had been lost. Hamlin crawled to his always-sympathetic mother to be shielded "from the just wrath of my father," who was away from the farm during the calamity. He was surprised at his father's reaction, for the normally stern disciplinarian knew when it was—and was not—appropriate to chastise an errant son. "He merely asked me how I felt, uncovered my burned feet, examined them, put the sheet back, and went away, without a word either of reproof or consolation."[32]

When Hamlin was fourteen, his sister Harriet died. The year before, she had persuaded her father to let her continue her education in the Cedar Valley Seminary in Osage, but in the spring of 1875 she became sick with what Garland called "a wasting fever" and which courthouse records show to have been "typhoid pneumonia."[33] For several weeks he watched her suffer from her bed in the living room. The diary he kept, a tiny notebook filled mostly with observations about the weather, on May 3 records, "Rain in the am in the pm cleared up. Plowed in the pm. Hattie was worse and I went after the doctor and up to uncle Davids." But on May 5 he recorded only that the weather was "Pretty pleasant. Went to town in the am." Without the eye for the significant event that would later mark his diaries, he did not think to record his sister's death on that day. Later, he would write that she whispered "be a good boy" before succumbing to her illness. "This was my first close contact with death," Garland remembered, "and it filled me with awe."[34] Deeply affected by the loss of her eldest child, his mother "never entirely returned to the jollity of her former years. . . . She had been youthful to that moment; after that she was middle-aged—even to her sons."[35]

When Hamlin was in his teens, he and his family began to attend the local Grange socials, held at the Burr Oak Grove school, a little more than two miles from the Garland farm. Officially named The Patrons of Husbandry, the Grange was founded in 1867 to improve the economic, social, and intellectual condition of farmers, but unlike most fraternal orders of the time, it admitted women.[36] As initially conceived, the Grange had the aim of improving the lives of farmers, many of whom were isolated by large distances from each other and from towns. But upon joining, farmers were likely to inquire about what pecuniary benefit they would receive for their dues, and so the Grange's mission soon expanded to cooperative buying and selling of farm goods. In the early stages, members of a local Grange contracted with local merchants for special prices for goods and services for members. But soon ambition spread, and state and eventually national Grange agencies sought to gain cooperative control over the manufacture of farm implements, transportation, and prices. Always the goal was the same: "to secure supplies at lower prices by bulking orders and dealing as directly as possible with manufacturers and jobbers; and to eliminate some of the profits of middlemen by shipping produce directly to the large markets instead of disposing of it to the local dealers and commission men."[37]

Young Hamlin, at age twelve through fifteen at the time of the Iowa Grange's growth, was scarcely aware of the pecuniary benefits of his father's membership in the local Grange. What did interest him was the organization's social functions. As its Declaration of Purposes spells out, the Grange was organized, among other things, "To develop a better and higher manhood and womanhood among ourselves; to enhance the comforts and attractions of our homes, and strengthen our attachments to our pursuits."[38] With a farmer's closest neighbor normally half a mile away or more, with communities and stores at even greater distances, with days occupied with lonely and unremitting toil, and with educational opportunities and reading material scarce, farm families eagerly embraced the Grange's social mission. To bring farmers together, the local Granges held regular meetings, usually monthly or semi-monthly but often weekly, at which "the farmers, with their wives, and sons and daughters of at least fourteen and sixteen years respectively, met in secret conclave to perform the work of a pleasing and appropriate ritual; a literary and musical program usually followed and then there was opportunity for games and general conversation."[39] At these meetings Hamlin learned a lesson he never forgot: that social organizations, formed to improve the lot of others while also providing pleasant company, can do as much for the social good as any overt political activity. This principle would inform every one of the many organizations he would eventually found or join.

In June 1875 Dick Garland returned from a Grange meeting with momentous news: the officers of the local Grange had asked him to become the county grain buyer for the elevator then under construction in Osage. He commuted from his farm, six miles away, to Osage, leaving fourteen-year-old Hamlin in charge of the farm and its hired hand. As a lad terrified of his father's wrath, Hamlin constantly worried about incurring his displeasure. "His uncanny powers of observation kept me terrified," he remembered; "if any tool was out of place or broken, he discovered it at once, and his reproof was never a cause of laughter to me or my brother."[40] That summer, on a rare visit to Osage to buy new clothes, Hamlin clashed with his father over his desire to have a more fashionable hat. His "Commander-in-Chief" denied his desire, arousing Hamlin's ire. "As I am not only doing a man's work on a boy's pay but actually super-intending the stock and tools," he argued, "I am entitled to certain individual rights in the choice of a hat."

"You'll wear the hat I provide," countered his father.

"I will not," Hamlin asserted, and then added ominously, "And you can't make me."

Garland records that his father seized him by the arm and they faced each other in a struggle for mastery. "Don't you strike me," Hamlin warned. And then, referring to past infractions of his father's will, he added, ominously, "You can't do that any more." Perhaps his father took note of his growing son's husky physique, for he handed him two dollars and dismissed him with a curt "get your own hat" and never struck him again.[41] From that point on, Hamlin grew in-creasingly independent, relishing his victory over his father's will but careful not to make too much of it, and he took on an even larger measure of managing the family farm.

In March 1876 Dick Garland decided to move to a rented house in Osage, tiring of the daily commute. Located at the edge of the town, the house came with a large plot, and soon Hamlin found himself caring for cows, horses, and a large garden. He was disappointed that town life did not bring an end to his daily chores, but now he could complete them more quickly.

And village life had its compensations. Founded in 1854, the year after the first white settlers had filed land claims when the U.S. government completed its removal of Native Americans from the region, Osage soon became the location of the government land office, busily catering to the needs of the 1,500 settlers, speculators, and surveyors who arrived in 1857. The town was named for Massachusetts capitalist Orrin Sage, who ironically never set foot in his namesake but whose representatives speculated in land and platted the town. By 1859 all of the land was sold, leaving a legacy of a support infrastructure—general stores, farm-supply outfits, hotels, sawmills, carpenter shops, and even an institute for higher education, the Cedar Valley Seminary. In 1869 the Illinois Central Railroad Company laid tracks through Osage, and in 1870 the town became the county seat, with a population of 1,400.[42] Hamlin records that his first visit to Osage occurred soon after the Garlands had arrived in Mitchell County, and they went to get outfitted for school, buying oversize new boots (with room to grow) and textbooks. As they traveled through the town on their lumber wagon, they marveled at the displays of candy, the array of ready-made clothing, and especially the exotic odors "of salt codfish and spices, calico and kerosene, apples and ginger-snaps."[43]

For the teenage Hamlin, Osage represented relief from farmwork and an opportunity to indulge his passion for education. But first he had to overcome his terror of "The Town-Boys," for even in 1876 Osage, he was reminded of the differences of class. The town boys viewed farm kids with disdain, for their disheveled appearance—rough haircuts from mothers and homemade clothing—marked them as a poorer, laboring class. For his part, Hamlin "hated and feared" the town boys, "knowing that they hated and despised me," and upon his move to Osage his first task was to defend himself against the town bullies and establish his willingness to fight.[44] Though not tall, he was powerfully made by his years in the field, and soon he had established his bona fides and thereby enlarged his circle of friends. For the rest of his life he would be fond of fine clothes and take care to be well dressed, and in his autobiographical writing he is careful to record milestones of haberdashery.

For part of that summer he worked for his father at the Grange elevator, where he weighed grain, kept books, and handled money. He also listened to the grumblings of the farmers as they dickered with grain buyers over the price of wheat. While his father tried to get them to understand that by banding together they could control supply and thereby the price they were paid, the farmers too easily succumbed to the lure of the individual deal. Hamlin therefore got his first glimpse of agrarian politics, an experience that would inform his first fiction.

In the fall of 1876 Hamlin enrolled in the Cedar Valley Seminary, an institution founded by Baptists to provide college-preparatory classes at a time when Osage had no high school. Its principal was Baptist preacher Alva Bush, who had helped found the school in 1862. Though established by Baptists, the school was organized to serve the greater needs of the county, as one county history explains: "The students are allowed the right of individual choice and judgment with respect to religious belief; so that while the college may be in one sense denominational, it is by no means sectarian, but a public institution of higher learning devoted to the interests of all the people in the neighboring country."[45] The Baptist congregation met in its chapel on Sundays; on school days the chapel served as the common meeting room. By 1881, the year Hamlin graduated, the seminary boasted ninety-three students, forty-five of whom were "unclassified"—that is, non-degree-seeking students "pursuing selected studies"—with the remainder divided into various levels of juniors and seniors, with fourteen in Hamlin's graduating class. Nearly all of the students came from relatively wealthy families, the sons and daughters of the business and professional classes, but compared to wealthy eastern families, their ambitions were low-key: to equip their sons and daughters to prosper in the Midwest. Few of the wealthiest seminary graduates went on to eastern universities; most went to "local [Iowa] colleges such as Grinnell and Cornell."[46]

For a small institution with only four or five faculty, the seminary offered a comparatively rich array of courses, which suggests the faculty were rather broadly trained. Juniors and "Junior-Middlers" took three classes in each of four terms in such subjects as arithmetic, physiology, geography, Greek, Latin, history, rhetoric, algebra, zoology, and botany. Senior-middlers and seniors progressed to the more difficult math of geometry and trigonometry, buttressed their lingual skills with French and German, and continued Latin declamations in Cicero and Virgil. Students crowned their final year with studies in astronomy, natural philosophy, geology, chemistry, mental and moral sciences, and logic and surveying. All students took part in Friday-afternoon recitals in "English Analysis, English and American literature, in addition to exercises in composition and declamation."[47] The seminary's curriculum was traditional and conservative in approach: courses emphasized practical training in rhetoric and applied sciences, with students reading standard textbooks and then meeting in recitation rooms to deliver what they had memorized. The school's mission reflected its practical orientation: "First to give such instruction as will be useful to the students in the practical affairs of life; and second, to give that general culture, to body and mind, which is more valuable than learning."[48]

In August 1876, to save money for the tuition fee of seven dollars per term, Hamlin had hired himself out at full wages (rather than at child's wages) to bind grain with a new Marsh Harvester. The hard work called on all the reserves of strength and endurance he could muster, but after a month of labor he had earned enough to buy a Sunday suit—his first—new boots, paper cuffs, a necktie, and textbooks. He was especially pleased with the clothes, for his homemade apparel had made him easy prey for the ridicule of the town boys.

When he first entered the seminary's chapel that September and saw "the stately professors on the platform" and heard the majesty of the choir, Hamlin "was reduced to a hare-like humility." "What right had I to share in this splendor?" he wondered. His shyness soon abated, but he never completely escaped feelings of inferiority when he compared himself to the wealthier students from the professional classes—indeed, most of his friends would remain those from the public schools. As he reflected years later, the seminary "gave farmers' boys like myself the opportunity of meeting those who were older, finer, more learned." But equally important, "it symbolized freedom from the hayfork and the hoe."[49] Mindful of his farm origins, he would never entirely lose his sense of social inferiority even after he had achieved renown and distinction.

While he struggled with mathematics, Hamlin excelled at oratory. He had always been fascinated by listening to the local preacher thunder forth during Sunday meetings, but at the seminary he heard, for the first time, skilled teachers declaim the classics. On Fridays, all students were required to recite lines from classic Latin, Greek, or English texts. Painfully shy among the more polished town boys, he worried about his performance. As the day approached for his first recitation, he was so overcome by fear that he could not eat. When alone in the barn or out in a field, he practiced at every opportunity until the appointed hour arrived. "I rose in my seat with a spring like a Jack from his box," he recalled. "My limbs were numb, so numb that I could scarcely feel the floor beneath my feet. . . . My head oscillated like a toy balloon, seemed indeed to be floating in the air, and my heart was pounding like a drum." But when he began his speech, a miraculous transformation occurred: "I became strangely master of myself. From somewhere above me a new and amazing power fell upon me and in that instant I perceived on the faces of my classmates a certain expression of surprise and serious respect. My subconscious oratorical self had taken charge."[50] That first declamation fired an ambition to become an orator, and soon he joined a debating society. On March 27, 1878, he would take the affirmative side in a debate entitled "Should the Negro Exodus Be Encouraged?" as part of an evening exhibition consisting of orations on "National Perils and Future Prosperity" and "The Discovery of America by the Norsemen," declamations on "The Battle of Concord" and "The Black Horse and His Rider," and other readings, recitations, and music. At the seminary, debates were commonly open to the public, with the town's leading citizens participating as judges and awarding medals.[51]

Today, the nineteenth-century's fascination with orators, oratory, and public reading has largely faded from cultural memory. Then, the public flocked to lecture halls to listen to such orators as Robert Ingersoll—perhaps the most famous orator of the time—address crowds on issues of religion, politics, even literary figures. Newspapers covered orations in detail, with articles parsing each line of the speech and reporters minutely describing the audience's response. As one historian of oratory explains, "People went to hear great speakers as they attended a concert or a play, hoping to be thrilled, enchanted, lifted out of themselves."[52] In his autobiography, Hamlin describes reading about one of Ingersoll's particularly controversial orations on agnosticism: "Under the light of Ingersoll's remorseless humor most of our superstitions vanished. I don't think my father's essential Christianity was in any degree diminished, he merely lost his respect for certain outworn traditions and empty creeds." One effect is that Dick Garland did not insist on church attendance, or "any religious observance on the part of his sons." Hamlin would forever be "grateful to him for his noninterference with my religious affairs."[53] He would remain an agnostic, inclining toward atheism after later study in Boston. Later he told Eldon Hill, who would write the first PhD thesis about his life and work, that "he frequently attended religious meetings merely to study the oratory, or to meet his friends, or to 'squire' one of the girls to her home."[54]

Hamlin's comparatively comfortable life in town lasted only a year, for news came that the renter of the Garland farm had failed, and so his father moved the family back to their former home. Hamlin's diary of entry for March 13, 1877, records the cryptic notation, "The folks got ready and moved [and] got away at noon," but the sixteen-year-old lad did not think to inscribe his impressions or the reasons for that move.[55] He remained in Osage to board with a neighbor until the end of the term on March 27, returning to the farm on weekends to help with the chores. His father might have remained in Osage and found another renter, but what likely contributed to his reasons for returning to the farm were a number of bad investments by the Iowa Patrons of Husbandry. In 1875, the year Dick Garland became manager for the Grange elevator, the Iowa Grange had invested heavily in the manufacture of farm implements, including a harvester factory in Osage. But when word spread that the Grange harvester was of inferior quality, the works failed, with the crash soon bankrupting the state Grange. For a time the Grange carried on seemingly unaffected, but membership began to decline as members found the Grange lacked sufficient capital to underwrite its investments.[56] The writing was on the wall, and Dick Garland likely returned to his farm to contain his expenses, and he continued, for a time, to work as grain buyer for the Grange by renewing his commute from the farm to Osage.

For Hamlin, the return to the farm was bittersweet. His year in town had served to magnify the differences between farm and town life, and in his eyes, life on the farm suffered badly by comparison. "All that we possessed seemed very cheap and deplorably commonplace" compared to the comforts of town, he would write. "Against these comforts, these luxurious conditions, we now set our ugly little farmhouse, with its rags and carpets, its battered furniture, its barren attic, and its hard, rude beds." Hamlin and Franklin both "loathed the smell of manure and hated the greasy clothing which our tasks made necessary." Portentously, both "vowed that when we were twenty-one we would leave the farm, never to return to it."[57]

For Franklin, the move meant the end of his formal schooling, for when Hamlin returned to the seminary at the end of October, fourteen-year-old Franklin was needed to supply his place in the fields and barn. Years later he would explain, "While Hamlin was attending the Seminary, I was at home doing the chores and keeping up the Farm work on the assumption that I was to have my chance when he had finished, but my chance never came. Conditions got so bad Father could not spare me or the money, then he sold the Farm and we moved to Dakota."[58] The move—and Hamlin's guilt over his brother's lost opportunity—would later inform the plot of one of his finest stories, "Up the Coulé," where Howard McLane returns home after ten years of success in Boston only to find that his younger brother's spirit has been broken by the struggle to save the family farm.

That summer Hamlin took on more responsibility for management of the farm, but while he bound, shocked, and stacked wheat he dreamed of returning to the seminary to fulfill his dream of becoming an orator. He went about his chores with a copy of Shakespeare at hand and "ranted the immortal soliloquies of *Hamlet* and *Richard* as I held the plow, feeling certain that I was following in the footprints of Lincoln and Demosthenes."[59] His brother remembered a more playful version of Hamlin's "ranting": "The Sword fights in Shakespeare made a great hit with both of us so we fashioned Broad Swords out of some tough elm timber we had then we engaged in some very lively fights, though probably very [in]expert. But we had loads of fun at it."[60]

Dick Garland was not sympathetic about Hamlin's proposed return to the seminary, believing that his son had education enough for a farmer. Besides, he himself had little formal schooling, and he was now one of the most prosperous farmers in Burr Oak Township, with some 290 acres under cultivation, more than any other farmer in the township, as well as possessing herds of cattle and swine.[61] To Hamlin's aid came his mother, who intervened to support her son's ambition. Hamlin recalled that "she responded helpfully to every effort which her sons made to raise themselves above the commonplace level of neighborhood life."[62] What he does not mention is that his mother raised and sold colts to help defray his seminary expenses.[63] Dick finally consented, provided Hamlin would agree to remain through the fall harvest, for the family depended on his labor. The effect of Hamlin's defiance of his father's will was to forever instill in him an unrelenting desire to succeed in an effort to show that the life of the mind is better than life as a farmer.

When plowing and corn husking ended in October, well after the start of school, Hamlin rejoined his classmates at the seminary, arranging to room with his friend Burton Babcock in a boardinghouse Monday through Friday at two dollars per week for room and board. On weekends, both returned to their respective farms. In April, Hamlin would cut short his seminary studies to engage in spring planting, and for the next several years this was the pattern—school during the winter months when he could be spared.

Seminary life offered Hamlin a welcome change of pace. Years later he would write of his education in a letter to the class of 1901: "I regard my years at the Cedar Valley Seminary as among the happiest of my life. I was a hard-working farmer boy at that time and the freedom from daily toil, the privilege of going to bed when I pleased and rising when my need of sleep was satisfied, would have made my return to school each autumn memorable, but in addition to these comforts I experienced each time a keener joy—the delight of shaking hands with classmates and friends many of whom like myself were fresh from the threshing machine or the corn-field. I remember too the tender sadness with which we parted each June some of us not to return at all."[64]

Hamlin seems to have thrown himself into his studies, devouring the few books in the school's rude library. The library was, he remembered, "pitifully small and ludicrously prescriptive, but its shelves held a few of the fine old classics, Scott, Dickens and Thackeray—the kind of books which can always be had at sets at very low prices." On its shelves he discovered Hawthorne's *Mosses from an Old Manse* and was soon completely absorbed by the author's "stately diction, the rich and glowing imagery, the mystical radiance" and thereby gained his first "literary touchstone" that, despite his later championing of realism, he would never abandon.[65] In 1895 he would help remedy the sparseness of the library's collection by sending it a complete set of his works to that time—*Main-Travelled Roads, Jason Edwards, A Member of the Third House, Prairie Folks, Prairie Songs,* and *Crumbling Idols.*[66]

He also tried his hand at acting. He was intimidated by the comparatively well-off seminary students, so he formed his closest friendships with students at the public high school. With them, during the winter of 1877–78, he organized a dramatic troupe with himself as stage manager and lead actor. The show, a typical late-nineteenth-century medley of orations and scenes from plays, seems to have consisted of pieces from Cicero, which Hamlin would declaim in "thunderous, rolling periods and passionate gestures"; a sketch about the death of a Revolutionary War veteran, in which Hamlin appeared in powdered wig as the veteran; and a portion of the play *His Brother's Keeper,* in which he played the "juvenile lover." He remembered two things about this inaugural performance. The first was that he accommodated himself easily to public performance; he was surprised to discover that he "had no fear at all" as he looked over the audience to see his parents, Franklin, and Jessie "all quite dazed (as I imagined) by my transcendent position behind the foot lights." The second was an early effort at extending this performance to other towns. He and his troupe booked their performance to the neighboring towns of St. Ansgar and Mitchell and achieved what he called "'an artistic success'—that is to say, we lost some eighteen dollars, which so depressed the management that it abandoned the tour."[67]

Hamlin returned to his place on the farm in April, with his memories of life in the seminary sustaining him through the long hours of toil. But late that summer—1878—the fields of wheat and corn withered. The chinch bug had arrived. A winged insect of about three-sixteenths of an inch, the chinch bug feeds primarily upon grasses such as wheat, corn, barley, and timothy. Most of the damage to crops occurs during the lymphal stage, when the emergent bug sucks juices from the stalk and leaves of the plant, which causes the host plant to become stunted (with accompanying reduced yields); and in heavy infestations, the plant withers and dies. In the Iowa of Garland's youth, it was common for chinch bugs to infest wheat first, and then, when the wheat ripened and the plant's fluids diminished, the bugs migrated to nearby cornfields to infest those plants.

Partly because of nascent chinch bug infestation but also because of declining prices for wheat and corn, Hamlin's father was reluctant to pay for his room and board at the seminary.[68] Finding that Burton's father also objected, the two hatched a plan: they, not their parents, would be responsible for the board. Additionally, Hamlin proposed a bargain: if his father would agree to pay for his schooling, upon graduation he would ask nothing further from him. His father agreed, and in October 1878 Hamlin returned to school, two weeks after his classmates.[69] He and Burton rented a room in a local boardinghouse, and by strict economy (and occasional raids on the house pantry) they managed to reduce the cost of their board to fifty cents per day—and it helped that Hamlin's mother supplied them with doughnuts and bread when they returned to their room on Mondays, and by Fridays, they were "starved out."[70]

His final year at the seminary was marked by his first foray into authorship: Hamlin, along with four other students, were editors of the *Cedar Valley Seminarian*, the quarterly magazine of the school. The June 1881 issue of the *Seminarian* was accompanied by several pages of advertisements from local businesses and included an essay from the principal extolling the virtues of the school; a column devoted to words of advice from departing professor David Call, who was leaving to become president of the University of Des Moines (a Baptist college which foundered during the depression); a number of essays on literary topics by students; alumni notes; and miscellaneous, often comic, observations about classmates. Because most of these pieces are unsigned, one cannot tell whether Hamlin had a hand in their composition, but the "Seminary and Town" page of his personal copy of the June 1881 issue bears the inscription "by Garland." The two dozen brief entries range from the flat announcement—"Fred Leonard, an old time student, is here on a visit. We knew him quick and easy"—to the aphoristic—"To talk politics well, is to conceal what you don't know, and draw out what the other man does know"—to sophomoric efforts at humor:

— Birds are singing, grass is springing, bees are stinging—er—our muse—a—fails us.
— Prof. in Moral Science class to Lady Senior, reciting:
  "Now I don't know that I am homely"—"You don't?"—It was
  the emphasis that crushed him.

Other comments reflect a more personal investment and even a barely concealed antagonism toward his father: "Fred Hall, a one-time 'Senior-Middler,' is pursuing his studies at home, on the farm. He may congratulate himself if they are all he is obliged to pursue. When we are on the farm we are compelled to pursue the harrow or corn-plow to the extreme detriment of studies." Elsewhere in the issue, a paragraph ascribes characteristics to each of the seven graduating men, reflecting the impression each has made on his peers. Hamlin seems to have been most impressive, not in his intellectual capabilities, but in his physical prowess. Whereas his best friend, Burton Babcock, is "the quiet man," Hamlin is "the athletic man." But there was hope for the future, for where Burton is "reserved," Hamlin is "reflective." When he later became famous, townspeople had difficulty reconciling the public Hamlin Garland with the awkward, sometimes arrogant youth they remembered. "Hamlin was always kind of tony," recalled Frank Jacobs, whose brother was Hamlin's classmate. "He always was wearing kid gloves when working." Jacobs remembered that Hamlin even plowed in a white frock coat. "How he hated farm work . . . and even more the dirt." Grace Bush Gardener, the daughter of the school principal, was even blunter: "Hamlin had a superiority complex."[71]

For the rest of his life, Hamlin would regard his seminary days as the formative experience of his life, for although he would for a time remain insecure in his abilities, he later recognized that his education in the seminary's rude classrooms equipped him for success. Years later he would describe the experience as "my social as well as my literary center. It was in truth my gateway to the sun."[72]

During his final year at the seminary, the chinch bug had returned in full force, seriously blighting the county's wheat and corn crops. "Not only had the pestiferous mites devoured the grain," Hamlin remembered of the infestation of 1880, "they had filled our stables, granaries, and even our kitchens with their ill-smelling crawling bodies—and now they were coming again in the added billions. By the middle of June they swarmed at the roots of the wheat—innumerable as the sands of the sea. They sapped the growing stalks till the leaves turned yellow. It was as if the field had been scorched, even the edges of the corn showed signs of blight. It was evident that the crop was lost unless some great change took place in the weather, and many men began to offer their land for sale."[73] With crop yields down, the number of farmers patronizing the Grange elevator slackened, and, discouraged, Dick Garland sold out his interest in the elevator as well as his principal farm (retaining his northern tract of eighty acres), and once again cast about for new lands, a place that would offer a fresh start: Dakota Territory.[74]

3

DAKOTA HOMESTEADER, 1881–84

In the 1870s Dakota Territory was still unsettled land. For years, the Yanktonais and other divisions of Sioux had been resisting, with little success, incursions of would-be settlers and government survey parties. By 1865 most of the Yanktonais had been removed to the Standing Rock Reservation, which straddles the border of present-day North and South Dakota, or to the Crow Creek Reservation in South Dakota. One band, however, headed by Magabobdu, or Drifting Goose, chief of the Hunkpati band of Yanktonais, remained in the James River valley, a fertile trough of fifty to seventy miles in width cutting through eastern South Dakota, running north to south for 250 miles. In 1873 General W. H. H. Beadle led a surveying party through the area but was turned back by Drifting Goose's band near present-day Redfield. Three years later, another survey party, this time in the charge of M. T. Wooley, met similar resistance. Not until 1878 did a survey party, this one under the command of Thomas Marshall, complete its mission, surveying the James River valley into southern Brown County. Although they too were menaced by Drifting Goose, Marshall convinced the chief that if the survey was held up Washington would send soldiers.

To remove this last obstacle to white settlement, in July 1879 President Rutherford B. Hayes established a reservation for Drifting Goose's band in three townships about eight miles south of present-day Aberdeen. But when it became apparent that white squatters had already settled in these townships, Hayes revoked his order, on July 13, 1880, and Drifting Goose agreed to remove his band to the Crow Creek Reservation in exchange for additional supplies. Surveys of the townships proceeded rapidly, for until the government of-

40

ficially accepted the survey the land could not legally be opened for settlement.[1] Hamlin would later base an early story—"Drifting Crane"—upon this incident.

Dick Garland apparently learned of this newly opened land from the many broadsides and advertisements boosting Dakota farms that flooded the newspapers. Perhaps he saw a broadside from the Chicago and Northwestern Railroad, then extending its tracks in Dakota, whose headline trumpeted "2,000,000 Farms of Fertile Prairie Lands to be had Free of Cost! In CENTRAL DAKOTA." Small print then explained: "The United States offers as a Gift Two Million Farms to Two Million Families who will occupy and improve them. . . . In the belt is 30 Millions of Acres of the Most Productive Grain Lands in the World." A map showing the location follows, with the railroad's line prominently displayed, and then the text continues: "YOU NEED A FARM! Here is one you can get simply by occupying it." Lest readers miss the point, the broadside advises, "It will be noticed that the Chicago and Northwestern Has Two Lines of Road that run through to these Lands. It is the only Rail Road that reaches them." And to remind the curious that country-building requires all sorts of people, the broadside notes, "Along the Lines in Dakota have been laid out a number of Towns in which are needed the Merchant, Mechanic and Laborer. CENTRAL DAKOTA is now, for the first time, open to settlement." Finally, to allay any worries about inhospitable country, the advertisement concludes cavalierly, "The Indians have been removed and their reservations offered to those who wish to occupy them."[2] In May 1881 Dick Garland embarked on a scouting trip to this newly opened land, intending to claim a homestead. To his experienced eyes, the James River valley seemed rich with promise. The newly melted snows had made the prairie bloom, and the rich clay loam soil was well suited for wheat farming. And the land was flat—so flat, as one geologist has remarked, "that it takes water three weeks to travel the length of the state in the James River."[3]

To encourage settlement in the territories, the U.S. Congress passed a number of laws designed to give away much of the public domain. In 1841 Congress had enacted the Preemption Law, which became the quickest means to enable settlers to own a quarter section, or 160 acres. The law recognized that many settlers were squatting on land prior to its being offered for sale and, in many cases, prior to its being surveyed. The law gave these settlers a preemptive right to acquire title to the land by filing a claim for the land, establishing residence upon it, and making some improvement to it. After six months and within five years, the settler paid $1.25 per acre and owned the land. Partly to encourage Union army enlistments, Congress passed the Homestead Act of 1862, which granted 160 acres to any U.S. citizen over twenty-one who resided on and cultivated the land for five years. An important stipulation excluded former Confederate soldiers, for a settler must never have "borne arms against the Government of the United States or given aid and comfort to its enemies."[4] The Homestead Act's main advantage over a preemption claim was that, aside from filing fees totaling eighteen dollars, settlers paid nothing for their claims. After five years, claimants "proved up" by providing two neighbors who would vouch for the improvements and sign the proof document. They then received a "patent," or deed to the land. And settlers could shortcut the process after six months by paying $1.25 per acre for the land. An important later amendment was to count Union military service toward the five-year cultivation period.

Settlers could also opt to file a "tree claim" as an addition to a homestead claim. Lumber was in short supply on the vast, treeless prairies, and to encourage tree production Congress passed the Timber Culture Act in 1873. The act granted 160 acres to settlers who planted 40 acres of timber (later reduced to 10 acres in an amendment of 1878). Many settlers filed multiple claims to acquire as much land as possible. A settler would first file a preemption claim, acquire title to it by paying two hundred dollars after six months, and then establish a homestead claim and often a tree claim as well; in many cases, particularly for early arrivals, settlers acquired three contiguous quarter sections in this manner.

To enable settlers to reach these newly opened lands—and to encourage commerce—the U.S. government gave away an astonishing one hundred million acres of public land to railroads in the form of land grants to make possible the various transcontinental rail lines. After a series of laws and amendments, the railroads eventually received up to forty miles of public land, twenty on each side in alternating sections, for each mile of track they laid in the states, and "double that width in the territories." Settlers could claim the "alternate sections retained by the government" in eighty-acre segments as either preemption or homestead claims; to help finance their tracks, the railroads then sold their sections at a government-mandated minimum of $2.50 per acre.[5] Naturally, "railroads moved aggressively to sell land to settlers or to speculators for resale, and even those lines without such a windfall promoted settlement to boost their freight business." To maximize their profits, railroads laid out town sites along their rights-of-way, and existing towns "lived or died according to whether the tracks came their way."[6] The railroads vigorously promoted the free land now opened to settlement and touted the conveniences of the new towns, and settlers rushed to claim their piece of the American dream.

At the time of Dick Garland's scouting expedition to Dakota, the Northwestern Railroad and the Milwaukee Railroad were both busily laying tracks through Dakota, with the Milwaukee reaching Aberdeen by July 1881 and the Northwestern arriving in nearby Ordway in October. "The rapidity of the settlement of Dakota is a marvel of the times," gushed Milwaukee Railroad president Alexander Mitchell in his report for 1883.[7] Dick Garland was determined to get in on the expected boom, and when he arrived at what was to become Ordway (founded later that summer of 1881) he promptly laid claim to a half section of land, one quarter (160 acres) as his homestead and an adjoining quarter in the name of his father (Hamlin's grandfather), two and a half miles northwest of Ordway. He also bought a lot in Ordway and filed a preemption claim on unsurveyed land eighteen miles west near the county line.[8] Eventually, he would amass about a thousand acres in landholdings and additional lots in the nearby town of Columbia. In semi-arid country like Dakota, where many acres were required to sustain a profitable wheat crop, it was common practice for settlers to grab as much land as possible. And the land went fast: the first claim was filed on April 23, 1880, and "by the end of the first year of filing, claims were filed for all but two of the townships open at that time."[9]

Meanwhile, Hamlin was busily preparing a speech for his graduation on June 15, 1881. The exodus to Dakota had given him his theme—"Going West"—but, ironically, he seems to have had no intention of following the legions heading there. He was determined that his oration would score a hit and probably overprepared as a result. "My opening paragraph," he remembered, "perplexed my fellows, and naturally, for it was exceedingly florid, filled with phrases like 'the lure of the sunset,' 'the westward urge of men,' and was neither prose nor verse." His initial stage fright dissipated, and "as I attained confidence my emotional chant mounted too high." The ornate writing needed simple expression, but, caught up in the moment, "I ranted deplorably, and though I closed amid fairly generous applause, no flowers were handed up to me." His only commendation came from a friend who observed wryly, "Well, that was an original piece of business!"[10]

His father had returned in time for the graduation festivities, as well as to celebrate his silver wedding anniversary, but then immediately returned, accompanied by eighteen-year-old Franklin, to begin plowing the Dakota sod. Hamlin was left in charge of the family farm and especially with bringing in the all-important harvest. The recent graduate, who had a bad case of postgraduate wanderlust, bitterly resumed his farm duties. "Help was scarce," he remembered, for many of the county's workers had left, tired of crop failures and eager for a new chance in Dakota. "I could not secure even so much as a boy to aid in milking the cows; I was obliged to work double time in order to set up the sheaves of barley which were in danger of mouldering on the wet ground. I worked with a kind of bitter, desperate pleasure, saying, 'This is the last time I shall ever lift a bundle of this accursed stuff.'" But then, in lifting some machinery, he strained his side so badly he was unable to work, which meant his father had to return to bring in the harvest. "For several weeks I hobbled about, bent like a gnome," he recalled, while his mother and sister prepared to move to Dakota.[11]

In September, as his family prepared to leave their fourth Iowa farm, Hamlin said good-bye and headed to Osage, where he would board his first train. Like many other recent graduates, he was filled with ambitious but vague plans. He knew he needed to find a job, but he wasn't sure what he wanted to do. Farming of any sort was out—he had had his fill of it. He had thought to read for the law, but a comment from friend Charles Lohr had stuck in his mind: "Don't do it," Lohr had counseled. "Whatever you do, don't become a lawyer's hack."[12] A devoted admirer of principal Alva Bush, Hamlin decided teaching was a noble profession—and teaching would allow him to indulge his passion for oratory. He had planned to ask Bush for a letter of recommendation, but his principal had died of a stroke only eleven days after graduation. Instead, he approached Edward Rands, the superintendent of Mitchell County public schools, for a letter, which, without the superlatives of later eras, read,

12 SEPT. 1881

To Whom It May Concern:

An intimate acquaintance with the bearer, Mr. H. Garland, permits me to say that he is a man of more than average ability. He possesses qualities which must insure his success as a teacher. Mr. Garland is energetic, persevering and has a rare command of language, which will materially aid him in explanation. These qualities accompanied with a love for the work should commend him to any school board desiring a superior teacher. Above all I know him to be honest and faithful, worthy of the confidence of any whom he may meet.

Very Respectfully,
Ed. M. Rands, Co. Supt.[13]

On the strength of this letter and a parting gift of thirty dollars from his father, Hamlin was confident he would soon find a job—but he seems first to have made a beeline to the home of a girl he calls "Alice" in Ramsey, Minnesota. In his autobiography he downplays the seriousness of his interest, recording only that he "greatly admired" her and that when he arrived he discovered he "was permitting myself an exaggeration of what had been to Alice only a pleasant association, for she greeted me composedly and waited for me to justify my presence."[14] He soon became aware that his affection for her was not returned, and left. But his interest in "Alice" was serious and long-lasting, and this rejection by his first love greatly affected him. His brother's wife remembered in 1950 that Hamlin didn't "talk of certain things that was [*sic*] close to his heart—it was hard to get him to say anything about 'Alice' his boyhood sweetheart—and after he was gone we could never find out her last name—she was a bankers [*sic*] daughter and that is all we could find—he had said very little about her to his wife, but I think he loved this girl very tenderly—and her death affected his life."[15] And in "How Will She Look? (Homeward Bound)," an unpublished poem written just before he returned to Osage for a short visit in 1887, six years after he had left "Alice" behind, Garland poignantly revealed his longing, regret, and hope:

> How will she look to me after long waiting?
> What will she do when she first meets my eyes?
> Will she start—and smile—the curving lips parting?
> Will she reach up to kiss me, or look down with sighs?
> > Now I am nearing her
> > So I am fearing her
> Longing for, fearing the flame of her eyes!
>
> Seven long years since we parted in anger,
> Seven lost years since that stormy good bye—
> O, could I relive them!—could I destroy them!—
> Ah God, the irrevocable years, how they fly!
> > I chide as I ride
> > The engine's slow stride,
> That bears me to Agnes, my sweet-heart, my bride! . . .
>
> Perhaps she is married—a mother—I know not!
> I've come back to see her, to see her again,
> To hold her dear hand while I say "O forgive me!
> A worn weary man with hot restless brain—"
> > I cry as I ride
> > To the engine's stern stride
> "O Agnes, forgive me my anger and pride!"[16]

Garland would never forget his first love, and her avatar would make an appearance in much of his fiction, most clearly in the short story "A Branch Road," which tells of a boy who, in jealous anger, abandons his girl and disappears in the wilds of Arizona. When he returns seven years later, he rescues Agnes and her child from her brutish husband, promising her a more fulfilling life with him.

From Alice's house Hamlin set out to divert his disappointment by finding a job, but he appears to have underestimated the tone of the superintendent's letter of reference, with its lack of superlatives, for in all the Minnesota towns at which he stopped—Faribault, Farmington, Chaska, Granite Falls—there was no job to be had. He was aiming generally for Ordway, for his parents would offer a temporary refuge during unsettled times. The rail line ended in Aberdeen, so he walked the twelve miles to Ordway, for the first time seeing "a landscape without a tree to break its sere expanse." At first the prairie's barrenness appealed to his romantic sentiments, and he would later write that "its lonely unplowed sweep gave me the satisfying sensation of being at last among the men who held the outposts,—sentinels for the marching millions who were approaching from the east. . . . My experienced eyes saw the deep, rich soil, and my youthful imagination looking into the future, supplied the trees and flowers which were to make this land a garden."[17]

In Ordway he found his father busy constructing the new town's first store. Named for the territorial governor, Nehemiah Ordway, the town was competing with other towns to become the territorial capital. And for a time, Ordway seemed destined to emerge as the victor: it was the northern terminal on the Chicago Northwestern Railroad, which meant that settlers traveling to the end of the line got off in Ordway and then set out to claim land. Ordway soon boasted all the accoutrements of a thriving territorial town: "a general store, two hotels, a lumberyard, a lawyer, a physician, and a druggist"—and, later, a blacksmith shop and two grain elevators.[18] In the fall of 1882, however, the railroad extended its lines through Columbia, six miles to the northwest, and Ordway soon lost the economic advantage of being a terminus. Today it is a ghost town.

But when Hamlin arrived in Ordway he found a bustling boomtown, electric with the excitement of profiteering. Speculators were grabbing land and settlers were pouring in—even his grandfather Garland arrived to take up a claim on a quarter section adjoining his son's claim. (His grandmother Garland had died in 1871, and his grandfather had tired of solitary life in Onalaska.) Land claim frauds were everywhere, for speculators recognized that the most desirable land was that which was near a reliable water supply and town conveniences, and settlers would pay for that convenience. Some claims were filed under fictitious names; other settlers, like Dick Garland, filed multiple claims under the names of family members, intending to exercise the buyout option after six months; and still others were rank speculators who filed claims, held them until all the nearby desirable land was claimed, and then "relinquished" their claims to new arrivals—that is, sold their right to the claim before proving up. And since relinquishments could only occur in the local land office, corrupt land agents often steered gullible new arrivals to speculators, who would then sell them a claim at prices ranging from fifty to four hundred dollars—and then the gulled settler was faced with two options: paying the government price of $1.25 per acre after six months of residence, or homesteading on the land for five years before securing title to it. The most common abuses involved preemptive and tree claims. South Dakota historian Herbert S. Schell describes typical fraudulent practices: "A packing box or a chicken coop might be called a house, and a weed patch with a few straggling sprouts would represent a cultivated tree claim. Sworn affidavits from 'witnesses' amounted to wholesale perjury, while lawyers who specialized in land cases availed themselves of every loophole to evade the law."[19] As soon as the six-month minimum "residency" had passed, these speculators paid the cash price of two hundred dollars for the 160-acre claim and then promptly jacked up the price for newcomers who, in many cases, were desperate to obtain desirable land. Even Dick Garland succumbed to the mania: at the height of the boom, in January 1884, he paid the inflated price of $1,200 for a parcel ten miles north of his homestead claim.[20] Abuses of the land grants were so rampant that Congress repealed the Preemption and Timber Culture acts in 1891. Schell concludes that our image of the homesteader patiently working his 160-acre farm for five years is incorrect for Dakota Territory, and he estimates that "The final homestead patents represent only about 15 per cent of the total area originally filed upon," with the remainder of the land having been secured "by direct purchase through the pre-emption law and the commuted homestead."[21]

While Hamlin was impressed with the rosy prospects for prosperity in Dakota, his wanderlust was not yet sated. He stayed only two weeks, working for his father at two dollars a day, shingling the roof of the combined houses, which shared a common wall. Hamlin was always adept at any physical labor. As his brother recalled, "the way that boy could lay shingles was something to see. He would fill his mouth with shingle nails[,] lay a row of Shingles[,] then with a one two tap of the hammer he would keep a continuous stream of nails from his mouth to the shingles til the row was all nailed down. He was always fast at any work that he undertook."[22]

With money in his pocket, Hamlin headed eastward, determined to see the country he had only read about in his schoolbooks, while also keeping an eye out for a teaching job. He first went to Hastings, Minnesota, where he experienced his first Mississippi steamboat ride, to Red Wing; from Red Wing he meandered to Wabasha, and then to Byron to visit one of his mother's cousins, William Harris. But before he reached his cousin's house he found his funds were exhausted and, hungry and in the midst of a rainstorm, resorted to begging a night's lodging from a reluctant farm wife, whom he later realized expected him to pay for the bed. Overcome by shame, he fled into the night, only to realize that, without shelter, he would likely die. He mastered his pride, knocked on a door, and confessed his poverty. In this moment of despair he learned about the power of money and vowed never to be caught without funds again.[23] He went to Onalaska to stay with his aunt Susan Bailey for two months and worked at a number of odd jobs, failing at each: he had no success as a book subscription agent, and as an accountant for a farm implement firm he bitterly chafed under the direction of his seventeen-year-old boss, a "chinless cockerel," a "pinheaded gamin" who ordered him to clean spittoons.[24] By February it was plain that he hadn't the patience to work for others on a steady basis: his seminary education got in the way. He next headed to Madison, where he met Franklin, who was on his way to Valparaiso, Indiana, where he planned to go to the Northern Indiana Normal School. Together the two brothers hatched a scheme that would indulge Hamlin's oratorical ambitions: Hamlin would become a lecturer. Franklin later recalled that they "promoted a little Amusement Company composed of Hamlin as Lecturer and myself as Manager, ticket seller, door keeper and all around flunky. I think we lasted three nights out in the County districts."[25] Hamlin attributed their failure to lack of planning: "We attempted to do that which an older and fully established lecturer would not have ventured. We tried to secure an audience with only two days' advance work, and of course we failed."[26] Ever after, when he came to make much of his living from lecturing, he made sure his lectures were well advertised.

After this adventure, Franklin went on to school while Hamlin halfheartedly looked for work as a teacher, but he was more interested in exploring. He continued in a series of temporary jobs: as a clerk, as a night watchman, and, oddly, as a singer for the Band of Hope, a religious arm of the YMCA carrying the Word to jailbirds. His experience shingling came in handy at his most lucrative position of carpenter, and as the spring of 1882 drew to close he chanced upon a performance of the Shakespearean actor Edwin Booth, whose passionate performance electrified him and gave him a new ambition: to hit the back trail to New England and see Boston and Maine, the latter the state of his father's birth.

When Franklin's term at school was over, they met in Chicago in July with a simple plan: to see Niagara Falls, tour New England, and visit the prosperous cities of Boston, New York, Philadelphia, and Washington. They figured when their money ran out, two strapping farm boys could easily find work, but, brought up on the expansive farms of the West, they miscalculated how much labor eastern farmers would need, and so they had difficulty in finding jobs. They toured on a shoestring budget, never far from hunger and occasionally resorting to sneaking a bed in an accommodating barn.

The cities overwhelmed them, but they marveled at the throngs of people, the pricey restaurants, and the electric lights of New York, the first they had seen. At last they had enough of tramping, and while Franklin returned to Ordway, Hamlin set out to find a teaching job with more earnestness than he had heretofore exhibited. Finally, in October, he found a position as a teacher in a county school in Grundy County, Illinois, at fifty dollars a month. While he admitted he didn't do well teaching mathematics, always his poorest subject, to his pupils, Hamlin thought he "helped them in their reading, writing, and spelling, which after all are more important than algebra."[27] More significantly, he had an opportunity to teach oratory at the Morris Normal and Scientific School in Morris, Illinois. When he left, he gained another letter of recommendation from the principal, Professor Kern:

30 NOV 1882

To Any Board of Education:

It gives me pleasure to testify of Prof. Hamlin Garland who taught in our school for a time, that he is a gentleman of more than ordinary ability, both as a scholar and teacher. He easily commands the good will of his students and by ambitious, thorough work holds a strong interest. I consider him an excellent elocutionist.[28]

His position as schoolteacher enabled Hamlin to realize two things about himself: that he liked public speaking, which gave him an opportunity to indulge his brain rather than his brawn; and that his seminary education had only shown him the way: further study was needed if he was to speak well about matters of substance. But how to further his education on fifty dollars a month?

Then came news that the land boom in Dakota had exploded, and a solution beckoned: he would become a land speculator. He could return to Ordway, preempt a claim near his parents', live with his parents while doing the minimum improvements to meet the letter of the law to prove up—and then sell out.

So many settlers were flocking to Dakota that by June 30, 1883, some twenty-two thousand homestead claims had been filed in Dakota Territory—and no wonder, for land in Wisconsin, Michigan, Minnesota, Illinois, Iowa, and other nearby states was selling for fifteen to twenty dollars per acre.[29] When he arrived in Ordway, Hamlin found the streets crowded with boomers. "All talk was of lots, of land," he remembered. "Hour by hour as the sun sank, prospectors returned to the hotel from their long trips into the unclaimed territory, hungry and tired but jubilant, and as they assembled in my father's store after supper, their boastful talk of 'claims secured' made me forget all my other ambitions. I was as eager to clutch my share of Uncle Sam's bounty as any of them."[30] When Hamlin arrived in Ordway he found that all available land in Brown County had been claimed by more than eight thousand residents, some of whom were selling their claims for five dollars per acre.[31] His father had gotten in early on the boom, and he planned to establish a branch store on his preemption claim in speculation that the railroad would extend its lines in that direction. In talking over his prospects with his father, Hamlin decided to head to neighboring McPherson County, twenty miles west and near where his father had established his preemption claim. There, with Charles Babcock, Burton's brother, he intended to claim three quarter sections—one for each of them and one for Franklin. Hamlin and Franklin would work in the branch store while holding—preempting—their claims. It was necessary to preempt because the land had not yet been surveyed, and they marked their claim boundaries by guesswork—measuring by means of wheel revolutions of their wagon and employing the rudimentary trigonometry from their school days. Because wood was scarce, the custom was to mark claims with a "straddle-bug"—three boards forming a tripod on which one inscribed one's name and date of the claim. Garland's claim—sw¼ of section 32, township 125N, range 67W—was about five miles west of his father's preemption claim and about nine miles south of present-day Leola, South Dakota.[32]

The landscape was like nothing he had ever seen—flat, treeless, empty of all life save short grass prairie and birds, the soil a rich product of glacial sediments. The years 1881 and 1882 had been uncommonly wet, and the accumulated moisture made the prairies bloom. "The prairie was covered with patches of snow and ice," Hamlin wrote, "the streams running bankful of posh and clear water, geese slowly winging their way against the wind, the ducks sitting here and there on the ponds, the sun bright, the wind cold and piercing, as we sped on over the unmarked prairie sod burnt bare as a bone."[33] And Franklin remembered, "When I first roamed those prairies Buffalo Carcasses dotted the plain like hay-cocks in a hay meadow. The ground was so smoothe you could drive anywhere with a Horse and buggy, regardless of roads, and the most invigorating air."[34]

The brothers' first task, to meet the conditions of preemption, was to establish a "residence"—though neither of them planned to do more than stay the obligatory one night per month since they preferred the comforts of their mother's cooking and the conveniences of town life. Hamlin described his shanty as a rude affair of rough pine boards, banked eave high with sod: "The roof was of tarred paper held in place with laths nailed down with shingle nails. . . . On the inside the rough boards were concealed from view by a kind of thick building paper, something of the same nature as the tarred paper but without the tar." The furniture consisted of packing boxes and a stove able to burn either coal or hay, whichever was available.[35]

While his father hired him to clerk in the branch store, five miles east of his claim, Hamlin turned out to be an inefficient storekeeper, for his sympathies lay with the newly arrived settlers who could scarcely afford to part with cash for supplies, and he was reluctant to charge them for the goods. Fortunately for the business, his father had set the prices. "Hamlin couldn't sell gold dollars for ninety cents a piece," his father would remark.[36] Franklin reports that his brother was so bad at business that "I ran the store and did the cooking for the outfit while Hamlin and Charles did the necessary improvements on our claims."[37] Hamlin found he had lots of time on his hands and he began to study, for the excitement of the land rush had not dulled his eagerness to fit himself to become a teacher.

He acquired standard reference works—John Green's *History of the English People* and Robert Chambers's *Cyclopedia of English Literature*—and set to work studying. More important was Hippolyte Taine's *History of English Literature*, which he devoured. Taine applied the methods of science to literature: by examining the circumstance of the composition of a particular work, Taine sought to derive more general laws of literary composition applicable to a national literature. He believed that one could best understand the emotive effect of a literary work and its expression of the "sentiments" of an age only by reconstructing the "causes" that led to its formation. A work of literature is therefore, in Taine's famous phrase, a product of race, environment, and epoch. Taine argued that heredity and physical environment shape the individual and his or her temperament and that these influences vary from people to people. Moreover, the physical distinctions of climate, location, and social customs create a dominant character for a given national literature. The "cold, moist lands" of Germany, for example, create a literature "beset by melancholy or violent sensations, prone to drunkenness and gluttony, bent on a fighting, blood-spilling life."[38] Finally, "historical currents," or "the long dominations of one intellectual pattern"—Taine's example is the Renaissance—also shape the mind and the literature of a people by providing a tradition for new writers to follow.[39] Taine provided Hamlin not only with a method for understanding literature, Donald Pizer observes, but also with a set of criteria by which to judge it. Garland accepted, with Taine, that "The highest function of literature . . . was to inform man about man, to tell the truth about a nation at a particular moment in its history, first of its way of life, but most of all its 'sentiments,' its inner nature and thought."[40] Believing that an indigenous American literature must likewise be a reflection of its land and people, Hamlin began to make meticulous notes about his reading, and especially of books that reflected American life, for in Taine he had found the key principle for what he would later advocate as the "local novel."

The thick building paper on his shanty's wall came in handy, for upon it he outlined his study of Taine. Franklin recalled that "during his leisure hours Hamlin, continuing his literary studies, covered the walls of our quarters with Charts of English Literature, from a way back up to then. He had it in periods, classes, epochs, cycles and what have you. As I look back upon it now it seems like [a] great performance."[41] And Hamlin remembered, "These charts were the wonder and astonishment of my neighbors whenever they chanced to enter the living room, and they appeared especially interested in the names written on the ceiling above my bed." Like Jack London's Martin Eden, he "had put my favorites there so that when I opened my eyes of a morning, I could not help absorbing a knowledge of their dates and works."[42]

His study of Taine also prompted him to try his hand at fiction and poetry, and Hamlin filled his notebooks with observations, many keyed to the harsh conditions he witnessed: "I staid over night in a little town in Dakota the other day. And was invited home to dinner by one of the small dealers, a pleasant jovial fellow. His wife was a remarkable woman. Once grandly beautiful she was still a fine looking woman despite the loss of one eye and the great scar on the temple. Her face while sad and reserved had something winning in its kind and matronly smile. Two attractive children called her mother. I was strangely interested in her face. Reflective and somber though it was a careless happy smile would sometimes light it into almost girlish beauty."[43] Some of these efforts he would read to his brother, and apparently he was so absorbed by his reading that he failed to pay attention to his surroundings. During one visit to his father's homestead house, Franklin explained, Hamlin sat on the doorstep to try out his latest composition:

> During his early writings, he always tried it out on me "as the Dog" he said I was of ordinary intelligence and if it went well with me, the general public would like it, well anyway while listening to his reading I was watching a big black cloud forming in the southwest, and being experienced in such matters I knew what was coming. One could see for many miles across those Dakota plains, and by the time he had finished the story, the storm, a young Cyclone no less, had reached to within a couple of miles of our place hitting a wheat field, and what it did to that wheat was something spectacu-

lar to be hold. I had been watching it carefully, and was sure it was
passing to the South of us, and as he finished I called his attention
to it and we went inside, closed all the doors and windows, and we
weathered it with little damage to our place.

On our way to town the next morning we saw a neighbors House
had been picked up bodily and set down again on its Roof, apparently with little damage. A cute little way with Cyclones.[44]

In early 1884 Hamlin came across Henry George's *Progress and
Poverty*, first published in 1879 and a national best-seller by 1883.
In four hundred carefully reasoned pages in his twenty-cent Lovell
Library edition, George examines a central paradox of American
economic life: Why, in the midst of so much prosperity, at a time
when industry is booming and when markets are expanding, is there
so much poverty? Why is it, he asks, that "where population is dens-
est, wealth greatest, and the machinery of production and exchange
most highly developed—we find the deepest poverty, the sharpest
struggle for existence, and the most of enforced idleness?"[45] After
exhaustive analysis of the economic interaction of land, labor, and
capital, richly developed by analogy and metaphor, George concludes that the cause of poverty is a system in which the products
of labor and capital are taxed more heavily than the land itself. In
a tax structure that levies taxes on the products of labor, the more
a laborer works, the more he produces—and the more his taxes increase. In contrast, the land gains value only because people make
"improvements" to it, yet the landowner pays comparatively little
in taxes for the land itself. As the land becomes more valuable in
proportion to the demand for it, the landowner's rent increases,
yet the landowner has contributed nothing to the goods produced
on the land that made it increase in value. The remedy to the problem of this "unearned increment," George argues, is a single tax on
the land, not the goods. Land would be taxed in proportion to the
average value of the land around it, as distinct from the improvements—buildings, factories, and so forth—on it. There would no
longer be incentive to acquire parcels of land and withhold them
from development: since taxes would be collected on the land itself,

the landowner would take no profit from speculation. With taxes removed, the laborer would be free to work to his utmost capacity and reap all of the benefits of his labor. Land prices artificially inflated by the goods produced on it would also decrease, and ownership of land would be possible for anyone willing to pay the annual tax on it.

As Hamlin read George's visionary rhetoric, his imagination was fired: "Unrestricted individual ownership of the earth I acknowledged to be wrong," he recorded, "and I caught some glimpse of the radiant plenty of George's ideal Commonwealth. The trumpet call of the closing pages filled me with a desire to battle for the right." He had long sought a cause, a great principle, and now he had found one: "Here was a theme for the great orator. Here was opportunity for the most devoted evangel."[46] Yet Hamlin would need to wait for his chance to fulfill his dream of oratorical glory, for he was in the midst of land speculation himself, seemingly unaware that he was currently locked into being part of the problem, not its solution. One has to wonder whether he recognized the irony of his current occupation as land speculator versus George's ringing denouncement of misuse of land that rightfully belonged to all of humanity. He certainly had seen the practical effects of such speculation in Ordway and on the Dakota prairie, where settlers bankrupted themselves to acquire a plot of semi-arid land. And how could he not have been aware of the manifest injustice of Dakota taxes applied to his own case? "Until he secured a patent to his claim," historian Herbert Schell explains, "the homesteader was relieved of any tax except on his improvements and personal property. Moreover, final proof might be deferred until the end of the seventh year." For his 160-acre preemption claim, with an assessed value of $575, Hamlin had paid a tax of $17.13 on the pine board shanty, his "improvements."[47]

During the summer of 1883, temperatures climbed beyond what they had been the previous two years, and signs of drought began to appear. The winter of 1881–82 had been unusually mild, and the early spring had prompted farmers to plant wheat early, producing in the summer of 1882 "a bumper crop of thirty-five to forty-five bushels per acre," which sold for eighty-nine cents per bushel in Aberdeen.[48] But when summer arrived and the rains failed to come, crops began to wither and settlers became discouraged. One settler wrote, "During the early years of settlement, there were a number of dry years. The effect on the newly established settlers can be imagined. Many settlers saw their dreams of owning their own land shattered, and returned to their first homes. Crops suffered also from too many gophers destroying a third of the grain."[49]

With an eye more toward profits than accuracy, boomers had promoted the land as fertile and as perfectly suited for agriculture, the towns as boasting all the conveniences of the East. An account by Elizabeth Perry, who held the quarter section adjoining Garland's claim, is typical: "Before we made the trip west, Maie [her sister] had sent me a newspaper with pictures and an elaborate writeup of the Methodist University at Ordway, Dakota, which gave us an idea of a wonderful institution to be found there. When we arrived in Ordway and looked for the University we found that it did not exist. There was only a hole in the ground and 'great expectations' which never materialized."[50]

The summer's heat furthered Hamlin's resolve to end his speculative ambitions, for the surveyors had not yet come, and he couldn't sell his claim until it had been surveyed and recorded. Later he described the summer of 1883: "The winds were hot and dry and the grass, baked on the stem, had become as inflammable as hay. The birds were silent. The sky, absolutely cloudless, began to scare us with its light. The sun rose through the dusty air, sinister with the flare of horizontal heat. The little gardens on the breaking withered, and many of the women began to complain bitterly of the loneliness, and lack of shade. The tiny cabins were like ovens at mid-day."[51]

And then winter came, which finally and forever stifled whatever pioneer ambition still remained after that brutal summer. "The blizzards were terrible," wrote one early settler. "Men used to string ropes or make fences from the house to the barn so they had something to hang onto to find their way back to the house after making the necessary trip out to feed the stock. The cold which followed these storms was so intense that every one had to dress for protection until the clothing donned was a burden. Frozen noses, ears, and fingers were so common a sight in the schoolroom that it didn't create much diversion when a child came in with a white nose. The teacher would send someone out for a basin of snow and appoint others to hold snow on the frozen places until they thawed out, while she went ahead with the classes."[52] Five years later Hamlin described the onset of a blizzard in "Holding Down a Claim in a Blizzard":

> It was a fearful scene. As far as the eye could penetrate, the stability of the prairie seemed changed to the furious lashings of a foam-white waste of waters. Great waves of snow met, shifted, spread, raced like wolves, joined again, rose, buffeted each other till puffs of fine snow sprang into the air like spray, only to fall and melt in the sliding streams. All was unreal, ghastly. No sky but a formless, impenetrable mass of flying snow; no earth except when a sweeping gust laid bare a long streak of blackened sod that had the effect, the terrifying effect, of a hollow, fathomless trough between the hissing waves, and over all the night and tempest were speeding like the flight of twin eagles.[53]

That terrible winter Hamlin experienced four full-scale blizzards as he trekked to his isolated shanty to meet the terms of his preemption claim. Compounding the screaming wind and driving snow were the subzero temperatures that his thin pine walls could do little to withstand. The scarcity of fuel on the treeless plains caused some settlers to resort to burning buffalo chips for fuel or exchanging bison bones (used in eastern fertilizer plants) for coal, but a more common expedient was simply burning hay—which was in ample supply. As one pioneer explained, "Because they had neither a place to buy fuel nor money with which to buy it, my people burned prairie hay that first winter in their tar papered shack. This was a tall tough stemmed coarse variety of grass and Father built a large stack of it near the door of the house. Evenings were spent twisting and tying handfuls of these stems into hard knots, which were then tamped into a large wash boiler until it was packed tight. The front lids were removed from the little Topsy stove and this boilerful of knots inverted over the opening. It lasted surprisingly well and sup-plied plenty of heat for the room and for cooking."[54]

The winter of 1883–84 marked Hamlin indelibly, and he would describe it in such novels as *A Little Norsk* and *The Moccasin Ranch*. More specifically, the hardship of his experience turned him firmly toward the city. As he explained in *A Son of the Middle Border*, "this experience . . . firmly chilled my enthusiasm for pioneering the plain."[55] But he lacked direction. "What can I do here?" he wrote a seminary classmate. "I am a failure as a trader and cannot resign myself to life on one of these bleak farms. Teaching [in] a country school is the only employment open to me, and there seems to be no immediate chance of that, for, like other preemptors, I am re-quired by law to visit my claim every thirty days. These trips are get-ting more dangerous, more depressing, every month, and yet they must be made."[56]

But then one day, a chance meeting with the Reverend James Whitford Bashford, who was guest preaching in an Ordway cha-pel, turned his sights eastward. Bashford, a Methodist minister from Portland, Maine, was in Dakota speculating in land. Like the Garlands, he was Wisconsin-born and apparently lent a sympathet-ic ear as Hamlin related his discouragement. With his own literary and oratorical ambitions, Hamlin must have been impressed by the young minister's credentials: after graduating from the University of Wisconsin, he went to graduate school at Boston University, where he received degrees from the Theological School in 1876, from the School of Oratory in 1878, and a PhD from the School of All Sciences in 1880. In 1889 he would accept the presidency of Ohio Wesleyan.[57] He advised Hamlin to go to Boston and study litera-ture and oratory at Boston University. While Hamlin was initially intimidated by the idea of living in a big city—his earlier spree with Franklin had convinced him that city dwellers were out to prey upon country folk—upon further reflection he realized that his life in Dakota was at a dead end and he needed to risk the journey. Bashford's offer to write a letter to one of the school's professors confirmed his resolve. Nevertheless, he dallied over the summer, torn between his parents' desire to keep him near and his own ambition to free himself from the frontier. His father, with his own westering ambition that prevented him from recognizing his son's dissatisfaction with farm life, counseled Hamlin to remain. Then, too, Dick counted on him to help with the harvest. More significant would be the effect of his leaving on his mother. Franklin had sold his claim earlier in the summer and fled to Chicago; if Hamlin also left, only fifteen-year-old Jessie would remain for companionship and help. Always closer to his mother than to his father, Hamlin was dismayed by the rough conditions of their frontier home, especially compared to the easier life on their Iowa farm. He bitterly resented his father for having forced her to leave Iowa; he begrudged his work in the field yet he was reluctant to leave his mother, for he saw himself as her protector. He therefore wavered. Finally, he decided: he would sell his claim and go to Boston.

So marked was Hamlin by his Dakota experience that while he would devote his writing to western themes, he never again lived in the "middle border." For the rest of his life he would identify himself as the son of pioneers, as being formed by the westering movement, and as being its legitimate spokesman. He would dedicate the next ten years to exploding eastern misconceptions of midwestern life, and his later work would focus on the Far West. Ironically, while he made his reputation as a midwestern writer, and traded upon it for the rest of his life, for the next fifty-seven years he would live in the nation's four largest cities: Boston, Chicago, New York, Los Angeles.

4

BOSTON MENTORS, 1884–85

On a cold and rainy day in October 1884, Hamlin Garland debarked from a train in Boston's Hoosac Station. In his pockets was $130, all that remained of the $200 he had earned from the sale of his Dakota claim. He had stopped in Chicago to buy a Prince Albert frock coat—his first made-to-order suit, a mid-thigh, double-breasted coat of heavy cloth—figuring the $20 investment in his future worth the extravagance. Travel expenses had consumed $50. He arrived with vague ambitions and large dreams: he considered returning to teaching and wanted more education to fit himself for a position, but he also was interested in exploring Boston, for his father had told him stories of his own youthful days as a teamster. Moreover, Boston was the home of the authors he had read in his McGuffey *Readers* and the occasional book that had come his way—James Russell Lowell, Oliver Wendell Holmes, Thomas Bailey Aldrich, William Dean Howells—and nearby were the homes of Longfellow, Hawthorne, Emerson, and Whittier.

But first he needed to find an inexpensive place to stay, for his earlier eastern tramp had shown him that money doesn't last long in the city. He found a lodging house at No. 12 Boylston Place, on the Boston Common near the public library. By strict economizing, he figured he could stretch his meager funds until May, allocating five dollars per week for room and board, which consisted mostly of coffee, bread, and doughnuts at the cheaper restaurants nearby. His immediate project was to gain admission to one of the universities. He sat in on a few courses at Boston University but found them dull, for the professors seemed "to teach what they had learned in books, and not what they had felt for themselves," Garland told an early interviewer.[1] He presented his letter of introduction from the Reverend Bashford to a literature professor, hoping to enroll as a non-degree-seeking student, but was so offended by the man's patronizing attitude that he stormed out. Next he tried Harvard, but regular tuition was beyond his reach, and Harvard was unwilling to make room for him on a course-by-course basis. It appeared his dream of furthering his education at Boston's leading universities was at an end, so he decided to enter upon an intense program of independent reading at the public library, striving to cram in as much reading as he could before his money ran out.

His reading at the Cedar Valley Seminary had largely been confined to classical texts in rhetoric and the standard British and American authors, and Hamlin had noted the contrast between life as he had experienced it and life as portrayed in fiction. That disparity confirmed his basic rationalist habit of mind, and his reading of Hippolyte Taine and Henry George in his Dakota shanty had awakened him to the writings of evolutionary thinkers. When he entered the Boston Public Library he eagerly sought out the work of those writers whom he had read in snippets in magazines and newspapers. "I read both day and night," he later recalled, "grappling with Darwin, Spencer, Fiske, Helmholtz, Haeckel,—all the mighty masters of evolution whose books I had not hitherto been able to open."[2] He read widely but haphazardly, for he lacked a mentor to help him distinguish the good from the mediocre, but at some point he stumbled upon Herbert Spencer. At the time, Spencer was all the rage among enlightened thinkers, for his application of Darwin's theory of evolution to all realms of human effort promised, as Donald Pizer has observed, to unlock "all the mysteries of the world, revealing their basic harmony and movement toward perfection for an age that was searching for a new faith either to replace or buttress the old."[3] In *First Principles* Spencer had articulated the thesis that was to organize his subsequent books: that simple and unified structures tend to evolve into complex, diverse, specialized, and interdependent units. Just as life evolves from simple cells to more specialized and complex forms, so too do social systems tend toward division of labor and increased complexity of commerce. As political systems develop, they produce more individual freedom, and even established art forms tend to grow into new ones. Spencer equated all evolutionary movement as signs of progress—indeed, he is responsible for the popular equation of "evolution" with "progress"—for in book after book he showed that, inevitably, evolution—in biology, social and political science, even art—is toward the better.

That Garland had the interest and patience to work through Spencer's abstruse language is remarkable, but Theodore Dreiser, Jack London, and other writers similarly record a transcendent moment when Spencer made everything make sense. For Garland, Spencer provided direction to his reading and led him to other evolutionary thinkers. "I became an evolutionist in the fullest sense," he remembered. "With eager haste I sought to compass the 'Synthetic Philosophy.' The universe took on order and harmony as, from my five cent breakfast, I went directly to the consideration of Spencer's theory of the evolution of music or painting or sculpture. It was thrilling, it was joyful to perceive that everything moved from the simple to the complex—how the bow-string became the harp, and the egg the chicken."[4] His immersion in Spencer transformed his outlook on literature, for Hamlin now understood that literature was becoming increasingly complex, and this complexity meant progress—improvement.

His other enthusiasm was oratory. He still held his youthful dream of becoming a great orator—though at what he was still unsure—and he attended a number of free lectures with the aim of picking up points on delivery. At the Young Men's Union he studied Boston's leading preachers, including Unitarian minister Edward Everett Hale, the author of *The Man without a Country*, and Cyrus Bartol, a Unitarian minister and transcendentalist who frequently lectured on Emerson. He was especially fond of Minot Savage, the pastor of Church of the Unity, who was an enthusiastic Spencerian and advocate of social reform and a frequent contributor to magazines; later, Savage would befriend the aspiring author. At other lecture halls Garland heard George William Curtis, the political editor of *Harper's Weekly*, lecture on social reform; he also listened to Henry Ward Beecher, a Presbyterian minister whose lectures on temperance and women's suffrage drew enormous crowds, and Frederic Douglass, perhaps the nation's most prominent speaker on behalf of African Americans. A signal moment in his lecture-going was an appearance by Robert Ingersoll. "I have just returned from hearing this celebrated man on his favorite subject," he recorded on January 18, 1885. "I am disappointed in his style of oratory. He has not the musical voice and graceful manner which I was led to believe he had. He is very funny at times and says many beautiful things but not eloquently." Hamlin had gone to the lecture expecting soaring heights of eloquence, but he left disappointed, "A dead waste of theological cant and dogma."[5] Only later, after more study of some "six or eight" performances, did he understand the reason for Ingersoll's eminence: "he visualized every word, every syllable. He thought each sentence out at the moment he gave it utterance. . . . He did not permit his organs of speech to proceed mechanically"—and Hamlin was impressed that Ingersoll spoke without a manuscript. The lesson would later inform his own lecturing, for Ingersoll "taught me the value of speaking as if thinking out loud."[6]

In November, at Chickering Hall, he saw Mark Twain and George Washington Cable on their "Twins of Genius" tour. He recorded his impressions of Twain in his notebook, taking care to note the details of Twain's delivery and mannerisms:

Twain appears on the stage with a calm face and easy homelike style that puts all at ease. His voice is flexible and with a fine compass. Running to the very fine deep notes easily. He hits off his most delicious things with a raspy, dry, "rosen" [*sic*] voice. He has a habit of coughing drily that adds to his quizzical wit. Passes his hands though his hair and wrings them. Never the ghost of a smile. Is an excellent elocutionist. Sighs deeply at times, with an irresistibly comic effect. His hair is gray and thick, his face a fine one. Wears no beard except a close clipped mustache. Is altogether a man whom you would take for any thing but the funny man he is.[7]

At one of the lectures at the Young Men's Christian Union, Garland heard Moses True Brown, head of the Boston School of

Oratory, lecture on the philosophy and laws of expression. When he went up to compliment the speaker after the lecture, Brown invited him to call on him at the school, a large room on the fourth floor of No. 7 Beacon Street. This meeting proved to have momentous consequences, for in Brown Garland found the mentor he needed, and Brown not only provided direction for his study but also assisted him materially in his ambition to teach.

Brown was born in 1827 in Deerfield, New Hampshire. After graduating from Dartmouth College, he became the principal of high schools in Manchester and New Britain, Connecticut, before becoming the superintendent of public schools in Toledo, Ohio. He married in 1863 and three years later moved to Boston, where he had been offered the new Chair of Oratory at Tufts University. While teaching at Tufts, he also taught elocution in Boston's public schools. His success led him to found the Boston School of Oratory in 1884, shortly before Garland met him. When Garland called on Brown, he discovered that they shared a deep interest in the application of evolutionary theory to oratory. As part of his program of self-education at the public library, Garland had been reading a number of elocution handbooks and treatises on the laws of expression. He had recently finished Darwin's *The Expression of the Emotions in Man and Animals* (1872) and was delighted to find at last someone with whom he could talk, for he had been starved for intellectual companionship. Brown was then in the midst of composing *The Synthetic Philosophy of Expression as Applied to the Arts of Reading, Oratory, and Personation* (1886), a work in which he sought to apply the laws of evolution to human expression and which would, upon its completion, become a basic textbook for the school. He found Garland to be well read in evolution and, more importantly, enthusiastic about his rather arcane project. When he learned that Garland could read French, he offered free tuition at his school in exchange for help with translation and transcription of a number of French articles for use in his book.

Garland's attendance at the Boston School of Oratory during the spring of 1885 and his work on Brown's book were instrumental in shaping his early career, for his study of the laws of expression deeply affected what he noticed at dramatic performances, at lectures, and in his reading; moreover, his early oratorical training influenced his own writing and lecturing. In 1884 and 1885 Boston was enjoying something of an oratorical renaissance. In 1872 Boston University had opened the nation's first School of Oratory, with Lewis B. Monroe as its professor of oratory and Alexander Graham Bell as its professor of vocal physiology and elocution. Upon Monroe's death in 1879 the university demoted his school to a department, and a number of his graduates went on to found private schools of oratory to carry on his legacy. In 1879 Anna Baright opened her School of Elocution and Expression, which later became Curry College; in 1880 Charles W. Emerson founded the Monroe College of Oratory, in honor of his mentor, later changing its name to the Emerson College of Oratory (today's Emerson College). To meet the needs of the students who flocked to Boston to study oratory, dozens of books advancing the latest theories of expression were published. The chief aim of all of these schools, Brown's included, was "the development of character and enrichment of personality." To achieve this end, students studied uplifting literature with periodic declamations; in voice training, students were taught to "free the voice from restricting habits and tension and to develop clear articulation and flexibility in the use of pitch, rate, volume, and quality." Physical training included exercises to "induce freedom and co-ordination" of gesture to "overcome habits which might interfere with the expression of thought and feeling."[8]

Brown rode the crest of this wave of interest in public speaking. At the time, the Delsarte system of oratory was the most popular method of training in public speaking in the United States. From 1839 until 1871, François Delsarte taught vocal music and operatic acting in Paris. Although he never published, never visited America, and did not specifically address the spoken word, he was the most influential theorist of expression in the United States from 1870 until 1900, largely through the efforts of dramatist Steele MacKaye, who had studied with Delsarte in Paris and later became his enthusiastic disciple. The Delsarte system was more philosophy than a system of expression, an attempt to organize arts and sciences along the lines of Catholic doctrine. Delsarte's aim was to establish the laws of art in correspondence to the Holy Trinity; all things in nature, Delsarte argued, had a trinitary organization. For example, man is divided into life, body, and soul, where vocal sound (i.e., tones, not words) expresses life, words express mind, and movement expresses soul. From this basic concept, Delsarte proceeded to organize all human artistic activity, from the mechanism and meaning of the voice, to the relative value of parts of speech, to the significance of gesture.[9] His system soon had enthusiastic converts, among them Lewis B. Monroe, Charles Emerson, and Moses True Brown. In an age that found in Spencer's synthetic philosophy a means to organize and apply Darwin's theory of evolution to all human endeavor, the attraction to Delsarte's system is easy to understand, for it similarly promised to organize all artistic activity according to natural law—one based on trinities rather than evolution.

When he heard MacKaye's lectures, Brown must have been thunderstruck, for here was a system that demonstrated a logical, systematic interconnection of movement and emotion, just what students of elocution and expression needed to succeed. But he was troubled by the emphasis on the Trinity, for Darwin had called into question such thinking. Why not substitute the laws of evolution for the "laws" of the Trinity? And in that idea was born the concept for his book: he would apply the laws of evolution to Delsarte's system of expression and arrive at a "synthetic philosophy" that would demonstrate the inevitable interconnection of mental activity with conscious, artistic expression.

Brown was still in the early stages of writing *The Synthetic Philosophy of Expression* when he engaged Garland's help. Since Delsarte's death, many of his students had published their notes and interpretations of his principles, but most were in French. Garland's task would be to translate these articles for Brown's use. Hamlin was flattered by his professor's confidence in his abilities, and he also saw an opportunity to brush up his rusty knowledge of the language he had struggled to learn at the Cedar Valley Seminary. While he was busy translating, he was also attending classes at the Boston School of Oratory, where he observed the Delsarte method in practice as well as in theory.[10]

The Synthetic Philosophy of Expression is a curious product of the nineteenth-century fascination for wide-ranging syntheses of all kinds, from Spencer's application of evolution to human endeavor, to Henry George's visionary economic analysis of the interconnection of progress and poverty, to the sweeping philosophical syntheses of John Stuart Mill and Karl Marx. Brown appears to have been a voracious reader of the latest works in evolution. Like Garland, he was enamored of Darwin's *The Expression of the Emotions in Man and Animals*, which "came as a draught from a living spring to men thirsting for new truth, and tired of teleological explanations of natural phenomena that did not explain," as he explained in the preface to his own book. He was also an enthusiast of Paolo Mantegazza, an Italian physiologist and Darwinian anthropologist who had attained fame as the first to isolate cocaine from coca leaves. In 1885 Mantegazza published *La physionomie et l'expression des sentiments*, which would not be translated into English (as *Physiognomy and Expression*) until 1890. In that work, parts of which Garland translated for Brown, Mantegazza had charted the expressions of humans around the world. The aim of his own book, Brown explained, would be to synthesize the theories of Darwin, Mantegazza, and Delsarte to arrive at a unified, "synthetic" application "to the conscious art technique by which the reader, actor, or orator enforces his thought and passion."[11] Moreover, he would be the first to apply the laws of evolution and Delsartean techniques to voice and articulate speech.

Like Spencer, Brown begins with "First Principles" before proceeding to show that all expression begins with consciousness of matter and spirit. Through exhaustive and painstaking analysis, he traces the evolution of matter and spirit into increased complexity and specialization as revealed through minute analysis of the correspondence of particular bodily movements to specific emotions. Movement of the elbow, for example, can be classified into three distinct gestures, each having emotive correspondences:

1. The elbow in poise indicates ease, self-possession, calmness, an equable temper, modesty.
2. The elbow eccentric (turned outwards) indicates strength, audacity, arrogance, abruptness.
3. The elbow concentric (turned inwards) indicates impotence, constraint, subordination, weakness, humility.[12]

In such fashion he cataloged every part of the body and its corresponding emotion—feet, legs, torso, arms, hands, fingers, eyebrow, nostril, lip, respiration, and so forth—concluding with a like application to vocal sounds and articulate speech. The result is a rather stilted tome that combines practical instruction in how to use a particular gesture to convey a given mood with a detailed philosophical analysis of the physiology that produces the gesture. Garland's class notes, preserved among his notebooks, reveal that Hamlin paid particular attention to the interconnection between voice and movement. "The voice is a product of gesture," he recorded. "Stress is a correspondence of the energy of the soul," while "Pitch is [the] place[ment] of a tone not musical scale. It is one of the three elements of tone. Note A. Pitch has for its correspondence height and depth in space."[13] The influence of the Delsarte method upon Garland's public readings may be seen in *Authors' Readings*, a volume of sketches of authors reading upon the platform by illustrator Art Young, who sketched "characteristic attitudes" of authors in the midst of their declamations. Garland, who was reading "Uncle Ethan Ripley," appears in a frock coat, book in hand, with arms, hands, and head assuming various dramatic positions as he personified the characters, with each gesture corresponding to a character's particular inflections.[14]

While Garland was going to classes and assisting with Brown's book, he occasionally splurged by attending plays, where he studied the art of dramatic expression. His chief enthusiasm was Edwin Booth, the Shakespearean actor who had electrified him three years before during his eastern jaunt with Franklin. Hamlin's thirty-five-cent ticket entitled him to a standing place on the balcony, and from that perspective he hungrily devoured the tragedian's performance, making detailed notes in his notebook when he returned to his room. At the time Booth was probably the most famous actor in America: prior to the Civil War he had skyrocketed to prominence for his sensitive, brooding performance of Hamlet. He retired from public view for a brief period after his younger brother, John Wilkes Booth, assassinated President Lincoln; when he returned, his performances were even more brooding and subtle. Later, Garland described how Booth's performances fired his ambition: "The art of this 'Prince of Tragedy' was a powerful educational influence along the lines of oratory, poetry and the drama. He expressed to me the soul of English Literature. . . . I said, 'I too, will help to make the dead lines of the great poets speak to the living people of today,' and with new fervor bent to the study of oratory as the handmaid of poetry."[15]

Garland's notes about Booth's performance, which he later developed into a series of lectures, reveal the influence of his work on Brown's *Synthetic Philosophy of Expression*. In one of these, "Edwin Booth as a Master of Expression," Garland compares the more restrained acting of Booth to the melodramatic acting of English tragedian Henry Irving.[16] "There are two great ways of studying a great actor," he begins. "One is to indulge in a great deal of Rhetoric. . . . The other is to seek by scientific reasoning to find the deep laid principles which make the artist great, principles drawn from the widest and best observation which make a science." One of these principles is the connection of emotion and the gesture of the arm. In *Synthetic Philosophy*, Brown had explained that "Gestures sweeping through long arcs, and ending in attitudes that draw the body upward along the vertical line, disclose the Emotive Being manifesting its highest moods or power and strength."[17] In describing Booth's ability to portray "outraged majesty," Garland explains how Booth's action conforms to Brown's principle: "The law is:—When the soul swells to meet a great occasion or rises with some grand conception then the hand as if seeking to uplift the body rises above the head. The whole frame is exalted along a vertical line. It is the most impressive of gestures and is usually but not always accompanied by a resonant voice." Booth also excelled at subtle expressions of emotion. Brown had written about the significance of the eye: "The eye is the center of expression both of the face and of the body. Whatever sensation or emotion stirs the other centres, some single muscle, or groups of muscles in the face, responds, and the eye becomes, as it were, the focal point toward which all the radial lines of feeling converge."[18] From the vantage point of a closer seat, Garland recorded his observation of Booth: "All action begins first and ceases last in the face and eyes, that is in those muscles most in use and nearest the nerve centers. The quiver of a nostril, the lightning flash of an eye does for Mr. Booth that which an inferior artist would put into a shoulder or elbow. He has an army in his eye which he commands. He dominates his subjects by mind not muscle. He is not obliged to move his body melodramatically." Garland's point is that more subtle methods of acting, grounded in psychology and physiology, are more effective means to convey character than are methods that rely upon an audience's familiarity with patterned types. Such quietism in acting, Garland argues, conveys more effectively the dramatist's idea, unlike the melodramatic actor's "shouts and ravings," which are not "true to the unity of the drama."

Booth's acting became for Garland the touchstone by which he measured virtually every play he saw. His many comments about plays in his published reminiscences and in his unpublished notebooks and diaries reveal a consistent pattern: Garland had a demanding and discriminating eye for acting. The content and form of a play, while important, mattered less than the quality of the acting. As he filled his notebooks with outlines of stories and plays, Garland sought to express what he admired in Booth: his ability to suggest the larger idea, the "abstraction," grounded in the evocative power of detail.

But Garland's first published story, "Ten Years Dead" (1885), which he probably wrote before he had absorbed Brown's synthetic philosophy, shows no influence of his reading of evolutionary theory. Rather, the story is influenced by the work of the hero of his seminary years, Hawthorne, and like most writers' early efforts, it is partly autobiographical, though he shifted the scene from Iowa to Illinois.[19] The story opens with the first-person narrator studying at a table in the Chicago Public Library. Across from him sits an apparently middle-age and melancholy man, Gregory. The narrator draws out Gregory's story. Born and raised on an Illinois farm, at age fifteen Gregory goes to a nearby college, working summers for his rather strict father. Upon graduation six years later, he quarrels with his father, who "had little respect for Greek and Latin." His father throws him out. He raises his arm to strike his father, "and then a swift dread blackness fell upon me and my brain melted under a searing heat." Ten years later, Gregory emerges into consciousness, Rip Van Winkle–like, with no memory of the years he had lost. All is changed: his appearance has aged, his mother grown old, his father dead. The most important loss is the girl to whom he was engaged. Clearly influenced by the memory of Hamlin's own lost love of his seminary days, "Agnes" had waited for Gregory for five years before marrying. Gregory is a doomed and shadowed man, mourning for his past and with no hope for the future, "a writhing worm beneath the remorseless heel of fate."

While clearly an apprentice work, "Ten Years Dead" foreshadows motifs that Garland would later develop in many of the stories that established his reputation: the stern, humorless farmer, made unimaginative by his years of labor; the narrator who feels guilt for having abandoned his overworked mother; the lost love, usually named "Agnes" or "Alice," whom the narrator has abandoned through a misunderstanding; and the movement of flight and return—all echoed in such stories as "A Branch Road" and "Up the Coulé" and the novel *Jason Edwards*.

In May 1885, when his meager funds were about gone, Garland told Brown he was planning to leave Boston and return to shingling. Brown offered him a job teaching in the summer term. His name would go in the catalog as "Professor Garland," and he would keep such tuition as he managed to attract. Eventually, he would become the director of the school's department of literature, where his courses on English and American literature served to refine his lectures and ultimately shaped the contents of *Crumbling Idols*.[20] Delighted at the good news, Hamlin wrote home for twenty-five dollars so he could pay his board and dye his suit—its seams were turning purple—and buy some shoes so that he would look more the part of a professor than of an impoverished student.

Shortly before this time, Hamlin had visited the Reverend Bashford in Portland, who gave him a letter of introduction to Dr. Hiram Cross in the Boston suburb of Jamaica Plain. When he got around to calling on Cross, he found they hit it off well—Cross reminded him of his old seminary principal, Alva Bush. Apparently, Cross took a paternal interest in the young Garland and, with his wife and children planning to go away for the summer, invited him to board with him in an attic room at 21 Seaverns Avenue in Jamaica Plain. These two acts of generosity—Brown's offer of a job and Cross's offer of a home—could not have come at a better time, for Garland now had a comfortable place to live with three square meals and the beginning of a profession.

With the prospect of summer school looming, Garland promptly set to work preparing lectures for his classes. His initial assignment was a course in American literature, and he would also offer a "special lecture" on "The Art of Edwin Booth." The neophyte teacher apparently impressed one of the students in his American literature class, Mrs. J. Wentworth Payson, who invited him to offer a series of three lectures at her suburban Hyde Park home in July. Garland promptly set to work drafting the lectures. While at Bashford's home in Portland he had submitted his first book review to the *Portland Transcript*, an impressionistic piece that surveyed Victor Hugo's *Les Misérables*, Jean Paul Richter's *Titan*, and Walter Scott's *Ivanhoe* as expressions of the sentiments of their respective countries, clearly a product of his reading of Taine's attempt to derive general laws of literary production by examining a work as a product of race, environment, and epoch.[21] He quickly set to work expanding his review into the first and third of his lectures, with a reworking of his observations of Booth forming the second, so that his course of lectures comprised "Victor Hugo and His Prose Masterpieces" (July 13), "Edwin Booth as a Master of Expression" (July 20), and "Some German and American Novels" (July 27). Students would pay fifty cents per lecture or a dollar for the whole course.[22]

Meanwhile, Mrs. Payson enlisted her friends to attend the lecture series. Among the audience were Garland's friends Brown and Cross, several professors of oratory, and reporters from the local papers. The *Hyde Park Times* called his Hugo lecture "brilliant, magnetic, masterly"; the *Norfolk County Gazette* praised his "large critical acumen and an ability to rise above a certain pettiness of criticism so often met with" that reveals "hidden sources of power instead of trifling with the obvious and commonplace." His friend Brown offered a sly dig: "Going back to shingling, are you?" while Cross pronounced, "You have no need to fear for the future." Garland afterward counted this lecture series as a signal moment in his career, for he had been "tested as teacher and orator," and his success set into motion additional introductions to the literary lights of Boston.[23]

Bolstered by this triumph at lecturing—and thereby fulfilling part of his dream for oratorical glory—Garland began to expand his lecture subjects, with the aim of extending his lecturing to other venues. Brown was so impressed by Garland's ability to command an audience that he hired him to teach for the next academic year. With Brown acting as his manager, Hamlin sent out his first professional lecture circular to lecture bureaus, schools, and literary societies, announcing a "Lecture Season of 1885–86," with the topic, "Studies in Literature and Expression by Hamlin Garland, Teacher of English Literature, Boston School of Oratory." He retained the first two lectures he had delivered at Mrs. Payson's, revised the third as "The Epic of the Age, the Novel—American and German," and added a fourth, "Poets of the New Eldorado." The four-page circular was filled with testimonials and press notices, with one praising him as "a man of insight, of fine powers both of analysis and generalization, of intellectual fairness, and of unusual clearness and forcefulness of statement," while another simply prophesied, "He is destined to become, in time, one of the prominent thinkers and lecturers in our day."[24]

His ten months in Boston had brought a remarkable change in his fortunes. He had arrived, full of eagerness to further his education, only to be disappointed when college doors remained closed to him. But his ambition and vitality were such that he did what few twenty-four-year-olds—then or now—have been able to do: he educated himself, convinced a stranger to employ him as a professor in a private school, despite his lack of credentials, and then persuaded some of the most eminent citizens in Boston to become his advocate and to pay money to hear what he had to say about literature. As one friend later remarked, "he had a genius for friendship," despite a manner that could often be abrupt.[25] For the next five years he was to support himself primarily through lecturing and teaching at the Boston School of Oratory.

THE EARNEST APPRENTICE, 1886–87

One important consequence of his decision to inaugurate a career as a professional lecturer is that Garland began to study literature even more intensely. In addition to borrowing books from the Boston Public Library, he was an avid reader of newspapers and magazines, from which he gleaned not only the latest discussions about literature but also the hottest literary gossip, for in the 1880s writers were celebrities, and newspapers tracked their movements with a devotion that matches our own fascination with Hollywood personalities. Late in 1885 he began to organize his lectures and notes into a larger scheme that he entitled "The Evolution of American Thought."

The title indicates his debt to Spencer and Taine as Garland developed lectures that he hoped eventually to publish as a book. He would revise and expand the lectures as his reading led him from one book to another—and as he gained experience testing the lectures on his audiences. Although the lectures today exist only in fragments, such titles as "The Colonial Phase," "The Revolutionary Age," "First Age of the Republic," and "The Literature of Democracy" suggest that Garland saw American literature as developing in parallel to political changes, from homogeneity of monarchy to heterogeneity of democracy—a schema that today underlies many college American literature textbooks.[1]

Like other evolutionary critics, Garland saw literature developing according to changes in social conditions—as inevitable "progress" from the simple to the complex, in Spencer's view, as responding to changes in race, environment, and epoch, in Taine's system. His extensive reading in evolution had taught him that everything changes; there are no absolutes in life or in art. Literature, like life itself, was evolving, and if an artist is to reflect the conditions of one's time and place, to express the "truth," he or she must look to the present, not to the past.

When he looked at contemporary literature, Garland therefore found that Whitman and the local colorists were at the head of the writers best expressing contemporary life. In his "Whitman" chapter, he explains that *Leaves of Grass* "is the spirit and prophecy of the modern, the incarnate spirit of democracy." Whitman's poetry embodies "the supreme movement of the age," which "has been the rise of the people, the growth of the average personality and the widening of sympathy."[2] He especially values Whitman's emphasis on the common man and common experience that served to unify Americans. The local-color movement, which included such writers as Bret Harte, Mary Wilkins Freeman, and George Washington Cable, was the other vital element in literature. In a country as large, diverse, and complex as the United States, only writers who attempted to describe particular regions could portray a particular area with accuracy. Garland had arrived at a core principle that was to inform all of his subsequent work: in accordance with natural law, the true artist depicts common life with fidelity to experience.

With the zeal of an eager convert, Garland began to correspond with those writers who best expressed the principles he was advocating in his lectures. Often, he wrote for information for use in his lectures, but he also sought confirmation of his judgments, for he was keenly aware that he lacked an academic pedigree. To his earliest enthusiasm, Edwin Booth, he enclosed "a very scanty and incoherent synopsis of a lecture" and summarized his thesis: "All writers are sooner or later dependent upon an artist of expression, whether they get a complete hearing or not. That is: *voice* and *action* can not be written, they are only indicated, and upon the degree of their expressiveness are the authors ranked." He explained that he intended to apply what he had learned about expression from Darwin, Spencer, and Mantegazza to Booth's performances, "analyzing the voice, cadences, rate, force, etc." And then he concluded, "if you are interested, I should be pleased to put into your hand sketches of my work and methods of study."[3]

Garland was nothing if not intrepid: here he was, at age twenty-five, presuming to critique the performance of America's greatest tragedian—and then sending the critique to the actor for comment. Small wonder that, as soon as he mailed the letter, he had second thoughts about the wisdom of his action. He was relieved when he received a cordial reply in which Booth expressed his gratitude for Garland's "mention of those seldom noticed effects of tone, eye and gesture." He was encouraged, too, Booth noted, "to know that such delicate lights and shades are appreciated and not wasted, as I often feared they were, than in loudest applause bestowed on the balder effects of one's art work."[4]

Emboldened by Booth's positive response, Garland soon began to send letters to other writers as he developed his lectures. To E. W. Howe, editor of the Atchison, Kansas, *Daily Globe* and author of the pioneering realistic novel *The Story of a Country Town* (1883), he wrote to introduce himself and ask for some biographical material. "I like your stories," he announced. "Your strong true delineation, of the monotonous and provincial life of the rural west compels my admiration, though it grieves me to think how unavoidable the most of its life is." And then, comparing his own experience on an Iowa farm to that depicted in Howe's novel, he added, "Has it not seemed to you a terrible waste of talent many times, when you have met men and women of fine powers, musical maybe, who were hedged by circumstances, walking a dull routine of petty duties, compelled to forget the outside world?" Garland's study of local-color writing had led him to conclude that few writers had been able to depict the reality of the life he himself had experienced on the Iowa prairie. But Howe was an exception. "You speak of these people not as one who coldly looks on them as 'picturesque' but in an earnest sincere tone *as from among them*," he continued. "Your work has an *indigenous* quality which appeals to me very strongly." Garland then explained he was at work on a chapter of "The Evolution of American Thought" in which he was describing "'local, scene and character painting'; in which you stand in solitary grandeur, in the midst of the great west"—but then he confessed his ambition: "myself your only rival, not having published yet."[5]

For Garland, writing to authors became an important means to clarify his thinking. In his letter to Howe, he first expressed a central tenet of local color that he would later flesh out more completely in *Crumbling Idols*: "Local color in a novel means that it has such quality of texture and back-ground that it could not have been written in any other place or by any one else than a native."[6] In his response Howe outlined his rural experience in Indiana and Missouri before admitting, "in confidence," that "I myself am the original of all the characters in the three books—at least, sometimes I fear that I am. I am so much like many of them."[7] Emboldened by Howe's response, and encouraged by Howe's example that one's own experience can become the material of fiction, Garland pressed on. "Dear Sir," he replied to Howe, "I have pondered much upon the singular life which you outlined to me in your letter and am more than ever convinced that the author of the 'Country Town' is the strongest writer the west owns—and more than that: from him is yet to come work greater than the *best* of anything he has now written." And then, revealing the fervor that would come to dominate his career, he brashly advised Howe to give up his job and devote himself to literature: "I want to see you enthrone that office cat in that editorial chair while you sit down to write that 'best book.' . . . I do not presume to offer advice," he concluded with all the naïveté of a man without a family to support, "but it does seem as though you could risk the relinquishment of that editorial chair."[8] Garland should have paid attention to Howe's response, for it sounded a warning that Garland was to discover for himself: local color seldom paid. After admitting he would like to write full-time, Howe told him, he could not do so because "My receipts from 'The Story of a Country Town' have amounted to something like $1,200 up to the present time, and yet it has had an unusual amount of newspaper booming."[9]

Despite his success at lecturing and the widening of his literary contacts, Garland was still pretty much on his own, with few close friends, partly due to his outsider status as a midwesterner but more because of his own standoffishness. As he realized much later, "I was an intellectual aristocrat," without much of a sense of humor and prone to serious conversation that must have rebuffed many.[10] Later he would grow more gregarious, more at ease in casual conversation, but during his earliest Boston years he was haunted with loneliness that he sought to subsume in study.

A summer visit from his old seminary chum Burton Babcock relieved his isolation. Like Garland, Babcock had tired of midwestern life, and he journeyed to Boston to enroll in the Harvard Divinity School to study for the ministry; like Garland, he too met with disappointment. The two Harvard rejects roamed the city for a week before Babcock returned home, seeing the sights and reminiscing about Osage friends who, like Garland and Babcock, had dispersed away from the farm.

Then a letter from Garland's father arrived with bad news: lack of rain in Dakota Territory had led to crop failures, and he was compelled to sell the store, return to the farm, and attempt to regroup. Franklin was planning to escape to Montana. The news aroused all the guilt lying dormant since his seminary days, for Hamlin was keenly aware of the sacrifices his family, particularly Franklin, had made to send him to school while Franklin assumed his place harnessed to the plow. As Hamlin later recollected, "I acknowledged once again that my education had in a sense been bought at his [Franklin's] expense."[11] With Franklin's departure into the unknown, his own family would fragment, leaving his mother isolated with only Jessie, now seventeen, to act as buffer to his father's stern resolve.

Although not in a position to send money, Garland believed his mother would rest easier if her sons were together. Accordingly, he called on a distant cousin, who owned a clothing store, and arranged for a job for Franklin. In October 1886 Franklin stepped from the train, wearied by the five-day journey, "so green," Franklin recalled, "that the Cows nibbled at me as I walked across the Common."[12] His arrival provided welcome relief from library tedium. The two brothers romped through the city, taking in the sights, with Hamlin playing tour guide. "Hamlin and I were together as much as we could be," his brother reminisced, "going to the beaches in the summer, and to Theatres and Symphony concerts, and during the Grand Opera season Each Saturday Night would find us each with his two bits clasped tightly in his right fist, waiting at the Gallery door for it to open when we made the mad rush up two or three hundred steps to the top gallery where we would sit and drink in That Glorious Music."[13]

While he was teasing out the threads of his thinking in letters to writers, Garland also began to review books for the *Boston Evening Transcript*. He had met Charles E. Hurd, the paper's literary editor, at Mrs. Payson's Hyde Park home in 1885. He soon made it his practice to call upon Hurd at his *Transcript* office, for he was starved for discussion about books—and Hurd seems to have found Garland to be a congenial conversationalist. Hurd introduced Garland to the works of Ibsen and other Scandinavian writers, and he often let Garland pick over the books that flooded his office. One day, eyeing the pile of books, Garland said, "I'll review some of those books for you—if you'd like me to."[14] Though it was unpaid work, publication gave him another outlet through which to try out his ideas—and practice expressing them in print rather than lecture.

Soon afterward, in preparing one of his lectures about the local novel, Garland chanced upon a copy of William Dean Howells's *The Undiscovered Country*. He had first encountered the novel in 1881 when he bought a secondhand copy from a post office clerk who mistook the novel for a travel book. A half hour's reading impressed him with the "grace and precision" of its style—but apparently not enough to finish the book, for, as he later recalled, Howells's style "made some of my literary heroes seem either crude or stilted" and aroused "resentment." As he noted wryly, "I was just young enough and conservative enough to be irritated and repelled by the modernity of William Dean Howells."[15] But this time he finished the novel and liked it enough to read another—*The Minister's Charge*—and then review it for the *Transcript* in January 1887. He commended Howells's treatment of character and situation, apparently somewhat to his surprise, for heretofore in his lectures Howells had not been a very bright light. His enthusiastic response to Howells's unconventional conclusion, in which Lemuel Barker achieves neither the success nor the marriage he had desired, reveals he had become a convert to the Howells camp:

To those who like to have all the villains killed and the honest men rewarded, the heroines all married to their respective lovers, and everything comfortably arranged in the last chapter, his ending of the "Minister's Charge" is aggravating, to put it mildly. . . . Art that can be verified is in the ascendancy, with heroes that are actual and heroines that are real. The time will yet come, if it has not already, when the public will recognize Mr. Howells as a public benefactor for replacing morbid, unnatural and hysterical fiction with pure, wholesome and natural studies of real life.[16]

The effect of this review, Garland later recounted, was far-reaching. The editor of the *Transcript*, Edward Clement, liked the review and called him into his office. "Was he about to offer me an editorial chair?" Garland hoped.

"That was an able article," Clement told him, "and I have sent a proof of it to Howells. You should know him personally." Clement offered to write a letter of introduction but warned the eager critic to wait until the smoke from the latest skirmish in the realist war had died down before acting upon it. In early 1886 Howells, the former editor of the *Atlantic Monthly* and one of America's foremost novelists, began to write the "Editor's Study" column of *Harper's Monthly Magazine*, from which he began a six-year stint as a literary career maker and breaker as he promoted the writers who agreed with his vision. The magazines were then embroiled in a debate over the virtues of realism, and if Garland were to meet Howells now, Clement cautioned, "his enemies would say that you had come under his magnetic influence."[17] Clement was prescient, for Garland would always be dogged by dismissive claims that he was little more than a Howells imitator.

But when Garland presented himself, letter in hand, to America's most influential writer in the parlor of Lee's Hotel in Auburndale, Massachusetts, on a spring day in 1887, he paid little heed to Clement's advice, for he was eager to meet America's foremost man of letters. Though initially intimidated by the novelist's fame, he wanted to try out on him his latest theories concerning realism. He described, apparently in some detail, his manuscript of

"The Evolution of American Thought." "In my judgment," he told Howells, "the men and women of the South and West and East are working, without knowing it, in accordance with a great principle which is this: American literature, in order to be great, must be national, and in order to be national must be spontaneous and deal with the conditions peculiar to our own land and climate. Every sincere writer must write of the life which he knows best and for which he cares most." Howells's response to the earnest tyro's declaiming was both supportive and flattering to a tender ego: "'You are doing a fine and valuable work,' he said, and I thought he meant it. 'Each of us has had some perception of this movement, but no one so far as I know has up to this time correlated it as definitely as you have done. I hope you will go on and finish and publish your book.'" Garland left this meeting exalted and eager to press onward with his ambition: "My apprenticeship seemed over," he later remembered. "To America's chief literary man I was also a writer, a literary historian, and with this recognition the current of my ambition changed. I began to hope that I too might some day become a novelist and put some part of the Middle West into fiction."[18]

Garland's recollection, coming thirty years after their initial meeting, might be suspected of egotism and fame seeking. But Howells similarly records being impressed with young Garland in a letter to Whitelaw Reid, the editor of the *New York Tribune*, written soon after their meeting: "A Mr. Hamlin Garland has called upon me, and has greatly interested and impressed me by his view of literature. He tells me that he has offered you a paper, and the present business is to bespeak your attention, not favor."[19] And thus began a thirty-year friendship, the most important one Garland was to form during his Boston years.

What accounted for that friendship? On Garland's part, he was no doubt in awe of Howells's achievement, flattered that this national leader of American letters deigned to converse with him, and grateful for his generosity of spirit aided by a penetrating intellect. He was also struck by Howells's humility, for few men of his stature could resist the pomp that attends celebrity: "He was always of a quiet, unassailable dignity and yet was unassuming, almost shy.

. . . He pretended to nothing," he later recorded in some lecture notes.[20] The fifty-four-year-old Howells later described his initial impression of the twenty-six-year-old Garland: "I suppose we were friends in the beginning, and never foes, because he had strong convictions too, and they were flatteringly like mine. . . . [T]here was nothing but common ground between us, and our convictions played over it as freely and affectionately as if they had been fancies."[21] He probably also respected Garland's energy and ambition, his enthusiastic and sincere efforts to promote a version of realism near to his heart. Perhaps he sought a protégé, for Garland clearly needed the guidance of an experienced writer to shape and focus his many enthusiasms.[22]

Howells's flattering attention nourished Garland's ambition to write, although preparing lectures consumed most of his time. With his deep fascination with Booth and his preparation in oratory, it was only natural that his first serious efforts at writing were in plays. Garland was particularly attracted to realistic and local-color dramas that exploited the details of regional American life, as suggested by a number of programs for popular dramas that he pasted in his 1886–87 notebook.

When Garland wrote "Love or the Law," his first completed creative work after the Hawthornesque short story "Ten Years Dead," he modeled it after the local-color melodramas he had been seeing in Boston and sought to embody in it the principles he had derived from Booth, Taine, and Moses T. Brown.[23] Subtitled "A Modern Play" and dated by Garland "Boston, Mar. 1887," "Love or the Law" is an early indication of the themes and methods Garland would later develop in his fiction. Although only the prologue and act 1 are extant, enough remains to suggest that melodrama, not realism, ruled his imagination, for the young writer was still exploring his many interests. The prologue begins with Hermann Lytle, a patent medicine "Doctor," viciously abusing his new wife, the former Ellen Loring. Because Ellen is young and pretty and sings well, Lytle has married her to entertain his customers with song while he manipulates them into buying his patent medicine, "The King of Pain." As Lytle tells Ellen, "That face and voice of your's [sic] are worth from fifty to a hundred dollars a day to me, on a day like this." Garland depicts Ellen as an unhappy wife exploited by her husband; as shill for a con man, Ellen is vulnerable to the rougher elements of frontier society. When Bill Green, Lytle's assistant, encounters Ellen weeping over her misfortune, he attempts to seduce her, only to be repulsed in typical melodramatic fashion:

ELLEN [*Comprehends now and springs up with a face of utter loathing mixed with surprise. She looks at him with out speaking till he begins to shake in fear.*] "If my husband knew of this he'd break every bone in your miserable body. I thought you a fool, a good natured creature but you are also a little villain. U-Ugh!" [*Shudders in disgust and turns away.*]

At this stage in his apprenticeship, Garland had few realistic models after which to pattern his own efforts. His principal concern was with learning how to avoid conventional plots; he had not yet figured out how to depict character or speech that accurately reflected his own experience, and the characters and language of the play reflect the melodramas familiar to him. Hermann Lytle is the dastardly villain; Bill Green the villainous opportunist; Ellen Loring the pure and innocent heroine; Rance Knapp the hero out to protect the heroine's virtue. The language of the principals is rendered almost entirely in the heightened rhetoric of melodrama. Only in the mouths of the rural folk does Garland achieve any verisimilitude; occasionally the depiction works, but mostly the dialogue seems strained. The plotting in the prologue is unified, but Garland loses the narrative thread in act 1.

What makes this apprenticeship work interesting is Garland's effort to apply his interpretation of Booth's acting to his characters. Much of "Edwin Booth as a Master of Expression" attempts to provide a physiological explanation of Booth's ability to convey changes of mood through facial gesture and through tonal variations in his speech. "Love or the Law" reflects this analysis through interpretive cues in the stage directions and occasionally through dialogue, although Garland has not yet discovered how to embody his analysis in dramatic action. For example, Ellen replies to Bill's suggestion that she run away from Lytle "*in a despondent tone which shows she had begun to think of it*"; Bill in turn responds to her "*in [a] confidential tone.*" When Rance explains why Ellen's face haunts him, he remarks, "There are lines on her face which tell she is a woman with a story, and the drooping lines of her beautiful mouth, show that it is a sad history. . . . She hardly said a word tonight and yet—yet she said much, by her gestures and the wonderful lines of her flower-like face." In his initial effort to write a local-color drama, Garland therefore combined his observations of Booth, his reading of evolutionary theories of expression, and his belief, derived from Taine, that literature should reflect and express the "sentiments" of its age.

"Love or the Law" suggests several patterns that Garland would later learn to depict more realistically: a male father figure (modeled on his own father) who exploits the heroine as a form of cheap labor; a heroine who is brutalized by marriage; and a hero who rescues the heroine from her exploitation. In "Love or the Law" Rance Knapp seeks to defend Ellen's honor from the crowd's slander; later, in *Main-Travelled Roads*, Garland would develop the pattern more masterfully. In "A Branch Road," Will Hannan returns to restore the woman he abandoned to her rightful place as a worshipped and protected icon. Will promises Agnes all the accoutrements of womanhood: she "can have a piano and books, and go to the theatre and concerts."[24] In "Among the Corn Rows" Julia Peterson trudges dejectedly in the cornfields, verbally whipped whenever she pauses in her exhaustion, prevented by her father's miserliness from enjoying the normal carefree life of youth. As she is dreaming that "Some one would come to release her from [the] drudgery" of field work, Rob Rodemaker fortuitously enters, promising her nothing more than housework—not the hard labor of a field hand—if she'll marry him.[25]

While he was at work on "Love or the Law" and teaching and lecturing, Garland continued to review books for the *Transcript*. In May 1887 he reviewed Joseph Kirkland's *Zury, the Meanest Man in Spring County*. He delighted in Kirkland's close study of the details of Illinois country life, his lack of sentimentality and freedom from convention, and concluded boldly, "To say that Joseph Kirkland has written the most realistic novel of American interior society is to state the simple fact."[26] Garland's review prompted a letter from Kirkland that praised the review as the one "that went straight to my heart." Then Kirkland asked, "How *could* you, an Eastern man, enter so completely into my views, aims, principles?"[27] Once Garland straightened Kirkland out about their common connection as sons of the middle border, a lively and important correspondence ensued. Kirkland, the son of the novelist Caroline Kirkland, was a successful Chicago lawyer. Coincidentally the same age as Garland's father, Kirkland would soon become the friendly, encouraging mentor Hamlin badly needed to shape his writerly ambitions into a productive direction.

Meanwhile, guilt at the three-year separation from his mother prompted Garland to plan a visit to Ordway, with a stop in Osage along the way to visit old friends. He planned to call on Kirkland in Chicago, for their correspondence revealed much common ground concerning the direction of American literature. One of their epistolary discussions involved how best to depict midwestern dialect. As his own efforts with "Love or the Law" had revealed to him, although he knew how midwestern speech sounded, he hadn't himself learned how to put it on the page. In spite of his own inadequacy, he nevertheless critiqued Kirkland's performance. Kirkland responded, "I recognize the justice of your criticism of my dialect; *but*—if this lingo—now spoken by some ten millions of people—is to be crystallized; it must be done by taking the average and *sticking to it.* It is a composite photograph, establishing a type." He went on to illustrate how to depict dialect by contrasting the poor performance of another writer with his own practice: "'this here' he renders 'this h'yuh,' instead of 'this h'yer' as I put it."[28]

Garland arrived in Chicago on July 2 and spent a congenial day and a half with the elder writer. They devoted much of their conversation to how best to write literature that reflected the current moment. In the midst of reading some of Garland's descriptive writing concerning the prairies, Kirkland looked up and asked, "Why don't you write fiction?"

"I can't manage the dialogue," Garland replied.

"Nonsense," he rejoined. "You're lazy, that's all. You use the narrative form because it's easier. Buckle to it—you can write stories as well as I can—but you must sweat!"[29]

Kirkland's rebuke opened Garland's eyes to the reason for his failure at dialect: while not exactly lazy—his voluminous notebooks bear witness to his industry—Garland had not heretofore approached dialogue with the same care and attention with which he had studied, say, evolution, or Taine. If he was going to succeed as a writer, he decided, he would henceforth need to direct his attention to learning the craft.

After leaving Kirkland, Garland went to Osage, and the journal he kept during his visit demonstrates the energy and care with which he applied Kirkland's lesson. He arrived in Osage on the Fourth of July, made incognito by his full beard. Notebook in hand, he stood unrecognized on street corners and in a hotel lobby, dutifully recording his observations. "I noticed many mistakes of grammar, but comparatively little dialect, properly speaking," he recorded in his notebook. "They said, 'I hadn't nothing,' and other such blunders. . . . I was keenly alive for the first time to their peculiarities." He compared eastern pronunciation to that of Iowans. "Uncle Billy Frazer, for example used the New Jersey dialect couw and nouw, etc. . . . He was full of the old kinds of curious phrases like, chingling. He said, 'The buggy wheel went chingling along the road.' Used the expression 'Bug out his eyes.'"[30] He filled page after page with similar observations, eavesdropping on Scots, Norwegians, and other groups to distinguish their manner of speech. When he left Osage three days later, he had learned how to use speech to distinguish characters.

His three years in Boston had refined his sensibility and magnified the differences between himself and his boyhood companions, and as Garland examined the lives of his former neighbors he was appalled by their insensitivity to the squalor of their surroundings. "The town seemed smaller, lonelier and more squalid," he recorded of his arrival that morning. And things got off to a bad start. He "went to the best hotel in town for my breakfast. It was a terrible breakfast." He took in the Fourth of July festivities and noted, "It was pitiful to see these people crowd to watch a miserable farce like this street parade. It was a revolution of the frightful monotony of the every day lives." He noted the poor clothes, the lack of keeping up with fashion. By noon his snobbery was in full flower, and he was relieved to talk with one of his former teachers, "a fine, strong, intelligent woman. She, among all the women I had met, had kept pace with me intellectually. I felt in speaking with her as though I were talking to one of my friends in Boston or Chicago."

The next day, he stayed with the family of William Frazer, one of his former neighbors, and his disillusionment deepened, for he was struck as never before by the crudity of farm life. At dinner that night, "the boys smelled of the stable and the whole scene was depressing and irritating," he recorded. "The mother scolded her boys harsh and petulant. Frazer shouted at the quarreling children with sudden rage. Manners were exceedingly rude and primitive." For page after page Garland poured out his disenchantment, describing in minute detail the meanness of living conditions, the effect on the people, making note after note with an eye for the telling detail: "The girl was fat, slatternly, and sloppy. She wore a mustache on her lip." Yet he was also aware of the striking contrast presented by a bountiful nature. In the evening, sitting in a pasture, he listened to the night sounds:

> Flies hummed all round, and the notes of a humming-bird far away; a robin chirped, and king birds and sparrows in the windbrake kept up a cheerful chatter. A blackbird broke forth at times into that unctuous wuree. The sounds from the farm yard completed the symphony. For a moment it made me forget the barrenness and monotony of this life. "How sweet it is to live in such peace," I said. . . .
>
> In that moment I became the boy of the past, and for a moment all that I was or had attained in the East was forgotten. I had the impulse to let all things else go by. "Here is all that is best and most lasting in life," I said.

These two motifs—the squalor of the midwestern farm set amid a contrasting scene of natural beauty—would dominate his writing for the next seven years. In Osage, he had discovered his material.

That discovery would be confirmed by his experiences on his parents' farm in Dakota. When he arrived at the train depot in Ordway, his father met him. All the resentment pushed back by three years' separation came to the fore. "In an instant I was back precisely where I had been when I left the farm," Garland would later write. "He was Captain, I was a corporal in the rear ranks." When he arrived at the family farm, he was overcome by the alteration in his mother's appearance. "The changes in her shocked me, filled me with a sense of guilt. Hesitation was in her speech. Her voice once so glowing and jocund, was tremulous, and her brown hair, once so abundant, was thin and gray."[31] Jessie, now a girl of eighteen, peered shyly at him, for her elder brother was almost a stranger and looked fierce behind his full beard. With guilt over his mother's decline pulling at him, combined with resentment of his father for subjecting his beloved mother to the privations of the Dakota farm, Garland resolved to remain for the summer. His presence would delight his mother, and his labor in the fields would help put the family on its feet. Nonetheless, he demanded—and got—full wages from his father.

With his mind filled with ambition for literary success, Garland took note of everything around him, with an eye for its use as literary material. Harvest time in the fields? Material for "Wheat Harvest," a lengthy descriptive article surveying various harvesting techniques in Wisconsin, Iowa, and Dakota, submitted on July 26 and syndicated in newspapers on July 31. Poems soon flowed from his pen: "Prairie Memories," "Beneath the Pines," "My Cabin"—these and many others composed that summer and published in the fall.[32] Ideas for stories filled his notebooks. In Boston he had roughly sketched out a story based on his homesteading experiences but had abandoned it for lack of inspiration. With the Dakota prairies firing his imagination, he returned to it and soon found he had a novel under way, "The Rise of Boomtown," in which he tells the story of the development of a typical western town.

He wrote to Kirkland to describe the flood of material he was producing. "I do not like your title 'Boomtown. *A Social Study,*'" Kirkland replied. "Our fiction *is* a social study, but we must conceal the study part. You might as well call it *an essay*, and so damn it at once. And if as I fear, your *study* of the subject is perceptible in your *treatment* of it, you must write it all over again to eliminate self and make your characters seem to act and talk with perfect spontaneity." Although they had known each other for only two months, Kirkland knew Garland well enough to recognize the strain of didacticism, no doubt reinforced by his lecturing, that he would never entirely succeed in eliminating. "The 'Art to conceal art' is the one indisputable thing in realism," Kirkland counseled. "Of course you have to throw light on your theme, but you must fool the reader with the idea that the light shines from within it, outward."[33] Garland returned to his manuscript with Kirkland's advice firmly in mind.

His return to Osage and Ordway became the culminating factor of his apprenticeship. He had learned that he could hold a crowd while speaking, and he had boundless energy and a far-reaching ambition to write. He knew he could construct plots, and Kirkland had pointed the way to how to handle dialogue. His observations at Osage and Ordway gave him his material: henceforth he would devote himself to depicting the truth of midwestern farm life as he himself had experienced it. "Obscurely forming in my mind were two great literary concepts," he would later write, "that truth was a higher quality than beauty, and that to spread the reign of justice should everywhere be the design and intent of the artist."[34] His immediate task was to learn what form—essay, poem, drama, story—would best express his ambition.

6

SINGLE-TAX REALIST, 1888

In September 1877 Garland returned to Boston and to his teaching, determined to introduce into his lectures his new vision of local color inspired by his western visit. At this point in his career he had not settled on a genre: he filled his notebooks with sketches, aborted stories, poems, fragments of plays, and autobiographical writing, exploring form as he sought a means to express his imagination. During the fall of 1887 a number of events occurred that would further his education and point him toward his calling.

In October Garland stopped by the *Transcript* offices, where Charles Hurd handed him a copy of James Whitcomb Riley's *The Old Swimmin'-Hole and 'Leven More Poems*, published in 1883. He was struck by Riley's unconventional subjects and dialect verse and "rejoiced in such phrases as 'the husky, rusty russel of the tossels of the corn,' and 'the moon a-hangin' o'er us like a yaller-colored slice,'" for he saw in Riley a kindred spirit attempting to render the truth of rural experience.[1] He promptly wrote to Riley to praise the poems and ask about more recent work. "The old feller is jes' plum' tickled to have his work appreciated for the reason of its fidelity and homely truthfulness to Nature," the Hoosier poet replied, and then promised to send him a copy of his forthcoming book, *Afterwhiles*, due out in December.[2]

When Garland received *Afterwhiles*, he promptly informed Riley that he was writing a "special article" for the *Transcript* and went on to praise the book as being "so genuine, so faithful to the lives and loves of the humble folk," for "it tells aloud what many humble folk think but can not put into words."[3] Riley's poems served an important function for Garland's own writing: they reminded him that readers, especially people of his own background, respond best to writing that addresses their lives in language they themselves use. As he remarked in his review of the book, after praising "When the Frost Is on the Punkin" in particular for being "plain, concrete and tangible": "I have read this poem and other of Mr. Riley's selections to men who never read any poetry and couldn't, for most poets had no connection with their lives and meant nothing to them, yet they felt as though their most silent emotions had been expressed by this little book of dialect poems."[4] With this exchange, Garland began a friendship with the Hoosier poet that would last until Riley's death in 1916.

That fall Garland began to write to other local-color writers with questions about their goals and practices. Part of his reason for doing so was to develop his lecture on "Local Novelists," but he was also seeking confirmation of his own judgment about the direction of the local-color movement, for at the time the movement had scarcely begun, and Garland would soon emerge as one of its leading theorists. He asked Mary Wilkins (who would add "Freeman" upon her marriage in 1902) about her purpose in depicting New England life. "You ask me whether I am trying to depict characters and incidents of the present time or of any particular region," she replied, "or whether I wish to deal with the past New England life." She explained that she hadn't thought about her broad goal before, "but I suppose I should as soon write about one time and one class of people as another, provided they appealed to my artistic sense, and I knew enough about them." About whether "the idea of being true" guided her writing, Wilkins noted that "making my characters *true* and having them say and do just the things they *would* say and do . . . is the only aim in literature of which I have been really conscious."[5]

To Kirkland he wrote to describe the poems he had written based on his Dakota trip, forthcoming reviews in the *Transcript*, and other work in progress. "I observe your literary industry," Kirkland replied on November 13. "While I am toiling over a chapter you rattle off a volume. You write—I rewrite." But he also thought his protégé wrote too quickly, for he had already observed that Garland's rush to get into print allowed little time for reflection and revision. "I envy you your facility," he remarked. And then, as if to illustrate by contrast, he noted, "Rarely does a chapter quite suit me or quite fit its place when I revise the whole work as I am continually doing." Garland had also described his other dream of attaining fame through his drama "Love or the Law." "Your play experiment is promising," Kirkland continued. "Your idea of acting in it is alarming. All my folks (experienced playgoers, critics and amateur actors) exclaimed at the idea. There is no road to the footlights except through the back of the stage." For two pages he counseled against performance, attempting to dissuade Garland, for the pages Hamlin had been sending him over the summer revealed little talent for stagecraft. And he pointed out that Garland's experience scarcely prepared him for the stage: "The lecture platform does not help; the elocutionary-declamatory experience positively hinders." What Garland needed, Kirkland concluded, was "A good professional playwright to prune and improve your play and some good professional players to represent it."[6]

Kirkland's advice may have encouraged Garland to renew his effort to capture the particulars of a region and its people in his writing. His first sustained effort at fiction, however, was unsatisfactory, for he hadn't yet figured out how to combine description of place with plot and character. He was hard at work on "The Rise of Boomtown," the novel based on his Dakota homesteading adventure. His preface reveals his own confusion about what he was attempting. "This is not a novel, neither is it a history," he began. Rather, his chief interest was recording the details of scene, applying what he had admired in the work of Wilkins, Riley, Kirkland, and Howe to his Dakota experience. "Its descriptions can be relied upon," he continued, "for I have aimed to be true to the scene and people."[7] Through the autobiographical character of newspaperman Albert Seagraves, who has arrived in "Boomtown"—Ordway—after graduating from an Iowa seminary, Garland describes the rapid growth of a typical boomtown and the rivalry between newspapers competing for a railhead in neighboring towns. There is little plot, little character interaction; Garland instead focuses on the details of land settlement and claim-holding.

He had much to learn about writing fiction based on his own experience, for in this early effort he had not yet learned how to remove himself from the events he described. In one section of the manuscript, for example, Garland draws a sketch of his claim shanty and then devotes a chapter to describing it, punctuated with numerous asides to the reader. "This picture, to which I point with pride as a fine bit of my own skill," he immodestly informs his readers, "represents the building when completed." He describes other objects for "the impatient reader who has been wondering" about items along the wall. "I flatter myself in thinking that I have given a little of the illimitable spaces of the sky and the plain," he continues confidently. "Had I been more of an artist (I have my limitations), I would have delineated the major sitting with coat off, smoking his cigar on the front side of the shanty."[8]

While he worked on the manuscript periodically over the next year, Garland seems to have made no attempt to publish it, though one excerpt, "Holding Down a Claim in a Blizzard," in which he describes the rigors of surviving a howling storm, appeared in *Harper's Weekly*, as did a poem inspired by the experience, "Lost in the Norther."[9] Instead, he would mine memories of his claim-holding as well as details of town life for later fiction.

One day as he labored at his desk he heard the sound of coal being shoveled in an alley. The scrape of the shovel reminded him of his boyhood on his father's farm, when he would shovel corn from wagon bed to crib, "and I fell a-dreaming, and from dreaming I came to composition," he later remembered.[10] The result was "The Huskin'," the first of six articles making up "Boy Life on the Prairie." In these articles he had more success with unifying recollections of his boyhood experience and narrative form. In "The Rise of Boomtown" he had struggled to combine memory with fiction, unable to divorce himself as narrator from the made-up events. But in the "Boy Life" sketches he abandoned the pretense of fiction for autobiography, choosing, as Donald Pizer has remarked, "the form that was for him, then and always, most direct and natural."[11] "The Huskin'," which appeared in *American Magazine* in January 1888, begins with the observation that other writers have portrayed corn husking through a romantic haze; his task will be to present "the latest phases of corn-husking in the West" with accuracy while also conveying the "poetry" of methods that have already passed into history. In this and the other sketches that followed, Garland largely succeeds in portraying the nostalgia of boyhood, drawing directly upon his own experience of life on the farm through the cycle of a year.[12] In "The Thrashin'," for example, he describes the moment the men set to work at the threshing machine: "Ah! That morning scene, that superb sky and air! As I write, I am once more in the faint gray light of dawn; the frost lies white as silver on every surface; the frozen ground rings like iron under the steel-shod feet of the horses. The breath of men and beasts rises in white puffs of cloud."[13]

While much of his narrative is appropriately nostalgic and excels at scene painting, Garland also applied the lessons he had been culling from his correspondence and promoting through his teaching: that realism required accurate depiction of the unpleasant as well as the beautiful. In "Between Hay an' Grass," for example, he interrupts his account of snaring gophers to comment on his own method, what he would later call "veritism": "I am often profoundly amused at the revelations which come to me in writing reminiscences of this nature. These genre pictures of boy-life in the West are intrinsically of no moment; their interest will be mainly due to the observer and his angle of vision; to one who (like myself) is a product of these scenes and incidents, a word or sentence concerning a common experience will assume great value, while at the same time, those reared among a totally different set of vulgar incidents will be amused merely."[14]

When Kirkland read the first two installments, he wrote to pronounce them "capital! It beats me in local color—description of scenery, times and places and persons and incidents—you show youth and freshness that are out of my reach." But he then admonished Garland for including "a few awkward, apologetic phrases" in the beginning of "The Huskin'": "I venture to present, therefore," "But the reader will ask for particulars," and others.[15] Garland was still struggling to find his narrative voice.

Garland also found occasion to include his poetry in the "Boy Life" sketches, typically when scenic beauty moved him to exaltation.

In "Meadow Memories" he describes the lush beauty of the open prairie, "in full flower, fragrant, green and yellow and white with blossoms and leaves, fresh from the rain, while a strong, cool wind is wafted from the clearing west." Yet prose is not enough to capture its beauty. "Words fail; song itself cannot express it":

> My Western land, I love thee yet!
> In dreams I ride my horse again,
> And breast the breezes blowing fleet
> From out the meadows cool and wet.[16]

On occasion Garland experimented with dialect, most often when recording phrases uttered by Iowa farmers, but his most successful use of dialect appeared in a poem that pays homage to one of Riley's best-known poems, "When the Frost Is on the Punkin." Riley began his rollicking verse with the lines

> When the frost is on the punkin and the fodder's in the shock,
> And you hear the kyouck and gobble of the struttin turkey-cock,
> And the clackin' of the guineys, and the cluckin' of the hens,
> And the rooster's hallylooer as he tiptoes on the fence;
> O, it's then's the times a feller is a-feelin' at his best.

In his review of *Afterwhiles*, Garland had asked of these lines, "What Western-born man could read the lyric . . . and not feel a thrill of exquisite pleasure?" Seeking to inspire a similar thrill in his readers, he imitated the rhythm and sentiment of the poem in "Then It's Spring." The first stanza reads:

> When the hens begin a-squawk'n'
> And a-rollin' in th' dust,
> When the roosters take t' talk'n'
> And a-crow'n' fit t' bust,
> When th' crows are caw'n' 'n' flock'n'
> An' the chickens boom an' sing—
> Then it's spring.[17]

With his work now appearing in magazines, Garland was eager for Kirkland's approval. "No, I did not see 'Lost in the Norther' and 'Holding down claims,'" Kirkland wrote in February 1888. "I should think you could do those splendidly." Garland had apparently described other work in progress as well. "Three novels at once underway!" Kirkland exclaimed and then added sardonically, "Your hands must be full." He then went on to chide the earnest student: "As to your 'occasional work'; I think that it is *good*; but that you are easily satisfied. You don't keep a thing revolving in your mind until some sharp, striking thought, dramatic or pathetic or humorous, starts into being, to compel the attention of the whole world."[18] Kirkland had identified a prime weakness in Garland's writing, one that Hamlin would never entirely eradicate: his too-hurried composition that often led to premature publication.

While Kirkland served as Garland's mentor at a critical moment of his apprenticeship and often rebuked his protégé for sloppy work, he respected Garland's judgment enough to enlist his aid in revising his second novel, *The McVeys*, for his publishers. He did not like the terms Houghton Mifflin offered and directed the firm to send the manuscript to Garland. Kirkland wanted to cut one hundred pages of the manuscript but "didn't want to blunder and leave in the poor parts," as he explained in a letter of March 20, 1888. Garland went to work blue-penciling the manuscript. Kirkland was pleased with the result. "All friendly reciprocal offices I willingly accept," he wrote on March 26, "but this 'lubbard labor' of reading 120 pp. of ms. and blue-penciling it for my benefit, I could scarcely ask of a professional litterateur—even if he were my own brother."[19]

Soon Kirkland returned the favor. Garland had been working on "Daddy Deering," his first sustained effort in fiction since the amateurish "The Rise of Boomtown." He took an incident described in "The Thrashin'"—an account of his teenage experience with a threshing machine during which Daddy Fairburn caws, "Never mind, sonny, they ain't pizen," as barley beards slide down the back of young Hamlin's neck—and expanded this brief scene into a full portrait of a strong though aging Daddy Deering, proud of his accomplishments as a master wheat stacker, hog butcher, and fiddler. He proudly sent off his latest effort to Kirkland.

He must have been surprised at the vehemence of Kirkland's response. "'Daddy Deering' has great strength—glorious in its main characteristics," Kirkland wrote. "Then it has what I call your faults. Subjectiveness amounting to egotism. You begin, not about Deering, but about yourself. 'I am perfectly certain' . . . 'So far as I know' . . . 'As I look back' . . . 'My ideas of his personality.' . . . All these on one page, and that the initial! An editor who began with that would be apt to cry 'too bad to use,' while one who began in the middle would say 'too good to lose.'" Once again, Kirkland pointed to Garland's chief flaw as a fictionist: the failure to remove autobiography from fiction. "Who cares whether *your* mind is working on the question why he was born at all?" he asked. "If I were you," Kirkland advised, "I would give up that damned typewriter that lends itself awkwardly to revisions. . . . Get a small page and stub pen and *work* over your work and you'll thank me for these criticisms." He then informed the nascent writer that he was going to rewrite the tale and submit it to *America,* a new Chicago weekly founded earlier that month, by way of demonstrating that attention to craft gets results.[20]

Two days later, Kirkland responded to "Paid His Way," Garland's effort to turn his parents' farming experiences into poetry. "Oh you heedless cuss!" he chastised the novice. "To discover a gem like 'He paid his way' and then half-ruin it in setting it!" He went on to rail against Garland's fumbling meter—"You begin with lines of three feet each—and then occasionally slip in one of four feet"—and concluded, "This is not genius; it is childish idleness—amateurish slip-shoddity. It is like grammar-school compositions."

Despite his impatience with what he perceived as Garland's sloppiness, Kirkland had a genuine fondness for the young man. As good mentors sometimes do, he rewrote the poem from beginning to end to demonstrate what Garland should be aiming for and sent the poem to *America,* prophesying that "it will make you famous. As soon as you learn to do justice to the public you'll have a public," he instructed, "and not be standing on a lonely little height, spouting good thoughts in poor words into vacancy."[21]

Kirkland's lesson was harsh, but it got results. Two days later

America promptly accepted "Paid His Way" and paid Garland fifteen dollars for the privilege of printing it.[22] But Garland seems to have resisted Kirkland's editorial efforts, for he complained about the revisions of his manuscripts, explaining his motives and sense of audience and purpose. Kirkland was by now exasperated at his truculent pupil and responded specifically to Garland's objections. "Who cares for your motives in writing?" he thundered. "You are not set up to be a teacher of men. After you shall have humbly written *facts* for twenty years then you can 'whack 'em over the head' with your preachment. 'They want to be preached to.' Yes, by Emerson and Tolstoi, but not by Garland and Kirkland." He returned both Garland's original and his revision and instructed the youth to compare "its present decent, proper, workmanlike, literary, professional, salable shape." "What's the result?" he concluded. "Fame and Fifteen Dollars."[23]

But Garland was not done: he apparently so resisted Kirkland's revisions that Kirkland concluded the matter by appealing to the editor of *America*. "In order to test the question of the value of the re-writing I had done," he wrote to Garland, "I sent 'America' the original, telling them that I had re-written it, that you preferred its original shape, and that I desired them to take their choice between the two forms. In reply they write 'The poem as you revised it is far better than the original, the latter being so faulty that had it been sent in in that state it would not have been considered at all.'"[24]

Kirkland's mentorship was instrumental in teaching Garland how to make the transition from lecturer to author. His two years of teaching classes of docile students had encouraged his tendency to pontificate, and the more experienced writer had correctly identified the element of condescension that it produced in his writing. Garland had not yet learned to trust and respect his reader, as revealed in his objection that readers "want to be preached to," so he had larded his prose with self-conscious reflections and autobiographical posing. By first railing against this tendency and then showing Garland how to revise, Kirkland provided a critical service in turning his student into a professional writer. Though he objected, Garland learned the lesson; henceforth he made a greater effort to restrict his personal interjections to autobiographical writing.

While he was learning the craft of writing, Garland became more directly involved in agitation for land reform. While in his Dakota shanty he had read Henry George's *Progress and Poverty*, and after he arrived in Boston he had sporadically attended single tax meetings, for he was busy developing his career as a lecturer. But when he returned to Boston after his visit west during the summer of 1887, he was full of bitterness at the wretched conditions of the farms and wracked with guilt at leaving his mother and sister in the squalor of their Dakota home. With his brother he began to attend Sunday-night meetings of the Boston chapter of the Anti-Poverty Society, which met at Horticultural Hall. Formed in New York in May 1887 after George's unsuccessful mayoral run, the Anti-Poverty Society sought to educate people about the single-tax remedy for unequal land distribution. The Boston branch was formed in August and attracted large audiences, but numbers began to decline after George was defeated in a bid for New York secretary of state. At the November 20 meeting the speaker acknowledged that no one was slated to address the next meeting. During a brainstorming session—an "'experience' meeting," as reported by the *Standard*, George's single-tax weekly—Garland stepped up to volunteer.[25]

In the week leading up to his November 27 address, Garland "agonized" in preparation. Before an enthusiastic audience of six hundred he delivered his lecture, which he entitled "The Social Aspect of the Land Tax." Because his address contains a number of points that Garland would later incorporate into his fiction, it is worth quoting in detail. He began by explaining that he would discuss the "social rather than pecuniary benefits" of the single tax, for "even if it were true that all men in this country had enough to eat, yet there were still things quite as necessary to social existence which they were unable to attain." Because of a tax system that rewards speculators for holding vast areas in anticipation of rising land values, he argued, "free land is a myth. We have squandered our inheritance. We gave it away in empires, we sell it now in counties." Warming to his topic, Garland went on to describe the effect of land speculation on the ordinary farm family: "Every foot of it was bought with blood and sweat and tears. It was and is bought with the loss of comfort, society, education. All that justifies and makes life sweet has been given by the settler for his lonely farm." He referred to his recent trip through Illinois, Iowa, Dakota, and Minnesota: "Higher education in the rural districts is a farce. The farm for the ambitious girl or boy is a living grave, a terrible solitude that eats out the life and hope and joy of life. Youth, gloomy and despairing, old age hopeless and fruitless."

The solution to the problem, he argued, "must do two things: it must concentrate the units of rural regions, and removing the pressure on the centres of population, must permit them to spread." By freeing the land—that is, by taxing land in proportion to the average value of the land around it, not in ratio to its improvements—"Business would expand naturally; empty lots would disappear. None could afford to hold the land idle. Monopoly would disappear." The result would be a more humane life for farm families, with hope and culture restored. "Land being held for use, not for sale," he concluded, "farmers would use it in the natural, civilized way; they would draw together in groups, and with the closer society would come the higher education, art, music, the drama, and the leisure to enjoy all these. . . . The reign of justice will have begun."[26]

As his address suggests, Garland's motive for promoting the single tax was deeply personal. When Hamlin arrived in Boston as an uncultured son of the prairie, he was particularly struck by the many cultural offerings in the East—and he availed himself of them at every opportunity. When he returned to the West, his newly acquired aesthetic sensibility made him sensitive to the mean, culturally impoverished life of the frontier farmer—a realization driven home by the effects on his own family, particularly on his mother, prematurely aged by hard work, and his sister Jessie, who could expect no other future than a life as an overworked farm wife.

With the zeal of a new convert, Garland immersed himself in the single-tax cause. In February 1888 he wrote to Henry George to offer his services. George suggested that "some of your Boston folks—the more prominent in the movement the better—write a letter to the *Standard* as a form of advertisement of Garland's wish to help out. "I am satisfied," George concluded, "that you will find quite a demand in New England for your services; our trouble is the want of speakers."[27] On March 31 the *Standard* announced that Garland, newly elected as vice-president of the Boston Anti-Poverty Society, was "open to engagements to speak in the cause of land reform at places not too distant from Boston." His only charge would be "actual expenses, which in most cases would be simply the railway fare."[28]

Soon Garland's political interests began to influence his writing and his criticism, for Hamlin was convinced that art should not only reflect present conditions but also work to improve them. Accordingly, he wrote two kinds of stories in early 1888: those prompted by nostalgic recollections of his youth, like "Daddy Deering" and most of his poetry, and those written in the mood of bitterness that his summer trip had aroused.

Kirkland's tutelage had shown him the error of expressing ideas in fiction through first-person addresses to the reader. When he completed his next story—"A Common Case"—he succeeded in communicating the ideas he had expressed in "The Social Aspect of the Land Tax" through characters rather than overt authorial statement. The story begins with two schoolteachers in Rock River, Iowa, discussing the "case" of Matilda Bent, who has declined from a vivacious girl into a worn-out farm wife dying of cancer. "I'd jest like t'ask you edgicated chaps what that woman's life is worth t' her—'r what any wife's life is worth on the western farm," asks one teacher. "The fact is, that woman is being murdered, just like thousands of others like her in this country." When she was young, Matilda "had a natural love for pretty things—flowers and pictures, and the like o' that—but she hasn't been able to have a single thing of that kind. Her time has been all taken up with cooking and washing and nursing children." Given the harsh reality of farm conditions, people have no time for culture, and any inclination has been beaten out of them by the grind of labor. "What are pictures and operas and dramas to her—or to the rest of us?" asks another. "Just the sunlight-

and-shadow play on the blank wall of our prison." In this early story, his second published, Garland had progressed in the art of fiction, but he still employs a mouthpiece character. Of Matilda Bent's case, one teacher concludes, expressing the point of Garland's single-tax address, "Yes, this is America. . . . The American farmer living in semi-solitude, his wife a slave, both denied the things that make life living. Fifty per cent of these farms mortgaged, in spite of the labors of every member of the family, and the most frugal living."[29] Though Garland would never entirely abandon the spokesman character, his mature fiction would better integrate the ideas into the fiction.

His new interest in the social effects of fiction influenced his review of Howells's *April Hopes*, published in February 1888. After praising the novel for its unromantic portrayal of love, its style, and its characters, Garland chastised Howells for not making the purpose clear:

> So far as I am concerned I believe in "novels of purpose." And my criticism upon "April Hopes" is that Mr. Howells has not made suf-ficient open statement of what I know he must have felt regard-ing this amiable, useless and heartless manner of life. So far from under-estimating his readers' intelligence, Mr. Howells's error is in over-estimating it. He takes it for granted that preaching about life is absolutely unnecessary and bad art, and that making a transcript of real life is enough. But the fact is the most of people enjoy easy, impassioned preaching. Just as the scent of human life escapes them, so in a novel approaching a transcript of real life the intent of the author escapes them unless the writer preaches a little.[30]

Howells, of course, was a strong advocate of unobtrusive, non-didac-tic instruction, as he remarked in an 1899 lecture: "The novel can teach, and for shame's sake, it must teach, but only by painting life truly."[31] Garland, filled with George's single-tax theories, in early 1888 primarily conceived of realism as a means to raise the social conscience of his reader. Moreover, his Whitmanesque romanticism led him to conceive of literature as an expression of the writer's per-sonality, and he chided Howells for writing *too* objectively. "Those who know Mr. Howells feel a loss in a book like 'April Hopes,'" he remarked in his review of the novel, "because he does not allow his strong, fine and tender personality to appear in overt fashion, feeling that his beneficial effect would have a wider reach."

Howells promptly wrote to respond to Garland's review, and his letter suggests that, like Kirkland, he quickly picked up on the younger writer's strain of didacticism that led him to believe readers "enjoy easy, impassioned preaching," figuratively walloping them over the head to make them understand the idea. "I read your criticisms with great interest and respect," Howells wrote on March 11, 1888.

> I supposed that the social intent of the book—the teaching that *love is not enough in love affairs*, but that there must be parity of ideal, training and disposition, in order to ensure happiness—was only too obvious. I meant to show that an engagement made from mere passion had better be broken, if it does not bear the strain of temperament; every such broken engagement I consider a blessing and an escape.—To infuse, or to declare, more of my personality in a story, would be a mistake, to my thinking: it should rather be the novelist's business to keep out of the way. My work must take its chance with readers.

And then, in pointed contrast to Garland's condescension of his readers, the more experienced writer added, "It was written from a sincere sense of the equality of men, and a real trust in them. I can't do more."[32]

Always receptive to Howells's opinion, Garland apparently pondered his remarks. In his review of *Annie Kilburn* later that year, he was less insistent on the necessity for an "open statement" of purpose and more cognizant of manifesting the "lesson" in the interaction of the characters. *Annie Kilburn*, he claimed, "is artistic in that it nowhere preaches. All shades of opinion are impartially represented." After a year of campaigning for the single tax on the lecture platform, he had a pretty good idea of the limitations of art and the advantages of more overt methods of swaying an audience. "The book might have appealed to a wider audience, perhaps," he noted, "had the author consented to be a little less artistic; that is to say, had he preached in person, his meaning might have been a little more obvious to the careless reader; but the artistic impartiality of the book is, after all, its strong point, its lasting value." Garland then concludes the point by showing he has thoroughly absorbed the master's lesson: "The author does not solve the problem; he is content to set it before us as it is in life, and let us draw our own conclusions. . . . He should teach, but concretely, objectively, not by stopping in the midst of his story to deliver harangues in the manner of the old school."[33]

During the spring of 1888 Hamlin grew more and more concerned about his family back in Dakota. His mother's letters were becoming despondent, for Dakota was undergoing drought, crops had been poor, and her health was failing. He decided to return to do what he could to alleviate their worries. "We are all well," his mother wrote on June 1, "but me I have a dizzy spell am some better this morn. . . . O I am growing old and ugly like all old folks." Referring to his labor in the fields during his previous visit, she promised that "we wont rush you in the harvest field this year" and assured him that he would eat better than he did on his last visit: "We are saving a pig to eat when you come and a veal so you wont have to eat Feasons old Beef."[34] To finance his trip, he announced in the *Standard* that he would be available to lecture on single-tax topics along the way. Accompanied by his friend and landlord, Dr. Hiram Cross, who wanted to see the Dakota prairie, he set off for Ordway, with stops to lecture in Indianapolis, Chicago, and Minneapolis.[35]

When he arrived at his parents' home in July, he was struck by how much conditions had deteriorated in a year. "The trees which my father had planted, the flowers which my mother had so faithfully watered, had withered in the heat," he later wrote. "The lawn was burned brown. No green thing was in sight, and no shade offered save that made by the little cabin." The grain had also withered, and clouds of dust rose with every footfall. His mother's letters had not adequately prepared him for her decline in health. Her speech was hesitant, her movements faltering, her complexion gray. "I bled, inwardly, every time I looked at her," he remembered. Jessie, now nineteen, further aroused his protective instincts. "She must be rescued at once or she will live and die the wife of some Dakota farmer," he told his mother.

Shortly after his arrival, as he was planning with Jessie her continued education, Garland heard "a short, piercing cry, followed by a low sobbing." He ran out into the yard, where he saw his mother in agony, tears streaming down her cheeks.

"I can't lift my feet," she cried. "I can't move."

Isabelle Garland had suffered a stroke.

Hamlin was wracked with grief and remorse, and all the latent guilt over his abandonment of his family rose to torment him. "I cursed the laws of man, I cursed myself," he would later write. But most of all he cursed his father for bringing his beloved mother into this godforsaken place, so remote from her relatives and so lacking in basic creature comforts.

Fortunately, Dr. Cross hadn't yet returned to Boston, and he came to Mrs. Garland's aid. "A minute blood vessel has ruptured in her brain, and a small clot has formed there," he told the suffering son. "If this is absorbed, as I think it will be, she will recover. Nothing can be done for her. No medicine can reach her. It is just a question of rest and quiet." But then Cross admonished Hamlin, "She should have been relieved from severe household labor years ago."

Cross's rebuke "stung like a poison dart" to the already guilt-ridden son, and his heart "filled with bitterness and rebellion, bitterness against the pioneering madness which had scattered our family, and rebellion toward my father who had kept my mother always on the border, working like a slave long after the time when she should have been taking her ease."[36] Above all else, he railed against his own selfishness in pursuing his ambition, first at the expense of Franklin's education, now at the cost of his mother's health. For his father his feelings grew more complex, a mixture of filial love and respect for his stamina but etched with a deepening resentment that would only diminish when Hamlin succeeded in "rescuing" his mother from the life to which his father's westering wanderlust had condemned her. But that was still five years in the future.

The immediate problem was how to ensure his mother's recovery. After talking matters over with Dr. Cross, Hamlin resolved to remain through the summer and return to Boston in September, for his career was gathering momentum and he could earn more in the East than in the fields and so help his mother. In a scene that would later find its way into "Up the Coulé," this Boston orator and teacher doffed his frock coat, rolled up his sleeves, and returned to his former occupation as field hand, laboring until exhausted at sunset. Nonetheless, he made time to write. He developed a lecture on "Dialect and Dialect Poets" for his fall lecture season and sent it, together with drafts of several poems, to Riley for comment. "I shall begin harvesting tomorrow," he wrote on August 5. "Already look brown and still '*Browning*.'"[37]

As August drew to a close, Hamlin tried to convince Jessie to accompany him to Osage, where he had been invited to be the "Speaker of the Day" at the annual country fair. He wanted to facilitate his sister's escape from Dakota by enrolling her in the Cedar Valley Seminary, but she resisted, for she knew her mother needed her. When her mother encouraged her to go—and when Garland hired some domestic help—Jessie reluctantly agreed.

At Osage, Garland was understandably eager to show off before his former schoolmates and neighbors. "It is customary at such times and places as this to deliver a political oration extolling one or the other of our presidential candidates," he began his speech. "I come to you today with a new message. I am non-partisan. A man of books. I have the audacity to talk to you upon social economy."[38] From this unpromising beginning his speech went downhill as he harangued his auditors with platitudes about his favorite topic of the single tax as remedy to unequal land distribution and falling wages. As Jessie watched her brother pontificate before the small, wind-blown crowd, she must have marveled at his confidence, his ease at addressing people. But for Hamlin, his address was "a defeat" as he watched the blank looks on his former neighbors' faces as they shuffled to escape from the lecturer.[39] Soon afterward, Jessie returned to Ordway, unable to master her homesickness, and Hamlin entrained for the East.

On his way home, Garland met Walt Whitman. He had first written to Whitman in November 1886, while preparing lectures for the Boston School of Oratory. At the time, Whitman did not enjoy his modern reputation of being a poetic innovator; rather, he was widely viewed as a poet who gloried in depicting the indecorous, even the obscene. On March 1, 1882, the Boston district attorney informed Osgood and Company, Whitman's new publisher, that its edition of *Leaves of Grass* contained obscene passages and would be banned from the mails.[40] The ensuing controversy filled Boston's newspapers as Whitman's critics exchanged barbs with his defenders. When Garland read *Leaves of Grass* in the public library, it was "double-starred" to restrict its circulation "only to serious students of literature."[41]

One November day in 1886, Garland learned that the sixty-seven-year-old poet had suffered another stroke, further limiting his ability to walk. "It is with profound sorrow that I read in the papers the news that you are again suffering from your old trouble," he began his letter. "I am everywhere in my teaching and writing making your claims felt and shall continue to do so." Though he noted that there was still "much opposition" to his poetry, "it was mostly ignorant or misled," he assured the poet. He went on to describe his planned volume "The Evolution of American Thought," enclosed an outline of it, and asked to use a paragraph from *Specimen Days & Collect* as a motto. He noted that he was "a border man" who had been "raised on the prairie frontier," and concluded, "your poems thrilled me, reversed many of my ideas, confirmed me in others, helped to make me what I am."[42]

Whitman seems to have warmed to Garland's enthusiastic letter, for he told his friend Horace Traubel in August 1888, shortly before Garland's visit, "Now, wasn't that a dandy letter from Garland? This was his first salutation . . . a first confession: not an obsequious obeisance made to the ground but just a manly shake of the hand." Garland's prairie roots also struck a common chord of sympathy: "That appeals to me," he told Traubel, "hits me hardest where I enjoy being hit." Though he was born near Long Island, Whitman saw the West as "my own country though I have mainly had to view it from afar."[43]

When Garland arrived at Whitman's Mickle Street house in

Camden, New Jersey, on September 26, he found Whitman ailing but still vigorous; his "powerful hand has an answering grip that tells of much vital force yet." He noted the poet's "magnificent head and snowy hair . . . like the sculptured head of Neptune," and was surprised to find that "He looks like his pictures, which cannot always be said of authors."

Although Whitman's doctor advised Garland to remain for only two minutes, the poet's interest in his young visitor was such that more than half an hour elapsed before the visit was concluded. In his fervent partisanship Garland asked whether Whitman would object if he carried his campaign to resurrect the poet's reputation to the newspapers. "I prefer to leave all that to time," Whitman responded. "Such things usually clear themselves up, and at any rate they deceive only the unthinking, whom your explanation might not reach." The conversation soon turned to contemporary writers, and Garland discovered that Whitman was unfamiliar with the work of two of his enthusiasms, Joseph Kirkland and Mary Wilkins, though he had read the works of other realists such as George Washington Cable, Mary Noailles Murfree, and Howells. Garland presented his thesis that regional writers best express the distinctive character of the American land and people. Whitman's response went home to the lecturer and budding author, for it confirmed Garland's sense of a nascent realistic movement that was celebrating the commonplace rather than the unusual. Today's writers don't seem to be "content with the common, normal man," Whitman told his interviewer; "they must take the exceptional, the diseased. They are not true, not American in the deeper sense." Garland responded that all young writers begin with "the abnormal rather than the normal, because the irregular startles, claims the attention first, makes the greater impression. . . . It is a preparatory stage, leading to something better." Whitman agreed with his analysis but urged that "the really heroic character of the common American man or woman be depicted in the novel and drama."

He then left Garland with a "friendly message" to carry to young authors in his lecturing and writing. "Tell them to go among the common men as one of them, never as looking down upon them.

Study their lives, find out and celebrate their splendid primitive honesty and what I am pleased to call their heroism. When our novelists shall do that, in addition to being true to their time, their art will be worthy [of] all praise from me or any other who is insisting on a native anti-class poem, novel or drama." Finally, he advised, "Don't let evil overshadow your books. Make it a foil as Shakespeare did. His evil is always a foil for purity. Somewhere in the play or novel let the light in."[44]

Whitman was pleased with his young visitor. "I am more than favorably impressed with Garland," he told Traubel. "He has a good voice—is almost Emersonee—has belly—some would say, guts. The English say of a man, 'he has guts, guts'—and that means something very good, not very bad. Garland has guts—the good kind: has voice, power, manliness—has chest tones in his talk which attract me."[45] To the end of his days, Whitman would express affection for his young advocate, telling Traubel that he admired Garland's "earnestness." "Garland is one of the fellows determined to be in the fight: in manner he is extremely quiet: has a low voice—speech toned down, way down. He does not give you the impression of a belligerent man at all, yet in his writing he is very aggressive."[46]

For his part, Garland was ecstatic about his encounter with the Good Gray Poet. Later he would remark that "His influence radiates like sun-shine" and "I find myself quoting his thought if not his words, many times—and I know very well that he has been to me a great force in ways difficult to trace."[47] For the next three years he would send Whitman regular reports about the favorable response to his lectures on Whitman's poetry. More immediately, he promptly went to work writing a review of Whitman's *November Boughs* for the *Transcript*, using the column to defend Whitman's poetry against detractors who objected to the poet's unconventional form and content. "There are not ten lines to which the ordinary reader of Shakespeare could consistently point as objectionable," Garland informed his readers; and "it still appears to me unreasonable to hold a prejudice against a most remarkable outpouring of exalted passion, prophecy, landscape painting, songs of the sea and, above all, calls for deeper love for Nature and for men." To those who protest that Whitman's lines are not "poetry," as commonly understood, he observed that evolution in the arts would inevitably take its course, for the "inertia of the average mind, whose thinking is necessarily along well-worn grooves, . . . can be but slowly and unwillingly turned aside."[48]

For Garland, hard at work organizing his lectures into the book he hoped to publish as "The Evolution of American Thought," Whitman served as an important figure. Indeed, the title itself derives from a line of Whitman's: "In nothing is there more evolution than in the American mind."[49] In a pivotal chapter of that projected work, titled "Walt Whitman: The Prophet of the New Age," Garland argues that Whitman represents "the idealization of the real" that "underlies and supports whatever is best and most enduring in every art now beginning in America." He valued Whitman's innovation in his choice of subject matter; to Garland, Whitman appeared to be part of the same general movement toward expressing the real that he saw in fiction. "He is then a realist and at the same time he is the greatest of idealists," he explained. "He . . . uses the real as the basis for the projection of the ideal. He is master of the real, nothing daunts him. The mud and slush in the street, the gray and desolate sky, the blackened walls, the rotting timbers of the wharf—the greedy, the ragged, the prostitute—vulgarity, deformity, all—no matter how apparently low and common, his soul receives and transforms into sweeping, mighty song."[50] As one Whitman scholar has remarked, "In the 1880s—when many people had argued that Irving or Cooper or Emerson himself was the father of American literature—no critic other than Garland looked ahead to argue that Whitman would influence not only American poetry but also fiction, music, and drama."[51]

For the rest of his life, Garland would value Whitman's inspiration, for he admired the poet as a true representative of the democratic spirit of America. "Walt Whitman has taught me two great and searching truths," he remarked at Whitman's seventieth birthday celebration on May 31, 1889. "These are, Optimism and Altruism—Hope for the future and Sympathy toward men."[52] In his proselytizing for the single tax and in his fiction, Garland would soon seek to embody Whitman's example. He would take from Whitman the title of his most famous book—*Main-Travelled Roads*—inspired by Whitman's long preface to *November Boughs*, "A Backward Glance O'er Travel'd Roads." And he would transform his father's Civil War service into a Whitman-inspired emblem of faith in the common man in one of his most famous stories, "The Return of the Private," directly applying Whitman's advice to celebrate the heroism of the common man. Worn out from his wartime service, his farm in a shambles, Private Smith and his wife plan for the future. "Here was the epic figure which Whitman has in mind, and which he calls the 'common American soldier.' With the livery of war on his limbs, this man was facing his future, his thoughts holding no scent of battle. Clean, clear-headed, in spite of physical weakness, Edward Smith, Private, turned future-ward with a sublime courage."[53]

Garland would also pay homage to Whitman in his first volume of poetry, *Prairie Songs*, by choosing prairie grass as its dominant organizing image. He expressed his veneration more directly in one of the poems in the collection, "A Tribute of Grasses," drawing upon details from his 1888 interview and dedicating it "To W. W.":

> Serene, vast head, with silver cloud of hair
> Lined on the purple dusk of death,
> A stern medallion, velvet set—
> Old Norseman, throned, not chained upon thy chair,
> Thy grasp of hand, thy hearty breath
> > Of welcome thrills me yet
> > As when I faced thee there!
>
> Loving my plain as thou the sea,
> Facing the East as thou the West,
> I bring a handful of grass to thee—
> The Prairie grasses I know the best;
> Type of the wealth and width of the plain,
> Strong of the strength of the wind and sleet,
> Fragrant with sunlight and cool with rain,
> I bring it and lay it low at thy feet,
> > Here by the eastern sea.[54]

Walt Whitman, with Joseph Kirkland, James Whitcomb Riley, and William Dean Howells, though in different ways, served as Garland's principal inspirations during his apprenticeship. From them Garland had learned to trust his reader's intelligence while celebrating the common man. He had learned to recognize his tendency to preach, and to attempt to diminish that inclination. He had enlarged his circle of literary acquaintances, and his name was beginning to appear before the public. He had gained a foothold; he was now determined to climb to the top.

7

LIFE UNDER THE WHEEL, 1888–89

Upon his return to Boston in September 1888, Garland began writing in earnest while also continuing his activities on behalf of the single-tax cause. The next three years would be among his most fertile, and his ambitions and energies were pulled in many directions. He wrote reams of fiction, much poetry, a number of book reviews, and several plays; he lectured widely; and he continued to enlarge his circle of friends among the writers, artists, musicians, and their patrons in Boston.

While he was still in Ordway, he had recorded in his notebook his impressions of Aberdeen: "Nothing is more dreary[,] stale and inhospitable than a small country town, far from anything and anybody. It is a good thing that I have written my work upon Boomtown for I am in too savage a mood to see any beauty in the thing this morning. It would kill me to live in such a filthy hopelessly petty and dreary place as this."[1] His four years in Boston, where he had enjoyed theater, concerts, and literary talk with writers and artists, had elevated his sensibilities; just as important, his association with other writers made him aware that literary depictions of the Midwest had failed to catch the truth of conditions as he had experienced them. Henceforth, he resolved, he would devote his art to portraying the Midwest truthfully, accurately.

His first effort was to expand his Aberdeen notes for a report on the deteriorating conditions in Dakota for Henry George's single-tax newspaper, the *Standard*. "Things are in a deplorable condition here," he lamented. "Every local paper is filled with notices of foreclosures. . . . In Brown county, there is but one live town; the others are grown up to weeds and are full of empty buildings. Vast quantities of land lie idle. . . . The people are discouraged, but they will not admit it. Many would go back if they could. But what could they do?"[2] Back at his Seaverns Avenue attic room in Jamaica Plain, he pondered the spirit-crushing conditions in Dakota, and especially the plight of his family. In short order he drafted "John Boyle's Conclusion," the bitterest story he would ever write.

"John Boyle's Conclusion" depicts the effects of harsh farm conditions and a disastrous storm upon two couples, the elderly Boyles and the younger Allings. Drought has come to Dakota, and the wheat—seared by hot winds and lack of rain—is blighted. In his portrayal of the Boyles, Garland emphasizes the farmers' hopelessness and bitterness, their dehumanization as they struggle in a life isolated from others and devoid of social amenities. John Boyle is without hope, crushed by what he feels is a vindictive environment. "If they *was* a God," he tells his wife, "seems t' me He'd send us rain when we needed it most. . . . I ain't done nothin' t' deserve such treatment." Burdened by a heavy mortgage and unable to sell because there are no buyers for the defeated land, Boyle has become disillusioned and believes that "all had conspired against him. God, Man, and Nature had assaulted him as if by preconceived plan."[3] When a hailstorm comes, flattening his crop and destroying his hovel of a home, his spirit breaks: he drowns himself, and his wife goes mad. Because the Allings are young, they rebound from their defeat and determine to begin again—but not in Dakota.

As in "A Common Case," written earlier that spring, Garland was still struggling to embody single-tax ideas in fiction. Reflecting Garland's interest in plays, John Boyle soliloquizes in the opening scene, and Porter Alling is a mouthpiece character who comments on the meaning of the action. On October 10, 1888, Garland submitted the story to *Once a Week*, a new illustrated newspaper founded in April of that year, but it declined. He tried other magazines before *Belford's*, a Chicago monthly founded in June 1888, accepted it in March 1889, but *Belford's* never published the story, which eventually was returned to Garland, probably in 1893 when the magazine ceased publication.

Garland's outrage at the busted Dakota land boom soon turned to more direct action. On November 11 the *Standard* noted that the Boston Single Tax League had been reorganized, with Garland as its new president. The immediate plan was to hold meetings in the suburbs to expand membership.[4] Soon Garland leapt into action, eager to get the movement going. "We have begun our new campaign in Boston with greater energy and certainly better methods than ever before," he noted in a letter to the *Standard* a week later. His lectures during his trip west had prompted ideas for more effective organization. He recommended drafting a simple petition, rather than "a long-winded manifesto," for circulation; he suggested printing cards with the names of officers and furnishing letterhead stationery for businesses with a statement of single-tax principles on the back. He recommended printing stickers and posters to advertise the cause, but above all he advocated establishing a lecture bureau to furnish speakers and advertising to all who requested them, noting that he was going to Southford and Concord to organize single-tax leagues and speaking in Cambridge, where a league had already been formed.[5]

Remembering his own favorable boyhood experience with Grange houses in Iowa, two months later Garland would urge that "'a single tax home' or headquarters [be] established in every town." "It is a sort of home," he explained, "where on every night in the week or once a week the comrades get together in an informal way and strike hands." The club would serve as a comforting refuge from the bustle of Boston life, with the room furnished with books and newspapers, its windows festooned with "placards . . . telling the weary wayfarer to come in and rest." And, as with the Grange houses, he urged gender integration: "The single tax men have made a mistake in not getting the women interested. By means of fairs or of some kind of entertainment, such as plays, the ladies can do a great deal to getting the means with which to furnish a suitable meeting room. . . . In many cases they are waiting to be invited to help. This crusade is their crusade, and we should let them feel it."[6] Garland had set in motion a lifelong pattern of forming clubs to bring together like-minded people in service of a cause, reflecting his belief in connecting a principle with concrete action.

Much later, his friend Joseph Edgar Chamberlin, whose column "The Listener" regularly appeared in the *Boston Evening Transcript*, described Garland at the time of his militancy:

> In appearance, in the 80's, Garland was a young man of certain singularities, but of great beauty. He was of medium height, of supple figure, with abundant brown hair, and wore a rather long, brown beard, that gave him an apostolic appearance. His grave, meditative manner heightened this apostolic effect. He would have made an excellent model for John, the Beloved Disciple. . . . I doubt if Garland has been as serious in his life as he was in 1887 or if he ever will be again. . . .
>
> He had, as he has now, a rather high-pitched, very clear voice, in which he spoke with due western regard for the r's and in that broadly cadenced way that seems to have been developed in the voices that ring over the rolling prairies. . . . He was like Garrison—he would not equivocate or compromise or deny anything that he really believed in. He would not write anything that his heart was not in.[7]

While campaigning for the Anti-Poverty Society, Garland continued to write, struggling to learn how to embed political idea into action. He had more success when he left single-tax ideas behind and focused on reminiscent fiction. While talking with his mother one day in Ordway, she told him about an Iowa neighbor who had returned to New York for a visit after an absence of many years. He was struck by the pathos of the story, he later told an interviewer, and "went into another room and began to write." "I read it to mother, and she liked it, and upon telling her I thought it was worth at least $75, she replied, 'Well, if that is so, I think you ought to divvy with me, for I gave you the story.'" When he finished "Mrs. Ripley's Trip" in Boston and *Harper's Weekly* accepted it in November, he promptly sent her half of the proceeds—but he received forty-five dollars for the story, not seventy-five.[8]

"Mrs. Ripley's Trip" marked a new advance in the art of fiction for Garland. In writing the story of an old woman's rebellion against domestic duties, he probed his memories of women's work in adapting his mother's tale. "I'm sixty years old," Jane Ripley tells her husband, "an' I've never had a day off to myself, not even Fourth o' July. If I've went a-visitin' 'r to a picnic, I've had to come home an' milk 'n' get supper for you men-folks. . . . For twenty-three years, Ethan Ripley, I've stuck right to the stove an' churn without a day or night off."[9] Her husband is "vanquished" by the vehemence of her determination in much the same manner that Adoniram Penn is surprised by his wife's "revolt" against her husband's will in Mary Wilkins Freeman's "The Revolt of 'Mother,'" published two years later.

Gone are the personal interjections that had so troubled Kirkland in Garland's earlier effort at a genre sketch, "Daddy Deering." Much of the story is told through interaction between characters, and the descriptive scenes are devoid of the authorial commentary through a mouthpiece character that had marked "John Boyle's Conclusion" as irretrievably polemical. Drawing on his knack for descriptive detail and his ear for dialect, Garland sketched the tale of a fiercely independent woman who embarks on a "spree" to return some weeks later to take up "her burden again, never more thinking to lay it down." He had found his narrative voice in the local-color tale, but he had yet to learn how to yoke a polemical idea to the narrative.

Garland was also busy expanding his lectures. In the back of his mind lurked the ambition to become self-supporting as a lecturer and author, and he was eager to establish himself in literary circles. In late 1888 he sent Riley his new lecture pamphlet, entitled "Studies in Literature and Expressive Art," listing nineteen lectures, the core of his planned book, "The Evolution of American Thought." He hoped to present them as a series to "literary clubs and schools in our suburban towns" but starred ten that were ready for separate delivery, among them his favorites:

9. Walt Whitman. The Prophet of the New Age.
10. The Epic of the Age. The Novel. The American Novel.
11. Americanism in the Novel. William D. Howells and
    Henry James.

"What is the name of your agent I talked with him while I was there about sometime handling my work?" he asked Riley in December.[11] While casting about for an agent, he established "a sort of connection" with the New England Conservatory of Music and hoped to be named one of its faculty. When he learned that Riley was coming to Boston, he tried to enlist the poet to join him in a dual program, perhaps thinking of his pleasure in the Twain-Cable "Twins of Genius" lecture he had witnessed four years earlier. "I would read 'Ladrone' and one or two other similar pieces, leaving to you the humor and pathos," he explained, referring to one of his early poems, about a faithful horse. "My connection with the Conservatory is teacher of American literature and I shall make *our* principles of art, shake the circumjacent atmosphere. And getting you there is part of my scheme. I hope to have Howells and other modern realists and Americans."[12]

So eager was he to establish himself that he was not above dropping names to achieve his goal. "When Whitcomb Riley was here he wanted me to meet you and it would have been brought about to my great pleasure, had you not been delayed in reaching the city," he began a letter to Samuel Clemens, then at the height of his fame; "but his name and the name of Mr. Howells will no doubt put me on proper footing with you." He enclosed his 1888–89 lecture circular as well as a new one for "Prairie Song and Western Story," four programs consisting of virtually every western poem, story, and sketch he had yet written. Included were excerpts from his "Boy Life" sketches, dialect poems, prose and poetry of his Dakota experience, "Mrs. Ripley's Trip," and four parts from "The Rise of Boomtown." "The Conservatory have made arrangements for me to teach these revolutionary American ideas of literature for the coming year and have also taken me into their [lecture] bureau, so far so good," he explained to Clemens; "but now we've got to get the public aware of me and interested in my matters." He asked Clemens for advice about reaching southern audiences: "This later group of novelists have large space in my book of lectures and I am enthusiastic over their future. I wish I could help them at the same time I help my-self." He asked for names of managers or other "advice as to procedure," and concluded by reminding Clemens once again that "We have mutual friends in Howells, Whitman, Riley and others, and I have wanted to meet you for a long time but have had no good opportunity."

Clemens, busy completing *A Connecticut Yankee in King Arthur's Court*, apparently was unimpressed with the brash young man's move, for he scrawled on the envelope, "Please tell him / Gone away to / finish a book, / & left no address. / SLC."[13]

Early in January 1889 the *Transcript*'s Charles Hurd gave Garland two tickets for a performance of James Herne's *Drifting Apart*. What Hamlin saw galvanized the habitual theatergoer and budding playwright, for he was entranced by the restrained quality of the acting, so different from the usual hyperbolic expression common on the stage. Immediately, he fired off a letter to Herne. "It was at once a surprise and an inspiration," he noted. "A surprise to find such work done by a man whose very name was unfamiliar to me; an inspiration, because I said he is a product of the new spirit of truth. Perhaps, without knowing it, you are linked with the new school of genuine realists; not the realists of the tank-drama and the fire-engine, but the school of artists who are trying to depict the essentials of the life common to us all of to-day."[14]

Drifting Apart is a melodramatic temperance play without the traditional didactic sermons preaching the evils of drink. Jack Hepburn, a sailor, marries Mary Miller, who is the usual long-suffering center of moral stability. One Christmas Eve Jack arrives home drunk, passes out, and then flees from home in his shame, abandoning his wife and new daughter. Five years later he returns to find that Mary is about to remarry; when her fiancé discovers her previous marriage, the Hepburns are cast into the streets and struggle to survive. In a

shocking fourth act, Mary and her child die of starvation while waiting for Jack to return with food. The act closes with Jack driven to
madness as a consequence of their deaths and his guilt. The curtain
rises in act 5 for the audience to discover that the preceding scenes
have been an extended dream; the cast assembles to sing "Turn Your
Glasses Upside Down" as the Hepburns celebrate Christmas.[15]

His letter continued to analyze each act in terms of the actors'
fidelity to truth, but Garland was especially impressed with the ability of the playwright's wife, Katherine Herne, to mimic life in the
second act: "The little caressing tones and gestures, the action of the
house-wife, sewing or moving about the room, the tones of mock
indignation, the fond admiration of Jack's jokes and actions, these
and a hundred other indescribable things make this act so real that
many are deceived into saying, 'that's not acting at all; its just what
any woman would do in her place,' and yet it is the perfection of
art."[16] With his training in oratorical expression and his admiration
for Booth's emotive gestures, Garland was alert to actors who could
express an idea with subtlety rather than with the exaggerated sentiment common to most melodramas of the time.

Herne responded on January 6, 1889, to express his pleasure:
"Your letter demonstrates the fact that as you saw my work, others will see it also, not so readily, nor so clearly—but they will see
it. . . . The opinions and convictions of a man like you carry great
weight. They are repeated. One says, 'Well if Mr. Garland endorses
such and such a thing, it must be meritorious. I will look into it' he
does so—prejudiced in its favor—he repeats your opinion to another—he to another and so on until all find themselves interested
in something they are the better for having known."[17] With this exchange of letters, Garland and Herne began a deep and satisfying
friendship that would last until Herne's death in 1901. They would
not meet, however, until May, when Herne returned to his Beale
Street home in the Boston suburb of Dorchester after fulfilling out-
of-town theater commitments.

Sometime that spring Franklin caught acting fever, perhaps as
a result of attending plays with his older brother. Employed as a
bookkeeper at a wholesale silverware outfit, he made time to take

acting lessons from dramatic coach Edith Stanhope. Hamlin recalls rehearsing Franklin "three nights in the week at his office," with Franklin adding that the rehearsals consisted of learning parts to thirteen plays, with six to be performed in any given week as part of the "kerosene circuit." When Hamlin attended his brother's first performance as a minor character in Edward Bulwer Lytton's *The Lady of Lyons*, he told Franklin that he "narrowly missed playing it well."[18] The tour "was extremely diverting but not at all remunerative," and when the "company went on a reef," Hamlin sent Franklin carfare, "crediting it to his educational account."[19]

Herne soon learned from Hamlin of Franklin's acting ambitions and offered the younger brother "the small but excellent character bit of the Old Fisherman" in his earlier success, *Hearts of Oak*, at twenty dollars per week and "*ostensible* charge of the stage" while learning "the artistic, mechanical and commercial parts of the dramatic profession from the back door to the front."[20]

One May afternoon Garland called on the Hernes. Katherine met him at the door and ushered him in to meet her three daughters—Julie, age eight, Chrystal, nearly seven, and Dorothy, three. He passed their scrutiny and went in to meet James A. Herne. Born in 1839, Herne was pulled out of school at age thirteen to work in a brush factory, his father, like Garland's, believing that education was unnecessary to make one's way in the world. After six years of hard labor, he left home as part of a traveling company playing *The Butcher of Ghent and His Dog*—with the dog the star of the show. He worked his way up in various stock companies, establishing a reputation as a skilled character actor. In 1876 he was the manager of the Baldwin Theater in San Francisco, with David Belasco as his assistant, when he met Katherine Corcoran. Born in Ireland 1856, Katherine soon immigrated with her family to the United States, where her father fought for the Union in the Civil War, later dying of injuries sustained while a prisoner of war. Her childhood was marked by destitution until an uncle helped her mother obtain a war widow's pension, and the family moved to California, where Katherine studied drama. Her coach arranged for Herne to observe Katherine run through a scene; immediately captivated by her beauty as well as her skill, he offered her a part in *Masks and Faces*. She became his leading lady while on tour, and they married in April 1878.[21] Herne later turned to playwriting, achieving his greatest financial success as coauthor (with Belasco) of *Hearts of Oak*, which opened in 1879. He wrote and acted in other plays, and when Garland saw him in *Drifting Apart* he was struggling to attract audiences, for the play's serious theme and realistic treatment failed to draw, and even the addition of the fifth-act dream device failed to overcome the public's perception that the play was depressing.

At the Hernes' home on that May evening, Garland soon found himself welcomed by the gregarious family, who marveled at his ability to converse easily about the latest scientific topics. Later he would write of that initial meeting, "I went away at last with the feeling that these people were my kind. I had never met such instant and warm-hearted sympathy. My head rang with their piquant phrases, their earnest and changeful voices."[22]

Herne's daughter Julie, who would later become an accomplished actress, remembered that "Hamlin Garland swept into that quiet household like a cyclone from his own prairies. He was about thirty years old, strong and broad-shouldered, and though of medium height, he seemed to fill Herne's study." She was especially struck by his commanding presence: "He was very handsome, with his pale face, dark beard, finely cut features and deep-set, flashing eyes. He had a pleasant voice, a strong Western accent and an infectious chuckle." Above all, his oratorical training held the young Julie "spell-bound as the words poured out, vivid, polished, perfectly phrased."[23] His visit lasted far into the night, she recalled, for Herne and Garland soon found they were "in general agreement about the drama, literature, religion and politics"—though Garland could be a difficult conversationalist. The earnest advocate had "a directness and forthrightness that amounted almost to brusqueness. He had no small-talk and abhorred trivialities. When the conversation did not interest him, he would get up and walk away. He was very much in earnest. . . . His humor was grim and ironic rather than genial. The hardships of his boyhood . . . had left their mark on him in a certain harshness of manner, a somewhat defiant attitude towards life. At the same time, he had an almost feminine tenderness and sympathy for suffering of any kind." Garland soon made a habit of riding his "safety bicycle"—the kind with the front wheel larger than the rear—out to the Hernes' Beale Street home, where he would impress the children of the neighborhood with the still relatively new invention, calling it his "fiery, untamed steed." Early on, Julie remembered, the Hernes called Garland "'the Dean,' partly in fun, partly in affection," for they were impressed with his education and his ability to hold forth on a variety of topics.[24]

Garland's earnest discussions of Spencer and Henry George soon converted Herne to the single-tax cause, and he, like Garland, began to speak on its behalf. They also introduced each other to their respective circles of friends—with Herne providing introductions to such actors as William Gillette, Mary Shaw, and Maud Banks, and Garland arranging for Herne to meet Howells and Charles Hurd, Edward Clement, and Joseph Chamberlin of the *Transcript*. More immediately, however, Garland's critique of *Drifting Apart* prompted Herne to make another round of revision. "If I do make fine work of it," he wrote to Garland concerning the revision, "it will be a reflecting of Hamlin Garland and his mentorship. I never saw my faults,—conspicuous as I know they must be to others. I could not see them, until you made them so clear."[25]

His friendship with the Hernes reawakened Garland's playwriting ambitions, and by June he had completed a draft of a single-tax play. *Under the Wheel* is Garland's most sustained effort to put into dramatic form the themes and characterizations depicted in the stories later gathered in *Main-Travelled Roads*. His purpose in the play, he later explained, was to "present first of all a picture of certain phases of American life, and secondarily a problem, because no section of life, carefully considered, fails to present phases of shortcomings, injustices, and suffering calculated to make the thoughtful man fall into deep thought."[26] The play portrays the social and environmental forces that, when coupled with land speculation, create a social "problem" for which George's single tax becomes, as Garland states in the preface, "the heroic cure for most—if not all—of the disease and deformity of our social life."

The play traces the struggle of the Edwards family to attain the American dream. Mired in the crowded tenements of the city, Jason Edwards is squeezed between increasing rents and decreasing wages. Lured by the railroad's advertisements for "free land" in Dakota, the Edwards family moves to the prairie, where they hope to start afresh with "wealth, health, and freedom" and therefore escape the vicissitudes of avaricious landlords and factory owners.[27] But the myth of the golden West soon collapses, for Edwards finds that the "free land" costs ten dollars an acre, his crops fail, and a violent hailstorm destroys both farm and home and leaves him physically paralyzed.

The play is, in part, a dramatization of Garland's November 1887 single-tax speech before the Boston Anti-Poverty Society, "The Social Aspect of the Land Tax." In his address Garland had outlined "the consequences of the insane policy" of encouraging land speculation, arguing that "for nearly a century free land has been a myth. Every foot of it was bought with blood and sweat and tears. . . . Our land policy has constantly opposed our social development by constant dispersion of men through the wilderness."[28] He also incorporated parts of "John Boyle's Conclusion," retaining both the central situation—a farmer lured west by promises of free land—and the denouement—the destruction of one's spirit before a harsh, indifferent nature. Portions of the narrative are transformed into the characterization and dialogue of *Under the Wheel*. For instance, Boyle's bitter reproaches against a seemingly vindictive God appear in Jason Edwards's mouth, and the depiction of the hailstorm and Boyle's cry "Hail, by the livin' God!" appear with little alteration.[29]

Garland had high hopes for his play. On July 20 the *Standard* reported that Herne planned to produce and star in the play, but the more reliable draw of an established play might have led him to change his mind. Or it might be that he found *Under the Wheel*'s realism undramatic for its time. Julie Herne remembers that her father once told her mother that "Garland's idea of drama is a scene in which two people discuss, for instance, the purchase of a ton of coal. One says, 'I think we are running short of coal.' The other replies, 'We have enough to last until next week.' To him, that is realism. To me, it is not drama."[30]

While working on *Under the Wheel*, Garland was also busy lecturing at the New England Conservatory, where he was doing his best to promote Whitman. "My class is composed of about fifty bright young girls studying music," he wrote to Whitman in April 1889. "You see I am not afraid to carry your word to anyone. To me there is not a line that has a downward tendency." But he acknowledged that propriety demanded protecting girls from knowledge of sex: "Still I recognize the fact that to many people 'A woman waits for me' is wholly inadmissible."[31] "A Woman Waits for Me," with its rich seminal imagery, was one of the poems specifically classified as "obscene" by the Boston district attorney in his 1882 ruling against *Leaves of Grass*. Whitman enjoyed receiving reports of Garland's promotional efforts, and the young advocate was invited to Whitman's seventieth birthday dinner in Camden. On May 31 Hamlin joined an assemblage of distinguished guests gathered to pay homage to the poet, including Julian Hawthorne, son of the author of *The Scarlet Letter*; Richard Watson Gilder, editor of the prestigious *Century* magazine; and other friends of Whitman's. Garland, seated second to Whitman's left, read his tribute, "The Teacher," in which he praised Whitman as "our great democratic poet" whose "sublime optimism spreads wings over" all misfortune. He then linked Whitman to the Spencerian doctrine of evolutionary progress, no doubt reflecting what he had been teaching his own students: "He caught long ago the deepest principle of evolution, of progress, which is, that the infinite past portends and prefigures the infinite future; that each age is the child of the past and the parent of the future; that nothing happens, that everything is caused; and that no age could conceivably have been other than it was." Whitman's faith in the future of humanity, Garland concluded, "is one of the great lessons of our poet-seer."[32]

By the summer of 1889 Garland had established a beachhead in the literary marketplace. Counting his first story, "Ten Years Dead," he had published three stories, and another, "John Boyle's Conclusion," had been accepted. His "Boy Life on the Prairie" sketches had confirmed his knack for descriptive writing, and more than two dozen poems, book reviews, and other miscellaneous writing kept his name before the public. In his remarkable industry he had drafts of several plays, a number of stories, and beginnings of novels under way simultaneously. As he explained to an interviewer in 1892, "I work exactly like a painter. I have, I may say, a number of canvases on the easel. I have at my elbow from five to twenty different things. I sit at my desk every morning. I take up sketch after sketch or a section of a novel. I read over what I have written, and when I come to the point where the day's work is to begin if I find myself unable to go on in the same mood in which I was writing when I stopped, I lay that aside and take up another; so that I have all the way from ten to twenty-five unfinished things on hand to work on when the mood is on me."[33] Most of his publishing successes had been with limited-circulation periodicals like the *American*, *Belford's*, and the *Boston Evening Transcript*, and although he had published three short items in the nationally circulated *Harper's Weekly*, he had his sights on bigger game. It was therefore with considerable delight that he cracked the *Century* with his first shot.

In June 1889 he submitted three stories to the most prestigious magazine of its time. "Dear Sir," he wrote to its editor, Richard Watson Gilder. "The only favor I ask for the enclosed stories is: that they be read with a due regard for the aims of the author. First I aim to be true to the life I am depicting and to deal not with abnormal phases so much as with representative phases. I am western born and the dialect and descriptive matter can be relied upon. Pardon me for bombarding you at wholesale."[34] Gilder accepted "A Spring Romance," an Iowa story about a hired man wooing a farmer's daughter against her father's wishes, and paid its author $75—more than $1,500 in today's money—the most he had yet been paid for his writing.[35] "It meant something to get into the *Century* in those days," Garland later remembered. "The praise of its editor was equivalent to a diploma. I regarded Gilder as second only to Howells in all that had to do with the judgment of fiction."[36]

The Century Illustrated Monthly Magazine was founded in 1881 from the ashes of *Scribner's Monthly*, after disagreement with the Scribner's book publishing house over the right to issue books caused a realignment of management and a change in the magazine's name and editorship. Gilder, who had been the associate editor of *Scribner's Monthly*, became editor in chief of the new magazine. The *Century* (named after the New York club at Gilder's suggestion) quickly soared to the top of American magazines after publishing a series of memoirs by Civil War generals, from 1884 to 1887, increasing its circulation from 127,000 to 225,000, lagging behind only the very popular *Youth's Companion* in numbers of subscribers.[37] It was known as America's best-printed magazine, with its excellent typography and well-executed illustrations. In addition to serial biographies and essays on topical issues, it boasted a roster of distinguished authors, among them Howells, Mark Twain, Henry James, Rebecca Harding Davis, Edward Eggleston, Bret Harte, George Washington Cable, and Helen Hunt Jackson. In the 1880s, three of Howells's novels appeared serially—*A Modern Instance, The Rise of Silas Lapham*, and *The Minister's Charge*—as did James's *The Bostonians* and expurgated selections from Twain's *Adventures of Huckleberry Finn*.

At the time of Garland's letter, Gilder was actively encouraging southern writers of local color, publishing, in addition to Twain and Cable, stories by such writers as Joel Chandler Harris and Thomas Nelson Page, which may be why Garland stressed the authenticity of his "dialect and descriptive matter." Like Howells, Gilder favored realistic writing, but he was also mindful that his magazine was aimed at families and did not want to shock or offend them by publishing stories that violated decorum. What counted was proportion. An editor with an eye always on the artistry of the submission, Gilder explained in an 1887 essay, "We do not want less realism, but more of it; and better, fuller than we now have! In some of our current realistic work a true method, used awkwardly by men freshly and deeply enamoured therewith, becomes obvious and ineffectual. The result is a straining after novelty; the elevation of the insignificant; in a word, a lack of proportion, a lack of art."[38]

"A Spring Romance" was just the sort of story Gilder was seeking, for the tale of an honest, hardworking hired man courting the daughter of a mulish, irascible farmer offered readers a pleasing picture of country ways while affirming the sanctity of home and the value of hard work. Garland soon sent another parcel of stories to Gilder. "If any changes will make them more acceptable," he noted in his letter of September 7, "be sure I will do all that is in reason. There may be some objection to the strong language—if so it can easily be softened down."[39] Gilder accepted the Dakota novelette "Old Pap's Flaxen"—a tale of two homesteading bachelors who adopt an orphaned girl—and paid Garland three hundred dollars for it, but he rejected "A Prairie Heroine," a grim story of a defeated farm wife. On a hardscrabble Iowa farm, Sim Burns has been made brutish by unending, backbreaking labor. He growls at his wife, kicks his children out of his way, and in general behaves more as an animal responding to conditions than as a man. Lucretia Burns is so despondent she contemplates suicide, not once, but twice.

Small wonder that Gilder rejected "A Prairie Heroine," for its depiction of human misery seemed all out of proportion to his eastern sensibility. In composing the story, Garland had learned much from the Hernes, particularly in depicting the human drama of a story to touch the emotions of his readers. While he wanted to be recognized as an artist, he also believed fiction was an effective means to move readers to action. After seeing Katharine Herne's moving evocation of pathos in *Drifting Apart,* Garland learned the persuasive power of sympathy as a means to elicit an emotional response. As he noted in an article about the Hernes, the suggestive subtlety of Katharine's portrayal of Mary Miller awoke in him a new understanding of maternal agony: "Mrs. Herne's acting of Mary Miller was my first realization of the compelling power of truth. It was so utterly opposed to the 'tragedy of the legitimate.' Here was tragedy that appalled and fascinated like the great fact of living. No noise, no contortions of face or limbs, yet somehow I was made to feel the dumb, inarticulate, interior agony of a mother. Never before had such acting faced me across the footlights."[40]

The stories Garland wrote after January 1889 show a new emphasis on sentiment enlisted to promote sympathy for the plight of the border farmer. Unlike his earlier fiction, "A Prairie Heroine" and "A Spring Romance"—like the later "Up the Coulé" and "A Branch Road"—demonstrate an increasing reliance upon sentimental emo-

tion and melodramatic plots, especially in depictions of downtrod-
den wives and redemptive conclusions. Believing in the inherent
goodness of the common man and convinced that emotions are a
moral index to character, Garland adopted the melodramatic strategy of explicitly indicating the value within a given situation through
gesture, pantomime, and tableau to convey the moral values of a
scene symbolically. In the climax of "A Prairie Heroine," for example, when Lily Graham gains Sim Burns's permission to comfort his
long-suffering wife, Lucretia, and to heal their shattered marriage,
Garland articulates the healing power of pity, rendered through the
fictional equivalent of the silent gesture: Lucretia "dropped her dish
as she heard Lily coming, and gazed up into the tender, pitying face.
Not a word was spoken, but something she saw there made her eyes
fill with tears, and her throat swell. It was pure sympathy. She put
her arms around the girl's neck and sobbed for the first time since
Friday night. Then they sat down on the grass under the hedge and
she told her story, interspersed with Lily's horrified comments. . . . It
helped her not to hate Burns; it helped her to pity and understand
him." Healed by Lily's sympathy, Lucretia forgives her husband's
cruelty and "become[s] a wife and mother again."[41] Because his goal
in this story was to show the Burns family—and particularly their
misery—to be a product of unjust land distribution, Garland adopted the rhetoric of melodrama so that readers could not help but
see the inequity of land speculation, which to him was the principal
cause of the impoverished conditions of the middle border.

In his reply to Gilder's rejection, Garland acknowledged that the
polemics of the story were out of proportion to its "art." "All you say
is very true," he wrote to Gilder. "'Prairie Heroine' in some phases
is a little too obviously preaching. My tendency is to present things
concretely and let others find the preaching. I know when I did
that final section that it was a falling off, from the artistic standpoint—but I wanted to 'let the light in' as Walt Whitman asked
me to do. I wanted to give hope, somehow."[42] Only rarely would
Garland manage to combine "art" and propaganda effectively, for
the two modes are diametrically opposed to one another in their
assumptions and methods. He wanted Howells and Gilder to rec-

ognize him as an artist on their terms—that is, to write fiction that conveyed what Howells called "the smiling aspects of life" in a manner in proportion to the average condition of people. But he was also a die-hard propagandist who wanted to move readers to action, and the most effective tool of the propagandist is hyperbole. There is artful propaganda, however—"A Prairie Heroine" demonstrates considerable skill in its use of melodramatic and sensational narrative strategies—and Garland's immediate challenge was to find the appropriate place to publish his polemical fiction.

8

MAIN-TRAVELLED ROADS, 1889–91

September 1889 proved to be a busy month. Word came that his sister, Jessie, had married. The fate Garland had feared and which he had delineated in "A Common Case" had come to pass: Jessie had married a Dakota farmer. The *Sentinel* of Columbia, Dakota Territory, announced the marriage of Bert S. Knapp and Jessie V. Garland on September 4: "The party was very lively and wide awake to be so Knappy," the paper breezily began. "None more than he appreciates the Garland of beauty and honor with which he has or-namented his happy future."[1] Her brother must have been pleased that his twenty-year-old sister had married and would remain in Columbia to keep his mother company, but he was no doubt dis-appointed that she had scaled no higher than a farmer's wife, for he had seen how badly farm life treated women. But Jessie would never find out whether her brother's forebodings would come true. Thirteen months later she was dead, a victim of malignant erysipelas, a bacterial skin infection that today is easily treated with antibiotics. Garland's only comment about the effect of her death appears in *A Son of the Middle Border*, where he records merely that "My little sis-ter died suddenly, leaving my father and mother alone on the bleak plain, seventeen hundred miles from both their sons. Hopelessly crippled, my mother now mourned the loss of her 'baby' and the soldier's keen eyes grew dim, for he loved his little daughter above everything else in the world."[2] With the deaths of both of his sisters and the crippling of his mother—all on isolated farms far from the comforts and security of cities—it is no wonder that Garland's early fiction is so marked by the grim specter of defeat. Later he would dedicate the novella *The Spirit of Sweetwater* (1898), the tale of a wealthy miner whose love for a sickly maiden restores her health, to both sisters.

On September 7 *Harper's Weekly* published "Under the Lion's Paw," one of Garland's finest stories; on that day, too, the *Standard* announced his offer to read the story for the benefit of single-tax clubs, in exchange for his expenses.[3] "Under the Lion's Paw" marked a notable advance for Garland. In this story he had at last figured out how to embody single-tax politics without overtly preaching his message. Farmer Haskins has been driven from his Kansas farm by voracious grasshoppers. Remembering all the vacant land he had crossed in Iowa—which he had bypassed because it was priced too dearly at ten or fifteen dollars per acre for bare land—he has arrived in Cedar County in desperation. The charitable Stephen Council arranges for him to take possession of a farm whose previous tenant has been driven off by a foreclosed mortgage. Jim Butler, Haskins's landlord—and the story's villain—is a former grocer turned land speculator, corrupted by the promise of easy cash. He agrees to rent the farm for $250 per year or sell it outright for $2,500. Three years later, when Haskins proudly shows Butler his $1,500 dollars worth of "improvements"—rebuilt farmhouse, new fencing, abundant livestock, rich fields of wheat—and offers to buy the farm, Butler jacks up the price, explaining that "The land is doubled in value, it don't matter how; it don't enter into the question; an' now you can pay me five hundred dollars a year rent, or take it on your own terms at fifty-five hundred, or—git out."[4] When Butler coolly explains that Haskins's sweat equity counts for nothing, that profiting from the unearned increment is the "reg'lar thing," Haskins becomes enraged and is saved by his baby's cry from stabbing Butler with a pitchfork.

Gone is the mouthpiece character who tells the reader the meaning of a scene; instead, Garland exemplifies in the interaction of the characters the point that speculation unfairly withholds land from use. Like "A Prairie Heroine," the story includes scenes designed to arouse his readers' passions and so move them to outrage, if not action. Indeed, the story was quickly enlisted in the single-tax cause. On September 28 the *Standard* reprinted the story along with an announcement from Garland that James Herne would read the story before "any single tax league" in Buffalo, Cincinnati, or Philadelphia during the next three weeks.[5] And for the next year, the *Standard* published frequent announcements of Herne's and Garland's reading of the story in various cities.

How do we explain the apparent unevenness of Garland's production, the appearance and non-appearance of preaching in stories written at about the same time? Part of the reason may lie in his method of working on any given story when prompted by a mood. But a more likely explanation is that, as he grew more experienced in the craft of fiction, Garland was better able to size up a magazine's requirements. He knew how to satisfy *Harper's Weekly*, but he also wanted to change the world through his fiction; in submitting "A Prairie Heroine" to the *Century*, he learned that the genteel magazine was not the right outlet. He had yet to discover a national magazine hospitable to polemical fiction.

Garland spent much of the fall revising "Old Pap's Flaxen" and attending plays. Dramatic interests soon took center stage. He promoted *Drifting Apart* by encouraging his friends to attend a revival and publishing a letter recommending it in the *Literary World*.[6] He collaborated with the Hernes on at least two plays, both never finished—composing alternate acts with Katherine of "Marrying a Title," a comedy of mismatched lovers, and, with James, "Fall River," a play about an adulterer. On October 30 he attended a performance of Ibsen's *A Doll's House*, "the first really noteworthy performance of an Ibsen play in America," with Beatrice Mansfield playing Nora. He immediately sent a letter to the *Transcript* proposing that an Ibsen club be formed to produce first Ibsen's plays and then radical American plays, thinking no doubt of his own *Under the Wheel*.[7] By January he had completed revisions of *Under the Wheel* and sent the play to Gilder. "Mr. Howells calls it a great play and Mr. Herne agrees from the actors standpoint," he told Gilder, hoping to influence his judgment. "These opinions make me courageous enough to send it to you." He then explained that he and Herne hoped to produce it in May and pointed to the mutual benefit of publication and production in sales of the magazine and tickets. "Please take the thing home on Sunday and spoil your only day of leisure look-ing at it."[8] Gilder declined.

Another success at *Harper's Weekly*—publication of the story "Old Sid's Christmas" in the December 28, 1889, issue—and the prospect of additional stories in the *Century* prompted Garland to act on a long-held dream: a room of his own. Since 1885 he had been room-ing in Hiram Cross's attic on Seaverns Avenue. In February 1890 he moved to 12 Moreland Street, three miles away in the suburb of Roxbury, where he shared an apartment with Franklin. "I went so far as to buy a couple of pictures and a new book rack, the first property I had ever owned," he recalled; "we glowed with such ex-ultant pride as only struggling youth can feel."[9] Seven months later, in September, the brothers would move to 9 Talman Place.

By the spring of 1890 Garland was growing frustrated with his ef-forts to get into print. Though he had now established a relationship with the *Century*, the magazine was so inundated with high-quality submissions that delays between acceptance and publication were lengthening. Indeed, supply overwhelmed demand at all the pres-tigious monthly magazines—*Harper's*, *Atlantic*, *Scribner's*—as well as the *Century*. Between January 1886 and January 1887, for instance, *Harper's* "received 12,024 manuscripts, half of them poems . . . and used a total of only 200 of these items."[10] Submission and acceptance figures for the *Century* were comparable. While Garland was highly gratified that his work had been accepted, he began to grow impa-tient at the delay in publication. "A Spring Romance" had been ac-cepted in June 1889 but would not be published until June 1891; "Old Pap's Flaxen," accepted in September 1889, experienced an even longer delay, not appearing in the *Century* until March, April, and May 1892. Gilder had also accepted "A Girl of Modern Tyre" in April 1890, but it would not be published until January 1897. Garland had written to his friends of his plans to collect a volume of his fiction and so enter the much-desired book market, but he could not do so until his stories had appeared in the magazine first. Little wonder that he complained to Gilder in November, "I've been looking with more (or less) than anxiety for the appearance of my stories a beginning of which was promised for October. I *hope* you havent put me off another year for I've got some other things I want to send you."[11]

Then in April 1890 came a letter accepting "A Prairie Heroine" from Benjamin Orange Flower, who had founded the *Arena* magazine four months earlier and intended his magazine to be a forum for controversial writing on current issues. "If satisfactory to you I will send you a check for seventy-five dollars," Flower wrote, no doubt surprising Garland by matching the *Century*'s payment for "A Spring Romance." But what followed must have pleased Garland even more, for Flower promised to mount a publicity campaign and call "attention to the publication of the story two weeks before it appears and will also call special attention in our Notes and Comments." But Flower's conclusion must have astonished the frustrated author:

> I notice you have seemed to suppress your thoughts in two or three instances and have erased some lines from your story. In writing for the Arena either stories or essays I wish you always to feel yourself thoroughly free to express any opinions you desire or to send home any lessons which you feel should be impressed upon the people. I for one do not believe in mincing matters when we are dealing with the great wrongs and evils of the day and the pitiful conditions of society and I do not wish you to feel in writing for the Arena at any time, the slightest constraint.[12]

Garland had met a struggling writer's dream: an accommodating editor who would publish virtually everything Garland cared to send him. Thus began one of the most significant professional relationships of his career, for Flower would publish thirty-three stories, articles, poems, and reviews by Garland, as well as his first three books, about one-third of his literary output during the years 1890 to 1894.

The son of an Illinois farmer-preacher, Flower was born near Albion, Illinois, in 1858. Raised in a home marked by religious and intellectual fervor, he studied for the ministry but soon quit to found a newspaper in Albion, where from his pulpit as editor he promoted a number of social reforms, primarily temperance. In 1882 he drifted to Boston, where his brother Charles, with a dubious medical degree, had founded a sanatorium to cure nervous disorders. After a stint as his brother's secretary, in 1886 Flower was put in charge of its house magazine, the *American Spectator*, whose primary mission was to advertise Dr. Flower's mail-order goods. As one student of the history of magazines has noted, Flower's "background of reformatory zeal, intellectuality, religion, and quackery are important in understanding the career of B. O. Flower's *Arena*," for the magazine immediately established itself as a forum for debate of contemporary social issues.[13] In its pages Flower trumpeted progress of all kinds. Early issues debated the intersection of science and religion, but soon Flower's zealotry spread outward. Contributors clashed over topics such as child labor, poverty, eradication of slums, birth control, eugenics, prostitution, women's rights, psychic phenomena, the single tax, and socialist politics. With his reform notions, Flower favored didactic fiction and decried the "Art for Art's Sake" movement as an "echo of a decaying civilization, . . . the shibboleth of a people drunken with pleasure; of a popular conscience anaesthetized."[14]

Garland soon found that Flower shared his interest in using fiction to improve the lives of others. He immediately sent Flower the manuscript of *Under the Wheel.* After reading only the opening pages, Flower paused to write, "We are in perfect accord as to the needs of the present hour and I am also impressed with the fact that we must depend as much on the drama and fiction as all other agencies combined in bringing about a higher civilization. There is nothing that so effectively carries home a lesson to the heart of the people as a realistic drama, conscientiously and ably acted, or a story true to life and strong in its moral emphasis."[15] He soon accepted *Under the Wheel,* paying Garland two hundred dollars, and the play appeared in the July issue. When they met that summer, Garland recalled, "I was surprised to find him of my own age, a small, round-faced, smiling youth with black eyes and curling hair. He was a new sort of reformer, genial, laughing, tolerant." In his diary he would remember Flower as "one of the most unselfish men I ever knew. 'Organized altruism' I have sometimes called him. He is a crank of course and a faddist but a brave and generous and high-minded eccentric after all is said."[16] Flower encouraged Garland's reform writing, suggesting he draft articles on the single tax and other controversial topics, as well as review books for the magazine.

It's hard to overstress the importance of Flower's encouragement, for the prompt publication—and equally prompt payment—soon put Garland on his feet financially and, just as important for his ambition, enabled him to reach an audience of like-minded readers. He thus crowed to Herne, "B. O. Flower and I are getting chums. He's one o' my kind. Dont smoke, chew, drink n'r fool away his time. He's indefatigable. A tremendous worker. . . . He's concentrated moral purpose." Equally important was the financial stability and growing circulation of the *Arena*. "And behind him stands that brother of his pouring out money wherever needed," Garland continued. "Mark my words these Flower bros. are going to be one of the great forces of the age. The *Arena* will print 30,000 copies as the first ed. this month. Nearly three times the circulation of the N. American Review—and twice the circulation of *Forum* and N. Am. Review put together—and all inside a year. Do you wonder I'm enthusiastic?"[17] In 1891 Garland would publish four short stories, two essays, and six book reviews in the *Arena*, more than half of his twenty publications for the year.

As he often did with works he regarded as important, Garland sent an advance copy of *Under the Wheel* to Howells. "The play mounts to a powerful effect that thrills, and it reaches an end that leaves me thinking most earnestly," his mentor wrote him. "It is *good*, and though I shall have some minor reproaches to make it when we meet, I wish now only to praise it."[18] When the play appeared in the July *Arena* it gathered a few press notices. In a lengthy, full-column review, the *Chicago Tribune* proclaimed Garland "an American Ibsen," "at his best" in depicting the western landscape. "The horror of drought—hopeless, persistent, unending, crushing, rainlessness in an agricultural district—is set forth with a degree of truth and unflinching boldness that no other realist could surpass." The *New York Independent* lauded the play as "undoubtedly one of the most vivid and promising pieces of creative literature put forth by a rising author in many years." The *Standard* printed an excerpt in its July 30 issue. The positive response soon prompted Garland to issue the play as a book, with the *Standard* announcing that it would cost only twenty-five cents per copy, "for the author desires it rather to be widely read than to be a paying production."[19] He appealed to Howells to introduce the play, but Howells declined, explaining, "I don't think it would be well for me to introduce or indorse your play. It has good legs of its own, and can stand on them without any sort of bolstering. I know the suggestion comes from your generous willingness to do anything and everything for your friends, and I love you for it; but I don't believe in it."[20]

Garland's first book was a vanity press production. He later told Barrett H. Clark that the play "was published by a young printer who was a fellow radical and willing to take a chance on the expense of the printing. It was not really published but an edition of a thousand was printed and I sold or gave away most of them."[21] It was printed from the *Arena* plates, and prospective buyers were directed to call for the book at 7 Beacon Street—the address of the Boston School of Oratory, where Garland was still a member of the faculty.

The publication of *Under the Wheel* soon led to larger ambitions for both Flower and Garland. Perhaps realizing he had missed an opportunity when Garland turned to a printer for the book publication of his play, in September Flower turned book publisher by establishing the Arena Publishing Company. Flower chose his first book wisely—or fortuitously. For the inaugural volume he recruited Helen Hamilton Gardener, a renowned feminist who gained considerable fame for her study "Sex in Brain," a carefully researched refutation of a claim by Dr. William Hammond, a former surgeon general of the U.S. Army, that women's brains are measurably inferior to men's. In November 1890, Flower published Gardener's novel *Is This Your Son, My Lord?*—an outspoken attack on the double standard that would in due course sell more than thirty-five thousand copies. But few of the Arena volumes ever attained that sort of celebrity. From 1890 to 1896 the Arena Publishing Company published an eclectic mix of 206 tracts, pamphlets, novels, and dry social studies with such titles as *The Money Question; A Spiritual Tour of the World in Search of the Lines of Life's Evolution; Christ, the Socialist; Deborah, the Advanced Woman;* and *Hypnotism: How It Is Done; Its Uses and Dangers.* The press's motto, which appeared on most covers, was "Art for Truth." Most books were issued in printings of a thousand, with cloth copies selling for a dollar and paperbound volumes for fifty cents. Many paperbound copies were sold in newsstands as part of the Arena, Copley Square, Present-Day Problems, Side Pocket, and Beacon Library series. Flower usually promoted the growing list with up to thirty-two pages of advertisements, promotional blurbs, and reviews in the *Arena.*[22]

Flower soon suggested to Garland that he collect a volume of his stories for publication by the Arena Publishing Company. This was Garland's dream: to be counted as an author of books, to have his fiction reviewed and discussed like that of Howells, Kirkland, Whitman, and other authors he admired. But there was a problem: a dearth of material for the volume. By March 1891 Garland had published nine stories, most of them unsuitable to make up a book-length collection. Some were out of the question: "Ten Years Dead" and "A Common Case" were embarrassing apprenticeship efforts. "Holding Down a Claim in a Blizzard" was, practically speaking, more autobiography than fiction. "Old Sid's Christmas" was a brief story about an aged convict's return home, only to be turned out at Christmas; while it was interesting, Garland rejected it because of its overt moralizing. "Drifting Crane," based on the stories he had heard about Drifting Goose and the settlement of the James River Valley, was out of synch with the four stories about life on midwestern farms that he wanted to form the core of the volume: "Mrs. Ripley's Trip," "Under the Lion's Paw," "Among the Corn Rows," and "The Return of the Private"—all save the last originally published in *Harper's Weekly.* He had other stories, but they had been accepted by magazines and could not be collected until they had appeared in print. The *Century* had two fine stories and a novelette—"A Spring Romance," "A Girl of Modern Tyre," and "Old Pap's Flaxen." *Belford's* was slated to publish two more—"Daddy Deering" and "John Boyle's Conclusion." And "A Prairie Heroine" was scheduled for the July *Arena.*

But lying in his drawer were two long stories—"A Branch Road" and "Up the Coulé," each containing some of his most effective descriptive writing—that Garland had been unable to publish, most likely because, at about fifteen thousand words each, they were of an inconvenient length: too long for the space most magazines had for short fiction, not long enough for serialization. Both are also infused with his sense of guilt at having left his family behind in the West to pursue his ambition. In each a protagonist returns home after an absence and bungles an attempt to rescue those he left behind. With these stories he led the collection he entitled *Main-Travelled Roads: Six Mississippi Valley Stories*, a volume that in truth is more a compilation of Garland's only available stories than it is a purposeful arrangement of stories organized around a controlling artistic principle.[23]

"A Branch Road" is a fictional retelling of Garland's breakup with his seminary sweetheart "Alice," named "Agnes" in the story. Will Hannan, a "seminary chap," has just arrived at a mutual understanding of love with Agnes. Abnormally sensitive to teasing from the fellows, he treats Agnes coldly at a threshing dinner and storms home. Three days later, not having spoken to her since the threshing and on his way to take her to the county fair, he is delayed by a carriage mishap; Agnes, thinking he has stood her up, goes to the fair with a rival. Will writes her an angry letter, carefully calculated to sear her heart, and leaves for Arizona. Seven years later he returns, having made his fortune, hoping to renew his romance with Agnes, despite not having written to her in the interim. He finds she has married his rival, who has verbally whipped her until she has become defeated and prematurely aged. In his guilt he vows to rescue her from her misery, pleads his case, and eventually wins her over—only to be caught short by the sound of a baby crying. Magnanimously, he agrees to take both mother and child, crying "Blue eyes, thank heaven!"—the eye color reflecting his own and not the father's, thus suggesting he will adopt the child as his own.[24]

"A Branch Road" contains some very good descriptive writing and excellent genre portraiture. What may have prompted its composition was news that "Alice" had died. In his autobiography, Garland remembers that he had recently learned of her death. "I had known for years that she was not for me," he mused, "but I loved to think of her as out there walking the lanes among the roses and the wheat as of old. . . . She had been a radiant and charming figure in my prairie world, and when I read the letter telling of her passing, my mind was irradiated with the picture she had made when last she said good-bye to me. Her gentle friendship had been very helpful through all my years of struggle and now, in the day of my security, her place was empty."[25] When he composed "A Branch Road," he recalled the poem about his lost love, "How Will She Look?" written just before his first return visit to Osage in 1887, and set out to capture its mood in his story. "A Branch Road" is thus in part a fantasy re-creation of Garland's bittersweet longing to rekindle his lost romance.

"Up the Coulé" is another story about a guilty return. Howard McLane has abandoned his family to a worn-out Wisconsin farm to pursue a successful stage career in New York. After ten years he returns, only to find the family displaced by a foreclosed mortgage, his mother prematurely aged, his brother broken and embittered, and his brother's wife regretting her marriage and longing to escape. Howard's first sight of his mother is particularly suggestive of Garland's guilt at having left his family in Dakota to pursue his ambition:

> A gray-haired woman was sitting in a rocking-chair on the porch, her hands in her lap, her eyes fixed on the faintly yellow sky, against which the hills stood dim purple silhouettes, and the locust-trees were etched as fine as lace. There was sorrow, resignation, and a sort of dumb despair in her attitude.
>
> Howard stood, his throat swelling till it seemed as if he would suffocate. This was his mother—the woman who bore him, the being who had taken her life in her hand for him; and he, in his excited and pleasurable life, had neglected her![26]

Garland's portrayal of Howard's brother Grant is also suggestive of his sense of culpability for having usurped his own brother's opportunities to succeed. As Howard fumbles an explanation for forgetting his family, he considers Grant and reflects, "Am I so much superior to him? Have not circumstances made me and destroyed him?" But then he rationalizes, "I begin to see it now. Being the oldest, I had the best chance. I was going to town to school while you were out ploughing and husking corn. Of course I thought you'd be going soon, yourself. I had three years the start of you. If you'd been in my place, *you* might have . . . been where I am."[27] All his life, Garland would attempt to make amends for his advantage over Franklin, as he did when he helped him find work in Boston and later arranged for Herne to employ him in his plays. Periodically over the years, Garland would continue to advance Franklin sums of money and otherwise assist him with employment opportunities. "Up the Coulé" suggests that, although his commitment to Spencerian ethics enabled him to rationalize his success, his sense of guilt was deeply ingrained.

Following these two poignant but ultimately bitter stories Garland placed the more lighthearted "Among the Corn Rows," which had appeared in *Harper's Weekly* on June 28, 1890. As he did for the other stories in the collection, he drew upon his prairie background. Rob Rodemaker is homesteading in Dakota Territory. Tiring of bachelor life and his terrible cooking, he sets out for Wisconsin, where the girls are "as thick as huckleberries." He runs across his old playmate Julia Peterson, whose father, as did Garland's, has harnessed her to the plow. Tiring of life as a human draft horse, Julia eagerly responds to Rob's offer to marry her—presented as one comrade to another, and not as a romantic proposal—and take her away from her burden.

"The Return of the Private," now one of Garland's most-anthologized stories, is based on his own father's return from the Civil War and had been published in the *Arena* in December 1890. The details so closely reflected his own father's return that Garland later used the story to begin *A Son of the Middle Border*, even leaving intact some of the lines, reworking it yet again into the conclusion of *Trail-Makers of the Middle Border*. "Under the Lion's Paw" and "Mrs. Ripley's Trip" completed the volume.

To provide a semblance of unity to the volume, Garland added an epigraph to the book and shorter epigraphs to each story in which he traced the metaphor of traveling over a western road. In his review of Whitman's *November Boughs* he had applauded the poet's use of a road metaphor in his preface—Whitman had cast "backward glances over our travel'd road" in assessing his poetic career; with the epigraph to and title of *Main-Travelled Roads*, Garland paid homage to Whitman's influence and, like Whitman, forecast the innovations of his stories, their reversal of the conventional depiction of rural life as nostalgically pleasant:

> The main-travelled road in the West (as everywhere) is hot and dusty in summer, and desolate and drear with mud in fall and spring, and in winter the winds sweep the snow across it; but it does sometimes cross a rich meadow where the songs of the larks and bobolinks and blackbirds are tangled. Follow it far enough, it may lead past a bend in the river where the water laughs eternally over its shallows.
>
> Mainly it is long and wearyful and has a dull little town at one end, and a home of toil at the other. Like the main-travelled road of life, it is traversed by many classes of people, but the poor and the weary predominate.

He dedicated the book to his parents: "To my father and mother, whose half-century pilgrimage on the main-travelled road of life has brought them only toil and deprivation, this book of stories is dedicated by a son to whom every day brings a deepening sense of his parents' silent heroism."

Main-Travelled Roads was published in June 1891 in a thousand paper and cloth copies, the third book issued by the Arena Publishing Company.[28] A myth has arisen, due in no small part to Garland himself, that upon publication "the outcry against it was instant and astonishing," as Garland wrote in his autobiography. "I had a foolish notion that the literary folk of the west would take a local pride in the color of my work, and to find myself execrated by nearly every critic as 'a bird willing to foul his own nest' was an amazement. Editorials and criticisms poured into the office, all written to prove that my pictures of the middle border were utterly false."[29] In fact, reviewers were remarkably balanced in their estimations of a book whose stories flew in the face of convention. Nearly all praised the volume for the high quality of its description and recognized that Garland wrote with the authority of one who had lived the life he depicted in his fiction. His friend Louise Chandler Moulton, reading advance sheets for her review in the *Boston Herald*, set the pattern for all of the reviews: praise for method mixed with a confession of distaste for the subject. "I have never before felt the desperate unspeakable pathos of the prairie farmer's struggle with life," she began, before confessing that the book "was far too minutely and baldly real to please my own taste." Perhaps it was the "overwhelming impression of grinding, unremunerated toil" that bothered the reviewer for the *Chicago Tribune* and other periodicals that Garland later exaggerated as an "outcry," particularly when writing about an event filtered through years of later critical abuse.[30]

As usual, Howells adroitly caught the tenor of the work: "These stories are full of the bitter and burning dust, the foul and trampled slush of the common avenues of life: the life of the men who hopelessly and cheerlessly make the wealth that enriches the alien and the idler, and impoverishes the producer." With his desire to be recognized as an artist, Garland must have been especially gratified to read that the collection "is a work of art, first of all, and we think of fine art." But then, reflecting his more decorous sense of what realism should include, Howells signaled what was to become a constant thread in commentary about Garland's work: his lack of attention to nuances of style. "He has a certain harshness and bluntness," he wrote, "an indifference to the more delicate charms of style; and he has still to learn that though the thistle is full of an unrecognized poetry, the rose has a poetry too, that even overpraise cannot spoil."[31] Garland had now arrived: America's foremost critic had praised his inaugural volume.

9

TABLE RAPPER, 1890–92

While Garland was busily at work establishing himself as a writer of fiction, he was equally engaged in attempting to alter the course of American drama, seeking to substitute contemporary issues and realistic characters for the clichéd conventions of melodrama. His friendship with the Hernes had introduced him to a number of actors, theater owners, and other drama enthusiasts, and as these friendship deepened he worked steadily on a number of play manuscripts as he simultaneously drafted fiction. On June 10, 1890, just three weeks before Garland published *Under the Wheel* in the July 1890 *Arena*, the Massachusetts Legislature erupted in a scandal that provided Garland with the plot and theme of "A Member of the Third House," his second attempt to bring his dramatic ideas before an audience. George F. Williams, the House representative from Delham, accused the West End Street Railway Company of using "unethical practices in an attempt to gain a franchise for an elevated street railway in Boston."[1] Williams alleged that the company's lobby—the "third house" of the play—engaged in bribery and coercion of Senate members, and he accused one Senator Fassett of taking a bribe. Fassett denied the accusation and promptly demanded that an investigation be launched into the matter.

Garland sat in on the hearings and apparently decided that the scandal—with its charges of corruption and profiteering—was the perfect subject for a radical play, for he copyrighted the title "A Member of the Third House: An American Play of To-Day" eight days after Williams levied his charges. By the end of the month the investigative committee had determined that, while the lobby had exerted pressure, it had not spent money to corrupt any legislator, and on July 1 the bill granting the West End franchise passed. Garland, however, did not accept the committee's findings and reversed its judgment in his play, which parallels the events of the scandal but alters the conclusion so that the accused senator (Ward in the play) confesses that he had been willing to take a bribe. His admission prompts the defeat of the bill, a rout of the lobbyists, and the suicide of the president of the railroad.

With "A Member of the Third House," Garland hoped to show Bostonians what a modern realistic play looks like: its subject was drawn from the headlines, so it was unabashedly contemporary; then, too, the issue itself mattered. While the melodramas and comedies currently on the stage offered familiar situations and always reaffirmed that all was right with the world, real life didn't work that way, and his play would show that, in his hands, drama could move people to action. The trick was to treat the matter convincingly while also rousing people's ire.

When he completed the play in August, he sent it to Flower, who shared his reform sentiments and had written in May to tell Garland that he thought free dramatic performances had enormous potential to make poor people "happy while they were being stimulated to think and also brought to touch with the best sentiments of the day."[2] Flower stayed up half the night reading the play and wrote its author on September 3, "I think it is immense; one of the finest dramatic creations I have ever read." But he was wary of the legal implications of publishing a play that followed events so closely "because you graphically portray so many individuals that will be readily recognized, then passing from that without changing your characters you picture individuals which in the first part of the play are well known personages as being criminals." He therefore advised consulting an attorney about liability.[3]

The lawyer Flower consulted advised against publication, and Garland had no luck persuading a dramatic manager to produce his play. But so committed was he to the "truth" of his dramatic convictions that he decided to invest his own money in staging a dramatic reading of the play, hoping that a positive reception would persuade balky managers. He hired Chickering Hall, a second-floor recital room of a piano manufacturer, and on October 30, 1890, he staged an "author's reading," charging fifty cents per ticket for the privilege of hearing his play. Even for this lone reading he toned down the play, writing Howells that he had "changed three acts already but it takes the vim out of the dialogue because making it so much vaguer." He invited his friends and even enlisted Howells into dragooning people to attend, with his mentor writing to Sylvester Baxter of the *Boston Herald* to arrange some prereading publicity.[4]

Garland's friend Charles Hurd, literary editor of the *Transcript*, offered an enthusiastic review, twice praising Garland as "courageous" in making legislative corruption the subject of his play. "The applause and attention seemed to indicate that the play took hold of the interest and admiration of the audience," Hurd wrote, and the play "certainly deserves the test of being acted."[5] In an apparent attempt to promote the play as controversial—and thereby demonstrate its draw—Garland drew up a program *after* the reading that included Boston press comments of October 31, carefully selected to portray the play as divisive. The *Boston Commonwealth* described the play as "a strong picture of the very worst influences that affect legislation," while the *Boston Herald* found it "reportorial in style, lacking in humor and movement." The *Globe* praised it as "stirring, theatric, and effective," while the *Home Journal* derided Garland for having "a conventional instinct for situation, but no power of developing character."[6] His promotional tactic failed to convince managers to stage the play, and he likewise failed to interest the *Century* in publishing it, so he consigned it to his "Developmental Bureau"—his desk drawer—as he told Gilder.[7]

While Garland was striking out with "A Member of the Third House," James Herne was making a similar attempt to extend the range of American drama with *Margaret Fleming*. The play's plot traces the exposure and decline of adulterer Philip Fleming, whose wife, contrary to dramatic conventions of the time, refuses to forgive him when she discovers he has produced a child with his mistress. "The wife-heart has gone out of me," she tells her husband, thereby conveying in the circumspect language of the time that she will henceforth forsake his bed; "only the mother-heart remains." When the play appeared in a three-day tryout in Lynn, Massachusetts—fittingly on Independence Day—Garland wrote an enthusiastic letter on its behalf for the *Transcript* in which he praised the play for its "intent to enforce a great social lesson" and commended the acting of Katharine Herne in the title role.[8] But, like Garland, Herne was unable to interest Boston or New York theater managers in the play, and it too languished.

Garland had great faith in the play as a notable example of modern realistic drama and soon volunteered as press agent on behalf of the play and the Hernes. He drafted a letter in support of the play and gathered signatures of fifty-five prominent Bostonians, mostly writers, journalists, and artists, among them his friends Howells, Moses True Brown, B. O. Flower, Charles Hurd, and Louise Chandler Moulton, but also other notables such as Thomas S. Perry, William Lloyd Garrison, and Mary Wilkins, and presented the petition to five Boston managers.[9] Like Herne, he too was rebuffed.

Then one day in the spring of 1891 Herne and Garland met Howells for lunch, and talk soon turned to their frustrated efforts to stage their plays. Howells, who himself had met with resistance in his attempts to have his one-act plays staged, had been following developments in the independent theater movement in Europe. At that luncheon he described the founding of the Freie Bühne and suggested that Herne and Garland form their own independent theater to stage their plays. "They brought the public to them by the sheer force of their dramatic novelty," Garland recalled Howells telling them. "Why don't you do as they did—hire a sail loft or a stable and produce your play in the simplest fashion? The people will come to see it if it is new and vital."[10] At the time, intellectuals were abuzz with the innovations of the independent theaters in Europe. In 1887 André Antoine founded the Théâtre Libre in Paris; in 1889 Otto Brahm established the Freie Bühne in Berlin; and in 1891 J. T. Grein launched the Independent Theater in London. Dedicated to staging imaginative plays considered too daring for the commercial stage, these theaters introduced audiences to the plays of Brieux, Ibsen, Hauptmann, Strindberg, the de Goncourts, and others. They also had a decided economic advantage: because commercial theaters typically sat large audiences, theater owners demanded plays that would guarantee full houses and so repay their investment. The effect on the selection of plays was predictable: managers chose plays that were familiar to their audiences and which featured stars, who in turn commanded star salaries, a condition no different from the modern Hollywood film industry and its penchant for stars and sequels. The independent theaters, playing to a house of only a few hundred, could take risks with radical plays that commercial theaters could not.

The Hernes rented Chickering Hall, went into debt to transform the recital hall into a more intimate theater space, and announced that *Margaret Fleming* would open on May 4, 1891. Garland sprang into action to promote the play. In a manifesto entitled "In the Interests of American Drama," bearing his signature and that of B. O. Flower, he declared, "we are on the eve of a great change in the drama commensurate with that already begun in the novel, that is, the change from the drama of plot and style to the drama of character and purpose." He confidently asserted his belief that a "growing number of people" were only waiting for an opportunity to "welcome serious studies of American life." Billed as "An American Play without a Soliloquy," *Margaret Fleming* would be a "first modest trial of the independent art theater," for there were "scores of plays in America waiting the establishment of a theatre freed from the necessity of compromise and whose production would be an honor and inspiration." Included as part of this circular were letters from Thomas S. Perry and Howells to Herne in which Howells predicted "an epoch-making effect" for the play.[11] Herne didn't have money enough for posters to advertise the play, so he had placards and circulars printed which his daughters distributed to businesses. Garland wrote scores of letters urging friends to attend, enclosing complimentary tickets in some. Six days before the play opened he wrote to the *Transcript* to educate the public about the play's innovations. "Boston is to see a trial of a radical play next week in Chickering Hall," he began, with implications for theater beyond the success or failure of this single play. If *Margaret Fleming* succeeds—thereby demonstrating the public's support of a "higher class of dramas"—small art theaters would need to be built to enable the performance of a new psychological drama, one "approaching the art of the novelist," "where it is very essential that the fine lines in the actor's face and the subtle inflections of his voice be easily perceptible to the auditor."[12] With this letter, for the first time in American theatrical history, Garland accurately forecast the future of noncommercial theater, which became known as the little theater movement of the 1910s and today flourishes as community theater. His study of the laws of expression, his minute observations of Booth, his own practice of fiction, and his acquaintance through the Hernes with the business of the theater showed him that the road to realistic, psychological drama required a small space so the nuances of character and expression could be perceived. Just as important were the economics of scale: small houses, few props, and minimal scene construction meant that fewer tickets needed to be sold to pay for it all.

When *Margaret Fleming* opened on May 4, Herne and his supporters were gratified by the audience of seventy-five to one hundred that barely filled a quarter of the converted recital hall. But the audience was largely composed of Boston's cultural elite, not the general public, who went to see *Hands across the Sea* in the Boston Museum, *A Night's Frolic* at the Park Theater, the comic opera *The Merry Monarch* at the Globe, or the military spectacle *The Soudan* at the Boston Theater.[13] While Garland had suggested an art theater sitting a house of five to eight hundred in his *Transcript* letter, the opening turnout should have warned him immediately that his estimate of enthusiasts of "radical" drama was askew. (By comparison, the Provincetown Players' Playhouse, the most famous of the little theaters of the 1910s, sat only two hundred and rarely filled.)

Reviewers were unkind, for Katharine Herne's quiet, non-sensational acting was an innovation that clashed with their expectations for florid theatrical entertainment. The *Transcript*'s reviewer, for example, complained that the treatment "was wearisome in its long-drawn-out monotony." But he reserved his knockout blow for the play's exposure of the double standard. In her refusal to forgive Philip's adultery, Margaret became a "monster of morality," for her standing on principle violated the nineteenth-century man's belief that a woman's femininity was inextricably linked with her ability to forgive. "One cannot help feeling," the reviewer concluded, "that the woman who was wronged, and who died breathing love and forgiveness to her betrayer, was a more lovable character than this unforgiving wife."[14]

Immediately, Garland replied. "I can't quite see her as a 'monster of morality,'" he wrote the *Transcript*. "'Margaret Fleming' . . . is intended to represent a fine intellectual but thoroughly domestic, every-day sort of woman with a moral nature strongly developed." When she discovers Philip's infidelity, "her whole moral nature revolts from the man." Though she retains a "lower and more organic feeling for him" because of their years together, "she has not the feeling of a true wife." He continued his publicity campaign, writing the *Transcript* two days later to quote comments from prominent citizens who had attended the play and calling for "a little generous effort on the part of the public and press to put this radical play on a paying basis, and so put new courage into the hearts of realists."[15]

Despite declining ticket sales, Garland and Flower were convinced they had found a public for an independent theater, for seeing the play soon became the thing to do. "To admit you have not seen 'Margaret Fleming,'" the *Boston Herald* remarked on May 12, "is to acknowledge you are 'not in the swim.'"[16] But after two weeks, ticket sales had dwindled, and Herne closed the play, his debts mounting. Still, a two-week run was not all that bad for an experimental production. Even Ibsen's *A Doll's House* would be played in single performances, mostly matinees, until after 1900.[17] But interest in the example *Margaret Fleming* had set remained high. On May 21 Garland and a number of Boston's cultural leaders met to form the First Independent Theater Association, whose prospectus was headlined "Truth for Art's Sake" and subtitled "A Society to Promote Dramatic Art in America" and reflected the ideals of its European progenitors. "The Objects of the Association," it began, are

> first and in general to encourage truth and progress in American Dramatic art. Second, and specifically, to secure and maintain a stage whereon the best and most unconventional studies of mod-

ern life and distinctively American life, may get a proper hearing. We believe the present poverty of Dramatic art in America is due to unfavorable conditions, rather than to a lack of play-writing talent, and it is the purpose of the Association to remove as far as possible, the commercial consideration and give the Dramatist the artistic atmosphere for his work, and bring to his production the most intelligent and sympathetic acting in America.

As secretary of the association and author of the prospectus, Garland made sure the document reflected his goals. The association outlined the scope of its intended plays along the lines of Garland's "Evolution of American Thought," with part 1 including "Studies of American Society"—social dramas and comedies of life—and part 2 representing "Studies in American History"—dramas of the colonial, revolutionary, "Border," and Civil War eras. Part 3 would include "Famous modern plays by the best Dramatists of Europe." Mindful of the rejections his own plays had received, Garland outlined a blind review process in which plays submitted to the association would be read by a reading committee, with only the secretary knowing the aspiring playwright's name until a decision had been reached. Tickets would be sold by subscription, and the committee began to plan a building with seating for five hundred.[18]

Notwithstanding favorable publicity in the press, funding could not be found and the project eventually died, although Garland was still stumping for the independent theater when he visited Chicago in January 1892. "I look to see an independent theater association organized in every principal city in America," he told an interviewer for the *Daily News*, but his visionary ideal was fourteen years too soon, for Chicago would not establish an independent theater until 1906 with Victor Mape's New Theatre—which would last barely a year before it too folded.[19]

Despite his enthusiasm and his tireless efforts to promote *Margaret Fleming* and the ideals behind the independent theater movement, Garland was not able to interest enough people in "Truth for Art's Sake" because he overestimated the public's willingness to be "improved." He believed that Boston possessed an audience interested in a more intellectual drama and needed only an opportunity to see a viable alternative to the pallidity of the commercial stage. Unfortunately, as he was to do in subsequent efforts to reform the stage, Garland misjudged the number of people who shared his interests in avant-garde drama. The literati of Boston packed the house the first few nights, but the audience dwindled to nothing in subsequent evenings. Garland and his supporters had made two disastrous errors in promoting *Margaret Fleming*. They overestimated the size of the audience already willing or able to appreciate the advanced ideas and challenging stagecraft of the drama they advocated. Worse, the elitist, highbrow tone of their promotions scared off potential auditors by advertising *Margaret Fleming* as a play that would "improve" them. Then, as now, few people wished to be improved by self-appointed proponents of culture. Consequently, the general public stayed away and *Margaret Fleming* played to a narrow circle of intellectuals, too narrow to meet costs. Garland had yet to learn that to become successful, an art theater must educate an audience gradually.

That May, while he was promoting *Margaret Fleming* and shaping his stories into *Main-Travelled Roads*, Garland discovered a new interest that would he would follow for the rest of his life: the scientific study of psychic phenomena. In 1848 Kate and Margaret Fox had become the subject of a nationwide craze when they reported a number of mysterious rappings at their Hydesville, New York, home. Soon, they were giving public performances of their ability to call forth the rappings, and the pseudoreligion of spiritualism, the ability to communicate with the dead through a medium, was born. By the 1880s, spiritualism was claiming more and more adherents, with newspapers and magazines devoting columns to the fad, and scientists and other intellectuals began to investigate the claims of mediums and spiritualists. At the time the study of abnormal psychology was in its infancy, and the workings of the mind were poorly understood. In the nineteenth century, neurologists generally conceived of mental activity to be directly connected to physical causes. When something went awry with the mind—for instance, excessive stimulation of the nerves, resulting in neurasthenia—physicians treated the body. S.

Weir Mitchell, the era's most influential specialist in nervous disorders, thus prescribed complete bed rest and fattening of the body to restore depleted nervous energy—a treatment immortalized in Charlotte Perkins Gilman's "The Yellow Wall-Paper." To many observers of psychic phenomena, it seemed eminently reasonable that the phenomena called forth in séances, if not the work of spirits, might be the product of some power of the mind not heretofore recognized. In 1882 the British Society for Psychical Research (SPR) was founded to study these mysterious phenomena and counted among its members some of Britain's most prestigious scientists and philosophers, including its first president, Alfred Sidgwick, the Knightsbridge Professor of Moral Philosophy at Cambridge. Other distinguished members included Alfred Russel Wallace, the co-discoverer of natural selection; William Crookes, the renowned chemist and future president of the Royal Society (1913–15); Arthur Balfour, a future prime minister; and Oliver Lodge, the physicist who made his reputation with innovations in radio.

In the United States, the American Society for Psychical Research (ASPR) was founded three years later, in 1885, with Harvard psychologist and philosopher William James the primary force behind its formation. Its first president was Simon Newcomb, head astronomer of the Naval Almanac Office, and illustrious members and associate members included psychologist G. Stanley Hall, Charles Sanders Peirce, Josiah Royce, Francis Parkman, and Theodore Roosevelt. The more pragmatic orientation of the U.S. academic researchers, however, and particularly their insistence that scientific protocols be established, led to much dissension, and the ASPR was absorbed into the British organization in 1889, not to become independent again until 1907.

As one historian of the subject has observed, psychical researchers were "part of a new thrust in psychology that resisted turning every discussion of conscious and unconscious mental states back toward the physical condition of the person being examined." In this pre-Freudian era, their research into the "supernormal" powers of the mind made important contributions to theories of the unconscious.[20] Frederic Myers, for example, a professor of classics at Cambridge and one of the original founders of the SPR, posited the existence of a "subliminal self," a vast subconscious region of the mind that produced sensations, thoughts, and emotions that occasionally revealed themselves to the conscious mind—through dreams, for example. This subliminal self, he suggested, may be responsible for supernormal phenomena. The psychic researchers, therefore, are in part responsible for developing psychological theories of the unconscious mind.

In 1891 Flower was the leading force behind the organization of the American Psychical Society, founded after the demise of the ASPR by a number of prominent Bostonians who wanted to apply scientific methods to the study of psychic phenomena. In *Forty Years of Psychic Research*, Garland recalls that Flower asked him to join the society's board of directors because his logical habit of mind, his background in science, and his general skepticism would serve as an effective counter to those members predisposed to believe. "Furthermore you are not bereaved as so many people are who go into this work," Flower told him, apparently unaware of the death of Garland's sister Jessie seven months before.[21] Flower was referring to the fact that most of those who went to mediums did so in hope of contacting the recently departed. The primary purpose of the American Psychical Society, its prospectus stated, was "to investigate the phenomena of Modern Spiritualism in accordance with scientific method, with a view to determining the facts and laws, and the most probable hypothesis which will explain the facts and laws."[22] At the organizational meeting on May 18, Garland was elected one of the directors of the fledgling society, and he would become its second president in January 1892.

The society's research agenda was ambitious but not very rigorous in the ordinary sense of basic scientific procedure. The two basic assumptions of the investigators were the following:

1. Man continues to exist after the change called death
2. There are laws in operation by obeying which spirits can communicate with mortals and produce many kinds of phenomena capable of being observed by the latter.[23]

To discover these laws, investigators were advised to examine phenomena with sympathetic skepticism. "It is not your business to play the part of detective nor to expose a swindler," the secretary of the society's Chicago branch advised in its journal. "You will do far better to leave that to others. The society is looking for truth, not fiction; for facts, not fraud." Investigators should take precautions to avoid trickery, but their prime duty is to record phenomena and not form hypotheses. "You are not bound to explain the causes of what you see, except to assure yourself that there is no possibility of mere jugglery of a physical character," he continued. Better to "hold your opinion in suspense" until one can "give the facts, duly authenticated to the thinkers of the age."[24] For the typical psychical investigator of the time, one historian has remarked, experiment meant "simply to put to the test, with as much rigor and observational control as the subject would permit, anyone who purported to be able to produce supernormal physical or mental phenomena."[25] Report after report described the existence of phenomena without probing the conditions that made them possible or attempting to form hypotheses and predict results.

Part of the difficulty in testing psychic phenomena, advocates claimed, was that conventional scientific procedures inhibited the production of the events. Hence the typical conditions favorable to the séance but antithetical to scientific methods: darkening the room to relax the medium and encourage spirits to come forth, joining of hands in a circle to increase the "magnetic current," playing music to "help the harmonious and receptive mood," and avoiding crossing limbs because "the circle is a battery, and such a position confuses the magnetic currents."[26] One might think that turning on a light would be the rational thing to do and so reveal the veracity of the medium at once, but one would be wrong, advocates explained, because light prevented communication between spirit and medium.

Representative investigations may be seen in the four reports Garland published in the *Psychical Review*.[27] In his most extensive report about a medium who could call forth voices and cause objects to move, Garland described thirty-two sittings over the course of five weeks and his elaborate precautions to prevent trickery. At the eighth sitting, on November 10, 1893, he bound the medium's arms to her chair with silk thread, fastened her ankles to the floor with tape, nailed her dress to the floor, pinned a newspaper to her dress, and nailed it to the floor. Then taps sounded from the table; he heard the movement of a pencil; books rained upon the table; and then the voice of "Wilbur" came from the tin cone lying on the table, which "for nearly two hours kept us roaring with laughter," the earnest investigator reported. "In the intervals, he played jokes upon us. He touched my cheek at a distance of six feet from the psychic." The mischievous "Wilbur" poked at them and teased them. "What made you jump?" "Wilbur" laughed after touching one investigator with the cone. When the session was over and the lights were turned on, the medium remained as before, her fetters still tightly fastened. Although the table had moved, Garland noted, "I cannot conceive how she could leave the table in the position in which it was found." Such are the bare outlines of "a very interesting and curious experiment," the researcher concluded.[28]

In the reports published in the *Psychical Review*, Garland was content merely to describe the phenomena without conjecture about causes, methods, or meaning. In later years, as he gained more experience, he believed that the phenomena were caused by hitherto unknown physical forces. As he told an interviewer in 1911, "I never in all my life have received a message that I was convinced was from the dead." Despite having received messages from deceased members of his own family, he concluded that "none of them has been convincing. I have been able to explain all of them on the hypothesis of mind reading." That is, one explanation popular among early psychical researchers was that mediums were extraordinarily receptive to the thoughts emanating from those attending the séance, and that sensitivity explained the psychic's seeming ability to communicate with the dead—she simply received the thoughts of an attendee, and thus was able to report things she could not possibly have known otherwise. After all, Garland explained, "the human body is a dynamo that throws off a variety of forces that we know little about at present." He went on to draw analogies about other invisible forces responsible for seemingly miraculous recent phenomena—Roentgen rays, radio waves—concluding that "spirit" phenomena are merely "different expressions of a physical force, concerning the true nature of which we are still in the dark." As for ghosts, "I am inclined to think that ghosts are liberated astral selves," the intrepid researcher remarked.[29]

As was typical for any organization he joined, Garland threw himself wholeheartedly into stumping for the cause of psychical research. As soon as he was elected president of the American Psychical Society in January 1892, he established branch societies in Washington DC, Los Angeles, Chicago, Denver, and Colorado Springs. Interest in psychic research was such that by 1893 the society had grown from the original 28 founding members to 245 dues-paying members and associates in Boston, plus another 106 members in the branch societies, for a total of 351 members.[30] Not all of Garland's friends approved of his activity. Julie Herne recalled that Garland would frequently arrive at the Herne home wild about a newly discovered medium whose exploits defied explanation. While Katharine inclined toward belief, James remained skeptical. One evening, when Garland reported observing a male medium who was able to balance an ordinary walking stick between his knees, "controlled only by the magnetism of the medium's wavering hands," James announced, "That's an old trick, Garland," and promised to reveal the secret after dinner.

Later, when gathered in a circle in the darkened room, Herne took his stick, rubbed it "to set the magnetic currents flowing," as he explained, and then placed it between his knees and removed his hands. The stick stood wavering, moving to the left and right as he waved his hands. "Garland was dumbfounded," Julie reports. When Katharine turned up the lamp, Garland saw a black silk thread fastened to Herne's trousers. "Garland took it in good part," says Julie, "but he attempted no more psychic experiments when Herne was about."[31]

Garland's interest in psychic phenomena was deep and long lasting. Although Hamlin would not turn his interest into literary material until 1905 with the publication of *The Tyranny of the Dark*, he would eventually publish two novels, three nonfiction books, and a number of articles about his psychic investigations. The depth of his interest is revealed in the Garland archive at the University of Southern California, which holds his transcripts of séances with more than fifteen mediums, including the famed Margery, as well as drafts of his published and unpublished writings about psychic phenomena. While Garland began as a skeptic—"and from the first refused to entertain the spirit hypothesis as a possibility," as Flower remembered—he became more credulous as he investigated further until, at the end of his life, he emerged as a believer, as revealed by his private correspondence.[32] Although he seems to have chased ghosts out of a genuine belief that he was making a contribution to knowledge, his amateur understanding of scientific methods, in particular his seeming ignorance of the experimental method, limited his ability to comprehend what he observed. But he was also aware of the apparent foolhardiness of his passion and retained a sense of humor about it. In later years, with the proceeds of the sale of one psychic article, he bought an automobile he named "Spook," and he once owned a cat he christened "Ectoplasm."

Garland was always receptive to causes that promised artistic, social, or economic uplift. Thus, when Flower suggested to his receptive ear that he write a novel about the Farmers' Alliance to be serialized in the *Arena* and then brought out by the Arena Publishing Company, Garland readily agreed, for he was eager to establish himself as a professional writer. It helped that Flower also promised to pay his expenses. Garland later recalled what Flower's largesse meant: "For the first time in my life I was able to travel in comfort. I could not only eat in the dining car, and sleep in the sleeping car, but I could go to a hotel at the end of my journey with a delightful sense of freedom from worry about the bills."[33] With Flower's advance in his pocket, Garland resigned as a full-time teacher at the Boston School of Oratory during the summer of 1891 (although his name would remain in the catalog until 1893), and for the next two years he traveled throughout the country, seldom remaining in one place for more than a month.

In the 1870s conditions for farmers nationwide had worsened as drought began to afflict many of the western states and wheat prices fell. A flood of eastern capital had led many farmers to mortgage their farms heavily to invest in machinery and extend their lands, and when crops failed, many farmers were ruined as banks foreclosed. And the railroads continued their stranglehold upon escalating transportation costs. Many farmers had left the Grange, which had done much to help farmers through educational and social programs and cooperative purchasing, because the organization specifically prohibited partisan politics, fearing that political dissension would jeopardize the community the Grange movement sought to foster. As farmers realized that direct legislative action was needed to redress conditions, they began to organize a number of associations with avowed political intent, leading to the founding of the National Farmers' Alliance in St. Louis in 1889.[34] As farmers rushed to join the Alliance—one newspaper reported in 1890 that a thousand were joining each week—politicians loyal to the farmers campaigned for national office. In 1890, fifty congressmen with Alliance sympathies were elected with the result that the Republican Party "lost 85 seats and its majority control in the House."[35] Soon farmers began clamoring for an independent political party, and in July 1892 Alliance supporters met in Omaha to settle upon a platform and candidates for national office in their newly formed People's (or Populist) Party.

Garland observed these developments with interest, but he seems at first to have distrusted the Alliance, for he believed the single-tax remedy was being ignored in the campaigning. "I was prejudiced against the Alliance before I went out to study it," he told the Chicago Single Tax Club on January 28, 1892. "Not that I questioned the honesty of its motives, or the general intelligence and patriotism of its adherents. But I regarded its methods as doubtful, and its aims as foolish, if not worse." But after interviewing a number of Alliance figures, among them the fiery orator Mary E. Lease, essayist Annie L. Diggs, Congressman Jerry Simpson of Kansas, and General James B. Weaver, former Greenbacker presidential candidate from Iowa and soon to be presidential nominee for the People's

Party, he came to their wholehearted support. "When I got among the farmers," he continued, "and really got an understanding of their position, I changed my mind. I found that they were not so far wrong after all. They are not pig-headed and reactionary. On the contrary, they are alive to new ideas and willing to be set right if it can be shown they are wrong. They eagerly heard me in advocacy of the single tax. . . . So I have cut loose from the old moorings and have thrown myself heart and soul into the farmers' movement."[36] He urged single taxers to withdraw their support of the Democratic Party and give it to the Alliance, which "is fighting three monopolies—the monopoly in land, the monopoly in transportation, and the monopoly in money," for the more politically successful Alliance was more likely to achieve their common goal.[37]

With Simpson, the most prominent of the Alliance congressmen, Garland campaigned for Iowa candidates. He traveled to Washington to observe Alliance politicians in action, reporting his impressions for the *Arena* in "The Alliance Wedge in Congress." These congressmen "are actual farmers; not landlords and speculators, but working farmers," he assured his readers. After profiling nine congressmen, stressing their efforts on behalf of working men, he concluded that "great forces are moving" and predicted a "popular upheaval similar to that of '61" would transform the nation.[38] In July he attended the first national convention of the People's Party in Omaha as a single-tax delegate. His friend Elia Peattie, at the time a columnist for the *Omaha World-Herald*, recalled that he read "Under the Lion's Paw" instead of making a speech. "I cannot forget the whirlwind of applause that greeted him," she remembered, "the whole audience rising and fluttering their handkerchiefs." Then, noticing "a sturdy old man who stared incredulously" at the hall's cries of "Garland! Garland!" she watched as the man "dropped his head on his arms and his body shook with sobs." It was Garland's father, who was at the convention as a South Dakota delegate. Dick Garland marveled as his son introduced him to General Weaver, the party's presidential candidate, and other luminaries. "I never thought Hamlin would make a success of writing," Dick told Elia Peattie and her husband, Robert, who were sitting next to him. "I couldn't believe that he would ever earn a living that way, but it seems that he is doing it." "For the first time in his life," the son recalled, "he deferred to me," and then added wryly, "He not only let me take charge of him, he let me pay the bills." Hamlin was proud that his father was able to see him feted by the party's leaders, but Dick's deference troubled him, for it was the son's first awareness of his father's advancing years.[39]

In 1892 Garland published four novels, three of them made up of recycled work, for his travels and speaking engagements on behalf of the Alliance left little time for the concentration writing demanded. On December 1, 1891, he had signed a contract for *Jason Edwards, An Average Man*, to be published by the Arena Publishing Company in January. He had high hopes for his first published novel, which is a slightly revised version of his play *Under the Wheel*. The contract specified that a full page of advertising would appear in the *Arena* for a minimum of six months and that the novel would appear in both cloth and paper, with a royalty of ten and five cents, respectively.[40] In its dedication, Garland showed his enthusiasm for his latest cause:

To the Farmers' Alliance

Whose mission it is to unite the farmer and the artisan, the north and the south, the blue and the gray under one banner, marching in a continent-wide battle-line against the denial of equal rights, I dedicate this story, with its implied hatred of all special privileges.

"Old Pap's Flaxen," the serial of two Dakota bachelors raising an orphaned Norwegian girl, which Gilder had accepted way back in 1889, finally began appearing in the *Century* between March and May. But Garland had grown weary of the delay between acceptance and publication, even though appearing in the pages of the *Century* was an authorial coup. Equally important, he was now dependent upon his writing for a large portion of his income, having resigned from teaching at the Boston School of Oratory, and delay in publication meant delay in getting paid. "I have decided to let Mr. Appleton bring out my little story," instead of the Century book division, he announced to Gilder. "I do this because he does it at once and because he is to give me place of honor in his summer series of American novels. I'm getting *old*," the thirty-two-year-old explained, "and I must make hay while the sun shines."[41] The story appeared as *A Little Norsk* in June.

In January, during his visit to Chicago, he met the publisher Francis J. Schulte, a German immigrant who had established a press in 1889. A year older than Garland, Schulte specialized in reissuing inexpensive editions of novels by famous writers whose sales had declined. In 1890 he scored a hit by publishing Ignatius Donnelly's dystopian novel *Caesar's Column*, which three other publishers had declined, and which eventually sold over a million copies.[42] Garland signed a contract with Schulte to publish a novelized version of the play Flower had rejected for fear of a lawsuit, and it appeared in April as *A Member of the Third House: A Dramatic Story*.

In January, too, the *Arena* began printing the serial of the novel it had commissioned, which Garland entitled *A Spoil of Office*. He had resurrected the unfinished manuscript of a novel entitled "Milton Jennings," an autobiographical rendering of his Iowa seminary experience featuring the title character and Radbourn, a radical lawyer.[43] The manuscript traces their parallel careers as they attend school and then enter county politics. To meet Flower's deadline, Garland created a composite figure he named Bradley Talcott, though he retained Jennings and Radbourn in lesser roles, and quickly revised the manuscript to focus on Bradley's growth from an intelligent but unsophisticated farmhand to an eager student with a pronounced interest in oratory. At a Grange picnic he meets the fiery speaker Ida Wilbur (modeled upon Mary E. Lease), whose oratorical skill inspires him to go to the seminary. With the ideal of Ida always before him, he escapes the drudgery of the farm and its twin fate, marriage to a shallow farm girl. Here, Garland first works out the motif he would later develop more skillfully in *Rose of Dutcher's Coolly*. A series of mentors advise Bradley to refrain from marriage until he establishes himself; he becomes a lawyer and is then drafted into county politics.

In the second half of the novel, Garland develops the rise and fall of Bradley Talcott as politician—first as a state representative, and later as an Alliance congressman who loses reelection because he refuses to kowtow to corrupt patronage. Eventually, Bradley marries his emancipated orator—but the unconventional couple agree to live apart so that each may devote him- or herself to the Alliance. As Donald Pizer points out, in Bradley and Ida's political involvement Garland "presented an accurate history of the progress of the farmers' movement from its loose, nonpolitical federation in the Grange to its complete political association in the People's party."[44]

Garland was understandably proud of his novel, the first he had written as a novel rather than as a play or a novelette, for in it he hoped to yoke his passion for realistic depiction of the West to serve the higher cause of political activism. When the serial appeared in book form in September, with a dedication to Howells, "the foremost historian of our common lives and the most vital figure in our literature," he waited to see how his effort would be received. Howells promptly wrote to express his pleasure—as well he might, for in the pages of the novel Garland has Ida Wilbur praise Howells specifically as the leading exemplar of the "modern novel." "I meant long ago to have told you how much I liked it," Howells wrote of *Spoil*. "The story interested me greatly; your hero was simply and strongly studied." He thought Garland was "brave" for having chosen to advocate women's rights, and he thought his protégé had finally hit the mark in depicting social concerns: "I think you have got very close to the *life of classes and kinds* as well as persons; the book is new in that, and I am proud of it for that reason."[45]

In a lengthy review for the *Arena*, Flower also praised the novel, seeing no impropriety in a publisher puffing his books in his own magazine, but more objective critics found little to commend. "As a delineator of social conditions, aspects of nature, types and classes of men, Mr. Garland excels," observed the *Chicago Tribune*. "In psychological portraiture, however, which modern writers regard as the highest achievement of the novelist, he is not so successful." The reviewer's astute recognition of Garland's chief virtue and weakness as a writer—his tendency to focus on the exterior rather than the interior, which would dog him for his entire career—was echoed in the *Nation*'s combined review of *Spoil* and *A Little Norsk*. "The bludgeon-like quality of his realism" is "true to the facts as the author has seen them," the reviewer opined, but "facts do not make art, nor do they make literature." The review likely cut Garland to the quick, for he wanted to be recognized as an artist and not a mere purveyor of verbal photographs. And matters weren't helped when the *Dial*, Chicago's foremost literary magazine, pirated the *Nation*'s observation: "The author handles a literary bludgeon, which is not exactly an artist's tool."[46]

Indeed, Garland's other novels were receiving similar comments. While reviewers lauded his pictorial realism, they preferred sunnier topics. The *Chicago Tribune* observed that in *Jason Edwards*, Garland "paints a terrible picture and he paints it well," and the *New York Times* asserted that in *A Member of the Third House* his "style is clear and robust, and he presents a true picture of one of the saddest phases of American life."[47] But on the whole, reviewers found Garland's fiction to be a "dreary world, which must seem . . . stale, flat, and unprofitable."[48] The *Nation* administered the coup de grâce over *A Member of the Third House*: "Its author," the reviewer intoned, "if he means to produce pictures instead of travesties of American manners, has still to learn to paint, not with the brush that furnishes the glaring figures of the advertiser, but with the touch and tone of the artist."[49]

Smarting from this critical abuse, Garland outwardly fostered a stoic demeanor. Inwardly, however, he must have been hurt, for at the very moment when he had finally arrived as a man of letters—with four novels, two serials, six stories, a half-dozen essays, and a number of miscellaneous pieces in print in 1892 and with his name frequently in the nation's magazines and newspapers—his novels were being panned. He had yet to realize that few writers have written successful artistic propaganda, for in most polemical fiction, the message, not the characters, dominates. But he certainly was aware of the problem. As he explained to a reporter for the *Los Angeles Herald*, referring to Whitman's earlier advice, "While I am a reformer I want to be an artist and I do not aim to teach obviously but to teach rather as light instructs us." But the year of largely un-favorable critical reaction to his novels had taken its toll, and he withdrew from the field. "I do not expect to write another political novel," he told the *Herald*. "I aim not to repeat, and as my ideas in this respect have been stated, it is improbable that I will ever write of politics again."[50]

10

THE CAMPAIGN FOR REALISM, 1893

With the defeat of the Populist Party in the 1892 elections, Garland withdrew from political activism. Part of the reason was no doubt his disappointment at the party's failure to convince voters that more governmental intervention was needed to improve farm conditions. He was also disappointed that the single-tax idea had gained so little sympathy in the party, for after the loss of 1892 the party shifted to become a free silver party—that is, agitating for unlimited coinage of silver as a solution to the economic collapse of 1893.[1] But another reason is that, once again, his interests shifted as his lecture career took off. From the fall of 1892 until the summer of 1895, Garland was deeply engaged in another reform, one that exercised people's emotions all out of proportion to its significance: the battle over realism.

On the surface, it seems like such a minor cause: with the nation entering its worst economic depression until the 1930s, with fifteen thousand businesses—including the nation's five largest railroads—going bankrupt in 1893, and with 20 percent of the nation's industrial workforce unemployed, a number of highly skilled writers devoted their considerable energies to debating in the nation's magazines whether realism or romanticism is the best form of American literature.[2] For many readers, Howells stood in the vanguard of proponents of realism. From his monthly "Editor's Study" column in *Harper's*, beginning in January 1886 and concluding in May 1892, when he resigned to assume the editorship of *Cosmopolitan*, he attacked romantic fiction, reviewed favorably those novels that agreed with his vision, and articulated the central principles of the movement. The publication of *Criticism and Fiction* in 1891, a gathering of his *Harper's* columns, amounted to realism's most influential manifesto.

As is common in such debates, the surface issue masked its true objective: envisioning what "America" means, what values it should seek to foster in its imaginative literature. At stake was national pride, a sense that American literature had at last arrived and could stand independent of European models. While magazinists had been scrapping over the issue since the 1870s, the outpouring of regional fiction, worsening rural conditions, and continued westward expansion raised the debate, after the crash of 1893, to its most strident level, when it also served as a welcome distraction from the economic chaos.

With his by now typically passionate vehemence, Garland promptly entered the fray in the November 1892 *Arena* with the publication of "The West in Literature," the first of his many essays arguing that American writers must throw off European models and form a distinctive national literature. "The question for America to settle is not whether it can produce something *greater* than the past," he announced, "but whether it shall produce something *different* from the past." Applying Spencer's notion of evolutionary progress to the argument, he observed that "life is always changing, and literature changes with it." With more than a hundred years of settlement, the nation now had distinct regions crying out for expression in literature; no need to depend on shopworn themes and characters imported from Europe. Any American literature worthy of the name would thus depict "the actual speech of the common people" and the manners and customs of its particular people. "Write of those things of which you know the most," he concluded, echoing Taine; "by so doing you will be true to yourself, true to your locality, and true to your time."[3]

Five months later he echoed these remarks in a second polemic in the *Arena*, "The Future of Fiction," in which he prophesied that local color would inevitably emerge as a dominant genre. Because the conventional reader still preferred the romances of the past, he observed, "destructive criticism is the most characteristic literary expression of the present and of the immediate future."[4] Behind his argument inevitably lurked some special pleading. The generally unfavorable reviews, and particularly the ad hominem nature of the attacks on his realism, had begun to take their toll. Like all zealots, he rationalized that his work was unappreciated because critics didn't understand it, so he sought to educate readers through polemical articles agitating for his brand of realism. But even more disheartening than the sneering criticism was the disappointing sales of his books. Garland's *Arena* account books show that from August 1891 to February 1893 he earned a total of $612.85 from royalties on *Main-Travelled Roads, Jason Edwards,* and *A Spoil of Office* and another $400 for the serial of *Spoil.* But he had also debited $1,067.85 from his *Arena* account, much of it in the form of cash advances for Franklin and himself.[5] Garland's sales were not out of line, however, with the typical book sales of other authors. As Daniel Borus has shown, "nearly three-fourths of the novels published" between 1891 and 1901 failed to sell more than 1,000 copies, the break-even point; and "only 6 percent of the fiction issued sold as many as 10,000 copies."[6]

Book authorship clearly was not paying—Garland had earned more from the serial of *Spoil* than he had from any one book. "The serial rights on my stories are something handsome," he told a reporter for the *Los Angeles Times* during his lecture tour in that city during the fall of 1892. "Where literature fails financially is in bookmaking. If I had to depend upon my books without serial rights on my newspaper and magazine stories, I could not live upon my income." ("Handsome" indeed. In today's dollars, the serial of *Spoil* was worth more than $8,500.)[7] Garland then pointed to a new market—McClure's newspaper syndicate, which had just syndicated "The Sociable at Dudley's"—as a writer's salvation, for prolific writers such as himself soon saturated the monthly magazine market, and he cited the delay in publication of his work at the *Century* as a primary example.[8]

One reason for his preoccupation with earning a living from his pen was that Garland was determined to "rescue" his mother from the privations of her South Dakota farm. His father's crop failures had led to a decline in the Garland family fortunes, and Dick

Garland was contemplating a move further west to Montana—which was utter anathema to Hamlin, who was deeply pained by his mother's ill health and her relative isolation and who still nursed a grudge against his father, whom he blamed for her illness. With Franklin, he talked over various ways to assist them. The most promising was relocating them back to West Salem, where their relatives could help look after them in their old age. He had his eye on a house but lacked the money to complete the deal. Franklin agreed to help as best he could on his meager actor's salary.

When Garland returned to Boston from his California trip, he realized that New York had become the nation's new literary center—Howells had moved there, so too had Herne. He soon followed, bunking at the Hernes' Convent Avenue home in Harlem while he made contacts with New York publishers and especially the McClure and Bacheller newspaper syndicates. Between January and March 1893 he shuttled frequently between Boston and New York as he tidied up loose ends and debated the merits of relocating to New York. For eight years he had lived in Boston and had a wide circle of friends, so leaving that security was a big step.

In February 1893 *Prairie Folks*, his second collection of stories, was published by F. J. Schulte of Chicago. Conceived as a companion volume to *Main-Travelled Roads*, the nine stories are united in place, in cast of characters, and by poetic epigraphs commenting on each tale. The stories were written contemporaneously with those in his former volume, but with more material from which to choose, Garland was able to unify the volume more successfully than he had *Main-Travelled Roads*. All save "Sim Burns's Wife," first published as "A Prairie Heroine," the story of a defeated farm wife too bitter for the *Century*, and "Drifting Crane," a story based on the conflict between Dakota cattleman and Drifting Goose, are local-color sketches, devoid of the polemics of his other fiction and chosen to illustrate the theories he promoted in "The West in Literature." All except "Drifting Crane" are set in Mitchell County, Iowa—fictionalized as Cedar County in the book.[9]

While he was in Los Angeles, Garland told a reporter that "I never have any plot in my stories." As a confirmed realist, he believed in depicting life accurately, and since "life has plans, but never any plot," fiction should also reflect that truth.[10] His statement accurately describes the local-color sketches of *Prairie Folks*, for there is little movement in the stories; Garland's concern is to depict as accurately as his craft would allow the typical incidents and characters of rural Iowa. In "Uncle Ethan Ripley," a sequel to "Mrs. Ripley's Trip," Ripley, who has never been sick a day in his life, is conned by a patent medicine salesman into letting him deface the Ripley barn with a garish ad. His payment: bottles of Dodd's Family Bitters. In "The Test of Elder Pill," a preacher loses his faith when his hellfire-and-damnation preaching is ridiculed by the skeptical William Bacon. "Village Cronies" is an excellent character sketch of old duffers playing checkers while joking about the degree of their baldness. Other sketches depict teenage courtship and saloon brawling.

On the whole, reviews praised the accuracy of Garland's realism while also observing that his method tended to focus on external rather than internal life. "There is no lack of local color in his sketches," the *Nation* opined; "in fact, there is little else." The reviewer singled out the one polemical story—"Sim Burns's Wife"—for detailed comment, observing that "the tale is devoid of incident; it is actionless and uninteresting; it is merely a description, a picture," and he advised the author to "take less concern for the setting" and "let us see more into the hearts of his prairie folk and less into their dwelling," for then "the value of his work would thereby be increased." Reviewing the volume for the *Arena*, Garland's loyal friend B. O. Flower proclaimed the book to be "powerfully written," "wonderful photographs or pen pictures of manners, customs, and the general atmosphere pervading life in the Upper Mississippi Valley."[11] Other reviewers echoed the praise for Garland's talent for local color, but missing was any superlative judgment.

In May Garland arrived in Chicago for a stay of five months. The opening of the World's Columbian Exposition, organized to celebrate the four hundredth anniversary of Columbus's discovery of America, had been delayed to May 1, 1893, because of the magnitude of construction. Builders constructed a veritable city in Jackson

Park, where over the course of six months its twenty-seven million visitors delighted in its sixty-five thousand exhibits, elevated railways, electric launches navigating its lagoons, and especially its gargantuan buildings sheathed in bright white staff—a form of stucco—earning the fair its nickname, the White City. In part to counter the celebration of material, industrial, and scientific progress that was a hallmark of the fair, the World's Congress Auxiliary was organized in October 1890 to recognize the achievements in the humanities and social sciences. Meeting at what is now the Art Institute of Chicago, the auxiliary hosted 1,283 sessions of 5,822 speakers delivering 5,978 addresses, with women's progress, education, religion, agriculture, and science and philosophy being the most numerous.[12]

Garland was eager for the Literary Congress, scheduled for the week of July 10. He wrote to Howells to ask if the elder writer was planning to speak. "I am not going to the literary Congress, and shall not write any paper," Howells replied. "If the authors assembled need guidance, *you* are the leader for them."[13] To his parents, Garland described the wonders he had seen. "Sell the cook stove if necessary and come," he wrote. "You *must* see this fair."[14] Franklin joined him in late May, and together they met the train conveying his parents. Wheeling his mother about in a chair to save her from undue fatigue, Hamlin delighted in showing his parents the sights—but soon he overwhelmed them in his exuberance. After three days they had had enough marvels, and the Garland clan entrained for West Salem, where the eldest son had dickered for a house in which he hoped to establish his parents.

Standing on four acres and surrounded by fruit trees, a cow pasture, a two-story barn, and a pigpen, the house was in poor condition and needed work before his parents could move in. It had been built in the year of Hamlin's birth by William Hull, a mason and carpenter, and after five years had passed into the hands of Rublee Hayes, from whom Garland bought the house.[15] Three large maples fronted the house (for which Garland named the place "Mapleshade"), and gardens rich in raspberries, asparagus, and grapevines, as well as plenty of flowers, appealed to his mother's greenery-starved eyes. "This is my choice," the son declared. "Right here we take root.

This shall be the Garland Homestead"—thereby confounding writers ever since who confuse this house with the place of his birth.[16] His father was less enamored with his son's usurpation of his former authority, but evidently the mother's wishes prevailed, and the aging wheat farmer agreed to relocate—but on the condition that he would return to his South Dakota farm during the growing season. "I'm no truck farmer," he would declare. "I turn this onion patch over to you. It's no place for me."[17] What clinched the arrangement was that Hamlin's aunt Susan Bailey, his father's widowed sister, agreed to help pay for the house if she could live in it too.[18] The elder Garlands returned to South Dakota to begin packing. Hamlin's mother would return on November 1, and his father would follow after crops were harvested in time for Thanksgiving. In the meantime, Hamlin had much to do: not only did he need to scrape together the balance of the purchase price, but some remodeling was needed. His years as a carpenter would prove handy, for he added a bay window, widened the living room, and generally restored the place. In time he would add a bathroom (the first in West Salem), furnace, and fireplace, and, to the marvel of his neighbors, a tennis court.

In "The Future of Fiction" Garland had prophesied that the local-color movement would soon encompass the cities, and in "The West in Literature" he had bemoaned the lack of a "magazine in the West that offers any encouragement to true Western Art. If I were starting a magazine in the West, I should aim to develop the art resources of my locality. I should fill it with local color."[19] Soon after he arrived in Chicago, he met with Schulte to plan just such a magazine. The poet Edwin Markham, who was present at the meeting, recorded in his notebook on June 6 that Schulte would publish the magazine, to be called *The Western Magazine*, with Garland serving as editor. Hamlin impressed Markham as "an earnest man—one who believes in his own work so thoroughly that he cannot fail to impress others."[20] But even belief in his own abilities could not withstand the lack of capital, for Schulte went bankrupt soon after this conversation. He had made an unsecured loan of twenty-five thousand dollars to his printer, Horace O'Donoghue, and when O'Donoghue committed suicide, Schulte was left with so little cash that he had to abandon his publishing firm. For the present, the Arena Publishing Company agreed to distribute Garland's two Schulte books along with his Arena books.[21]

Garland must have been dismayed at this news, for *Prairie Folks* had just been released, and now he no longer had a publisher to promote the volumes already printed and bound. One consequence was that *Prairie Folks* was inadequately reviewed and didn't make the splash he had hoped for. In March he had written to Melville E. Stone, founder of the *Chicago Daily News* and later first president of the Associated Press, to describe his plan to publish two more books, "one of my verse and one of my western landscapes in prose," which he hoped to have illustrated and "brought out in fine style."[22] Stone passed Garland's letter to his son Herbert, who was a student at Harvard and who, with his classmate Hannibal Ingalls Kimball, had just entered the publishing field with a pamphlet, *Chicago and the World's Fair: A Popular Guide*, and a bound book, *First Editions of American Authors*. Although still in college, Stone and Kimball were nothing if not enterprising—both were staff members of the Harvard *Crimson*, and Stone served as a stringer for a number of Boston papers—and they planned to open a Chicago branch of the firm to capitalize on the attention the world's fair had brought to Chicago. Stone wrote his father, "I wish I had enough of a 'pull' to get a chance at publishing them myself. I would see that they were as prettily gotten out as any books in the country." But he doubted that an established author like Garland would let "a new firm . . . much less a boy" take on his books.[23]

But Stone got his chance when Schulte went under, although it is astonishing, given his difficulty with Schulte, that Garland would gamble on a new house helmed by Stone, age twenty-two, and Kimball, age nineteen, rather than approaching a more established publisher. Of his decision, Garland recorded only that "having cast in my lot with Chicago, it was inevitable that I should ally myself with its newest literary enterprise, a business which expressed something of my faith in the west."[24] By the end of May he had contracted with the fledgling firm to bring out a new edition of *Main-Travelled Roads*, together with a volume of poetry, scheduled for the fall.

On July 14, the last day of the Literary Congress at the world's fair, Garland got his chance to promote his ideas to a national audience when he became a substitute for Thomas Nelson Page, who had to withdraw. The weeklong Literary Congress had aroused much attention among fairgoers and the press. It had begun on Monday, July 10, with a general session celebrating American authorship, followed by an important Tuesday session devoted to copyright, a hot issue for American authors who had remained unprotected against international piracy until 1891, when the United States became a signatory to an international copyright law.[25] Copyright addresses spilled over to Wednesday, which was devoted to "The Rights and Interests of Authors," followed by a Thursday session on "Criticism and Literature." Friday's session, with the most attendance of any of the literary topics, was devoted to "Aspects of Modern Fiction."

George Washington Cable chaired the Friday session and opened with "The Uses and Methods of Fiction," in which he offered the traditional argument that beauty is the proper province of authors and that truth should always be subservient to its greater glory. The popular romancer Mary Hartwell Catherwood followed on "Form and Condensation in the Novel," in which she argued that readers "want intensified life" to show "the beauty of the human soul." With the conservative position stated, Garland's friend Alice French, who wrote local-color tales under the pen name Octave Thanet, spoke on "The Short Story," and Anna B. McMahan discussed "The New Motive in Fiction."[26] Then, as Lucy Monroe described events, Garland stepped to the podium "with his accustomed felicity of phrasing and intensity of manner" to speak on "Local Color in Fiction." As he had done in his two *Arena* articles, he prophesied that "local color is demonstrably the life of fiction," the only American literature destined to prevail. Joseph Kirkland then began to speak on "The Ebb-Tide in Realism," in which he lauded contemporary novelists, when, through the chairman, Catherwood interrupted the proceedings "to say a few words in defense of the old heroes she admired so much and whom she seemed to think had not been accorded due reverence by some of the speakers."[27] What followed, the *Chicago Tribune* reported, was a "joust" between Catherwood and Garland, with Catherwood defending "the dead past" and Garland championing "the living present."[28]

What made this minor skirmish in the realism war notable was the subsequent furor in the press. Eugene Field, then writing a "Sharps and Flats" column for the *Chicago Record*, amused Chicagoans by printing humorous verse and satiric commentary on current events and people. Although Garland records that he and Field were "something more than acquaintances" at the time, he was well aware that no one—not even friends—escaped Field's jesting when events lent themselves to his brand of satire.[29] Field wasn't present at the Literary Congress, but he apparently received a report of the Catherwood-Garland brawl. Adopting the *Tribune*'s joust metaphor, he proceeded to roast Garland for his "wonderful photography," but Catherwood "hath chosen the better part," for "she loves the fanciful in fiction." In "the intellectual wrestling match" between Catherwood and "the apostle of realism," Garland's "'in hoc signo' is a dung fork or a butter paddle," while Catherwood's "is a lance or an embroidery needle. Give us the lance and its champion every time."[30]

The combative author soon responded. "I had my share in the general hearty laugh over your most excellent fooling yesterday," he wrote to Field, who printed his letter in his column, "for I realized (as no doubt others did) that a layer of serious meaning ran under it all." While Garland attempted to match Field's tomfoolery, his evangelism soon mastered his humor. He informed Field that "lords and ladies are in dire straits" and assured him that "realism or veritism or sincerity or Americanism (at bottom these words mean practically the same thing) is on the increase." Although realists might be in the minority for the present, "we're fighters, and we've got Truth on our side." "Do you want to know what we contend for—we disturbers of the dreamers and breakers of graven images?" he asked. "We stand for Sincerity: we are warring against Effectism." Then, adopting Field's metaphor, he concluded, "then let the battle begin, the pitchforks and the butter-ladles be couched and ready, and their eager bearers cry 'Let death be the utterance—the battle-ground the west!'"[31]

For the next week the battle continued daily in Field's column, with Catherwood and Garland both contributing letters while Field served as the referee who fixed the fight in Catherwood's favor. In his letter of July 31, Garland defended himself against Field's sneer that he wrote "wonderful photography"—then a common epithet applied to realists. His explanation of his method was his clearest statement to date of his notion of "veritism," his fusion of Howellsian realism with literary impressionism, a term coined from his study of the aesthetic theories of Eugene Véron. Later he would elaborate the idea in *Crumbling Idols,* but one important effect of Field's criticism is that it pressed him to clarify his aesthetic theory. "The veritist does *not* 'write of things as they are,' but *of* things as he *sees* them: which is the whole width of art and the world from the position ascribed to him. His writing is *not* photography nor the statement of things as the casual observer sees them. His writing is of nearly [*sic*] things *plus* his interest in them—things *plus* his selection of them and distribution of values *plus* his irresistible desire to state his view of things which has never been uttered by any one else."[32] In short, the veritist differs from the realist in that his depiction is colored by his individual perception and selection of detail to convey that perception.

That summer Garland interviewed Eugene Field and James Whitcomb Riley for *McClure's Magazine.* Samuel S. McClure, who had published Garland's "The Sociable at Dudley's" through his newspaper syndicate in November 1892, had just founded the magazine, with its first issue appearing in June, just when the financial panic hit. To make it competitive with the big three—*Century, Atlantic,* and *Harper's*—and survive the economic collapse, he tapped a number of well-known writers to send on assignments, counting on their proven mastery of language to draw readers. Among them was Garland, whose interview with Field for the magazine's "Real Conversations" series would appear in the magazine's third issue.

The Field interview took place in June, before the Literary Congress debacle. Cast as a dialogue between interviewer and subject, where Garland himself becomes a character in the interview being recorded by an "objective" observer, Garland used the occasion to reinforce the themes of his two *Arena* articles, where Field exclaims, "I tell you, brother Garland, the West is the coming country. We ought to have a big magazine to develop the West. It's absurd to suppose we're going on always being a tributary to the East!"[33] Elsewhere in the interview, Garland took pains to describe Field's appearance and habits of speech. In the Riley interview, which took place in August, he lobbied for the value of local color and dialect, with Riley as America's foremost exemplar. In this interview he dropped all pretense of objective recording and pressed his case directly. "We've been so afraid the world would find us lacking in scholarship, that we've allowed it to find us lacking in creative work," he told Riley. He then proceeded to demonstrate for his readers the specific ways in which Riley transmuted the raw materials of country life into work of "genius."[34]

Again, Garland's promotion of western writers riled the eastern press. Soon after the Field interview appeared, the *Critic* blasted Garland for self-aggrandizement. "[Garland] has never put his pen to paper but to exploit himself," the writer declared. He objected to the impropriety of Garland's description of Field, citing as particularly offensive to eastern readers the line "He was stripped to his shirt-sleeves and sat with his feet on a small stand" as well as Garland's depiction of the dialogue itself. Field, the *Critic* claimed, "deserves a better fate than to be held up to the readers of a magazine as a living example of all that is 'wildest and woolliest.' If this be the realistic way of treating one's friends, let us pray to be interviewed by romanticists."[35] Field later got his revenge by circulating a rumor that Garland had become engaged to "Miss Birdie Smilax, the belle of East Salem [*sic*]," who had won distinction for winning "first prize for butter-making at the competitive exhibition of the Patrons of Husbandry at Oshkosh." The daughter of the owner of "the biggest red barn in the country," she had at last succeeded in ensnaring this most prominent of "the few invincible, impregnable bachelors."[36]

Then, in October, Garland loosed his most vehement fusillade to date when he published "Literary Emancipation of the West" in the *Forum*. Then the most respected magazine of comment of the time, the *Forum* specialized in printing articles by important writers on reform movements of all sorts. More balanced in treatment than the *Arena*, it was the magazine readers relied upon to discern trends in contemporary affairs. Garland could not have chosen a better magazine to attract attention to his plea for western art, and attention he soon received.

He began with a factual observation that the growth of the West, and particularly Chicago, meant that the East no longer dominated commerce. With the shift in the production of goods also comes a shift in the production of art, for, as he observed prophetically, "the material always subtends the intellectual"—that is, art follows money, a principle he would rely on when forming the Cliff Dwellers' Club in 1907 and other clubs designed to bring together artists and patrons. Prophesying that Chicago was destined to become the new literary center of the United States, with concomitant publishing houses and literary magazines, he proceeded, perhaps designedly, to insult his eastern readers. "The blight upon the literature of the West, like that of all provinces," he blithely asserted, "has been its tendency to work in accepted modes, its childish desire to write for the applause of its masters in the East." Though he later claimed he was surprised by the unfavorable response from eastern critics, how could he have been surprised when he proceeded to heap opprobrium upon the East? Accusing the East of harboring a "sterile culture" in contrast to the "creative work" of the West, Garland called for writers to abandon eastern models and turn to the West for inspiration, for the East is "essentially aristocratic and un-American."[37]

The reaction was immediate and predictable. Responding to an advance copy of the *Forum*, the *Chicago Tribune* announced the thesis of the "aggressive young writer, Hamlin Garland"—"that the East is too English to be American, and that only from Chicago Westward can real Americanism be found." Rather than "dispute so pugnacious a young man as Mr. Garland," the critic presented large extracts of Garland's essay and concluded, in the idiom of the Field fiasco, "there is nothing left for the West to do but gird its loins and prepare for the championship."[38] The *Critic* similarly chided Garland for the "noise" of his argument. "Do be a little more reasonable and less violent, and you will be much more convincing," the writer admonished. "Don't fall into that pernicious habit of calling everything that is blatant, American, and everything that is refined, un-American." Finally, the *Critic* concluded, "the American who goes about with a chip on his shoulder, who spreads his coat-tails, and shouts from the house-tops that he is a 'genuwine Amurricun,' is not the one who reflects most credit upon his country or in whom the better class of his countrymen take the most pride."[39] More salvos appeared in other magazines, including a lengthy, thoughtful point-by-point response from George Hamlin Fitch in the *Californian Illustrated Magazine*, which one would have thought would be more sympathetic to Garland's call to arms. But not so. Although recognizing Garland as a "man of great force" and "the most eloquent 'boomer'" of the "new literary movement," Fitch deconstructed Garland's every point, concluding that he stood for "a colossal conceit, a hard, material instinct and a scorn of leisure that are absolutely opposed to any true work in literature."[40]

Garland later recalled that *Forum* editor Walter Hines Page, grateful for the controversy that sells magazines, told him "with glee" that his article "had brought forth nearly a thousand editorial comments, commendatory and otherwise."[41] But while Garland was never averse to criticism that focused on his work (for he too recognized the sales value of publicity), he was pained at comment that attacked him personally. An editorial in the *Dial*, Chicago's most prestigious magazine, called Garland "a strong-lunged but untrained product of the prairies" who "is straightway hailed as the apostle of the newest and consequently the best realism," prompting the pugnacious author to fire off an angry letter to its editor, Francis F. Browne.[42] "I don't mind how much your editors pound away at my theories but hard words are not argument," he wrote. He blasted the *Dial* for being a "conservative rear-guard" journal and, in a reply to Browne's six-page typed counterargument, retorted that "I have never said a word in public reflecting upon anybody. . . . Careful reading of my *Forum* article will show that I am fair."[43]

Thirty-seven years later, in musing about his campaign for realism, Garland recalled that "it was in truth a most astonishingly bitter war, quite as bitter as any sectarian conflict of recent years," and he justified his vehemence because he "had suffered so much criticism from sentimental critics that I was savage."[44] Add to that motive his conviction that he was speaking the truth, his contentious personality, and the exuberance of youth, and it was clear that this was only the opening engagement of what would become a protracted battle.

More salvos would follow, but first he needed to tidy up eastern commitments.

11

THE ICONOCLAST, 1893–94

In November, soon after the *Dial* flap, Garland returned to Boston. He intended to settle permanently in Chicago, since he was convinced the city was destined to become the cultural center of America, but first he needed to tie up loose ends. One was his involvement with the American Psychical Society, for he had arranged for a particularly noteworthy psychic in Los Angeles to come to Boston for testing by the society. For five weeks, from November 3 to December 10, in thirty-two sittings, he puzzled over the phenomena called forth by the psychic, Mrs. Mary Curryer Smith. He marveled over table rappings, moving furniture, disembodied voices, and flying objects. While not ready to "admit of supernatural origin for the phenomena," at this point he was not able to discern the physical causes he suspected responsible and remained receptive to further exploration.[1]

By December 15, 1893, he had moved to New York, where he shared an apartment with Franklin at 107 West 105th Street. Herne's *Shore Acres* had opened on October 30 at Miner's Fifth Avenue Theater, destined to become a smash hit and eventually make Herne a millionaire. Franklin had an important role as the land speculator Josiah Blake, and, with faith in the play's audience appeal, had written to ask his elder brother to help share the expense of a flat rather than live in a lodging house. With his customary laxness about chronology in his autobiography, Garland attributes the move to a sudden realization that "New York was about to become the Literary Center of America"—a surprising statement given his similar claim for Chicago in "The Literary Emancipation of the West," published in October, and his statement to Field in July that he planned to establish his headquarters in Chicago. And no small part of that decision was his desire to be near his beloved mother in West Salem, a trip of eight hours by train.[2]

What likely prompted Garland to put off his move to Chicago was his desire to be in on the theatrical action surrounding the New York run of *Shore Acres*, which had already had a very successful tryout in Boston during the summer. Then, too, while he wanted to establish Chicago's potential eminence in publishing, he also realized that, for the time being, New York was the home of the editors and magazines who were publishing his work, particularly Samuel S. McClure, whose newly established *McClure's Magazine* and his McClure Newspaper Syndicate would shortly replace the *Arena* as his most important publishing venue, and Irving Bacheller, whose newspaper syndicate similarly distributed much of the prolific author's work.

Garland settled into a cramped flat of "only twelve-and-a-half feet wide and about forty-eight feet long," where, as was now his habit, he devoted mornings to writing.[3] Much of his attention was devoted to arranging terms with his new publishers, Stone and Kimball. While still in Chicago during July, he had, through the efforts of Stone's father, Melville E. Stone, consented to give the Harvard undergrads his next book, which he had entitled *Prairie Songs*, and arranged for them to reissue *Main-Travelled Roads*. In going over his plans with Howells, he asked whether the elder writer would allow his highly laudatory review to stand as an introduction to the volume. "A fellow who stands as strong upon his legs as you, wanting a hand from a dotard like me!" exclaimed Howells. "I think the public would say, 'Who is this paltering fool, who introduces a book of Garland's to us?'"[4] Nonetheless, he gave his consent, and his review served as the introduction to all subsequent editions during Garland's lifetime.

Garland soon became irritated by the precocious schoolboys' lack of business acumen. His arrangements were surprisingly loose for an author of his experience. Rather than establishing a formal contract calling for a set royalty, Garland made an agreement in which he essentially entered into partnership with the firm. In exchange for the rights to *Main-Travelled Roads* and the manuscript of *Prairie Songs*, he would receive half of all profits above the expenses of manufacture and advertising.[5] On their part, Stone and Kimball were counting on the controversial author's name to bring attention to their firm. In October a steady stream of letters began in which Garland instructed Stone in the business of publishing and marketing. He lectured Stone about the need for more descriptive advertising—"goodly paragraphs" rather than the brief notes of the prospectus. "I think it is customary to put at least one or two of an authors books on the title page," he suggested in a second letter. For Garland, with the two Schulte books essentially off the market because of the failure of the firm, this was no small matter. "I own these books and you would be helping me rather than some other firm," he told him.[6] Stone, who was as much of an iconoclast as Garland in terms of book design, wanted his press to become famous for its artistically designed books, with distinctive covers, typography, and illustrations, and he ignored Garland's wishes when the books were published.

By December Garland was thoroughly exasperated at the delay, for he had turned over *Main-Travelled Roads* and the manuscript of *Prairie Songs* in August and had yet to receive copies; the books had been announced in September, and he naturally hoped to capitalize on the notoriety stemming from his campaign for realism.[7] Then, too, he expected that his poetry would show his critics that he was extending his artistic range and that he could no longer be dismissed as a prairie muckraker. "The reason I do not care to promise another book, just now, is because I feel your facilities are inadequate for doing the work of distributing the books," Garland announced. "This delay has been very disastrous to me. It has cut me off from any proper attention from the critics and has made the success of the whole enterprise doubtful." He was especially bothered that the distractions of the season would mean that *Prairie Songs* would "go into the ruck of Christmas books and will not get ten lines of notice." He chided Stone for the lack of proper advertising and noted that "your time is divided between your studies and your business, this is a great objection." Finally, he told him, "I want to aid you to build up a fine publishing house in Chicago but until you get settled and know what you are going to do and how to do it, I dont feel safe in letting you have my essays. I have been deeply worried and chagrined by this delay and to take on myself more such distress would not be just to myself."[8]

His letter prompted quick action, for three days later Garland had received copies of both books and a letter that must have allayed his concerns, for he then sounded Stone out about reissuing *Prairie Folks* as a "companion volume" to *Main-Travelled Roads*. Since he owned the plates, he offered the book on "the same co-operative rates" and estimated the manufacturing cost of a thousand copies to be three hundred dollars.[9]

When he finally saw the two books, Garland was, as the historian of the firm has remarked, "extravagantly pleased" with them. The design of the books was stunning. The trade edition was bound in green buckram with an illustration of three cornstalks stamped in gold leaf so that the front and back covers were identical; the design was carried to the spine as well. The type, on wove paper, was Modernized Old Style, with the title page carrying a publisher's device stamped in red, as was the title and name of the publisher. In his negotiations with Stone, Garland had urged that the books be illustrated, and he retained Horace T. Carpenter to do the cover design and illustrations for the volumes. The artist provided a frontispiece and six illustrations for *Main-Travelled Roads* and fifty-four illustrations for the eighty-four poems of *Prairie Songs*. The firm also issued large-paper editions of both books—that is, with the text printed on heavy paper with conspicuously wide margins—limited to 110 copies, bound in cream buckram with the same cover design. (Today, both editions are highly valued by book collectors, who admire their innovative bindings.) Stone took extraordinary care with the manufacture of these books, for they were the first two real books the firm issued and he was counting on them to draw attention to his developing list. The first printing of *Main-Travelled Roads* by the Craig Press of Chicago was unsatisfactory, so Stone had it redone by the Wilson Press of Cambridge, which is likely the reason for the delay that so displeased Garland.[10]

While negotiating with Stone, Garland also began corresponding with Johnson Brigham, who was just starting the *Midland Monthly*, a magazine in Des Moines, Iowa. To help promote *Prairie Songs* and Brigham's magazine, Garland arranged for Brigham to publish nine poems from advance sheets in the inaugural issue. He also included the manuscript of another ("Massasagua") to be reproduced in fac-simile and arranged for Carpenter to illustrate the Riley-influenced opening poem, "Horses Chawin' Hay." Deeply interested in any mag-azine devoted to western culture, Garland sold a number of pieces at reduced rates after it became clear that Brigham couldn't afford his usual price. From his drawer he pulled an unpublished "Boy Life" sketch, selling it for thirty-five dollars while trying hard to con-vince Brigham to take a novel for serialization, a "story of Iowa town life," for which he had refused six hundred dollars "for serial rights alone." He assured the editor that his story "contains no politics no reforms," for he did not intend to repeat his polemical fiction. "I want you to understand I am not grasping for myself," he explained to Brigham, but he had a payment to meet on his "little fruit farm" and his aging parents to support too. If the novel didn't interest him, he had a number of novelettes of "my very best work" for sale at two hundred to four hundred dollars. If these were too costly, he had "a number of curious and unusual studies of men and nature" priced from twenty to eighty dollars. Finally, he had still more "Boy Life" sketches available.[11]

Brigham ultimately accepted "Mount Shasta" and "A Night Land-ing on the Mississippi River," two of the "curious and unusual stud-ies" that are descriptive sketches of places rather than tales, for which he paid twenty dollars each. "I cant let you have the Garland-ish things for $25," the author would later inform his editor when he balked at Garland's much higher prices for his more desirable fiction.[12] By 1894 Garland had arrived as an author: in demand as a lecturer and with his name exciting controversy in the press, the prolific author was finally in a position to command premium rates for his work.

When *Prairie Songs* was published, the reception was, as Garland feared, muted by its poor timing, and the volume garnered few re-views. Flower loyally praised the volume in the *Arena* but predicted that the poems would occasion "another attack of mental hydrophobia among some conservative critics, who are always affected distressingly when a volume appears which is too strong, true, and original to be conventional. These little men have been lonely since Whitman died."[13] The reference to Whitman was apt, for Garland was indeed influenced by Whitman's free-verse form, as he was by Whitman's organizing image of grass. Other influences were the dialect poems of James Whitcomb Riley and the lyrics of Joaquin Miller, "the poet of the Sierras," whose verse Garland much admired.[14] In the foreword, Garland described the grasses of the prairie and the plains and offered the collection as his memorial to the carefree days of boyhood in which he and Franklin romped over the fields of northern Iowa and, later, Dakota Territory. The predominant tone of the volume is of a reminiscent nostalgia for a land that has irrevocably changed.

Garland is best at descriptive, nondialect verse. In poems such as the oft-reprinted "Color in the Wheat," the opening stanza describes the wheat's color in terms of movement:

> Like liquid gold the wheat field lies,
> A marvel of yellow and green,
> That ripples and runs, that floats and flies,
> With the subtle shadows, the change—the sheen
> That plays in the golden hair of a girl.[15]

In "A Dakota Harvest Field" he pictures the look of the field after harvest: "The golden stubble stretches, / Looped and laced with silvery spider's webs" while overhead "The over-arching majesty of purple clouds grows brighter / Soaring above in seas of green and blue."[16]

Not all of the poems celebrate the majesty of the landscape and the fecundity of the natural world. Some, like "A Human Habitation," share with his short fiction a pattern of depicting human misery within a glorious natural setting. Beneath a beautifully colored sky sits a "settler's shack," which is not quite "a prison" but rather "solitary confinement," for "to some worn woman / Another monotonous day was born."[17]

In "Horses Chawin' Hay" Garland captures the essence of Riley's evocation of sentimental nostalgia through a speaker musing on memories called forth by a mundane event—here, the sound of horses chewing hay:

> I love t' hear 'em chankin',
> Jest a-grindin' slow and low,
> With their snouts a-rootin' clover
> Deep as their ol' heads 'll go

Such sounds evoke a memory of sleeping on a prairie schooner listening to the night sounds. The speaker marvels that such a minor sound can "float a feller backwards . . . an' start his throat a-achin'."[18]

As Flower prophesied, conservative critics pounced on Garland's realism. "Must we call it poetry?" the *New York Tribune* asked. The *Chicago Evening Post* observed that *Prairie Songs* "mark his limitations sharply as none other of his works has done" and complained that Garland's uneven rhymes and "infelicitous choice of language"—with "such harsh words as 'rattle,' 'squeal' and 'bustle'"—are needlessly offensive. The *Chicago Tribune* dismissed the volume as "diluted Whitmania" that "misses . . . the music of poetry just as one misses in many pieces the magic of rhyme."[19] By this point in his career, Garland had become amused rather than perturbed by critical controversy, for he regarded his poetry as a passing phase rather than his important work. To Stone he wrote, "It is amusing to read the contention about P. Songs."[20] And to Brigham he explained phlegmatically, "it was a foregone conclusion that certain critics should say ironical things. You will soon find—if you have not already done so, that there is a literary war in progress—the same old war between the new and the old—and critics of the traditional school read the new to condemn. This does not disturb the new."[21]

Soon after he arrived in New York, Garland renewed his acquaintance with Stephen Crane, whom he had first met during the summer of 1891 and again in 1892 while teaching at the Seaside

Assembly in Avon-by-the-Sea, New Jersey, a school similar to Brown's Boston School of Oratory in curriculum and methods. There, Crane had reported Garland's lecture on Howells for the *New York Tribune*, and the two struck up a friendship, discussed literature, and played baseball.[22] Crane had sent Garland a copy of *Maggie: A Girl of the Streets* (1893) when it was published, and, impressed with its innovative style, Garland had reviewed the novel for the *Arena* as an excellent example of local color of the slums whose words "illuminate like flashes of light."[23] When he next met Crane, in December 1893 or January 1894, he learned that the younger author was finding it difficult to publish his work. Garland promptly provided introductions to a number of editors, among them Samuel McClure, Irving Bacheller, and Herbert Stone.[24] He also inspired one of Crane's most-anthologized pieces of reportage. Howells had suggested to Garland that he write an article about the midnight breadlines that were then forming in the city. "It isn't my field," Garland told Crane, "but it is yours. You could do it beyond anybody."[25] The result was "The Men in the Storm," which, together with "An Omnibus Baby," Garland mailed to Flower for publication in the *Arena*.[26] Garland was so impressed with Crane's talent that earlier he had arranged an introduction to Howells in April 1893, hoping that the senior writer could help Crane place his poetry with *Harper's Monthly*.

Garland was intensely interested in Crane's distinctive style and especially his method of composition. One day in March 1894 Crane stopped by Garland's apartment with a sheaf of poems, "at once quaintly humorous and audacious, unrhymed and almost without rhythm, but the figures employed with masterful brevity were colossal."[27] With his own volume of poetry fresh from the press, Garland was acutely tuned to other innovative poets. He had followed Whitman's and Riley's lead in challenging conventional poetic diction, but now he saw someone who had apparently answered his call to throw off literary masters, for Crane's style was unique. Indeed, Garland would never tire of quoting examples of Crane's distinctive style, and he seems to have been at a loss for how to account for its origin. He knew from his own experience how difficult creative composition was—he had a long apprenticeship full of false starts to prove it—and he always labored to revise his work. So he was prepared to accept Crane's assertion that he composed in his head and had only to "draw off" the lines, without revision, for how else to account for a style so radically at variance with his own? "According to his explanation," Garland recounted, "the composition of these lines was an entirely automatic, subconscious process." Still the president of the American Psychical Society and with five weeks of daily tests of the Los Angeles psychic fresh in his mind, Garland was certain that a psychic force was channeling through this new poetic medium. "There is a ghost at your shoulder," Garland told him in "mock seriousness," but he took Crane's assertion seriously enough to "test" him.[28] He asked Crane to sit at his desk and "do one for me." Crane took Garland's pen and "wrote steadily, composedly, without a moment's hesitation, one of his most powerful poems. It flowed from his pen like oil, but when I examined it, I found it not only without blot or erasure, but perfectly correct in punctuation." Writing twenty years after the event, Garland couldn't remember which specific poem flowed from the force transmitting through Crane's brain, but after several sittings during which Crane penned a number of poems, the flow ebbed, and Crane told Garland, "That place in my brain is empty."[29] Partly as a result of this encounter, Crane dedicated *The Black Riders and Other Lines* to Garland when the volume appeared in May 1895.

In April 1894 Crane called on Garland again with another manuscript. "The first sentence fairly took me captive," Garland recorded. "It described a vast army in camp on one side of a river, confronting with its thousands of eyes a similar monster on the opposite bank." Reading the opening of *The Red Badge of Courage* filled Garland with "the thrill of the editor who has fallen unexpectedly upon a work of genius." But how to explain the startling imagery, wondrous similes, and unusual diction coming from the work of a mere boy, and one with disheveled clothes, nicotine-stained fingers, and hair badly in need of a haircut? "It was as if the youth in some mysterious way had secured the cooperation of a spirit, the spirit of an officer in the Civil War," Garland decided. "How else could one account for the boy's knowledge of war?"[30]

Crane explained that his knowledge of war had come from the football field, not the spirit world, but he might have gone on to say that the effects Garland admired were in part due to Garland's own theories about the nature and methods of realism. During their frequent meetings that spring Garland was busy preparing the essays he would gather in *Crumbling Idols*, and central to them was his notion of "veritism," a blending of the realist's insistence upon verisimilitude of detail with the impressionist's tendency to paint objects as they appear to his or her individual eye. The impressionists, Garland wrote in one of the most significant of these essays, "cannot sacrifice color for multiple lines. They do not paint leaves, they paint masses of color; they paint the *effect* of the leaves upon the eye."[31] Living in a rooming house occupied by painters and illustrators, Crane no doubt considered the elder writer's pronouncements seriously, for *The Red Badge of Courage* is filled with the impressionistic effects of color that Garland admired. But when Garland asked where the second half of the manuscript was, Crane explained that it was in hock to his typist. Garland loaned the youth fifteen dollars to redeem the manuscript and, after performing some editorial emendations, left for Chicago.[32] Crane was forever grateful for Garland's timely encouragement at this early stage of his career. "I've been to see Garland," he told the painter Corwin Knapp Linson. "He tells me I am a Genius! That's what he said 'Genius.'"[33] But the influence was not all one-sided.

Even as he was in the midst of stumping for Populist candidates in 1892 and at the height of his campaign for realism, Garland had been working to extend his artistic range. As he traveled he had been jotting down in his notebooks descriptive sketches of places and objects. Typically devoid of human actors, these sketches were his attempt to apply the painterly techniques he had observed at the easels of his Boston art friends, particularly the impressionist landscape painter John J. Enneking, whom he had met during his 1885 lectures at Mrs. Payson's Hyde Park home. Through his talks with and observations of Enneking, Garland became well acquainted with impressionism, and he had studied the psychology of color, being especially influenced by Spencer's "The Valuation of Evidence," in which the philosopher offered a "scientific explanation for colored shadows, one of the most noticeable and notorious impressionistic practices."[34] By February 1894 he had drafted a lecture on impressionism that became one of the most important essays in *Crumbling Idols*, what one historian of the movement has called "probably the first all-out defense of the movement to be written in English."[35] Occasionally, Garland had interspersed in his fiction descriptive scenes marked by impressionistic color, as in this example from "Up the Coulé": "Over the western wall of the circling amphitheatre the sun was setting. A few scattering clouds were drifting on the west wind, their shadows sliding down the green and purple slopes. The dazzling sunlight flamed along the luscious velvety grass, and shot amid the rounded, distant purple peaks, and streamed in bars of gold and crimson across the blue mist of the narrower upper Coulés."[36] In the fall of 1892 he had begun publishing some of the sketches, the most effective of which are the prose word paintings of "Western Landscapes" in which Garland sought to portray the color and emotion conveyed by a particular place. Here is "San Francisco Bay (December)":

A tossing spread of dull green water, lined here and there with white waves caught up by the powerful north wind. Out of this dull green level the brown and rounded hills lay, landlocking it. Behind this semicircular wall of hills, the mountains rose not quite to the region of snows.

Gulls wheeled and dipped plenteously, and the yellow-green waves sounded a brisk, not entirely angry note.

The mountains were a royal blue, but the hills and islands were stern and forbidding in color; barren and treeless except where the live-oaks and chaparral lay in patches, like cloud shadows.

It was all crisp, strong, invigorating; nothing soft, nothing rich. A flare of clear sunshine, and a pushing, sounding wind.[37]

After his encounter with Crane in the spring of 1894, Garland turned to new experiments with prose, consciously attempting to apply Crane's striking style to his own work. He seems to have been especially struck by what one scholar calls Crane's ability to find "the verbal equivalents of sensory experience and the subjective values of that experience" as perceived by the observer.[38] In a series of sketches he titled "Chicago Studies," Garland departed from the objective point of view of "Western Landscapes" to convey a more darkly subjective impression of Chicago life in language remarkably like Crane's. His admiration for *Maggie* shows in "Election Night," where "Men shook their quavering hands above their heads in white frenzy and beat each other in an insane congratulation," and in "The Streets in Winter," where "The buildings stood against the gray-white vague sky in grim, darkly-blue masses."[39] In "Lake Front at Night," Garland's descriptive technique echoes Crane's in *Red Badge of Courage*:

> Out of the green-black water, foam-flowers bloomed in gigantic impulses. Urged from the outer deeps, smooth swells came shore-ward to burst into leaping, voice-ful breakers, flinging their spray in the freezing air.
>
> The roar was keyed higher than that of the ocean, sharper, more spiteful, with less lion-like majesty, and yet deadly and ravenous, as if it called for human flesh.[40]

Garland revised "Chicago Studies" intermittently over the years, and it remained unpublished at his death. But he applied the same approach to a number of other sketches published in 1894, the best of which is his account of the Carnegie steel mill at Homestead, Pennsylvania. In a first-person narrative describing the steel-making process and its effect on workers, Garland effectively combines description of the visceral effect of the process with social commentary, with most of that commentary appearing in the mouths of those he interviewed. Here, for example, is his description of the cutting process: "The furious scream of a saw broke forth, the monstrous exaggeration of a circular wood saw—a saw that melted its way through a beam of solid iron with deafening outcry, producing a gigantic glowing wheel of spattering sparks of golden fire. While it lasted all else was hid from sight."[41]

While Garland was advising Crane and nudging Stone to follow through with the publication of *Main-Travelled Roads* and *Prairie*

Songs, Stone was busy trying to convince Garland to let him bring out his volume of essays, for publication of "Literary Emancipation of the West" had made the controversial author a hot commodity. For his part, Garland dangled the essays as a carrot to encourage Stone to publish the volume on his terms. By January 16 matters had progressed to the point where Garland issued four conditions for giving the book to Stone and Kimball:

1st Can you assure me a profit of 15% or $187.50 on first edition.
2nd Can you sell a limited edition.
3rd Do you intend to make it uniform with the other books.
4th Do you expect to make head-quarters in Chicago during the year.

For Garland, the collection of essays was his most important work to date, and he wanted assurance that it would be handsomely print-ed and actively marketed. Stone was still enrolled at Harvard, so he couldn't devote his full energies to the enterprise; and while Garland had been approached by several more-established firms who were "willing to pay unusual royalties and make unusual con-cessions," he wanted to promote Chicago as a literary center and saw Stone and Kimball's success as an important step toward that goal—provided Stone could meet his conditions.[42]

Two days later, after a satisfactory reply, Garland consented to allow the firm to publish *Crumbling Idols,* which he intended to be his last controversial work. "I am ready to send out purely literary books hereafter," he informed Stone. "I shall not repeat either my economic writing or this literary and art reform. Having said my say I shall proceed on to other things," keenly aware that his po-lemical writing had resulted in comparatively few sales. He outlined a number of books he had nearly ready—among them "Western Landscapes," a collection of his sketches—and promised, "you need not fear repetitious or monotonous work. You dont know my plans and resources."[43] By the end of January he had sent Stone the vari-ous essays for the book, explaining, "As you can see I have knitted the whole thing together and improved it very much," but he also worried that Stone "might exalt the casket above the contents."[44] During February and March, as Garland shuttled from New York to Chicago to Memphis delivering lectures, he took great care with proofreading the book, pestering Stone for galleys and sending a copy to his brother as an additional check, for, as he explained, "I dont want to be hurried about this book. It must be perfectly proof-read."[45] Garland expected controversial reaction in the press, and he didn't want to give his detractors any opportunity to skewer him over slovenly prose, as they had done for some of his earlier books. Indeed, in the interest of wider sales, he wanted to promote controversy, advising Stone to include a page with "the names of my other books and also some of the critical opinions for this reason. It will provide controversy and will be read by people who do not know the names of my books, and weight will be added to these essays by the evidence of my successful work."[46]

Crumbling Idols: Twelve Essays on Art Dealing Chiefly with Literature, Painting, and the Drama was published in May 1894 and was dedicated "To Those Men and Women of America Who Have the Courage to Be Artists." Garland may have taken the title from a comment he made to Eugene Field in which he referred to the realists as "we disturbers of the dreamers and breakers of the graven images."[47] Of the twelve essays, seven were revisions of four previously published essays, three were lectures he had recently delivered in Memphis and Chicago, and two were apparently written specifically for the volume.[48] In recasting his material, he seems to have acted deliberately to provoke conservative critics, revising essays to match the strident tone of "Literary Emancipation of the West." Relying on his training in oratory, he pointed his rhetoric to inflame through attacking the values dear to the East. In "Provincialism," for example, the opening chapter, which had its genesis in "The West in Literature," he added a number of paragraphs that challenged eastern cultural supremacy. "It can almost be stated as a rule without an exception," he asserted, "that in our colleges there is no chair of English literature which is not dominated by conservative criticism, and where sneering allusion to modern writers is not daily made. The pupil is taught to worship the past, and is kept blind to the mighty literary movements of his own time."[49] Relishing the fray to come, he told an interviewer in February:

> If the essays are in key with the essay in the *Forum* there will be the most delightful rumpus we have seen in the literary press for a long while. Oh, dear, how I do love to be in a good old literary Donneybrook Fair—it clears the atmosphere!
>
> There have been a good many sharp criticisms made upon the position I have taken, and so long as a man deals with the principles I advocate, criticism and disapproval do not bother me. But I confess to feeling some disgust and bitterness when I see so-called criticism resorting to slurring personalities. It almost makes me despair, and I never despair, for I am an optimist.[50]

When the volume appeared in May, Garland sat back and awaited the ruckus. He didn't have long to wait.

While Garland had fully expected the book to arouse controversy, he had to be hurt by the jeering tone and ad hominem attacks of the reviews. One called him "a trifle hysterical" and derided the identical covers of the book as "fitting, since you can read the essays from either side you like and find them equally entertaining"; another accused him of possessing "sophomoric rhetoric." His old enemy, the *Dial*, dismissed him as "bellicose, obstreperous, blatant. Nobody could possibly agree with him, whatever he said." And the *Independent* accused this former "professor of American literature" of lacking knowledge of his subject and overwrought expression: "We do not find Mr. Garland a clear reasoner; he does not seem to be familiar with the history of literatures; he evidently speaks from the emotional centers, not from rich treasures of knowledge."[51] Early in the controversy, Howells wrote to reassure him: "You are getting plenty of abuse from the critics these days, but you are getting respect, too. They all know there is an honest man inside your book, and a strong one. You go further than I do, but you are in the right way, and you will arrive! You *have* arrived, in fact."[52]

Following the controversy in the press was Theodore Roosevelt, at the time U.S. Civil Service commissioner and himself the author of dozens of books and hundreds of essays. Although he would later become one of Garland's important friends, at the time he thought Garland was "a man with some power and with half an idea, but he is such a hopeless crank that nothing can be done with him," he wrote to Brander Matthews. "He is one of the very few men who give us most trouble in producing a spirit of sane Americanism, because his excessive foolishness creates a reaction against us." What exasperated Roosevelt was Garland's extremist rhetoric, in particular his call to cast off all masters, including Shakespeare. Though he thought that Garland was "in his main thought . . . entirely right. We must strike out for ourselves," Roosevelt believed "his ignorance, crudity, and utter lack of cultivation make him entirely unfit to understand the effect of the great masters of thought upon the language and upon literature."[53]

Later, after a summer's worth of abuse that included a barb from the *Critic* indicting Garland for "second-class work," Howells again consoled him: "The kites that draw the electricity are the kites that go up. The kites that stay down are safe. You have written a book that has made people talk against it; if it were not a strong book they would not talk of it. Of course it was very bold, and it was largely true, and people like neither courage nor truth; yet they are the things that are worth while. You will not lose either—I know you!"[54] In throwing down the gauntlet to the eastern critics, Garland had miscalculated the effect of his rhetoric. Intending to inspire while challenging complacency, he instead came off as a rustic boob, blind to the accomplishments of the East and too willing to accept any mediocrity as art—so long as it practiced local color or was written by a westerner. His response to the vituperation, he later noted, was to quit reading reviews, for they embittered him.[55]

12

WESTERN HORIZONS, 1895

In the midst of the controversy concerning *Crumbling Idols*, Garland discovered yet another enthusiasm: bringing American art to the masses. The 1893 Columbian Exposition had awakened great interest in the visual arts, and among its exhibitions were a number of paintings by Scandinavian impressionists that had aroused much discussion among fairgoers. For Garland, the interest in the arts was further evidence that Chicago was to become a great literary and cultural center, and he soon began to promote the visual arts in his lectures. During a visit to the city in February 1894 he gave a lecture on impressionism at the home of Franklin Head, a banker and patron of the arts. After the lecture he met the sculptor Lorado Taft, who was to become a lifelong friend. Born in the same year as Garland, Taft had studied at the École des Beaux-Arts in Paris, and when he returned to Chicago he opened a studio that soon became the focal point for a number of artists, writers, and others interested in the arts. In 1886 he became an instructor at the Chicago Art Institute. His first major commission was to design two companion pieces for the Columbian Exposition, *The Sleep of the Flowers* and *The Awakening of the Flowers*, which fronted the entrance of the Horticultural Building and brought him much attention. Like Garland, Taft had been influenced by the ideas of Hippolyte Taine, who taught at the École des Beaux-Arts while Taft was a student there.[1]

Taft introduced Garland to a group of artists who met in his or fellow sculptor Bessie Potter's studio on Friday afternoons after the matinee performance of the Chicago Symphony. They dubbed themselves "The Little Room," after Madelaine Yale Wynne's story of an intermittently appearing room. Later, when the Fine Arts Building at the corner of Michigan and Van Buren was completed, they shifted to meet at the studio of painter Ralph Clarkson. When he was in Chicago, Garland was one of the regulars at this informal club, and there he formed many lasting friendships, none more important than that with Henry Blake Fuller. Shortly before he moved to Chicago, Hamlin had read Fuller's *The Cliff Dwellers*, a grim satire of life amid the Chicago skyscrapers. "In you Chicago has found her first indigenous novelist," he immediately wrote to Fuller after finishing the novel, certain that he had found the western writer he had prophesied in *Crumbling Idols*.[2] He likely met Fuller though Taft at the Little Room, for Fuller was one of its most loyal participants. Aloof, impatient with pretension, highly intelligent and erudite, seemingly indifferent to reform or the uplift measures Garland advocated, Fuller was in many ways Garland's opposite. "Every human soul is at the final touch elusive," Garland recorded two years after meeting Fuller, "but Henry Fuller's is more so than any I have ever known. It is a ghost in flesh, a wraith in pantaloons." Fuller would become Garland's closest friend, his literary confidante, whose judgment he respected "second only to Howells'."[3]

In their discussions about the future of art and Chicago's role in the developing culture of the Midwest, Garland and Taft soon concluded that the uplift they envisioned could only occur through an educational program. Garland returned to New York, but Taft was busy interesting others, among them Mrs. T. Vernette Morse, an artist, philanthropist, and editor of *The Arts*, a Chicago magazine founded shortly before the exposition. In March, Morse, Taft, and others met to plan an arts organization that would, through lectures, exhibitions, home-study courses, and the magazine (later retitled *Arts for America* to reflect its new goal), educate the public about the potential of American art in its broadest sense—painting, sculpture, music, literature, architecture. When Garland returned to settle permanently in Chicago in April 1894 at 474 Elm Street, just three doors from the lake, he joined with them to form the Central Art Association of America. On May 1 the association issued a prospectus naming their goals and officers. Garland was president, Taft first vice-president, Morse secretary, and Franklin Head treasurer, and a group of twelve "counselors"—most of them wealthy patrons—functioned as advisers. With the motto "For the promotion and dispersion of good art among the people," the association sought to encourage appreciation of American art and to aid artists by educating a public to buy their work.

During the summer the association gathered together an alliance of art clubs throughout the Midwest, formed study courses, and prepared a chautauqua system of printed lectures. On October 25 Garland delivered the first lecture, on the goals of the association, to Chicago's Friday Club, with lectures by Eugene Field, Alice French, and the actors Joseph Jefferson and Sol Smith Russell following.[4] In October, too, the association was ready with its first exhibit of American impressionists, held at the Art Institute. In December the association sponsored an exhibit of sixty paintings by Indiana artists. From these exhibits Taft organized a series of traveling exhibitions to a number of western towns, while Garland produced two pamphlets, in dialogue form, by "The Critical Triumvirate"—a novelist, sculptor, and conservative painter (Garland, Taft, and Charles Francis Browne, respectively)—which provided a witty discussion of the exhibits.[5]

As Lucy Monroe pointed out in her review of the December exhibition for the *Critic*, Garland was an ideal choice as president: "No better man could have been found to execute the purposes of the Association, for he has all the indomitable energy of a pioneer, with a faith in the present and future of American art which will move any mountains that may venture to get in his way."[6] Garland at last had found his niche, and in the years to come he would become increasingly involved in social and artistic improvement schemes that drew on his talent for organization. Between the summer of 1894 and the spring of 1895 he devoted much of his energy to furthering the association's goals as exhibits traveled to Memphis, La Crosse, Madison, Topeka, Lincoln, and Kansas City. In an article for the *Forum* he revealed that much of his motive stemmed from his own impoverished cultural experience in the Midwest: "The walls of American homes are, as a rule, hung with pictures of the crudest sort. Even in the fine homes of the cities, it is the exception to find pictures worth a second glance. Taste has not really been considerably raised by reading. The thing most needed is contact with the actual work of the artist."[7] His comment about the lack of effect of reading on uplifting taste suggests that he was reacting, in part, to the lack of critical appreciation of his own work. Just as he had sought to educate readers about the kind of literature they should value through essays in the *Arena* and the *Forum*, so too did he now seek to foster an appreciation for American art that leaned toward impressionistic landscapes. As he noted in an introduction to an exhibition catalog in January 1895, applying the argument of *Crumbling Idols* to art, "Our art and our criticism alike should be founded, not upon tradition, not upon a school, but upon the individual perception of nature's vivid and subtle coloring." To do otherwise—to seek acceptance in the East—is "intellectual timidity"; the true artist "must not repeat; must not imitate."[8]

In his work with the Central Art Association, Garland did not neglect his literary career. For much of 1894 and 1895 he divided his efforts between fiction and the descriptive sketch, interviewing the sculptor Edward Kemeys for *McClure's* and contributing a sketch of the poet Joaquin Miller, whom he had met during his west coast visit of 1892, for the Bacheller Syndicate.[9] He had tried to extend his range by composing tales of northern Wisconsin, but his most significant effort was a serial based on his homesteading experience in the *Chap-Book*, a magazine conceived as a house organ to advertise Stone and Kimball's books but which soon emerged as a leader among the avant-garde. The *Chap-Book* began publication in May 1894, and soon Stone tapped his most important writer for a contribution. Garland published "The Land of the Straddle-Bug" serially from November 1894 to February 1895, apparently accepting a reduced price to help encourage the firm. In the midst of publication, Garland dashed off an angry letter to Stone, expressing his exasperation at Stone's delay in payment, which he needed to meet a note due on his West Salem home.[10] "The Land of the Straddle-Bug" shows Garland at the height of his fictional powers. Arriving during the Dakota land boom of 1884–85, Blanche and Howard Burke set out to establish a homestead in McPherson County, where they endure a harsh summer and even harsher winter with two bachelors, Jim Rivers and Robert Bailey. As the winter misery piles up, Blanche becomes increasingly disenchanted with her weak husband and enters into an affair with Rivers. When she learns she is pregnant, she and Rivers flee to establish a life together, but before they get very far they are trapped by a blizzard and seek sanctuary in Bailey's store. Bailey struggles with his conscience about whether to prevent or aid their escape and eventually decides the decision is Blanche's.

Unlike much of Garland's earlier fiction, the economic themes and gender politics are integrally wedded to the local-color backdrop. As his friend James A. Herne had earlier suggested in *Margaret Fleming*, Garland's point is not to suggest that unsatisfactory marriages justify adultery but that a woman has the right to choose the conditions of her life. To convey that point forcefully, as Donald Pizer has observed, "he used the example of adultery, in which every social and fictional convention called for either society or the wronged man to determine the fate of the woman."[11]

With the Central Art Association humming smoothly, during the summer of 1895 Garland undertook a tour of the West accompanied by two friends from the association, the painter Charles Francis Browne and the sculptor Hermon Atkins MacNeil, artists who had never been west of the Mississippi River and who were searching for new subjects for their art. Garland was to serve as their guide, and he would pay for his portion of the trip through articles about the experience published through the Bacheller Syndicate. Although he had passed through the West several times and had spent some weeks exploring Colorado in 1893 and 1894, the summer of 1895 marked his first extensive tour of the high country of Colorado, as well as of the Indian reservations of New Mexico and Arizona. The effect of this trip on his life and subsequent work, he later recalled, was pivotal, for the scenic majesty of the natural surroundings filled him with awe and cemented his decision to cast aside his focus on social reform. Then, too, he noted, "All my emotional relationships with the 'High Country' were pleasant, my sense of responsibility was less keen, hence the notes of resentment, of opposition to unjust social conditions which had made my other books an offence to readers were almost entirely absent in my studies of the mountaineers. My pity was less challenged in their case."[12] To that one might add that, with his mother now settled in West Salem, he no longer had the burden of guilt to motivate his fiction.

After devoting his career thus far to depicting the squalid conditions of farm life, Garland was particularly sensitive to the grandeur of the mountains and valleys, so unlike the steep valleys of his native Wisconsin and the flat farmlands of Iowa and South Dakota. "From the dry hot plains, across the blazing purple of the mesa's edge, I look away to where the white clouds soar in majesty above the serrate crest of the Uncomphagre," he recorded in his notebook. "Twelve thousand feet! I am brother to the eagles now!"[13] His rapture over the splendid vistas of the natural surroundings extended to his encounter with Indians at the Southern Ute Reservation, in the southwestern corner of Colorado. He had seen Indians during previous trips through the West, but this visit marked his first extensive study of the life, customs, and future of Indians living on reservations. Immediately Garland noted the irony of applying white values to the Utes and that current government policy was both unjust and likely to fail in its intent of "civilizing" Indians. "It requires a peculiar mind to understand the Indian," he wrote in "Among the Southern Utes," his first extensive essay on the subject. "First, his inherited habits of thought must be understood and, second, the power, the almost infrangible power of his environment. He must be considered as a man born of a certain race, and situated in a certain environment—he must be considered relatively in all questions of morality. It is absurd to apply to him the measures of Saxon virtues."[14]

Like many of those sympathetic to Indians, Garland tended to see Native Americans as less-evolved human beings who were products of their environment. It was therefore incumbent upon the more civilized white race to help them adapt to the dominant Anglo-Saxon culture. "They need instruction, not in religion, but in living, in working, in daily habit," he noted later in this essay. "In the war of political factions they have been neglected in the matter of schooling. In the war of greed and political brigandage they will probably be sacrificed in the end. Such is the process concealed under the glib phrase, 'the war of the races.'"[15]

By 1895 government policy toward American Indians had begun to change, partly because of the westward expansion of white settlers. Until the 1870s the United States accepted Indian sovereignty upon reservations, and tribes acted as autonomous nations with their own legal and political structures. Before the 1870s the buffalo—the foundation of Plains Indian culture—seemed inexhaustible, and official government policy was to maintain a separate but wary coexistence. But with the expansion of the nation's railway system in the 1870s came an explosion of white settlements, for the railroad corporations early understood that the key to financing the roads was local service, not cross-country shipments, and that expanding local service, by transporting farm and ranch products to market, was the crucial means.[16] As a result, the population of white settlers in the West expanded rapidly in the 1880s. Accompanying the influx of settlers was pressure to occupy land held by the tribes, which to the white perspective seemed "empty" and therefore available for settlement. Even Theodore Roosevelt, who had a greater understanding than most other politicians of Indian-white relations, believed that the land by rights belonged to those who cultivated it: "Let sentimentalists say what they will, the man who puts the soil to use must of right dispossess the man who does not, or the world will come to a standstill."[17]

The pressure to open up Indian lands for settlement sparked a ferocious political debate that culminated in the passage of Henry Dawes's General Allotment Act of 1887, which guided government policy until 1934, when it was replaced by the Indian Reorganization Act. The goal of the Dawes Act was to open up "unused" tribal land for settlement after the tribes become self-sufficient members of society. In theory, the process of acculturating Indians to hold white values and become productive citizens would work fairly swiftly. First, portions of reservations, on the fringe away from Indian communities, would be opened to white settlement. The money from the sale of this land would then be used to teach white methods of farming to the Indians, and once they became self-sufficient, land adequate to sustain a family would be apportioned out to individual Indians as "allotments," or homesteads. Each tribe would approve each change in its borders by majority vote. With self-sufficiency would come citizenship. All "leftover" land would then be opened to white settlement.

The Dawes Act quickly and effectively disfranchised Native Americans. When the act was passed in 1887, tribal landholdings in the United States amounted to 139 million acres; by 1934, those acres had dwindled to a mere 48 million.[18] The Dawes Act reflected the culmination of a paternalistic conception of Indian-white relations: the Indian was a "savage," a child of the Stone Age dwelling in barbarism; it was therefore incumbent on the whites, as a "superior" race, to lead the "backward Indian" to the light of civilization. In 1881, Hiram Price, the commissioner of Indian Affairs, captured the prevailing attitude in his annual report: "To domesticate and civilize wild Indians is a noble work, the accomplishment of which should be a crown of glory to any nation. But to allow them to drag along year after year, and generation after generation, in their old superstitions, laziness, and filth, when we have the power to elevate them in the scale of humanity, would be a lasting disgrace to our government."[19] The architects of the nation's Indian policies accordingly sought to remake Indians after their own image and took steps to eradicate Native American culture. Value lay in the productive use of land, measured by the products it produced. Therefore, Indians should become farmers or ranchers living on individual homesteads, which would have the added result of dispersing potential for resistance. To become "civilized," Indians needed to be taught to farm, to be educated in schools, and to give up all aspects of their culture that "held them back" from following the white man's road—from language to traditional dress to long hair to communal hunting: anything that would impede a smooth transition.

Such was the backdrop when Garland began visiting the reservations in 1895. Like his artist friends, he went in search of material, eager to record the stories of a people whose traditional way of life he believed to be threatened with extinction. As he notes in "Among the Southern Utes," "Whether they will survive the complete break-up of their tribal manners, customs, and laws is a grave question. One man whose opinion was authoritative said to me gravely and emphatically, 'they are disappearing from the face of the earth,' and undoubtedly they are fewer today than ever before in their known history; yet it may be that if justice is done them, if they are properly instructed, they may increase in numbers rather than diminish." But in 1895, still smarting from criticism of his reform-minded fiction, Garland was more interested in the potential of Indian life for use as literary material than he was in seeking to redress injustice. "It is not my purpose to enter into any controversy on this question," he continued. "The art side of their life, its dramatic and pictorial aspects are nearest to me at this time."[20]

From the Southern Ute Reservation, Garland and his friends traveled to the Tiwa pueblo of Isleta, near Albuquerque, where Garland witnessed an ancient means of threshing wheat, with ponies trampling the wheat and the wind carrying off the chaff. In an essay about his experience, Garland described the Tiwas' daily life, emphasizing its peaceful, wholesome characteristics, delighting in detailing the customs while also noting the disconnect between the official view of the Indians and his own observations. "Why disturb this peace—why 'civilize' these kindly folks?" he asked. "I could not see that we had anything to give them. Why disturb them? Why harass them with our problems?"[21]

From Isleta they made their way to the Hopi reservation north of Winslow, Arizona. Garland was most interested in observing the snake dance at Walpi, near Keams Canyon. He had the good fortune to stumble upon an ethnological field camp, where he met Jesse W. Fewkes, who was a Bureau of American Ethnology archaeologist studying the Hopi for the Smithsonian, and Frederick W. Hodge, whose *Handbook of the American Indian* (1907, 1910) would become the basic reference source in the field. Fewkes helped Garland gain access to parts of the ceremony, which was normally off-limits to whites, and enabled him to understand the significance of what he witnessed. In his article "Among the Moki Indians," Garland produced one of the earliest popular accounts of the ceremony. He especially delighted in the rituals of the portion of the ceremony he was allowed to see: the procession of the dancers, the songs, the details of snake handling, the dignity of the participants. The days Garland spent living with the Hopi (called "Moqui" at the time) impressed him with their fellow humanity, an essential corrective to his prior understanding of them as "inferior peoples." "It would be impossible to see elsewhere in America another such scene," he wrote. "It humanized these people. It took away all feeling of savagery from these men. They were priests. They were performing in a traditional ceremony. The ceremony itself had in it something of the barbarity of the olden time, but their pleasant and smiling faces as they received water from the hands of their women had no trace of ferocity left."[22]

At Walpi Garland met Dr. Theophil Mitchell Prudden, a bacteriologist and the head of the Department of Pathology at Columbia University, and with him he traveled to the Zuni, Laguna, and Acoma pueblos in New Mexico, taking pages of notes about Indian customs and the effect of white encroachment upon Indian lands. A persistent theme in the essays that resulted from these visits is a respect for Native American culture and a growing awareness that the loss of that culture means a lost opportunity to understand the similar roots of western society. As he concluded in an essay about his 1895 visits to the pueblos of Arizona and New Mexico, "There is sorrow ahead for them all—but there is also enlightenment, and enlightenment, we are accustomed to hear, is worth its cost. Possibly to us—but it will not be altogether a joyous thing to see these kindly, quaint and fascinating folk become booted and hatted citizens of Arizona. . . . The study of their manners and customs will throw a vivid light upon the early Greek and Roman and German people as well as upon races less advanced on the scale of development."[23] In later reflections upon the significance of his 1895 trip, Garland remarked that "all my later work was influenced by the concepts and emotions of this inspirational outing."[24]

But the stories would wait, for first he needed to complete the novel he hoped would make his reputation.

Rose of Dutcher's Coolly, Garland's most important novel, traces the development of a motherless girl from her childhood on a small farm in a Wisconsin coulee through her student days at the University of Wisconsin to her emergence in Chicago as an aspiring poet. It ends with her marriage to a prominent Chicago newspaperman and literary critic. Garland had conceived its plot in 1890, when he had recorded in his notebook the outline of a story entitled "A Father's Love": "Story of a man whose child, a girl, started to school from a narrow valley. How her mind expanded and her home narrowed. The father, seeing he was losing her, tried to make the home so pleasant she could stay at home. He bought new furniture. Built a new house while she was away at school. . . . She was made all the more miserable. It made her seem like a criminal, but she couldn't stay in the valley."[25] He made extensive notes about the Wisconsin scenes of the novel during the summer of 1892, mostly outlining Rose's reaction to Madison and recording snatches of dialogue. During the summer of 1893 he sketched Rose's adolescence, which formed the basis of chapter 2:

> From 10 to 15 was a period of fundamental experience. She developed the desires of a woman without her restraining modesty. She did unnamable things mostly out of a curiosity. She ranged through every experience within her reach. She inquired into everything she saw. She would not be hushed or turned aside.
>
> She fed potato bugs to toads and being interested in their tongues held them and pried their mouth open while her companions cried out in horror. She squeezed grass-hoppers to see them emit green froth and work their mandibles. She watched animals giving birth to young and ran to her father with a dozen questions concerning the great mystery.
>
> She was strong and brown and generally dirty with the dirt of the fields—good wholesome dirt.[26]

In the background, of course, was his own boyhood on prairie farms, and particularly the memory of the hardship his mother had faced and his own struggle to fashion a career. So he imagined for Rose quite another future, one in which she escaped conventional expectations to find fulfillment in the city.

This future would involve the full blossoming of her sexuality and individuality. During his early years in Boston, Garland had become a devotee of Walt Whitman's advocacy of what one scholar calls "the healthy, wholesome physical," and that consciousness of the body lies behind Rose's early awareness of her own body, her frank curiosity about naked boys, her pleasures in sensory experience.[27] Whitman's celebration of comradeship between men and women had also long influenced Garland. He had also been following developments in the debate over the rights of the "New Woman," as she was then called in the nation's magazines, to take equal part in society. In "A New Declaration of Rights," an 1891 essay advocating the single tax, he argued that once men recognize a woman's right to work and to receive equal pay, she will become "the free agent of her own destiny. Then marriage will be a mutual co-partnership between equals. Prostitution will disappear, and marrying for a home, that first cousin of prostitution, will also disappear. It is a woman's dependency," he concluded, "her fear of the world, fear of want, of the terrible struggle outside that enslaves her."[28]

Garland had expressed this theme in "The Land of the Straddle-Bug," and he likely discussed his ideas with his friend B. O. Flower. Among the *Arena*'s many essays about the rights of women was Flower's own "Prostitution in the Marriage Bond," published in June 1895. At that time Garland had completed only the first third of the novel, having stalled at the point where Rose departs for Chicago.[29] These early chapters already showed Flower's influence, and, as a frequent contributor to the *Arena*, Garland likely overcame his writer's block by reading Flower's essay, for its solution to the "marriage problem" bears a striking resemblance to the one offered in *Rose of Dutcher's Coolly*.

Flower offered several remedies for women's prostituting themselves through marriage, the first being knowledge. "Children should be taught the mystery of their being at their father's knee," and wives should understand they don't have to satisfy their husband's lust. Moreover, Flower continued, the child whose imagination was "filled with pure, inspiring, and exalted ideals" would, "even though cursed with inherited passion," be lifted "from the cellar of being into the realm of higher life." Finally, after discussing the need for liberalizing property laws, Flower concluded that less-restrictive divorce laws would enable women to escape "a life of prostitution under the sanction of law and respectability."[30]

When he returned to his manuscript, Garland shifted the emphasis from her physical and mental awakening to the question of whether Rose would marry, the central concern of the Madison and Chicago portions of the novel. At a time when marriage meant subservience of wife to husband, both legally and socially, his challenge was to portray realistically a girl who was not compelled to marry but who could choose to do so. Such a girl would need to be unconventional, and from the first Rose is a remarkably ungirlish girl. She is active, imaginative, a natural leader; she beats boys in many games and spies on them when they skinny-dip. She swings in trees and runs naked through the corn, her vigorous outdoor life leaving her face "brown and red as leather, and her stout little hands . . . always covered with warts and good brown earth." Yet she does not lose her femininity, for while her feet might be "brown as toads," they remain "graceful and small."[31] This is no big-footed, mannish girl—only a tall, strong, healthy adolescent who contrasts markedly with the clean, pale, and sickly girls who faint at the sight of insects.

Rose is naturally inquisitive, and, as Flower had counseled, she learns at her father's knee "that babies were not brought by the doctor, and that they did not come from heaven." When she is thirteen, passion stirs on a picnic with her playmate Carl. In a scene that prompted reviewers to accuse him of immorality, Garland describes Rose's awakening desire:

> She felt a terrible hunger, a desire to take his head in her arms and kiss it. Her muscles ached and quivered with something she could not fathom. As she resisted she grew calm, but mysteriously sad, as if something were passing from her forever. The leaves whispered a message to her, and the stream repeated an occult note of joy, which was mixed with sorrow.

The struggle of wild fear and bitter-sweet hunger of desire—this vague, mysterious perception of her sex, did not last, to Rose. It was lost when she came out of the wood into the road on the way homeward. It was a formless impulse and throbbing stir far down below definite thought.[32]

Later, Rose again throbs with desire when a young coquette of a teacher unleashes a "storm of passion" among her students. While the older boys fight with "a sudden savagery of rivalry" to win her smiles and caresses, the teacher "gathered the larger girls around her as she flirted with the young men, until children like Carl and Rose became part of it all." Fortunately, the town's fathers awaken to their children's danger in the nick of time and promptly send the teacher packing. Rose and Carl are gently interviewed by Rose's father, who determines that she "would outgrow" what Garland calls "the touch of thoughtless hands."[33]

As Flower had argued that children need an inspiring ideal to lift them "from the cellar of being," Rose begins to yearn for the "higher life" when she finds an ideal that stirs her imagination and aspirations, a circus acrobat whose "naked limbs, his proud neck, the lofty carriage of his head" make the boys of her acquaintance pale by contrast. As Garland notes, "This ideal . . . lifted her and developed her. It enabled her to escape the clutch of mere brute passion which . . . leads to destructive early marriages."[34] Here Garland sounds a recurrent theme of the novel: if women are to take equal part in society, they need to delay marriage and childbirth. During her college years and her early days in Chicago society, Rose finds a series of mentors who all warn against early marriage—Mrs. Spencer, the "famous woman lawyer" she meets on the train to Madison; Dr. Thatcher, with whom she lives during her college years; and Dr. Isabel Herrick, who introduces her to Chicago society. Having already witnessed the disaster that "brute passion" has brought to young women like her back in the coulee, Rose readily takes this advice to heart. Isabel Herrick, herself engaged and concerned mostly that Rose not marry for money, tries to convince her that "one primal event"—motherhood—will bring out her domestic instincts:

"I've seen it transform a score of women. It will make you domestic and will turn sewing into a delight." At that, Rose shrinks "as if a doom had been pronounced upon her."[35]

In Josie, Dr. Thatcher's niece and Rose's fellow student at the university, Garland provides a stereotypical young woman who serves as a foil to his heroine. Unlike the imposingly robust Rose, Josie is small and has pale, dainty hands. For Rose, college means escaping from the farm and early marriage. She is temporarily drawn to an admirer in college but eventually turns him down, proclaiming, "I don't want to marry any one just yet. . . . I want to be free." Although she doesn't say it in so many words, she, like Flower, considers marriage a form of prostitution. Realizing that men are drawn to her body, especially her "splendid curve of bust," she later explains to Isabel Herrick, "I hate to think of marrying for a home, and I hate to think of marrying as a profession. . . . I get sick and tired of the whole thing." For Josie, in contrast, college means attracting a husband, and graduation simply offers "the chance to wear a fetching gown, and be looked at by an immense crowd—and one extra man."[36]

Still, Rose longs for love, and she grows increasingly lonely after college. Garland's central problem was how to introduce the almost obligatory love plot without trapping his New Woman in a conventional marriage. His solution was to invent a New Man as companion to his New Woman, one who could revel in her emancipation. That Warren Mason is so thinly drawn and unconvincing suggests the difficulty in overcoming gender stereotypes. Garland viewed most men as "polygamous by instinct, insatiable as animals," so he made Mason something of a father figure and deemphasized his sexual desire.[37] Mason is much older than Rose and largely cerebral; though he duly notes Rose's beauty, he is drawn mostly by her "imagination," which promises variety and "endless charm," instead of the stagnation of most traditional marriages. Yet he questions whether he can commit to one woman, and she is jolted to think that she needs him to approve her poetry and that marriage will limit her freedom: "She rebelled at the implied inferiority of her position in relation to him and also at the physical bondage implied."[38]

To resolve the conflict, Garland has Mason propose through a pointedly unromantic letter in which he lists all the reasons she should not marry him, among them his inability to compromise and to promise eternal faithfulness. While he expects nothing from her—not cooking, not housekeeping, not children—he promises her complete liberty. "I want you as comrade and lover, not as subject or servant, or unwilling wife," he avows. The word "comrade" moves her to accept, for it "promised intellectual companionship never before possible to her."[39]

For Garland, the publication of *Rose of Dutcher's Coolly* was a momentous event. The idea for the novel had been fermenting since 1890, and he had spent more time on its composition than he had on any other work, for in it he sought to embody the literary theories he had been advocating for years. When he finally sent off corrected proofs for publication, he expected—or at least hoped—that his years of toil would pay off in public acclaim, but when the novel was published in December 1895 he must have been shattered by the vehemence of the attacks. "There can be no possible excuse for the writer who uses filth in the making of fiction," thundered the *Philadelphia Press.* "It is in the power of any reckless amateur scribbler in the world to-day to make himself notorious if he so wishes. He has only to put into print a sequence of such facts or imaginings as shall tend to make pure women blush, and label the thing, Smut, a Novel, by Seekfame; and all the impure minds in the world will welcome it gladly." The *Dial* objected to the novel's "wanton nastiness"; the *Chicago Daily Tribune* complained that Garland was "stubbornly and childishly nasty"; and the *Independent* charged him with having "chosen animal coarseness, and chosen it defiantly, as his source of appeal to his audience." And the *Chicago Times-Herald* lamented, "The book almost makes one want to preach suicide to all young girls—country or city—every kind." Even William Dean Howells, friend and father figure to Garland, gently upbraided his disciple for inadequate characterization in a review for *Harper's Weekly.*[40] Clearly, Garland had miscalculated.

No one noticed that *Prairie Folks*, that orphaned child of the Schulte firm, was published simultaneously with *Rose* in matching covers.

FIG. 1. Hamlin Garland in 1872. Courtesy of University
of Southern California, on behalf of the
USC Specialized Libraries and Archival Collections.

FIG. 2. Richard Hayes Garland at the time of Hamlin's
graduation from the Cedar Valley Seminary. Courtesy of
University of Southern California, on behalf of
the USC Specialized Libraries and Archival Collections.

FIG. 3. Isabelle McClintock Garland. Courtesy of University
of Southern California, on behalf of the
USC Specialized Libraries and Archival Collections.

FIG. 4. Harriet Garland in the only known photo. Courtesy of University of Southern California, on behalf of the USC Specialized Libraries and Archival Collections.

FIG. 5. Jessie Garland. Courtesy of University of Southern California, on behalf of the USC Specialized Libraries and Archival Collections.

FIG. 6. Franklin Garland (*left*) and Hamlin, ca. 1881.
Courtesy of University of Southern California, on behalf of the
USC Specialized Libraries and Archival Collections.

FIG. 7. The Garland farm in Mitchell County, Iowa, looking pretty much as it did in the 1870s. Courtesy of www.jonmorrisphoto.com.

FIG. 8. The Cedar Valley Seminary graduating class of 1881. Standing at far right is Garland; seated at far left is Burton Babcock, who would accompany Garland to the Klondike; seated in front of Garland, with chin in hand, is Anna J. Kelly, who may have been the "Alice" of *A Son of the Middle Border*. Courtesy of University of Southern California, on behalf of the USC Specialized Libraries and Archival Collections.

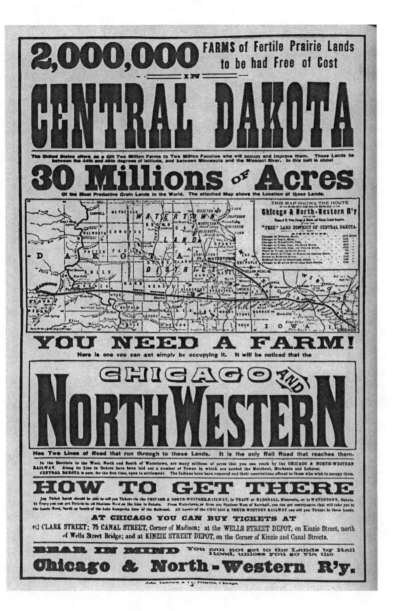

FIG. 9. Dakota homesteading advertisement, ca. 1881.
Shown as reproduced in *Pioneer Railroad: The Story of the Chicago
and Northwestern System*, by Robert Casey and W. A. Douglas
(New York: McGraw-Hill, 1975), 182.

FIG. 10. Moses T. Brown, head of the Boston School of Oratory.
Courtesy of University of Southern California, on
behalf of the USC Specialized Libraries and Archival Collections.

FIG. 11. Hamlin Garland in 1887. Joseph E. Chamberlin
would describe his appearance on the lecture platform as "apostolic."
Courtesy of University of Southern California, on
behalf of the usc Specialized Libraries and Archival Collections.

FIG. 12. Joseph Kirkland, the Chicago novelist whose mentorship came at a critical time. From William Morton Payne, "Literary Chicago," *New England Magazine* 13 (February 1893). Courtesy of Matthew S. S. Johnson.

FIG. 13. Benjamin O. Flower, the *Arena* editor who published so much of Garland's early work. Courtesy of University of Southern California, on behalf of the USC Specialized Libraries and Archival Collections.

FIG. 14. Cover of the Stone and Kimball edition of *Main-Travelled Roads*. Courtesy of Gary Culbert.

Garland Homestead, West Salem Wis. 1893

FIG. 15. (*top*) The Garland home in West Salem, Wisconsin, in 1893. Courtesy of University of Southern California, on behalf of the USC Specialized Libraries and Archival Collections.

FIG. 16. (*bottom*) Garland posing for a sculpture by Bessie Potter Vonnoh in 1895. Courtesy of University of Southern California, on behalf of the USC Specialized Libraries and Archival Collections.

FIG. 17. Lorado Taft in his studio. Courtesy of University
of Southern California, on behalf of the
USC Specialized Libraries and Archival Collections.

FIG. 18. Henry B. Fuller, Garland's closest friend. Courtesy
of University of Southern California, on behalf of
the USC Specialized Libraries and Archival Collections.

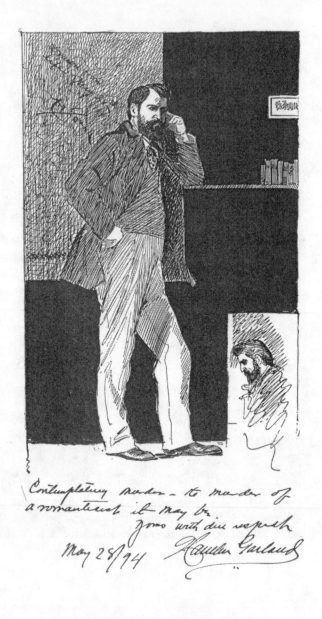

FIG. 19. Sketch of Garland at the height of the realism wars,
by Art Young, May 28, 1894. Garland has written:
"Contemplating murder—the murder of a romanticist
it may be." From Art Young, *Authors' Readings* (New York:
Frederick A Stokes, 1897).

FIG. 20. Garland hiding from mosquitoes in the Klondike.
Courtesy of University of Southern California, on behalf of the
USC Specialized Libraries and Archival Collections.

FIG. 21. William Dean Howells. Photograph "Mr. W.D. Howells"
by Zaida Ben-Yusuf, ca. 1900. Courtesy of Library of Congress, Prints
and Photographs Division, LC-USZ62-66951.

FIG. 22. Zulime Maune Taft, photographed in 1893 at the Columbian World's Exposition. Courtesy of University of Southern California, on behalf of the USC Specialized Libraries and Archival Collections.

FIG. 23. Caricature of Garland at the height of his reputation. From *The Philistine*, August 1899. Photo courtesy of The Newberry Library, Chicago.

FIG. 24. Garland in 1909 at the height of what Henry B. Fuller called his "club-carpentering." Courtesy of University of Southern California, on behalf of the USC Specialized Libraries and Archival Collections.

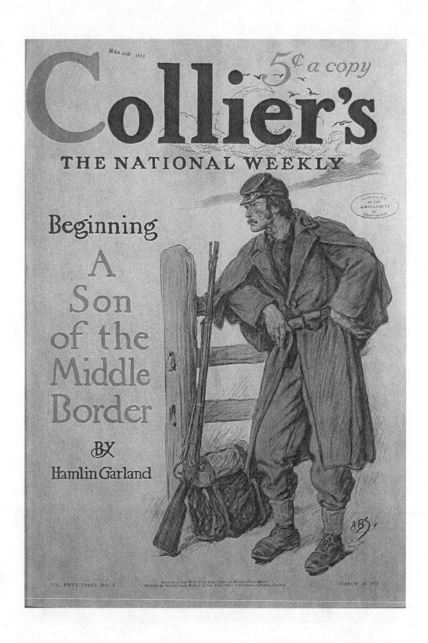

FIG. 25. *Collier's* magazine, the serial that launched Garland's comeback.
Courtesy of MagazineArt.org.

FIG. 26. Mary Isabel Garland in costume for a play.
Courtesy of University of Southern California, on behalf of
the USC Specialized Libraries and Archival Collections.

FIG. 27. Constance Garland. Courtesy of Victoria Doyle-Jones.

FIG. 28. Garland at fifty-six. Courtesy of University of Southern California, on behalf of the USC Specialized Libraries and Archival Collections.

FIG. 29. Illustration for *Trail-Makers of the Middle Border* (p. 244), by Constance Garland. Represented are Richard, Isabelle, Harriet, Hamlin, and Franklin. Courtesy of University of Southern California, on behalf of the USC Specialized Libraries and Archival Collections.

FIG. 30. Garland at his Hollywood home. Courtesy of
University of Southern California, on behalf of the USC Specialized
Libraries and Archival Collections.

FIG. 31. Garland and his
psychic, Sophia Williams,
digging for buried crosses.
Courtesy of University
of Southern California,
on behalf of the USC
Specialized Libraries and
Archival Collections.

Hamlin Garland unearthing a cross

FIG. 32. The crosses today. Courtesy of the West Salem
Historical Society, West Salem, Wisconsin.

13

"HO, FOR THE KLONDIKE!" 1896–98

Reeling from the critical cudgeling over *Rose of Dutcher's Coolly*, one day Garland was talking over his troubles with Samuel S. McClure, who was then hustling to increase the circulation of *McClure's Magazine*. When the first issue appeared in June 1893, few would have predicted its meteoric rise. In 1885 the four leading monthly magazines—*Century, Harper's, Atlantic, Scribner's*—averaged a circulation of one hundred thousand or more and were aimed at an educated, middle-and upper-class readership, which was reflected in their single-copy price of twenty-five or thirty-five cents. In the 1890s a number of new ten-and fifteen-cent magazines debuted that were marketed to the general population by featuring more articles concerned with science, personalities, inventions, and progress, accompanied by many illustrations and much advertising to pay for it all. The development of photoengraving—the halftone illustration—led to an explosion of inexpensive illustrations. Even the staid *Century* climbed aboard the illustration bandwagon. Whereas it had paid up to three hundred dollars for a full-page woodcut, it could buy a halftone for twenty dollars. Postage rates had decreased from three cents to one cent per pound, and advertising quickly replaced subscriptions as the primary source of revenue. The result was that the number of magazines had increased from 3,100 in 1885 to more than 5,100 in 1895.[1]

McClure was an innovative player in the rise of the ten-cent magazine. With his magazine filled with pages of well-printed illustrations, lively and fresh nonfiction articles, serious treatment of contemporary affairs, and keen interest in invention and progress in general, he sought to make *McClure's* the leading magazine of its time. When he began he relied on the files of fiction he had accumulated for his newspaper syndicate, and from the beginning *McClure's* published a disproportionate number of English authors, among them Kipling, Stevenson, Conan Doyle, and Hardy. To increase his circulation, McClure approached a number of writers like Garland to send on assignment, counting on their proven ability to write well about topics of current interest to draw readers to his magazine. At the time, readers were fascinated with illustrated biographies of great leaders and people in the news—Garland's Field and Riley interviews for *McClure's* "Real Conversations" series are representative of this type of article, as was "Homestead and Its Perilous Trades" an example of the magazine's brand of investigative journalism. By 1895 McClure had tapped Ida Tarbell to write a life of Abraham Lincoln, and when it began serialization in November 1895, circulation reached 190,000. The next month it climbed to 250,000.[2] Clearly, McClure was on to a good thing.

In January 1896 Garland accepted a commission from McClure to write a biography of Ulysses S. Grant for serialization in *McClure's*, with a book to follow. The diary he kept intermittently reveals the seasoned writer debating the wisdom of accepting an assignment that would divert him from the path he had been treading for so long. If he accepted McClure's offer, Hamlin recorded on January 6, "it will be to enter upon a great change in my work. I shall lay aside fiction for a year and take up the study of a great personality in real life. Whether I succeed or not, it will be a fruitful year, no doubt of that. It will bring me into contact with people of a different class from those I have met. Historical characters—old men soon to pass away." After working on the project for a month, he came to terms with the magnitude of the job, and decided, "I dont suppose I shall really lose anything by the year's work upon Grant. A character so great, so dramatic, so western surely can not be a waste of effort. The truth is I am beginning to take exquisite delight, perhaps serious delight in reminiscing over the glory of days gone by."[3]

Garland was attracted by the commission for several reasons. First, he was supporting his aging parents and needed the cash. He was also ready for a change of literary direction, for while his books had occasioned considerable comment, sales had been poor. Then, too, he was tired of the realism wars and of polemical comment in magazines and vowed to retire from the battle. Grant had also been his father's commander and Hamlin's boyhood hero, and Garland greatly admired what he called Grant's "pioneer spirit," seeing in him the qualities he so admired in the westerner. For the next year and a half, Garland traveled widely, interviewing family members and men under Grant's command, probing their memories of the famed Civil War general and president, who had died in 1885. He visited scenes of significant battles, journeyed to the various places Grant had lived, went to Mexico to better understand Grant's role in the war with Mexico over the annexation of Texas, and ensconced himself in the Library of Congress studying papers related to Grant's presidency. With his mind largely focused on Grant, Garland devoted little time to fiction; instead, to keep the pot boiling, he wrote a number of sketches based on his observations of western characters and Indians that he placed with newspaper syndicates headed by McClure, Bacheller, and Albert Bigelow Paine.

Garland made time to return to Colorado during the summer of 1896, where he again visited the Southern Ute Reservation, and to Dulce, New Mexico, where he went to the Jicarilla Apache Reservation in the company of John L. Gaylord, the agency clerk, who was his interpreter and informed him about the history of the reservation. There he was distressed by the impoverished conditions brought on by the poor land and scarce water. "They seemed to be making a desperate attempt to secure a living in conformity to the law of the awe-compelling white man," he wrote in an essay about his trip.[4] The inability of the government to understand its wards aroused his passion, as he recorded in his notes:

> I left Ouray with a disgust of the men who were connected with the service. They are not able to comprehend the real state of the Indian's mind. The trader is more nearly just. He finds it to his interest and also he naturally inclines to being fair and just to them, and they trust him. The deep-seated distrust of the whiteman

yields only after the severest test. It does not do to *say* "I am your friend"—it must be demonstrated. He must be tried, tried hard. His words must be studied. A man who is good today and swears at the "damn Indian" tomorrow may win the silent toleration of the Indian but not his confidence.[5]

While he took notes for stories based on his observations, the Grant project left little time to develop them, and so he filed them away for a later day.

In November Garland pressed McClure for a contract for the Grant biography. His compensation was generous: fifty dollars per thousand words, paid out at fifty dollars per week, up to a maximum of five thousand dollars, plus expenses and, later, book royalties. It was, Garland remarked, "more money than I had ever hoped to earn," and in today's dollars it amounted to $1,150 per week, or a maximum of nearly $115,000. But such generosity came with a price: *McClure's* reserved the right of "editorial suggestion and supervision." If Garland and McClure could not agree about revisions, the contract called for the matter to be referred to "an arbitrator—Mr. Howells, if he will act for us."[6]

When the first two installments of the Grant serial appeared in *McClure's*, Garland discovered that the magazine's editors were drastically cutting his material. At stake was not just his integrity as a writer but also his compensation, for his contract stipulated payment by the number of words *McClure's* published, not the number he wrote. For advice he turned to Howells, who had noticed that his friend's prose had become less polished than usual. "If the papers have been cut," Howells wrote, "that accounts for a certain roughness and abruptness that troubled me. You have got some newspaper diction in your penpoint, and you must shake it out. . . . It is a shame for McClure to touch your work. You ought to make a mighty row whenever he does it."[7] To demonstrate the butchery *McClure's* was performing on his carefully researched text, Garland sent Howells the proof of another installment, "Grant's Life in Missouri." Howells noted a marked falling off from Garland's usual style and wrote to guide him back to the true path:

This is very interesting, and lets one see the man plainly. But it lacks texture, and compared with your work in fiction I find a poorness in the diction which I do not like. No doubt you feel the McClures sitting on your head, but you must be good and strong in spite of them. Read Taine's French Revolution a little, and see how he *packs* his material, and yet makes every word tell. You ought to have put that long Fishback interview into your own language. The effect of it is to cheapen your page as it now stands. How could a newspaper have done worse?

But he also reminded Garland to maintain his integrity, and of the importance of this book to his career:

About the personal matters which the McCs. have marked out, you must use your judgment. I think them interesting, but you know best your own point of view, and how much you are bound to the sources of your information and to the Grant family, whose feelings, if they are open and kind to you, must be regarded. You must not consider my *stets* as final opinions. They are meant rather to remand the question to your farther reflection.

Your very best is the least you can give to this work. It is a great chance for you, and you must take yourself by the collar and rise to it. You are man enough to excuse my bluntness.[8]

The squabble over the editing continued to worsen, and on May 1, 1897, Garland was disenchanted enough to write to Brander Matthews, "My Grant matter is cut to smithereens, dont read a word of it." By June, Garland and McClure had come to an impasse, and in July a notice appeared that the current installment would be the last. The matter did not quite end there, however, for three more installments later appeared, likely to settle up on monies advanced.[9]

In February 1897, while conducting research in Washington DC, Garland was in turn preoccupied with family matters and basking in unexpected professional success. Achievements in sound recording had progressed to where phonographs were becoming affordable.

He bought a Columbia Graphophone and, in tinkering with it, soon realized the device was just what he needed to assuage his guilt at so many absences away from his mother. He arranged to send "a cheap machine, about $50, all fixings" to his mother and promptly began recording messages to her, advising his brother to do the same.[10] At the same time, he learned that Stella Esther Burkhart, whom Franklin had married in 1895, had died. "I don't know what I can say to comfort you," he wrote. "You and I have talked these things over before and you know my thought. It is only a space between her going and the going of us all. We are both of an age when Death must be an expected visitor." He then counseled his brother to lose himself in work: "It seems cruel to say this but your philosophy will help you see the virtue of it."[11]

On the heels of this calamity came encouraging news: Garland was approached by a representative of D. Appleton and Company, the firm that had published *A Little Norsk* in 1892, with an offer to bring out a uniform edition of four books—*Jason Edwards, A Spoil of Office, A Member of the Third House* (which he now owned under terms of his contracts), and a new collection of stories, eventually entitled *Wayside Courtships.* To Franklin he announced optimistically, "I will then issue books as rapidly as I think the public will stand it." He signed contracts on February 19 and 26 that gave him a 15 percent royalty.[12] Garland had had terrible luck with his publishers: the Arena books had sold poorly, the Stone and Kimball books more poorly still, and the Schulte firm had died before his two books with them had had a chance. He was understandably elated when he announced the Appleton deal to Taft and crowed, "Also I am to be in 'The Library of the World's Best Literature' both in my own right and as the biographer of Grant. Slowly we approach Homer!" He signed off, "Regards to all inkwiring friends—even enemies."[13]

During the spring, as he took breaks from his Grant research, Garland prepared the Appleton books. *Jason Edwards* and *A Member of the Third House* were simply printed from the plates of the old editions, but apparently in response to reviews of the novel, he revised *A Spoil of Office,* muting Ida Wilbur's political speeches and revising the final scene to make the self-imposed separation between Ida and Bradley Talcott more plausible.[14] For *Wayside Courtships* he wrote no new work but rather assembled stories published as far back as 1888. The thirteen stories vary considerably in length and skill, and while he wrote Franklin that it would be "about women, . . . 'The Ways O' Women' or 'The Ways That Women Tread.' Something like that," they are collectively only loosely about the "courtships" of the eventual title.[15] "A Stop-Over at Tyre," originally sold to the *Century* in 1890 but not published until January 1897, is among the collection's best. It is the tale of two college book agents who devote a summer's campaign to Tyre, Wisconsin, one of whom moves on to the next conquest while the other forgoes his education to marry the girl he met. "The Owner of Mill Farm," originally published as "A Graceless Husband" in 1893 in *Northwestern Miller,* is of a piece with Garland's best reform fiction of his *Main-Travelled Roads* days. The other stories range from impressionistic prose poems of brief meetings to sketches of divorce and prostitution to two romances designed to appeal to the readers of the *Ladies' Home Journal.* On the whole, the collection shows a side of Garland of which few of today's readers are aware.[16] The books were attractively designed, with the corn motif that had graced his Stone and Kimball books now embossed in gold as a single corn plant in panels on the front cover and spine.

With his commitments to Appleton completed, and while waiting for the Grant installments to finish publication in *McClure's,* Garland returned to the West, accompanied by Franklin, intending to visit the Sioux and other Indians of the Northwest with the aim of gathering material for a new direction in his fiction, now that it had become abundantly clear that his middle border fiction had failed to win an audience. His interviews and observations at Standing Rock Reservation in Dakota Territory proved to be of signal importance for his burgeoning interest in the American Indian, in particular deepening his perception of the inevitable erosion of Indian customs in the face of an overpowering white culture.

Armed with a letter of introduction from General Nelson A. Miles, Garland arrived at Standing Rock in July. Then the commanding general of the U.S. Army, Miles had led the army forces that sup-

pressed the Sioux during the Ghost Dance uprising, which had culminated in the massacre at Wounded Knee in December 1890. Part
of Garland's purpose in visiting Standing Rock was to learn the Sioux
perspective about the arrest and death of Sitting Bull, who had been
portrayed in the media as a villainous and cowardly warmonger.
His letter from General Miles opened agency records, and Garland
compared official accounts of Sitting Bull's internment and death
to what he had learned from the Sioux he interviewed, among them
Rain-in-the-Face, who was with Sitting Bull at the battle of Little Big
Horn and who was, for a time, credited with killing Custer. The idea
for the novella "The Silent Eaters" had been planted, but Garland's
interviewing was interrupted by news that the Northern Cheyennes
on the Tongue River Reservation in Montana were in revolt. The
eastern boundary of the reservation was in dispute, with white settlers occupying much of the disputed land and allowing their cattle
to range over the reservation. The Cheyennes had been raiding the
cattle, and when the body of a white sheepherder was discovered
just off the reservation, the settlers blamed the Cheyennes for his
death and armed themselves for revenge. Troops had been sent in
to restore order.[17] Later, Garland would base *The Captain of the Gray-
Horse Troop*, his most popular novel, upon this incident.

The Garland brothers hurried to Fort Custer, where they met
George P. Aherne, the government meat inspector for the Crow
Agency. From him and the trader R. W. Cummings, Garland learned
more about the army's perception of Sitting Bull and of the battle at
Little Big Horn, as well as details about Sioux and Crow social customs. Continuing next to the Lame Deer Agency, Garland spent two
weeks with the agent, Captain George W. H. Stouch, who became a
close friend and would later provide many details about Indian life
that Garland worked into his stories. At Lame Deer, aided by the
interpreter Wolf Voice, Garland learned details of the "outbreak"
from White Bull, the chief of the Tongue River Cheyennes, and his
headmen Spotted Elk, Bull Thigh, White Shield, Spotted Hawk, and
White Hawk.[18] In "A Typical Indian Scare: The Cheyenne Trouble,"
his report about the incident, Garland sounded a new reformist

note in his thinking about Indians: he accused settlers of exploiting the weak for their own selfish ends. "It is the self-interest and local barbarism of the whites which keep the Indian continually alarmed, suspicious and revengeful," he concluded his essay.

> The settlers are remorseless, vindictive, and accept every lying re-
> port with eagerness and joy.
> There is but one thing to do and that is to fence in these reser-
> vations. Keep the whites off the Indian's land and the Indian on his
> own land. It should be perfectly plain that this land is the Indians'
> and that no scheming of greedy ranchmen and pliant politicians
> can ever take it from them. Then these murders will cease and the
> Indian lay aside his knife and gun. Till then he has need to be as
> well armed as the white rustler—his neighbor.[19]

While at Lame Deer, Garland also interviewed Two Moon, who had been with Sitting Bull at Little Big Horn and whose account of the battle portrayed the Sioux as a disorganized yet ultimately triumphant defensive force, in contrast to the prevailing account of Custer's defeat as a deliberate and carefully orchestrated attack by the Sioux. Garland's "General Custer's Last Fight as Seen by Two Moon," largely in Two Moon's words, appeared in the September 1898 *McClure's* and has been a resource ever since for subsequent accounts of the Custer battle. Garland also interviewed American Horse, who was a signatory to the Crook Commission treaty of 1875, which reduced Sioux lands by half. American Horse was also one of the "progressives" who persuaded the Sioux to end the Ghost Dance "rebellion," and in 1891 he headed the Pine Ridge delegation to Washington to secure rations and better treatment of the Sioux. From American Horse Garland learned still more about Sioux social customs and collected details about the history of the army's suppression of Sioux culture. Garland filled his notebooks with interviews and notes describing the landscape and Indian customs. Story ideas were flooding the pages, and when he returned to Washington after two months of research into Native Americans, he recalled, his imagination was "teeming with subjects for poems, short stories and novels. . . . Aspiring vaguely to qualify as the fictionist of this region, I was eager to be at work."[20]

But his plan was interrupted by the tantalizing news that gold had been discovered in the Klondike. Here was a new opportunity for fresh literary material, and the newspapers were filled with accounts of the fortunes to be made. In July, on the back trail to Washington from the reservations, the intrepid traveler entrained for Seattle, where Garland found the city awash in gold seekers clamoring for passage to the Klondike. Determined to be a part of the grand adventure, he made plans to go to the goldfields with his boyhood friend Burton Babcock, who was proving up on a timber claim near Seattle. In *The Trail of the Goldseekers*, his book about the experience, Garland records that his motivation for going was the adventure itself: "I believed that I was about to take part in a most picturesque and impressive movement across the wilderness. I believed it to be the last great march of the kind which could ever come in America, so rapidly were the wild places being settled up. I wished, therefore, to take part in this tramp of the goldseekers, to be one of them, and record their deeds. I wished to return to the wilderness also, to forget books and theories of art and social problems, and come again face to face with the great free spaces of woods and skies and streams."[21] But his public record of his journey glosses over the motivations and, in this instance, masks the inner torment that led to his decision. About this time he began keeping an intermittent diary, and his notes reveal that he was afflicted with neurasthenia—whose symptoms include lassitude, irritability, and hypochondria—and suffered occasional bouts of depression, all the while undergoing considerable soul-searching and casting about for meaning and direction in his life. His Klondike adventure would become the means to restore his mental and physical health, to blow the scholar's cobwebs from his brain. His experiences on the trip—and more especially, the five months of introspection afforded by the journey—would enable him to take stock of his ambitions and achievements and to make decisions concerning the direction of his writing and life. In short, the trip became a life-changing experience that turned him decisively away from hard-bitten stories about Midwest deprivation and toward novels celebrating the mountain West.

But with the summer drawing to a close, Garland would have to wait until the next year before he could leave for the Klondike, and he needed to finish his Grant biography. When he arrived in Washington, he threw himself into turning the serial articles into book form, working at his desk for long hours. He treated Grant as a character in a novel, presenting the events of his life chronologically, without the usual prevision of later significance so common to biographies. In this way Garland remained true to his realistic credo, for the events of Grant's life unfolded without what Garland called "false emphasis," the authorial comment that calls attention to the later significance of an event. He drew on his knowledge of rural life and knack for descriptive writing to dress the scene, which helped readers visualize the events, and he cast many of his interviews into dialogue, which emphasized the humanity of his subject and stepped up the narrative pace. The result is a biography that blends factual detail with fictional techniques into a narrative that is highly readable—even today. Though he did not know it at the time, in writing the Grant biography Garland had perfected the techniques that would enable him to excel in his most accomplished genre—life writing.

By October 1897 he was in New York, chiefly to attend the mayoral convention at which his idol Henry George accepted the nomination of the United Labor Party. The fiery passion of George's acceptance speech was still able to rouse Garland's enthusiasm, as he recorded in his journal: "Such a speech was never before heard on the political platform. In a few words he lifted it all to a height from which the toiling ones of the whole earth could be seen. It became a movement of the world and from a strife for offices, the Municipal Campaign of 1897 is likely to be the next great step in the evangelization of the world in behalf of the landless and disinherited of the whole earth."[22] But the enthusiasm was short-lived, for George died unexpectedly of a stroke on October 29. For a week, Garland was overwhelmed. "Henry George's death has come to me with more of sorrow than that of any man in my life," he recalled. "I knew him so well and he meant so much to me. I have given up all my engagements, all my letters, my work and my other friends to visit with the family and the various committees to do honor to this great man."[23]

For solace Garland sought companionship at the Players Club, founded in 1888 by Edwin Booth to promote social interaction among members of the dramatic professions and those in the other arts. While on his western tour with Franklin, Hamlin had written Brander Matthews to ask him to nominate the Garland brothers for membership.[24] For Hamlin, membership not only provided access to the gentlemanly talk of other writers and artists, which he craved, but also allowed him to use the club as a mail drop and temporary office—a tremendous bonus for one who traveled to New York as often as he did.

In October he attended the liquidation of Stone and Kimball. The firm he hoped would be a beacon for western publishing had fallen on hard times. The two partners had dissolved the company in March 1896 over disagreement about the firm's expansion. Stone had taken the *Chap-Book* and remained in Chicago to start his own firm; Kimball had purchased the backlist and moved to New York. But Kimball had gotten into financial difficulties and had begun to sell copyrights. An auction of all copyrights and printed stock took place on October 21, with Garland attending in the company of E. C. Stedman and G. E. Woodberry, editors of the ten-volume Stone and Kimball edition of Poe. The failure of the firm hit him hard, as he recorded in his journal:

I have just returned from a sheriff sale of the books of Stone and Kimball. A rather melancholy affair. . . .

Kimball "the corpse" kept up a cheerful show and laughed with Mr Stedman[,] Mr Woodberry and myself with apparent insouciance—alluding to me as "chief mourner." Alert attorneys were there to protect the interests of the leading creditors and authors. . . .

Everything went absurdly low as they always do at such a sale. The most of the buyers were too ignorant to know the name of the books and were there to buy *any* book at 3¢ or 5¢. It was not a cheerful scene. Mr Stedman said to Mr Woodberry and myself, "If we could but contrive to have Kimballs insouciance put up at auction we would be all but paid in full."[25]

The months of work on the Grant biography—poring over dusty newspapers in libraries and fielding reams of letters, but especially the almost continual travel to interview witnesses before they died—began to exact a toll on his health and spirits. Always introspective, Garland began to brood over his successes and failure. His habit of recording his observations now shifted to noting his changing moods in his journal (and on January 1, 1898, he began a daily diary that he would keep for the rest of his life):

Nov. 25 [1897] *Thanksgiving Day*
After two months in the city I am feeling the effect of it in my weak muscles and seeing it in the increasing pallor of my face. There is no place for me here. I need the outdoor life. I must have a horse and a chance to get out where the sky can be seen.

I am feeling already a growing restlessness. I would like to start next spring across the land to the Klondike—just for the wonder and the grandeur of the ride over a thousand miles of untracked land.[26]

Dec. 19. 97 *Gray hairs.*
Today in brushing my beard I was struck by the increase of gray hairs therein. I am past middle life that is evident. I am on the western slope. I have done so little of what I had hoped to do. How much shall I be able to do of the work I *now* hope to do?[27]

As was by now his custom for major changes in his life and career, Garland visited Howells to outline his planned trip to the Klondike. He went over his itinerary and maps of the largely unexplored region, remarking to Howells, "At this point I go in, and at this point I come out, over a thousand miles of unknown territory." Garland describes Howells's response as a look of "wonder. In his glance I saw my action reflected as a dangerous as well as a foolish project. . . . Suppose I broke an ankle? Suppose I fell sick in that wilderness?"[28] This meeting, though Garland did not know it at the time, was to be a career maker, for it set into motion a series of events that would lead to his best book, a Pulitzer Prize, and national fame. His realization that, at age thirty-seven, he was about to undertake a potentially life-threatening trip prompted him to begin dictating his autobiography to a shorthand stenographer, an account he began on February 27, 1898. Now skilled at adopting techniques of fiction to tell the story of Ulysses S. Grant, he cast his life under the title "The Story of Grant McLane," wedding the name of his most recent enthusiasm to his own life.[29] In April, when he departed for his wilderness adventure, he took comfort that if he did not return, a "record" would be preserved for posterity.

In 1897 little was known about the remote Klondike region. Maps were rudimentary, and reports of conditions were wildly inaccurate. Soon after the *Excelsior* and *Portland* docked in San Francisco and Seattle in July 1897 with their holds full of gold, the nation's newspapers and magazines sent reporters scurrying to the region. Garland took another tack. On behalf of *McClure's Magazine*, on December 30, 1897, he traveled to Canada to interview Clifford Sifton, Canada's minister of the interior, and William Ogilvie, the engineer who surveyed the Yukon Territory and who became commissioner of the Yukon in 1898. From them he gleaned details about the location of the goldfields, mining techniques, living conditions in the region, and most importantly the various routes, publishing the result as "Ho, for the Klondike!" in *McClure's* in March 1898. In this article, billed by the editor as containing the "latest and most authentic general information regarding the Klondike and the roads to it," Garland quoted heavily from Canadian officials to describe the general inhospitality of the region's climate before moving to discuss the advantages and disadvantages of each route.[30] The "all-water" route (also known as the "rich man's route"), by steamship from Seattle through the Bering Sea to St. Michael at the mouth of the Yukon, and thence by riverboat to Dawson, more than 4,700 miles, was the longest, most time-consuming, most expensive, but easiest route. Garland estimated the fare would cost $150 to $300, with ten cents per pound for baggage, but the chief problems were that the river was only navigable from June to September and the voyage would consume valuable time, for each miner was trying to beat the others before all the claims were staked.[31] The common routes, less expensive and less time-consuming and therefore more appealing to argonauts, commenced by steamship from Seattle to Skagway or Dyea, and thence overland up over the Chilkoot or White passes and then downriver by boat to Dawson, a distance of about 1,600 miles—roughly 1,000 by sea, more than 500 by river, and less than 50 by land. And finally there were the various overland routes, from Edmonton or Ashcroft or Kamloops, up the various watersheds and over the Stikeen and Skeena mountains and down to the headwaters of the Teslin and Yukon rivers, thus avoiding the formidable Coast Range and the necessity of dealing with Canadian customs officials.

In the fall of 1897, conditions at Skagway and Dyea were more horrible than Garland or others knew. While the steamship fare from Seattle to Skagway at the onset of the stampede was not all that expensive—about twenty-five dollars—as soon as the intrepid miner arrived, the expenses began to mount. There were debarkation fees and fees to ferry one's gear from ship to shore (wharves had not yet been built), where one's outfit was simply dumped at the mercy of the incoming tide, as well as duties if the outfit was purchased in the United States—at times as high as 30 percent.[32] But the passes themselves presented the first of two major financial impediments. By the fall of 1897 the Canadian government required each miner to bring along one year's supply of provisions and gear, amounting to about one ton and costing between six hundred and a thousand dollars, depending on when and where it was purchased.[33] That ton of gear needed to be carried over one of the two passes, which varied from twenty-six to thirty-six miles in length. Conditions at White Pass, as E. Hazard Wells, the correspondent for the Scripps-McCrae newspaper syndicate, described them in August 1897, were already extremely dangerous: horses had worn the paths away to bare rock, and, without secure footing, many horses had fallen and their carcasses lined the trail, which was now negotiable only by foot.[34]

At first many miners hired packers, but demand soon caused skyrocketing inflation, from about eight cents per pound before the rush to twenty-two cents per pound during the first week in August (incidentally, the price Jack London paid), rising to as much as a dollar per pound two weeks later.[35] A miner transporting one ton of gear would therefore pay between $160 and $2,000, depending upon when he chanced to arrive at the pass. Small wonder most miners opted to pack in their gear themselves—and thereby added pressure to race along the trail before all the claims were taken and the snows began to fall. Wells explained the process: "A miner portaging 1200 pounds of provisions for the winter must make 12 round trips of 52 miles each, a total of 624 miles over precipitous mountains, carrying a 100-pound pack for that entire distance." Once over the pass, the miner somehow needed to acquire a boat to ferry himself and his outfit downriver five hundred miles to Dawson. Early in the boom, three enterprising souls packed in a sawmill and sold boats for seventy-five to one hundred dollars each, but they were soon overwhelmed by demand, so most miners either packed in knockdown boats or whipsawed lumber and built their own.[36] And with thousands of miners crossing the pass, soon the trees were gone.

With this dismal picture as his backdrop, Garland concluded, based on his interviews, that the Telegraph Trail, abandoned after only one hundred miles when the North Atlantic undersea cable made it unnecessary, beginning in Ashcroft and following the Frazer, Bulkley, Skeena, and Stikeen riversheds to Glenora, was the most favorable and least expensive way to approach the goldfields. At a time when four or five horses would be needed to pack in the ton of supplies required to sustain a person for a year, securing adequate feed was paramount. Official reports described the Ashcroft route, though long, as being "a comparatively cheap and pleasant route, with no duties and no toll to pay."[37] For the first 223 miles it followed an established wagon road to Quesnelle; the next 125 miles crossed "nearly level country with good grass," and though "there are hundreds of creeks, none are deep or hard to pass." The trail was filled with "over 300 good hay swamps," and the longest portion without good feed was a mere 15 miles. Garland was sketchy about the remaining 525 miles to Telegraph Creek and the 150 miles to his ultimate destination, Teslin Lake, but he assured his readers that "The trail has been traveled for thirty-five years, and the Canadian government has spent thousands of dollars to keep it in first-class condition."[38] He estimated that, at most, the thousand-mile trip would require fifty days, though by sending supplies to Hazelton and Glenora (which Garland did himself) one might make the trip in forty days because of the lighter load. Grass would be available by late April. "The Ashcroft Trail is alluring," Garland concluded. "The climate is genial and the land full of game. There are frequent stopping places, and the Indians are friendly and helpful. . . . It is estimated that $200 would enable a man to go through from Ashcroft to Teslin Lake, but no one should undertake the journey with less than $500 in hand."[39] He apparently chose not to heed Ogilvie's warning, duly recorded in his notes: "Every dollar found there is the product of pain and misery."[40] At the back of his mind was a resolution to take the overland route, the most difficult of the routes, to restore strength to his flabby muscles and prove he could take it, in emulation of the romantic, self-reliant westerner that so appealed to him. Armed with his notebook and eager to record his adventure for a series of articles and a book he hoped to write about the experience, he arranged to meet Burton Babcock in Ashcroft in April 1898.

As the time neared for his departure, Garland took stock of himself, his recent writing project, and his growing sense of alienation, recording on February 23, 1898: "The last two years of historical work have wrought a great change in me. My mind has turned inward. I find it less easy to observe men and nature. I find it less easy to mix and merge in the clouds, in the wind, in the woods. This may come back to me. I should be grieved if I thought I were cut off from the exquisite pleasure I once had in the physical." He then wrote of his hopeful expectation for his northern adventure, before turning to verse, the form he felt most suitable for exultation, and dashed off what would become the first stanza of "Anticipation," the opening poem of *The Trail of the Goldseekers*:

It may be that my trip will do much for me. The release from the historical will be like the setting free of a captive eagle.

> I will wash my brain in the splendid breeze,
> I will lay my cheek to the burning sun.
> I will drink the breath of the mossy trees
> And the clouds shall meet me one by one.
> I will fling the scholar's pen aside
> And grasp once more the bronchoe's rein,
> And I will ride, and ride and ride,
> Till the rain is snow and the snow is rain![41]

Once his journey began, Garland delighted in the scenic landscape, and from the ease of the wagon road he reveled in the daily routine of breaking camp and covering miles, "thoroughly enjoying the trip." Into the journey by 160 miles, he began hearing reports of onerous conditions ahead, of clouds of flies and poisonous grass that limited forage for their horses. "All these I regarded as the croakings of men who had never had the courage to go over the trail, and who exaggerated the accounts they had heard from others," he wrote, naively confident of his own courage and hardihood.[42] But as he tramped farther along the trail, Garland soon found that his sources were terribly wrong: there was very little grass available; and far from passing through a dry climate, akin to eastern Washington, as he had been informed, the trail was filled with mud bogs and drenching rain, the rivers overrunning their banks and requiring considerable logistics to ford—something he had never encountered in American forests. By June 10, when he reached his cache at Hazleton, the halfway point, after battling clouds of ravenous mosquitoes, Garland realized that he "had been led into a sort of sack, and the string was tied behind us," for he had little choice but to press onward.[43] From Hazleton he and Babcock climbed upward through the dark and wet forests of the Skeena Mountains, oppressed by the gloom, the incessant rain, and lack of grass for the horses. During a rare moment of sunshine, Garland paused to reflect on his achievement thus far, proudly recording in his diary on June 28, "I am dirty, ragged and lame, my hands are calloused and seamed with dirt but I am strong and healthy—I am standing the west better than I thought I could. I feel like one who had been travelling in sub-aqueous regions for weeks."[44] And then conditions through the unsurveyed land became more trying: the mosquito problem worsened, and the rain continued, turning the trail into a long mud pit. And weighing heavily upon Garland's conscience was the continuing hardship his horses faced: lame, bruised, ridden with pack sores, and starving from lack of grass, they had little choice but to eat noxious weeds, which poisoned them. Still Garland and Babcock limped onward, now on half-rations, sharing part of their meager supplies with even less fortunate trailers until finally, seventy-nine days after leaving Ashcroft, they emerged at the "ratty" town of Telegraph Creek, half-starved, footsore, filthy, but triumphant at having survived a brutal trek.

At Telegraph Creek a discouraged Garland bought passage down-river to Glenora, where he concluded enough was enough—he had proved he could take it. To his brother Franklin he boasted, "We have made 1000 miles of hell's own trail. I am as hard as nails. . . . It was a tremendous experience. I had only one pair of shoes and one pair trousers hanging on to me when I reached Telegraph, but I could swing 50# sacks like dumb-bells."[45] He quickly filed a report of his journey, and his hardships along the trail made front-page headlines in a number of newspapers.[46] After a few days' rest he mulled over his achievement, a bit disappointed by the lack of literary material the trip had provided. He had expected, based on promotional brochures then flooding the public, that the trail would be picturesque, with an opportunity to observe the wildlife and mountain plants he so loved. He mused on August 7, just before leaving Babcock to journey downriver: "I do not feel that I have secured so much literary material but I have gained in mental and physical health. The thousand miles of trail are milling together—soon they will shorten and I will recall only the most striking pleasures and pains connected with it. It has given me a genuine taste of the wild life and the expedients of the trail. I wanted a touch of the real thing, something which could not be questioned and I have had it." But then, as if to prove to himself his own hardihood, he recorded, "I am not satisfied though. I wish I could have a few weeks in the Kalispell mts with some good man."[47]

Mindful that fall was fast approaching, he knew he would need to hurry if he wanted to see the goldfields before he had to return to Chicago. He booked passage to Skagway, and with thirty days' supplies and in the company of the town's newspaper editor, he hiked over White Pass while stumbling over the thousands of carcasses of rotting horses that littered the trail to Lake Bennett. There he became a tourist, hiring a series of boats and packers to get him to Lake Atlin, where a new strike had been reported. He observed the miners, panned for gold, took pictures and made notes for articles, and then returned via Chilkoot Pass to Skagway, where he determined to end his adventure. "Henceforth I intended to ride," he remarked; "nevertheless I was pleased to think I could still walk thirty miles in eleven hours through a rain storm, and over a summit three thousand six hundred feet in height. The city had not entirely eaten the heart out of my body."[48] Mindful of the fate of prospectors' horses when they were no longer needed—they were typically abandoned and left to starve—he booked passage to West Salem for his faithful steed, Prince (which he renamed "Ladrone" after his early poem about a faithful horse sold and abandoned after years of devoted service), figuring the freight charge would be amply repaid by a clear conscience.

What was the harvest of Garland's Klondike adventure? Clearly, Hamlin did not undertake the "poor man's route" to save money, for a twenty-five-dollar fare from Seattle to Skagway would have enabled him to avoid seventy-nine days of toil along the trail. No, as he records in *The Trail of the Goldseekers*, he went in search of adventure and literary material and took "the hard way through" to prove to himself that he could be as hardy as the cowboys he had come to admire, despite his eastern flab.[49] Near the end of his chronicle, he summarizes his achievement in "The Toil of the Trail":

What have I gained by the toil of the trail?
I know and know well.
I have found once again the lore I had lost
In the loud city's hell.

I have broadened my hand to the cinch and the axe,
I have laid my flesh to the rain;
I was hunter and trailer and guide;
I have touched the most primitive wildness again.

I have threaded the wild with the stealth of the deer,
No eagle is freer than I;
No mountain can thwart me, no torrent appall,
I defy the stern sky.
So long as I live these joys will remain,
I have touched the most primitive wildness again.[50]

His trip did not immediately provide the literary bounty for which Garland had hoped—from it came one book, four articles, some poems, and one novel—but his firsthand experience in the wilderness gave him the authority he needed, as a "veritist," to write about the mountain West.[51] Thereafter he wrote no more stories of the middle border. For the next eighteen years his fiction focused on the westerner and the Indian, and in this work he largely abandoned the reformist strain that had proved so unremunerative.

14

THE END OF THE TRAIL, 1899–1902

When Garland returned from the wilderness in September 1898, his physical health was renewed by his experience and he threw himself into his writing, producing more creative work in the twelve months following his experience than during any other year in his career. But still the depressions plagued him. The Klondike trek had temporarily sated his wanderlust, but he remained dissatisfied and unhappy, worried about earning a reliable income and sensitive to his wavering public reputation. On his thirty-eighth birthday, he looked in the mirror and wasn't pleased: "I can not reasonably call myself young any longer. The gray is in my hair and the lines of care are on my face. My joints are no longer supple and free. True I have no loss of limb, scarcely a scar. I am undeniably middle aged."[1] While still on his Klondike trek, he jotted down a number of poems about a topic to which men away from civilization often turn. A stanza deleted from the published version of "Here the Trail Ends," the concluding poem of *The Trail of the Goldseekers*, suggests the direction his introspection was taking him:

> And you my sweet girl—my secret ideal,
> My grand splendid wife whom I never quite found
> Do I lose you too? Am I always to wander
> In search of your face in the dark over there—
> That is hardest of all. For you I wrought daily
> For you I kept honest—you[,] you alone.
> And now I must go from the plain and the mountain
> And never more hope for the light of your face—
> To you where you dwell I send greeting—

238

And homage—and a long fare well—
For here the trail ends.[2]

During those long, silent days in the saddle he took stock and decided, as this stanza suggests, that his problem was loneliness. When he returned to civilization, he decided to cast fortune to the winds and marry. His writing was now bringing steady though modest returns, and by careful management he thought he might be able to support a wife. But he knew that his temperament, so often dogmatic and insistent, would demand a woman with mammoth understanding, and so he was not hopeful.

On September 26, copies of *Ulysses S. Grant: His Life and Character*, the book over which he nearly ruined his health, reached him in West Salem. "I am not at all sure that it is what I intended it to be, but I did my best and there it stands," he noted in his diary, but his concern was unwarranted, for he had at last managed to write a book that was almost universally acclaimed—a feat he would not repeat until the publication of *A Son of the Middle Border*, nineteen years later. "The story is exceedingly well told, and no pains seem to have been spared to ensure accuracy in every essential particular," opined the *Critic*, the journal that had so often castigated his work and personality. "He gives a book which will be long read for its human interest," *Book News* informed its readers, and in a lengthy column of lavish praise the *New York Times* offered what must have particularly pleased Garland, given his early struggle to remove didacticism from his writing: "Mr. Garland writes admirably, is content—a thing rare among biographers—to keep his own personality in the background."[3] His two years of labor, thousands of miles of travel, and exhaustive research had finally paid off. Ironically, the preoccupation of the public with the Spanish-American War had given it a new set of heroes. The papers were filled with the dispatches of Richard Harding Davis trumpeting the achievements of Commodore George Dewey (soon promoted to admiral) and Theodore Roosevelt and his Rough Riders, and interest in Grant temporarily waned. The result was disappointing sales.

His mood brightened on November 3, when during an evening

with his friends Browne, Taft, and Fuller he dined with Taft's sister Zulime, who had just returned from four years of studying art in Paris. Garland had first met Zulime in 1894, just before she left. At the time, filled with the ideals of the Central Art Association, he admonished her for leaving the United States to study European masters. Predictably, she had bristled at his harangue, and Garland retained an impression of her as a spoiled, "coldly-haughty young person running away from her native land, not to study art but to have a pleasant time in Paris." During her four years abroad she had matured into a sophisticated, charming twenty-eight-year-old woman, and Garland took note, remembering that "while Miss Taft did not betray keen interest in me she did not precisely discourage me," and thereafter he sought out her company.[4]

The Taft family patriarch, Don Carlos, formerly a professor of geology at the University of Illinois and recently a banker in Hanover, Kansas, also had a penchant for classical literature, saddling his children with names drawn from his favorite works—Lorado Zadok, Zulime Maune, Florizel Adino, and Turbulance Doctoria. As a child, Zulime (from the play by Voltaire, pronounced "zoo-lah-mee," according to her granddaughter) would burst into tears when her name was called in school, but by adulthood she appears to have accepted the inevitable questioning. Like her brother Lorado, she was a gifted artist. For the Columbian Exposition she sculpted *Learning* for display in the Art Building, as well as a statue of *Victory* for display in the interior of the Manufacturers' Building. As a result, she was featured, with a striking engraving of her, in an issue of the *Illustrated American* as part of a story on exposition sculpture by women artists.[5] She scored a hit with the colossal figure of *Freedom Breaking Her Chains*, which caused one reviewer to marvel, "One can scarcely believe that the slender girlish figure has the physical endurance, or the small white hand the strength to model those great forceful figures, but all unaided she has accomplished that which will crown her with honor, for she has embodied in plaster much of the grace and dignity of her own soul."[6]

During the fall, as he worked sporadically at his manuscripts, largely adrift and dejected, Garland recorded in his diary his progress in searching for a companion. Although he was by nature formal and reserved when it came to inscribing such personal details, his entries nonetheless offer a portrait of a morose man eager for companionship yet unable to avoid offending others. During a visit to the Little Room, for example, he found it difficult to adopt the persona of a cavalier: "As for me, I was there and made my usual number of enemies by blurting out my real mind instead of being gallant and lying. I called on Miss [Anna] Dorsey in the evening and managed to make her feel miserable by telling her I pitied her among the 'elite' yesterday. So it goes. I manage to make enemies right and left and before and behind."[7] Their spat didn't last, and he squired Anna to other events, while accompanying Zulime to still others, all the while contemplating the effect of his wanderlust on his ability to settle down.

In December he was back in New York to meet with his editors and cast about for a new book publisher for two volumes he planned to write, one based on his Klondike trip, the other on the autobiographical manuscript he had dictated before he left. In January, over several lunches at the Players Club, he met with George Platt Brett, head of the American branch of the newly reorganized house of Macmillan, which in 1899 led the nation in the number of new books published, 615.[8] Brett offered to take over three of the failed Stone and Kimball titles—*Main-Travelled Roads*, *Prairie Folks*, and *Rose of Dutcher's Coolly*—if Garland would also give him the two new books he had planned—*Boy Life on the Prairie* and *The Trail of the Goldseekers*. Brett was interested in Garland's work, as he explained to Frederick Macmillan, head of the parent firm, "chiefly because he has so much influence with the younger writers in this country," and he hoped the controversial author would attract new writers to the developing list.[9] The five volumes would be published in a uniform edition of brown cloth with a variation of the Stone and Kimball corn motif—now a single ear of corn radiating in four spokes surrounding the title—embossed in gold on the cover and spine. The terms were sweet: an advance of one thousand dollars for the three Stone and Kimball books and two thousand dollars for the two new ones, for a total of three thousand dollars—in today's dollars, seventy thousand. "I shall be freed from care for a year anyway," he confided to his diary—then adding, dolefully, "that kind of care."[10]

Macmillan planned to publish *Rose* and *Goldseekers* in May, with the other three books to follow in the fall, so Garland settled down to prepare the books. With the sneers of its critics still stinging, he revised *Rose* by altering some of the scenes and much of the language, though he did not change his fundamental conception. His primary intent was to excise some of the more overt references to sexuality. The brakeman who ogled Rose "with the glare of a sex maniac"—the phrase that so troubled reviewers—now eyes her "with an insolent glare." He muted many of the references to Rose's body, added a brief scene depicting Rose and Mason after their marriage, apparently in an attempt to make the remote and stiff Mason a more believable character, and polished many loose expressions that had come to embarrass him. The result was a more professionally written novel.[11] *The Trail of the Goldseekers* was based on the daily journal he kept during the trip as well as other notebooks filled with observations and poetry. Its subtitle, "A Record of Travel in Prose and Verse," accurately describes its contents, for interspersed among the daily record of his activities are forty-three poems, nearly all original.

To satisfy Macmillan's desire to advertise the slim *Main-Travelled Roads* as an expanded edition, Garland added three stories: "The Creamery Man" (from *Outlook*, December 1897); "A Day's Pleasure," which had appeared in the *Ladies' Home Journal* as "Sam Markham's Wife" (July 1898); and "Uncle Ripley's Speculation," which he took from *Prairie Folks* and placed following "Mrs. Ripley's Trip" as "Uncle Ethan Ripley." He devoted more time and care to *Prairie Folks*, dropping a second story and revising, mostly to improve style, four others that had been published through Bacheller's newspaper syndicate.[12] No one was more thrifty than Garland in maximizing the return of his literary capital. Since Macmillan had no plans for *Prairie Songs* and because he liked the effect in *Goldseekers*, he decided to disperse the poems among the stories, adding thirteen to the volume.

Garland devoted considerable time to *Boy Life on the Prairie*, which Macmillan intended to be the standout of his books, accompanying the text with six full-page illustrations and forty-seven line drawings by the popular illustrator E. M. Deming. He combined his earlier "Boy Life" articles (published in the *American* and *Midland Monthly*) with the autobiographical manuscript he had dictated before leaving for the Klondike and a few other scattered pieces, in the process expanding the time frame from a single year to chronicle the growth and maturation of Lincoln Stewart, based on himself. "It is not my intention to present in *Lincoln Stewart* the details of my own life and character," Garland disingenuously remarked in the preface, for he indeed did so, though he intended his characterization to "depict boy life, not boys," with the characters standing as types. He also interspersed thirty-two poems, nearly all from *Prairie Songs*, and thus put about half of his orphaned book back into print. He largely succeeded in his aim of creating a nostalgic depiction of a past that was rapidly fading, and the book went on to become a steady seller, under different publishers and revisions. Today it is highly regarded by scholars of the American boy book, who place it in company with Twain's *Tom Sawyer* and Howells's *Boys Town*, books aimed at adults reminiscing about childhood.[13]

At the end of January Garland met Juliet Wilbor Tompkins, who had come to New York to edit the *Puritan*, a short-lived illustrated women's magazine that had just absorbed *Godey's Magazine*, part of the Frank Munsey empire. Born in California in 1871, Tompkins would go on to a successful career as a novelist and magazine essayist. She soon caught Garland's attention: "I do not know a more strenuous and vivid personality than Juliet," he wrote in his diary. "She is not pretty—at least her beauty is of the inner and intellectual sort. She radiates with wit, her smile is lovely and her movements bird-like. It is hard to think of her as the editor of a cheap magazine."[14] He soon began taking her to plays and lectures, all the while pondering whether he was ready to settle down.

Garland wound up his business in New York during February, foremost of which was attending the first meeting of the National Institute of Arts and Letters on February 11. Founded in 1898 as an offshoot of the American Social Science Association, the institute was formed to recognize and promote distinction in literature, music, and the fine arts. Its membership eventually numbered 250 of the nation's most illustrious writers, musicians, artists, and architects. Though its early years were marred by squabbling about the institute's purpose—Henry Fuller once asked Garland, "Another Institute dinner?—Don't they do anything *but* eat?"—once the organization acquired an endowment, it began to confer prizes for excellence and thereby acquired a purpose other than merely being another exclusive club.[15] Garland was naturally quite pleased to be asked to become a charter member, and at the direction of the institute's first president, Charles Dudley Warner, he and playwright Augustus Thomas drafted the organization's constitution. Although his active participation in the institute was limited because of his Chicago residence, Garland was an enthusiastic proponent and would later take a more active role.

He also renewed an acquaintance with Israel Zangwill, the British writer he had met earlier in Chicago. Author of a number of volumes concerning Jewish life, Zangwill was in New York to arrange for the dramatic adaptation *Children of the Ghetto* (1892), which would appear in October under the direction of James Herne. Zangwill encouraged Garland to visit England and offered to be his guide. Garland, his pockets now comfortably lined with the Macmillan advance, was tempted.[16]

On March 1 the inveterate traveler was back in Chicago, where he began accompanying Lorado and Zulime Taft to exhibitions and other gatherings. At mid-month he went with them to Eagle's Nest Camp, an art colony founded by Lorado that year at the estate of Wallace Heckman, the financial administrator of the University of Chicago and an art patron. Located one hundred miles west of Chicago on the banks of the Rock River near Oregon, Illinois, at the time the colony consisted of only one frame building to serve as the kitchen—guests stayed in tents, though that summer Taft, Browne, and the painter Ralph Clarkson began to erect cabins. Garland's carpentry skills were in demand, and he helped Taft raise his roof.[17] As a trustee for the colony, Garland envisioned erecting a summer cabin for himself—instead, two years later, he raised a tepee made for him by the mother of Antelope, one of his Cheyenne friends. (He was fond of lying before its fire, the play of firelight evoking memories of his Indian friends, which he then turned to fiction amid the suggestive atmosphere.)[18] Garland's growing interest in Zulime soon attracted the notice of Taft. Familiar with Garland's obstreperous temperament, Lorado was not keen on the writer as a prospective brother-in-law, so to discourage his interest, he told Garland that Zulime was engaged.[19]

Crushed, and without speaking to Zulime, Garland abruptly decided to go to England. He entrained for New York, where he called on Juliet Tompkins on April 16, apparently deciding to encourage her interest since he believed Zulime had spurned him. On April 19 he sailed for Liverpool on the *Teutonic*, not very excited about his prospects in England: "I had no elation—almost no emotion concerning the trip. It was not much different than taking the train for New Orleans. Nothing like so important to me as my trip last year to the wild."[20] The next day his ennui suddenly changed, for he found himself afflicted with a serious case of seasickness. "The Scotch doctor on the steamer said I was the worst sailor he had ever known in his experience of nearly a quarter century," he remembered, and he endured the seven-day passage confined to his bunk, barely managing to keep down a meal when the seas abated on the third day—and then promptly losing it when the seas built back up.[21]

When he regained his land legs he met with Zangwill, whose first order of business was to take Garland to a tailor, for Garland believed his western wear would not do for calls on English society, and particularly a meeting of the Author's Society, where he would be a featured guest. In *Roadside Meetings* Garland makes much of the comedy surrounding the acquisition of his first swallow-tailed coat, which he had hitherto rejected on principle. He was also well aware that his shoddy wardrobe limited his social options—especially calls on marriageable young ladies. But a letter to his mother reveals that he—not Zangwill—insisted on the formal coat. "It's all bosh, this talk about the rigid rule of dress," he explained. "The Zangwill brothers laughed at the idea," for "Americans are greater sticklers for conventions than Londoners themselves."[22] Suitably equipped in a fine

English suit, Garland spent the next month calling on James M. Barrie, George Bernard Shaw, Arthur Conan Doyle, Bret Harte, and others. He delighted in showing Conan Doyle, who shared his interest in psychic phenomena, the mysteries of the curve ball—done with a cricket ball and bat—and noted that he and Shaw "were good friends at once."[23] Twice the local colorist recorded his response to streetwalkers, apparently more out of curiosity than any desire to patronize them. English whores repelled him: "They prowled like hyenas, lying in wait like cats. Some sang to advertise their trade, others called 'Hello, darling!' A few sauntered insolently, all were haggard and painted. Poor, thin, angular, undersized creatures for the most part, bent and hatchet-faced. Some were like walking sepulchers—all white without—disease within—an appalling army!" On May 30 he was in Paris, whose prostitutes were "much more attractive than English women, more allurement in the glance, more mystery, less vulgarly wanton. They had style and grace, even in the plainest of them."[24]

By June 24 he was back in New York, and his first order of business was to call on Juliet Tompkins. He took her to a play and read to her from the manuscript of a novel he then called "The Hustler"—the comic story of a cowboy who goes to England in a "big canoe," suffers terrible seasickness, and amuses socialite London with his rustic slang and western customs. In search of backers for a Colorado mine, Jim Matteson falls in love with a wealthy English maiden but eventually realizes they can never mesh in each other's worlds. Fortunately, a beautiful western girl is waiting for him back home; he returns to Colorado and, torn between two loves and after several misunderstandings, convinces her to marry him. Garland obviously relied on his own travel and romantic experience—and a vague nod to Mark Twain's *A Connecticut Yankee in King Arthur's Court*—in his portrayal of this Colorado cowboy in London society. But one looks in vain for details of his wooing of Juliet Tompkins in New York, for the pages for June 28 to July 7 have been torn from his diary, where Garland might have remarked more specifically about his interest. His daughter remarks that upon his return to Chicago "a flood of letters followed him, full of rapturous admiration and

girlish yearning." Later, "Aunt Juliet" became one of Zulime's closest friends and told Mary Isabel Garland, "You know, I might have
been your mother." Mary Isabel considers her mother's indifference
to Garland's attention as the decisive factor in the writer's turning
away from Juliet to Zulime.[25]

When the diary resumes on July 8, Garland is back in Chicago,
morose and contemplating a bleak future. "I find myself filled with
doubt of my ability to settle down here in the west," he wrote. "I have
not been so restless and dissatisfied for years. How it will all end I
do not know. Perhaps my restlessness may wear itself out by and
by. . . . I have felt as never before the crowding in upon me of life's
problems. My old people, my growing sense of age and fear of the
future. . . . I am no longer young!"[26] For the remainder of July he
moused about Chicago and West Salem, struggling to concentrate
on the manuscript of *Boy Life on the Prairie*, which he had promised
to deliver by October 1, distracted by worry about his mother's and
aunt's health and by searching for a home for them in Chicago. His
mother decided to remain in West Salem, and so the dutiful son
promptly engaged in home improvement, expanding the house and
remodeling the interior.

A letter from Fuller suggesting he come to Eagle's Nest Camp provided the impetus to escape his growing boredom with West Salem.
Then, too, Zulime would be there. At some point, Garland learned
that Lorado was mistaken in telling him Zulime was engaged.

In August he went walking or horseback riding nearly every day
with Zulime while also working on the manuscript of "The Hustler,"
which would appear in book form as *Her Mountain Lover*, his only
comic novel. In *A Daughter of the Middle Border*, Garland has left a
charming account of their courtship, full of romance and self-dep-
recation, where Zulime is the prize too good for the hapless suitor.
It is also an account Zulime "steadfastly refused to read," Mary Isabel
maintains, because, her mother told her, "it isn't true."[27]

In fact, their courtship was fraught with difficulties, for Zulime
needed much convincing, and Garland was operating under a mistaken assumption that his close friend Henry Fuller was his rival. "We
are seeing a great deal of each other on a friendly basis," he noted

soon after he arrived. "A very good loyal girl. I am taking Fullers [*sic*] place for the time being. That he greatly admires her is certain." Although he was envious of his friend's attentions to Zulime, he need not have worried: later he would learn that his best friend was homosexual and romantically uninterested in Zulime. At the time he knew only that Fuller was an intensely private man who invited no one—not even his closest friends—to his home, nor would he reveal much about his own past. Living at a time when homosexual behavior was a criminal offense in most states, Fuller naturally remained in the closet; then, too, Garland's own reticence about sexual matters did not invite confidences. Garland would eventually find out about Fuller's sexual proclivity, and even, after a fashion, reluctantly tolerate it, but that was years in the future. Now, as Hamlin walked with Zulime, his thoughts turned to the other woman in his life for some inevitable comparisons about matrimonial potential, as he recorded with some surprise, "For a 'confirmed old bachelor' I seem to be doing my share of 'beauing.'"[28]

During September and October, Garland fielded letters from Juliet and Zulime, but the distance separating New York from West Salem soon gave Zulime the advantage. He oscillated between West Salem and Eagle's Nest, attending to his ailing mother and courting Zulime. By October he had decided to ask Zulime to marry him, partly nudged by his mother, who had urged him to "hurry"—for her health was declining and she wanted to see her elder son married.[29] At Eagle's Nest, for the first time, they walked and talked alone, a sign of their growing seriousness, for on previous visits they had been chaperoned by one of the Heckman daughters. By October 10, matters had come to a head: "Z and I walked and talked nearly all day—to some purpose. . . . 'Mauna' comes to interest me more and more and grows more certain of her feelings toward the question in hand. We still walk to and fro on the wood road. Days of gentle debate and serious question. It is a solemn moment for us both—solemn and sweet at the same time." He popped the question the next day, but Zulime requested time to consider, and Garland entrained for West Salem, where he continued his wooing through the mails.

That Zulime wanted time to contemplate is understandable, for Garland's personality was nothing if not forceful, and she knew that the compromises required by marriage were certain to be difficult for Hamlin. Then, too, according to Mary Isabel, "Zulime Taft was not in love with Hamlin Garland when she married him. . . . Mother said she had admired Hamlin, liked him but love as a physical passion had no part in it." She was no doubt attracted by the celebrity surrounding the controversial writer, in an age when writers were feted like movie stars. "I don't know quite why I did it," Zulime told her daughter. "Except he was handsome, distinguished, much talked about. And Lorado liked him." And, Mary Isabel adds wryly, "Father was a strong character and I imagine his wooing was pretty hard to withstand."[30]

Finally, on October 20, Zulime accepted his proposal, and Garland rushed to Howells to tell him the good news. "He was profoundly interested in Z. and made most minute inquiries about her," he recorded in his diary four days later. The next day, he brought Zulime to meet his benefactor. Howells proffered his congratulations and then remarked, Garland later wrote, "Your husband-elect is one of my boys. I am particularly concerned with his good fortune." Garland could not have hoped for a better benediction, as he noted: "In a literary sense this was my paternal blessing, for 'Mr. Howells' had been a kind of spiritual progenitor and guide ever since my first meeting with him in '87. . . . We both went away, rich in the honor of his approval of our prospective union."[31] And Zulime certainly recognized the shared warmth of the friendship, recording in her diary about a subsequent luncheon: "He is Hamlin's hero, in a way—and I admire the personal side equally much. His evident fondness for Hamlin—has quite won my heart."[32]

For Garland, the next step was to convince Lorado that he would make an acceptable brother-in-law. He went to Chicago to plead his case to the sculptor and protective brother. "Lorado . . . confessed himself very jealous of Zulime but was satisfied in this case," Garland recorded after the interrogation. "He was unusually serious for him and spoke with considerable feeling. We know each other very well and there seems little doubt but that we will continue good friends as before."[33] Lorado had good reason for concern: in May 1898 his youngest sister, Turbulance (called "Turbie" by friends), had married Charles Francis Browne, one of the "Critical Triumvirate" of the Central Art Association days and Garland's good friend and western travel companion of 1895. So now two of his closest friends would be married to his sisters, and he must have worried about the effects of propinquity. How many brothers want their friends to marry their sisters?

With benedictions from the two people who mattered most, the decks were clear to plan the wedding. As Warren Mason's proposal letter in *Rose of Dutcher's Coolly* suggests, Garland had pretty liberal ideas about marriage and the duties of husband and wife. He was relieved to find that Zulime would accept a civil ceremony, writing his brother that "We are both averse to publicity. I am very glad to find that she cares nothing about a public wedding or the use of the church and minister. She is a mighty fine liberal girl. She is as free from the usual prejudice as any woman I know."[34] They decided to be married at her father's home in Hanover, Kansas, on November 23, enabling Hamlin to meet his father-in-law, before going to West Salem to meet his parents for Thanksgiving, always an important day for the Garland clan.

By October 31 the impatient groom was getting underfoot and interfering with the dressmaking. Exasperated, Zulime pleaded with him to vamoose. "I dont really know why I am doing this," Garland noted as he headed to New Mexico, "but she said 'You'd better go' and so here I am rushing into the wild country."[35] Amid his visit among the Navajos at Gallup and Ganado, he picked up some blankets and pottery for gifts. As he traveled in the Southwest, all his love for the western landscape returned, and he persuaded Zulime to move the wedding date up to November 18, which would allow a lightning trip to the Colorado mountains before returning to West Salem on the thirtieth. Zulime agreed, and Garland entrained for St. Joseph, Missouri, where he figured he would arrive in time to surprise her at the train station.

As the wedding approached, Garland worried himself sick and took to his bed. "In order to relieve me," he remembered, "my friends put me into a vapor bath and when I came out of it I was immediately seized with dizziness and at last fell into a state of catalepsy [i.e., muscular rigidity] which seemed to me to be paralysis. My feet and legs became set like marble—my hand clutched inward with most excruciating pain." Gamely, he gritted his teeth and resolved not to let his bride down. On his wedding day, he duly recorded, "Though weak and lame I determined to get through the ceremony as Zuliema [*sic*] wished it and so at 1 o'clock like one risen from the dead I went down in my long pack coat and we were married by Judge Sturgis in the simplest way possible." The civil ceremony over, the groom miraculously recovered and they boarded the four o'clock train to Colorado Springs.[36]

With boyish pleasure, Garland delighted in showing Zulime via horseback the trails he loved through the Colorado mountains, fully aware that to some "this wedding trip will seem a lunatic, extravagant fantasy on my part; but Zulime declared herself grateful to me for having insisted upon it."[37] Zulime may have told her eager husband she was glad for the western honeymoon trip, but to her daughter the city girl confided that "she was in tears a good part of the time." "Hamlin wanted me to see everything and he thought nothing of a thirty or forty mile ride," she told Mary Isabel. "He was always assuring me that there was an even better view around the next corner and all I wanted to do was get off that stupid horse and sit down beside the trail and cry. One time I did just that and Hamlin disgustedly rode on alone and looked at his view before he came back to me. It was not my idea of a honeymoon."[38]

At dawn on Thanksgiving Day the newlyweds arrived in West Salem, where Dick Garland was waiting with a horse and carriage. "It wasn't in the least the tender meeting I had expected to witness," Hamlin remembered, but at last the former borderman "was able to reach his hand down to Zulime" and welcome her into the family. Hamlin's mother also hesitated, before the two "met in an embrace of mutual love and confidence."[39] Contrary to the portrait Garland paints in *A Daughter of the Middle Border* of joyous parents eagerly welcoming his bride, his mother soon became jealous and possessive, for her son did not curtail his constant travel, and only later did she come to accept her daughter-in-law. "I tried my best," Zulime recalled, "but she couldn't bear to have us alone together. She was always coming to the foot of the stairs and calling, 'Hamlin, aren't you coming down?' and usually Hamlin went."[40] Zulime's recollection is borne out by Garland's diary, which describes their contentment in isolating themselves in their room, only to be interrupted by Hamlin's mother, who "is jealous of our companionship and often comes to the door if she thinks we are staying up stairs too long. She likes to have us sit where she can see us."[41]

With family introductions completed, the Garlands journeyed to Washington and New York for the winter, where the proud groom introduced his bride to his eastern friends, among them the Hernes, Howells, Stedman, Matthews, composer Edward MacDowell, publishers Edward Bok and Frank Doubleday, and Frank Norris, with whom they quickly developed a close friendship.[42] "It is great, meeting all of these distinguished men, in this simple fashion," Zulime reflected, "and it makes me very happy to know that they seem to approve of Hamlin's choice."[43] But the social whirl was not enough to stave off homesickness, and soon Zulime pleaded to return to the familiarity of Chicago. Shortly after their arrival in February, Garland received a letter summoning him home: his aunt Susan was near death.

Susan Bailey died on February 25, 1900, leaving her brother, Dick Garland, as her only heir. Though her estate was valued at only a few thousand dollars, for the first time it offered the Dakota wheat farmer "a sense of security, a feeling of independence, a freedom from worry."[44] No longer dependent upon his son for security, Dick put his South Dakota lands up for sale and resolved to remain in West Salem, soon becoming president of the village council. But even his father's newfound prosperity did not diminish Hamlin's sense of obligation to care for his mother. In his mind, he had largely replaced his father in terms of financial support; though he sorely needed to cut the apron strings, he was constitutionally unable to do so.

During the spring, Garland traveled between Chicago and West Salem as his mother's letters grew more imperious, demanding his presence by noting her failing health. Some of the dutiful son's weary resentment emerges in his diaries, where he writes in March, "Mother is a weight on my consciousness all the time. For thirteen years I have thought of her and what I could do for her almost without cessation. She is so helpless—so without resource. Zuliema [*sic*] is a great help to me now but no one can release me. I do not seek release. I want to do all I can for mother every day—it is only when I feel my writing pangs that I become uneasy."[45]

In February 1900 Garland finished the manuscript of *The Eagle's Heart*, a serial romance he had begun while on his Klondike journey and into which he poured all his love of the western mountains. It was to be the first of six novels set in Colorado, and it marked a new direction for his fiction. By now Garland had mastered the conventions of writing for a national audience of magazine readers drawn to plots that featured stalwart heroes on lonely quests for manhood amid a myriad of adverse challenges. The novel formed a natural bridge between his stories of the middle border and his new interest in the West. As he explained to one correspondent, he intended the novel to be "the epic of the prairie people merging into mountaineers."[46] As he would do whenever he ventured into new genres, he turned first to his own experience, setting the action in Rock River, Iowa, where his protagonist, Harold Excell, is the son of a minister noted for his oratorical excellence and from whom Harold has inherited a formidable temper and propensity toward violence and for whom he nourishes a rebellious spirit. Harold develops into an archetypal "bad boy" of dime-novel fiction and is soon jailed for knifing, in self-defense, the slanderer of a girl to whom he is attracted.

When he gets out of jail, Harold changes his name to "Moses N. Hardluck" and flees to the West, where he is, by turns, cattle driver, sheep rancher, cowboy, and professional bad man as he retraces the route Garland took on his 1895 western visit. Harold becomes the "eagle's heart" of the title, unwilling to be restrained by civilization, his desire to taste the freedom of the unsettled lands always prodding him westward, as suggested by the poem "Anticipation," which prefaced *The Trail of the Goldseekers* and served as the impetus for the novel.

Harold takes special delight in the snake dance at Walpi and earns a reputation as a defender of the Indians against their exploiters. But his too-ready temper and an unwillingness to suffer any insult, coupled with a deadly accuracy with a firearm, soon earns him the moniker "Black Mose," and he becomes a feared desperado. Eventually, after drifting into such occupations as wagon guard and lawman, Harold tires of the lonely life of the saddle and dreams of settling down with Mary Yardwell, the beautiful maiden who had attempted to reform him through an outreach program of song while he was in jail. After a number of missteps they eventually wed, and the novel closes with Harold accepting an appointment as Indian agent at Sand Lake.

Delighted when he succeeded in selling the serial to the *Saturday Evening Post* for two thousand dollars, Garland promptly presented the check to a surprised Zulime as her birthday present.[47] When Appleton published *The Eagle's Heart* in October, Garland was pleased by this foray into romance: "Sometimes I think it will sell largely," he mused, "and then as I analyze it I see that it lacks the 'ingredients' of the successful novel. I pleases me however. It is well made and fairly well written so let it stand."[48] The reviewers, however, were divided in their response. The *Chicago Tribune* believed Garland to be "at his best" in this novel, for he had succeeded in softening "his realistic faults and mannerisms" with "just enough romantic exaggeration to lend color and spirit" to his tale. Some complained of tepid characterization of his hero—a problem he would rarely resolve. Most, however, praised Garland's ability to describe the western setting convincingly. As the *Brooklyn Daily Eagle* concluded, despite the inadequacies in characterization of Harold Excell, "on the side of fidelity to nature and picturesqueness of description it is the best novel of the range and the round-up and its civilizations and its barbarisms that has yet been published."[49]

In April 1900 Garland and Zulime left for the Darlington Agency at the Cheyenne and Arapaho Reservation in Oklahoma, at the invitation of George Stouch, the former agent at Lame Deer, who had just been transferred and who wrote to ask whether the Garlands would like to accompany him on his inaugural tour of the reservation.[50] Garland's imagination immediately responded to the Indians he interviewed and to Stouch's stories of his adventures, and Hamlin began drafting many of the stories that would be collected in *The Book of the American Indian* and would further clarify his perception of the Indian "as a man of the polished stone age trying to adapt himself to steam and electricity."[51]

Garland returned to West Salem in late May, determined to devote his art to capturing the beauty of the West. At first his imagination responded to the West as another form of local color, but in the Indians he soon found reason to awaken his dormant reform spirit. While in West Salem he attended the Old Settlers' Reunion, a gathering to celebrate the village's founders, who had wrested the land from the Indians. During the meeting, a newspaper reporter recorded, the author intemperately "declared the Indians in the Black Hawk war entirely right and the whites entirely wrong. He said the name of Black Hawk should ever be revered and remembered." Of course, this did not go unchallenged: "He was greeted by boos and hisses from hundreds, who gave a tremendous demonstration of disapproval." After listening to the crowd cheer a defender of the settlers "for several minutes," Garland "left in disgust"—and then wrote a letter to the paper's editor in which he first noted that a number of old settlers "listened courteously and cheered me heartily" and then asked that the reporter be dismissed. When the affair made headlines in the *Chicago Tribune* and *New York Times*, he vowed to be "more careful of my words" and resolved to "speak no more except to . . . people who will at least grant me the right of being myself."[52]

While Garland was in New York on November 25, the telegram he had been dreading arrived: his mother was dying. Frantic, he rushed to make the last train to Chicago only to receive word en route that she had died. For twenty years his mother had served as the primary impetus to his craft, for the complex web of guilt, ambition, and desire to please had prompted his earliest short fiction and later encouraged his relocation to Chicago. When he arrived he could not bring himself to look upon her face in the open casket, preferring to remember her in life and not death. "That day was the longest, bitterest, I had ever known," Garland remembered, "for the reason that, mixed with my grief, my sense of remorse, was a feeling of utter helplessness."[53] For days he wandered around the Homestead, overcome with memories of his mother, wishing he had been able to do more for her. "Zulime thinks my regret morbid," he recorded in his diary, "but I can not but dwell on the things I might have done for her and did not."[54] For consolation, in an act of catharsis, he began drafting "The Wife of a Pioneer," his memorial to his mother. In it he offered a moving account of his mother's sacrifices for her children, her physical deterioration brought on by the hardships of pioneering, all tempered by a painful awareness that he could have done more to ease her burden but had not. But he also acknowledged that his mother had inspired his best writing. "I write in the hope of making some other work-weary mother happy," he concluded his chronicle. "There is nothing more appealing to me than neglected age. To see an old father or mother sitting in loneliness and poverty dreaming of an absent son who never comes, of a daughter who never writes, is to me more moving than Hamlet or Othello. If we are false to those who have given us birth we are false indeed."[55]

Drafting this tribute purged his remorse, and on December 6 Garland began writing *The Captain of the Gray-Horse Troop*, his most popular novel, which was based on the conflict between the Cheyennes and ranchers about which he had written while at Lame Deer in 1897. Increasingly, his reservation experience began to occupy his imagination, and he contemplated a volume of stories about the Indians that he was to call, at various times, "Our Red Neighbors," "The Changing Heart of the Red Man," and "The Red Pioneer." Garland knew his portrayal would be at odds with that of other writers, and he was wary about interesting publishers in his sympathetic depiction. "I am an impressionist and these tales spring from my personal impressions of red life and red character," he remarked. "To me a Cheyenne village is like any other collection of people, a mixture of good and bad. . . . I have drawn the tender and humorous side of their lives as well as the patiently heroic side. If you don't want such interpretations, it is your privilege to return them."[56]

In April a letter from George Lorimer, the editor of the *Saturday*

Evening Post, arrived with an offer of two thousand dollars for the serial rights to *Captain*. "I shall try to secure more," he duly recorded, mindful of the responsibilities of marriage.[57] Zulime was pregnant, and Garland began to plan for the increased expenses children bring. By 1901 he had thoroughly probed the multifaceted magazine market, and his years of experience had given him not only the ability to write for a specific type of magazine but also the confidence of an author who could demand—and get—top prices for his work. After all the years of scrimping, Garland suddenly found himself awash in cash: the sale of the serial rights to *Her Mountain Lover* and *Captain* had garnered $3,500, and he had received an advance of $500 for the book version of each novel.[58] Feeling the need to revisit the West to reconnect with his material, he departed for Oklahoma on May 3, leaving Zulime behind.

In Oklahoma he met with George Stouch, the agent who served as the prototype for Curtis in *Captain*. The trip not only provided details for his novel but also awakened in Garland a serious case of land hunger. Throwing off his earlier commitment to the single tax, he decided to invest part of his savings into 320 acres near Colony. "Like Henry George," he explained to his father, "we both understand the value of the unearned increment."[59] In time he would amass a thousand acres, which he would rent on shares. Unlike the rascally landlord Butler in "Under the Lion's Paw," however, Garland paid for improvements to his farms—barbed wire, posts, staples, labor. A 1902 statement shows his rent income from four farms to be a mere $119.01. Later he would add to his investments additional lots, houses, and acreage 220 miles west in and near Muskogee, Oklahoma, in time amassing a respectable portfolio that would help him survive the lean years of the Great Depression. Although he defended Indians in stories and essays, he was not above profiting from their land: records show, for example, that in 1904 he bought two lots in Muskogee (established in 1900) for six hundred dollars, which had originally been sold to the previous owners the year before by the chief of the Muskogees, Pleasant Porter, for a mere ten dollars. He understood Henry George all too well.[60]

While in Oklahoma he learned that James Herne, his stalwart companion of his Boston days, was dying. "He was a man of great power, and of great charm even when in liquor—which he used in-frequently," Garland recorded in his diary. "He was, after all is said and done, the most original of our dramatists."[61] Upon Herne's death, on June 2, Garland wrote to console Katherine: "Dear friend, remember that he would not have you falter at this moment or sor-row over him. He did a good work—and had reached a time when he could go without a sense of failure. Had he died in 1890 how much sadder it would have been! . . . If there is anything I can do let me know. If there is anything he wished me to do, tell me." He then drafted a memorial article for the *Arena* in which he traced Herne's achievement as the foremost dramatist of his age.[62]

He returned to West Salem to be with Zulime for the birth of their child, but their son was stillborn. So painful was the memory that the normally dutiful diarist never mentioned the calamity in any of his published writings and only recorded the event circumspectly in the note, "This morning at about 4 am Zulime called me. She was in great pain and Father went for the Doctor. Before he came the worst was over. She must be in bed for a week and our plans are all awry again."[63]

After Zulime had recovered, the Garlands went on yet another tour of Colorado. When Hamlin returned to West Salem in October, his father astonished him by stating that he intended to remarry, after only eleven months as a widower. "I don't like this—but I have no right to oppose it," Garland recorded, the reason obvious: "It isnt easy to rid myself of a feeling that Mother would not have liked this."[64] Garland never mentions his father's remarriage in his mem-oirs, and he did his best to keep the fact from public knowledge, partly because, like many children, he felt remarriage disloyal to his mother, but also because his father's second wife violated the fam-ily myth that he constructed in his memoirs. Never as close to his father as he was to his mother, he seems to have been insensitive to his father's growing loneliness in West Salem, with his two sons so often away. In November, Dick Garland, seventy, married Mary M. Bolles, sixty, a widow.[65]

Meanwhile, Garland continued to practice his craft, although he was becoming bored with romance stories, lucrative though they were. By the fall of 1901, as he became more deeply involved in the composition of his Indian fiction, and as he went over his notes and meditated upon his themes, the reformist spirit that had lain dormant since the ridicule of his polemical remarks about literary realism of the early 1890s became fully aroused. Increasingly, he began forming connections with men who were attempting to improve reservation life. With George Bird Grinnell, Charles F. Lummis, and C. Hart Merriam, all of whom had traveled among and written about the American Indians, he formed the Sequoya League, whose motto was "to make better Indians." The league was dedicated to improving conditions on the reservations by lobbying government officials and publicizing concerns through Lummis's magazine, *Out West.* Garland's intentions may be seen in a draft of the organization's constitution, which he sent to Lummis on December 24, 1901:

1. To promote the welfare of the red man. To defend him against aggression. To foster legislation in his behalf.
2. To instruct him in ways of living. To teach him to be self-supporting along the lines of his natural aptitudes. To revive and perfect his native industries.
3. To secure a market for his products.
4. To educate and ennoble him as a red man preserving all that is fine and picturesque in him, so that his progress will be an unbroken evolution from his past as a hunter to his future as a craftsman and industrialist.
5. To unite in a non-partisan, non-sectarian league all those who have the redmans happiness and good cheer at heart.[66]

When Theodore Roosevelt became president in 1901, Garland began to lobby actively for changes in government Indian policy, trying at times to guide the appointment of officials who shared his point of view, relying on a warm friendship based on their common interests in literature and the out-of-doors. They had first met during the fall of 1896, when Roosevelt was the New York City police commissioner. They found they had much common ground in their mutual admiration of western authors and for the strenuous life.[67]

Roosevelt respected Garland's firsthand experience and relied upon his advice, eventually appointing him, unofficially, to take charge of a project to regularize the "renaming" of the Indians according to white patrilineal custom in an effort to protect inheritance rights.[68] In the midst of his politicking came news in January 1902 that Commissioner of Indian Affairs William Jones had issued an order to selected agents in which he identified "a few customs among the Indians which . . . should be modified or discontinued," among them long hair, traditional dress, body paint, dances, and feasts. "It was not that long hair, paint, blankets, etc. are objectionable in themselves," Jones wrote in a letter to Secretary of the Interior Ethan Allen Hitchcock, "but that they are a badge of servitude to savage ways and traditions which are effectual barriers to the uplifting of the race."[69]

This "hair-cut order" immediately prompted outrage from the nation's newspapers, and Jones backed off. But it also prompted Garland to write "The Red Man's Present Needs," an eloquent and passionate argument to rid the Department of Indian Affairs of its "foolish policies" and replace them with those more conducive to "make better Indians, and to make the transition from their old life to the new as easy as may be, to lessen rather than to add to the weight of their suffering."[70] This essay, in closely reasoned argument and blunt, even at times bitter, language, is Garland's most incisive discussion of American Indians. It is also particularly illuminating of the issues that underlie his Indian fiction, among them the deep ties of Indians to the land; the need to encourage Indian arts and traditions; the destructive effects of the boarding school system, which disrupts families and creates animosity; and the desirability of conferring full citizenship upon those Indians who had taken allotments. It marks his fullest public statement of his perception of the American Indian's relationship to society and dominant culture's moral obligation to treat him as a brother.

These concerns are echoed in *The Captain of the Gray-Horse Troop*, which was published in March 1902. In the most complex plotting of any novel he had yet written, Garland tells the story of Captain George Curtis, the newly appointed agent for the Teton Sioux (called "Tetong" in the novel), who arrives in time to prevent a war between his wards and a group of savage cattlemen who want to exterminate the Indians so they can grab their land. In a narrative enlivened by rich depictions of the landscape, Garland makes clear that it is the cattlemen, not the Indians, who are "savages," and that the dominant culture has a moral obligation to treat the Indians humanely and as equals. Onto this theme he grafts a double romance plot so necessary for serial fiction, basing his artist-heroine, Elsie Brisbane, upon Zulime, which enables him to incorporate some discussion of impressionism and the role of the artist. While academic readers have disparaged the novel for its paternalism and especially for its adherence to romantic conventions, contemporary readers were more approving.[71] Upon receiving an autographed copy, B. O. Flower wrote to praise his old friend's novel as "your best work. It combines the excellencies of your more recent long books with the strong altruistic and moral motive which was so marked a feature of your earlier novels."[72] Reviewers were extravagant in their praise—a first for a Garland novel. The *Chicago Tribune* summed up its achievement: "It has fairly good construction, extraordinarily good characterization, an honest purpose, a clear and appropriate style, and it furnishes plenty of interest." The *New York Times* praised the novel as "a thoughtful study of the Indian problem" whose author, "better than in his previous stories, has caught the atmosphere of the plains." Even the love subplot, typically his weak element, was lauded as "well told and happily solved." He must have been gratified when the *Dial*, which had formerly ridiculed his work, described the novel as "a capital story" that successfully combined argument and story to create a novel with a "charm of style beyond what Mr. Garland has hitherto attained."[73]

For the first time, Garland had an acclaimed novel that was vigorously promoted, for his publisher, the prestigious Harper and Brothers, gave the book a big send-off, with weekly advertising in the *New York Times*, full-page ads in magazines, even "an almost life-size portrait" of the author "on the bill boards of all the elevated roads." And to his pleasant surprise, the firm published a full-page photo of Zulime in *Harper's Weekly*, capitalizing on her beauty to draw readers to the novel. It was with a sense of earned satisfaction that the author remarked, "It really looked like a second arrival of Hamlin Garland."[74]

That fall, after yet another trip to Colorado, Garland returned to West Salem to find that, in his absence, his father and stepmother had decided to move into their own house. No doubt the increasing friction between the jealous son and the stubborn father had combined to make the house very crowded indeed. For the first time, Garland was the sole possessor of the Homestead, having bought out his brother's share earlier that year when Franklin quit the stage to gamble on a coffee and rubber plantation in Mexico. "This is our first chance at real housekeeping," Garland recorded. "We are at last householders."[75]

The timing was certainly apt. Zulime was pregnant again.

15

ADRIFT, 1903–7

On July 15, 1903, Garland witnessed his daughter's violent birth, the memory of which would haunt him forever. After three days of labor, Zulime was exhausted and close to death. A young, inexperienced doctor, Edward Evans of La Crosse, had at last been called in and performed a forceps delivery, disfiguring the infant with a "blazing purple scar that covered half [her] face." Horrified by the trauma, the new father turned to his diary. "No man has the right to put a woman through such torture!" he raged. "The whole idea of birth is animal, obscene. It must not happen to my wife again." His self-reproach filled the pages.[1] The next day, when he had composed himself, Garland sat down to write a letter to the president of the United States. "Every woman who passes through the maternity battle should be sainted," he told Theodore Roosevelt. "After seeing Zulime in her agony sweat—I am not prepared to follow you in your advocacy of large families. It really is a wonder that they live through it." In his reply, the president defended his position by arguing that a "woman who flinches from childbirth stands on par with the soldier who drops his rifle and runs in battle. . . . If . . . a man or a woman refuses to do his or her duty, why they are contemptible creatures and have no right in the community." In a subsequent letter, Garland agreed to disagree.[2]

As soon as she had recovered from her ordeal, Zulime set to work to make wide-ruffled baby bonnets to hide her child's scarred face. The scars eventually faded, but Garland's memory did not, and his daughter attributes his later antipathy to any writing that touches upon sex to the trial of her birth. And also, perhaps, to its aftermath. Three months later, Zulime would undergo an unspecified operation, likely to correct damage from the birth, that left her "moaning with anguish of mind and body . . . her face livid, her eyes wild and strange." While the doctors were "repolishing their weapons" in a room "almost as ferocious as the scene after her delivery of the child," the horrified husband blamed himself for having "caused all this and my heart was wrung."[3]

Garland wanted to call his daughter "Isabel," after his mother, but Zulime objected, and so they compromised by naming the baby after Zulime's mother, christening her "Mary Isabel," which throughout childhood would be shortened to "Mebbsie." As an adult, Mary Isabel would drop her first name when she began playing bit parts on the professional stage.

Early in their marriage, Garland hoped his wife would continue her career as an artist, for as he had indicated in *Rose of Dutcher's Coolly*, he was a firm believer in women continuing their careers during marriage. Before long, however, Zulime found that the demands of motherhood and the social duties as wife of the peripatetic author claimed all her energy. "I *wish* Zulime had kept on with her career," he told Mary Isabel. "She is enormously gifted. She could have made a real name for herself." When Mary Isabel asked her mother why she had abandoned her career, Zulime told her, "Because I'm not good enough. I'm a copyist, not a creator. In Paris I saw so much real genius that I became discouraged."[4]

While awaiting the birth of his daughter, Garland had been finishing *Hesper*, a novel he had begun in July 1902, ultimately revising it three times before he deemed it ready for publication.[5] Set amid a miners' strike in Colorado, *Hesper* tells the story of an eastern woman visiting the West with her consumptive younger brother, who in turn develops a hero worship for a cowboy-turned-miner with a mysterious past. Against her better judgment, she falls in love with the miner while coming to love the majesty of the western landscape. To symbolize her acceptance of the West and the cowboy, she takes the name "Hesper," the name her West-loving father originally intended for her.

As he had for *The Captain of the Gray-Horse Troop*, Garland hoped for serial publication, for bitter experience had taught him to rely on the cash from the serial rather than book royalties. Immediately, he encountered difficulties. Frederick Duneka, his editor at Harper's, thought the story's plot was too cohesive and lacked the segmentation necessary for a serial, and pushed for immediate publication as a book. "If I published direct and sold only five or six thousand I would be in bad temper," Garland told Duneka, and then threatened to take his book elsewhere.

> If I am not of prime importance to Harpers I cant afford to publish with them. This is a disagreeable and low-minded business-like way of speaking and I ought to be ashamed of it—but I'm not. The fact is I have no other way of making a living. I've written the best book I could conceive at the time—it is now in printable form and I am going out as you would do to do the best I can for it and for myself. This necessitates a serial publication and if a serial publication can only be arranged by disposal of the book rights also you can not blame me for making such a trade. Of course you may be right that the book is not a good serial story—if that develops then I shall certainly want to publish this fall.[6]

He then turned to the services of Paul Revere Reynolds, who had established America's first literary agency in 1895 and counted among his clients a number of prominent American authors, including Frank Norris, Stephen Crane, Willa Cather, and Jack London. Garland had first employed Reynolds's services in 1897 but had grown increasingly irritated with the agent's inability to negotiate a higher price than Garland could on his own. He turned the manuscript of *Hesper* over to Reynolds, with the instruction to seek at least two thousand dollars and to "hustle."[7] His concern was well founded, for with a 15 percent royalty on a $1.50 book, he would have to sell 8,888 copies to earn that sum, and few of his books had enjoyed such sales. For years Garland had relied on income from a serial priming the public for later book sale, and the serial publication of his last three books— *The Eagle's Heart, Her Mountain Lover,* and *The Captain of the Gray-Horse Troop*—had enabled him at last to enjoy a comfortable living. But Reynolds was unable to interest a magazine, and the book was published on October 8.

Garland's concern, however, turned out to be unwarranted, for *Hesper* was widely and for the most part extravagantly praised, collecting more reviews than had any of his previous novels. "'Hesper' represents the best work that Mr. Garland has done," judged the *Dial* in a typical review. "In it he has sloughed off most of the earlier defects of thought and expression; his asperities have become softened, and his rawness has undergone a transformation into something very like urbanity." "*Hesper* is a thrilling romance, a vigorous work of literary art worthy of the author's reputation," offered the *Independent.* Even Howells stayed up until midnight to finish the book, and then wrote to Garland, "It is a fine book, full of a manly poetry, and a high ideal."[8]

With this novel, Garland had finally figured out how to wed his enthusiasm for the West to the romantic plots that readers desired, and worries over the lost income from serialization must have been assuaged when the royalty checks began rolling in. In its first year, *Hesper* sold more than twenty-three thousand copies, earning its author $5,137.38—more than $112,000 in today's dollars—the most he had ever received for a novel, and an achievement he would never repeat for a work of fiction.[9] Garland had arrived: from 1902 to 1904 he was one of Harper's most successful authors. He had now surpassed the earnings of Howells, who earned $3,341 for *Heroines of Fiction* (1901), $3,258 for *The Kentons* (1902), and $3,059 for *The Son of Royal Langbrith*—but neither could match the first-year sales of Booth Tarkington, who would earn $15,645 (62,590 copies) for *Cherry* (1903), or of Katherine Cecil Thurston, who would earn an astonishing $47,153 (163,426 copies) for *The Masquerader* (1904).[10]

His new success as an author certainly came at a propitious time, for his world changed with the birth of his daughter. Immediately, Hamlin became a doting father, filling the pages of his diary with her every advance, noting her first steps, her first words, recording every achievement, no matter how small. As he would later write, "It was a sweet period of my life, one of the most satisfactory of my entire history." But the distractions that come with having an infant in the house soon affected his ability to conceive plots. "The baby is taking a great deal of my time and is a presence in my brain that prevents concentration," he noted. "I would not have her away but she is not conducive to great new work."[11] As his attention turned to his family, he found himself unable to focus the drive that had hitherto made him so prolific. Ironically, the publication of *Captain* and *Hesper* had brought him financial reward and, for the first time, public acclaim. Poised to capitalize on his newfound reputation, which he had been working to achieve for the past fifteen years, he instead turned away, unable to muster enthusiasm for writing. While he would henceforth crank out on average a book each year, they were mostly minor efforts, often written more out of habit than enthusiasm, as he sought a subject that would engage him. For the next twelve years he would flit from one project to another, striving to find something that would rekindle his former interest.

One such project envisioned by this former advocate of the single tax was his dream of acquiring enough land so that he would not have to rely upon his writing for security. In early 1902 his brother wanted him to help underwrite his dream of owning a Mexican plantation. The land cost only a dollar an acre—but the owners wanted to sell the entire fifty-thousand-acre parcel in one lump. Garland attempted to interest a number of his literary friends, among them Irving Bacheller and Albert Shaw, editor of the *Review of Reviews*. He was unable to convince Shaw, and when Franklin contracted yellow fever and nearly died, the venture fell through.[12] When he recovered, Franklin next turned gold speculator and negotiated for the purchase of a Mexican mine. Garland would supply the capital, and Franklin would manage the actual mining operations.

Franklin had landed in the state of Zacatecas, on the flanks of Pico de Teyra near the town of Camacho, about 350 miles southwest of Brownsville, Texas. The region had long been mined for gold and silver, and Franklin had a chance to purchase the El Porvenir ("The Future") mine. He wrote to his brother for help. Garland was interested, and by December 17, 1903, he seems to have supplied funds sufficient to buy into a partnership with three other men already at work at the mine. "If my mine turns out," he noted in his diary, "I will stop writing for a year and see what comes of it."[13]

Franklin and his band of Mexican laborers were extracting ore by chasing the vein from the surface, what Garland would later refer to as "gophering." At the end of January, Franklin sent his brother a progress report. He was optimistic about the percentage of gold in the ore, and though he had been liberal with Garland's bank account, he believed the mine would soon be showing a profit. "The entire mine is concentrating ore running about 20 grams gold and 10 grams silver—and 30% iron," he wrote. "This figures out about $38.00 per ton gross, and cost to concentrate about $6.00 leaving a profit of about $32.00." If the ore did pan out, Franklin explained, they would need to invest six thousand dollars in a stamp mill.[14] Garland's reply must have been vehement and worried, for Franklin chided, "You need not worry! I'm not buying a mill yet. You evidently did not read my letter carefully, and as is your habit you did not refer to it again in answering it. It is not time yet to put in a concentrator, and will not be for some months." He encouraged Garland to attract some investors to help finance the mine and buy out the current ownership, for they "are getting more hard up every day and can be bought out now pretty cheap."[15]

Garland learned in March that Franklin's estimates of profits had been too optimistic. "The high grade ore only runs about $92.00 per ton, gross," Franklin told him, "instead of $400.00 as Ossolinski [an assayer] confidently asserted it would." Nonetheless, Franklin believed that, after labor and freight costs, the mine could still turn a profit—the operation had posted a loss of only two hundred dollars for February.[16]

On April 9 Garland was in Camacho, accompanied by Irving Bacheller and Archer Brown, a Chicago investor. After eighteen miles—and three arduous hours in a donkey cart—they arrived at El Porvenir to survey the diggings for themselves, bedding down that night in Franklin's "cave," a new and memorable experience for the seasoned camper and his wealthy, comfort-loving friends. When morning dawned, the practical-minded Brown took one look at the mine and its environs and dashed the brothers' hopes. "There is no water to work the ore," he told them, "no roads to transport it to the smelter, and the cost of production is more than the ore will bring."[17] In the five months of Franklin's speculation, Garland had sunk $8,132.05 in the mine.[18] Disheartened, he withdrew from the venture.

But the eager land speculator did not give up, for May found him in Oklahoma Territory, where he installed Franklin as his on-site manager of his Oklahoma properties and began buying lots in and near Muskogee. By the end of the year he had accumulated property worth ten thousand dollars.[19] Franklin recalls that the idea was to capitalize on the oil boom getting under way just then: "He bot some Farm Land which we hoped would prove to be Oil bearing, as that was Oil territory, but we found no oil." Later, "he also bot some City lots, and built one Business Bldg., and four Dwelling houses."[20] The investments would, over the years, provide a small but steady income.

Amid his speculations, Garland was seeing another novel to publication. *The Light of the Star* had appeared as a serial in the *Ladies' Home Journal* from January to May 1904, and as soon as the final installment appeared, Harper's issued the book version on May 15. He had begun the story in July 1902 under the title "The Glittering Woman," basing it on his experience with the Boston First Independent Theater Association. The events in the novel closely follow Garland's excursions into the drama. Born in the West, George Douglass is an egotistical architect who dabbles in dramatic criticism. He has won notice for his observations of actors, first published in magazines, and then gathered them into a controversial volume entitled *The Modern Stage*. To demonstrate his theories, Douglass writes an *Under the Wheel*–like play entitled *Lillian's Duty* for the famous romantic actress Helen Merival. The play fails because it "instructs in sociology." Smarting from his critical roasting, he writes another, *Enid's Choice*, and tells Helen, "We will create our own audience."[21] Though calculated to produce "happy tears" in the audience, *Enid's Choice* fails to attract an audience because its characters and especially its acting are too realistic for the public. To make money and to save the reputation of the actress who is staging his plays, Douglass casts aside his principles and writes a costume melodrama, *Allessandra*, which wins the favor of the dramatic managers who had mocked his earlier work. Douglass is saved from having to compromise his principles, however, because, unknown to him until the night of *Allessandra*'s planned opening, *Enid's Choice* has at last succeeded in finding its "thoughtful audience" and is now playing to a full house.

The Light of the Star suggests that Garland's retreat from realism to romance is more closely linked to his failure in the theater than is generally acknowledged. When he began writing plays, Garland was confident of success; his failure embittered him for years. This bitterness is particularly apparent in one diary entry. When the dramatic agent Elizabeth Marbury approached him about having his novels *The Eagle's Heart* and *Her Mountain Lover* adapted for the stage, Garland noted in his diary, "I permitted myself no illusions. Nothing is so shifty as a dramatic manager."[22] Writing *The Light of the Star* gave him the opportunity to vindicate his dramatic ambitions through the creation of an alternative biography; it also allowed him to portray his shift to the more lucrative romance in terms that enabled him to salvage his pride. As Helen Merival tells Douglass when his romantic melodrama *Allessandra* pleases the managers, "We have both made a fight for good work and failed. No one can blame us if we yield to necessity."[23]

But reviewers did blame Garland for betraying his principles, for concocting a sentimental love story with a mild theme of reform and calculated to cater to the public's desire for romance. As an astonished reviewer for the *Chicago Tribune* put it, "We are all doing it! Garland, too—heaven help us all—Garland too!"[24] The novel was scarcely noticed, and after the success of *Hesper*, Garland must have been disappointed in the first year's royalties: $1,730.84.[25] It was a sign of things to come.

By fall Garland was back in New York to negotiate with Harper's for his next novel. But he was wearying of plotting conventional tales of romance and worked only halfheartedly at his manuscripts. He was feeling middle-aged, as he dourly noted being fitted for his first pair of reading glasses: "My daughter will never know her father as a young man." For the first time in twelve years he cast a vote, for his friend Theodore Roosevelt, who was up for reelection.[26] With his interest in fiction waning, he turned toward the organizations that increasingly commanded his attention and energy, further depleting his creative drive.

One of these was the National Institute of Arts and Letters. During a January 1904 meeting, talk turned to how best to raise an endowment so that the organization would have a fund to award prizes for distinguished accomplishment in the arts. The composer Edward MacDowell suggested a membership divided into two classes might better attract donors, and the poet E. C. Stedman proposed selecting that membership from within as a sort of senate and calling it, along the lines of the French Academy, the American Academy of Arts and Letters. During the spring, a labyrinthine procedure for selection was worked out: the 150 institute members would elect the first seven academicians, and these seven in turn would choose eight more; these fifteen would then elect five, and these twenty would choose the final ten members, for a total of thirty (in 1907, to redress the disproportionate number of members in the literature section, membership was expanded to fifty, and in 1908 the institute enlarged to 250). Henry Fuller was characteristically skeptical about the plan, asking, "Will biggening its body give it more reality, when what it needs is a definite endowment of spirit?"[27] On December 2 Garland acted as teller at the meeting that elected the initial seven members. Howells easily led with fifty-three votes, followed by the sculptor Augustus St. Gaudens, Stedman, the painter John LaFarge, Samuel Clemens, Secretary of State John Hay (coauthor of a ten-volume biography of Lincoln), and MacDowell. Sometime during the monthly dinner meetings, the initial reason for the academy's existence—raising an endowment—became submerged beneath the election procedures and self-congratulations of those elected. While the academy was founded to recognize distinguished achievement in art and letters and thus serve as a model for younger artists and writers, its early years were marked by petty squabbling over procedures and purpose—and by elections of new members as the generally elderly academicians died. Later, after he himself was elected to the academy, Garland would make a heroic effort to make it more than an exclusive gentlemen's club.[28]

The other event commanding his attention was a dinner celebrating the twenty-fifth anniversary of the publication of the book that had so influenced his early work, Henry George's *Progress and Poverty*. The purpose of the banquet, which was held on January 24, 1905, at the Astor Hotel, was "to have representative speakers review the influence of 'Progress and Poverty,' and consider the probable future trend of public thought and action." As chairman of the organizing committee and as toastmaster, Garland took charge of invitations and the program. He secured acceptances to speak from William Lloyd Garrison Jr., son of the abolitionist leader; William Jennings Bryan, three-time democratic presidential candidate and later the prosecutor in the Scopes trial; and five others. After the ten-course meal, Garland toasted the speakers as he and three hundred guests heard Garrison speak on the book's "Plea for Justice," Bryan on "Equal Opportunity," and other speakers on its economic, political, and literary influence.[29] One wonders whether Garland, with his lands in Oklahoma and his gold mine in Mexico, was aware of the irony of presiding at a dinner honoring the man who advocated the end of land speculation and whose cause he had championed in his early fiction.

In July he was in Colorado Springs gathering local color about western jails and convicts. He asked the warden of the state penitentiary to lock him in a cell for thirty minutes so he might experience prison life. The minutes dragged into hours, as the warden forgot about him while visiting with friends from the East. Garland endured the jeering of the prisoners, with one convicted murderer taunting, "What the hell are you in for? When are they going to stretch your neck?" Three hours later, the absent-minded turnkey remembered his guest and set the veritist free. Once out, Garland sent the warden a box of cigars and asked him to keep the event quiet. But his escapade was picked up by the *New York Times*, which headlined the front-page story "Hamlin Garland in Cell."[30] If imitation is a sign of influence, Garland's scrape with the law had at least one copycat, inspiring another page-one story: six months later, a shoplifter was apprehended in New York. Her excuse: "Like Hamlin Garland . . . she was getting material for an article on 'How Easy It Is to Steal in a Department Store.'"[31]

Meanwhile, Garland had been working in desultory fashion at his writing. Casting about for ideas, he at last returned to an old enthusiasm, the study of psychic phenomena. Surely there was a theme for a novel in the mysterious rappings of séances and mediums. He reflected on the three most convincing mediums he had interviewed and recognized a pattern: all considered themselves in bondage to the dark forces commanding them and were weary of the constant suspicion and endless testing of debunkers and investigators like Garland himself. And he had mediums in his own family, for both his mother and an aunt had gathered around the séance table. He recalled the words of his aunt, who told him, "For two years these spirit forces made my life a hell," and from that remark he derived his theme and title: *The Tyranny of the Dark*.[32] The story involves a Colorado girl, Viola Lambert, whose parents exploit her psychic ability. Vying for her attentions are a clergyman who has left his church to become a devotee to spiritualism and a skeptical scientist who eventually rescues her from the tyranny of the shadow world.

Garland was initially reluctant to put his psychic interests to fictional use, fearing he would be branded a crank, but with twenty books behind him, an established reputation, and a publisher who believed he was golden, he decided to risk it. He argued that his subject and treatment did not depart in any significant way from his earlier books, writing to his publishers, "I regard this theme as a legitimate and interesting literary problem. 'The Tyranny of the Dark' is based on accurate observation. . . . Every test which I therein describe, I myself have employed." Harper's was persuaded, and the novel was serialized in *Harper's Weekly* from January to May 1905, with the book appearing on May 4, before the final installment appeared on May 13. Reviewers were disappointed with the novel, not because of the subject, but because Garland didn't satisfactorily resolve the problem of whether psychic forces are manifestations of the spirit world or some form of "unexplored biology." While Garland later claimed much interest from readers and quoted pages of approving letters from leading scientists, actual sales were only moderate, with the first year's royalties amounting to $2,162.29—less than half of what he received for *Hesper*.[33]

While in New York correcting the proofs of *Tyranny*, Garland had dined occasionally with his friends Edward and Marion MacDowell. One evening that April, Garland and English publisher John Lane noted that MacDowell appeared to be sick. "His mind wandered and his hands were nerveless," Garland remembered. "He was so little himself that I was shocked and yet his wife seemed not to notice it. . . . All his old time brightness was lost." By November, MacDowell's condition had deteriorated. "Edward is hopelessly insane," Garland recorded.[34] To help Marion in her time of despair, Garland moved into their hotel to assist with his friend's care.

Born in 1860, MacDowell studied in Paris and Frankfurt and so impressed Franz Liszt that the elder composer arranged for the publication of the student's first compositions. After marrying Marion Griswold Nevins, one of his students, MacDowell returned to Boston in 1888, where Garland first heard him perform. MacDowell soon gained a reputation as America's foremost composer with a number of impressionist pieces such as *Woodland Sketches*, *Sea Pieces*, *Fireside Tales*, and *New England Idyls*. MacDowell had admired Garland's comments on music in *Crumbling Idols*, and when they met in 1896 the two found they had much in common: both sought to break with established conventions, both were interested in the application of science to the arts, and both found common ground between painting and their respective arts. In 1896 MacDowell was the obvious choice to become the first professor of music at Columbia University's newly established Department of Music, and Garland made it his practice to call upon his friend whenever he was in the city. A skilled painter himself, MacDowell wanted to establish a school of the arts, believing that the beneficial influence of interdisciplinarity would lead to creativity in all the arts. But he soon ran afoul of academic bureaucracy. When he returned from a sabbatical in 1904 he found that Columbia's new president, Nicholas Murray Butler, had relegated music course offerings to the teacher's college. Amid a furor that found its way to the newspapers, MacDowell resigned.

Garland and his friends attributed MacDowell's nervous collapse to the pressures brought on by his fight with the Columbia bureaucracy. When the composer died in January 1908, his death

certificate listed as cause of death "Paresis (Dementia Paralytica)."[35]
Back in 1905, when MacDowell's growing insanity became obvious,
Garland worked out a plan to aid Marion in creating a memorial
to her husband, writing to Richard Watson Gilder, "A few of us are
forming a 'MacDowell Club' with the purpose of spreading a knowledge of the fine arts and to make a special study of his theories of
music and its relation to the fine arts."[36] Garland quickly drafted
a plan for the organization and wrote its constitution; its purpose
was to carry out MacDowell's dream of promoting "a sympathetic
understanding of the correlation" between "the arts of music, literature, the drama, painting, sculpture, and architecture," and to
"contribute to the broadening of their influence."[37] The club was
incorporated on January 16, 1906, and Garland presided at the first
annual dinner meeting in March. As vice-president of the club he
campaigned on its behalf in the newspapers and in lectures, and by
the close of its second year the MacDowell Club boasted more than
four hundred members. In its first five years the club presented
or sponsored concerts, plays, readings, and exhibitions of painting
and sculpture; funded student scholarships; and formed branch
clubs in sixty-six cities. Its most enduring legacy was contributing
funds to establish in 1907 the MacDowell Colony at the MacDowell
estate in Peterborough, New Hampshire, whose purpose was to provide what MacDowell himself could never find: sanctuary from outside pressures that interfered with creativity. Since its inception the
prestigious retreat has sponsored more than 4,500 individuals in
residence.

By March 1906 Garland had grown tired of bouncing between
Chicago and New York. The practicalities of publishing meant that
he frequently needed to travel to New York to negotiate terms and
to attend to revisions and proofreading, and while ten years before
he had urged Americans to recognize Chicago as the nation's new
literary center, he had long given up that illusion. Aside from the
homestead in West Salem, he had no permanent residence—he
and Zulime would alternate stays in West Salem with renting flats
in Chicago and New York or rooms in hotels—and with an infant

daughter, he wearied of the nomadic life. He pressed Zulime to move, hoping to build near Irving Bacheller's estate in Riverside, Connecticut, but Zulime couldn't bear to leave friends and her brother, sister, and father, the last of whom who had moved to the city in his declining years.

The frequent traveling took its toll on the Garlands' marriage. Hamlin's frequent absences left little time for his family, and when Garland was at home he tended to focus on Mary Isabel rather than Zulime. In May he began to complain of ill health, recording in his diary the onset of chills, an upset stomach, severe headaches, fever, and "sore kidneys"—flu symptoms. Then, abruptly, on May 24, Garland packed his valise for Toronto, where he intended to catch a boat to Liverpool, hoping that the shorter trip would decrease his seasickness. His reasons for going are obscure. He omits any mention of the trip in *A Daughter of the Middle Border*, and in *Companions on the Trail* he writes only that his doctor, "with a fine understanding of my wishes," "ordered" him to go for the sake of his health, for he had been complaining of being "worn down with writing and lecturing."[38] To Zulime he wrote, "I have just been to see Dr Small who examined me and said he thought the trip would do me good." And then he added, "it may do me a lot of good—make me much better to live with. You hope so don't you."[39] One wonders how four months of constant sightseeing, visits with celebrities, and eating unfamiliar foods would have rested the intrepid traveler.

But Mary Isabel suggests another reason why the doting father might have torn himself away from his beloved three-year-old daughter for fifteen weeks. Years later, when she discussed her own marital difficulties with her mother, she learned that Zulime had fallen in love with a man who "was from out of town, dynamic, handsome, vastly rich, with just one idea in the world: to take Zulime away with him." "I was tempted, horribly," Zulime told her daughter. "I had never felt anything like that before. It was as if I were—another person. I couldn't think what to do. Hamlin was away a great deal, lecturing, attending to business in the East." She debated leaving her husband but could not give up her child, and "the thought of robbing Hamlin of the light of his life was intolerable." Thoroughly miserable, she sent her lover away. "It was worse than—dying," she admitted. "The long, empty years seemed to stretch on forever."

When asked whether her husband knew, Zulime replied, "Yes . . . but we have never spoken of it since." Once she had heard her mother's confession, Mary Isabel recalled, "many things about my father became clearer to me. He was a proud, self-centered man. It must have turned his world to dust and ashes."[40] Amid this domestic turmoil, coupled with arguments about whether to move to New York, Garland may have decided that a trip abroad, alone, would allow time for distance to mend broken hearts. As soon as he departed, he regretted the decision: "It came over me again in the night how far I am from my baby—and how foolish to take the risk of losing her. What is the use? Why not stay with her—in my own land." Three days later, he added, "I felt weak and disgusted with myself for coming on this trip."[41] No mention of Zulime in the weeks following.

When Garland returned to his Chicago flat on September 2, it was with a renewed determination to settle down and buy a house in Chicago. But first he needed to replenish the exchequer, for he had deliberately avoided drafting any travel essays to pay for the trip. In July, while in Venice, an idea for a novel had occurred to him. "I think I have a scheme to make the trip pay—Jim and Bessie may take the trip for Lorimer," he wrote to Zulime, referring to George Lorimer, the editor of the *Saturday Evening Post.*[42] He had thought to mine his travel experience for a sequel to *Her Mountain Lover* in which Jim Matteson brings an American perspective to comment on the famous sights of Europe. By October 8 he had grown disillusioned with the novel. "It seems more and more like a dusty thorofare," he reflected. "I am keenly conscious that it has been done before and done better and yet there are pages of comment on Venice, Naples, Carcassone which are true and vital." To make the narrative work, he had to "arrange chance meetings and other co-incidences which I dislike." Although he did complete the work, the result was unsatisfactory, and he seems to have made no effort to publish it.[43]

Garland's fading creative imagination can be seen in his next two novels as he reworked old books. If a sequel to a successful novel would not work, perhaps enlarging shorter ones would. He took *The Spirit of Sweetwater*, an 1897 serial in the *Ladies' Home Journal* published as a slim novelette of one hundred small pages in 1898, and to it added a new opening section, additional scenes, and fairly extensive stylistic revisions, publishing the result as *Witch's Gold* in September 1906. But the enlarged novel was still slim, which his publisher, Doubleday, tried to conceal by printing its 223 pages in a large font with only twenty lines to a page. (By contrast, his Harper's novels averaged thirty lines or more per page and were nearly twice as long.) He next turned to his Klondike adventure and rewrote his travelogue as a juvenile novel for serialization in the *Youth's Companion*. In *The Long Trail* his boy hero follows his own route along the Telegraph Trail but encounters various bad men, enabling Garland to add the thrills of pursuit, escape, and actual mining to the story. When the book appeared in April 1907, it enjoyed only modest sales.[44]

Then, on October 30, three-year-old Mary Isabel fell sick. For ten days Garland watched in agony as she declined, anxiously recording her rising fever. Zulime too was ill. On November 11 the worried father finally realized this was no ordinary illness and ordered his doctor to call in another physician and nurse. When the physician arrived he took one look, diagnosed diphtheria, and asked permission to administer the antitoxin, warning Garland that without it his daughter would not live out the night. Three days later, Garland recorded jubilantly, "The baby will live! . . . The whole world seems renewed." By November 19 she had recovered much of her former health, and Garland, who had put aside the manuscript of a new novel about the power of money to effect change, reflected, "Here is 'money magic' in truth, for with the means to employ the best available medical and nursing skill I have saved my child. Had I been as poor as most farmers are, she would have passed into the shadow never to return to us."[45]

The novel was *Money Magic*, another romance set in Colorado. It would appear as a serial in *Harper's Weekly* from August to October 1907 before coming out in book form in October. This time Garland varied his usual theme of an eastern beauty drawn to a western outdoorsman by drawing upon his own family triangle to write a novel about adulterous love. Mart Haney, a sometime gambler and saloonkeeper who has struck it rich with a gold mine, has fallen for Bertha Gilman, the eighteen-year-old daughter of a poor widow. Bushwhacked by an old enemy who shotguns him, Haney, near death, convinces Bertha to marry him so she'll inherit his money. But he rallies, though his wound leaves him crippled and prematurely aged. Soon, Bertha falls in love with another man and, partly to escape this new temptation, the Haneys travel eastward, where her education is advanced in the bohemian art circles of Chicago and New York. After she is propositioned by a libertine painter who uses his art as a lure, she and Haney flee to the more wholesome Colorado, where Haney, after realizing that Bertha loves another man, in a final act of self-sacrificing love, commits suicide to free her.[46]

Money Magic is unusually complex in its development of character and motivation—by far the best of Garland's novels in terms of psychological development. That may be due in part to his personal awareness of the effects of a love triangle, and Garland avoids the easy melodramatic resolution of casting one man as a villain: both lovers have much to recommend them; both are fundamentally good people. Bertha's quandary—whether to remain with the man whose money provides for her care, a man who wholeheartedly loves and depends upon her, or to leave to pursue her soul's passion—is convincingly sketched and realistically presented. While the *New York Times* claimed it to be "the best novel that has come from his pen"—a claim echoed by the *Bookman*, which also praised it as "far and away the best and most significant novel that Mr. Garland has written in many years"—the damage had already been done by the mediocre novels that had dribbled out since *Hesper*. Few newspapers or magazines bothered to review the novel, and sales were sluggish.[47]

Mary Isabel's brush with death renewed her father's determination to buy a house in Chicago, for Garland wanted no more of West Salem's isolation. In December 1907 he found a house, a narrow, three-story building at 6427 Greenwood Avenue in the neighborhood of Woodlawn, just a few blocks south of the University of Chicago. Once more, the move came at a propitious time: Zulime was pregnant again.

16

"A BORN PROMOTER," 1907–14

On June 18, 1907, just nine months after Garland had returned from Europe, and despite his vow at the time of Mary Isabel's birth not to put his wife through the trauma again, a second daughter was born. The new parents could not immediately agree on a name for the infant, and her birth certificate recorded "no name female Garland." Henry Fuller was appalled at the delay in naming the infant, and he later told her, "when you were quite new I looked you over and told your undecided parents that they were at liberty—a mighty narrow liberty—to choose between 'Lucy' and 'Constance.' They wisely chose the latter."[1] Whether intended or not, the baby's name symbolized the new constancy of her parents' marriage. Unlike Mary Isabel, little Constance was a fussy, sickly baby with an allergy to milk that caused her to cry continuously for months. Tired of the endless wailing, Garland withdrew from the infant, much preferring to indulge the companionship he had developed with his elder daughter. His diary largely ignores his youngest daughter: in the weeks after her birth he continues to list Mary Isabel's daily achievements—even her nickname for her sister, "Marjorie Christmas," after her two favorite words—but of Constance, whose name doesn't appear until December 18 in the diary, he recorded only that she "seems to be coming along very nicely but does not appeal to me the way Mary Isabel did. She is quite a different girl—I dont see why she should be but she is."[2]

Soon, he came to play favorites. Mary Isabel remembers her father telling her mother, "This is *my* child," drawing her near. "The other is *your* child."[3] In his memoirs, Garland admits he largely ignored Constance, because spending more time with her would mean "neglecting her sister whose comradeship with me had been so close. . . . A second child is—a second child." Only later, after she outgrew her allergy and ceased crying, would he begin to record his second daughter's accomplishments. Constance's daughter believes that her grandfather's "rejection of my mother as a sickly infant, toddler, and young child left her emotionally scarred for a lifetime," that her mother spent much of her childhood seeking her father's approval, and that Garland did not pay much attention to her until Constance was twelve and he discovered she could draw.[4] Later, Constance would take "Hamlin" for her middle name in an attempt to attract her father's attention.

Zulime's pregnancy and Hamlin's subsequent decision to remain in Chicago ended, for a time, his desire to move to New York. But Garland missed the congenial association of creative folk at the Players, MacDowell, National Arts, and other New York clubs. Although he has been derided as an inveterate clubman—even his friend Henry Fuller once called him a "club carpenter and joiner"—clubs were as necessary to his craft as pen and ink.[5] He did not work well in isolation, and he relied on the stimulation provided by other writers and artists—he once remarked, "I need the aid of dignified surroundings and appreciative friends in order to keep up my 'illusion of grandeur.'"[6] Then, too, he never forgot the lesson he had learned in Iowa at the monthly Grange meetings—that social organizations, formed to improve the common good while also providing pleasant company, can do as much for social and artistic achievement as any overt political activity—a guiding principle for every organization he had joined since youth. For Garland, clubs and their activities were a key means of uplifting the arts, a way to put into action the principles he had advocated in *Crumbling Idols* and from the lecture platform. As Mary Isabel once observed, "Daddy was a born promoter"—once an idea caught fire, he couldn't rest until he had striven to bring it into existence.[7]

Because the birth of his second daughter discouraged his idea of moving to New York, Garland came up with a plan of bringing to Chicago a club that would emulate the Players. On June 6 he met with Taft, Fuller, Clarkson, Browne, and others to plan the club.

Provisionally naming the group the Midland Arts Association, they drafted a prospectus and sent letters of invitation to the male members of the Little Room. "Broadly speaking," Garland explained, "this club will bring together men of artistic and literary tastes who are now widely scattered among the various social and business organizations of Chicago, and unite them with the artists, writers, architects and musicians of the city in a club whose purposes are distinctly and primarily aesthetic."[8] Over the summer, as responses from interested invitees arrived, the details were worked out. Early on, to enhance the club's exclusivity, Garland proposed limiting membership to 250 resident members and dividing the membership into two classes: professional workers in the arts and "lay" members who were distinguished in some other field but who tended to be wealthy bankers, businessmen, and other patrons of art. Though his avowed purpose was simply to provide a congenial place for creative people to congregate, the practical effect was to bring together artists and those with the money and power to support artistic endeavor. Although the purpose of the club was not to promote the arts, it did so nonetheless though its collegial atmosphere and the interaction of its members.

The question of a name for the club soon dominated planning meetings. Earlier, in 1895, Garland had been part of a similar effort to form a Chicago club for creative folk when Herbert Stone founded the Attic Club, named for its plan to secure a headquarters at the top of a building, where rents were cheapest, for elevators were not then in wide use. Though a charter member, Garland resigned within a month of its founding because of disagreement over the procedure to elect members, and apparently the club foundered too.[9] Since the new club also intended to take lodgings on the upper floors and counted among its members a number from the original Attic Club, on August 13 they hurriedly incorporated under the name "The Attic Club" in order to make a deadline for filing legal papers.[10] But Garland wanted to distinguish this club from the earlier effort, and at the next meeting he proposed a change in name—to the Cliff Dwellers—which the ninety-five members present adopted unanimously.[11] Most accounts of the club explain that

Garland proposed the name to honor his friend Henry Fuller, whose novel by that name examines life among Chicago's tall buildings. And Garland himself fostered that notion in his memoirs. But the name originated in its founder's love for the cliff-dwelling Indians, as early press accounts of the club's founding explain.[12] Indian-themed accoutrements dominated the club's appointments and ceremonies, from the name of its central room (the Khiva) to decorations on its tableware to its gavel (a war club) to its opening ceremonies, which included Indian costumes, poems, and pipe-and fire-lighting rituals. Garland no doubt played up the double reference in homage to his friend, who, though listed among the charter members, soon withdrew and thereafter never set foot in the place.[13]

One December evening, while dining with John O'Hara Cosgrave, the editor of *Everybody's Magazine*, Garland regaled the guests with tales of his psychic experiences. After observing the rapt attention of the guests, Cosgrave asked Garland to write a series of articles for the magazine. On December 27 Garland began drafting *The Shadow World*, an account of his psychic investigations in Boston and elsewhere. To make the story cohere, he cast the events of his *Psychical Review* articles in conversational form, giving fictional names to the principals but retaining himself as chief participant. In March he was in Indianapolis at the home of his friends John and Mary Judah. He had received word of an amazing psychic who not only did not enter the trancelike state in darkened rooms so common among mediums, but instead held séances in daylight and dispensed with trumpets and other accoutrements. His friend Edward MacDowell had finally succumbed to his illness on January 23, 1908, and, looking for material to flesh out the "Shadow World" series, Garland proposed an attempt to contact MacDowell's spirit. Armed with fresh slates and a receptive attitude, for three hours he watched as mysterious lines, some appearing to be the signature "E. A. McDowell" (without the *a*) and the suggestive "Isinghere," appeared on the slates. Garland was accompanied by Fuller, who was more skeptical than Garland but also could read music and play the piano. In another session, in response to Garland's request for some bars from MacDowell's uncompleted *Tragic Sonata*, musical notes appeared on the slates.

At the direction of the slates and "MacDowell's" whispers, Garland and Fuller labored mightily to complete the sonata. Garland was convinced he had finally found the proof of individual survival he had long been looking for—until he saw a framed photograph at the MacDowell home bearing the variant signature and Marion dismissed the composition as being uncharacteristic of her husband's work. Perhaps the psychic was reading Garland's mind rather than communicating with the dead? Garland chalked this up to another puzzle from the fourth dimension.[14]

But the experience, in exhaustive detail, went into the series. *The Shadow World* was serialized in *Everybody's* from April to September 1908, and immediately letters recounting similar experiences began pouring in. Confronted with this obvious sign of readerly interest, Garland and Cosgrave decided to sponsor a contest "to encourage practical experiment, and to further a cold, keen, calculating analysis of spiritualistic phenomena." Although they received hundreds of submissions, few "were conducted systematically, with careful notations at the time of the happenings."[15] In November 1908, four of the six winning essays appeared in *Everybody's*. When the book appeared in October, reviewers were either dismissive ("[who would have] dreamed that a man of his intelligence, ability, and experience could have written it") or resoundingly supportive ("Every detail of this remarkable experience is well worth reading"), reflecting the popular division over the veracity of psychic phenomena.[16]

While his interest in fiction flagged, Garland returned to an earlier enthusiasm and began devoting more evenings to the theater. Among his favorite performers were the Donald Robertson Players, who were then presenting an ambitious program of European plays, most of which had never before been staged in the United States. Robertson interested Garland because Robertson's dramatic ambitions so clearly reflected his own. A Scottish immigrant, Robertson first acted in the companies of Lester Wallack, Kate Claxton, Dion Boucicault, and Steele MacKaye, and he later toured with Mary Shaw's troupe presenting Ibsen's plays. As Garland had done in Boston, Robertson sought to cultivate an appreciation for "intellectual" drama that disengaged itself from the standard melodramatic and social comedy fare of the commercial theater.

Robertson believed that audiences remained bound to the commercial theater because they were not aware of the variety of drama available; he therefore designed his first season's repertoire as an educational smorgasbord. The seventeen plays, presented in eight months in nearly two hundred performances, included dramas by Molière, Ibsen, Hauptmann, Maeterlinck, Bjornson, Gogol, and others. By exposing audiences to the variety of "literary" drama, Robertson hoped to encourage a taste for more intellectual plays. As part of his educational program, he extended performances to college audiences at the universities of Chicago, Michigan, Illinois, Wisconsin, Minnesota, and Indiana and to Northwestern University.

By most accounts, this first season was a critical though not a popular success. For the 1908 season Robertson gained the backing of Ira Nelson Morris, a millionaire meatpacker, to subsidize the theater. Freed from financial worry, Robertson included four new American plays as part of his program to encourage native drama, among them Garland's *Miller of Boscobel*, a play Hamlin had been working on intermittently since 1892 and which had been inspired by the events of the Homestead Strike of that year.[17]

Miller of Boscobel is the culmination of Garland's efforts to write an American version of the "play of ideas" in the form of a protest melodrama that anticipates the open-ended resolutions of contemporary drama. Set in Marvinsburg, a representative factory town, the play opens in the library of Lillian Warner, a recent widow who has inherited the Warner Mills. Amid declining profits, the factory owners have begun to squeeze the workers by cutting hours and pay. Faced with potential starvation, the workers organize an industry-wide labor alliance suggestive of the International Workers of the World. When "Anarchist" Jay Miller, the leader of the impending strike, calls on Warner to beg her not to join the Employer's Trust and lock out her employees, they recognize each other as having been lovers when Miller was studying for the ministry in the idyllic Boscobel, Wisconsin. Moved by his account of the desperate plight of the workers as winter approaches, Warner agrees not to join the Employer's Trust, even though she is being pressured to do so by General Marvin, the powerful owner of the Marvin Mills and the play's designated villain. As the lone holdout from the Employer's Trust, Warner is flooded with displaced workers and struggles to keep them employed, while General Marvin, true to his threats, has cut off her supplies. The conflict between labor and capital is heating up, and both sides threaten armed resistance.

In the last act, the situation has deteriorated. Marvin's mill is an armed camp, Warner's mill has been destroyed by arson, and Miller is brought to Marvin's mill under arrest. Suddenly, a series of explosions rocks the building, and Sarah Schmidt, a foreign radical armed with a bomb, throws herself at Marvin's feet. In a gesture of self-sacrifice, Miller saves Marvin by grabbing Schmidt, whose grasp on the bomb he cannot break, and throws her into another room, where the bomb explodes. Miller is killed, and the curtain descends with the closing line, "Labor has slain its one loyal leader."[18]

Designed to explore the current debate over the competing demands of capital and labor, *Miller of Boscobel* is the most dramatically effective play Garland wrote. In constructing a play of ideas, he succeeded in depicting the conflicting motivations of his characters rather than assigning a single motivational cause as he had done in his earlier protest play, *Under the Wheel.* Through its discussion of the place of sentiment in business, the play questions whether the conflict between capital and labor can ever result in justice for the laborer.

Garland's extensive diary notations concerning *Miller of Boscobel* reveal how much a successful production mattered to him. No other manuscript receives this much comment in his diaries—his typical notation records only his progress with or completion of a manuscript, but seldom any difficulty in the composition itself. Yet Garland was never confident of success, as he wrote five days before the first production: "I spent nearly the entire day helping at a rehearsal of 'Miller of Boskobell,' my play. It is pretty intense but I do not see any success for it. Some of the people read it beautifully. Others were hard or soft according to their nature."[19]

The public reception of the play, however, was better than Garland had hoped, although the reviewers' comments are more indicative of public attitudes toward the theater in general than of the merits of *Miller of Boscobel*. The play was presented in two tryouts in Madison and Appleton, Wisconsin, on January 29 and 30, 1909, and then at Fullerton Hall at the Art Institute of Chicago on February 3. The circumstances of the first production were unfavorable, for a howling blizzard in Madison kept many people at home and the company played to a house only one-third full. Reviewing the first production, the *Wisconsin State Journal* noted the initial nervousness of the actors and praised the acting of Robertson (Miller) and Marion Redlich (Warner). "There is a fineness of quality and lofty purpose in Mr. Garland's dialogue that commands the attention of the cultured among the audience," the reviewer observed. "He shows a wonderful range of sympathy, understanding and sentiment." However, the reviewer betrays his unfamiliarity with plays of ideas, preferring more traditional melodramatic fare with its ranting villains and neatly encapsulated moral lessons—the very thing Garland had labored so hard to make less obvious: "The two crying needs of 'Miller of Boskobell' are, definite action, and a bit of light comedy. William Owen, an actor of worth, plays Gen. Marvin, the head of the trust, and his character is the only one that clearly and distinctly stands unhampered to the brain. Mr. Garland could make his meaning, his lesson, definite so that every theatre goer would carry away with him the text of a lesson learned."[20] Snow delayed the company's arrival at Appleton, so the play didn't get under way until 9:30; however, the audience waited, and Garland "sat in front and took notes and set my wits to work to smooth the play out."[21] The reviewer of this production was more appreciative of Garland's intentions but wished for "possibly another love entanglement." For the conclusion, however, the reviewer had nothing but praise: "Here is where Garland's powers shine at their best. It is artistic, moving, overwhelming as a grand orchestral crash. As reflecting the grim tragedy of labor the play is a masterly piece of work, not grotesquely overdone as are some of its kind, and ending in the triumph of justice and right."[22]

After these tryouts, Garland was eager for a good show in Chicago, where his friends would be in the audience; moreover, *Miller of Boscobel* was the first modern realistic American play Robertson staged, and a successful production would, they hoped, encourage additional American plays and therefore fulfill Garland's long ambition to pioneer a modern American drama. But given the previous performances, Garland was practical enough not to set his hopes too high. As he confided to his diary, "A big crowd came to see the play[,] many more than could get in. I was not much excited by the event, in fact I had made up my mind beforehand that the audience would not care for it, and that the critics would 'nail' it. It held the audience to the end, held them very still and tense. No one went away—not one—before the curtain fell but I am not sure that they went away pleased. Zulime and my close circle of friends were much affected by this play but that of course proves nothing as to its larger appeal."[23] In a lengthy review for the *Chicago Tribune*, Burns Mantle concurred with Garland's perception of the play's effect on the audience, but he also identified what had long been bothering Garland: "His trouble has been in clouding his original intention with too many incidents and in blanketing his theme in an effort to keep all angles of the story in view." After observing that it seemed as though Garland "practically began a new play with each act," Mantle concluded that the play is therefore "forced to depend on its incidents, its characters, and its dialogue rather than a cumulative interest in its plot. These are not sufficiently strong to stand the strain and hence it falls apart." And in what must have particularly wounded the old veritist, Mantle concluded, "Mr. Garland also is inclined to make his characters more fanciful than real and his dialogue bookish rather than natural."[24]

After this lukewarm critical reception, Robertson returned the play to Garland for further revision. During the month of February Garland attempted to improve the third act, noting in his diary that "I tried very hard to raise it all to a higher level. I fear it can not be done & it is essentially a labor play and I can't make it anything else." He enlisted the aid of Fuller, who helped condense the second and third acts and outlined a synopsis for another. By March 9 Garland had given up, and he withdrew the manuscript.[25]

While expending his creative energy in the Cliff Dwellers and his play, Garland struggled to find something to write about that would engage his imagination. For an author who had formerly published dozens of stories, articles, and books each year, the years 1909 through 1912 marked a creative descent. In January 1909 his contracts with Macmillan expired, and he bought the plates and unsold stock of his five Macmillan books and transferred them to Harper and Brothers, who next year would issue *Other Main-Travelled Roads*, a culling of the best selections from *Prairie Folks* and *Wayside Courtships*, whose publisher, D. Appleton, had since entered bankruptcy.[26] In mining his back file, he resurrected "The Land of the Straddle-Bug," a tale of adultery on the Dakota prairie that had appeared in the *Chap-Book* in 1894. After polishing its sentences, he sent it off to Harper's, who published it in September as *The Moccasin Ranch*. At least one reader thought Garland's tendency to reissue old work in new covers wasn't cricket and wrote to the *New York Times* to protest. He noted the prior publication of *Moccasin Ranch* and *Witch's Gold* and asked, "One wonders to just what extent things of this sort are legitimate."[27]

His ambition revived slightly with *Cavanagh, Forest Ranger*, published in March 1910. Garland had long been interested in the growing conservation movement, particularly in his beloved West, and in the past he had campaigned to establish a national park in Colorado.[28] For this novel he created a forest ranger hero who, amid a standard love subplot, intercedes in the growing conflict between cattle ranchers and sheep ranchers, both of whom want to exploit the forests and grasslands for their own use without regard for the future. With topical references to Roosevelt, his forestry policies, and especially to the nation's chief forester, Gifford Pinchot (who was fired by Roosevelt's successor, Taft—an event grafted to the plot of the novel), Garland hoped his novel would tap into the public's interest in the political controversy. He even secured an introduction to the novel by Pinchot. Although the novel enjoyed good sales, Garland's waning interest in writing fiction, particularly in composing the love plots demanded by readers of popular fiction, was now painfully evident. Then, too, he had allowed himself to be bullied by his publisher, who wanted the book in time for the spring list.[29] For

Garland, disengaged from romantic fiction and fearing he was written out, the few months he spent drafting the novel caused him to hurry the action and compress his theme—a fact Howells was quick to point out: "You might indeed have made more of it; you had most interesting people in hand and a prodigious scene, and I wish you had given us the drama of the epoch more deeply and largely than you have done." He then gently pointed Garland back to the true path: "One day, I hope you will revert to the temper of your first work, and give us a picture of the wild life you know so well on the lines of 'Main-Traveled Roads.' You have in you greater things than you have done, and you owe the world which has welcomed you the best you have in you. 'Be true to the dream of thy youth'—the dream of an absolute and unsparing 'veritism'; the word is yours."[30]

In his reply two days later, Garland acknowledged the truth of Howells's judgment, for it accorded with his own:

> I have *not* measured up to my opportunity but perhaps waiting would have been of no avail. The plain truth is I watched the Forestry Service develop for sixteen years and it was only last summer that the motive to use it came. I'm running low on motives. I don't care to write love-stories or stories of adventure and I can not revert to the prairie life without falling into the reminiscent sadness of the man of fifty.
>
> My own belief is that my work is pretty well done but as I remember the cordial endorsement of men like yourself and Gilder I have no reason to complain. I have had in way of honor (and pay) all I deserve—probably. I am dissatisfied only on the artistic side. Why does not our literature tally with the big things we do as a people? I had hopes of doing it once but that was only the foolish egotism of youth.[31]

Perhaps out of kindness to his friend, Howells did not review *Cavanagh.*

Early in February 1911, Robertson met Garland at the Cliff Dwellers to tell him about his new plans to establish an art theater in Chicago.

The result of this discussion—the establishment of the Chicago Theater Society—was to sap Garland's creative energy and imagination for the next two years to the exclusion, as Garland would note repeatedly in his diary, of more remunerative work. Organized along the lines of the group he had founded in Boston in 1891, the First Independent Theater Association, the Chicago Theater Society clearly reflected Garland's interests and agenda. As a guarantee organization rather than as a producing company, the society hoped to avoid the financial and management problems that had plagued the Robertson Players. It was composed of about one hundred subscribers who established a fund sufficient to cover the expenses of a season of ten weeks. Previous attempts to establish a noncommercial theater had foundered in part because the manager had to look after the financial management of the theater as well as the details of production; the society therefore contracted with the Shubert Brothers, who would take over the business end of the theater and thereby enable the manager to concentrate on the plays. The society would submit a list of thirty plays to the Shuberts, of which the Shuberts would select ten for production in the Shubert-owned Lyric Theater by the Drama Players, headed by Robertson, and guarantee "the productions as satisfactory in every respect." In turn, the society would guarantee "about $7000 a week to cover all expenses."[32]

Garland's only published comment about his involvement in the Chicago Theater Society appears in *Companions on the Trail*, where Hamlin dismisses his role as secretary as a passing whim: "I should not have accepted this position, but I did. I saw in it a chance for diversion."[33] His extensive diary notations concerning his participation in the society, however, belie this posture of nonchalance. For more than two and a half years he meticulously noted his daily activities as he vigorously promoted the society. Elected chairman of the committee of organization on April 27, 1911, Garland began to solicit potential donors for the guarantee fund as well as to draft the prospectus. On May 11 he became the society's corresponding secretary and began a flurry of correspondence with playwrights who hoped to have their plays chosen by the society, issued publicity releases to the Chicago papers, wrote to other repertory theaters to arrange performances under the society's auspices, and acted as liaison between the Shuberts and the society.

By mid-July a serious rift had developed concerning the choice of plays, brought about by the competing interests of the members, Robertson and Garland in particular. In a review of the first season, the *Dial* noted that "The Society was formed, not to take chances with untried material, but to present works of approved merit and unquestionable significance."[34] Robertson, as dramatic director, wanted more decision-making authority and wished to continue staging the great plays of Europe, as he had been doing in his former company, the Robertson Players. Garland, however, saw the Chicago Theater Society as his best chance to prove his long-held theory that American authors had not achieved prominence because commercial considerations led managers to favor plays with proven audience appeal. In drawing up a tentative list of plays for consideration, Garland had leaned heavily toward American authors, and in particular plays by his good friends William Vaughn Moody (*The Faith Healer*, 1909), Augustus Thomas (*Arizona*, 1899), and James Herne (*Shore Acres*, 1892). Garland prematurely leaked his proposed list to the press before the society had made the final selection; in response, Robertson gave his list to James O'Donnell Bennett of the *Chicago Record-Herald*. The resulting controversy nearly shattered the fledgling society. "The Chicago Theater Society is finding Donald Robertson difficult—and my duties as secretary are to be unpleasant I fear," Garland recorded in his diary on July 12.[35] He wrote to Robertson and chastised him for what he saw as Robertson's deviation from the goals of the society. In response, Robertson fired off two angry letters to Garland protesting what he felt to be Garland's usurpation of his position as dramatic director.

To settle their differences, Garland, with business secretary Arthur Bissell and treasurer Frank Logan, conferred with the society's president, Edith McCormick, the daughter of John D. Rockefeller and wife of businessman Harold McCormick, who then became a member of the play selection committee to resolve the issue. Their decision: add eight more plays to the list of thirty, these eight plays presumably satisfactory to Robertson.[36] Garland left for Greeley, Colorado, soon after this meeting, but matters had deteriorated so badly that he contemplated resigning. As he wrote to Logan, "I am writing Mrs. McCormick to say that if she has anyone in mind to represent her, who thinks the production of American plays less important than the production of foreign plays, I shall be very glad to resign. If my theories prove to be a source of friction to the Society, and if the Board think that the guarantors are not in sympathy with what I am trying to bring about, I certainly will withdraw. It may be that I misjudge the temper of our members."[37] The repercussions of this squabble were greater than those involved anticipated. After learning of the many grievances in the newspapers, the public—and especially the critics—became confused about the society's purpose. Depending upon whose list they read, reviewers wrote that the society would produce either intellectual, "highbrow" drama, American plays, or the best plays of the Continent.

Hoping to eliminate the confusion, Garland sent a letter to the *Nation* and to the *Chicago Record-Herald*. Echoing statements he had made in Boston so long ago, he wrote,

> It is our plan to present the most unconventional and truthful comedy obtainable, but it is not easy to make up a programme. . . . Personally (and as the secretary of the society) I am more profoundly concerned with the question of how this organization can be of use to the American dramatist who wishes to write character plays without the "arm of coincidence." . . .
>
> It may be that we are mistaken, but we believe there are plays of this character already written (and, perhaps, thrice refused by managers who must consider their "stars"), and that a repertory stage would furnish a hearing for such pieces. It may be that we are being cheated of plays which would be a credit to our literature and a joy to the theatre-goer. Anyhow, that is my own belief. It cannot be that we are so lacking in observation and invention as to be obliged to borrow all of our high-class comedy from the old world.[38]

Garland's letter ended the controversy, for the reviewers now understood that the society's aim was not to "exploit the esoteric drama, or the drama of the cult," or to revive plays that had failed in the commercial theater. Moreover, "It is not, most emphatically not, to stage American plays because they are the work of American writers . . . irrespective of those broad standards of excellence that alone should determine selection," as the *Dial* wrote.[39] Other reviewers praised the society—and Garland in particular—for seeking to foster new plays by American playwrights. Responding to Garland's letter in his July 22 column in the *Chicago Evening Post*, Frederick Hatton declared, "Mr. Garland's stand seems to us to be characterized by the element of vision which the enterprise must have if it is to be progressive. A program given over entirely to revivals means that we shall go back to the ancient and honorable American theatrical occupation of marking time. So long as we do that we shall remain provincial in all things dramatic."[40] The tone of all these columns was that of high expectation: the reviewers were eager for the society to succeed, and an extensive and interesting dialogue took place in the letters columns, with such luminaries as Walter Prichard Eaton, Barrett H. Clark, and Constance Skinner suggesting plays for the society to sponsor.[41]

Finally, on August 18 the society announced its selection of seven plays by foreign authors: *The Learned Ladies* (Molière), *The Thunderbolt* (Pinero), *The Lady from the Sea* (Ibsen), *The Stronger* (Giacosa), *The Passing of the Torch* (Hervieu), *The Coffee House* (Goldoni), and *The Voysey Inheritance* (Granville-Barker; subsequently dropped). It would also produce three plays by Americans, to be announced at a later date.[42]

Garland embarked upon an extensive, time-consuming search for three American plays that would illustrate his theories. He wrote to Augustus Thomas, who agreed to write a play specifically for the society, but prior commitments later caused him to decline. Plays began pouring in from authors responding to the society's play contest, but Garland found few of them satisfactory. As he explained during an interview about the contest,

The plays thus far submitted seemed to lack the individuality, the self-expressive quality, which the society is seeking. . . .

Of course, we are not hoping for masterpieces in this early stage of the movement, though we will call the man blessed who gives us one. We are eager for a play that is significant, whether it be in one or five acts. In short, the executive committee has agreed that its stage shall be open to the most self-expressive, the most original, and the most American of dramatists. . . . We have already found good reason to believe that there is an intellectual stirring among American dramatists which will soon result in work as significant of our own time and people as that of the young dramatists who have been associated with the Abbey theater of Dublin and the Court theater of London.[43]

Garland went to New York in September and spent six days at the Shubert office reading plays. Clearly exhausted by his task, he noted in his diary, "I went back to the club very tired and not at all willing to go to the theater or anywhere else." He later added to this entry the note, "I have a feeling that I am wasting my time in an unworthy position. Why should I be Secretary of the Chicago Theater Society? I decided to go home at once."[44] By December the play selection committee had chosen the American plays. Two—*Gold*, by Ancella Hunter, and *June Madness*, by Henry K. Webster—had been rejected by commercial theaters; *The Maternal Instinct*, by Robert Herrick and Harrison Rhodes, was written expressly for the society.[45]

Despite much earnest boosting by the Chicago papers, the Chicago Theater Society had consistent difficulty in attracting audiences to its productions. After a series of tryouts in New York and other cities to mixed reviews, the Drama Players opened in Chicago with Molière's *The Learned Ladies* on February 5, 1912. "Robertson and his company succeeded in over-turning the feeling of distrust," Garland recorded in his diary. "They pleased the audience with a classic comedy and that is something to say. There was a fine audience and many curtain calls. I was immensely relieved."[46] Two days later, however, he noted that the audience was dwindling, and his daily notations depict his despair as he realized that, for play after play, the subscribers turned out in force for the openings but few people came for subsequent productions. On March 8 the board of directors met and decided to reduce ticket prices in hope of attracting students. The strategy proved ineffective, however, as Garland noted on March 13, "The Drama Players are doing no business at all. I feel we are in for it." By the season's end, it was clear to all those involved that, as Garland put it, "nothing we do can win an audience. We've lost our chance—if we ever had any."[47]

The reasons for this failure to interest an audience can be traced, as Robert Morss Lovett explained in his review of the season, to the poor selection of plays. The society was formed to offer the best plays of Europe and America, plays that would demonstrate the highest standards of craftsmanship, innovation, and intellectual content, yet the plays chosen were "unprepossessing" and "already memories," "already out of date."[48] Moreover, the *Dial* noted, entrusting the selection of plays to a committee perverted "the singleness of aim which was absolutely imperative" and promoted "the confusion that comes from compromise, and working at cross-purposes, and the effort to reconcile conflicting views."[49] Of the American plays, only *June Madness* created any audience support. However, the *Dial* questioned whether this play "came within the scope of the Society's endeavors," for its sensational treatment of illicit love merely replicated what could be found in the commercial theaters. The result was more confusion, for the public could not "understand how the declared objects of the Society were being furthered" by this play. Lovett also observed that other theater groups were offering plays in Chicago that better illustrated the society's aims; the production of *The Playboy of the Western World* by the visiting Irish Players in particular showed what a small theater could—and should—do.[50]

Although the Drama Players did not succeed in attracting a substantial audience, their failure did provide a valuable lesson in theater management. Garland and his associates proved that enough people were interested in alternative theater to support one on a subscription basis, and their publicity activities on its behalf succeeded in educating the public about the aims of an art theater. Critics were united in praising the quality of the acting and particularly the Drama Players' departure from the "star" system, with its emphasis on personality, in favor of the ensemble. Moreover, although the society's board of directors and the Shuberts were understandably concerned about the return on their investment, the society did not fare too badly when their losses are compared to those suffered by the Chicago and New York Little Theater ventures. As one reviewer noted, receipts amounted to "about fifty per cent of the sums pledged by them. This is not a bad outcome for the first season of what was confessedly an experimental enterprise."[51]

Faced with the fact that their own Drama Players were not attracting an audience, the society decided to dissolve the Drama Players and to sponsor other theater groups for the 1912–13 season. The society's new goals were to bring to Chicago "plays of artistic merit and interest" and "to organize all the people of the city who are interested in such plays."[52] In this new purpose the society was remarkably successful. Over the next two years, Chicagoans were able to see an astounding variety of dramas, ranging from the classics to the most recent innovations of Europe to American regional drama. New York's Coburn Players produced *Electra*, *Iphigenia*, and *Macbeth*; Winthrop Ames's reorganized New Theater (New York) offered Schnitzler's *Anatol*; the society sponsored the Hull House Players in *The Tragedy of Nan*, *Justice*, and *The Pigeon*; Dublin's Abbey Players appeared for four weeks in twenty-two plays; the Horniman Players of Manchester presented four weeks of classical and modern English comedy; the Wisconsin Dramatic Society offered four short plays, including Zona Gale's *Neighbors*; the society also sponsored individual productions of Stanley Houghton's controversial *Hindle Wakes* and George Hazelton and J. H. Benrimo's *The Yellow Jacket*, a play inspired by the conventions of Chinese theater; finally, B. Iden Payne, the former stage director of the Manchester Players, began his long and distinguished career in America by offering a repertory of plays under the society's auspices.[53]

As early as 1892 Garland had prophesied the role of the independent theater in overcoming commercialism on the American stage, telling an interviewer for the *Chicago Daily News* that the independent theater "should aim at the encouragement of American drama. It should be a school to educate the public as well as the dramatist and the actor."[54] That he consistently overestimated public receptivity for noncommercial theater and did not sufficiently appreciate the amount of dramatic education necessary for his ambitions to succeed is one of the great ironies of his career. Although his first effort, the Boston First Independent Theater Association, did not achieve its aims, the Chicago Theater Society provided a wealth of data about theater management and advertising, play selection and ensemble acting, that both encouraged other theater groups and focused public attention upon the little theater ideal. Innovators learned from the society's example to emphasize the importance of the director's unified artistic vision and to take risks with the choice of plays, rather than attempting to play it safe with a repertory governed by committee decisions that both pandered to commercial needs and simultaneously sought to uplift the masses. Garland was a key player in this historical moment, and although he was too embittered by the society's immediate failure to understand or appreciate his role, he was largely responsible for the society's direction and influence.

In the midst of his involvement with the theater, Garland had turned to another pot-boiling novel, once again mining his interest in the occult for material. In *Victor Ollnee's Discipline* (1911) he tells the story of the son of a medium who is "disciplined" by spirits for his lack of belief. After undergoing a series of punishments orchestrated by vindictive voices, including public ridicule, sickness, and eventually the death of his mother, who becomes a martyr for her belief, the titular hero resolves to believe but hopes that the voices will henceforth leave him alone. Reviewers were unkind and dismissed the novel as spiritualistic propaganda, with the *New York Times* mourning, "There was a time when Hamlin Garland could write a good story, when he was looked upon as the Western hope of American fiction," and lamenting his novels' "steadily deteriorating quality." While the novel may be defensible as a tract, the reviewer concluded, "as fiction it is deplorable." Sales were tepid, with the fewest sold of any of his Harper's books.[55] Garland was so embarrassed by the novel that in all the volumes of his reminiscences, including *Forty Years of Psychic Research*, he nowhere mentioned the book.

Garland had long desired that outward manifestation of affluence and influence—the collected edition—and in December 1911, with a faith in its author's popularity that belied the tepid sales of *Victor Ollnee's Discipline*, Harper's published the Sunset Edition, eight volumes of Garland's best work: *Main-Travelled Roads, Rose of Dutcher's Coolly, The Eagle's Heart, The Captain of the Gray-Horse Troop, Hesper, Money Magic, Cavanagh, Forest Ranger,* and *Other Main-Travelled Roads.* The edition was sold as a set, with a subscription to three Harper periodicals, for thirteen dollars, and Garland agreed to accept a fifty-cent royalty for each set, a decision that, more than any other of recent years, set his books before the public, for by June 30, 1915, Harper's had sold 26,417 sets.[56] Knowing his critical standing needed a boost, Garland asked Howells to write an article about his collected novels. To his delight, Howells agreed, and "Mr. Garland's Books" appeared in the *North American Review*, where his mentor praised Garland's novels "as indigenous, in the true sense, as any our country had produced," while also tracing the broad outlines of his career. Of the novels, he chose *Money Magic* "as possibly the most masterly" because "it expresses constancy to his old ideal of veritism."[57]

Casting about for something to do after the release of *Victor Ollnee's Discipline*, Garland dusted off an old manuscript he'd been pecking at over the years. Shortly before leaving for the Klondike, he had dictated a fictionalized version of his autobiography as "The Story of Grant McLane," later mining it for use in *Boy Life in the Prairie.* On October 22, 1911, he settled down to revise what he had written, hoping that a change to nonfiction would reengage his creative energy. Soon he became absorbed as he slipped into the past and relived former triumphs. By March a chapter had come back from the typist. "It reads very well, plain and direct as it should be," he recorded in his diary about this early version of *A Son of the Middle Border.* "It is a difficult job this writing an egotistic story in a way that shall seem frank and yet not prove offensive."[58] By June 1912 he had completed a manuscript of one hundred thousand words and approached Harper's. But Frederick Leigh, Harper's vice-president, worried about the effect of a Garland autobiography on the sale of future Garland novels, fearing that it would spell the end of a book-a-year property. Garland wrote to Howells, his old counselor, for advice. "I think it highly probable that I shall never write another novel," he told Howells, "for the reason that love stories no longer seem to me worth while." He asked for Howells's opinion and concluded, "I don't think it is an egotistical book, because I have gone beyond that stage. It is rather an attempt to catch for my children some part of the beauty and significance of the life of the border during the forty years of my remembrance." Howells replied that he thought the book "would be important and delightful, and would add to the interest of your other books."[59] Encouraged, Garland returned to the manuscript.

One October morning, Garland was awakened by the sound of Zulime screaming and the smell of smoke in the air. The Homestead was on fire. They grabbed the children and bolted for the door. While Zulime phoned for help, Garland returned with the garden hose, but its feeble stream was useless. Earlier they had formed a fire evacuation plan, and while Zulime gathered her jewelry and family photographs, Garland ran to his study, tossing what manuscripts he could gather from the second-floor window, with a neighbor bundling them into a blanket, before leaping out as the flames came into the room. In moments, the house was ablaze. Fern Fox, their servant, had left the valve open on the gasoline stove the night before, and when she lit it the stove exploded into fire, engulfing her with flame and burning her severely. Garland could not bear to watch the house that contained so many memories go up in smoke, so he turned away. Later, when it was all over and the neighbors had found clothes for the Garland family, they rallied to assess the damage. The west wing and sleeping porch were badly burned, but the east wing and roof were largely intact. Many of his treasured autographed books had burned, as had paintings by his friends John J. Enneking and T. S. Steele. His collection of Navajo blankets and other souvenirs of his excursions among the Indians were charred. Some of their furniture had been salvaged, thoroughly waterlogged, but most of the contents of the house was a dead loss. News of the fire made the front pages of the *New York Times* and the *Chicago Tribune*. Garland resolved to rebuild.[60]

For much of the fall he labored to restore their home, and that Thanksgiving the family toasted its survival. As soon as he could, he returned to the manuscript of his autobiography, with the expenses of rebuilding acting as additional motivation. But he was baffled by how to tell his story. In the "Boy Life" articles of 1888 he had narrated largely descriptive sketches in the first person, and when he mined them for *Boy Life on the Prairie* he cast them as a third-person fictional tale of a boy on the plains. But he was now fifty-two years old and the prairie had passed, the events now filtered through a nostalgic haze. He had written his narrative in the first person, but it seemed like a work of monstrous egotism, though he was convinced that the events, if not the life, were worth preserving. He queried Robert Underwood Johnson to see if the *Century* would be interested in "partial serialization and book publication afterwards," explaining that Harper's had passed on the serial. "Of course I am under no hard and fast agreement with *Harpers*. I can go elsewhere at any time but they have most of my work and I gave them first 'look.'"[61] Johnson declined.

In December Garland sent the manuscript to his good friend Edward Bok, editor of the *Ladies' Home Journal*, the magazine that had published so many of his romances. But Bok declined, explaining that, despite knowing Garland well, "I had no idea of the . . . privations that you have gone through." But as for publication, "I think that your belief in realism has led you to go too much into details. . . . I cannot get away from the intimate quality of it all, and on that ground I shouldn't like to see it published." Bok suggested he carve out two smaller books, one on "A Prairie Boyhood," the other on "A Prairie Mother." Offering salve to the wound of rejection, he passed the manuscript on to George Lorimer of the *Saturday Evening Post*, which, like Bok's magazine, had published many of Garland's fictions. But Lorimer also turned it down.[62]

By January 1913, Garland was both dejected and desperate for money to restore their West Salem house. He offered a section of the manuscript to Wilbur Cross, editor of the newly formed *Yale Review*, noting that he would accept a reduced rate. Cross wasn't interested. Next, in hopes of ameliorating the egotism of first-person narration, he decided to present the story as an "abandoned auto-biography" left by one Lincoln Stewart that he, Garland, has edited and offered as "the study of a family and an epoch."[63] In his guise as a "conscientious historian," Garland alternated first-person "quotations" from this manuscript with his third-person commentary. The result was a tale still largely in first person interspersed with occasional passages in third person. He sent it to Edward Wheeler, the editor of *Current Literature*, who found the narrative "very interesting" but was also jarred by the alternation of point of view.[64] In April Hamlin tried Harper's again, hoping that the new form might persuade his publisher to accept it. Duneka offered to publish the book only if Garland would forego the customary advance on royalties. Garland was partly to blame for the condition, because he had grown so depressed over the book's prospects that, as Duneka reminded him, "In all our talks . . . you voiced your belief (and ours) that the book would never sell in paying quantities, and that we might even be out of pocket on the venture." Now thoroughly discouraged, Garland decided to forego publication, for "it is sure to expose me to unfriendly criticism and I do not feel like opening myself to the scoffer."[65]

By summer he had rallied and sent it to the *Century*, hoping that Robert Sterling Yard, its new editor, might be receptive. In its original form, *A Son of the Middle Border* included a preface in which Garland explained his motive in writing and warned readers "against believing that this book contains all the facts of my world." Indeed, thinking it undignified for a man of fifty-three to talk about his youthful loves, he had sidestepped the issue:

> The story of my life truthfully implicated would give larger space to my loves but as no reminiscence these days is without an over-frank confession of sexual passion it will be more distinguished for me to admit that I never had a "love affair" and that my admirations (of which I have had many) never came to anything more than a shy glance and stammering word. I was never a "squire of dames" and my adoration remained in almost every case wordless as well as worshipped. Though a powerful man physically, athletic

and passionate, I was brought up to regard women as beings to be shielded not abused. This is very old-fashioned and absurd I admit but so it was. When tempted to forget my teaching I thought of my own sisters and said "Every maid is somebodys daughter, somebodys sister."

Therefore the reader will find no erotic details in this chronicle.[66]

That he was now desperate for a sale can be seen in his proposal to sex up his manuscript for contemporary readers. "Should I fetch up the sexual side of the subject by putting in Lincolns very remote and shy relationship with women?" he asked Yard. "Of course I could manufacture a continuous love-story but it would not be true—it would be introducing a fictional strand but my publishers (I mean *Harpers*) think it would help. My own feeling is against it. You come at the problem freshly and I shall be aided if you put down your candid judgment. I have a notion that the book is more distinguished as it is, but naturally as Riley says 'Thats jist Because I'm prejudiced.'" Yard advised him to "leave the book as it stands," for Garland's contemplated changes would introduce "a foreign element into a perfectly consistent and dignified work of art and literature." Yard then noted that "a lot of magazinists seem to have lost their heads" about the current "sex craze" afflicting magazines. But he declined the manuscript nonetheless.[67]

Meanwhile, amid his depression over his inability to interest any of his former publishers in his work, Garland sought distraction in helping form yet another organization, this time the Authors' League of America. Formed "as an urgent necessity, for the mutual protection and information of authors in their dealings with publishers," the league's avowed purpose was to advise authors about their legal rights and to serve as a professional resource for practicing writers. Garland needed no convincing about the need for such an organization, for his dealings with publishers had, over the years, been fraught with difficulties—from making unwise choices in selecting a publisher (Schulte) to accepting publication on terms that favored the publisher rather than himself (Stone and Kimball) to disagreements over serial and book rights (Harper's). The four principal aims of the Authors' League, as stated in its constitution, were to attain adequate domestic and international copyright legislation, to protect the rights of all authors, to advise authors about how best to sell their work at adequate compensation, and to inform authors about their legal rights.[68] The league was incorporated on December 18, 1912, and 350 writers had joined by the time of its first official meeting on April 8, 1913. Before that meeting, Garland was one of ten writers nominated to serve on the advisory council, and although he wasn't present at the first official meeting, he was elected to fill one of the thirty council slots. Three years later he would become one of six honorary vice-presidents, serving in that capacity until 1917.

Another distraction came in the form of the National Institute of Arts and Letters. In 1907 Garland had been elected one of its vice-presidents, representing the Midwest, and he had been clamoring for the annual meeting to take place in Chicago rather than New York, the better to demonstrate the national scope of an organization he believed would chart the course of American letters. After much debate, it was decided to hold the combined meeting of both the National Institute of Arts and Letters and the American Academy of Arts and Letters in Chicago. This would be the third time the annual meeting was held outside New York (they had met in Washington in 1909 and Philadelphia in 1912), for members were eager to dispel the illusion that the two organizations were little more than an exclusive old boys' club. As chairman of the committee on arrangements, Garland threw himself into a letter-writing campaign as he gathered together the leaders of Chicago's artistic clubs, with the Cliff Dwellers serving as the official host. Foremost on his mind was whom to ask to be the meeting's chief speaker, for he expected the nation's eyes to turn to Chicago.

His first choice was Theodore Roosevelt, and he proposed that the former president address "some subject like THE INFLUENCE OF THE MIDDLE BORDER ON AMERICAN LETTERS, or THE VALUE OF THE OPEN AIR SCHOOL OF FICTION AND POETRY." He urged Roosevelt to accept, for "this meeting can be made and *must* be made the most important meeting the Institute ever held."[69] For a time it appeared Roosevelt would attend, but in July he withdrew because he was sailing to Rio de Janeiro in October. Garland next turned to President Woodrow Wilson, who, like Roosevelt, was a member of both the institute and the academy, but Wilson too was unable to attend and instead sent a letter to be read at the formal banquet. Academy secretary Robert Underwood Johnson wrote to congratulate Garland on progress made. "I'm glad you feel so kindly about what I'm trying to do here," Garland replied. "When the Institute is able to pay me a salary of at least $50 per month, I shall be very glad to be invited to serve as its Secretary. I'm a great little Secretary, without pay. Think what I would be if I were getting $55 per month!!!"[70]

Garland arranged for a special train of Pullman cars to carry the aged members of the organizations to Chicago in comfort, and for two days, November 13 and 14, the joint meeting captivated Chicago papers. "American Genius to Forge Ahead, 'Immortals' Say," trumpeted the *Chicago Tribune*, before outlining the public program of events. Later, Garland would write that although at the time he counted this meeting as "the most successful session the Institute ever had," in reality, the distinguished visitors felt sorry for the provincial Chicagoans and, when the festivities concluded, "hurried into their Pullman cars with perfectly evident relief."[71]

With his duties as organizer completed, Garland returned to the manuscript of his autobiography, this time, at the suggestion of Edward Wheeler, putting it all into third person. "My fear of being called egotistic led me to this change," he noted.[72] In January he was in Pittsburgh lecturing, on his way to New York with the hope that a personal visit would interest editors in his story. The lecture went badly, putting Garland in a foul mood—which only intensified when he missed his train. "I had a feeling that my whole trip was to be a failure," he somberly recorded. "My life seems a failure. For a ten dollar bill I would have returned to Chicago with my ms. and in despair. I went to bed a defeated man. It was one of the darkest hours of my life."[73]

Two days later, his optimism restored, he called on the Harper's office. His editors were still not interested in his life story, but William Briggs, one of the editors, referred him to Mark Sullivan of *Collier's*, an illustrated weekly that had made its fame through its commentary on social and governmental affairs. Sullivan, a member of the magazine's editorial staff since 1906, specialized in political commentary, and when Garland went to the *Collier's* office, Sullivan had just been promoted to editor and was looking to set his stamp on the magazine. In 1913 *Collier's* had reduced its price to five cents, and circulation soared; it would reach the one million mark in 1917, putting it near the top in terms of copies sold. Sullivan was seeking American material to offset a spate of British pieces and agreed to read the manuscript, referring it to his assistant, Edgar G. Sisson. For fourteen days Garland was on tenterhooks as he awaited Sullivan's verdict. Finally, on February 2, Sisson offered $2,500 for a six-part serial, later augmented to $3,100. "I got thrills all the way through it," Sullivan later told Garland. "It will make a very important serial for us. I shall print it to please myself. If our readers don't like it so much the worse for them."[74] For three years, Garland had been revising his story. Six editors—all of whom were friends—had rejected the manuscript, their rebuff also indicating to Garland that his life, his rags-to-riches climb up the professional and social ladder, all his struggle and achievement, were not worth reading. In his spiraling depression he had lost interest in fiction, and at fifty-four he had little to look forward to but the trivial details of club management and doting on his daughters. Sullivan's acceptance put wind back in his sails. And then in quick succession came other sales. Two days later Sullivan offered four hundred dollars for a story, and the *Century* offered three hundred dollars for an article on James A. Herne. "We owe a debt of gratitude to Mark Sullivan which we can never repay," Garland wrote to Zulime. "He has given me a chance to 'come back,' as they say of a temporarily defeated prize-fighter."[75]

17

His morale boosted by Sullivan's acceptance of "A Son of the Middle Border," Garland set to work preparing six installments for serial publication. Meanwhile, in February 1914 Harper and Brothers published *A Forester's Daughter*, another novel about the forestry service. Tired of the conventional romance plot that readers expected, Hamlin reversed the formula. The daughter of a forest supervisor, Berea McFarlane is an outdoorsy Amazon who takes command of sickly easterner Wayland Norcross as she introduces him to the life of the trail in Colorado's high country. Although apprehensive of the physical demands of outdoor life, Norcross gamely follows Berea's instruction, in time falling in love while also recovering his health. Along the way, Garland indulges his love of the mountains through detailed description of the mechanics of making and breaking camp. In a preface to the novel, he excuses the absence of his customary sociological theme by stating that Berea simply took control of the narrative—a dodge to conceal his own halfhearted attention to novel writing. His publishers sought to forestall readers' disappointment in this falling off of Garland's usual approach by picking up on his reversal of plot in an advertisement repeated throughout February and March in the *New York Times* and other papers: "Mr. Garland announces that he would like to have it understood that this is *not* the greatest novel of the year, that it is *not* the latest and the strongest work of the author; it is *not* a gripping study of elemental passions, it is merely an idyllic story of *youth* for *youth*. . . . It can be read by every one in the family circle. Ask for it."[1] It was the last novel he would write.

In March the first installment of his autobiography appeared in

Collier's, bolstered by a full-cover illustration of a Civil War veteran leaning against a fence and prominently headlined, "Beginning A Son of the Middle Border By Hamlin Garland." Sullivan spared no effort to feature the serial and secured noted illustrator Alice Barber Stephens to do the illustrations. Stephens had spent much of her early career illustrating Harper's magazines and books before branching out to illustrate leading magazines such as *McClure's, Cosmopolitan,* and *Ladies' Home Journal.* Soon she had achieved "'world-wide fame' and semi-celebrity status" as the most accomplished woman illustrator of the time.[2]

Garland still worried about the presumption that his life was significant enough to warrant an autobiography. To forestall criticism, he prefaced the first installment with an elaborate explanation. "It is now a quarter of a century," Garland opens the preface in the guise of Lincoln Stewart, "since I began to write of the West, and here (midway on the trail) I am minded to pause and look back on the long, hard road over which I have trudged, eager to make a final record of my joys before they escape me, and in order that I may preserve for my children some few of the intimate details of a life which is already passing if not completely vanished." After warning his readers that the story will not contain the "whole truth" about an author or a man, Garland notes that the chronicle should be read as "the study of a family and an epoch." In this awkward guise the first installment opens, "In beginning this story of Lincoln Stewart, I am almost wholly dependent upon the man's own words in order to account for his boyhood. He says: 'All of this universe known to me in 1865 was bounded by the wooded hills of a little Wisconsin coulee.'" The narrative then proceeds in blocks of first-person quotation introduced rather clumsily by brief introductory phrases.[3] Five installments of "Son" appeared from March to August, carrying the story to "Lincoln Enters Hostile Territory"—Garland's fifteenth year in Osage, where he is tormented by the "town boys"—when publication was interrupted by the outbreak of the Great War. Garland's story could not compete with the news from Europe, and Sullivan filled the September and October issues with features on the conflict, assuring the disappointed author that he would resume publication at a later date, and so Garland put off searching for a publisher for the book version.

Hard of hearing but still spry at age eighty-three, Dick Garland had been reading the installments as they appeared, easily recognizing himself as "Duncan Stewart," the husband who uproots his wife from a comfortable farm to thrust her onto the frontier, the father who turns his eight-year-old son out to work in the fields at dawn. "Aren't you a little hard on me?" he asked his author-son, with some resentment. "I don't think so, Father," Hamlin replied. "You must admit you were a stern disciplinarian in those days."[4] With his novelist's eye, Garland knew that any good narrative needs a conflict, and he had settled upon his rebellion against his father's authority to provide structure for the first part of his autobiography. In this way he had finally settled an old grievance.

With some excess cash from the sale of "Son" in his pocket, and recognizing that "Son" was also his father's story—and also to make amends for his depiction of Dick Garland—on September 1, his father's eighty-fourth birthday, Garland paid off his father's two outstanding notes on some Oklahoma property, leaving him to begin his eighty-fifth year debt-free. Seven weeks later, Dick Garland was dead, his body discovered on the floor of the barn. In marked contrast to the outpouring of grief that had infused his diary entries upon his mother's death, Garland recorded merely, "This ends a good man's life. A soldier and a pioneer. He lies so still and natural in his room that I feel like walking softly as I enter." Later, Garland would write that with the passage of time and his own success, memories of his father's tyranny over his family, his "mistakes, his weaknesses, faded from my mind" as he contemplated his father's "dignity, his manly grace."[5] On November 20, Dick's widow, "Aunt Mary," signed a quit claim deed to his West Salem property, conveying title to seven lots to Hamlin and Franklin, in exchange for one dollar. By the terms of Dick's will, she would receive the household goods and, for the remainder of her life, the use of their house, but Dick's six West Salem houses were to go jointly to Frank and Hamlin.[6]

When Hamlin returned to Chicago, it was with the awareness that his last tie to the region had been severed, and he again longed to move to New York. But Zulime balked—during the last fifteen years her roots had sunk deep, and, by nature reserved, she did not relish the whirlwind of New York social activities expected of the wife of the gregarious Hamlin Garland. The prospect of accompanying her husband to his innumerable dinners filled her with apprehension, for she could not bear to hear him speak. "Hamlin speaks very well, I know," Zulime told Mary Isabel. "He's never awkward or tasteless. It's just that it—makes me so nervous." Mary Isabel speculates that her mother may have feared witnessing some platform failure but was most likely bored, having heard it all before.[7] But more likely is that Zulime, who was highly self-conscious, feared her husband would let drop some intimate detail of their family life, and all heads would turn to her.

Again, Garland turned to his customary club-carpentering as he sought to establish what he so missed in New York, this time in the form of the Society of Midland Authors. In November, John M. Stahl, the master of the Writer's Guild of Chicago, had called a meeting to form an organization of Illinois writers with the aim of fostering camaraderie. When a committee on organization met at the Cliff Dwellers on December 9, Stahl was unable to be present, and in what followed Garland effectively hijacked the organization and altered its purpose to conform to his vision of the "middle border." "Bent upon broadening Mr. Stahl's parochial idea," wrote Hobart Chatfield-Taylor, the society's first president, "this doughty champion of the Middle West orated unabatingly until the domain of the proposed society had been so extended as to include within it all that vast region of the land lying north of the Ohio River, and between the Alleghenies and the Rockies." Its objectives now were to foster "a closer association among the writers of the Middle West, the stimulation of creative literary effort, and the establishment of a library of books and manuscripts by members of the organization."[8] The society soon boasted a distinguished roster of members, including George Ade, Clarence Darrow, Edna Ferber, Zona Gale, Ring Lardner, Vachel Lindsay, Edgar Lee Masters, and Harriet Monroe. Still in existence today, the Society of Midland Authors continues its founders' purpose of fostering camaraderie among writers and awarding prizes to distinguished books.

Meanwhile, trouble was brewing at the Cliff Dwellers. Czar Hamlin the First, as he was known to members, had become increasingly imperious in his management of the club. He refused to permit alcohol on the premises; he issued a directive that no women were permitted in the club until after 6 p.m. (for fear of upsetting the business lunches that had become commonplace); and at one point he "demanded that a house rule be passed forbidding public smoking of cigarettes by females in the club rooms. One of the directors softly remarked he hoped no action would be taken that would exclude his wife from coming to the club."[9] The members wearied of Garland's imprimatur, and on December 14 plotted a coup: they passed an amendment to the bylaws to restrict the president's term of office to no more than two successive terms. Deeply wounded, Garland noted, "At the Club I saw [the architect Irving K.] Pond and other of the 'Insurgents' busy making plans for my undoing. . . . It looks like the end of the Club for me. After having done more than any other man to build it up—I am now to be shelved unless I make a fight—and that, of course, I shall not do. If my friends will not do anything for me, then it is time I got entirely out of the Club and the town."[10] At the annual meeting on January 11, 1915, which Garland did not attend, for he had fled to New York, the reign of Czar Hamlin came to an official end; on that date he was replaced by "Czar Charles the Bold"—so called for being willing to replace Garland—his good friend Charles Hutchinson, president of the Art Institute of Chicago.[11]

Garland's friends attempted to smooth over his hurt feelings by hosting a testimonial dinner at which Hamlin would be presented with a "loving cup"—a ceremonial punch bowl. "I hope that only those who are genuinely interested in the testimonial will be included," Garland wrote to Karelton Hackett when he learned of the plan. "It would be ludicrous to have the men who were so active in the opposition campaign appear as cordial admirers now."[12] The luncheon was scheduled for March 1, but Garland begged off because the new president—who had suggested the testimonial—was out of town. Some disaffected members met anyway, set up a bar beneath Garland's portrait, and installed Roswell Field as bartender. Field turned the portrait face to the wall and hung a large sign that read, "THIS PLACE HAS CHANGED HANDS."[13]

Garland, who had resolved to leave Chicago, tried to put the best face on it when the testimonial finally took place on May 4. "I am going East because there is more game in New York," he began as he accepted the loving cup.

> Confiding editors and unsuspecting publishers abound in the wilds of Manhattan. Consider me therefore as a joyous wolf going among timid and juicy sheep.
>
> I go now because the hunting is good. Why, even on the Main-Travelled Road between my hotel and Gramercy Park, I have brought down three fat editors in a single day, and yet the "close season" may shut in at any time and it stands me well . . . to improve the present opportunity. Being fairly active on my feet and a moderately good marksman, I hope to send back occasional cheerful notes of my success. If, however, the chase is reversed and the slayer is slain, put a line on your wall, saying: "He was a busy hunter and valiant till the deer turned and cast him out."[14]

The affront of having effectively been kicked out of the club still rankled years later. In 1931, when he returned to the Cliff Dwellers to attend a dinner in his honor, he penned a note that is framed and displayed on its wall to this day: "I expected and predicted that the Cliff Dwellers would bust up when I relinquished the helm much against my will—But I admit I'm wrong—Hamlin Garland."

Garland again tried to convince Zulime to move to New York, but she was understandably reluctant to leave family and friends. "Zulime is all torn up over the thought of leaving and it is evident that she will never leave of her own free will and I do not intend to coerce her," he confided to his diary. "It means that she and the children will remain here and I will go on to New York to do my work."[15]

In January 1916 Garland was back in New York, resigned to a commuter marriage. Adding impetus to his decision to relocate was an offer by the Vitagraph Company to film his novels. In 1913 and 1914 Garland had begun testing the waters of the infant film industry by sending out feelers to various film companies. The Authors' League had recently been trumpeting the potential of film, and especially the need for writers to turn their novels into scenarios. As a vice-president of the league, Garland no doubt read a provocative article in its *Bulletin* by J. Stuart Blackton, the president of Vitagraph and fellow member of the league, that outlined the easy-money promise of film. "The short story writer who gets from one hundred to five hundred dollars for magazine stories can get a similar amount from the picture manufacturers," Blackton asserted, and what likely caught Garland's eye was the greater sum that established writers could command: "The authors of international fame, who make thousands in royalties, can make thousands more from picture royalties—and in every case without interfering with their book or magazine rights."[16] In February 1916 Garland began negotiations with Vitagraph to film four of his novels—*Hesper, Money Magic, The Captain of the Gray-Horse Troop,* and *Cavanagh, Forest Ranger.*

Blackton and Albert E. Smith formed the Vitagraph Company in 1896. They had been presenting a series of entertainments in vaudeville and had delighted in the audience's response to Thomas Edison's Kinetoscope, a combination film camera and peephole viewer. Soon they were producing their own shorts, and by the time Garland encountered them Vitagraph was the largest and most important of the early film companies. While Garland dreamed of striking it rich in film, he had seen enough of the early films to know that most were poorly made and full of stereotypes, particularly in Westerns, which were in vogue. He therefore insisted on the right to approve scenarios. "I want to co-operate as fully as I can without being a hindrance," he wrote to Jasper Brady, Vitagraph's scenario director. "It is not a side issue with me—it is one of the most important ventures of my life."[17]

For days Garland worried over the details of the potential sale of film rights, in part lured by Blackton's promise of easy profits but more by the awareness that film promised a new audience for his books. "I am at that point of life when a turn of this kind is needful," he mused. "I want to reach the young people and there is no better way than the pictures. It is the universal medium."[18]

His concern that his novels be filmed accurately demanded his presence at the Vitagraph studios in Brooklyn, and he urged Zulime to sell the house and move to New York. He peppered Blackton with suggestions for the filming of *Hesper*, filling pages with descriptions of scenery, clothing, and nuances of characterization. All the while he was writing Zulime, singing the praises of New York and urging her to come, apparently ignoring his resolution not to coerce her. Finally, on March 24, Zulime relented and agreed to sell the house. What her husband did not appreciate was the emotional cost of the decision. Mary Isabel describes her mother reduced to tears by a telegram more peremptory than the others: "To have our mother now prostrated, sobbing like a heartbroken child was appalling." Zulime knew she "was going to have to surrender," for "it was easier to let Hamlin have his own way" than to argue.[19] One wonders whether Garland appreciated the irony that in this coercion of his wife, he had reenacted his father's similar pressure on his mother in his many relocations on the middle border, which had become a dominant theme of Garland's early fiction and of his autobiography.

The Garland family arrived in New York in May, where they took rooms at the Schuyler Arms while Hamlin searched for a flat. On June 28 Garland took the children to see a pre-release version of *Hesper*. He was crushed. "The play is so drab and uninteresting that it cant possibly succeed," he recorded in his diary. "I came home deeply disheartened by the cheap and uninspired way in which the play was done." To Blackton, he explained, "All the romance and beauty of the mountain life is left entirely out of it."[20] Garland had advocated filming on location in the Colorado mountains, but Blackton chose the more cost-effective option of setting *Hesper* amid the hills of New Jersey. Garland was also troubled by the extras, Pennsylvania coal miners "whose lamps and blackened faces were ludicrously out of place" and contrasted mightily with the high-country gold miners of his story.[21] He resolved to take a more active role in future productions, but he would continue to be disappointed in the films as they were released, despite his best efforts to ensure they accurately reflected his novels. His dreams of sudden wealth also vanished, for his royalties amounted to three or four thousand dollars and not the tens of thousands he had envisioned.[22]

While Garland was involved with Vitagraph, Harper's published *They of the High Trails,* a collection of his Rocky Mountain short stories. He had proposed the collection in July 1915, for he did not have the energy to produce a novel for the spring list. In looking over his files, he realized he had accumulated a number of western stories and proposed issuing them as two books—for spring, *The Outlaw of Blizzard Basin and Other Stories of Wyoming,* and in the fall, *The Grub-Staker and Other Stories of Colorado*—thereby maximizing his literary capital.[23] Harper's vetoed the double-volume idea, and when the book was published in April 1916 it contained nine stories, all of them originally published in magazines between 1899 and 1915, and all retitled for the collection to emphasize each piece as a story about a western character type.[24] The volume was for the most part pleasantly received, with the *New York Times* observing that "there is a charm and versatility about the volume which make it a veritable find"—a sentiment echoed by other reviewers. And then, in September, Howells reviewed the collection for *Harper's Monthly* and offered lofty praise. "By virtue of these, and of those other tales and novels of his dealing with life in the region of mountain-time," he magisterially asserted, "Mr. Garland has measurably succeeded to the place in the sunset held by Bret Harte and Mark Twain." He lauded the "artistic conscience which still prevails with him" and commended "his feeling of proportion, his love of beauty in nature [that] keeps him from betraying his reader with any such falsehood to human nature."[25] After his disappointments with Vitagraph, Garland was understandably pleased. "Did you see the article about your Daddy in the Sept. Harper's?" he asked his daughters. "It makes me feel like less of a failure when I read it."[26]

As he had for *Main-Travelled Roads,* Garland recognized a promotional opportunity and asked Howells if he would allow his review to stand as an introduction to a new edition of the collection. Howells agreed, and in 1917 Harper's reissued the volume with an "appreciation" by Theodore Roosevelt, a preface by Howells, and an additional story, "The Tourist," which had appeared as

"Emily's Horse Wrangler" in *Collier's* in August 1916. Ironically, despite Howells's judgment that Garland had at last attained the artistry for which he had striven so long, at age fifty-six he retired as a fiction writer. "Emily's Horse Wrangler" was the last story he would publish.

Meanwhile, the Garlands continued their search for a permanent home. The key question was where to send their daughters to school. In spite of his American boosterism, Hamlin was developing a serious case of xenophobia that would intensify as he aged. He was appalled by the influx of eastern European immigrants on New York streets. "I ought to be democratic enough to send my girls to our public schools," he later wrote, "but when I see the mob of children of all colors and conditions pouring out of their doors, I can not bring myself to put my daughters among them."[27] One evening, while dining with John O'Hara Cosgrave, his *Everybody's* editor, Jessica Cosgrave offered to enroll the Garland girls at the Lenox School for Girls, a preparatory school for Finch College that she had just founded. As an additional incentive, she offered half-price tuition. In July, after much searching, the Garlands leased a seventh-floor flat at 71 East Ninety-second Street.[28] Although the apartment was only a short walk from school, Hamlin's cramped study and the noise from neighbors would bother him for years, greatly hampering his ability to concentrate.

Once settled in New York, Garland found that he was increasingly in demand as a speaker and as an organizer. "Calls for meetings, for subscriptions, for the use of my name come in every mail," he complained.[29] But seldom could he turn them down. When John Agar offered him a life membership in the National Arts Club in exchange for boosting the club's literary activities, Garland couldn't refuse.[30] Although New York had many organizations devoted to individual arts, the National Arts Club had been founded in 1898 to promote and stimulate interest in all the arts by providing what many of the other organizations lacked: exhibition space and membership that included both men and women. The 1,200 resident and nonresident members who joined in the year of its founding soon enabled the club to aspire to its ambition of representing a national membership.

Garland accepted Agar's offer and soon was busy revamping the club's annual book exhibit. Each November the club would host what amounted to a publishers' bazaar—a display of new books that emphasized their colorful bindings. Garland was in charge of the 1916 exhibition, and by the following year he had transformed it into a juried exhibition of three hundred leading books as selected by a panel of fifty distinguished reviewers and university professors. With his organizational appetite whetted, Garland soon turned to forming another body to provide what no single organization could: an "official" reception committee, representing American literature broadly conceived, for visiting writers. With himself as chairman and *Current Literature* editor Edward J. Wheeler as secretary, Garland invited the heads of seven New York arts clubs to form the Joint Committee of the Literary Arts: the National Arts Club, the Society of American Dramatists, the Authors' League of America, the MacDowell Club, the Pen and Brush Club, the Author's Club, and the Poetry Society of America. As he explained to a reporter, "At present there is no organization to give expression to literary America, no club to further any big literary movement or entertain a visiting author." Other organizations had limited space and represented only a segment of American authorship; the Joint Committee existed to confer a wider recognition, "to congratulate, to express the approval of literary America to a fellow author."[31]

Garland was motivated in part by nationalistic fervor amid the Great War as well as his growing sense that contemporary literature was in decline as younger writers, with less reverence for the past, began to displace the old guard. On February 7, 1917, the Joint Committee sponsored a dinner for South American writers, many of whom had relocated to the United States because of war blockades that had cut them off from Europe and turned them to writing about their own countries. Garland was especially interested in the work of Brazilian local colorists.[32] On March 21 the Joint Committee held a dinner to commemorate Howells's eightieth birthday. Howells was unable to attend, but Garland gathered testimonial letters from the elder writer's contemporaries and had them bound into what Howells called a volume of "obituary testimonials."[33]

While he was doing his part to make American literature visible amid the tumult of the war, Garland offered his services to the Vigilantes, a group organized to further American war interests by disseminating propaganda to the nation's newspapers. The Vigilantes was founded during a November 1916 meeting at the Players Club by Hermann Hagedorn, an author who, like many others of German descent, sought a more active way to declare his allegiance to the United States. As their letterhead, emblazoned with the image of a lantern-bearing minuteman astride a galloping horse, explained, the Vigilantes was "A Non-Partisan Organization of Authors, Artists and Others for Patriotic Purposes." Their avowed purposes were

1. To arouse the country to a realization of the importance of the problems confronting the American people.
2. To awaken and cultivate in the youth of the country a sense of public service and an intelligent interest in citizenship and national problems.
3. To work vigorously for preparedness; mental, moral and physical.
4. To work with special vigor for Universal Military Training and Service under exclusive Federal control, as a basic principle of American democracy.

Among its more than ninety contributors were George Ade, Gertrude Atherton, Irving Bacheller, George W. Cable, Douglas Fairbanks, Charles Dana Gibson, Joyce Kilmer, Mary Roberts Rinehart, Theodore Roosevelt, Mark Sullivan, and Booth Tarkington. Members contributed short articles advocating various patriotic causes, without charge, for syndication through the Wheeler Syndicate and the American Press Association.

When Hagedorn invited Garland to become involved in March, he promptly responded with "The Volunteer Soldier," an article that began by extolling his father's volunteer service during the Civil War.

But the times had changed and universal service was now necessary. "Every man must feel his obligation to serve the government which protects him and educates him," Garland argued. "Service should be universal and then it will be just and equitable."[34] In 1918 he would contribute a number of other pieces, among them "Our Duty to Our Citizen Army," "Our Alien Press," "Universal Military Training," "The Crime of Profiteering," and "No Negotiated Peace."

Meanwhile, three more installments of "Son of the Middle Border" began appearing in *Collier's* in March, accompanied by a blurb from Theodore Roosevelt. "Hamlin Garland is a man of letters and a man of action, a lover of nature and a lover of the life of men," Roosevelt began before praising the accuracy and compassion of Garland's writing. "For thirty years he has done good work; and never better work than he is doing now."[35] To make room for articles on the Great War, Sullivan had encouraged Garland to condense the story and to put the narrative back in first person. "No one will criticize it on the score of egotism," he reassured him. "Most readers will want to know that Hamlin Garland is telling the story of his pioneer relations and friends."[36] When the installments concluded in May, he had carried his story from his Cedar Valley Seminary days to the close of his Dakota homesteading experience.

Garland had also finally found a publisher for the book version. Frederic Duneka, his editor at Harper's since 1902, who had faith even in Garland's psychic books, had little confidence that readers would be interested in Garland's autobiography and had passed on the customary advance against royalties. Frank Doubleday was willing though not eager to publish the book but was more interested in a future Garland novel: "This is a book," Doubleday explained, "which we cannot expect will have a great sale (very few autobiographies do), but we think very well of it, and shall be glad to publish it with the understanding that you do not expect it to sell like a popular novel . . . and also that when you write a novel you would naturally bring it to us."[37] But George Brett of Macmillan—the publisher to whom Garland had brought four books in 1899—was more enthusiastic and saw in the autobiography an opportunity to bring Garland back to the firm. His editor was Edward C. Marsh, who made the mistake of offering the standard Macmillan contract to the sensitive author, who was accustomed to working so closely with his publisher that his presence was necessary prior to publication. "You publishers have everything your own way on these printed forms," Garland wrote. "I usually make out a type-written copy that makes us that [*sic*] we are PARTNERS in the transaction. I cant afford to publish with any firm on the old-fashioned basis. I want to feel that I am a part of the house. At Harpers I have been that and I want Macmillans to take a friendly interest in my affairs. I want to be consulted on all vital points."[38] Finally, after much negotiation over the amount of royalty and the number of illustrations (and being chided for being "difficult"), Garland signed a contract that gave him a royalty of 15 percent, rising to 20 percent on sales above ten thousand copies. And what also pleased him was that Macmillan would also issue a limited, autographed edition with special binding and additional illustrations. Unlike the lukewarm Duneka, Brett was a Garland partisan who wanted to take over all of Garland's books and reissue them in a uniform edition. Too late, Harper's saw their prolific property defecting and tried to corral Garland back into the fold. "They seem to have suddenly wakened to the value of my work and name," Garland reflected after a meeting with William Briggs of Harper's. Like Brett, Briggs attempted to persuade him with "talk about making a new edition of my books."[39] But Garland had lost faith in his longtime publisher, and especially with its luke-warm marketing campaign, and anyway he had already contracted to give *Son* to Macmillan.

Amid his many committee responsibilities and negotiations over his autobiography, Garland was struggling to cope with increasing pain from a general malaise that he typically referred to as "lame-ness," the symptoms of which first appeared in early 1915. At first the trouble seemed connected to diet—"Nothing that I eat seems to go off just right," he noted. "I get lame if I eat meat and lamer if don't—and so it puzzles me." Doctors initially thought he might have contracted an infection due to bad teeth. One July morning he was awakened by severe cramping that was "like the clutching of a giant hand under my arm and across my breast. It stopped my breath every time it came."[40] The pain soon became so acute that he was unable to concentrate on writing, and for months he filled the pages of his diary with his symptoms and attempted treatments. Mary Isabel recalled that "some nights the torture was so overwhelming that he would walk the floor, tears streaming down his cheeks, while Mother or I walked behind him, pounding his back with all our strength to counteract the pain."[41] He tried changes in his diet and underwent several physicals, but still the cramping, the joint pain, the weakness persisted. Only aspirin offered temporary relief.

None of the specialists he consulted were able to palliate his condition. He tried Christian Science, but while he enjoyed the hospitality of the meeting, he found, despite his belief in psychic forces, the accounts of miraculous cures to be illogical.[42] Then came a glimmer of hope. His doctor recommended that Garland go to the famed Battle Creek Sanitarium for treatment, for he found "no organic weakness in my heart lungs or kidneys. I'm run down and need running up." Bemusedly, Garland noted that he was "in a trap. I cant exercise without getting lame and if I don't exercise I get flabby and nerveless."[43] For advice, Garland wrote to his friend John Burroughs, whom he had met shortly after his first visit to Whitman in 1888 and who was similarly afflicted. Burroughs told Garland he had found relief at the Middletown, Connecticut, branch of the Battle Creek Sanitarium. "The only effectual remedy I found was heat and electricity, and a meatless diet," wrote Burroughs, who was "baked and sweated and electrocuted, and dieted, and got relief at the end of a week or ten days." Burroughs described Dr. John Kellogg's theories that most illness originated in the "clogged and unsanitary condition of the colon" and concluded, "I think if we could keep this drain pipe well cleaned and sterilized that two thirds of our illnesses would vanish." He was now careful to keep his "anatomical sewage pipe" flushed weekly "with warm salted water," he told Garland, abjured coffee, tea, and alcohol, and dosed himself with "sanatogen"—a protein powder composed of casein and glycerophosphate—and his neuritis had disappeared.[44]

Encouraged by Burroughs's report and desperate for relief,

as soon as he had delivered the manuscript of *Son* to Macmillan, Garland boarded the train to Michigan, where he limped into the Battle Creek Sanitarium on April 7. Like all new arrivals, he underwent a complete physical exam, including chemical analysis of the blood, urine, and stools; X-ray examination of the chest, heart, and lungs; culminating in the administration of the famed "test meal"—a laxative designed to thoroughly clean out the gastrointestinal tract. Once Garland was cleaned, prodded, and rested, his doctor designed a program of diet and exercise. The governing assumption of Battle Creek was that "Nature creates and maintains; therefore she must be able to heal." People became sick because their daily habits interfered with natural bodily processes; by removing the causes of illness—bad diet, slothful living—the body would naturally heal itself. Patients were put on a low-protein and high-roughage diet, the better to stimulate frequent emptying of the bowel, "to prevent the stasis which gives rise to putrefaction, retention of body wastes, and consequent intestinal toxemia."[45] The diet excluded meats, animal fats, pepper, mustard, vinegar, spices, and other irritants, as well as alcohol, coffee, and tea. In many ways years ahead of its time, the sanitarium and its menu countered the prevailing meat-rich diet by insisting upon pure food and plenty of fresh fruits and vegetables, all accompanied by calorie counts. With their digestive system thoroughly cleaned, patients underwent a series of exercises designed to restore out-of-shape bodies—long walks in fresh air and sunshine and a program of gymnastics and hydrotherapy, mechanical therapy, and light therapy, followed by massage.

Garland left an amusing account of his experience at this early fat farm in an unpublished manuscript entitled "The Good Ship Sanitas," named for the sanitarium's main building's resemblance to an ocean liner and the custom of ringing bells on the hour. In it he devotes much space to the single aspect of the "cure" that most bothered the "incapables": the diet. "No hint or suspicion, much less a smell of beef, turkey or fish or coffee was on the bewildering menu which I found beside my plate," he recorded. "Instead I read of 'nuttose cutlets' 'protose steaks' 'iron brew' 'Sanitas Cocoa' 'bran buns' and 'mock chicken soup'—and to confuse the situation still more each item was carefully analyzed and estimated into its carbohydrates and proteins and basic salts." His doctor, one Riley, seemed overwhelmed, bored, and discouraged by his chronically sick patients and looked like a man "who could do [with] a cigar and a whisky and soda."[46] Some patients, growing tired of the fare, slipped out to "Chicken Jo's" for a snack, and Garland observed another nip at a smuggled bottle of whiskey, and he once interrupted another indulging a forbidden cigar. Garland himself once escaped to enjoy a "regular" meal at a friend's house. By April 13, Garland had had enough and resolved to leave, but Dr. Kellogg convinced him to remain, and he gamely stuck it out, enduring arc-light treatment for his spine and the assaults of the machines in the mechanical gym, which he confessed "did me good"—as did a few rounds with a punching bag. But by April 28 his lameness had returned and he felt worse off than when he arrived. Although he recognized the "many excellencies" of the institution—"it gives tired old men and debilitated men new leases on life. It awakens atrophied muscles and restores hope"—he concluded that "it did nothing for me." When he left as soon as he could travel, on May 2, he staggered out "so weak that I could scarcely carry my bag."[47]

When Garland returned to New York he found proofs of *A Son of the Middle Border* waiting for corrections. As he bent to his task he became edgy, apprehensive of how his life story would be received, aware of the high stakes of his gamble. He recorded in his diary, "As I near the end of the last chapter of 'the Border' I am in a panic. At times I have a feeling that the book is of no value whatsoever. Then I think of certain passages and find them good. Probably it is good in spots and bad in spots. My brain is pretty clear now—too clear I am afraid—enabling me to see the faults in the book."[48] He asked Marsh to send advance sheets to Howells, Roosevelt, Burroughs, Brander Matthews, and Brand Whitlock, hoping for a favorable word to be used for promotion. "I am getting old and shameless as you can see," he admitted. "Of course I wouldn't do this if I did not feel sure of the sympathy of these men. They will feel the power of the vanished Middle Border just as you and I do."[49]

As soon as he finished correcting the proofs, Garland began looking for a summer residence to escape the city's heat and to comfort his daughters, who sorely missed rural life at the Homestead in West Salem. On July 29 he found one near Tannersville, New York, about 125 miles away in the Catskills. While visiting his friend the artist Orlando Rouland, in Onteora Park, an exclusive residence community, Garland discovered an unoccupied cabin adjacent to Onteora and arranged to rent it. When his family arrived they delighted in its rusticity, its quiet setting, but most of all its coolness. Just as important to Garland was the fact that his neighbors included some of his friends—the most prominent of whom was John Burroughs, in nearby Roxbury. Best of all was that the cabin could be had for less than a thousand dollars, and as soon as Garland's offer was accepted he named the place "Camp Neshonoc," after the Wisconsin village of his family.[50]

Meanwhile, letters arrived from the advance readers of *Son*. "Unless the first 24 pages deceive me," Howells wrote, "you have written one of the truest and greatest books in the world. Now indeed our life is getting into our literature. But now and then [y]our literosity gets the better of your life, and then I want to kill you. More anon."[51] Two days later Howells finished the book and had high praise indeed, though tempered with his characteristic admonition about Garland's lack of attention to details. "So far as I know your book is without its like in literature," he wrote. "It is perfectly true to life, and beautiful with right feeling, from first to last. I wish every American, every human being might read it. Never before has any man told our mortal story so manfully so kindly. I would like it to go on forever. But I miss two galley slips, 160–161, and where are they? It often needs proof reading."[52]

Pleased by this tribute from America's foremost man of letters and aware of the effects of such praise on the sales of the book, Garland immediately wrote to ask whether he could use Howells's letter in the marketing of the book. He must have been abashed at Howells's reply: "I have most decidedly refused to let MacMillans quote from my letter to you. I hope to be your friendliest critic, but not their advance agent. To let a publisher advertise from such a letter as I like to write to a brother-writer would take all heart and trust out of friendship, and I *never* do it."[53] While he might not want his private correspondence used to market his old friend's book, Howells did contribute a lengthy and highly laudatory review to the *New York Times Review of Books*. Appearing on the front page and accompanied by a distinguished portrait of Garland, Howells's review began, "In all the region of autobiography, so far as I know it, I do not know quite the like of Mr. Garland's story of his life, and I should rank it with the very greatest of its kind in literature." Howells ranked *Son* above the autobiographies of Goethe, Rousseau, and Franklin in its "grasp of the great serious, elemental things, the endeavor and the endurance which have constituted us as a people." He described Garland's method of making his personal story stand for a nation's westering movement as "a psychological synthesis of personal and general conditions in a new country, such as has not got into our literature before. That in itself, if it were nothing else, is a precious contribution to human knowledge." After noting the minor "fault" of Garland's lack of accounting for his father's "iron persistence ready, if not willing, to sacrifice the youth of wife and children to the realization" of his westering dream, he concluded that the story is both "the memorial of a generation, of a whole order of American experience," and "an epic of such mood and make as has not been imagined before."[54]

Ever without confidence in his abilities, Garland dourly noted in his diary that day, "Howells beautiful article was in the *Times* and the publication of this review undoubtedly marks an epoch in my literary life." Yet even high praise from Howells was not enough, for the concluding lines reveal his perennial dissatisfaction, the constant striving for artistic perfection that he would seldom achieve: "To have won a place with Howells and his like ought to satisfy me—but it doesn't. I had hoped to go farther and do better. . . . Howells is too kind in his judgment. I am still the learner."[55]

Other, equally laudatory reviews arrived, and Garland was surprised to discover he had scored a hit. All his years of revision, of ceaseless fretting over the manuscript, of refining style and deepening his story amid considerable physical pain and bouts of depression, had paid off. But what to do next? In crafting his story, Garland had left open the possibility of a sequel with the closing lines:

As I was leaving next day for Chicago, I said, "Mother, what shall I bring you from the city?"

With a shy smile she answered, "There is only one thing more you can bring me,—one thing more that I want."

"What is that?"

"A daughter. I need a daughter—and some grandchildren."[56]

He had thought *Son* would be his last book, given the tepid response by publishers. But publication had come at a propitious time, for the horrors of the Great War had led Americans to revalue their country and its traditions, and Garland's celebration of the pioneer spirit, his rags-to-riches climb from obscurity to prominence, had struck a responsive chord. His chief counselor in his autobiography, Mark Sullivan, urged him to continue the story, and that November Garland set to work, worried about the challenge facing all sequels—that of measuring up to the original.[57]

And then came a completely unexpected honor. His friend Brander Matthews telegraphed that Garland had been elected to the American Academy of Arts and Letters, chiefly as a result of the publication of *Son*. "All this is deeply gratifying," the new academician noted. "In a very real sense it crowns my career."[58] He was now an "immortal," a member of the most prestigious organization to which he could aspire. For the remainder of his life, he would be its most untiring advocate.

18

OUT OF STEP WITH THE MODERNS, 1918–30

A Son of the Middle Border, Garland's greatest financial success, would go on to sell more copies during his lifetime than any of his other books. In addition to the regular trade edition, it appeared in five editions marketed to various groups, as well as being issued as a set with *A Daughter of the Middle Border*, besides being published in England by John Lane and reprinted in 1928 by Grosset and Dunlap. It was vigorously promoted and critically acclaimed. By 1947 Macmillan had sold 177,201 copies, a whopping number for a Garland title.[1] Yet Hamlin writes that sales were "relatively small," that the book "made no wide appeal," and that "it was the kind of book which people read without buying."[2]

Part of the reason for his disconnect with the facts is that for his whole life Garland was afflicted with a terrible case of what Thorstein Veblen calls "invidious comparison," the tendency to measure one's success by comparing one's material wealth with others'. His friends were often better off financially—in some cases, truly rich—and many of his writer friends wrote novels selling in the hundreds of thousands. He envied now mostly forgotten writers like Irving Bacheller (*Eben Holden*, 1900), Winston Churchill (*The Crisis*, 1901), Owen Wister (*The Virginian*, 1903), Rex Beach (*The Spoilers*, 1906), and Booth Tarkington (*Penrod*, 1914), whose initial best-selling novels led to additional financial successes. His diary is full of mournful notes recording his lack of earning power in comparison with his friends'. Despite the fact that for most of their married life the Garlands enjoyed the services of a maid, enrolled their children in a private school, and kept a house in the country, Garland was never able to appreciate his own achievement. One day, after noting Zulime at routine housekeeping, he groused, "I sensed once again the humiliating realization that my 'success' is a very weak and helpless honor. So long as my wife must scrub floors and my children wear threadbare garments, I am a failure." But he also recognized the relative nature of such comparisons. "Measured by the rewards my fellows enjoy," he continued, "my condition is disgraceful—measured by my Iowa playmates—I am a marvel. The vexing fact is I am not comparing myself to them but to Bacheller and [Ernest Thompson] Seton and [Albert Bigelow] Paine. The worst of it is that at fifty eight one does not make any great change in ones fortunes."[3]

But another reason for his sense of failure amid his greatest success was that his long preoccupation with the past had led to a singular myopia concerning contemporary literature. One effect of his move to New York was to expose him to the mixing of cultures that immigration had brought. As fate would have it, this exposure came at exactly the wrong time, for in 1918, at age fifty-eight, Garland was in ill-health, his body aching from what eventually was diagnosed as arthritis, very much aware of the infirmities that come with age, and prone to the carping that often accompanies extended illness. His novels had ceased to sell in appreciable quantities, and he had retreated into reliving the past—a time in which, in his nostalgic recollection, the country was unified in its goals and values. In the Wisconsin and Iowa of his remembrance, his neighbors had hailed from New England or Scandinavia or Germany and had made it a matter of pride to assimilate into the nation. But the eastern Europeans he saw on the streets of New York struck him, in his now conservative outlook, as alien to the traditions he was daily describing in his writing. During a walk in the park with Mary Isabel, for example, he "got among the Lithuanians" and returned "much depressed by them. My daughter does not like runty little foreigners—and I confess they seemed a good deal like vermin as they sprawled about on the benches."[4]

Then, too, cultural changes in entertainment, brought about by movies and the rise of magazines with circulations in the millions, served to increase his disdain for the immigrant. He perceived contemporary writers as tradesmen rather than artists, who were writing for a magazine industry whose primary goal was to sell advertising and not to publish works of literary merit. The story was only the incidental hook, full of sensation and violence, provided to lure readers to buy soap and underwear. To these magazines and their lowbrow readers Garland attributed the change in literature. As he told Joyce Kilmer in an interview for the *New York Times*, "we are called upon to write for readers who are not only unreflective but crudely sensual, many of whom have brought to America the moral laxity and passionate intensity of the South of Europe." Ironically, the literary evolutionist who in his youthful iconoclasm had called upon writers to break with the idols of the past now called for shoring up those idols when they were threatened. Although he was aware of the irony, telling Kilmer "it does not become the author of 'Crumbling Idols' to pose as an old fogy," he had "small sympathy with the materialistic ideals of our young writers"—all the while secretly coveting and envying their success. "Theoretically I am a democrat," he told Kilmer, in a statement that would surface repeatedly in his essays and books during the coming decade. "Actually I am an intellectual aristocrat. I believe in 'an aristocracy of mind, of character, of will,' as Ibsen puts it. It is not enough for me to write for the masses. I want to have the approbation of my intellectual superiors."[5]

In his nostalgia for the past, Garland was blind to the innovations of the modernists. Their linguistic inventiveness, disruption of chronology, sense of alienation, and invention of new narrative structures marked a perception of reality markedly at odds with his own. He was especially galled by the modernist assault upon decorum, the frank depiction of sex, of adultery, of violence seemingly for its own sake, all of which he dismissed as "pornography." Nowhere in his voluminous reminiscences, correspondence, or diaries does Garland mention Hemingway, Fitzgerald, Faulkner, Stein, Eliot, Williams, or Stevens, though he does write about those whose lives intersected with his own, such as Dreiser, Lewis, O'Neill, Pound, and Frost. He seems unaware of the contributions of the writers of the Harlem Renaissance. Everywhere he turned he heard jazz—but to his ear, accustomed to the soothing melodies of folk songs or the stately rhythms of classical symphonies, the music was raucous and jarring, inflaming desires better kept under wraps. A voracious reader all his life, he was likely aware of the modernists but chose not to record their names, believing their work pandered to the desire for titillation and was only a temporary phase. As he told one correspondent,

> I am an evolutionist and I do not enjoy seeing men and women returning to the morality of monkeys. The morals of the barnyard are not something to enter upon but to leave behind. The Great War brought as its aftermath a period of licentiousness like that which followed the Napoleonic wars and we are still in it but slowly emerging. That is the way it appears to me. Nearly all the popular successes of the last twenty years have been the result of pandering to this taste for the illicit. Stories which used to be confined to saloons and brothels are now printed in regular book form and brought into the drawing room.[6]

Garland was gratified by the success of *A Son of the Middle Border*, for discerning readers had at last validated his life and work, and he hoped his example would provide an antidote to the incursion of modernism that so distressed him. The publication of the book brought renewed demands for lectures, and he delivered a program he entitled "Memories of the Middle Border" to a number of university audiences in addition to lectures on the writers he had known in America and in England. "Garland was a superb lecturer," a friend recalled. "He cultivated accents, inflections, idioms, timing, delivery, tones, pauses, rhythms of speech and such vocal nuances with the same loving care and aura of perfection as a dedicated rose grower exhibits for the blooms in his garden."[7] In February 1918 he signed a contract with Macmillan for a sequel to his autobiography, its working title—"The Sunset Regions"—reflecting his perception that it would be his final book, a legacy for his daughters. With a daily diary to guide him, the writing went quickly, though he was chagrined to discover that some of the entries, particularly for the years 1912 to

1916, were so "elliptical and monotonous in expression" that they failed to prod his memory. Aware that he could no longer count on his memory, henceforth he resolved to be more detailed in his notations.[8] He completed a draft by August 2, although already he saw "a thousand places which need change," primarily "enriching by small additions here and there" and the removal of "certain parts which are too personal."[9] He took great pleasure in the manuscript, for his daily retreat into the past enabled him to forget the pain of his lameness, which seemed to be intensifying, so much so that he could not bear to sit and wrote while lying on his couch. At times the pain in his shoulder was so severe that "I dip my pen in the ink with my left hand. Once the pen is filled and in my right hand I can move it but I can not lift my arm. It is not very comforting," he wryly observed, "to see my right hand helplessly waiting for its fellow to furnish the pen." And his doctors warned him that soon he would be confined to a wheelchair.[10]

Then, in late August, relief came in the form of one Dr. Fenton B. Turck, whom Garland had met casually in 1905 and who had noted his deteriorated condition during a call at Camp Neshonoc. Turck was a biologist and physician who had won acclaim for his research in cell biology. His investigation into the causes of crop failure led him to conclude that each plant has its specific "cell-sap," which he termed "cytost," an overabundance of which caused the plant to break down. But when one extracted the cells and injected a weak solution of them into healthy plants, one could gradually build up an immunity to the toxic substance through the action of "anti-cytost," the serum derived from the immunizing agent. By experimenting with the amount of "cytost" and "anti-cytost" reacting in cell division, Turck was able to raise the plant's resistance to disease. He applied his research to animal and human biology, determining that "many disorders in animal tissue, as in plants, are due to abnormal cell breakdown and the liberation of excessive quantities of cytost in the cell media." Administration of cytost and anti-cytost, which were tissue extracts, both stimulated the growth of tissue and built up the resistance to disease. As a member of the U.S. medical corps during the Great War he developed a serum for the treatment of shell shock, wounds, and other injuries and attracted wide attention.[11]

One week after Turck injected him with cytost, Garland noted a near-miraculous recovery, walking seven miles.[12] The treatments continued for several months, though Garland does not specify what constituted Turck's therapy. During one office visit, Turck "said that my whole trouble was auto-poisoning and that it could be cured by a system of diet and exercise"; but Garland also reports receiving a number of shots of serum as well as at least one injection in his shoulder of chloroform, apparently to produce autolysis, or the enzymatic digestion of diseased cell tissue, which produced the desired cytost.[13] And while a firm friendship soon developed, Turck wasn't above exploiting his patient: the daily office visits often lasted two hours or more, during which Turck held forth about his discoveries and shoved pages of his articles at his now captive patient, who sometimes transformed Turck's turgid prose into less abstruse language but more often acted as coach. The result of this odd collaboration would be published after Turck's death as *The Action of the Living Cell* (1933). Adopting a role he had performed so often in the past, Garland soon became Turck's enthusiastic booster and in 1926 would help found the Turck Foundation for Biological Research to enable Turck to continue his research.

Whatever they were, Turck's treatments worked, and after three years of debilitating pain Garland found his body pain-free, his vigor returned, his mind cleared, and he felt renewed confidence in life. Feeling at last his normal self, Garland wasted no time in launching a counteroffensive against the assault of modernism upon the genteel tradition that had shaped his aesthetic. Earlier in 1918, Frank D. Fackenthal, who as the secretary of Columbia University was responsible for the administration of the Pulitzer prizes, asked Garland to serve on the drama jury for the 1918 prize. Garland was naturally gratified by the recognition such service conferred, and he saw in it an opportunity to counter the incursion of journalistic standards in literature by rewarding those plays that strove for the highest artistic standards. Fackenthal apparently held Garland's judgment in high regard—or perhaps he recognized Garland's conscientious organizational talents—for he went on to appoint Garland to serve on the drama jury from 1918 to 1922, as the chair in 1919 and 1920, and as the chair of both the drama and fiction juries in 1921. In some ways, Garland was an odd choice for a drama juror, for his frequent travels on the lecture circuit often made him unavailable to see the plays he was to judge. His credentials as a drama juror were also suspect: despite his long interest in drama, he had, after all, made his reputation in fiction, his intense involvement with the Chicago Theater Society had ended badly, and his fellow jurors were established playwrights or drama critics. Nonetheless, he saw his position as Pulitzer juror as an opportunity to promote the "aristocracy of mind, of character, of will" that, as he had informed Joyce Kilmer, marked the true artist.

Though later the standards would change, in these early years of the Pulitzer administration Garland took seriously the drama prize's stipulation that the award go to the American play "which shall best represent the educational value and power of the stage in raising the standard of good morals, good taste and good manners." He recommended against conferring the award for 1919, because "most of the plays of the year in question are either very light entertainment or so crudely melodramatic as to be of very little literary value."[14] The one action the committee accomplished that year was to change the award period to coincide with the dramatic season (fall through spring) rather than the calendar year.

When the 1920 season began, Garland was ready to recognize a striking play that would serve as a model of taste and decorum and inspire audiences and other playwrights. But soon he found he had little time to see plays and wrote to friends for recommendations. He was taken aback to discover that Eugene O'Neill's *Beyond the Horizon*, a tragic drama about two brothers in love with the same woman, soon emerged as his correspondents' favorite. While he recognized the superiority of O'Neill's play, he couldn't get past the dramatist's subject, which offended his sense of propriety. He much preferred *Washington: The Man Who Made Us*, by fellow National Institute member Percy MacKaye, although he had only read the play and had not seen it performed. When the other two jurors, Richard Burton and

Walter Prichard Eaton, also voted for O'Neill's play, he attempted to direct the award to *Abraham Lincoln*, a play by the Englishman John Drinkwater. By doing so, he wrote to Eaton, "perhaps we can emphasize the pettiness of our native output by giving a prize to this serious and noble work." And to Fackenthal he added that "perhaps a lively 'row' would call attention to the failure of our writers or producers or who ever is to blame in the matter."[15] Earlier, he had written to Nicholas Murray Butler, the president of Columbia University and chair of the Pulitzer Advisory Board, about the legitimacy of offering the prize to an Englishman. Butler, who as a fellow member of the American Academy shared Garland's outlook and preferred Drinkwater's play, had replied that "if the book or play was on an American subject, it would not be disqualified in competition although the author was himself a foreigner."[16] Garland immediately encountered opposition from drama critic Clayton Hamilton, who had served on the previous year's drama jury and to whom he had written because Burton had left town after sending in his recommendation. "I am violently opposed to giving the Pulitzer Prize to an Englishman," Hamilton wrote. "The donor intended this prize for the encouragement of American authorship; and nothing could be more discouraging than to hand it to a foreigner, however eminent," especially since there were "an unusual number of meritorious native plays." Moreover, *Beyond the Horizon* was "one of the very best American plays ever written."[17] When Garland received a similar recommendation from Montrose Moses, perhaps the most eminent drama critic of the day, that "There is no doubt in my mind that the outstanding play of the season by an American is Eugene O'Neill's BEYOND THE HORIZON"—and Moses went on to enumerate its many virtues—Garland caved in, reluctantly voting to award the prize to O'Neill, the first of his four Pulitzers, though personally, he explained to Butler, "I can not regard O'Neill's play as 'Noble' or 'Uplifting' which are I believe the expressed terms of the bequest."[18]

Other letters to Fackenthal reveal that Garland recognized O'Neill's power of expression and the play's significance but wished the play "did not go quite so far in its depressing delineation of a decaying family."[19] His reluctance to confer the award to O'Neill stemmed from the fact that Garland, like the terms of the Pulitzer bequest, was out of step with the emergence of modernism in American drama. Marked by relentless experiment with form and by innovations in subject matter, the plays being produced were written, for the most part, by a generation far more liberal in its treatment of sex than the author of *Rose of Dutcher's Coolly* could tolerate. Garland consistently lobbied against voting the prize to O'Neill's plays. For *Anna Christie*, the tale of a prostitute and O'Neill's second prize-winning play, he had nothing but scorn. "I do not see how we can vote a prize to the morbid kind of play that O'Neill writes," he railed to William Lyon Phelps, the chair of the 1922 Pulitzer drama jury. "He has had one prize on those lines and to give him another would be to emphasize a kind of thing which is essentially unwholesome. . . . It seems to me we have had too much pornographic literature this year. The Pulitzer Prize should not add to its vogue. I hate the whole school which is essentially unAmerican."[20] And when *Desire under the Elms* appeared, a play in which a son sleeps with his father's wife and fathers a son-brother, staged with innovative Freudian symbolism so at odds with the realism upon which he had been nurtured, Garland was appalled. "This play is not drawn from American life, but from the study of a pessimistic European philosophy," he wrote to the *New York Times*. It is "not only un-American in tone and method but equally cynical and subversive" and does not "represent the normal wholesome life" that literature ought to represent.[21]

As chair of the 1921 novel jury, Garland was in a pickle, for he didn't really like any of the novels under consideration and believed none met the Pulitzer criteria that the prize be awarded to the novel that best presents "the wholesome atmosphere of American life and the highest standard of American manners and manhood." The leading contenders were Sinclair Lewis's *Main Street*, Edith Wharton's *The Age of Innocence*, Floyd Dell's *Moon-Calf*, Zona Gale's *Miss Lulu Bett*, and Lee Wilson Dodd's *The Book of Susan*. To fellow juror Stuart Pratt Sherman he complained that Wharton's novel "stirred me not at all" and seemed "rather arid"; he dismissed *The Book of Susan* as "pornographic" and therefore not worth considering; *Moon-Calf* "left me tired of unimportant details in the life of a youngster who represents Newspaper English and Small-town Radicalism."[22] While he recognized the power of *Main Street*, he thought the characters were "too much like clay figures—types rather than individuals." He much preferred *Miss Lulu Bett*, a short novel by his friend and fellow Wisconsin writer that examined the economic exploitation of women against a backdrop of small-town prejudice. "I tried to reread MAIN STREET and failed," he wrote Sherman. "It gave me a curious disgust. . . . Will anyone re-read it?"[23]

Sherman was strongly for *Main Street*, as was the other juror, Robert Morss Lovett. In a series of letters during the spring, Sherman lobbied hard on behalf of *Main Street*, striving to convince Garland to overcome his prejudice and recognize the superior claim of Lewis's novel. As it had for Garland, *The Age of Innocence* "left me cold," Sherman wrote. But *Main Street* not only kept him up until 1 a.m., but "it is packed and crammed with the reality of this life that we know so well. And it is saturated with criticism." Sherman was rather surprised that Garland didn't recognize *Main Street* as the logical descendant of his own *Main-Travelled Roads*. "I'm hanged if I can understand why the author of 'A Son of the Middle Border' doesn't warm up to" Lewis, Sherman chided Garland. "I shall not change my opinion between now and the first of May," he concluded, referring to the committee's deadline. "Please record my vote as unhesitantly given for Sinclair Lewis's 'Main Street.'"[24] (Ironically, Lewis had written to Garland in 1915, "If I ever succeed in expressing anything of Minnesota and its neighbors, you will be largely responsible, I fancy; for it was in your books that the real romance of that land was first revealed to me.")[25]

But when Garland conveyed the jury's vote to Fackenthal, he did so in so halfhearted a manner that the "recommendation" was more a complaint about the current crop of novels than it was a committee decision. And in a footnote he added, "It would in a way be a tribute to the magnificent work which Mrs. Wharton has done to vote the prize to her."[26] When the Pulitzer Prize for the best novel of 1921 was awarded in May, it went to *The Age of Innocence*. "I inadvertently allowed to stand the statement indicating that the jury had recommended the 'Age of Innocence,' Fackenthal sheepishly explained to Garland. "I am sorry for the error, and trust that it is not sufficiently serious to annoy the members of the jury."[27] But annoy them it did. Fackenthal "is extraordinarily naive," Lovett complained to Garland upon receiving a copy of Fackenthal's explanation. "In the first place, I do not think the Committee—I speak for Sherman and myself at least—had any idea that its decision was not to be final. In the second place, why should it not annoy the members of the jury to be placed on record as recommending one book when in fact, they recommended another?" So incensed was Lovett that he publicly castigated the prize-awarding process in an editorial in the *New Republic*, of which he was editor, and in which he quoted correspondence and revealed the vote of the committee for *Main Street*, which, he added, "I believe was unanimous."[28]

By late 1924, when Fackenthal once again pressed him to serve on the Pulitzer drama jury, Garland was reluctant, for none of the plays upheld the standards he admired. By March he was fed up with the year's crop of "experiments in pornography" and asked to be released from the jury. Fackenthal talked him into remaining, and Garland agreed to do so only if his dissent would be published with the committee's report. When it became clear that the other two jurors preferred Sidney Howard's *They Knew What They Wanted*, a play in which a young woman marries an old man for economic convenience but becomes pregnant by the older man's younger friend, Garland had had enough. "I will not vote for any pornographic drama," he told Fackenthal, and quit in disgust.[29]

Garland wasn't having much luck shaping the future of American literature though the Pulitzer prizes, but he had more effect with the American Academy of Arts and Letters. Ironically, while he was the old fogy on the Pulitzer juries, he was the Young Turk of the academy. His passion for the academy's mission and his evident organizational prowess led to his being elected temporary secretary when its permanent secretary, Robert Underwood Johnson, was appointed ambassador to Italy. Garland assumed his post in April 1920 and promptly set out to mold the academy into an agency that would arrest the incursion of the moderns.

In 1920 the American Academy was an institution with a vague purpose, without a permanent home, and with a membership largely over sixty years of age whose aesthetic was solidly based in the nineteenth century. Among its most ardent members were Robert Underwood Johnson, born in 1853, who had assumed the editorship of the *Century* upon Gilder's death in 1909 and who had been elected on the strength of his (now forgotten) poetry. William Milligan Sloane, born in 1850, was a Columbia University history professor and author of a four-volume *Life of Napoleon* and other works. Nicholas Murray Butler, a relative youth, born in 1862, was president of Columbia University, author of scores of books on education and politics, and later would be the co-winner of the 1931 Nobel Peace Prize. Brander Matthews, born in 1852, was a dramatic critic, novelist, and the first professor of dramatic literature in America at Columbia University. These men looked with disdain upon the new crop of writers and artists. To Johnson, modernist poets such as T. S. Eliot, Ezra Pound, Wallace Stevens, and E. E. Cummings "wish to exalt into poetic association words that heretofore have not been considered poetic," which was anathema to the true purpose of poetry, which is "to express the pervasive and permanent spiritual forces of all time." To counteract this pernicious influence, "The Academy's chief influence will come from what and whom it recognizes, what and whom it praises, and what and whom it puts forth."[30]

Garland was deeply committed to the academy's mission, which he expressed in three lines that he hoped would become the organization's motto:

> To conserve the best in America's past
> To promote the best in America's present
> To insure the best in America's future.

He wanted the academy to be not merely a warehouse of past accomplishments but "a progressive urge, a force making for more original art, a finer citizenship, a loftier conception of life." It should not just promote the best of the present creative artists; it should also "condemn the bad" by speaking out against artists whose work becomes a corrupting force; above all, it should act "to uphold standards, to boldly make distinctions between the merchandiser and the conscientious craftsman." If the academy did not do so, he warned, "we are in danger of becoming a nation of intellectual hoodlums, a mob of polyglot opportunists, caring nothing for the past and careless of the future."[31]

But the other members were singularly inert and so little inclined to action that, at times, hardly anyone showed up to conduct business, such as it was. At one board of directors meeting convened to nominate a new president upon the death of Howells, only Garland (as secretary) and two others—Sloane and Butler—showed up. What followed, according to the minutes, has all the elements of farce: "Mr. Garland suggested that in his opinion Chancellor Sloane should be elected to the presidency and Dr. Nicholas Murray Butler should then be elected Chancellor. For obvious reasons Mr. Garland's suggestions were not supported by those present."[32]

Elected to the academy's board of directors in November 1920 (on which he would remain until 1931), Garland promptly began to agitate for the group to take a more active role in American culture. While as part of its educational program the academy had offered occasional public lectures at the Chemists' Club in New York, Garland proposed to designate one or two persons as official academy lecturers, with an expense account, and send them to the hinterlands. By way of example, he pointed out that in January and February he had extended his official academy lecture, "Americanism in Literature and Art" (chiefly about Howells), to a number of university audiences in Rochester, Buffalo, Pittsburgh, and Philadelphia, while Sloane had lectured on "Personality and Politics" to similar audiences in Syracuse, Albany, and Brooklyn, and together "they had reached six or seven thousand persons who knew more about the Academy than they did before." The board deferred the proposal to a committee, which never met.[33]

Garland had more success promoting the organization on March 1, 1921, in an invitation-only meeting to memorialize Howells, who had died on May 11, 1920. At this meeting, held at the New York Public Library, Garland coordinated an exhibit of Howells materials, organized a slate of speakers, and publicized the event to honor the foremost influence on his life and career. While he was pleased with the meeting itself, he was disappointed that it didn't make more of a splash in the press. He had invited more than eighty-five publications to send representatives, gave interviews to the leading papers, and sent a publicity packet totaling forty-seven typed pages to the newspapers and the Associated Press. He had hoped for "an aftermath of special articles in the Sunday papers" but believed it had been crowded out by news reports of Warren Harding's presidential inauguration.[34] Or it may be that the democratic newspapers merely snubbed the aristocratic, invitation-only event.

Garland wanted to make the academy a more visible part of the literary scene. To promote and inspire younger artists, he recommended forming an advisory committee of people outside the academy to award prizes, together with a public address explaining the reason for the award. Mindful of the advanced years and lethargy of most academy members, he suggested that the committee be "made up of a selected group of the leading critics on the magazines and periodicals of the country, men whose daily business it is to keep in touch with the advances in each of the arts."[35] The board failed to act upon his recommendation. By a provision in the Pulitzer plan of award, the American Academy and the National Institute were already charged with selecting members of the Pulitzer Prize juries; now Garland proposed turning over the entire process to the academy. "It would be a source of power and influence if the Academy could administer the Pulitzer Prize Fund," he wrote to Sloane, who was now the president of the academy. "I don't see much life to the Institute.—This is another of my suggestions at present." "Who of all of us will give the time to read and decide?" Sloane replied.[36] The administration of the Pulitzers remained with Columbia.

What most worried Garland was the advanced age of the academy members. As he pointed out to Sloane, "As Thomas says I am 'the ebullient youth of the Board' which is comical considering that I am sixty one. I have pushed hard because I saw a superb opportunity to make a ten-strike—and we are going to do it."[37] Aware of the reluctance of his fellows to elect more progressive artists, he proposed offering associate or honorary memberships to "men of distinction who are sympathetic with our purpose but whose work is not precisely of the character which we require for regular membership." Doing so, he added, would also be one way to admit women, for with the exception of Julia Ward Howe, who had been elected to the institute in 1907 and elevated to the academy in 1908 (dying in 1910), no woman had entered this organization of elderly chauvinists.[38] Honorary memberships would come, but not until 1929.

In 1917, as chair of the institute's literature selection committee for nominations, Garland had advocated electing Mary Wilkins Freeman, Edith Wharton, and Margaret Deland, committed to the principal of recognizing distinctive work irrespective of gender yet also aware that his fellow members' chauvinism would mean an uphill fight. When the institute met formally on January 26, 1918, a furor promptly erupted. Surprisingly, Johnson was one of Garland's chief allies, urging the election of Wharton, who won sixty-four affirmative and only six negative votes, with Freeman winning fifty-six affirmative and ten negative and Deland sixty-one affirmative and seven negative votes. But the specter of women's eligibility for elevation to the academy, should they be elected to the institute, derailed the proceedings. In subsequent balloting, members vetoed the proposition to admit women by a vote of twenty-three to seventeen.[39] For the next eight years the issue continued to resurface, but resolution became mired in procedural squabbles until 1926, when, after consulting a lawyer who advised there was no legal way to exclude women, the power brokers gave up. Surprisingly, after starting the imbroglio by proposing women for election in 1917, Garland abruptly changed tack in an effort to avoid discord. As he somewhat disingenuously explained to fellow board member Archer Huntington, who was also the academy's chief benefactor, "I am for the rights of women, as a general proposition but I do not advocate their admission to either the Institute or the Academy just now. I fear the effect of a dissension in the Institute as a result of this election."[40] In 1926 Freeman, Wharton, Deland, and Agnes Repplier became the first women elected to the institute since Julia Ward Howe's election nineteen years before.

In later years, mindful of the growing influence of radio, Garland proposed instituting an academy medal for good diction on the radio. He had received a radio for Christmas in 1922. "I had never manipulated one before and it quite absorbed me," he remembered, though he then remarked crankily, "I was most impressed however with the sad fact that the mystery of the process did not transform cheap and empty words into poetry." Public radio broadcasts had debuted in 1920, and by 1922, sales of the new invention amounted to 60 million dollars, soaring to 842 million in 1929 as the influence of this technological marvel began to pervade American life.[41] The former local colorist had become increasingly impatient with "our 'grinding r's,' our 'barbarous nasals' and our 'distorted vowels'" that marked the regional speech patterns of announcers and radio actors, and as he observed the mass of immigrants utter their own dialectal variations he bemoaned the erosion of the "purity" of English speech. He saw the radio as a "nation-wide school" that could teach proper English "to our lately arrived European immigrants," thereby performing a valuable service of enculturation.[42] In 1929 he would present the academy's first Gold Medal for Good Diction on the Radio to Milton J. Cross of NBC, lauding him for his "beauty of voice, and a quiet naturalness of expression."[43]

In 1920, with Robert Underwood Johnson abroad in Italy, Garland saw an opportunity to redirect the course of the academy by plotting a coup: his target was none other than Johnson himself. As the academy's permanent secretary, Johnson, more than any other member, was responsible for the organization's direction, and his resistance to change had long bothered Garland. To Matthews he explained, "the weakness of the Academy lies in the sad fact that we are all growing old. Johnson as well as the rest of us. We must strengthen ourselves with youth.—How *can* we relieve Johnson gracefully."[44] Perhaps remembering the Cliff Dwellers' means of orchestrating his own ouster as president of the club, he convinced the board to amend the constitution to remove the permanency provision for the office of secretary. Soon, he advocated the removal of Johnson altogether. "We need a young, vigorous managing secretary," he wrote to Matthews, "a man not a member, a man who will be in the office all the time. . . . We cant be run by a volunteer member seventy years of age. . . . I can not be a party to a passive policy. I am for war. The Academy should be a progressive force in American Arts and Letters. We must not be senile. We are called 'an old man's Home'—and 'That Johnson Thing.'"[45]

Upon his return, Johnson was deeply wounded when he learned of the amendment. "The change of my title was unethical," he protested to Sloane, "besides exposing me publicly to the implication that I was not any longer *persona grata* to my associates of the Academy."[46] "Johnson has no real grievance," Garland blithely wrote to Sloane. "If instead we had ousted him from the office he might complain but we have merely changed the designation of his office."[47] Letters continued to bounce back and forth. At stake was more than a petty squabble over a title, for the issue was who would bear responsibility for charting the future of the academy. As with many other organizations, the secretary did most of the active work, with the president serving primarily as a figurehead. Garland wanted to make clear, once and for all, that executive power should reside with the president and not an elderly secretary with little motivation to change. By December he was worn out with the squabble. Upon learning that Johnson planned to show the board documents in which Garland had urged his replacement, Garland resolved to avoid the unpleasantness by not attending the next board meeting. "I am so out of patience with Johnson's tactics that I don't want to sit through any more of his prosy harangues," he told Sloane.[48] Johnson retained his office as permanent secretary, a position he would occupy until his death in 1937.

Relieved of the stress associated with this politicking, Garland continued to agitate for the academy to assume a larger presence. As he had done for the Society of Midland Authors, he developed an archive of members' books, manuscripts, and memorabilia so that the collection "should become indispensable to the historian of such subjects and it should offer library facilities for the critic and special student of the arts." He wanted rooms in the new academy building, then under construction, to be set aside as temporary studies for members "in need of quiet places to work."[49] Tired of the haphazard manner of election, he wanted nominees to file applications so that members could be informed about the merits of those they were called upon to evaluate. "Edwin Markham for example does not have to be explained," he noted by way of example. "He is in Whos Who. Some of the Academy elections have to be explained even to the members," far less the public. And then, in pointed reference to his fellow board members, he added, "There is always the danger of electing too many men who are merely college professors. The Academy cannot afford to elect a classicist in preference to the man of original genius."[50]

So who were these "original geniuses" being squeezed out by college professors like Sloane, Butler, and Matthews? Candidates for election to the American Academy first had to be elected to the National Institute. In January 1913 Garland had nominated Theodore Dreiser for election to the institute. Earlier, he had read and been impressed by *Sister Carrie* and had dined with Dreiser and feted him at the Cliff Dwellers. Though he was a bit put off by Dreiser's lack of polish, he admired his "largeness of perception and honesty of purpose."[51] But in June Johnson wrote that he had resigned from the *Century,* in part because of an editorial dispute over the magazine's forthcoming publication of extracts from Dreiser's *A Traveler at Forty.* "I found it contained accounts of the author's illicit relations with five different women, with disgusting details," Johnson complained. "More than this he told the cost of his adventures amorous in Venice, gave a list of the most notorious houses of ill-fame in Paris and made defense of his conduct from the moral point of view—the most unblushing and immoral thing I have ever read."[52] Garland was taken aback. "Can we postpone his election?" he asked. "I feel as you do about these things and I do [not] wish to seem to sanction for a moment any such baseness as he seems engaged in. I am willing to publicly withdraw my nomination if it seems nescessary [*sic*] but you would need to stand behind me as my source of information. I certainly shall oppose his election on the basis of your letter."[53] Dreiser never was elected to the institute, and by 1916, when his novel *The "Genius"* was condemned by the New York Society for the Suppression of Vice, Garland's antipathy to Dreiser's brand of modernism had deepened to the extent that he refused to sign a formal protest against the suppression circulated by the Authors' League, of which he was then an honorary vice-president.[54] When H. L. Mencken, the principal organizer of the protest, learned of Garland's refusal, he wrote to urge the reluctant veritist to reconsider. "Your own experience with 'Rose of Dutcher's Coolly' . . . no doubt gave you an insight into the methods of the moralists who strive to keep American literature at a level of chemical purity," he reminded Garland, unaware of Garland's earlier rearguard action in engineering Dreiser's ouster from election to the National Institute.[55] But Garland was resolute. Dreiser never forgot the snub. Three days after Garland's death, he wrote to Edgar Lee Masters, who had similarly suffered from Garland's disapproval: "What a meaningless person! He was so socially correct and cautious. I met him several times, dined at his home in Chicago and each time came away with a feeling of futility—wasted minutes or hours. He was careful of his words—almost fearful of what he might say or think."[56]

Shortly after the *Main Street* Pulitzer Prize debacle, Garland proposed Sinclair Lewis for election to the institute. Though he did not believe the novel met the criteria for the award, he recognized the general merit of Lewis's work. But when Lewis was elected in 1922 he declined the honor, in part because of the Pulitzer snub, deeply wounding Garland, who thereafter never passed up an opportunity to slur Lewis. Garland's friends Albert Bigelow Paine (elected 1918), Irving Bacheller, and Vachel Lindsay (both elected in 1920) easily made it into the institute, but when Garland nominated Carl Sandburg in 1926, Johnson torpedoed the nomination. "I shall oppose him with all my force," Johnson replied. "He is the worst representative of the eccentricities of free verse that the country has afforded. . . . We are too prone to accept the vogue of a work like 'Main Street,' and rush the author into the Institute. I feel very strongly about the Institute as related to the art of poetry and I do not look with complacency on a reinforcement of its membership from those who, in my judgment, are conspicuously degrading that art."[57] Sandburg had to wait for the votes of more progressive members in 1933.

Although Garland often pronounced that a candidate needed to be a person of distinguished achievement to become one of the immortals of the academy, he wasn't opposed to bending the rules occasionally for those he admired—even if it meant electing another college professor. Of his friend William Lyon Phelps, a professor of English at Yale University and a prolific author of books on literary topics, Garland wrote to explain his nomination: "Wm. Lyon Phelps is not a great writer but he is a most appealing lecturer and a personality of charm and distinction. I am disposed to join in nominating him."[58] Phelps was elevated that year. For others, Garland's judgments have stood the test of time. Twice he nominated Edward Arlington Robinson. As he explained to Brander Matthews in 1924, "I am inclined to favor Robinson. After all he's the outstanding poet today. His election would be hailed as logical."[59] But Robinson would have to wait for a third nomination, in 1927, before Garland's fellow academicians would see the logic. Garland much approved the election of Robert Frost in 1930, and though he didn't like O'Neill's plays, he recognized his talent. "What about O'NEILL?" he asked Johnson when they were canvassing a slate of potential candidates in 1926. "He is our outstanding dramatist. . . . He would carry IF he were properly sponsored."[60] But O'Neill would wait until 1933.

Clearly, Garland was by now a man out of sync with the times. His long preoccupation with his own past, with reliving his former triumphs, and especially with retracing the battle for realism in his autobiography had served to cement more firmly the value of that movement. One effect was to leave him utterly incapable of recognizing the significance of the burgeoning modernist movement. In 1923 and 1924 Garland issued a spate of articles complaining about the current state of American letters and extolling the virtues of the American Academy as a counteractive force. In one of these, "Current Fiction Heroes," he expanded upon the theme of his Kilmer interview, blaming the loss of decorum and decency in literature on "unrestricted immigration from the Old World" that had led to "huge masses of undigested alien citizens" who clamor for sensation, jazz, and tales of sex. He deplored the influence of French, Russian, and Norwegian writers and British decadence on younger writers, whose work was marked by "an overinsistence on sex themes and by a kind of sad egomania." Only by returning to the values of the past, he argued, could traditional American values be restored.[61] When he sent a copy of the article to Fred Lewis Pattee, a professor of English at Pennsylvania State College who was at work on *The New American Literature* (1930), Pattee chided Garland for his loss of perspective, reminded him of his own youthful iconoclasm in *Crumbling Idols*, and suggested that rather than condemn the new literature outright he should attempt to "understand the psychology" of the movement. "Something has come over America," he prodded Garland; "what is it? Don't damn the new creators. . . . We old ones may be making asses of ourselves by damning the oncoming tide of the future," he warned, "and trying to sweep it back with our tiny brooms of later-Victorian adjectives."[62]

Garland must have been surprised when Pattee published a rejoinder to "Current Fiction Heroes" entitled "Those Fiery Radicals of Yesteryear: A Letter to Hamlin Garland on Generations and Literary Manners," in which he took Garland to task for being out of touch with the modernists, quoted Garland's own words from *Crumbling Idols* that "Youth should be free from the domination of the dead," reminded him of the furor *Rose of Dutcher's Coolly* had caused in its break with tradition, and suggested that "these 'young radicals' of today are precisely what your generation has made them." He lauded Garland's veritism for blazing a new trail in literature, and he reminded the elder writer that the current generation of writers are "your disciples [who] have pushed on as far beyond you as you and Crane pushed on beyond Howells and James." If Garland couldn't recognize the effects of his own youthful iconoclasm, Pattee concluded, then he should retire from the fray and "leave New York that so depresses you . . . and go and live with the men you understand and are wholly at home with."[63] Garland might well have remembered his earlier advice to Johnson Brigham when *Prairie Songs* was being cudgeled by the critics in 1894: "You will soon find—if you have not already done so, that there is a literary war in progress—the same old war between the new and the old—and critics of the traditional school read the new to condemn. This does not disturb the new."[64]

19

THE HISTORIAN, 1919–29

While mounting his rearguard action against the incursion of the modernists, Garland was busy revising the manuscript of *A Daughter of the Middle Border*. Relieved of the pain from his arthritis, he was once again able to spend extended hours at his desk, going over the flaws of the manuscript and laboring to revise it to fit with the method and style of *Son*, all too aware that few sequels measure up to the original. Macmillan, his publisher, pushed for an early release of the book, but Garland was wary of letting the manuscript go too soon, all the while knowing that his primary readers—his father's generation and the one following—were quickly passing. Adding motivation to his revision was an unpleasant meeting with William Briggs, of the Harper's firm, who untactfully told Garland his Harper's novels were "dead ducks." "I suspect that this is true," Garland mournfully reflected. "All my material is now 'history.' . . . I see nothing ahead now but reminiscent books."[1]

He tested the waters for serial publication, hoping to follow the financial windfall of *Son*, but all the magazines he tried—among them the *Saturday Evening Post, Everybody's, Delineator, Century, Atlantic,* and *McClure's*—turned him down. For advice, he sent the manuscript to Mark Sullivan, who had revitalized his career by publishing the serial of *Son*. Sullivan diagnosed the problem: for *Son*, Garland had relied primarily upon his memory and a few letters, notebooks, and manuscripts, which forced him to unify his impressions by combining related events. His daily diary, begun in 1898, five years after *Daughter* begins, had become a compositional crutch, for Garland had fallen victim to the pitfall facing every biographer: allowing chronology, and not the story, to dominate. The great charm of

Son, Sullivan perceptively explained, was its creation of "moods" centered around pivotal events that enabled readers to partake in Garland's nostalgia for the past. But with the present manuscript, "you have what is practically a diary, events being taken in order as they came. The result, so far as moods is concerned, is to give an effect of scrappiness." He advised Garland to combine related events into chapters, in effect to dispense with the diary form.[2]

Garland set about rewriting the entire manuscript. As he did so, as was his habit, he began another manuscript, a sort of prequel, a semi-fictional "history" of his father's westward migration that would end with his return from the Civil War and the beginning of *A Son of the Middle Border*. He would turn to it periodically over the next few years, eventually publishing it as *Trail-Makers of the Middle Border* in 1926.

On January 6, 1919, his old friend Theodore Roosevelt died. Garland was incredulous. "Death and Roosevelt do not seem possible partners," he confided to his diary. "He was life, abounding, restless life. It is almost beyond my powers to imagine him lying still. He was the biggest, the most vital, the most versatile man I ever saw or met. He was a half-dozen great men in one."[3] As he would do more frequently as he aged and his contemporaries passed on, Garland set to work writing a number of memoirs.[4] He also helped form the Roosevelt Memorial Committee and served as head of a subsidiary committee charged with soliciting "brief characteristic personal stories of Roosevelt." The resulting volume appeared in 1927 as *Roosevelt as We Knew Him*, edited by Frederick S. Wood.[5]

Meanwhile, Mary Isabel, at age sixteen, was beginning to date, and in the process nearly drove her father to distraction. One night she and her beau were delayed from returning from the Palisades Amusement Park across the Hudson River by a ferry breakdown. When they arrived at 2 a.m., Garland was waiting at the door, his eyes blazing. He seized his daughter by the arm and shoved her toward the door. "You go upstairs," he told her. "You can tell me about it later." He turned to the unfortunate young man. "As for you!" he thundered. "Never come to this house again!" Slamming the door, the upset father trudged up the stairs. He "looked at me in a way to chill my soul," Mary Isabel remembered. "I thought I could trust you," he muttered, before going to his room. Garland did not speak to Mary Isabel at breakfast or dinner the following day. Zulime advised apologizing to her father. "What for?" Mary Isabel asked. "I told the truth. It was in the paper tonight about the ferry breaking down—"

"I know—"

"He's unfair! He should apologize to me!"

"He never will," her mother explained. "It is constitutionally impossible for Hamlin to apologize. Oh, he'll make it up to you in many ways but he just can't say the words." Eventually, Mary Isabel did apologize, and her father took her in his arms. That night he took her to see William Gillette in *Sherlock Holmes*.

Of this episode, so traumatic to the daughter whose moods and fiery spirit so resembled his own, Garland dourly recorded, "We have been very happy together Mary Isabel and I but I see she is now to take her divergent path. . . . This was a very painful night for me."[6]

As Mary Isabel began to spend more time at the fashionable parties common among her wealthy classmates, and with Constance, at age twelve, soon to follow, Garland began to cast about for ways to economize. When the Players Club, of which he had been a member for twenty-two years, raised its annual dues to $120, he decided to resign. "I cant stand the expense, particularly as I hope to go into the Century," he explained to Robert Underwood Johnson. "I hate to leave the old club where I have been at home for so long but the truth is, no one goes there any more—I mean none of my special friends and associates." Besides, "the food is cheaper at the Century and most of my friends go there. It seems the natural place for me to loaf."[7]

Founded in 1857 by the poet William Cullen Bryant and others, the Century Association took its name for its one hundred members—artists, authors, and amateurs devoted to letters and the fine arts. By the time Garland approached the club, membership had expanded to a thousand resident and three hundred nonresident members. Candidates for membership in this exclusive club went through a rigorous vetting process. To be admitted, Garland needed a formal letter of nomination, with a second, which then went to the admissions committee. Two negative votes would strike his name from candidacy. Once he survived the admissions committee, the membership at large voted. No more than twenty names could be proposed in a given year, and if one-fifth of the votes cast were negative, the candidate's name would be struck.

Garland called on his friends to put his name forward. With his desire for this sort of institutional recognition, he was understandably pleased to survive the voting process. To Henry Fuller he crowed, "I have resigned from the Players and am now a member of the Century Club. This is the top. I cant get any higher until I seek the Gates of Pearl. . . . I am a 'Senator' now!"[8] But he was disappointed upon his first visit as a Centurion. "It was rather depressing. The men were nearly all gray-haired and many were bald. I felt like a youth in the midst of so much age and dignity," he complained. "I dont regret my action in joining but it was a little less inspiring than I had hoped it would be."[9] Nonetheless, for his remaining years in New York, a visit to the Century would form a part of his daily routine—a habit Zulime would count on. "Whatever you do," she would tell her children with relief as Hamlin went out the door, "don't marry a man who works at home. Marry one who goes to work at eight every morning and doesn't come home till five."[10]

In January 1920 Garland received a check for five hundred dollars for "The Spirit World on Trial," an article discussing the advances of science in confirming the existence of psychic phenomena. He had been commissioned to write the piece for *McClure's*, which wanted to capitalize on the wave of interest in spirit communication caused by the bereavements of the Great War and the forthcoming U.S. tour of Sir Oliver Lodge, the eminent British physicist whose book *Raymond, or Life and Death* had been a sensational success in 1916 (the book traced his spirit communication with his son, who had been killed in the war). With the proceeds Garland bought a new seven-hundred-dollar Ford and promptly christened it the "Spook," with Constance painting its name on the doors. His decision had been prompted in part by the example of John Burroughs, who, at age eighty-three, one day coolly drove up to Camp Neshonoc.

Garland marveled at the advent of this new technological marvel and at age sixty, after a lifetime astride horses or traveling by train, was determined to master the machine and enjoy the freedom of travel it offered. "Daddy spent hours each day polishing it and 'tinkering,' as he called it, 'with the mixture,'" Mary Isabel recalled, "which was possibly why it was always so reluctant to start." She and her father received driving lessons from a neighbor's chauffeur, but when Garland's erratic driving prompted his teacher to yell "Damn you, Garland! Get your foot off that gas!" he delegated most of the driving to his more proficient daughter. And matters weren't helped when, out driving a mere month after having bought the car, he tipped the "Spook" over after meeting another vehicle on the road. Nothing was hurt but his pride—"It was a sad blow to me that I should have an accident the first time I go out at night," he reflected. "I had a hard time to get to sleep." Neighbors marveled at the sight of the "Spook"-emblazoned car pulling into Garland's Cheyenne tepee, which had become the garage.[11]

In January he also met Edward Marsh with a copy of his Grant biography tucked under his arm, hoping that Macmillan would be interested in reprinting it, reminding readers of Grant's importance to the nation's history. The formerly prolific author had not published a book in three years, and he was mindful that his name was fading from public awareness. Marsh readily agreed to the venture, for he seems to have greatly admired Garland's writing. As soon as he secured Marsh's consent, Garland made his way to the headquarters of the *Mentor*, an education magazine that published a single article in each issue; its motto: "Learn One Thing Every Day." Its editor, William Moffat, agreed to publish an excerpt. Garland also lined up an article on his friend Irving Bacheller for *Red Cross Magazine*.[12] Jubilantly, Garland jotted down his progress in the restoration of his reputation: "I am to be in the March Mentor 400000 Red Cross Magazine 1000000, McClures 600000"—the numbers referring to the magazines' circulation. "As the children say, people are going to hear about me one of these days."[13] He was immensely gratified when *Ulysses S. Grant* was published in October, for at a Chicago book fair he signed copies for two and a half hours, bemusedly noting, "I never before had the sense of having a really popular book. We must have sold two hundred copies."[14]

In June 1921, after putting off his publisher for three years while he labored to revise his prose, Garland finally delivered the manuscript of *A Daughter of the Middle Border* to Macmillan. Despite his years of authorship, of having proved time and again that he could deliver the goods, he still worried about his manuscript's reception. "I have a sense of panic lest it shall turn out not to be good enough," he recorded, "but it seems as a thing accomplished now."[15] By August, when the first proofs arrived, he was more encouraged. "As I run rapidly over the proof I began to realize that to many readers it will seem a notably wide arc of activity," he reflected. "To go from the Skeena to Surrey, to write three volumes of fiction in the same year, to study Cheyennes and Navajoes, and to take a wife on a honeymoon in the Rockies and then to Washington [and] to New York is to be active—to put it modestly. . . . I begin to think the book may succeed!!"[16]

He labored over page proofs in September, uncertain whether readers would find interesting this continuation of his life story, which begins the day after the Thanksgiving feast that concluded *Son* and ends with the death of his father in 1914. After reading the proofs cover to cover in an eight-hour stint, he found many passages he still wanted to revise, even after seven complete revisions, but realized it was too late: the manuscript now "must take its chances." For four years he had been struggling to turn his personal biography into an emblem of the American myth that anyone—even a plowboy from Iowa—can succeed if he or she has determination enough, all too aware that the process was complicated by the entrance of his family into his chronicle, for the myth worked best for lone strugglers on the upward trail. But he thought he had largely succeeded, for "when I get away from its transitory personal aspects it takes on something of the character of History. Whether it is noble or trivial will depend upon the reader," he mused. "Some will find it unduly personal, no doubt, others will wish the revelation had been made more complete. So far as I am concerned—I, the writer, I wish it were better in a literary sense. Not all of it has that final unchangeable character which I find in my best work."[17]

Even amid his doubts about the public's interest in *Daughter*, he had broached to Macmillan the idea of taking up a number of his Harper's books and reissuing them in that venue so flattering to an author's ego, the uniform set. As he explained to Henry Hoyns, a vice-president at Harper's, "I am merely trying to keep them in print and in a uniform edition."[18] Macmillan was willing to gamble on the venture on the strength of the continuing sale of *Son*, but Garland would have to pay for the plates and existing stock, which effectively derailed the plan. As he told Harold Latham, his Macmillan editor (who would later edit Margaret Mitchell's *Gone with the Wind*), "No doubt the offer you have made is all you can afford but as it is only half of what I get now without any expenditure at all is seems the part of wisdom to let the books stay where they are." Besides, he added, in a typically unsavvy coda, "there is very little sale in any of the books and you are not missing anything."[19]

A Daughter of the Middle Border was scheduled for publication on November 1, and Garland eagerly awaited the first ads. In June he had met with Latham, who had promised "a wide—and vigorous campaign of advertising." But when Garland scanned the publishers' announcements of new books in the Sunday papers of October 2, he failed to find any mention of *Daughter*. "The Macmillan Co has lost interest in it and no longer considers it an important book," he concluded, and promptly telephoned Latham to complain.[20] "The best time for advertising and promoting a book is on the book's publication," Latham patiently explained. "If advertising appears prior to its issue much of its effect is lost through the inability to make immediate sales."[21]

By December 18 only three reviews had appeared, and those were by friends. "It is clearly evident to me," he wrote to Latham, "that Macmillans do not consider my book of sufficient appeal to warrant featuring it in their advertising and so I wish you would come tomorrow prepared to tell me what it will cost to give the book a quick sharp campaign of advertising in the *Times*, the Boston Transcript, the Chicago Tribune and the Los Angeles Times. I have put too many years of work into this book to allow it to fade out."[22] What pained Garland was that in the ads he had seen, Macmillan's advertising did not feature his book in the manner to which he had become accustomed: large ads devoted solely to his book, with prominent display type, illustrations, and quotations from eminent writers. Instead, Macmillan had merely listed his book—in the *New York Times*, for example—as one of a number of Macmillan titles.[23] When he met Latham for lunch the next day, he made it plain he was "desperately dissatisfied" with the Macmillan promotional campaign and offered to waive royalties, "provided those royalties were put into advertising." "The plain truth is my sales are pitiful," he told Latham. "With the aid of Howells, Roosevelt, Burroughs and all my good friends we have sold less than fifteen thousand copies of the Son—and less than ten thousand copies of the Daughter. This is no sale at all."[24]

By January Garland was thoroughly demoralized. "It seems as if all interest in me had suddenly ceased," he mourned. "All I had won by thirty five years effort seems of no value whatsoever."[25] Desperate to pump life into what he perceived as a flaccid marketing campaign, he spent the next day at the Macmillan office, where he learned that the company had indeed done little by way of prepublication publicity and that current efforts had ceased. Determined to rescue his book—and his reputation—he wrote to a number of editorial friends to solicit reviews, each time suggesting that the writer be sure to promote the book as a companion to its more successful predecessor. He went over Latham's head to complain to the president of Macmillan, George Platt Brett: "I am deeply disturbed and humiliated by the failure of my second volume to meet the expectations of your editors," he wrote on January 23, nearly three months after the publication of *Daughter*. "The fact that you are not willing to advertise it individually and that you have ceased to advertise it in any way proves that you have no faith in it." He asked about issuing a lower-priced edition of *Son*, which sold for $2.50, hoping that a reissue might revitalize the sales of *Daughter*. "I am heart-sick over the whole situation," he concluded. "I would think the book worthless if it were not for the opinions of a few men whose judgment I trust."[26] In his reply, Brett reassured the despondent author that Macmillan was "pleased to have published so notable and so interesting a book." He reminded Garland that few sequels sell as well or command as much attention as the first book and told him that he had complete faith the book would, with time, find its market. "If I recollect rightly," he reminded Garland, "you were somewhat similarly discouraged with the sale of the earlier volume shortly after it was published but that book did, in the end, sell pretty well."[27]

Amid the *Daughter* advertising debacle, Garland's spirits rallied somewhat by an offer from Harper's to publish twelve of his books in a uniform set in May. Macmillan's tentative interest in taking over Garland's books had apparently caused Harper's to revalue their property. Reissuing the books involved little financial risk, for Harper's would simply print from the existing plates and bind in a uniform cover. It helped that Edward Marsh, his editor at Macmillan, who had resigned in May 1920 to take an editorial position at Harper's, would be his editor for the project—and promised to make a strong push in publicity, which is what Garland really most desired. Hamlin agreed to contribute a new foreword to each volume, which would simply be added to the existing sheets, and he was quite willing to accept a reduced royalty of 10 percent if it meant getting his work back before the public—for he hoped that a uniform edition would revive sales of his autobiographies. As he went through his Harper's titles, evaluating each book, he realized his strongest books concerned western subjects, and so he and his publishers settled upon a dozen titles for the "Border Edition": *Main-Travelled Roads, Other Main-Travelled Roads, Boy Life on the Prairie, Rose of Dutcher's Coolly, The Eagle's Heart, The Captain of the Gray-Horse Troop, Hesper, Money Magic* (retitled *Mart Haney's Mate*), *Cavanagh, Forest Ranger, They of the High Trails, The Long Trail,* and *The Forester's Daughter*. To this collected edition, Harper's promised to add a volume of Garland's collected Indian fiction as well as another installment of his autobiography (for he had given up on Macmillan), both to be published at a later date.[28]

In the midst of work on the Border Edition, Garland was puzzling over what to do about Mary Isabel. She was due to graduate from the Finch Academy in May. She had inherited her father's interest in drama and had become a talented actress in school plays. When she announced that she intended to pursue a career on the stage, her protective father, well aware of the casual morality common among acting folk, offered to send her to England if she would postpone her decision, hoping that a delay would lead her to other enthusiasms. He wasn't sure how he would pay for the trip, but he was hopeful that, somehow, royalties from *Daughter* and the Border Edition would make the trip possible. As he mulled over the proposed trip, he began to think of taking the whole family abroad for an extended visit. He was in part prompted by the need to refresh his lectures on English authors, for it had been some sixteen years since he had last been to England, and he had just signed a two-year contract with the Keedick Lecture Bureau to manage his lectures. But another reason was that the years of mining his past for literary material had become an agreeable habit, and he thought of bringing his autobiography up to the present. "In arguing it to myself," he recalled, "I spoke of it as a farther exploration of 'Back East' country—an extension of the family back-trailing," for his and Zulime's ancestors had emigrated from England.[29] He secured berths on March 6 and then "visited the bank to see how much money I had left," all the while worrying about the wisdom of the expenditure.[30]

Then on April 6, during a meeting at the American Academy, Garland learned unofficially from Maurice Eagan, the chair of the biography jury, that *A Daughter of the Middle Border* had been awarded the Pulitzer Prize for biography. Naturally, he was enormously gratified by this recognition of his book, the product of so much toil and despair, but even more satisfying was the thousand-dollar prize money that, he noted, "comes opportunely" like "something found in the grass."[31] While Garland nonchalantly plays down the award in his memoirs, in truth he was privy to the backstage maneuvering surrounding the prize. His friend William Allen White, the editor of the Emporia, Kansas, *Gazette* and one of the jury members, had written Garland on March 20 to inform him that he had voted the prize to him, enclosed a copy of his letter to Eagan recording his vote, and vowed to "yell like a coyote" if "Columbia University goes to monkeying with these awards" as it did the previous year when the Pulitzer board "rather ruthlessly took the award away, and gave it to

Edith Wharton for her novel." One wonders how Garland reacted to White's promise, since it had been he who was instrumental in denying the award to Lewis's *Main Street*.[32]

Added to this accolade was a call by an enterprising graduate student, who came to interview Garland for her master's thesis about his work. Garland was gratified by this recognition, the first academic treatment of his work, but he was also bemused by being "the subject of a careful historical monograph—precisely as though I were a personage in the past. . . . It is hard for me to get that sort of view of myself and my work. I have been so long a 'promising writer.'"[33]

On May 31 Garland sailed to England in advance of his family, his chief task being to secure a home for the next four months, for he wanted his daughters to experience life in England and not merely to become tourists. He was also mulling over how to write the third volume of his autobiography, which would cover the years 1915 to the present. On the one hand, he had the evidence of the *Daughter* debacle to show him that the public had little interest in his later life; on the other, the Pulitzer Prize suggested, notwithstanding sales, that his life story had merit to discerning readers. Then he was struck with an idea: why not make his planned luncheons with English authors the centerpiece of the volume? He knew from his lectures that people were always interested in the doings of celebrities, and his account would also demonstrate his own importance to literary culture and serve as an antidote to his increasing sense of displacement from current literature. The trick would be to tell the story in such a way that the egotism of his motive would be concealed; he would therefore focus the narrative on his daughters' reactions to the famous and cast himself as the bemused father enjoying his daughters' coming-of-age. Who could object to that? He also planned to make the book a family project. Constance had inherited her mother's artistic talent and already, at age fifteen, was an accomplished illustrator. While in England he would introduce her to Arthur Rackham, the famed illustrator of children's books. From her father Mary Isabel had inherited an attraction to the written word, and with her help in typing and editing and Constance's drawings, he hoped to make an appealing book. "If we can 'rough-out' a frame-work for it while I am a long way from my diaries," he mused from his London flat, "I can fill it in from the records after I return."[34]

In July and August Garland and his family made the rounds of English society, calling on old friends such as George Bernard Shaw, Arthur Conan Doyle, James Barrie, and Rudyard Kipling, and meeting new authors, such as Joseph Conrad and A. A. Milne. When they returned to the United States on October 22, Hamlin had filled his notebooks with fresh impressions for lectures and made a start on the manuscript that would evolve into *Back-Trailers from the Middle Border*, a generous section of which was devoted to this English summer.

Shortly before he sailed to England, Garland had arranged the contents for the promised collection of his Indian fiction, which would be published as *The Book of the American Indian*. He had selected five stories previously published in periodicals ("A Spartan Mother," "Nistina," "The Iron Khiva," "The New Medicine House," and "Drifting Crane") and an unpublished story, "Hotan, the Red Pioneer," as well as "The Silent Eaters," a novella that traces the life and death of Sitting Bull, in particular his efforts to resist cultural disenfranchisement and to protect and prolong the Sioux way of life. Garland had based his account on his interviews with Sioux chiefs and white traders and agents at Standing Rock in 1897 and 1900, as well as on a detailed examination of agency records. "The Silent Eaters" had lain in his drawer for twenty years, and he was eager to see it, at long last, published. He revised the stories, left them with Edward Marsh, and departed for England.

But on August 14, 1922, he received disturbing news from Marsh: "Hotan" was unsatisfactory and would have to be omitted. Worse, the estimate of the volume's length was seriously off: "All of the stories, but particularly 'The Silent Eaters,' are considerably shorter than we estimated," Marsh wrote. "You must have cut more than I supposed. The book is really too short as it stands. We should have to pad it out to get the requisite number of pages, and the appearance of padding will hurt it. . . . This book must look right and it is a matter of great importance, in my judgment, to have a few thousand more words. If the original copy is not accessible, can we not dig out some copy from some of the old magazines in which certain stories appeared?"[35]

Garland directed Marsh to go to his New York apartment and raid his files in search of additional material. On September 6 Marsh wrote to say that he had "succeeded in burglarizing your apartment and taking out the Indian material from the two files which you designated."[36] From those files Marsh selected nine stories to supplement Garland's original selection. Six had appeared previously in magazines: "The Outlaw" (revised as "The Story of Howling Wolf"), "Lone Wolf's Old Guard," "Big Moggasen," "The Storm-Child," "The River's Warning," and "Rising Wolf—Ghost Dancer." Three—"The Blood Lust," "The Remorse of Waumdisapa," and "A Decree of Council"—saw publication for the first time in *The Book of the American Indian.* By the time Garland returned from England in October, Marsh had arranged the contents, and proofs were waiting for Garland's approval.

When he and Garland had first planned the volume, Marsh had proposed including extensive illustrations by Frederic Remington to increase sales. Like Garland's stories, the illustrations had previously appeared in *Harper's Magazine* or *Harper's Weekly,* periodicals published by the Harper firm, so the material would be available without payment of permission fees to another publisher.

At first, Garland opposed including Remington's work because he detested the man and was deeply opposed to the manner of his sketches, which he believed to be markedly at odds with his own perspective. Years later he summarized his objection: "My design was directly opposite to that of Remington, who carried to the study of these hunters all the contempt, all the conventional notions of a hard and rather prosaic illustrator. He never got the wilderness point of view. His white hunters were all ragged, bearded, narrow between the eyes, and his red men stringy, gross of feature, and cruel. I recognized no harmony between his drawings and my text."[37] Marsh apparently convinced Garland that the firm's bottom line needed the illustrations, for they planned a handsome, oversize book ($12\frac{1}{2}$" x 9") with a generous page size (a text block of $7\frac{1}{2}$" x 4"), both to set off the illustrations and to compensate for the shortness of text, which would sell for $6.00, rather than the $2.50 of the Border Edition books. Harper's was also busily building a list of books about the American Indian, with such titles as *Adventures of Buffalo Bill*, William Cody's autobiography; *Crooked Trails* and *Pony Tracks*, Remington's collections of illustrated essays (both reissued in 1923); and a number of other novels and collections. The large-format *Book of the American Indian*, marketed as an art book (with the authorial credit reading "Written by Hamlin Garland/Pictured by Frederic Remington"), would be the standout book of the list.

The inclusion of Remington's illustrations proved to be a wise marketing decision. Although the book was not a best-seller, it did sell "more than ten times the number of copies" Garland anticipated, and today good copies are in demand in used-and rare-book stores.[38] When the book was published in October 1923, reviewers praised the stories as an important event in the nation's literary history. The *New York Times Book Review*, for example, lauded Garland for his "service to American literature." Of the stories, the review concluded that "If they do no more than prick our conscience as to a national responsibility toward an ancient race which, as the Indian Bureau reminds us, is slowly increasing, then they will bring their greatest honor to a distinguished American writer."[39] The *New York Evening Post* called the book "an American document of distinct value," and Henry Fuller, reviewing for the *New York Herald*, praised Garland's "full knowledge of the various human elements involved" and his spirit of reform: "He writes with indignation and with a strong emphasis on special cases." Fuller certainly well understood Garland's aims, for as Garland's closest friend he had read the drafts of "The Silent Eaters" in manuscript and knew the pains Garland had taken to make his stories an accurate reflection of the life he had witnessed. Indeed, the review focuses on the accuracy of Garland's portrait of Sitting Bull. "Here at last," Fuller remarked, "is a detailed account of the affair and its culminating catastrophe from the Indian viewpoint.[40]

As a volume designed as a "gift book"—what today we would call a "coffee table book"—*The Book of the American Indian* has a certain appeal, for it was indeed a handsomely executed volume. As Garland later realized, the book would not have been published if it hadn't included Remington's illustrations, but he also appreciated the irony of their inclusion, for they have virtually no connection with the stories themselves, having been selected largely because of their availability and the appeal of Remington's name. Indeed, Garland must have been aghast at the disjunctive effects of some of the illustrations. For example, the illustration "A Kiowa Maiden" appears within "Wahiah—A Spartan Mother," a story about Cheyenne Indians at the Darlington Agency in Oklahoma, not the Kiowa. Worse, the illustration's caption is markedly at odds with the plot of the story. "Wahiah" is about the subjugation of Cheyenne children to the white man's desire to put them in school. The focus of the story is the headmaster's discipline, which involves whipping a child who refuses to attend school until his spirit is broken. And the whipping is no mere show whipping: the headmaster wears two rods to a frazzle before spanking the boy, the shame of which finally breaks him. The parents are ready to kill the teacher but finally come to respect the headmaster, who points out that the children are doomed unless they learn English and adapt to conditions; in response, the mother snaps in two her son's bow and arrows, the boy's "symbols of freedom." But the caption of the illustration ignores the plot and theme and substitutes instead a fantasy of wish fulfillment: "That Indian parents are very proud of their children's progress is evidenced by the eagerness with which they send their sons and daughters to the schools established by the Government on the different Indian reservations. The Kiowa maiden here pictured is one of the many Indian girls and boys who are more and more availing themselves of the opportunity to obtain an education and thus fit themselves to take their places in civilized society." The illustration was originally published as an accompaniment to Richard Harding Davis's "The West from a Car Window," in *Harper's Weekly* of May 14, 1892. That illustration included no caption, as indeed did none of the illustrations in their original magazine publication. When assembling *The Book of the American Indian*, some functionary at Harper's, with an eye out the window rather than on the text, apparently wrote this and the other captions without reading the stories themselves.

Similar effects occur elsewhere in the volume, suggesting that the uncredited caption writer had devoured popular accounts depicting Indians as bloodthirsty savages. The sketch "An Apache Indian" is placed within "The Iron Khiva," a story of the Hopis, and its caption describes the "hideously cruel" Apache of the title as a "red-handed murderer." Occasionally, the caption writer had better luck: "The Medicine Man's Signal," originally illustrating Remington's report "The Sioux Outbreak in South Dakota," appropriately appears within "Rising Wolf, Ghost Dancer." And the writer may have been familiar with Garland's stories about the Wisconsin coulees, for the caption to "Footprints in the Snow," illustrating "The Storm-Child," a story about a child lost in the snow, warns about Indians "popping out of some coulee." Sometimes, too, the caption writer simply gave up and confessed his or her ignorance. The caption to "An Indian Trapper," incongruously placed within "The Story of Howling Wolf," reads, "This Indian trapper depicted by Remington may be a Cree, or perhaps a Blackfoot." Ironically, although Remington did illustrate "Drifting Crane" for its original 1890 publication in *Harper's Weekly*, that illustration did not appear in *The Book of the American Indian*.

At the time they were composed, the stories in *The Book of the American Indian* marked a significant departure from stories and journalism by white authors depicting Indians as treacherous and barbaric savages. Even though his attitude toward Indians reflects the cultural paternalism of the times, Garland also respects Native Americans as people with developed cultures that ought to be preserved and protected from exploitation and racial eradication. In "The Redman as Material," one of the earliest essays treating the Indian as a figure in literature, he indicts writers who have shaped public opinion through their misrepresentations of Indians. "All this would be harmless enough if the reader only understood that the novelist doesn't know anything about 'Injuns,'" he notes, "but the gentle reader is part of a great public, and reading this kind of thing leads to false notions of human life. Such fiction has helped to make the English-speaking peoples the most ruthless conquerors the world has ever seen."[41] Garland's stories about American Indians are his attempt to correct false representations of Indians by showing the shared humanity among all people who occupy the American West.

In November 1922 Garland set out on a lecture tour with nineteen-year-old Mary Isabel, hoping her participation on the platform would sate her desire for the stage. Together they delivered a program entitled "Memories of the Middle Border" in which they took turns reading excerpts from Garland's stories, poems, and autobiographies, with Mary Isabel costumed alternately as her mother and grandmother. While Garland remembered the tour as being an unqualified success, Mary Isabel recounts moments of success and failure. "We were doing one-night stands and it was hard and exhausting work," she explained to a correspondent in 1963. After a snowy February performance in Pennsylvania, "Daddy said in deep dejection, 'Well, daughter, we were a failure that time.' At which point I burst into tears."[42] The strain of measuring up to her father's high expectations took its toll in occasional quarrels, and soon Mary Isabel reminded her father of his promise to let her pursue a stage career. Garland wasn't about to set his favorite daughter loose among the laid-back morality of the thespians he railed against in his campaign against the modernists, so he arranged a spot for her in the National Theater Company, where she would be under the supervisory eye of his close friend Augustus Thomas. But Garland's effort to protect his daughter was in vain, for during the first week of rehearsals she "learned more of the seamy side of life than I had learned before or since," in particular "the modern connotation of the word 'fairy.'"[43] Later, in March 1923, Garland would make a similar arrangement for her in the acting company of his friend Walter Hampden, where she played bit parts in *Cyrano de Bergerac*.[44] With Mary Isabel busy on the stage, sixteen-year-old Constance stepped into her place on the lecture platform.

Meanwhile, Garland was delivering a set of lectures entitled

"Personal Reminiscences of Famous English Authors," the harvest of his 1922 trip to England.[45] Seeking to repeat the success of the previous summer, in 1923 he returned with his family for another summer in England, where he entered into another round of luncheons with English authors. He would make similar trips, without his family, in 1924 and 1925, each time returning with reams of notes to vitalize his lectures.

He kept plodding away at the twin manuscripts of *Trail-Makers* and *Back-Trailers*, the former a mostly fictional and romantic account of his father's pioneering, the latter his ongoing life story. He confessed doing so to be "a fond and foolish desire on my part," but "I still have a feeble impulse to do something to which posterity will refer"—all too aware that "posterity wont do it, of course."[46] He trudged on, more out of habit and the human desire for recognition that his achievements mattered than out of any expectation of financial return. For a while, the usually decisive author couldn't decide which manuscript to complete: he was dismayed by the thinness of his diaries and struggled to retrieve the memories he had intended his notes to evoke. "When I set them down," he recalled, "I had the notion that a line, a word, a phrase would bring back the complete picture—but they do not." But the "Pathfinder," as he then called *Trail-Makers*, had similarly bogged down—until Henry Fuller read the manuscript and suggested turning the semi-fictional novel into a prologue to *Son* and calling it "A Pioneer of the Middle Border." "If it can be read in this way I shall immediately set to work to expand the present m.s. and fit it into the scheme," Garland decided.[47] A prequel was born, and *Back-Trailers* went into the drawer.

In October a letter arrived from Macmillan offering a contract for *Trail-Makers*. "I am reluctant to sign any contract with any firm which will leave me helpless," Garland wrote to Harold Latham, alluding to the lack of distinctive advertising for *Daughter*. "I'll quit publishing altogether rather than go through another such period of disappointment. . . . My work must be treated with distinguished emphasis or remain unpublished. It may not be worthy of such honor," he admitted, "but I shall put my best into what I publish and the publisher must put his best into the advertising and sale of the finished product."[48] He and Latham could not agree on terms, and Garland set the manuscript aside for the year. Later he turned to setting one publisher against the other, telling Latham that he was going "to make a test of its quality with Harpers." He was encouraged by a favorable report from the Harper's readers, who believed *Trail-Makers* "to be an important book" and wanted to feature it in their advertising, and he turned with renewed interest to revision—but in no hurry to publish, for he was baffled by how to link his father's mostly fictional war service, which concluded the book, with the largely factual account of his pioneering. The facts as he knew them served to check his ability to create fiction.[49]

While Garland delighted in the comparative quiet that Camp Neshonoc, his retreat in the Catskills, provided for his writing, as he approached age sixty-five he wearied of the inconveniences of a rough, drafty cabin without electricity. One cold May morning he felt the discomfort more keenly and complained, "each morning I get up in a cold room, wash in cold water and go into a cold kitchen to make my break-fast—then I shiver in my study with an oil stove feebly trying to take the chill off the air. . . . Havent I had enough of pioneering?"[50] He spent the weeks on either side of his monthlong trip to England remodeling the house, adding two bathrooms, a new roof, and electric lights, proud that at nearly sixty-five he could rely on his carpentry skills. But then in August 1925 came an opportunity to buy a larger, two-story home situated on a ledge above Camp Neshonoc, near the top of Onteora Mountain. For days he debated the expense, for he would need to become a dues-paying member of the Onteora Corporation, a homeowners' association within whose domain the house fell. In the end, lured by creature comforts, Garland bought the house (for four thousand dollars), christened it "Grey Ledge," and wallowed in the luxury of the largest study he had had since the one in the West Salem homestead. It helped that, in the midst of moving into Grey Ledge, he learned of a pirated film version of *Cavanagh*; he demanded—and got—ten thousand dollars in royalties.[51] Ironically, the royalty for this pirated film was more than twice what he received for his four Vitagraph productions. Two months later, the Garlands moved from their Ninety-second Street apartment to a flat at 507 Cathedral Parkway, the former home the victim of a wrecking ball. With an eye for future historians whom he hoped would read his diaries, Hamlin noted, "For nine years I have lived and wrought in this row of rooms in the top middle story of a run-down smelly apartment building known as Holland Court—I set this down for any one interested hereafter"—and then described the books he had composed in the flat.[52]

On November 19, 1925, Mary Isabel took her father aside to announce her plans to marry Hardesty Johnson, first tenor and leader of the Jean de Reszke Singers, whom she had first met in England in 1922. He had urged her to pursue a career, if not college, but Mary Isabel was more interested in marriage than in earning a living. Earlier, Garland had headed off a potentially disastrous liaison with one "Bill," an actor Mary Isabel met in the Hampden troupe, and in her memoir she confesses it was a near thing. Even her limited experience with acting had introduced her to actors' casual attitude toward marital fidelity, and she agreed to marriage only on the condition that "Bill" give up acting. But when she discovered that "Bill" had returned to the stage, she broke off the relationship. Garland much admired Hardesty, impressed with his singing ability, and when the de Reszke Singers returned to the United States in a program that featured Will Rogers, to be headquartered in New York, Garland was resigned to the inevitable, taking comfort that his daughter would remain near.[53]

Mary Isabel and Hardesty Johnson were married on May 12, 1926, at the home of Fenton B. Turck. While Garland had the normal father's concern for a singer's ability to provide for his daughter, he soon became his son-in-law's eager booster, adding him to his lecture program, where Hardesty would sing songs of the middle border with Mary Isabel accompanying him on the piano. The bride was twenty-three and eager for married life. "There was nothing abandoned about our wedding night," she remembered. "I had experienced almost nothing and tossed and turned and finally got up and sat in a chair by the window for the rest of the night," while her husband slept, unaware of his wife's dissatisfaction. The next morning, he told her, "You know, darling, we mustn't make a habit of this" as he spurned her attentions.[54] Hardesty, whose heart had been weakened by rheumatic fever, worried that sexual activity would endanger his health. For the next ten years, Mary Isabel would keep secret her marital dissatisfaction and eventual separation even as Garland sent her monthly "allowance" checks of one hundred dollars to make up for Hardesty's intermittent paychecks.

Meanwhile, Garland continued to revise *Trail-Makers*, struggling to find a way to combine "what I know from the talk of my relatives and what I imagine" about his father's pioneering, for he was convinced that his father's story represented the westering impulse that had created America. Harper's was no longer interested in the book, he wrote to Latham, because it was too closely linked to the middle border saga published by the rival house; they would have much preferred "a long manuscript which could be treated entirely by itself and not as an introduction to 'A Son of the Middle Border.'"[55] He was still dissatisfied with the second half of the manuscript, the section treating his father's war service, despite eight years of work on it. "It is too shrewd a trade between truth and fiction to be successful," he decided, realizing he could do no more with it. And then he gloomily concluded, "I doubt if the book will enhance my reputation. Probably it will be sharply criticized as a decline in creative power."[56]

Eventually, after much dickering about terms, which included Macmillan's promise to publish five thousand copies of a one-volume edition of *Son* and *Daughter*, *Trail-Makers* was scheduled for publication in October 1926. Cementing the deal was a commission of $350 for Constance to illustrate the volume—"a most joyous outcome of my plan," the proud father recorded, "for she will not only go on my title page—but she is to help me on the side where I am weakest. She will give charm and youth to my book."[57] Ever the devotee of veritism, he and Constance repaired to the New York Public Library, where they spent several hours poring over back issues of *Harper's Weekly* of 1859 to 1863, studying the illustrations.

As publication drew near, Garland was again on tenterhooks. The recognition conferred by the Pulitzer Prize for *Daughter* led him to worry that this prequel to his story would not live up to the expectations created by the previous two volumes of his saga. Then, too, he had not published a book since 1923 and was wary of a repetition of the humiliation he had suffered over the promotion of *A Daughter of the Middle Border*. Suddenly, he was sure the book would fail and was convinced the critics would pounce. "It is an unassuming little book," he wrote to Brett; "I am asking your publicity department to 'sing small' in its praise. I should be sorry to have my readers approach it in too expectant a mood."[58] Brett, who hadn't yet read the book, replied that "the publicity department is making this book their most important book of the year, placing it in all the advertisements and anticipating a very considerable demand for it."[59] Then, on October 15, came good news: the entire first printing of fifteen thousand copies had already sold out before the official publication, and a new printing was in the works. "It seems incredible that this plain, unexciting little book should outsell my other books," Garland mused.[60] One wonders whether Latham had the grace to admit he was wrong, and Garland right, about the effect of prepublication publicity.

Four days later, Brett had finally made time to read the book. "He thinks it one of the best things you have ever done," Latham told Garland. "He says he can sell fifty thousand copies of it almost at once."[61] Brett directed Latham to devote the whole energies of the Macmillan Company into promoting the book in a "'best seller' campaign"—provided Garland would agree to an amended contract that offered him a smaller royalty in exchange for "at least" ten thousand dollars in advertising.[62] In addition to a big push in newspaper advertising, the firm issued a lavish publicity pamphlet entitled *Hamlin Garland, Memories of the Middle Border*, with illustrations by Constance and reprints of favorable reviews of his work. Macmillan was especially proud of Garland's latest accomplishment: an honorary doctorate from the University of Wisconsin, which he had received on June 21, 1926, the first of his four honorary degrees. The pamphlet began by quoting the conferral address and touting Garland as "a native son receiving the highest literary distinction his State could give him."[63] Brett's faith in the appeal of Garland's latest book was not misplaced, and while it did not sell the number of copies the firm had hoped for, it did garner respectful and for the most part positive reviews.

For the first time since *Hesper*, Garland had a popular success; indeed, in terms of copies sold during the year following its publication, *Trail-Makers* was Garland's best-selling book—a fact that truly astonished him. Even in the midst of the boom, Garland could not "believe that there is enough in the book to warrant a larger sale," but he attributed any interest to "the psychology of the hour" in which readers sought escape from the incursion of the modernists by "developing an appreciation of the romance of our early history."[64]

While Garland was enjoying an unexpected best-seller, Constance was dating Joseph Wesley Harper, a great-grandson of one of the founders of Harper and Brothers. On July 28, 1927, she announced her plans to marry. She was barely twenty. "I am not happy over this decision," Garland wrote, as much bothered by the prospective loss of his illustrator as by the pitfalls of early marriage. Despite his earlier advocacy of women continuing to work after marriage—as indicated in *Rose of Dutcher's Coolly*—he seems to have assumed that Constance would abandon their partnership after her marriage. But he realized his wishes could not trump love: "She must do as her mother did—abandon her father's tribe for the tribe of the alien."[65] The couple was married on September 12 at Grey Ledge, leaving shortly thereafter for Hollywood, where Joe's mother had a home on DeMille Drive, near the palatial estate of Cecil B. DeMille. Constance would return for Christmas, but the Harpers planned to live in Hollywood where Joe was an enterprising land developer. A doting father, Garland was morose about the breakup of his family, although he recognized its inevitability.

The success of *Trail-Makers* revived interest in Garland's work, and Macmillan wasted little time in pressing Garland to finish the concluding volume of his family saga. On May 1, Brett told Garland he wanted *Back-Trailers* for fall publication. "I want to make it our big feature non-fiction book," he informed the sixty-seven-year-old writer, who had now grown accustomed to a more leisurely pace of composition. But Brett also wanted Garland to transform his diaries "into a literary autobiography and make it my final and biggest work." Garland "came home shaken out of my easy attitude." The prospect was so overwhelming "that I could hardly sleep."[66]

His apprehension is easy to understand. Earlier, in casting about for a project to take up after *Back-Trailers*, it had occurred to Garland that his diaries still contained still plenty of unmined material about literary celebrities; he had therefore selected a number of key entries, transcribed them, and sent a trial manuscript to Macmillan. He envisioned publishing a selection of his encounters with authors and presenting them as dated entries, with occasional supplementary comment—a method that would involve some expansion but not the wholesale recasting necessary for a full literary autobiography. Since 1898 Garland had been keeping a daily diary, a book-size notebook specifically printed for that purpose into which he had crammed his observations of celebrities and reflections about the events of his life. He had now accumulated some thirty volumes, filled with his crabbed, barely decipherable script. Then, too, because the entries tended to be composed of brief, fragmented impressions, often entered at odd moments on trains or late at night, Garland would need to expand his comments considerably. After he conceived the project and began editing his diaries, in 1925, the character of his diaries changed and he began to record his impressions with an eye for their eventual public audience, which affected not only the details he set down but also the style and tone of his prose.

Brett wanted a book that would encompass the whole of Garland's literary career, beginning with his arrival in Boston in 1884, one that would offer Garland's perspective on the leading literary figures of the day. From Brett's standpoint, such a volume would have an obvious appeal to readers who delighted in gossip about famous writers, timed to appear shortly after *Back-Trailers* had directed readerly interest to Garland; for Garland, the venture was attractive because the volume would further ensure his legacy by showcasing his importance to literary culture.

When he warned Brett that such a project could easily fill several volumes, Brett appeared undaunted. For the first twenty-four years of his career, Garland had only occasional dated records, so he would have to rely primarily upon his memory—and upon his enormous archive of correspondence, lecture notes, offprints, manuscripts, and other ephemera of a man of letters. No one knew better than Garland how extensive his field of literary acquaintance was, and the sheer magnitude of the job was overwhelming. At first he was perplexed about how to proceed, for his middle border saga had interwoven his career with his family history, and he was wary about the necessary repetition. Latham argued that few readers would compare the twin series. And Garland was reluctant to give up his fixation on presenting the book as a series of dated entries. Only after Latham repeatedly cajoled him about the necessity for a connective narrative thread—and after he ran the plan by Henry Fuller, his chief literary adviser now that Howells was dead—did Garland agree to what amounted to a complete rewriting of his four middle border books with the emphasis on his literary, and not family, life.

With his next project on the horizon, Garland bent to the task of a final revision of *Back-Trailers*, laboring mightily to repeat the tone and artistry of its predecessors. For a time he had called the manuscript "Granddaughters of the Middle Border," seeking to carry on the family metaphor of the previous volumes. Beginning with his removal to New York in 1915, it carried his story forward to the marriage of his daughters and treated honestly his successes and failures. "If I have succeeded, even measurably, in the purpose of this final volume," Garland wrote in an afterword, "the experiences of my family on its backward-tracing pilgrimage will be seen as typical of the present as the explorations of my father's family was of the past."[67] But while he periodically punctuated his narrative with references to the representative nature of his family's adventures, the story remains focused on the particular events of an extraordinarily fortuitous family: the father, who, through sheer strength of will rather than native genius, nudged his way into prominence; the daughters, enjoying the opportunities brought to them by their father's activities, blissfully unaware of their privilege. Zulime has a curiously minor presence, a bit player hovering in the background in a narrative suffused with the nostalgia of a man keenly aware that his heyday has passed.

Back-Trailers from the Middle Border was published in October 1928, accompanied by illustrations by Constance, who, to her father's delight, did not let marriage interfere with her part of the family project. Reviewers were respectful but tepid, noting Garland's shift from the representative nature of the earlier volumes to focus on the personal. "While the new volume is not so valuable as historical material," the *Los Angeles Times* observed, "it is rich in personal reminiscences of a man who has lived long and actively." Reviewers rightly pointed to the rich vein of "reminiscences and sketches" of literary celebrities that make the book "the fascinating volume that it is," noted the *Milwaukee Journal.* And while the *Brooklyn Daily Eagle* thought it "a very pedestrian book," it was nonetheless full of "great charm, . . . a soothing finale in which little melodies in a minor key are sung by the old master," made all the more charming by "the numerous pen-and-ink illustrations" that fill the book. Garland's old friend Joseph Edgar Chamberlin concluded his lengthy review for the *Boston Evening Transcript* by observing that the four books "are an important and very interesting addition to American literature" that deserved to "be all in one binding, expressive of their unity of effect," but he wondered whether another would follow, for "Mr. Garland, at sixty-eight, is younger, more buoyant, than he was at fifty. The End of the Trail," he prophesied, "is not yet."[68]

With his latest book in print, Garland turned to reworking the events of *A Son of the Middle Border.* Much was simply rewritten, the events expanded to comment on his encounters with a literary *Who's Who.* He quoted his correspondence with Howe, Booth, Kirkland, Herne, Howells, and others; he tapped his lecture notes and drew upon early articles; he mined his travel notebooks and concluded with a travelogue of his 1899 trip abroad. Casting about for a way to finish this first volume, he shifted his meeting with Henry James, which had occurred during his 1906 visit, to appear as a chapter near the end of his chronicle. The writing went rapidly, and within a year he had completed the manuscript. He struggled over what to call the book, alternating among "Sign Posts and Stepping Stones," "Wayside Meetings," "The Literary Nomad," "Literary Trade-Winds," "Currents of Influence," and "Esthetic Invasions" before settling on

"Roadside Meetings of a Literary Nomad" as a worthy continuation of the road and travel metaphors that had dominated so many of his titles.

While he was preparing the manuscript, changes were under way in his family circle. January 1, 1929, found Hamlin and Zulime in Hollywood, visiting Constance and Joe Harper. In February 1929 Mary Isabel wrote to announce that she and Hardesty were planning to move to Hollywood so that he could test the waters of employment in the film industry. "Reproach was in their eyes and voices," Mary Isabel recalled of the effect of this news on her parents. "That means a lonely life for Zulime and me unless we come too," Garland recorded. A month later, as Garland contemplated "the bright air and cheerful homes of California," he "wondered whether it was worthwhile to come back to New York."[69]

20

FORTUNATE EXILE, 1929–40

When Garland arrived in Hollywood in January 1929, he marveled at the temperate climate: "Weather is like June, cloudless, windless and serene." Everywhere he turned he noted blossoming flowers, verdant shrubs, and green trees, all bathed in warm sunlight that played over the tasteful gardens and Spanish architecture—"The view was all so strange, so beautiful, so unlike anything else in America that I am 'stumped' for adjectives with which to describe it."[1] When he thought of the cold New York winters, the depths of snow and icy winds, he wondered why he should bother to return to the East when he could enjoy the warmth of California. Joe Harper, whom Mary Isabel characterized as tied too closely to his mother's apron strings, had come into an inheritance and was then engaged in building a house next door to his mother's home on DeMille Drive, named for the famed movie director whose mansion graced the top of the hill and faced Griffith Park, named in honor of another famous director, D. W. Griffith. As he explored the neighboring hillsides and faced the prospect of returning to an empty New York flat, Garland began to think of spending winters in California. But he was troubled by the distance from his beloved club life and the comparative lack of literary culture in Los Angeles. As he entrained for New York on March 5, he realized that "in spite of all the charm out here, I have a desire to get back and into the thick of things intellectual—back at the center of discussion. I am in exile here—remote from my fellows, an army officer on leave."[2]

Soon, however, he had second thoughts as he pondered the implications of a three-thousand-mile separation from his beloved daughters. Constance was pregnant, and he planned to return to

Hollywood to celebrate. Then on July 29, 1929, came word of the death of his closest friend, Henry B. Fuller. "He carries with him a large part of my life for we have been intimate friends for more than a third of a century," he confided to his diary. "Next to Howells he was my most trusted literary advisor. His judgment was so swift and so acute that I went to him in all matters where I felt at a loss." Garland couldn't get to Chicago in time for Fuller's funeral, so instead he contributed a letter to the *New York Times* lauding his friend's achievement.[3] Fuller's death served to remind Garland of the transitory nature of life, and if he needed any further prodding to cast off the East in favor of relocating to Hollywood, the impending birth of his first grandson facilitated the decision. August 10 found him at 2018 North Hobart Boulevard, where Mary Isabel and Hardesty had rented a house, a convenient two blocks away from the Harper home on DeMille Drive.

John Wesley Harper was born on September 6. Garland enjoyed his new position as grandfather, but he also realized that tearing Zulime away from her family to return to New York would devastate her. For days he debated what he would lose by relocating to Hollywood even as he was enticed by the temperate climate. "This country allures me now," he mused. "I like its brightness and newness and freedom from winter but I suffer when I think of abandoning all that New England has meant to me. I remember its hills and storms and deep snows as I remember poetry or song. As I grow older I shall recall it still more wistfully—but here are my daughters and grandson! It is a hard decision to make."[4] Finally, on October 19, he decided to build a house for Mary Isabel and Hardesty, with a wing reserved for himself and Zulime, and spend winters in Hollywood. What clinched the matter was that Joe Harper agreed to sell the lot next door. With a five-hundred-dollar deposit as earnest money, he and Zulime left for New York, with a promise to return in two months to begin construction.

Construction began on January 2, 1930, at 2045 DeMille Drive. For the first time in his life, Garland had the pleasure of designing a house with his needs in mind, and foremost among them was a sumptuous study, his "workshop," lined with built-in bookshelves and windows overlooking the garden. The house was completed on April 18. To pay for it he sold some bonds, but then a sudden windfall appeared in the form of B. George Ulizio, the president of the New Jersey Investment Realty Corporation and a book collector, who learned that Garland had a rare first edition of Stephen Crane's *Maggie*. Ulizio had completed his collection of Crane editions except for *Maggie*, he told Garland, and he planned to "present" it to the Princeton University library once the collection was complete. Garland was reluctant to dispose of his copy but informed Ulizio that Franklin also had an inscribed copy that he thought his brother would sell. Eventually, after much correspondence, Garland arranged to sell Franklin's copy for four hundred dollars, together with Hamlin's inscription about the circumstances under which Crane gave the book for another one hundred dollars. Recognizing a golden opportunity to finance the construction of the house, soon Garland was offering Ulizio inscribed copies of Crane's *The Black Riders and Other Lines*, Riley's *The Ole Swimmin' Hole*, and other books.

In May Garland was back in New York accompanied by a bundle of books for appraisal. "What is the use of hoarding them?" he wondered. "Why not have the benefit of their sale while I am alive?"[5] One dealer offered $1,500 for *Maggie*, another offered $2,000, and still another told him he should expect $3,000. And then he learned that another copy had just sold for $2,100. Garland was incensed. "That man Ulizio is a crook," he wrote to Zulime. "He took advantage of my ignorance of the [Crane] boom and 'chouselled' me." More temperately, he wrote to Ulizio, "In all your correspondence you said 'I am willing to pay the fair market price for the book.' . . . You assured me that you were buying the book for Princeton University and that you had no intention of reselling the book but even so the payment to my brother might very justly be increased." Ulizio did not add to the payment, and eventually Garland sold five autographed books to another dealer, grumbling, "They are all without any conscience when it comes to getting a book cheap."[6]

Garland had gone east primarily to conclude arrangements for yet another edition of *Main-Travelled Roads*, one that included an additional story—"The Fireplace," a reprinting of "Martha's Fireplace," which had originally appeared in the *Delineator* in 1905, and one which he hoped would give his most celebrated volume an elegiac close. More important were the illustrations by Constance that he hoped would attract a new generation of readers more accustomed to illustrated magazines. Viewing the dummy of the book, he was a bit disappointed with the quality of the printing but decided, "It does what I had hoped for, it gives me a definitive edition."[7]

His other task was to read proofs of *Roadside Meetings*, which had been serialized in the *Bookman* from October 1929 to March 1930 and which Macmillan was planning to publish on his seventieth birthday. When Latham presented him with two copies at the Century Club, adorned with Constance's portraits of his literary acquaintances on the endpapers, Garland was pleased with its appearance, but ever doubtful of the appeal of his work to younger readers, he wondered, "will anybody be interested to read it? I do not expect many to do so. Faithful friends will buy it for a Christmas present but not many will know the men and women mentioned in the book." Four weeks later he was surprised when Brett told him, "'It is the best book of the year—and one of the best books of a decade'—and as the judgment of a cold keen, commercial publisher, this remark had weight with me."[8] Even as he was awaiting the publication of *Roadside*, Garland had been pressing on with transforming his diaries into his literary autobiography and had completed revisions for the second volume, *Companions on the Trail.* As a publisher of many of the day's leading authors, Brett enjoyed Garland's presentation of literary history, part chronicle of the development of American literature and part high-toned literary gossip. As he later told Garland, "I don't see why this series of yours should not become in time a literary history of modern-day America as you have seen all the worthwhile people and taken part in all the prominent events."[9]

Garland returned to Hollywood in time to celebrate Thanksgiving with his daughters and to be with Constance, who was expecting another child, to be born on December 31 and christened Constance Garland Harper. While he was awaiting the occasion, Sinclair Lewis was awarded the Nobel Prize for literature, an event that proved deeply troubling for some members of the American Academy and would end with a surprising sobriquet for Garland.

Earlier, Lewis had deeply offended members of the National Institute when he had declined election after Garland proposed him for membership in 1921. Worse, he had refused the 1925 Pulitzer Prize for *Arrowsmith* to avenge the slight for *Main Street,* and he publicly castigated the institute and academy as part of "the inquisition of earnest literary ladies" that compelled "writers to become safe, polite, obedient and sterile. . . . [B]y accepting the prizes and approval of these vague institutions, we are admitting their authority, publicly confirming them as the final judges of literary excellence, and I enquire whether any prize is worth that subservience."[10] When Lewis was announced as the first American recipient of the Nobel Prize for literature, Princeton professor Henry van Dyke, a founding member of the institute and a member of the academy since 1908, promptly condemned the choice of an author whose novels "scoff at America and its traditions" as "a back-handed compliment" to America.[11]

Van Dyke's public condemnation provoked Lewis to retaliate at length in his acceptance speech, and he took aim directly at the American Academy of Arts and Letters. While the academy's members did include "a really distinguished university president as Nicholas Murray Butler, so admirable and courageous a scholar as Wilbur Cross," and such "first-rate writers and poets" as Edward Arlington Robinson, Robert Frost, Hamlin Garland, Owen Wister, Brand Whitlock, Edith Wharton, and Booth Tarkington," it had failed to elect such important and innovative writers as Theodore Dreiser, Eugene O'Neill, Willa Cather, Carl Sandburg, Edgar Lee Masters, H. L. Mencken, and George Jean Nathan. "While most of our giants are excluded," Lewis complained, "the Academy does, however, include three extraordinarily bad poets, two very melodramatic and insignificant playwrights, two gentlemen who are known only because they are university presidents, . . . and several gentlemen of whom, I sadly confess my ignorance, I never heard."

Lewis then went on to vilify Howells, whose genteel realism had influenced a generation of writers. "His influence is not altogether gone today," he continued. "He is still worshipped by Hamlin Garland, an author who should have been in every way greater than Howells, but who, under Howells's influence, changed from a harsh and magnificent realist into a genial, insignificant lecturer." Garland must have been pained by Lewis's contemptuous reference and Lewis's misconstruing of his relationship with Howells, for the surviving correspondence does not indicate that Howells shaped Garland's literary practice in any significant way, though Garland readily admitted Howells's influence as a model he always strived to emulate. Twenty-five years younger than Garland and representing a modernism so radically at odds with the elder writer's own practice, Lewis went on to describe his disappointment in the trajectory of Garland's career, for he noted that *Main-Travelled Roads* and *Rose of Dutcher's Coolly* had "made it possible for me to write of America as I see it and not as Mr. William Dean Howells so sunnily saw it. And it is a completely revelatory American tragedy," he concluded, "that in our land of freedom men like Garland, who first blast the roads to freedom, become themselves the most bound." But pained though he must have been at Lewis's denunciation and depiction of him as a has-been sell-out, Garland also accepted, as if it were his due, Lewis's passing of the mantle. "Mr. Garland is, so far as we have one," Lewis proclaimed, albeit with scorn, "the dean of American letters today."[12]

Garland made no mention of Lewis's speech in his diary, though later he told one interviewer that a number of his friends had called his attention to the speech, "thinking I'd feel flattered; but I am not," he remarked. "Why should Lewis patronize me? The whelp!"[13] But columnists were quick to pick up on Lewis's remark about Garland as the reigning "dean of American letters." Two weeks later, the *Los Angeles Times* noted that Garland, "the dean of American letters," would address a dinner of the Iowa Association of Southern California; and soon afterward the *Chicago Tribune* announced that Garland, "the dean of American authors," would present the academy's medal for good diction on the radio to Alwyn Bach, its second recipient. All this mention of Garland as "dean" prompted Lee Shippey, a columnist for the *Los Angeles Times*, to solidify the title.

"Has anyone thought of giving Hamlin Garland the unofficial title of dean of American letters?" he asked. "Mr. Garland is 70 years old and for forty years has been a force."[14] Thereafter, until he died, Garland was billed in lecture circulars and periodical notices as "The Dean of American Letters."

Another accolade came on June 24, 1931, when Garland read his morning paper and discovered he had been awarded the Roosevelt Medal for Distinguished Service by the Roosevelt Memorial Association, an organization he had helped found shortly after the former president's death. "His fiction and his autobiographical writings alike are history transposed by the understanding of a poet and lover of mankind," the citation read, "and fulfill in rare measure the demand for imagination in historical writing eloquently phrased by Theodore Roosevelt in his address as president of the American Historical Association." Garland was tremendously pleased by this tribute to his long career as novelist and historian, and when he received the medal in October he wrote to his daughters that "We shall have it on the parlor table—under glass!—and padlocked!!"[15]

But on the heels of this award came calamity. In August Zulime developed a tremor in her hands and feet and was unable to control the shaking. Garland feared she had suffered a stroke and consulted physicians, but they were unable to diagnose her malady. "It depresses me beyond expression to see her so sad and so irresolute," he mourned, realizing their summers in New York were about to end. Years later she would be diagnosed with Parkinson's disease, and, embarrassed by her condition and in continual fear that the tremor would extend to her head, she refused to go out in public and only occasionally received visitors at home. As soon as he finished reading proofs for *Companions on the Trail*, due to be published in September, Garland gave up their Cathedral Parkway flat and packed his books, resolved to move permanently to Hollywood, where his daughters could assist with Zulime's care. "In giving up a residence in New York City," he realized, "I am ending my active literary life and separating myself from many friends of more than twenty five years of association."[16]

When he arrived in Hollywood in 1931 in time for Thanksgiving and announced that henceforth he and Zulime would live in the DeMille Drive home, Garland had little idea that his move would effect a profound change in his moods and activities and that his relocation would provoke a growing estrangement from his favorite daughter. "What were we to say?" Mary Isabel recalled. "Fond as we were of them and grateful for their generosity, it was impossible to lead any life of our own while they were there. Guests had to be carefully screened, early hours observed, menus adjusted to their needs and likes."[17] A controlling and domineering parent, Garland made Mary Isabel feel guilty and ungrateful whenever she would go out—matched by Joe Harper's mother, Olive Grismer, "a handsome, dictatorial ex-actress" who similarly attempted to direct the lives of her son and daughter-in-law.[18] Naturally, Mary Isabel soon became resentful—while also recognizing her obligation to her parents. The poisonous mix of generations began to affect her marriage, and to avoid her parents' criticism she began censoring her growing marital unhappiness.

As Zulime's condition grew worse, Garland began to curtail his lectures to spend more time with his wife. "Father was bewildered, miserable," Mary Isabel recalled. "He haunted her bedroom, sitting by her hour after hour, sometimes reading aloud or listening with her to symphonic music on her bedside radio that was never turned off, day or night. Often he would lean forward and take her poor, quivering hand in his big paw, holding it for as long as she would permit him. In her own wretchedness, Mother was cool, almost unkind to Father." For diversion, Mary Isabel would take them on long drives to neighboring attractions and to polo matches at the Uplifters Club, during which "Father always sought Mother's hand, humbly, almost pleadingly, as if in shame for some past injustice, yet I knew that Father—stubborn, unreasonable, emotionally mercurial—was at the core all warmth and tenderness."[19]

Cut off from his friends, from the clubs that had formed so large a part of his life, Garland soon became introspective, morose, prone to dwelling on past accomplishments and lost opportunities—all magnified by his morning stint at revising his diaries for *My Friendly Contemporaries*. With *Companions* he had brought his story to Mark Sullivan's acceptance of *A Son of the Middle Border* in 1914; in *Contemporaries* he brought it to the close of his 1922 trip abroad. Both volumes suffer in comparison to the more reflective *Roadside Meetings*, for he had come to depend on his brief diary entries. A procession of luncheons, meetings with authors, and brief accounts of the various organizations he helped form flood the pages, but there is little reflection and only modest elaboration of the context or effect of his meetings with the famous and near-famous. The result is a tedious and surprisingly dull narrative. While Garland revised practically all diary entries, he largely revised for style and rarely augmented an event with substantive details. In part this is due to the flagging creative energy of a man in his seventies, but it is also due to his own stubbornness. When Harold Latham, the editor for all of his Macmillan books, warned him that his dependence on his diaries was dominating *Contemporaries* and would "scare off readers," Garland replied testily, "It is essentially a diary form and cant be done in any other way without entirely rewriting it. . . . Furthermore it is the diary note which gives it authenticity and value. Its individual character arises from the fact that the characters come and go like characters in a novel."[20] In a lapse of editorial acumen, Latham backpedaled, "It is certainly not my intention to urge upon you any suggestion as to format," he wrote. "Having put before you the reminder that there is some general objection to the diary form, and having also reminded you that this form has not been used quite so consistently in the previous books, . . . I am content to leave the matter with you for the final handling. Whatever you do will be quite all right."[21] Like Brett, Latham was deeply impressed with the range of Garland's literary acquaintances and was committed to publishing the memoirs because he believed they were "going to be a valuable source work in the social and literary history of our times."[22] Perhaps he also recognized that a complete recasting of the narrative was now beyond Garland's capabilities.

My Friendly Contemporaries was published in September 1932. As Garland pressed ahead with what would become *Afternoon Neighbors*, he felt his isolation keenly. In October he resigned from the academy's board of directors and the chairmanship of the radio medal committee, explaining in a letter to the president of the academy that it was necessary because "I shall never be able, probably, to spend another winter in New York City. . . . I deeply regret this necessity but my wife's health is precarious and I doubt if she will ever go back even to Onteora for the summer."[23] He resigned from the Century Association and canceled his eastern lecture dates. A writer who formerly was at the vanguard of literary events, he now saw that his self-imposed California exile meant that he was on the road to literary oblivion. He reflected, "I recall going in to see Mr. Howells once in his later years—when he was beginning to feel 'out of it'—and during my call he said, 'I have outlived my vogue.' I could not believe this at the time but I understand it now. I have never reached the 'vogue' but I begin to realize that people are no longer interested in my books or in me."[24] Occasionally, he was bemused and pleased to receive letters from enterprising graduate students who wrote to probe his memories about writers he had known, none more important than Eldon Hill, who was then busy with what would become the first dissertation devoted to Garland's life and early career.

Hill had begun corresponding with Garland in 1928 when, as a twenty-two-year-old student at Ohio State University, he wrote to commend the writer's middle border books. By 1931 Hill had chosen Garland to be the subject of his doctoral thesis, and over a span of nine years he would write nearly two hundred letters to Garland in which he asked questions about his works and influences. Garland was extravagantly pleased with Hill's interest, coming at a time when he felt he had largely been forgotten by younger readers, and he patiently responded to the queries of his "Young Advocate" and sent him bundles of correspondence from his literary acquaintances, even as he solicited Hill's aid to help with the details of his occasional eastern lecture engagements. Hill was a patient and methodical researcher who doggedly sought to classify every scrap of information about Garland; the Eldon Hill archive at Miami University in Oxford, Ohio, is filled with his painstaking transcriptions of large sections from Garland's writings and correspondence. Hill's procedure for collecting data is understandable in an era before photocopy machines, but it came to irritate Garland, who feared the young scholar would never complete his study. Hoping to expedite matters by giving Hill a period of direct access to his subject, the Garlands invited Hill and his wife for an extended visit, but here too Hamlin soon became impatient. "I began to feel the burden of Hills observation," he confided to his diary in 1936. "He is so ceaselessly alert to catch something important falling from my lips that I dislike his eagerness." Worn out by the Hills' visit, which lasted a month, Garland complained, "He eyed me so closely and asked so many questions that I grew restless under it. It bored me. The longer he stayed, the harder it was to talk with him. I felt that I was being perpetually interviewed, and worst of all I lost confidence in the little man. I doubt if he ever does anything worth while with the material."[25] Nonetheless, with few others interested in his life and works, Garland continued to supply Hill with material, leaving unmailed the last letter he would write, challenging Hill to follow his psychic exploration as a vital component of his work. Garland would not live to see Hill's study, completed in 1940 as "A Biographical Study of Hamlin Garland from 1860 to 1895," a thesis that incidentally established the precedent of regarding only the writer's formative years as deserving of academic interest.

Other signs that Garland had not been entirely forgotten appeared in the form of professors at the University of Southern California who, realizing that a man who had personally known many of the authors they were teaching lived nearby, promptly invited him to address their classes. The most important of these was the coincidentally named Garland Greever, who asked Garland to address Epsilon Phi, the English honor society. Soon, Garland was a frequent guest lecturer in Greever's classes. "He often asked who among the students showed promise of creative achievement in writing," Greever remembered. "He asked that such students be brought to his home; he discussed with them the problems of authorship; he exhorted them to revise what they wrote and then revise again and again until they had captured the exact meaning, the precise emotional nuance. Nothing pleased him better than to confer face to face with talented and eager younger writers."[26]

In June 1933 a letter from Latham arrived postponing publication of *Afternoon Neighbors* until 1934. Earlier, he had written that book sales were suffering because of the nation's economic collapse and that sales of *Companions* had still not earned Garland's advance of three thousand dollars, and the debit against *Roadside* was "a little more than" a thousand dollars. "None of us here have the slightest doubt whatsoever in our minds as to the outstanding merit or importance of these books of yours, nor have we any serious apprehension as to their ultimate earnings," he reassured Garland. By way of consolation, he added, "This information should not discourage you; it does not discourage us."[27]

During the spring, Garland had turned to an old enthusiasm when he met Dora Drane, a friend of Zulime's from Chicago, who was an accomplished medium. For weeks he conducted séances during which the ghosts of his past would emerge from a cardboard megaphone that floated around his study. Accustomed to reliving conversations as he revised his diaries into his memoirs, it was but a short step to hearing the voices of friends during the séances, and chief among them was the voice of Henry B. Fuller, whom he sorely missed. Accustomed to a daily stint of writing, and casting about for something to do, on the day he received Latham's letter postponing *Afternoon* he recorded, "I turned away from the task and began to go over the records of my psychic experiences to see what unused material I had in my files."[28] As he went through his records of séance transcripts and previous articles, he realized he had material enough to form a book. Accustomed to transforming his diaries into a narrative, Garland now turned to doing the same thing with his psychic experiments.

His diary entries reveal that he wavered between believing the voices were genuine and fearing that they were "a blending of the thought (conscious and unconscious) of the sitters and the psychic."[29] During one sitting, for example, he asked to speak to his parents. When the "personalities" came, he asked for confirmation of their identities, suggesting that his "mother" say her name. "Isabel," he heard, then "gentle sobbing." "If I could believe this it would be the most momentous event of my life," he concluded. "If my mother could whisper a single word it would mean more than all of Millikan and Einstein's so-called discoveries. Father also came but could not speak." Fuller and Henry James then "discussed the fourth dimensional concept." But then he noted, apparently ignoring its significance, "As the cone sank, it seemed partly upheld by an elastic cord."[30]

For months Garland enjoyed the nightly diversions of psychic sittings as he tinkered with the manuscript of what would become *Forty Years of Psychic Research*. He devoted two chapters to recounting the events of his séances, but whereas he formerly had sought to test the veracity of his medium though various controls, he was now content to carry on conversations with the shades of his friends, a psychic substitute for the talk of his New York clubs. He concluded the volume convinced that the phenomena existed but unconvinced that their source lay in the spirit world. Mary Isabel remembered that the séances were "absorbing, breathtaking but inconclusive. . . . Nearing the end himself, he said he would like to be convinced but nothing he had experienced in his forty years of psychic research had given him the slightest conviction of life after death."[31] "I am still the experimenter, the seeker," Garland concluded; "I find myself most in harmony with those who say: 'All these movements, voices, forms, are biodynamic in character. They are born of certain unknown powers of the human organism. They are thought-forms—resultants of mind controlling matter. They all originate in the séance room and have not been proven to go beyond it.'" Of his many conversations with "Fuller," he admitted it likely that they were "a product of my own brain," but "I can not tell you how he came to speak nor why his thought persisted in opposition to ours."[32]

In June 1935 a letter from Latham arrived confirming that Macmillan wanted to publish *Forty Years* the following spring. "I have a very real enthusiasm for your book on Psychic Research," Latham wrote. "I think it promises to be an important contribution to this subject, and one which we can publish with real pride." But then he explained that Macmillan did not expect a very large sale of the book, despite Garland's stature, and offered the smallest royalty Garland had yet received from the firm: 10 percent on sales up to 2,500, 15 percent thereafter, with a trifling five-hundred-dollar advance.[33]

Meanwhile, changes were under way in the lives of his daughters. Unknown to Garland, both Mary Isabel and Constance were growing increasingly dissatisfied in their marriages. In 1934 Mary Isabel met the writer Mindret Lord and his wife, singer Marguerite Namara, a former flame of Hardesty's when they had both been students of Jean de Reszke in Nice. Soon the couples began to spend much time together, each flirting with the other's spouse. By June, Mary Isabel and Mindret had fallen in love, and she and Hardesty, who seems to have been unusually understanding and agreed to a separation, moved to New York, both agreeing not to reveal to Garland the true reason for the relocation. Knowing of her father's possessive love for her, his deep admiration for Hardesty, his antipathy to the morality of a generation far more casual than his own, as well as being dependent on his monthly check for one hundred dollars, she greatly feared his reaction. On November 2 Garland learned that Mary Isabel and Hardesty had separated. He was devastated. "This was an appalling revelation to me for I had no suspicion of it," he confided to his diary. "I could not believe it for it involved a long period of duplicity on Mary Isabels part."[34] Four weeks later he learned of her involvement with the married Mindret and promptly fired off an angry letter: "Your sister tells me you have left your husband and are involved with another man. I need not tell you what this means to me but I want to say I will never see this man or take him by the hand. Your monthly allowance will continue but do not expect anything else from me."[35] What must have crossed Garland's mind at this time was the memory of Zulime's own love affair far in the past and its wrenching effects on their marriage, but they had persevered and made the marriage work, and he urged his daughter to do the same. Mary Isabel at once wrote and poured out her heart to her father, trying to make him understand. His reply was curt: "I understand you are contemplating divorce. You will have no help from me in this matter. I have always stood for honesty and decency and I wish no part in this dangerous venture you embarked on.

From now on, the subject is closed between us."[36] Thereafter, his letters, usually effusive in expression of his love for and interest in his favorite daughter, were brief and impersonal. For consolation, Mary Isabel turned to her mother, who was far more supportive and acted as intermediary to temper Hamlin's wrath. As soon as the couple could save enough money for a lawyer, Mary Isabel arranged for an absentee Mexican divorce, and she and Mindret were married on December 21, 1936.

While Garland was fretting over his disappointment in his eldest daughter, Constance was dealing with her own marital difficulties. In 1930 Joe Harper had been an usher at the marriage of Cecil B. DeMille's daughter Cecilia to Francis Calvin, and the Calvins lived in the mansion atop DeMille Drive. The Calvin and Harper children often played together, and soon the parents developed a warm friendship too. One day in 1936 Joe announced that he wanted a divorce so he could marry Cecilia. Again Garland was devastated at this crumbling of his world and mourned, "Constance informed us today that she and Joe—after eight years of wedded life, had agreed to separate and so—I who have stood for decency and loyalty in social life find myself with two daughters seeking divorces!" Adding to his pain were fears that the sensation-loving press would learn that the daughter of the famed director was now involved with Garland's son-in-law. Two days later, he added, "If ever I have a biographer he can take this as one of my darkest weeks. Both my daughters separated from their husbands, my wife an invalid, myself threatened with pneumonia and unable to see even the few friends I have left."[37] By January 18, 1937, Garland had rallied and accompanied Constance to her lawyer's office to sign the divorce decree. Joe Harper and Cecilia DeMille Calvin were married one year later, on January 21, 1938, and promptly settled in to live in his mother's house, next door to Constance's. Little wonder that the ménage on DeMille Drive soon led to Constance's decision to sell her house. As her father reflected, "These are the complications of divorce, deeper yet are the complications in the minds of the children. They can not understand why their father and mother do not live together as they used to do."[38]

Garland's seventy-sixth year was singularly fraught with disappointments. Not only was his family world crumbling, but Latham soon rejected the fifth installment of his memoirs, "The Fortunate Exiles," a portion of which Garland had sent him for preliminary comment. Garland had doggedly pushed on with his life story, taking up where *Afternoon Neighbors* had left off—his move to California—and continuing to the present. Far away from his literary acquaintances who had formed the core of the previous volumes, he now recorded his daily activities as he discovered southern California in the heyday of its development. Chapters are full of comment on his reaction to movies, his meetings with celebrities such as Will Rogers, Douglas Fairbanks, John Barrymore, and Zane Grey, and the minor triumphs of honorary degrees and the occasional invited lecture. But now coming to dominate are the cranky reflections of a man preoccupied with the growing infirmities of age and the vivid awareness that his moment in the sun is now long past, but who still faces the future with courage and curiosity. Ultimately, he prefaced the volume with the note that "The Fortunate Exiles" was "the final comment of a man who once aspired to be a great writer and who now admits his failure to achieve anything more than a mediocre success." Of the manuscript, Latham wrote, "it seems to me that there is too little that is really significant, really important for the present length. It is all very pleasantly written, all very agreeable reading, but it has not the social significance or the power of anything else of yours."[39] In part, the falling off was due to Garland's estrangement from the eastern literary circles that had formerly resonated with readers, but it was also due to his by now complete dependence on his diaries and his inability to augment them in any substantial way.

Even as he was dealing with the disappointment of Latham's rejection, Garland was taking steps to ensure that his contribution to American literary culture would not be forgotten. By now he had established close ties with the University of Southern California's Doheny Library, which was busy courting him in an effort to secure his papers. On April 2, 1936, the Doheny opened an exhibit entitled "Hamlin Garland and His Literary Friends," which consisted of a number of cases containing letters from Barrie, Shaw,

Kipling, Hardy, Crane, Howells, Whitman, Norris, Burroughs, Riley, Roosevelt, and others, in addition to cases of photographs, manuscripts, books, and other memorabilia. After a summer's exhibition, the collection went on tour as "The Makers of American Literature" to a number of state, public, and university libraries in California, Iowa, Indiana, Illinois, Ohio, Wisconsin, and elsewhere. Part of his purpose was publicity for the American Academy, but Garland also hoped the exhibit would remind viewers of his own contributions and, ultimately, secure younger readers for his books.

That fall he was delighted when independent filmmaker Guy D. Haselton approached him with a proposition to make a biographical film showcasing his life and works. When Haselton met with Garland on September 28, 1936, he spent three hours filming Garland walking amid his garden at his DeMille Drive home, romping with his two grandchildren, and drinking from a mysterious bottle with his brother, Franklin—what the extant continuity calls his "special beverage." Garland naturally was flattered by the attention, but he was not optimistic about the marketability of the film, as he confided in his diary: "It is the first time such colorful and thorough film has been taken of me and it may be that someone will be interested in it as a record when I am only a memory. The defect in this and similar films is lack of significant action."[40] The challenge of the film, eventually entitled *Hamlin Garland, Dean of American Letters*—Garland was pleased by the tribute, Lewis's derision notwithstanding—was how to convey a biography of an elderly writer without sound, for Haselton was recording on sixteen-millimeter film, and not until the next year would a sound-on-film sixteen-millimeter camera become available. Haselton's solution was to open with several title screens summarizing Garland's career, followed by a montage of the *Collier's* magazine illustrations of *A Son of the Middle Border* to illustrate Garland's youth, then photographs of the writer in his heyday together with shots of some of his most significant acquaintances, and concluding with title pages of his most recent Macmillan books. Following the biographical segment appears the section nearest to Garland's heart—contemporary scenes of the elderly writer in action, making coffee, at work at his desk, and strutting his vigor by raking leaves, much as contemporary presidents cut brush for the media. For this and many of his occasional lectures Garland donned a white suit to emphasize his resemblance to Mark Twain, for with his bushy mustache and flowing white locks he delighted in the inevitable comparisons. "If this goes on," he once remarked to his family after an interviewer called attention to his resemblance, "I shall be almost as much a figure as Sinclair Lewis." Garland was much amused by this hoodwinking of the public. During one dinner party, a man approached him and began conversing in German. "I have been related to Mark Twain and Hawthorne," Garland recorded bemusedly, "but to Einstein is a new experience."[41]

Part of the reason for his interest in the film project was the coincidence of its timing. Early on Garland immediately saw that the film would enhance the traveling exhibit and help ensure his legacy. By January 1937 he was writing to George Steele Seymour, the founder of the Order of the Bookfellows, a Chicago literary and publishing club, for help in coordinating showings of the film with exhibits. He also enlisted the aid of Eldon Hill, who was by now a member of the English faculty at Miami University and who would serve as Garland's agent; Hill traveled to Bloomington to show the film in its first public exhibition in March 1937 at Indiana University.

Garland believed the film was the first attempt at a film biography, and indeed a surviving brochure promotes it as "The First Cine-Biography!" and describes it as "an intimate motion picture study of Hamlin Garland as he is today—a priceless document in living pictures of the head of America's First Family of Letters in his Los Angeles home." For Garland this must have gone down like honey, since, as he confided to his diary, "At one time I had such sense of power that I imagined myself going on to international fame but as son, as husband and later as father I was not able to concentrate as before. Some men can be all these things and yet do great deeds like Grant, like Lincoln. I had not the power I thought I had. Now I can look back on my books and speeches and see their weaknesses and their mistakes, too late to better them or replace them with new expressions."[42] The Haselton film thus served to remind Garland (and the world) of his former glory, though he was realistic enough to recognize the limited interest in the film, explaining it to his old friend Grace Vanamee, administrative secretary of the American Academy, as "a record which I am glad to have made even if no one but my immediate family and friends are interested."[43]

With *Forty Years of Psychical Research* published and "The Fortunate Exiles" stalled, Garland cast about for another project. For his entire adult life he had spent each morning laboring at one book or another, and he felt at a loss without a manuscript under way. Four years earlier he had received a letter from a man by the name of Gregory Parent who had written with a wild tale: his wife, a psychic who had died five years before, had discovered many hidden objects at the direction of spirits and had taken a number of spirit photographs. Was Garland interested in examining the collection? Perennially interested in psychic problems, Garland called on Parent and surveyed his collection of ectoplasmic photographs. He was intrigued but was unable to investigate further because of a looming deadline for *Afternoon Neighbors*. But in the fall of 1936, with his latest book wrapped up, Garland remembered Parent's collection and decided to take up the investigation. But Parent had since died. When Garland succeeded in locating Parent's sister and the collection of photographs and more than 1,500 objects, he embarked on one of the oddest undertakings of his long and varied career: an attempt to verify the legitimacy of the Parent collection, an investigation that was to culminate in his last, and certainly strangest, book— *The Mystery of the Buried Crosses*—and which was to become an obsession that consumed his final years.

Between October 1936 and March 1937, Garland studied the photographs and objects, which were metallic crosses, many embossed with figures or encrusted with adobe. Parent had kept careful records, some twenty-two notebooks and a bundle of manuscript in which he had attempted a narrative of his wife's history and the conditions of discovery—in all cases the Parents had been led to the objects by spirit voices which directed them to dig at locations over a wide swath of southern California. According to Parent's notes, the spirits, padres of the eighteenth-century San Juan Capistrano

Mission, told his wife, "When our mission was threatened by hostile forces we advised our people to hide their trinkets in balls of adobe, for these when dried would be indistinguishable from common rocks. This they did and now they are eager to have these 'sacred rocks' recovered. We will show you where to find them."[44]

Garland was struck by the story. Parent had recorded the names of others who had witnessed the proceedings, and Garland sought them out and interviewed them. The more he learned, the more he was intrigued. He sent the objects to several museums for authentication. His friend Frederick W. Hodge, whom he had known since his efforts on behalf of the Indian renaming project in 1901, now with the Southwest Museum, soon replied. After pointing out a number of historical inaccuracies in Parent's account of the conditions of discovery, Hodge turned to the objects themselves, many of which "no doubt . . . came from a five-and-ten-cent store." "I might go on indefinitely," he concluded, "to show that the whole collection was conceived in fraud or in some diseased brain but this is not necessary, as everything points to the ungenuineness of the articles." Of the spirit photographs that so impressed Garland, "every one . . . is an obvious fake as anyone can see." The Smithsonian replied that the designs on the objects were "obviously made with a mold taken from an impression of an original design," and "the objects seem to be of recent origin."[45] Despite the contrary reports, Garland could not believe the Parents "possessed the wit or the means to carry out such an elaborate and costly hoax."[46] More important, nearing the end himself, he desperately wanted to believe in the existence of psychic phenomena that would make one's mortality more palatable.

He therefore determined to duplicate the conditions of discovery by invoking psychic aid himself, for if he were able to find buried crosses at the direction of spirits, he would at last have proof of the survival of personality he had sought for more than forty years. Eventually, through a Chicago friend he located a nonprofessional medium, one Sophia Williams, and beginning in March 1937 he conducted daily séances, guided as ever by the spirit of his good friend Henry B. Fuller. Garland conversed with the spirits of his former literary acquaintances, who urged him forward in his inquiries, and he devised a series of experiments to test his medium's validity, as well as recording and photographing the visitations in an attempt to gather scientific evidence of continued survival. As part of his investigation, Garland eventually discovered some fifteen buried crosses, guided by spirit voices who told him where to look.

What so impressed Garland about Williams was that she seemed to convey the voices in a brightly lit room with surprising ease and without the usual claptrap of the typical séance: red lights and other paraphernalia, ritual incantations, trancelike states, and so forth. The voices appeared to emanate from her body and not her lips—confirmed, Garland believed, by his methods of preventing speech: taping her mouth shut, placing an all-day sucker in her mouth to prevent ventriloquism, and similar methods akin to his practice in the 1890s. In his efforts to prove the validity of these voices, Garland placed a microphone against Williams's chest and strung a wire between it and the receiver located in other rooms of the house, and even next door, at times some 150 feet away, the idea being that she would not be able to hear his questions but he would be able to hear the voices.

Soon Garland was convinced he had finally found the means to demonstrate the existence of life beyond death while also occasionally doubting the "evidence" itself. At one troubled moment he mused, "The whole thing is astounding and yet I cant rid myself of a feeling that it is all coming out of our own minds."[47] With all the enthusiasm of his former youth, the seventy-six-year-old writer began to plan a book about his investigations. He kept Harold Latham informed of his progress, and at one point Latham attended a sitting. "We gave Latham the shock of his life," Garland noted. "He heard 'Fuller' and 'Father Serra' talk through the transmitter. He feels that we have a very vital book here."[48] Before long, Garland had finished a draft of his psychic adventures, entitled it "Mechanical Proofs of Human Survival," and shipped it off to Macmillan. Meanwhile, he continued the séances.

On August 6, Amelia Earhart spoke.

Earhart, the most famous woman aviator of her time, with her navigator, Fred Noonan, had left New Guinea on July 2, bound for

Howland Island on the next leg of her attempt to become the first woman to fly around the world. She had disappeared en route, and the world's press eagerly covered the ensuing search. On August 5, "Fuller" appeared during one of Garland's séances and explained he had spoken with Earhart, who had described the crash and their efforts to survive. Garland dutifully recorded the details, sent them to Latham, and the next day had a lengthy interview with "Earhart," who encouraged him to communicate with her husband, George Palmer Putnam, grandson of the founder of the Putnam publishing company. "ALL THIS TO BE A DEAD SECRET. We dont want to be troubled by reporters," Garland wrote to his daughters, who were in New York.[49] Garland immediately wrote to Putnam, explained what had happened, and sent him a five-page transcript of the séance. Putnam apparently took Garland seriously, for by August 14 he had arrived for a sitting. Though skeptical at first, he returned for additional sittings, spoke with "Earhart," and accompanied Garland and Williams on cross-hunting expeditions, at one point unearthing a cross himself and photographing it. By October 20 he had apparently become resigned to his wife's death, for on that day Garland recorded that Putnam was making a play for Constance, who had since returned to the household, and while Garland questioned the suitability of a romance between his daughter and a man of fifty, he realized that "Constance is a grown woman and I do not feel it nescessary [sic] to tell her what to do."[50]

While Garland was busy with the Earhart affair and trying to work it into his story of the crosses, Latham had received the manuscript and sent it out for review. "I know that this letter is going to be a great disappointment to you," he tactfully began his letter of August 5. Although personally he thought the story was "exciting" and "absorbing," he wrote in his role as Macmillan editor, "we simply don't believe in it. We do not know what the explanation is, but that you have really established communication with the departed, we gravely question. We think the book would be greeted in two ways—respectful skepticism from those who know and love you and your work, and entirely disrespectful guffaws from those who are no respecters of persons, however distinguished. It is our honest conviction that the publication of the book will do you no good." He enclosed the report from the reader, who opined that the story "is so amazing as to pass any ordinary possibilities of belief." The reader noted that Garland had quoted as voices of spirits two individuals "both of whom are (or were yesterday) very much alive" and concluded, "Were Mr. Garland not Mr. Garland, I should think the book an amazing hoax, believable in its main parts only by a lunatic. . . . If Mr. Garland wants to risk the odium of having his bewildering yarn exploded, . . . I see no reason why the book should not be published. It is certainly weird and exciting enough to keep the stupidest reader wide awake."[51]

Garland realized he had made a tactical error in presenting the book as a factual record of his investigations. "I am too old to care very much for what happens to me now," he wrote to Constance, asking her to remove the foreword and "any direct argument for the theory of survival," and see if Latham would reconsider the book as a mystery story.[52] In the meantime, he would shop it around to other publishers.

While he revised the story that fall he continued his sittings with Williams. During one séance he discovered she was cheating. "Constance in fiddling with the transmitter discovered that she could produce some of the sounds which we have been hearing in the receiver," he recorded on September 17, "and while she could not reproduce the whispers which come from Mrs. Williams, she threw doubt on some of the happenings. The mystery of the buried crosses remains but much of the material gained in listening in my adjoining room is doubtful." For days Garland wrestled with the implications for his project. "It is inconceivable that she should deliberately set out to fool me," he reflected. "One naturally says if she will cheat in this, she will cheat in the other more important things."[53] For her part, Constance was incensed, for she had begun as a believer and had herself dug up a cross. "I am so convinced Mrs. Williams is a fraud—in part at least," she began a letter to Mary Isabel, "that my comment will necessarily be biased." She described her discovery of the medium's fraudulent production of whispers and her suspicion that Williams had to have an accomplice who planted the crosses.

She had surreptitiously checked Williams's purse, and the medium could not have hidden the objects on her person, she argued, because "she wears a pair of skin tight overalls—she is very plump and you never saw anything fit so quick." As for her father's credulity, "Daddy asks leading questions. He has trusted her so that he has unconsciously given her all the help in the world"; during one séance when Constance wouldn't let her father ask the questions, "we got nothing."[54] Later, when Mary Isabel and Mindret returned to California, they manufactured a cross to show the old man how easy it was to fabricate the "evidence." Nonplussed, Garland simply observed, "In that case, I guess we'll have to call it 'The *Mystery* of the Buried Crosses' and let it go at that."[55]

Garland now had evidence that his psychic was a fraud, at least in part, but he nonetheless continued his experiments. Part of his reason for doing so is that Zulime apparently was more convinced than he and spent hours in rapt attention to the floating cones and mysterious whispers. But he also reverted to his earlier belief that while the phenomena may not come from the dead, they may come from some element of "unexplored biology," and he believed that finding the crosses was the one sure way to demonstrate the existence of the phenomena, whatever the source. He continued to correspond with his patient editor, Harold Latham, who was inclined to some level of belief and at one point wrote, "I am afraid I don't believe that she [Williams] is actually putting you into communication with these men and women who have gone on. On the other hand, I don't think she is producing these whispers herself or of her own volition through any chicanery or apparatus. I think I incline to believe that there is some physical explanation"—and then he quoted Garland's comment in a recent letter that the voices "may all come from the same source, our subconscious minds." Much later Latham recalled, "I know from talks with him that he was honestly puzzled. He could not believe and yet, as he put it, he couldn't 'not believe.'"[56]

Convinced he had a worthwhile book, Garland shopped the manuscript. Harper's, the publisher of so many of his other books, declined. So did Farrar & Rinehart and Scribner's. George Putnam tried to interest Harcourt, but to no avail. Finally, Garland succeeded in interesting John Macrae of E. P. Dutton, who in 1937 had published *The Betty Book: Excursions into the World of Other-Consciousness*, by Garland's good friend Stewart Edward White. In the book White chronicles the development of his wife's mediumship and encounters with "the invisibles," who guided her development. Macrae seems to have been receptive to books on the paranormal, for he published a number of others, including White's sequel, *Across the Unknown* (1939), and Harold H. U. Cross's *A Cavalcade of the Supernatural* (1939). When he accepted *The Mystery of the Buried Crosses* in May 1938, Macrae told Garland, "I feel this is an extraordinary piece of work, quite out of the ordinary run of books on the subject of psychic manifestation. Your thesis is a hard one for the layman to accept wholeheartedly, and yet unless you have been deceived by a carefully planned and efficiently carried out conspiracy, it is impossible to see how one can put aside the evidence which you have so painstakingly piled up." Because photographs would be essential to the story, making for a higher-priced book, and because of the limited appeal of the volume, Macrae offered to take the book on the condition that Garland waive royalties on the first 1,500 copies and accept a 10 percent royalty on copies thereafter; but if the book sold three thousand in its first year, Dutton would pay royalties on all copies sold.[57] Garland accepted with alacrity.

Several events occurred in the 1930s that made it a propitious time for Garland to conceive of and publish *The Mystery of the Buried Crosses*. While people had long been fascinated with spiritualism and mediums, the scientific study of psychic phenomena was in its infancy. Before 1934 psychical research was divided between the spiritualists (like Garland), who sought to verify spectacular mediums, and the experimentalists, who typically explored mental phenomena such as telepathy and clairvoyance. The public was periodically tantalized by press reports of each group's discoveries, with the spiritualists garnering most of the public's attention though their sensational "triumphs"—and through equally spectacular debunkings (the magician Houdini, one might recall, gained much of his fame through exposés of fraudulent mediums).

But in 1927 devotees of spiritualism suffered a setback from which they never really recovered. In that year a young psychologist named Joseph B. Rhine accepted a position at Duke University, from which he inaugurated a series of experiments designed to measure the existence of telepathic communication. By using "Zener cards"—cards embossed with distinctive symbols of triangles, circles, and the like, designed by his colleague Karl Zener—Rhine was able to demonstrate statistically significant evidence for the existence of psychic phenomena. The publication of the results of these experiments in 1934 as a monograph entitled *Extra-Sensory Perception* prompted a wave of popular interest in psychic phenomena and decisively shifted the study of psychic phenomena into the camp of the experimentalists.

Upon its publication, Rhine's book was widely reviewed, and articles championing the validity of ESP appeared in the nation's magazines. In 1937 Rhine launched the *Journal of Parapsychology* at Duke, which offered scientific legitimacy to psychical research. And in October 1937 Rhine published *New Frontiers of the Mind*, a popularized account of his discoveries, which became a Book of the Month Club selection. ESP cards were offered for sale in every bookstore. The Zenith Radio Corporation broadcast a yearlong series of heavily promoted programs concerning psychic phenomena. These programs, aired nationwide, began by dramatizing historically significant cases of science pioneers and then moved to chronicling the evidence for psychic activity—including, for the bulk of the programs, tests of telepathic ability conducted live on the air.[58]

Garland thus undertook his investigation into the buried crosses at a time when the public's appetite for accounts of psychic investigation was unsated. Indeed, that appetite has never really diminished; it has only altered forms. People have always been drawn to extra-rational explanations for the unusual, and these explanations appear to occur in cycles. One need only recall the transcendental meditation and reincarnation fads of the 1960s and 1970s, the accounts of near-death experiences in the 1970s, the alien-invasion fantasies of the 1980s, or the New Age preoccupations of recent years to see that, for many people, the cold logic of science does not provide comforting answers to the most fundamental questions concerning life's purpose. And as a confirmed believer that the human mind had unrecognized powers, Garland was certainly receptive to phenomena that seemed to offer these answers.

Despite its seeming lunacy, *The Mystery of the Buried Crosses* was better received than one might suppose. Reviews were either politely skeptical or enthusiastically supportive—none dismissed Garland as a crank. The reviewer for the *New York Herald Tribune*, for example, praised his objectivity and skeptical conclusion and called the book a "walloping good story" that was "as racy and as exciting as a mystery thriller, despite Mr. Garland's efforts to slow it down and give it the tone of a doctor's thesis." Edward Wagenknecht, who would later become a prominent professor at Boston University and the author of a number of books on literary subjects, concluded that "this is simply a most absorbing book," while believing that Garland's "skepticism [is] overdone. If he were to apply the same standards he applies to psychic problems in the ordinary affairs of life, I doubt if he could prove that he digests his breakfast."[59]

Soon Garland mounted five touring exhibits of his discoveries—consisting primarily of the objects he had discovered, with mounted placards describing the evidence he had gathered and a list of reasons for their legitimacy—to more than twenty-four libraries and museums across the country. He made a nationwide radio broadcast on his seventy-ninth birthday concerning the book—a dramatization with an interview that appeared as part of CBS's *Strange as It Seems* series—and he contracted with the North American Film Corporation to do an educational film about his investigation.[60] But his efforts had little effect on sales. Soon after the book was published in May 1939, he received a disheartening letter from Macrae, who informed him that "the book-sellers had refused to purchase the book and that no advertising could be done without adding to the indebtedness of the book."[61] By October 31 only 850 copies had been sold. He had promised Sophia Williams one-third of the royalties in exchange for her aid, but by the terms of his contract, he received nothing for his two years' labor on the book.[62]

The elderly writer was to have one last hurrah. As he was revising

The Mystery of the Buried Crosses, worrying about the final distribution of his immense archive of manuscripts and inscribed books, and bemoaning the increasing debilities of age, he was invited to address the American Academy's annual meeting on November 10, 1938. He was immensely gratified by the honor, which came at a time when he believed he had been forgotten by the literary world, but he worried that his declining health—in particular the loss of teeth that affected his speech—would disappoint his auditors. "I feel that I am an old fellow with very little authority or mental vigor left," he wrote to Grace Vanamee. "I fear I shall be just another dull reader of a dull paper." For weeks he labored over his speech, determined to "write something that will hit hard."[63] When he stood before his fellows—most of whom, like Garland, were men in their seventies—they welcomed the old trailer with thunderous applause as he returned to an old theme. "As an evolutionist," he proclaimed, "I welcome the analysis of new relationships, new characters, but I find a large percentage of current books, magazines and plays worthless or detestable. I do not feel in them anything permanent or beneficial." But he was hopeful that the salaciousness of contemporary literature would be supplanted by new forms with a succeeding generation, for he believed that "No fashion of any kind—even this shameless kind—can long endure, for each generation coming to expression demands a literature of its own kind."[64] Garland's final address to the organization that had dominated his life for the last twenty years merely repackaged the themes of "Current Fiction Heroes," published in 1923. But his audience of like-minded men applauded thunderously—largely because the speakers preceding him "were lifeless and almost inaudible" in comparison, Garland thought—yet Garland believed the address to be "a most brilliant ending of my career in the East."[65]

His final months were filled with the details of preparing his estate for his inevitable departure, for every day the mirror reminded him that he was on the sundown trail. Garland faced his waning creative ability and his body's inevitable decay with dignity, with curiosity, and often with humor. "As I was dressing this morning," he recorded one day, "I had a disgusting concept of what my ageing body requires.

It is not only a poor, fumbling, tremulous machine, it is a decaying mass of flesh and bone. It needs constant care to prevent its being a nuisance to others. It stinks, it sheds its hair. It itches, aches and burns. It constantly sloughs its skin. It sweats, wrinkles and cracks. It was a poor contrivance at the beginning—it is now a burden. I must continue to wash it, dress it, endure its out-thrusting hair and finger nails and keep its internal cog-works from clogging. The best I can do for it is to cover it up with cloth of pleasing texture and color, for it is certain to become more unsightly as the months march on."[66] He made amends with Mary Isabel by welcoming her new husband to the family—indeed, Mindret soon became the son he never had, for Garland appreciated his "lively mind" and enjoyed discussing books with a fellow writer, so much so that, Mary Isabel remembers, she "became a little resentful" of her father's habit of dragging Mindret to his study to talk "without the womenfolk interrupting." Soon he was engaged in planning to build a house for them.[67]

Then one day in late February 1940, Garland experienced a sudden wave of dizziness. The habit of a lifetime was with him to the end, as he turned to his diary to record the progress of his body's decline: "For some obscure reason, I am suddenly unsteady on my legs and as I was feeding the fire tonight, I nearly fell into the fireplace. This dizziness may be due to indigestion and temporary but it is very disturbing nevertheless." He paused to take stock: "As a man dying on his feet I have lost all pride in my books and all expectation of further reward."[68] Not wanting to worry his family, he concealed his condition even as waves of dizziness affected his ability to walk. To his surprise, his mind was unaffected and, writer to the end, he plugged away at "The Fortunate Exiles," hoping to complete the manuscript for posthumous publication even if no one was interested in publishing it. He put the manuscript aside and took up his pen to write a letter to Eldon Hill, still hopeful that Hill would complete his study of a subject that Garland by now thought held little interest to anybody. About his own approaching death, Garland explained, "I am neither awed nor rebellious—I am curious, just as I used to be when crossing a range into an unknown valley. Each year lessens my regret at leaving the third dimension behind for my friends and relatives are now mainly in the unknown valley—and my work is less and less valuable to the public."[69] He then turned to make a final, cryptic note in his diary, as if to remind a future biographer to record his life as he himself had faced it, a celebration of uncommon achievement tempered with a recognition of inevitable limitations: "No man's biography is complete without a record of his moments of doubt and despair."[70]

On March 1 Zulime discovered Garland collapsed but conscious, complaining that for the past half hour he had been shouting for help, unable to move owing to paralysis on his left side. He had suffered a cerebral hemorrhage. When the power of speech also failed, he resorted to the skill that had sustained him through a lifetime: he inscribed his final words on notepaper. When that ability too failed, with his mind still active despite his body's betrayal, he turned to Indian sign talk with his good friend and business adviser of his California years, A. Gaylord Beaman. Finally, at noon on Saturday, March 2, he lapsed into a coma. Ever curious about what waited over the horizon, perhaps eager to join Henry B. Fuller and other long-departed friends, on March 4, 1940, at 6:10 p.m., the old trailer crossed over into the fourth dimension.[71]

NOTES

ABBREVIATIONS

Academy American Academy of Arts and Letters, New York
City. Items reproduced courtesy of the American
Academy of Arts and Letters.

Afternoon Hamlin Garland, *Afternoon Neighbors: Further Excerpts
from a Literary Log* (New York: Macmillan, 1934).

Back-Trailers Hamlin Garland, *Back-Trailers from the Middle Border*,
illustrations by Constance Garland (New York:
Macmillan, 1928).

Companions Hamlin Garland, *Companions on the Trail: A Literary
Chronicle*, decorations by Constance Garland (New
York: Macmillan, 1931).

Contemporaries Hamlin Garland, *My Friendly Contemporaries: A
Literary Log*, decorations by Constance Garland (New
York: Macmillan, 1932).

Crosses Hamlin Garland, *The Mystery of the Buried Crosses*
(New York: Dutton, 1939).

Daughter Hamlin Garland, *A Daughter of the Middle Border* (New
York: Macmillan, 1921).

Diary Hamlin Garland's diary, 1898–1940, items GD 1–43.
The Huntington Library, San Marino, California.
Items reproduced by permission of the Huntington
Library.

Forty Years Hamlin Garland, *Forty Years of Psychic Research* (New
York: Macmillan, 1936).

Huntington The Huntington Library, San Marino, California.
Items reproduced by permission of the Huntington
Library.

Main-Travelled Roads Hamlin Garland, *Main-Travelled Roads*, ed. Donald
Pizer (Columbus: Merrill, 1970). A facsimile of the
1891 Arena edition.

Miami	Eldon Hill Collection, the Walter Havighurst Special Collections, Miami University Libraries, Oxford, Ohio.
NYPL	Manuscripts and Archives Division, the New York Public Library, Astor, Lenox and Tilden Foundations.
Roadside Meetings	Hamlin Garland, *Roadside Meetings*, decorations by Constance Garland (New York: Macmillan, 1930).
Selected Letters	Hamlin Garland, *Selected Letters of Hamlin Garland*, ed. Keith Newlin and Joseph B. McCullough (Lincoln: University of Nebraska Press, 1998).
Son	Hamlin Garland, *A Son of the Middle Border* (New York: Macmillan, 1917).
"This Loving Daughter"	Isabel Garland Lord, "This Loving Daughter" (an unpublished memoir of her father). Copy courtesy of her granddaughter, Victoria Doyle-Jones. Another copy is deposited in the Huntington Library, item FAC 1285).
Trail-Makers	Hamlin Garland, *Trail-Makers of the Middle Border*, illustrations by Constance Garland (New York: Macmillan, 1926).
USC	Hamlin Garland Papers, Specialized Libraries and Archival Collections, University of Southern California.

PROLOGUE

1. "Hamlin Garland Rites Held at Neshonoc," *West Salem Nonpareil-Journal*, March 14, 1940, 1.

2. Diary, February 18, 1940.

3. Garland to Zulime Garland, April 25, [no year], item GD 335, Huntington; "Hamlin Garland Returns; Admirers Besiege Author," *Chicago Daily News*, [October 1938], clipping, Miami.

4. Horace Traubel, *With Walt Whitman in Camden*, vol. 3 (New York: Rowman and Littlefield, 1961), 438.

5. Booth Tarkington, "Hamlin Garland," in *Commemorative Tributes of the American Academy of Arts and Letters, 1905–1941* (New York: American Academy, 1942), 400; Robert Morss Lovett to Eldon Hill, November 27, 1934, Miami; Henry James, "American Letter," *Literature*, April 9, 1898, 422; S. S. McClure's recollection of Howells's comment, bound in a memorial volume celebrating

Garland's seventy-third birthday, as quoted by Eldon Hill in "Hamlin Garland: The Writer as Citizen" (unpublished biography, Miami), 309; Eldon Hill's transcription of Robert Peattie's unpublished autobiography, Miami; Theodore Roosevelt to Brander Matthews, May 21, 1894, in *The Letters of Theodore Roosevelt and Brander Matthews*, ed. Lawrence J. Oliver (Knoxville: University of Tennessee Press, 1995), 81; Charles Lummis, "That Which Is Written," *Land of Sunshine*, November 1886, 248.

6. Diary, April 9, 1899.

7. Harold Latham in "Centennial Tributes and a Checklist of the Hamlin Garland Papers in the University of Southern California Library," in *University of Southern California Library Bulletin 9*, ed. and comp. Lloyd Arvidson (Los Angeles: University of Southern California, 1962), 13.

1. RETURN OF THE PRIVATE

1. *Contemporaries*, 519.

2. James D. Jones, "The Garland Heritage" (unpublished typescript, West Salem Historical Society, West Salem WI); Hamlin Garland, "Biographical Notes of R. H. Garland," item 504, USC. Jones is a descendant of the McClintock branch of the family. During the composition of *A Son of the Middle Border*, Garland asked his father about his early memories and noted, "He had a clear notion of it all up to his Civil War experience. I realized that he must soon pass and that I should get as much of his history as I could" (Diary, December 27, 1911). Garland would later mine the "Biographical Notes" for much of the early family history in *A Son of the Middle Border* and *Trail-Makers of the Middle Border*.

3. *Trail-Makers*, 54–55.

4. Garland, "Biographical Notes of R. H. Garland," 3.

5. Hamlin Garland, "A Son of the Middle Border," pt. 1, "Half Lights," *Collier's*, March 28, 1914, 6.

6. Garland, "Half Lights," 6–7.

7. *Son*, 24.

8. See Errol Kindschy, *Leonard's Dream: A History of West Salem* (privately printed, 1981), 11–16.

9. Garland, "Biographical Notes of R. H. Garland," 4.

10. *Trail-Makers*, 224.

11. Garland, "Biographical Notes of R. H. Garland," 4.

12. Garland, "Biographical Notes of R. H. Garland," 5.

13. John A. Stanley, *From Then Until Now* (privately printed, 1948), 5–6.

14. From Richard Garland's Civil War certificate of service, issued March 8, 1920, in Madison, item 712, USC.

15. Garland, "Biographical Notes of R. H. Garland," 5.

16. Letter by Captain B. F. Cooper, provost marshall, Sixth District, La Crosse, January 16, 1864, cited in Jones, "The Garland Heritage," 10.

17. Garland, "Biographical Notes of R. H. Garland," 5.

18. Land deeds filed in October 1865 show that Richard Hayes Garland paid $165.66 for 118.55 acres on December 31, 1864, for NE NW and W½NE¼ sec. 3, T16 R7. On May 28, 1865, he paid $27.97 for 20 acres located N½ SE NW¼ sec. 3 T16 R7. Cited in Jones, "The Garland Heritage," 10.

19. See Jones, "The Garland Heritage," 10; Jones compiled the details of Dick Garland's service from division records.

20. Garland, "Biographical Notes of R. H. Garland," 5.

21. *Son*, 92.

22. *Son*, 7–8.

23. *Son*, 31.

24. "1894—A Visit to the West," notebook 42, USC. In this notebook, Hamlin records his earliest memories, many of which would eventually become part of *A Son of the Middle Border*.

25. Hamlin Garland, "The Wife of a Pioneer," *Ladies' Home Journal*, September 1903, 8, 42.

2. BOY LIFE ON THE PRAIRIE

1. *Son*, 42.

2. See Jones, "The Garland Heritage," 10. Jones records that "on 24 March 1868 Richard and Isabelle sold their farm to James A. Spier for $3,500.00 subject to a mortgage of $500.00 to Jacob Tourtlotte dated June 1866." In *A Son of the Middle Border* Garland notes that his family moved to Hesper in February (58).

3. In his notes to the Penguin edition of *A Son of the Middle Border* (New York: Penguin, 1995), 378, Joseph B. McCullough identifies the song as a ballad by George T. Morris entitled "Westwart, ho!" originally published in *Godey's Lady's Book* in January 1839. Garland's version differs from the original in several of the verses, reflecting the changes as the song passed from pioneer to pioneer.

4. *Son*, 63.

5. *Son*, 75.

6. Garland, "The Wife of a Pioneer," 8.

7. The *Mitchell County Press* for July 14, 1870, records a real estate transfer between Michael Clark to R. H. Garland for $1,700 for the quarter section (160 acres) of SW 30-99-16. Later tax records, however, show the land was actually 132.7 acres. See Thomas G. Schuppe, "Hamlin Garland of Iowa," *Annals of Iowa* 44 (1972): 847. The next day, July 15, Dick also bought a lot in nearby

Osage—lot 7, block 135, at Ninth and Main streets—from his father-in-law, Hugh McClintock. See Jones, "The Garland Heritage," 11. In the *Collier's* version of *A Son of the Middle Border* (but not the book version), Garland writes that Hugh had relocated to Osage, but later in both magazine and book version Hamlin returns to Onalaska in 1881, where he visits Hugh. Perhaps Hugh had merely invested in land in Osage. In both versions, Hamlin remembers the farm as being "rented," but his memory is in error.

8. *Son*, 82.

9. *Son*, 83.

10. Population counts from the 1870 census as cited in *History of Mitchell and Worth Counties, Iowa* (Springfield IL: Union Publishing, 1884), 68. By 1880 Mitchell County had grown to 14,361 citizens while Winneshiek had gained only 367, for a total population of 23,937.

11. See Schuppe, "Hamlin Garland of Iowa," 841; the data are derived from *Iowa Agricultural Census* (1870), *Iowa Population Census* (1870), and *Platt Book of Winneshiek County Iowa* (1886).

12. Allan G. Bogue, *From Prairie to Corn Belt: Farming on the Illinois and Iowa Prairies in the Nineteenth Century* (Chicago: University of Chicago Press, 1963), 70.

13. "Gossip about Hamlin Garland." *Los Angeles Times*, August 8, 1897, 21.

14. *Son*, 88. See also *Boy Life on the Prairie* (New York: Macmillan, 1899), where Garland describes a breaking plow in this fictional memoir (79).

15. *History of Mitchell and Worth Counties, Iowa*, 177.

16. Christine Pawley, *Reading on the Middle Border: The Culture of Print in Late-Nineteenth-Century Osage, Iowa* (Amherst: University of Massachusetts Press, 2001), 50.

17. *Son*, 95, 92. For Garland's slate, see item 715, USC.

18. *Son*, 100.

19. Hamlin Garland, "Boy Life on the Prairie," pt. 4, "Between Hay an' Grass," *American Magazine*, June 1888, 149. The series of six articles describing his Iowa boyhood appeared between January and October 1888 in *American Magazine*. In them, Garland describes life on a prairie farm filtered through a consciousness that the events of only ten years past are already disappearing; he therefore describes that life with an eye toward documenting a bit of passing history. He later thoroughly revised the articles, cast them as fiction, considerably deepened the nostalgia of the sketches, and published the result as *Boy Life on the Prairie* (1899). When he came to write his autobiography he again revised them, even shifting the scene of "The Thrashin'" from the Iowa of his adolescence to Wisconsin of his preteen years, and deepened the nostalgia appropriate to a man of fifty-four.

20. Franklin Garland to Eldon Hill, July 19, 1940, Miami.

21. The Garlands' farm was the quarter section located at section 6, township 98, range 19, Burr Oak Township, Mitchell County, Iowa (Schuppe, "Hamlin Garland of Iowa," 848); the deed is dated February 21, 1871 (Jones, "The Garland Heritage," 11).

22. Solon Justus Buck, *The Granger Movement* (Cambridge: Harvard University Press, 1933), 27.

23. Average crop prices are from Buck, *The Granger Movement*, 29.

24. In 1871 his farm was taxed at $6.10 per acre, compared to an average of $20.12 per acre for all other Burr Oak Township farms. Since these are the acres that the young Hamlin plowed, the low taxation suggests they were not as productive as Dick Garland had hoped and is likely the reason he bought another tract (Schuppe, "Hamlin Garland of Iowa," 848–49).

25. *Son*, 115.

26. *Son*, 112.

27. Garland to Harvey C. Minnich, April 2, 1936, in *Selected Letters*, 376. In 1936 Garland would be one of twelve board members of the William Holmes McGuffey Memorial Association responsible for selecting 150 "old favorites" to commemorate the McGuffey centennial. The volume appeared as *Old Favorites from the McGuffey Readers*, ed. Harvey C. Minnich (1936).

28. Franklin Garland to Eldon Hill, July 19, 1940, Miami.

29. Hamlin Garland, *Prairie Songs* (Chicago: Stone and Kimball, 1893), 147.

30. Hamlin Garland, "Boy Life on the Prairie," pt. 3, "The Voice of Spring," *American Magazine*, April 1888, 686.

31. Hamlin Garland, "Boy Life on the Prairie," pt. 4, "Melons and Early Frosts," *American Magazine*, October 1888, 716.

32. *Son*, 157–58.

33. See Bill Webb, "Osage Has Forgotten Author," *Mason City (Iowa) Globe-Gazette*, November 24, 1956, 18.

34. Garland's 1875 diary, item 10, USC; *Son*, 171.

35. Hamlin Garland, *A Pioneer Mother* (Chicago: Bookfellows, 1922), 12.

36. Buck, *The Granger Movement*, 41.

37. Buck, *The Granger Movement*, 240–41.

38. "Declaration of Purposes of the National Grange," 1874, http://www.geocities.com/cannongrange/declaration_purposes.html.

39. Buck, *The Granger Movement*, 280.

40. *Son*, 174.

41. *Son*, 177–78.

42. Pawley, *Reading on the Middle Border*, 10. The population of Osage is de-

rived from the 1870 census as reported by Schuppe, "Hamlin Garland of Iowa," 850.

43. *Son*, 91.

44. *Son*, 189–90.

45. *History of Mitchell and Worth Counties, Iowa*, 443.

46. Pawley, *Reading on the Middle Border*, 20. While Garland would later state in *A Son of the Middle Border* and elsewhere that the students came from the surrounding farms, Pawley's study of census and seminary records suggests that most students came from comparatively well-to-do families (17–20). The numbers of seminary students come from the school magazine, *Cedar Valley Seminarian*, June 1881. Eldon Hill reports that 187 students enrolled in 1877–78: "The total received tuition was $1,947.25, or an average of little more than ten dollars per student" ("A Biographical Study of Hamlin Garland from 1860 to 1895" [PhD diss., Ohio State University, 1940], 23). And during that term, there were only three full-time teachers.

47. *Cedar Valley Seminarian*, June 1881, 10.

48. *Cedar Valley Seminarian*, June 1881, 1.

49. *Son*, 196–97.

50. *Son*, 198–99.

51. See exhibition program for March 27, 1878, item 709d, USC; and Gladys Diana Chatman, "An Historical Study of Cedar Valley Seminary" (master's thesis, Drake University, 1941), 34–35.

52. Barnet Baskerville, *The People's Voice: The Orator in American Society* (Lexington: University of Kentucky Press, 1979), 86.

53. *Son*, 192, 207.

54. Hill, "A Biographical Study of Hamlin Garland," 22.

55. Garland's 1877 diary, item 10, USC.

56. A plan was hatched to issue stock to gain capital—the Grange hoped to garner twenty-five thousand dollars by issuing shares at ten dollars per share—but the plan failed and members rapidly abandoned the Grange. On October 1, 1875, there were 51,332 members of the Iowa Grange, but that number had fallen to 32,019 by July 1, 1876. See Buck, *The Granger Movement*, 243, and table, "Statistics of the Patrons of Husbandry," between pp. 58 and 59.

57. *Son*, 205–6.

58. Franklin Garland to Hill, July 19, 1940, Miami. Schuppe reports that Osage public school records show the last date of Franklin's attendance at school as February 1, 1877 ("Hamlin Garland of Iowa," 850).

59. *Son*, 207.

60. Franklin Garland to Eldon Hill, July 19, 1940, Miami.

61. Tax records for 1873 show Richard H. Garland paying more in taxes, based on acreage, than his neighbors. See Schuppe, "Hamlin Garland of Iowa," 850.

62. *Son*, 209–10.

63. Ida Ewell Tilson, a longtime West Salem neighbor, told Eldon Hill that Isabelle Garland "put Hamlin through Osage Seminary by 'raising colts.'" Hill, notes entitled "I Go on a Pilgrimage to Garland's Coulee Country," October 20, 1929, Miami.

64. Garland to Editor, *Junior Annual*, Osage, Iowa, ca. 1901 (courtesy of Monte J. Kloberdanz, Osage, Iowa).

65. *Son*, 219–20.

66. Pawley, *Reading on the Middle Border*, 42.

67. *Son*, 213–14.

68. The national average price for wheat had dropped from $1.06 per bushel in 1877 to $0.78 in 1878, and the price for corn had dipped from $0.35 in 1877 to $0.32 in 1897 (Buck, *The Granger Movement*, 29).

69. *Son*, 216, 238.

70. *Son*, 223. For raids on the pantry, see Chatman, "An Historical Study of Cedar Valley Seminary," 38.

71. Quoted in Webb, "Osage Has Forgotten Author."

72. Garland to the Osage Public Library, June 26, [1929], Osage Public Library, Osage, Iowa.

73. *Son*, 229.

74. The October 14, 1880, *Osage Press* records the sale of SE 6-98-16 to Johnson and Allis for $3,200. Apparently, Dick Garland had previously sold a portion of SW 30-99-16, for the *Iowa Agricultural Census* for 1880 shows that he owned 240 acres, so after the sale of SE 6-98-16 he was left with 80 acres. Neither the *Census* nor Hamlin clarifies where the family lived for the next year, so either they moved back to their former farm or reached an agreement with Johnson and Allis to remain in their residence. See Schuppe, "Hamlin Garland of Iowa," 851.

3. DAKOTA HOMESTEADER

1. *Brown County History* (Aberdeen SD: Brown County Museum and Historical Society, 1980), 18–21.

2. Broadside reproduced in Robert J. Casey and W. A. S. Douglas, *Pioneer Railroad: The Story of the Chicago and North Western System* (New York: McGraw-Hill, 1948), following p. 182.

3. E. P. Rothrock, *A Geology of South Dakota* (1943), quoted in Herbert S.

Schell, *History of South Dakota*, 3rd ed., rev. (Lincoln: University of Nebraska Press, 1975), 5.

4. *United States Statutes at Large*, 37th Cong., 2nd sess., ch. 75 (1862), 392.

5. David M. Ellis, "The Homestead Clause in Railroad Land Grants," in *The Frontier in American Development: Essays in Honor of Paul William Gates*, ed. David M. Ellis (Ithaca: Cornell University Press, 1969), 53, 48.

6. Robert C. McMath Jr., *American Populism: A Social History, 1877–1898* (New York: Hill and Wang, 1993), 22.

7. Quoted in August Derleth, *The Milwaukee Road: Its First One Hundred Years* (New York: Creative Age Press, 1948), 133.

8. Land Office records show that Richard Hayes Garland proved up on a homestead claim filed for sw¼ of section 28, township 125N, range 63w. Other records show his homestead to occupy the south half of the section—320 acres. Since the terms of the Homestead Act limit claims to one 160-acre parcel, at some point Dick Garland acquired the title to the contiguous quarter section. In *A Son of the Middle Border*, Hamlin notes that his grandfather filed an adjoining claim to his father's homestead (248), so Dick likely filed the claim in his father's name and, after his father's death in 1886, acquired title to the land. Dick Garland's preemption claim has not been located. While in *A Son of the Middle Border* Hamlin says the claim is thirty miles west (302), in *Roadside Meetings* he extends the distance to forty miles (3). But the county line—and Garland's own claim—is about eighteen miles from Ordway.

9. *Brown County History*, 36.

10. *Son*, 231–32.

11. *Son*, 235.

12. *Son*, 228. The comment stuck with him, for he used the scene, and the line, in *A Spoil of Office*, where Radbourne tells Bradley Talcott, "[Lawyer] Brown wants to see you. He wants to make you a 'lawyer's hack'!" (*Arena*, February 1892, 392).

13. Item 710, USC.

14. *Son*, 241.

15. Alice Field Garland to Eldon Hill, May 11, 1950, Miami.

16. The poem exists in three states (item 274, USC). I have restored the canceled penultimate stanza (the last one quoted here) of one of the versions. "Alice" or "Agnes" remains unidentified.

17. *Son*, 246–47.

18. *Brown County History*, 97.

19. Schell, *History of South Dakota*, 171–72.

20. Dick Garland's parcel is SE¼ of section 4, township 126, range 63, land records cited in e-mail from William Aisenbrey, Aberdeen, South Dakota.

21. Schell, *History of South Dakota*, 174.

22. Franklin Garland to Eldon Hill, July 19, 1940, Miami.

23. *Son*, 252–54.

24. *Son*, 259.

25. Franklin Garland to Eldon Hill, July 19, 1940, Miami.

26. *Son*, 261.

27. *Son*, 299.

28. Item 710, USC.

29. McMath, *American Populism*, 24; *Early History of Brown County: A Literature of the People* (Aberdeen SD: Brown County Territorial Pioneers, 1965), 13.

30. *Son*, 301–2.

31. *Brown County History*, 89. The population boom in Brown County was staggering: in 1880 there were 353 residents; by 1885 there were 12,241 (Schell, *History of South Dakota*, 165).

32. Land records show that Garland's claim was filed on March 24, 1884, and that he paid the government cash price for his 160 acres—two hundred dollars—which suggests that the survey was not completed until a year had passed. Garland incorporated his claim as part of the manuscript of "The Rise of Boomtown." See Hamlin Garland, "'The Rise of Boomtown': An Unpublished Dakota Novel by Hamlin Garland," ed. Donald Pizer, *South Dakota Historical Collections* 28 (1956): 345–89. The novel was begun shortly after his claim-holding experience, in mid-1886, and relies for much of its texture on his actual experiences. As the preface to the novel explains, "Its descriptions can be relied upon, for I have aimed to be true to the scene and people." I shall therefore occasionally refer to Garland's descriptions to illustrate the details of his Dakota experience.

33. Garland, "'The Rise of Boomtown,'" 376.

34. Franklin Garland to Eldon Hill, July 19, 1940, Miami.

35. Garland, "'The Rise of Boomtown,'" 371.

36. *Son*, 305.

37. Franklin Garland to Eldon Hill, July 19, 1940, Miami.

38. Hippolyte Taine, *History of English Literature*, vol. 1, trans. H. van Laun (Philadelphia: David McKay, n.d.), 19.

39. Taine, *History of English Literature*, 23.

40. Donald Pizer, *Hamlin Garland's Early Work and Career* (Berkeley: University of California Press, 1960), 9.

41. Franklin Garland to Eldon Hill, July 19, 1940, Miami.

42. *Son*, 307. In "'The Rise of Boomtown'" Garland notes that "with a fiendish purpose and a lazy purpose I covered the ceiling in the same way and whenever

a visitor came in, he nearly broke his neck trying to read the words which I read with the greatest ease" (371).

43. Notebook dated "1884, McPherson County, Dakota," item 12, USC, quoted in Hill, "A Biographical Study of Hamlin Garland," 36.

44. Franklin Garland to Eldon Hill, July 19, 1940, Miami.

45. Henry George, *Progress and Poverty* (New York: John W. Lovell, 1883), 9–10. For a lucid explanation of George's theory see Louis Wasserman, "The Essential Henry George," in *Critics of Henry George: A Centenary Appraisal of Their Strictures on Progress and Poverty*, ed. Robert V. Anderson (Rutherford NJ: Fairleigh Dickinson University Press, 1979), 29–43.

46. *Son*, 313–14.

47. Schell, *History of South Dakota*, 187–88. For Garland's tax for the year 1884, paid on September 29, 1885, see Garland, "'The Rise of Boomtown,'" 378–79; also South Dakota Writers' Program, *Homesteaders of McPherson County*, American Guide Series (Pierre SD: n.p., 1941), 14. However, the *Leola Centennial Anniversary Book* (Leola SD: Leola Centennial Committee, 1984) notes that tax records for 1884 show that Garland paid a tax of $1.43 for his quarter section, assessed at $575 (http://www.odessa3.org/collections/towns/link/leola84.txt). Despite this discrepancy, the point remains that Garland paid more tax for his meager possessions than he did for his land.

48. *Brown County History*, 89.

49. Oscar S. Kotila, in *Early History of Brown County*, 166.

50. As told by Mrs. John H. (Elizabeth Van Buren) Perry to Paul W. Kieser, *Early History of Brown County*, 177.

51. *Son*, 308.

52. Ethel Nemeyer, in *Early History of Brown County*, 69.

53. Hamlin Garland, "Holding Down a Claim in a Blizzard," *Harper's Weekly*, January 28, 1888, 66.

54. Ethel Nemeyer, in *Early History of Brown County*, 69.

55. *Son*, 312.

56. Hamlin Garland, "A Son of the Middle Border," pt. 3, "A Prairie Outpost," *Collier's*, May 26, 1917, 14.

57. *National Cyclopedia of American Biography*, vol. 4 (Ann Arbor: University Microfilms, 1967), 160.

4. BOSTON MENTORS

1. Alpheus Cody, "Hamlin Garland, Author," *St. Louis Republic*, February 11, 1894, 27.

2. *Son*, 322.

3. Pizer, *Hamlin Garland's Early Work and Career*, 11.

4. *Son*, 324, 323.

5. Hamlin Garland, "Notebook begun Oct./6/84," 138, item 13, USC.

6. *Roadside Meetings*, 45, 46.

7. James B. Stronks, "Mark Twain's Boston Stage Debut as Seen by Hamlin Garland," *New England Quarterly* 36 (March 1963): 86. Garland recorded his impression of Twain's performance, which occurred on either November 13 or 15, 1884, in his Boston notebook, item 13, USC.

8. Edyth Renshaw, "Five Private Schools of Speech," in *History of Speech Education in America*, ed. Karl R. Wallace (New York: Appleton, 1954), 321.

9. Claude L. Shaver, "Steele MacKaye and the Delsartian Tradition," in Wallace, *History of Speech Education*, 208.

10. In *A Son of the Middle Border* Garland mentions that at the school he "was introduced to the pretty teacher of Delsarte, Miss Maida Craigen," and that in assisting Brown with his book he "read every listed book or article upon expression, and translated several French authorities, transcribing them in longhand for his use" (335).

11. Moses True Brown, *The Synthetic Philosophy of Expression as Applied to the Arts of Reading, Oratory, and Personation* (Boston: Houghton Mifflin, 1886), iv, vi.

12. Brown, *The Synthetic Philosophy of Expression*, 170.

13. Hamlin Garland, "Notes on lectures at Boston School of Oratory," December 12, [1885], item 15, USC.

14. Art Young, *Authors' Readings* (New York: Frederick A. Stokes, 1897).

15. *Son*, 329.

16. "Edwin Booth as a Master of Expression" (584a, USC) has been edited and made available in Mark Rocha's unpublished dissertation, "The Feminization of Failure in American Historiography: The Case of the Invisible Drama in the Life of Hamlin Garland" (University of Southern California, 1988). Part 1 of Rocha's study summarizes and comments briefly upon all of Garland's play manuscripts; part 2 is a selected edition of Garland's dramatic criticism and the text of *Rip Van Winkle*. Rocha's dating of play manuscripts, however, is unreliable, for many entries in Garland's diaries (located at the Huntington Library), which Rocha apparently did not consult, contradict his speculations.

17. Brown, *The Synthetic Philosophy of Expression*, 192.

18. Brown, *The Synthetic Philosophy of Expression*, 231.

19. Hamlin Garland, "Ten Years Dead," *Every Other Saturday*, March 28, 1885, 97–99. *Every Other Saturday* was a Boston periodical that appeared from 1884 to 1885. See also C. E. Schorer, "Hamlin Garland's First Published Story," *American Literature* 25 (1953): 89–92.

20. See the Boston School of Oratory's 1893–94 catalog, which lists Garland's courses. Among the American literature offerings are courses in "The Modern Age" and "Logical Prophecy," which formed the basis of "The Future of Fiction" and which would be published in *Arena* in 1894 and would later form chapter 6, "The Local Novel," and chapter 4, "Literary Prophecy," of *Crumbling Idols*. I am indebted to Robert Fleming, archivist of Emerson College Library, for kindly supplying me with a copy of the Boston School of Oratory's catalog.

21. See "Three Great Novels," *Portland Transcript*, May 20, 1885, 60. The review has been introduced and reprinted in Seth Bovey and Gary Scharnhorst, "Hamlin Garland's First Published Essay," ANQ 5 (1992): 20–23.

22. The invitation card for the lectures is pasted in Garland's May 15, 1885, notebook, item 16, USC.

23. The newspaper quotations are from Garland's 1885–86 lecture circular, item 670, USC; *Son*, 344; *Roadside Meetings*, 21.

24. Garland's 1885–86 lecture circular, item 670, USC.

25. Julie Herne, "James A. Herne, Actor and Dramatist" (unpublished biography, Herbert J. Edwards Collection, Folger Library, University of Maine, Orono), 246.

5. THE EARNEST APPRENTICE

1. Garland never published "The Evolution of American Thought," which remains in manuscript (item 465, USC). Additional titles of extant chapters are "Walt Whitman," "The Epic of the Age," "The Present and the Future," and "Logical Prophecy." For the fullest discussion of the genesis and content of the work, see Pizer, *Hamlin Garland's Early Work and Career*, 13–21.

2. Kenneth M. Price, "Hamlin Garland's 'The Evolution of American Thought': A Missing Link in the History of Whitman Criticism," *Walt Whitman Quarterly Review* 3 (Fall 1985): 5. Price's article includes the text of Garland's "Whitman" chapter.

3. Garland to Booth, January 22, 1886, in *Selected Letters*, 12.

4. Booth to Garland, n.d., pasted on flyleaf of notebook 50, "Literary Notes," USC. The letter is Garland's copy, with Booth's mounted signature. Garland quotes the letter in *Roadside Meetings*, 48.

5. Garland to Howe, July 2, 1886, in *Selected Letters*, 13–14.

6. Hamlin Garland, *Crumbling Idols* (Chicago: Stone and Kimball, 1894), 64.

7. Howe to Garland, July 7, 1886, USC.

8. Garland to Howe, July 15, 1886, in *Selected Letters*, 15–16.

9. Howe to Garland, July 23, 1886, USC.

10. *Son*, 327.

11. *Son*, 348.

12. Franklin Garland to Eldon Hill, July 19, 1940, Miami. In *A Son of the Middle Border* Hamlin places Franklin's arrival in the summer of 1886 and says Franklin got a job as an accountant with a railroad (349); in his letter to Hill, Franklin describes at length his job in the clothing store; after his cousin fired him, the cousin arranged a job with the Shawmut Avenue Street Car Company.

13. Franklin Garland to Eldon Hill, July 19, 1940, Miami.

14. *Roadside Meetings*, 23.

15. *Son*, 227. Compare with an 1896 interview: "One day I happened to pick up 'The Undiscovered Country.' I glanced at it at first, supposing that it was a scientific work of some sort. I read it and became attracted at once. 'This,' I said to myself, 'is what I've been looking for.' I couldn't afford to buy the book, so I had to content myself with what I could get at the counter. It made an indelible impression on me, though it didn't immediately affect my literary ideals. It stole insidiously into my mind. I knew it was the best English I had ever read, but I wouldn't admit that then, as I was fresh from Hawthorne and Victor Hugo. I afterward grew very indignant over some statement of Mr. Howells concerning Hugo's faults" ("A Chat with Hamlin Garland," *Illustrated American*, March 21, 1896, 367).

16. Hamlin Garland, "Lemuel Barker," *Boston Evening Transcript*, January 31, 1887, 6.

17. Hamlin Garland, "Meetings with Howells," *Bookman*, March 1917, 2–3.

18. Garland, "Meetings with Howells," 4–5. Garland published several accounts, with slight variations, of his initial meeting, which was also a favorite topic of his lectures. "Meetings with Howells" provides the most detail; see also *Roadside Meetings*, 24–25, 55–61, and *Son*, 384–90.

19. Howells to Whitelaw Reid, May 2, 1887, in *Selected Letters of W. D. Howells*, ed. George Arms et al., 6 vols. (Boston: Twayne, 1976–83), 3:187.

20. "Meetings with Authors. Lecture Notes," in *Hamlin Garland's Diaries*, ed. Donald Pizer (San Marino CA: Huntington Library Press, 1968), 152.

21. "Mr. Garland's Books," *North American Review*, October 1912, 523.

22. Howells's estimation of Garland may be gleaned primarily from the more than 130 letters he wrote to him, held in USC, a portion of which have been published. Howells seems not to have retained Garland's letters to him (only twelve are extant), nor did he keep a diary, and he detested lecturing. One must therefore reconstruct the nature of the friendship largely from Garland's many published and unpublished remarks as well as from Howells's letters to Garland.

23. The manuscript of "Love or the Law" (item 203, USC) was typed with the uppercase typewriter Garland used between 1886 and 1888. I have not pre-

served the idiosyncrasies of Garland's typewriter in my transcriptions. Garland was also inconsistent in the conventions of underlining staging cues, enclosing dialogue within quotation marks, and placing periods and commas within quotation marks. I have therefore regularized my transcriptions but have not corrected his punctuation, spelling, and use (and non-use) of the apostrophe.

24. Garland, *Main-Travelled Roads*, 69.

25. Garland, *Main-Travelled Roads*, 185.

26. Hamlin Garland, "Zury, 'The Meanest Man in Spring County,'" *Boston Evening Transcript*, May 16, 1887, 3.

27. Joseph Kirkland to Garland, May 23, 1887, USC. Garland's letters to Kirkland have not survived.

28. Kirkland to Garland, May 31, 1887, USC.

29. *Son*, 354.

30. Garland, transcript of 1887 notebook describing his western visit, item 19, USC. In the transcript, Garland has considerably expanded the notes he made in notebook 18, USC. The transcript would later form the basis of chapter 28, "A Visit to the West," of *A Son of the Middle Border*.

31. *Son*, 368–69.

32. Hamlin Garland, "Wheat Harvest," *Louisville Courier-Journal*, July 31, 1887, 13; "Prairie Memories," *American*, October 1887, 653; "Beneath the Pines," *American*, November 1887, 87; "My Cabin," *American*, December 1887, 232.

33. Kirkland to Garland, July 30, 1887, USC.

34. *Son*, 374.

6. SINGLE-TAX REALIST

1. *Roadside Meetings*, 97. Garland refers to Riley's "When the Frost Is on the Punkin" and "Wortermelon Time"; for the latter poem, Riley's line reads, "And the new-moon hangin' ore us like a yeller-cored slice."

2. Riley to Garland, October 10, 1887, in Florence French, "'Dear Man!': Bluff Letters of Literary Friendship from James Whitcomb Riley to Hamlin Garland," *Ball State University Forum* 20 (1979): 39.

3. Garland to Riley, December 17, 1897, in *Selected Letters*, 23.

4. Hamlin Garland, "James Whitcomb Riley," *Boston Evening Transcript*, December 21, 1887, 6.

5. Freeman to Garland, November 23, 1887, in *The Infant Sphinx: Collected Letters of Mary E. Wilkins Freeman*, ed. Brent L. Kendrick (Metuchen NJ: Scarecrow Press, 1985), 83.

6. Kirkland to Garland, November 13, 1887, USC.

7. Garland, "'The Rise of Boomtown,'" 352.

8. Garland, manuscript of "The Rise of Boomtown," item 165b, USC.

9. Garland, "Holding Down a Claim in a Blizzard," 66–67; Hamlin Garland, "Lost in the Norther," *Harper's Weekly*, December 3, 1887, 883.

10. *Son*, 351.

11. Pizer, *Hamlin Garland's Early Work and Career*, 54.

12. The entire series of "Boy Life on the Prairie" in *American Magazine* is as follows: pt. 1, "The Huskin'," January 1888, 299–303; pt. 2, "The Thrashin'," March 1888, 570–77; pt. 3, "The Voice of Spring," April 1888, 684–90; pt. 4, "Between Hay an' Grass," June 1888, 148–55; pt. 5, "Meadow Memories," July 1888, 296–303; pt. 6, "Melons and Early Frosts," October 1888, 712–17. Garland later reworked the series to form the core of *Boy Life on the Prairie* (1899), and he used some of the sketches in *A Son of the Middle Border* as well.

13. Garland, "The Thrashin'," 571.

14. Garland, "Between Hay an' Grass," 150.

15. Kirkland to Garland, March 20, 1888, USC.

16. Garland, "Meadow Memories," 300.

17. Garland, "The Voice of Spring," 687. The poem was later collected in *Prairie Songs*.

18. Kirkland to Garland, February 13, 1888, USC.

19. Kirkland to Garland, March 20, 26, 1888, USC.

20. Kirkland to Garland, April 27, 1888, USC. Subtitled "A Journal for Americans, Devoted to Honest Politics and Good Literature," *America* was founded on July 5, 1888, by Slason Thompson. After *America* rejected "Daddy Deering"—Kirkland speculated the magazine was reluctant to print stories about hog butchering—the story was submitted to *Harper's Weekly* and was ultimately accepted by *Belford's* in October 1888. When it was published four years later in *Belford's* (April 1892, 152–61), Kirkland's revisions remained. The story was later revised and included in *Prairie Folks*.

21. Kirkland to Garland, April 29, 1888, USC.

22. In two letters to Kirkland, Slason Thompson, the magazine's editor, confirmed details of payment. See Thompson to Kirkland, May 1, 2, 1888, USC. "Paid His Way" appeared in *America* on May 19, 1888, 6; it was later reprinted in *Prairie Songs*.

23. Kirkland to Garland, May 3, 1888, USC.

24. Kirkland to Garland, May 16, 1888, USC.

25. Pizer, *Hamlin Garland's Early Work and Career*, 45–46. See also Pizer's more detailed discussion, "Hamlin Garland in the Standard," *American Literature* 26 (1954): 401–15.

26. "Anti-Poverty Lecture in Boston," *Standard*, December 10, 1887, 5.

27. George to Garland, March 19, 1888, USC.

28. "Interesting to Massachusetts Anti-Povertyites," *Standard*, March 31, 1888, 2.

29. Hamlin Garland, "A Common Case," *Belford's*, July 1888, 190–91, 192. The story was reprinted in the *Standard* on July 28, 1888, 6. Garland later reprinted it in *Wayside Courtships* as "Before the Low Green Door" without its didactic first part.

30. Hamlin Garland, "April Hopes," *Boston Evening Transcript*, March 1, 1888, 6.

31. W. D. Howells, "Novel-Writing and Novel-Reading," in *Selected Literary Criticism*, vol. 3, *1898–1920*, ed. Ronald Gottesman (Bloomington: Indiana University Press, 1993), 222.

32. Howells to Garland, March 11, 1888, in *Selected Letters of W. D. Howells*, 3:220.

33. Hamlin Garland, "Annie Kilburn," *Boston Evening Transcript*, December 27, 1888, 6.

34. Isabelle Garland to Hamlin Garland, June 1, 1888, quoted in Hill, "A Biographical Study of Hamlin Garland," 88–89.

35. Hamlin Garland, "Professor Garland's Western Trip," *Standard*, June 23, 1888, 3; "Prof. Garland's Western Trip," *Standard*, October 13, 1888, 3.

36. The foregoing account of Garland's arrival in Ordway and his mother's stroke is from *Son*, 399–402.

37. Garland to Riley, August 5, 1888, in *Selected Letters*, 30.

38. "At the Fair," Garland's 1888 notebook, item 21, USC.

39. *Son*, 407.

40. Jerome Loving, *Walt Whitman, the Song of Himself* (Berkeley: University of California Press, 1999), 414.

41. *Roadside Meetings*, 127.

42. Garland to Whitman, November 24, 1886, in *Selected Letters*, 19–20.

43. Horace Traubel, *With Walt Whitman in Camden*, vol. 2 (New York: Rowman and Littlefield, 1961), 162–63.

44. Hamlin Garland, "Whitman at Seventy: How the Good Gray Poet Looks and Talks," *New York Herald*, June 30, 1889, 7. Soon after he worked up his notes from his interview, Garland sent them to Whitman, who added several phrases to clarify his meaning. Garland later incorporated this interview into *Roadside Meetings*, 131–38.

45. Traubel, *With Walt Whitman in Camden*, 2:384.

46. Traubel, *With Walt Whitman in Camden*, 3:437.

47. Garland to Traubel, May 24, 1901, in *Selected Letters*, 140. For discus-

sion of the Garland-Whitman relationship, see B. R. McElderry Jr., "Hamlin Garland's View of Whitman," *The Personalist* 36 (1955): 369–78; and Nancy Bunge, "Walt Whitman's Influence on Hamlin Garland," *Walt Whitman Review* 23 (1977): 45–50.

48. Hamlin Garland, "Whitman's 'November Boughs,'" *Boston Evening Transcript*, November 15, 1888, 6.

49. See Garland to Whitman, November 24, 1886, in *Selected Letters*, 20. The line appears in Whitman's "Foundation Stages—then Others," part of *Specimen Days & Collect* (1882).

50. Price, "Garland's 'The Evolution of American Thought,'" 14.

51. Price, "Garland's 'The Evolution of American Thought,'" 3–4.

52. Hamlin Garland, "The Teacher," in *Camden's Compliments to Walt Whitman*, ed. Horace Traubel (Philadelphia: David McKay, 1889), 40.

53. Hamlin Garland, "The Return of the Private," *Arena*, December 1890, 113. Garland later deleted this passage in the 1893 edition of *Main-Travelled Roads* and all editions thereafter, probably because he sought to remove didactic expression.

54. Garland, *Prairie Songs*, 116. The poem also appears, with minor changes in punctuation, as "Walt Whitman," in *In Re Walt Whitman*, ed. Horace L. Traubel (Philadelphia: David McKay, 1893), 328.

7. LIFE UNDER THE WHEEL

1. Garland's 1888 notebook, item 21, USC.

2. Hamlin Garland, "Work in New Fields," *Standard*, August 25, 1888, 8.

3. Hamlin Garland, "'John Boyle's Conclusion': An Unpublished Middle Border Story by Hamlin Garland," ed. Donald Pizer, *American Literature* 31 (1959): 62.

4. "Boston Single Tax League Reorganized and Ready for a New Campaign," *Standard*, November 10, 1888, 4.

5. Hamlin Garland, "Cheering Words from Professor Garland—Some Capital Suggestions," *Standard*, November 17, 1888, 32.

6. Hamlin Garland, "For Club Houses at Small Expense," *Standard*, January 12, 1889, 2.

7. Joseph Edgar Chamberlin, "Hamlin Garland—the Hardy of the West," in *Hamlin Garland: A Son of the Middle Border* (undated promotional pamphlet published by Macmillan), 10–11. The article is reprinted from the *Transcript*.

8. "Gossip about Hamlin Garland," *Los Angeles Times*, August 8, 1897, 21. Garland was fond of retelling this story: it appears in *A Son of the Middle Border* but is misplaced as occurring in 1887 (371–72) and in *Roadside Meetings*, 115–16.

Garland's Harper and Bros. account file (item 669j, USC) records payment for the story.

9. Hamlin Garland, "Mrs. Ripley's Trip," *Harper's Weekly*, November 28, 1888, 894–95.

10. "Studies in Literature and Expressive Art, by Hamlin Garland. 1888–89," enclosed in an undated letter to Riley, Lilly Library, Indiana University, Bloomington.

11. Garland to Riley, December 19, 1888, in *Selected Letters*, 38.

12. Garland to Riley, February 17, 1889, in *Selected Letters*, 43–44.

13. Garland to Clemens, [after March 21, 1889], in *Selected Letters*, 45–47.

14. Garland to Herne, [before January 6, 1889], in *Selected Letters*, 38.

15. The manuscript of *Drifting Apart* is no longer extant; the foregoing synopsis is from the play's earlier version, *Mary the Fisherman's Child*, printed under the title *Drifting Apart* in Arthur Hobson Quinn, ed., *The Early Plays of James A. Herne* (1940). The play underwent much revision before Garland saw it in January 1889. In "Mr. and Mrs. Herne" (*Arena*, October 1891, 543–60), Garland quotes extensively from the version he saw.

16. Garland to Herne, [before January 6, 1889], in *Selected Letters*, 39.

17. Herne to Garland, January 6, 1889, USC.

18. *Son*, 382; Franklin Garland to Eldon Hill, July 19, 1940, Miami.

19. *Son*, 383.

20. Herne to Garland, undated, USC.

21. Herbert J. Edwards and Julie Herne, *James A. Herne: The Rise of Realism in the American Drama* (Orono: University of Maine Press, 1964), 20–25.

22. Hamlin Garland, "On the Road with James A. Herne," *Century*, August 1914, 574.

23. Herne, "James A. Herne, Actor and Dramatist," 244.

24. Herne, "James A. Herne, Actor and Dramatist," 245–46, 250.

25. Herne to Garland, June 4, 1889, USC.

26. Hamlin Garland, *Under the Wheel* (Boston: Barta Press, 1890), preface. *Under the Wheel* was originally published in the July 1890 issue of *Arena*. When the Barta Press reissued the play in book form in late August or September, using the *Arena* plates, it deleted the header, thereby also removing the page numbers. Garland added a preface to the front and a page of press comment to the back. Since the Barta edition has no page numbers, my citations are to the *Arena* printing. Garland tried several titles, among them "Jason Edwards," before settling on *Under the Wheel*. When Garland published the play in novel form in 1892 he entitled it *Jason Edwards: An Average Man*.

27. Hamlin Garland, "Under the Wheel: A Modern Play in Six Scenes," *Arena*, July 1890, 195.

28. "Anti-Poverty Lecture in Boston," *Standard*, December 10, 1887, 5.

29. Hamlin Garland, "John Boyle's Conclusion," 68; Garland, "Under the Wheel," 217. Portions of Garland's novel manuscript "The Rise of Boomtown" were also incorporated into scene 2 of *Under the Wheel.* The segments describe the rivalry of the *Boomtown Daily Spike* and the *Belleplain Argus* (cf. Garland, "'The Rise of Boomtown,'" 364–67; Garland, "Under the Wheel," 196–97).

30. Herne, "James A. Herne, Actor and Dramatist," 248–49.

31. Garland to Whitman, [April 3, 1889], in *Selected Letters*, 47.

32. Garland, "The Teacher," 40–41. For events of the dinner, see Horace Traubel, *With Walt Whitman in Camden*, vol. 5, ed. Gertrude Traubel (Carbondale: Southern Illinois University Press, 1964), 246–51.

33. "An American Author: How Mr. Hamlin Garland Got His Start in Literature," *Washington Post*, May 8, 1892, 12.

34. Garland to Gilder, [June 1889], in *Selected Letters*, 52. Garland's account notebook (item 23, USC) records that on June 10 he submitted "A Vernal Romance" (published as "A Spring Romance"), "The Sociable at Dudley's," and "A Moving Accident" (Pizer, *Hamlin Garland's Early Work and Career*, 182n21).

35. "A Spring Romance" appeared in *Century*, June 1891, 296–302; it was reprinted as "William Bacon's Hired Man" in *Prairie Folks*. For the relative value of the U.S. dollar see Samuel H. Williamson, "What Is the Relative Value?" *Economic History Services*, http://www.eh.net/hmit/compare. The estimate is based on the Consumer Price Index for 2005.

36. *Son*, 412.

37. Frank Luther Mott, *A History of American Magazines*, vol. 3, *1865–1885* (Cambridge: Harvard University Press, 1957), 468. For circulation figures, see pp. 6–7.

38. Richard Watson Gilder, "Certain Tendencies in Current Literature," *New Princeton Review* 4 (July 1887): 6, quoted in Herbert F. Smith, *Richard Watson Gilder* (New York: Twayne, 1970), 142.

39. Garland to Gilder, September 7, 1889, in *Selected Letters*, 52–53.

40. Garland, "Mr. and Mrs. Herne," 545.

41. Hamlin Garland, "A Prairie Heroine," *Arena*, July 1891, 243, 246. The story was reprinted as "Sim Burns's Wife" in *Prairie Folks* and as "Lucretia Burns" in *Other Main-Travelled Roads*.

42. Garland to Gilder, October 10, 1889, in *Selected Letters*, 54.

8. *MAIN-TRAVELLED ROADS*

1. "Married," *Sentinel (Columbia, Brown County, Dakota Territory)*, September 12, 1889 (clipping courtesy of William Aisenbrey).

2. *Son*, 414–15. Jessie Garland died on October 11, 1890. She is buried in the Parkview Cemetery, Columbia, Brown County, South Dakota.

3. Hamlin Garland, "Under the Lion's Paw," *Harper's Weekly*, September 7, 1889, 726–27; "A Story of Single Tax Clubs," *Standard*, September 7, 1889, 3.

4. Garland, "Under the Lion's Paw," 727.

5. Hamlin Garland, "An Interesting Announcement," *Standard*, September 28, 1889, 3. The same issue also reported that Garland had read *Under the Wheel* to an audience in New York (2).

6. Hamlin Garland, "Truth in the Drama," *Literary World*, September 14, 1889, 307–8.

7. Robert Herndon Fife and Ansten Anstensen, "Henrik Ibsen on the American Stage," *American-Scandanavian Review* 16 (1928): 220; Hamlin Garland, "An Ibsen Club," *Boston Evening Transcript*, November 9, 1889, 5.

8. Garland to Gilder, January 10, 1890, in *Selected Letters*, 61.

9. *Son*, 413.

10. Charles Johanningsmeier, *Fiction and the Literary Marketplace: The Role of Newspaper Syndicates, 1860–1900* (Cambridge: Cambridge University Press, 1997), 113.

11. Garland to Gilder, November 1, 1890, in *Selected Letters*, 68.

12. Flower to Garland, April 30, 1890, USC.

13. Frank Luther Mott, *A History of American Magazines*, vol. 4, *1885–1905* (Cambridge: Harvard University Press, 1957), 402.

14. B. O. Flower, "An Epoch-Marking Drama," *Arena*, July 1891, 247.

15. Flower to Garland, May 3, 1890, USC.

16. *Roadside Meetings*, 176; Diary, October 4, 1900.

17. Garland to Herne, November 21, 1890, in *Selected Letters*, 68–69.

18. Howells to Garland, June 6, 1890, USC.

19. "Literature of the Day," *Chicago Tribune*, August 2, 1890, 12; the quotation from the *New York Independent* appears on the inside front cover of the Barta Press edition. The *Standard* printed an excerpt on pp. 6–7 of its July 30, 1890, issue; the announcement appeared on August 27, 1890, 6.

20. Howells to Garland, August 27, 1890, in *Selected Letters of W. D. Howells*, 3:289.

21. Garland to Clark, March 7, 1934, in *Selected Letters*, 371.

22. See Roger E. Stoddard, "Vanity and Reform: B. O. Flower's Arena Publishing Company, Boston, 1890–1896, with a Bibliographic List of Arena Imprints," *Papers of the Bibliographical Society of America* 76 (1982): 273–337.

23. For a contrasting discussion of the volume's unity in terms of its road metaphor, see Donald Pizer's introduction to *Main-Travelled Roads*, v–xviii; and also

Pizer's "Hamlin Garland's *Main-Travelled Roads* Revisited," *South Dakota Review* 29 (1991): 53–67.

24. Garland, *Main-Travelled Roads*, 73.

25. *Son*, 419–20. "Alice" may have been fellow Cedar Valley Seminary graduate Anna J. Kelly, who served with Garland as a coeditor of the *Seminarian*. After graduation, Kelly married a man named Taneyhill and died in 1889, according to a tombstone in the Osage cemetery. While Garland recalls that he learned of her death in 1891, given his frequent misdating of events in the volume, it is likely he remembered the mood rather than the specific date.

26. *Main-Travelled Roads*, 87–88.

27. *Main-Travelled Roads*, 142–43.

28. In 1891 the press published Flower's *Lessons Learned from Other Lives* and six pamphlets (Stoddard, "Vanity and Reform," 330).

29. *Son*, 415.

30. Chandler's review is unsigned: "A Drama of the West," *Boston Herald*, May 31, 1891, 22; "'Main-Travelled Roads,'" *Chicago Tribune*, June 13, 1891, 12.

31. W. D. Howells, "Editor's Study," *Harper's Monthly*, September 1891, 639, 640.

9. TABLE RAPPER

1. Quoted in Pizer, *Hamlin Garland's Early Work and Career*, 84. I am indebted to Pizer's discussion of "A Member of the Third House" for details of the genesis of the play. Because the manuscript of the play is no longer extant, my discussion is based on the novel version, published in 1892.

2. Flower to Garland, May 5, 1890, USC.

3. Flower to Garland, September 3, 1890, USC.

4. Garland to Howells, October 29, 1890, in *Selected Letters*, 67; Howells to Garland, October 27, 1890, in *Selected Letters of W. D. Howells*, 3:289n2.

5. "The Listener," *Boston Evening Transcript*, November 1, 1890, 6.

6. Program circular, reprinted in Lars Ahnebrink, *The Beginnings of Naturalism in American Fiction* (Cambridge: Harvard University Press, 1950), 455–58.

7. Garland to Gilder, November 1, 1890, in *Selected Letters*, 68.

8. Hamlin Garland, "Mr. Herne's New Play," *Boston Evening Transcript*, July 8, 1890, 6; also reprinted in Donald Pizer, "An 1890 Account of *Margaret Fleming*," *American Literature* 27 (1955): 264–67.

9. Herne, "James A. Herne, Actor and Dramatist," 301, 309–10.

10. *Roadside Meetings*, 75–76. See also Hamlin Garland, "William Dean Howells's Boston: A Posthumous Pilgrimage," *Boston Evening Transcript*, May 22, 1920, pt. 3:4.

11. Part of the circular is reprinted in Ahnebrink, *Beginnings of Naturalism*, 454–55.

12. Hamlin Garland, "The Question of an Independent Theater," *Boston Evening Transcript*, April 29, 1891, 6.

13. John Perry, *James A. Herne: The American Ibsen* (Chicago: Nelson-Hall, 1978), 154–55.

14. "Chickering Hall—'Margaret Fleming,'" *Boston Evening Transcript*, May 5, 1891, 4.

15. Hamlin Garland, "The Morality of Margaret Fleming," *Boston Evening Transcript*, May 7, 1891, 6; "The New Drama," *Boston Evening Transcript*, May 9, 1891, 12.

16. Quoted in Perry, *James A. Herne*, 161.

17. Fife and Anstensen, "Ibsen on the American Stage," 218–28. Herne went on to revive the play in a number of short runs, each time altering its structure in an effort to make it more palatable to theater managers. It achieved its greatest popular and monetary success in 1907, six years after his death, when his daughter Chrystal starred in the title role under Katharine's direction. See Edwards and Herne, *James A. Herne*, 68–73.

18. "A Prospectus of the First Independent Theatre Association," item 690c, USC; also reprinted in Ahnebrink, *Beginnings of Naturalism*, 451. See also Theodore Hatlen, "*Margaret Fleming* and the Boston Independent Theatre," *Educational Theatre Journal* 8 (1956): 17–21; Alice M. Robinson, "James A. Herne and His 'Theatre Libre' in Boston," *Players* 48 (1973): 202–9; and Barnard Hewitt, "*Margaret Fleming* and Chickering Hall: The First Little Theatre in America?" *Theatre Journal* 34 (1982): 165–71.

19. "For a 'Theatre Libre': Prof. Hamlin Garland's Plans," *Chicago Daily News*, January 30, 1892 (morning issue), 1; James L. Highlander, "America's First Art Theatre: The New Theatre of Chicago," *Educational Theatre Journal* 11 (1959): 285–90.

20. R. Laurence Moore, *In Search of White Crows: Spiritualism, Parapsychology, and American Culture* (New York: Oxford University Press, 1977), 138.

21. *Forty Years*, 2.

22. Prospectus and Constitution, American Psychical Society, Boston, 1891, Miami.

23. T. E[rnest] A[llen], "Editorial," *Psychical Review* 1, no. 1 (1892): 87.

24. Miles Menander Dawson, "Suggestions to Investigators," *Psychical Review* 2, no. 5 (1893): 81, 83.

25. Seymour H. Mauskopf and Michael R. McVaugh, *The Elusive Science: Origins and Experimental Psychical Research* (Baltimore: Johns Hopkins University Press, 1980), 7.

26. Giles B. Stebbens, "Suggestions as to Psychical Research and 'Circles,'" *Psychical Review* 2, no. 5 (1893): 43.

27. "Psychography. Mr. Garland's Report," *Psychical Review* 1, no. 1 (1892): 43–44; "An Experiment in Psychography," *Psychical Review* 1, no. 2 (1892): 136–37; "Sounds, Voices, and Physical Disturbances in the Presence of a Psychic," *Psychical Review* 1, no. 3 (1893): 226–29; and "Report of Dark Séances, with a Nonprofessional Psychic, for Voices and the Movement of Objects without Contact," *Psychical Review* 2, nos. 6–7 (1893–94): 152–77.

28. Garland, "Report of Dark Séances," 157, 158.

29. "No Proofs of Existence of Spirits—Hamlin Garland," *New York Times*, sec. 5, November 19, 1911, 3.

30. List of members for 1893, *Psychical Review* 2, no. 5 (1893): 89–96.

31. Herne, "James A. Herne, Actor and Dramatist," 265–66.

32. B. O. Flower, "Garland in Ghostland," *Arena*, August 1905, 207.

33. *Son*, 423.

34. McMath, *American Populism*, 83–107.

35. Quentin E. Martin, "'This Spreading Radicalism': Hamlin Garland's *A Spoil of Office* and the Creation of True Populism," *Studies in American Fiction* 26 (1998): 33.

36. Quoted in "Single Tax News . . . Illinois," *Standard*, February 3, 1892, 8.

37. "Urges Democrats to Leave," *Chicago Tribune*, January 29, 1892, 3.

38. Hamlin Garland, "The Alliance Wedge in Congress," *Arena*, March 1892, 448, 457.

39. Elia Peattie, unpublished memoirs as transcribed by Eldon Hill, Miami; *Son*, 424. For Garland's reading of *Under the Wheel*, see "They Believe in Henry George," *Chicago Tribune*, July 4, 1892, 2.

40. Contract for *Jason Edwards*, item 669c, USC.

41. Garland to Gilder, [before March 1892], in *Selected Letters*, 77.

42. John Tebbel, *A History of Book Publishing in the United States*, vol. 2 (New York: R. R. Bowker, 1975), 448–49.

43. See Pizer, *Hamlin Garland's Early Work and Career*, 104, to which I am indebted for details about the genesis of *A Spoil of Office*. In *A Son of the Middle Border*, Garland refers to this manuscript as "Bradley Talcott" (422).

44. Pizer, *Hamlin Garland's Early Work and Career*, 105.

45. Howells to Garland, September 14, 1892, in *Selected Letters of W. D. Howells*, 4:24–25.

46. B. O. Flower, "Books of the Day," *Arena*, October 1892, xli–lv; "'A Spoil of Office,'" *Chicago Tribune*, September 16, 1892, 12; "Recent Novels," *Nation*, October 6, 1892, 262; William Morton Payne, "Recent American Fiction," *Dial*, February 16, 1893, 114.

47. "Brief Mention," *Chicago Tribune*, March 12, 1892, 13; "Four New Novels," *New York Times*, March 20, 1892, 19.

48. "Fiction," *Literary World*, May 7, 1892, 166.

49. "More Novels," *Nation*, May 12, 1892, 363.

50. "He Criticizes His Own Books," *Los Angeles Herald*, November 27, 1892, 3.

10. THE CAMPAIGN FOR REALISM

1. Pizer, *Hamlin Garland's Early Work and Career*, 96. See also McMath, *American Populism*, 180–85.

2. Figures from McMath, *American Populism*, 181.

3. Hamlin Garland, "The West in Literature," *Arena*, November 1892, 671, 674, 675, 676.

4. Hamlin Garland, "The Future of Fiction," *Arena*, April 1893, 519.

5. Garland's *Arena* royalty statements, item 669c, USC. Garland's *Arena* contract called for a royalty of five cents per paper copy and ten cents per cloth, and most of the sales were in paper. By February 1, 1893, *Jason Edwards* sold 2,378 in paper and 212 in cloth; *Spoil* sold 2,326 in paper and 168 in cloth. Records for *Main-Travelled Roads* are incomplete. From March 1, 1892, to February 1, 1893, the book sold 1,124 in paper and 309 in cloth; the account shows additional royalty payments of $96.80, $78.95, and $76.80 for *Main-Travelled Roads* prior to March 1—clearly, that volume was the only one with any significant readership.

6. Daniel Borus, *Writing Realism: Howells, James, and Norris in the Mass Market* (Chapel Hill: University of North Carolina Press, 1989), 41. Borus's figures are based on his study of the Harper and Brothers records and estimates in *Publishers' Weekly*.

7. See Williamson, "What Is the Relative Value?"

8. "Hamlin Garland, the Western Writer Who Is Just Now Attracting So Much Attention," *Los Angeles Times*, December 3, 1892, 8. "The Sociable at Dudley's" appeared in a number of newspapers, among them the *Los Angeles Times*, November 27, 1892, 10, before being collected in *Prairie Folks*.

9. Garland retitled several of the stories for *Prairie Folks*; all were also revised, mostly minor changes in wording and punctuation. The stories and their original serial publication are as follows: "Uncle Ethan's Speculation" (*Arena*, December 1891, 125–35); "The Test of Elder Pill" (*Arena*, March 1891, 480–501); "William Bacon's Hired Man" (as "A Spring Romance," *Century*, June 1891, 296–302); "Sim Burns's Wife" (as "A Prairie Heroine," *Arena*, July 1891, 223–46); "Saturday Night on the Farm" (as "At the Brewery," *Cosmopolitan*, May 1892, 34–42); "Village Cronies" (as "An Evening at the Corner Grocery," *Arena*,

September 1891, 504–12); "Drifting Crane" (*Harper's Weekly*, May 31, 1890, 421–22); "Daddy Deering" (*Belford's*, April 1892, 152–61); "The Sociable at Dudley's" (McClure Syndicate, *Los Angeles Times*, November 27, 1892, 10).

10. "He Criticizes His Own Books," 3.

11. "Recent Fiction," *Nation*, June 1, 1893, 408; B. O. Flower, "Prairie Folks," *Arena*, April 1893, xiii–xiv.

12. Rossiter Johnson, *A History of the World's Columbian Exposition*, vol. 4, *Congresses* (New York, Appleton, 1897), 6.

13. Howells to Garland, May 28, 1893, in *Selected Letters of W. D. Howells*, 4:47–48.

14. *Son*, 458.

15. *Hamlin Garland—As West Salem Knew Him* (West Salem WI: West Salem Journal, 1951), 14.

16. *Son*, 462. Indeed, the house today is a National Historic Landmark and is promoted through advertising, brochures, and websites as "The Garland Homestead."

17. *Daughter*, 13.

18. *Son*, 443.

19. Garland, "The West in Literature," 676.

20. Jesse Sidney Goldstein, "Two Literary Radicals: Garland and Markham in Chicago, 1893," *American Literature* 17 (1945): 153.

21. Sidney Kramer, *A History of Stone and Kimball and Herbert S. Stone and Co., with a Bibliography of Their Publications, 1893–1905* (Chicago: University of Chicago Press, 1940), 19–20; "Books of the Day/Notes," *Arena*, June 1893, xix; Tebbel, *A History of Book Publishing in the United States*, 449.

22. Hamlin Garland to Melville E. Stone, March 5, 1895, Stone and Kimball Papers, Midwest Manuscript Collection, Newberry Library, Chicago.

23. Kramer, *A History of Stone and Kimball*, 17.

24. *Daughter*, 24.

25. Indeed, Garland himself suffered at the hands of pirates. In 1892 the British firm of T. Fisher Unwin published a pirated edition of *Main-Travelled Roads*, apparently oblivious to the recent law.

26. Johnson, *A History of the World's Columbian Exposition*, 168. See also "The Literature Congresses," *Dial*, July 1, 1893, 5–7; and "The Congress of Authors," *Dial*, July 16, 1893, 29–32. For a thorough account of events see Donald Pizer, "A Summer Campaign in Chicago: Hamlin Garland Defends a Native Art," *Western Humanities Review* 13 (1959): 375–82. Garland would also address the Congress of General Education on July 24, speaking on the topic "What Should the Public Schools Teach?" See "They Defend Fads," *Chicago Tribune*, July 25, 1893, 8.

27. Lucy Monroe, "Chicago Letter," *Critic*, July 22, 1893, 60.

28. "Octave Thanet on the Short Story," *Chicago Tribune*, July 15, 1893, 8.

29. *Roadside Meetings*, 241.

30. Eugene Field, "Sharps and Flats," *Chicago Record*, July 27, 1893, 4.

31. Garland to Field, July 27, 1893, in "Sharps and Flats," *Chicago Record*, July 28, 1893, 4.

32. Garland to Field, July 31, 1893, in "Sharps and Flats," *Chicago Record*, August 1, 1893, 4.

33. Hamlin Garland, "Real Conversations," pt. 2, "A Dialogue between Eugene Field and Hamlin Garland," *McClure's*, August 1893, 204.

34. Hamlin Garland, "Real Conversations," pt. 4, "A Dialogue between James Whitcomb Riley and Hamlin Garland," *McClure's*, February 1894, 221, 234.

35. X. Y. Zed, "Realism with a Vengeance," *Critic*, September 2, 1893, 158.

36. As reported in "Hamlin and Birdie," *Aberdeen Daily News*, August 16, 1894 (clipping courtesy of William Aisenbrey).

37. Hamlin Garland, "Literary Emancipation of the West," *Forum*, October 1893, 160, 161, 164.

38. "From East to West," *Chicago Tribune*, September 24, 1893, 26.

39. "The Lounger," *Critic*, September 30, 1893, 213–14.

40. George Hamlin Fitch, "Is the West in Literary Bondage?" *Californian Illustrated Magazine*, January 1894, 235, 241.

41. *Roadside Meetings*, 251.

42. "The Literary West Once More," *Dial*, October 1, 1893, 174.

43. Garland to Browne, October 12, 1893, October 21, 1893, in *Selected Letters*, 78, 80. For fuller discussion of the exchange, see Joseph B. McCullough, "Hamlin Garland's Quarrel with 'The Dial,'" *American Literary Realism* 9 (Winter 1976): 77–80.

44. *Roadside Meetings*, 248, 255.

11. THE ICONOCLAST

1. Garland, "Report of Dark Séances," 174.

2. *Son*, 429. For his statement to Field about moving to Chicago, see Field, "Sharps and Flats," *Chicago Record*, July 27, 1893, 4, where Field remarks that "we are glad to hear that there is a prospect of Mr. Garland's making his home here in Chicago."

3. *Son*, 429–30.

4. Howells to Garland, August 23, 1893, in *Selected Letters of W. D. Howells*, 4:49.

5. Agreement for *Main-Travelled Roads* and *Prairie Songs*, August 11, 1893, and addendum to contract for *Rose of Dutcher's Coolly*, item 6600, USC.

6. Garland's comments about more descriptive advertising appear in an undated letter to Stone, Miami; his comments about listing his books on the title page appear in Garland to Stone, October 16, 1893, Miami.

7. See Lucy Monroe, "Chicago Letter," *Critic*, September 30, 1893, 215–16.

8. Garland to Stone, December 16, 1893, in *Selected Letters*, 82–83.

9. Garland to Stone, December 19, 1893, Yale Collection of American Literature, Beinecke Rare Book and Manuscript Library, Yale University. Stone and Kimball did not publish an edition of *Prairie Folks* until 1895.

10. See Kramer, *History of Stone and Kimball*, 18, 197–98. See also the illustrated bibliography of Garland's books at http://people.uncw.edu/newlink/garland/books/.

11. Garland to Brigham, [November 25, 1893], Miami. The extracts from *Prairie Songs* appeared in *Midland Monthly*, January 1894, 23–27; "Boy Life in the West—Winter," with illustrations by H. T. Carpenter, appeared in *Midland Monthly*, February 1894, 113–22.

12. "Mount Shasta," *Midland Monthly*, December 1894, 481–83; "A Night Landing on the Mississippi River," *Midland Monthly*, February 1895, 142–33; Garland to Brigham, October 10, 1894, Miami.

13. B. O. Flower, "Prairie Songs," *Arena*, January 1894, viii.

14. Garland later interviewed Miller at his home near Oakland and syndicated his article. See "A Pacific Tolstoi," *Los Angeles Times*, June 17, 1894, 13.

15. Garland, *Prairie Songs*, 26.

16. Garland, *Prairie Songs*, 87.

17. Garland, *Prairie Songs*, 75.

18. Garland, *Prairie Songs*, 139.

19. *New York Tribune* as quoted in the *Midland Monthly*, February 1894, 196; "Books of the Week," *Chicago Evening Post*, January 13, 1894, 12; "Two Books of Verse," *Chicago Tribune*, January 13, 1894, 10.

20. Garland to Stone, January 26, 1894, Hamlin Garland Papers, NYPL.

21. Garland to Brigham, January 26, 1894, in *Selected Letters*, 90.

22. Garland taught for two summers at the Seaside Assembly and was put in charge of the School of Literature in 1892 ("Seaside Assembly," *Brooklyn Eagle*, July 8, 1892, 3). For Crane's report of Garland's lecture, see "Howells Discussed at Avon-by-the-Sea," *New York Tribune*, August 18, 1891, 5. Garland described his friendship with Crane in "Stephen Crane: A Soldier of Fortune," *Saturday Evening Post*, July 28, 1900, 16–17; "Stephen Crane as I Knew Him," *Yale Review* 3 (April 1914): 494–506; and *Roadside Meetings*, 189–206. All accounts are riddled with inaccurate dates. For an effort to straighten out Garland's chronology, see Donald Pizer, "The Garland-Crane Relationship," in *Realism and Naturalism*

in Nineteenth-Century American Literature (Carbondale: University of Southern Illinois Press, 1966), 114–20.

23. Hamlin Garland, "An Ambitious French Novel and a Modest American Story," *Arena*, June 1893, xii.

24. Garland hoped McClure would syndicate some of Crane's work (Garland to McClure, January 8, 1894, in *Selected Letters*, 84). He also wrote to Julius Chambers, managing editor of the *New York World*, for a similar purpose (Garland to Chambers, February 2, 1894, in *Selected Letters*, 91); and in an unpublished letter to Herbert Stone, who was coming to New York to meet Howells, Herne, and Stedman, Garland noted, "I've got something very interesting to show you, beside, of Mr. Crane's. He's a great boy" (Garland to Stone, January 27, 1894, #1407-z Miscellaneous Autographs from the Rare Book Collection, Southern Historical Collection, Wilson Library, University of North Carolina at Chapel Hill).

25. Garland, "Stephen Crane: A Soldier of Fortune," 17.

26. *Roadside Meetings*, 197. "An Omnibus Baby" was published in *Arena*, May 1894, 819–12; and "The Men in the Storm" in *Arena*, October 1894, 37–48.

27. *Roadside Meetings*, 193.

28. Garland, "Stephen Crane as I Knew Him," 502.

29. *Roadside Meetings*, 194, 195.

30. *Roadside Meetings*, 196.

31. Garland, *Crumbling Idols*, 124.

32. For Garland's influence on *The Red Badge of Courage*, I am indebted to Stanley Wertheim, "Crane and Garland: The Education of an Impressionist," *North Dakota Quarterly* 35 (Winter 1967): 23–28. For a précis of events in the Garland-Crane relationship, see Stanley Wertheim and Paul Sorrentino, *The Crane Log: A Documentary Life of Stephen Crane, 1871–1900* (New York: G. K. Hall, 1994), 97–104.

33. Linson to Garland, January 26, 1926, USC.

34. Pizer, *Hamlin Garland's Early Work and Career*, 135.

35. John Rewald, *History of Impressionism* (1946), as quoted in Pizer, *Hamlin Garland's Early Work and Career*, 133.

36. Garland, *Main-Travelled Roads*, 81–82.

37. Hamlin Garland, "Western Landscapes," *Atlantic Monthly*, December 1893, 806.

38. James Nagel, *Stephen Crane and Literary Impressionism* (University Park: Pennsylvania State University Press, 1983), 29.

39. James B. Stronks, "A Realist Experiments with Impressionism: Hamlin Garland's 'Chicago Studies,'" *American Literature* 36 (1964): 50.

40. Stronks, "A Realist Experiments with Impressionism," 49.

41. Hamlin Garland, "Homestead and Its Perilous Trades," *McClure's*, June 1984, 5. The article was also syndicated in a number of newspapers by the McClure Syndicate. For a comparison of Garland's technique in the Homestead article with Crane's method in "In the Depths of a Coal Mine," see Donald Pizer, "Late Nineteenth-Century American Literary Naturalism: A Re-Introduction," *American Literary Realism* 38 (2006): 189–202.

42. Garland to Stone, January 16, 1894, in *Selected Letters*, 86.

43. Garland to Stone, January 18, 1894, in *Selected Letters*, 89.

44. Garland to Stone, January 22, 1894, MS/Letter File, Rare Book and Manuscript Library, University of Illinois at Urbana-Champagne.

45. Garland to Stone, February 1894, MS/Letter File, Rare Book and Manuscript Library, University of Illinois at Urbana-Champagne. The date is obscured on this postcard.

46. Garland to Stone, [ca. March 1894], in *Selected Letters*, 92–93.

47. Garland to Field, in "Sharps and Flats," *Chicago Record*, July 28, 1893, 4. In his comment to Field, Garland was likely repeating Howells's directive that the realist should "break the images of false gods and misshapen heroes, to take away the poor silly toys that many grown people would still like to play with" ("Editor's Study," *Harper's Monthly*, May 1886, 973).

48. The essays and their sources follow. For some of these details I am indebted to Pizer, *Hamlin Garland's Early Work and Career*, 190n51. (1) "Provincialism," from "The West in Literature"; (2) "New Fields," no published source, though extensive notes exist in notebook 32, USC; (3) "The Question of Success," from "The West in Literature"; (4) "Literary Prophecy," from "The Future of Fiction"; (5) "Local Color in Art," delivered as a lecture in Memphis; (6) "The Local Novel," from "The Future of Fiction"; (7) "The Drift of the Drama," delivered as a lecture in Memphis; (8) "The Influence of Ibsen," from "Ibsen as a Dramatist"; (9) "Impressionism," delivered as a lecture in Chicago; (10) "Literary Centers," from "Literary Emancipation of the West"; (11) "Literary Masters," from "Literary Emancipation of the West"; (12) "A Recapitulatory After-Word," partly from "Literary Emancipation of the West."

49. Garland, *Crumbling Idols*, 9.

50. Walter Blackburn Harte, "Hamlin Garland, a Virile New Force in Our Literature," *Chicago Inter-Ocean*, February 18, 1894, 31.

51. "On Various Topics," *Book Buyer*, July 1894, 308; "'Crumbling Idols,'" *Literary World*, June 2, 1894, 164; Edward E. Hale Jr., "Signs of Life in Literature," *Dial*, July 1, 1894, 11; "Mr. Hamlin Garland's Essays," *Independent*, June 21, 1894, 801.

52. Howells to Garland, May 30, 1894, in *Life in Letters of William Dean Howells*, vol. 2, ed. Mildred Howells (1928; repr., New York: Russell and Russell, 1968), 51.

53. Roosevelt to Matthews, May 21, 1894, June 29, 1898, in *Letters of Theodore Roosevelt and Brander Matthews*, 81, 82.

54. "'Crumbling Idols,'" *Critic*, September 15, 1894, 169; Howells to Garland, October 28, 1894, in *Selected Letters of W. D. Howells*, 4:79–80.

55. *Daughter*, 25.

12. WESTERN HORIZONS

1. John Pilkington, "Fuller, Garland, Taft, and the Art of the West," *Papers on Language and Literature* 8, supp. (1972): 41; see also Sarah J. Moore, "On the Frontier of Culture," *Chicago History* 16, no. 2 (1987): 4–13.

2. Garland to Fuller, January 17, 1894, in *Selected Letters*, 88.

3. Garland's 1895–1899 journal (typed transcript), October 6, 1897, item 7a, USC; *Daughter*, 209. Garland devotes a chapter to Fuller in *Roadside Meetings*, 262–75.

4. "Just a Nice Affair," *Chicago Tribune*, October 26, 1894, 3. I am also indebted to Donald Pizer's discussion of Garland's involvement in the association in *Hamlin Garland's Early Work and Career*, 136–40.

5. The pamphlets are *Impressions on Impressionism, Being a Discussion of the American Art Exhibition at the Art Institute, Chicago, by a Critical Triumvirate* (Chicago: Central Art Association, 1894) and *Five Hoosier Painters, Being a Discussion of the Holiday Exhibit of the Indianapolis Group, in Chicago* (Chicago: Central Art Association, 1894). On his copy Garland penciled in the names of the triumvirate.

6. Lucy Monroe, "Chicago Letter," *Critic*, December 29, 1894, 450.

7. Hamlin Garland, "Successful Efforts to Teach Art to the Masses," *Forum*, July 1895, 606.

8. Hamlin Garland, "Art Conditions in Chicago," in *Catalogue, United Annual Exhibition of the Palette Club and the Cosmopolitan Art Club* (Chicago: Art Institute, January 24, 1895), n.p.

9. See Hamlin Garland, "Edward Kemeys: A Sculptor of Frontier Life and Wild Animals," *McClure's*, July 1895, 120–31. The sketch was serialized by the McClure Syndicate in September 1894; see, for example, "Kemeys: A Visit and Talk with Our Pioneer Sculptor," *Los Angeles Times*, September 19, 1894, 5. The Joaquin Miller sketch appeared under a number of titles; see, for example, "The Poet of the Sierras," *Washington Post*, June 17, 1894, 22; "A Pacific Tolstoi," *Los Angeles Times*, June 17, 1894, 13.

10. Garland to Stone, January 26, 1895, in *Selected Letters*, 97–98. "The Land of the Straddle-Bug" later appeared as the novel *The Moccasin Ranch* (1909).

11. Pizer, *Hamlin Garland's Early Work and Career*, 155. For contrasting views see Robert F. Gish, "Desertion and Rescue on the Dakota Plains: Hamlin Garland in the Land of the Straddle-Bug," *South Dakota Review* 10, no. 3 (1978): 30–45; Quentin E. Martin, "Agricultural Awakenings: Hamlin Garland's *A Little Norsk* and 'The Land of the Straddle-Bug,'" *American Literary Realism* 37 (2005): 141–58.

12. *Daughter*, 31.

13. Quoted in *Daughter*, 29.

14. "Among the Southern Utes" was originally syndicated in the "Over Indian Trails" series; it is reprinted in *Hamlin Garland's Observations on the American Indian, 1895–1905*, ed. Lonnie E. Underhill and Daniel F. Littlefield Jr. (Tucson: University of Arizona Press, 1976), 62.

15. Garland, "Among the Southern Utes," 65.

16. For discussion of the railroads' influence on government Indian policy, in particular the cession of tribal lands, see Frederick E. Hoaxie, *A Final Promise: The Campaign to Assimilate the Indians, 1880–1920* (1984; repr., Cambridge: Cambridge University Press, 1989), 45–48.

17. Quoted in William T. Hagan, *Theodore Roosevelt and Six Friends of the Indian* (Norman: University of Oklahoma Press, 1997), 6.

18. Underhill and Littlefield, *Garland's Observations on the American Indian*, 167n5.

19. Quoted in Robert M. Utley, *The Last Days of the Sioux Nation* (New Haven: Yale University Press, 1963), 30–31.

20. Garland, "Among the Southern Utes," 71.

21. Hamlin Garland, "A Day at Isleta," in Underhill and Littlefield, *Garland's Observations on the American Indian*, 78. The sketch was originally syndicated in the "Over Indian Trails" series. For my account of the chronology of Garland's visits to reservations, I am indebted to Underhill and Littlefield's "Introductory Survey."

22. Hamlin Garland, "Among the Moki Indians," *Harper's Weekly*, August 15 1896, 801–7; reprinted in Underhill and Littlefield, *Garland's Observations on the American Indian*, 108.

23. Hamlin Garland, "The Most Mysterious People in the World: The Cliff Dwellers and Pueblo People of Arizona," *Ladies' Home Journal*, October 1896, 5–6; reprinted in Underhill and Littlefield, *Garland's Observations on the American Indian*, 128.

24. *Roadside Meetings*, 298.

25. Quoted in Pizer, *Hamlin Garland's Early Work and Career*, 155.

26. Garland's summer 1893 notebook, "Summer and the West," item 38, USC.

27. Kenneth M. Price, "Whitman's Influence on Hamlin Garland's *Rose of Dutcher's Coolly*," in *Walt Whitman of Mickle Street: A Centennial Collection*, ed. Geoffrey M. Sill (Knoxville: University of Tennessee Press, 1994), 197.

28. Hamlin Garland, "A New Declaration of Rights," *Arena*, January 1891, 183.

29. Pizer, *Hamlin Garland's Early Work and Career*, 156.

30. B. O. Flower, "Prostitution in the Marriage Bond," *Arena*, June 1895, 68, 69, 70.

31. Hamlin Garland, *Rose of Dutcher's Coolly* (Chicago: Stone and Kimball, 1895), 17, 19.

32. Garland, *Rose of Dutcher's Coolly*, 31–32.

33. Garland, *Rose of Dutcher's Coolly*, 37, 39.

34. Garland, *Rose of Dutcher's Coolly*, 55, 62.

35. Garland, *Rose of Dutcher's Coolly*, 329.

36. Garland, *Rose of Dutcher's Coolly*, 148, 327–28, 133.

37. Garland, *Rose of Dutcher's Coolly*, 288.

38. Garland, *Rose of Dutcher's Coolly*, 335.

39. Garland, *Rose of Dutcher's Coolly*, 380, 383.

40. "Hamlin Garland's Latest Fury," *Philadelphia Press*, sec. 3, January 5, 1896, 22; William Morton Payne, "Recent Fiction," *Dial*, February 1, 1896, 80; "Hamlin Garland's Latest," *Chicago Daily Tribune*, December 14, 1895, 9; "Literature," *Independent*, February 6, 1896, 189; "Literature of Today," *Chicago Times-Herald*, December 9, 1895, 10; W. D. Howells, "Life and Letters," *Harper's Weekly*, March 7, 1896, 223.

13. "HO, FOR THE KLONDIKE!"

1. Mott, *History of American Magazines*, 4:5, 8.

2. Peter Lyon, *Success Story: The Life and Times of S. S. McClure* (New York: Scribner's, 1963), 137.

3. Garland's 1895–1899 journal, entries for January 6 and February 14, 1896, item 7a, USC.

4. Hamlin Garland, "The Jicarilla Apaches," in Underhill and Littlefield, *Garland's Observations on the American Indian*, 133.

5. Quoted in "Introductory Survey," in Underhill and Littlefield, *Garland's Observations on the American Indian*, 19.

6. Garland's contact for *Grant*, dated November 14, 1896, item 669k, USC; *Daughter*, 35. For dollar equivalents see Williamson, "What Is the Relative Value?"

7. Howells to Garland, January 8, 1897, in *Selected Letters of W. D. Howells*, 4:139. The two installments are "The Early Life of Ulysses S. Grant," *McClure's*, December 1896, 125; and "Grant at West Point," *McClure's*, January 1897, 195–210. These and other installments were also syndicated to newspapers.

8. Howells to Garland, January 24, 1897, in *Selected Letters of W. D. Howells*, 4:143. "Grant's Life in Missouri" appeared in *McClure's*, April 1897, 514–20. When he revised the series into book form, Garland heeded Howells's advice and put the Fishback interview into his own language.

9. Garland to Matthews, May 1, 1897, Brander Matthews Papers, Rare Book and Manuscript Library, Columbia University; the articles were published in the August 1897 and April and May 1898 issues.

10. See Garland to [Albert B.] Brady, February 2, 1897, MSS 6324-d, Clifton Waller Barrett Library of American Literature, Special Collections, University of Virginia Library; Garland to Franklin Garland, February 6, 1897, USC; *Daughter*, 35.

11. Garland to Franklin Garland, February 3, 1897, in *Selected Letters*, 108.

12. Garland to Franklin Garland, February 6, 1897, USC. Garland's Appleton contracts are in the Lilly Library, Indiana University.

13. Garland to Taft, March 9, 1897, USC. Garland's "Ulysses S. Grant (1822–1885)" appeared in vol. 16 of *The World's Best Literature, Ancient and Modern*, ed. Charles Dudley Warner (New York: International Society, 1897), 6593–6600. A brief introductory sketch of Garland, the poem "A Summer Mood" (from *Prairie Songs*), and "A Storm on Lake Michigan," an excerpt from *Rose of Dutcher's Coolly*, appear in vol. 15, 6195–6204.

14. See Eberhard Alsen, "Hamlin Garland's First Novel," *Western American Literature* 4 (1969): 91–105.

15. Garland to Franklin Garland, February 6, 1897, USC. See also "Notes on Books," item 668f, USC, in which Garland tries out dozens of titles for the proposed collection.

16. Garland retitled all but one of the stories and made superficial revisions to all save "Before the Low Green Door," in which he omitted the didactic first section of the original story. "A Meeting in the Foothills" also reveals many additions to descriptive matter. The stories and their original serial publication are as follows: "At the Beginning" (as "Before the Overture," *Ladies' Home Journal*, May 1893, 10); "A Preacher's Love Story" (as "An Evangel in Cyene," *Harper's*, August 1895, 375–90); "A Meeting in the Foothills" (as "The Girl from Washington," Bacheller Syndicate, *Chicago Tribune*, January 19, 1896, 37, 39); "A Stop-Over at Tyre" (as "A Girl of Modern Tyre," *Century*, January 1897, 401–23); "An Alien in the Pines" (as "Only a Lumber Jack," *Harper's Weekly*, December

8, 1894, 1158–59); "The Owner of Mill Farm" (as "A Graceless Husband," *Northwestern Miller*, extra Christmas number, December 1893, 57–62); "Of those Who Seek": (1. "The Prisoned Fool" [as "Under the Dome of the Capitol: A Prose Etching," *Arena*, September 1892, 468–70]; 2. "A Sheltered One" [as "Opposites," *Bookman*, November 1895, 196–97]; 3. "A Fair Exile" [as "A Short-Term Exile," *Literary Northwest*, July 1893, 308–15]; 4. "The Passing Stranger" [as "In the Glance of His Face," *Penny Magazine*, May 1896, 57–60]); "Before the Low Green Door" (as "A Common Case," *Belford's*, July 1888, 188–99); "Upon Impulse" (*Bookman*, January 1897, 428–32); "The End of Love Is Love of Love" (as "Forgetting," *Ladies' Home Journal*, December 1892, 17).

17. See "Introductory Survey," Underhill and Littlefield, *Garland's Observations on the American Indian*, 21, 143–44.

18. "Introductory Survey," Underhill and Littlefield, *Garland's Observations on the American Indian*, 148.

19. "A Typical Indian Scare," Underhill and Littlefield, *Garland's Observations on the American Indian*, 157.

20. *Daughter*, 52.

21. Hamlin Garland, *The Trail of the Goldseekers: A Record of Travel in Prose and Verse* (New York: Macmillan, 1899), 8.

22. Garland's 1895–1899 journal, October 6, 1897, item 7a, USC.

23. Garland, journal entry, November 4, 1897, in "Literary Notes," 23, item 50, USC.

24. Garland to Matthews, July 12, 1897, in *Selected Letters*, 112.

25. Garland, "Literary Notes," 17–18, item 50, USC. For an account of the firm's dissolution, see Kramer, *History of Stone and Kimball*, 74–89.

26. Garland, "Literary Notes," 29, item 50, USC.

27. Garland, "Literary Notes," 49, item 50, USC.

28. *Roadside Meetings*, 373.

29. Garland's dictated "The Story of Grant McLane" is preserved as item 8c, USC. Before his Klondike trek Garland kept diaries intermittently. He made a transcript of his journal for 1895–99 (item 7a, USC) when he was preparing *Roadside Meetings*, and this transcript records his dictation of his autobiography. "Grant McLane" is also a character in "Up the Coulé."

30. Hamlin Garland, "Ho, for the Klondike!" *McClure's*, March 1898, 443.

31. *Klondike: The Chicago Record's Book for Gold Seekers*, appearing in late 1897, estimated that the voyage from Seattle to St. Michael would take fifteen days, with a potential several week layover while awaiting passage upriver to Dawson, and the seventeen-hundred-mile voyage up the Yukon River would take fifteen

or twenty days (repr., Tucson: Tombstone Nugget, 1965, 10). Pierre Breton reports that the typical $150 fare to St. Michael had skyrocketed to $1,000 by the winter of 1897 (*The Klondike Fever: The Life and Death of the Last Great Gold Rush* [New York: Knopf, 1958], 127).

32. Dianne Newell, "The Importance of Information and Misinformation in the Making of the Klondike Gold Rush," *Journal of Canadian Studies* 21, no. 4 (1986–87): 104.

33. See Breton, *The Klondike Fever*, 165–66; and Newell, "Klondike Gold Rush," 104.

34. Wells left for the Klondike on July 26. His newspaper reports, combined with diary entries, were published as *Magnificence and Misery: A Firsthand Account of the 1897 Klondike Gold Rush*, ed. Randall M. Dodd (Garden City NY: Doubleday, 1984). See also the memoir of Tappan Adney, the *Harper's Weekly* correspondent, *The Klondike Stampede* (1900; repr., Vancouver: University of British Columbia Press, 1994).

35. See Franklin Walker, *Jack London and the Klondike* (San Marino CA: Huntington Library Press, 1966), 57.

36. Wells, *Magnificence and Misery*, 39, 43–44.

37. Garland, "Ho, for the Klondike," 446.

38. Garland, "Ho, for the Klondike," 445–46.

39. Garland, "Ho, for the Klondike," 446, 447.

40. Ogilvie's warning appears on page 43 of the first of two notebooks (item 51, USC) in which Garland recorded the notes from his interviews of Canadian officials.

41. Garland's 1895–1899 journal, item 7a, USC.

42. Garland, *The Trail of the Goldseekers*, 26.

43. Garland, *The Trail of the Goldseekers*, 100.

44. Diary, June 28, 1898. Years later, Garland revised the diary entries for publication in his memoirs. Unless otherwise indicated, my transcriptions are of the initial, unrevised entry.

45. Garland to Franklin Garland, July 22, 1898, in *Selected Letters*, 116–17.

46. Garland's report about the trail conditions, filed from Hazelton on June 27, was syndicated as "In the Klondike: The Grim Realities of the Overland Trail," *Cleveland Leader*, July 31, 1898, 20. For news reports concerning his ordeal, see the September 19, 1898, issues of the *Brooklyn Eagle* (p. 1), *Chicago Times-Herald* (pp. 1, 2), and *Chicago Tribune* (p. 5), which printed the syndicated story under versions of "Hamlin Garland's Peril."

47. Diary, August 7, 1898.

48. Garland, *The Trail of the Goldseekers*, 237.

49. Robert Gish finds an element of "camp" in Garland's seeking a "master's degree in hardihood" only to bail out when the going got rough and describes Garland as "a zany and unconscious parody of the ideal, heroic trailer and man of the wilderness which Garland never authentically and convincingly becomes" ("Hamlin Garland's Northwest Travels: 'Camp' Westering," in *The Critical Reception of Hamlin Garland, 1891–1978*, ed. Charles L. P. Silet, Robert B. Welch, and Richard Boudreau [Troy NY: Whitston, 1985], 412). True, Garland felt homesick for more comfortable conditions, but Gish seems unaware that Garland entered the Northwest, not as a goldseeker determined to stick it out until he found his fortune, but as a chronicler of the movement, under a deadline. He remained until prior commitments required his return; indeed, when he heard of the Atlin Lake strike, he delayed his return for as long as possible.

50. Garland, *The Trail of the Goldseekers*, 193. In the manuscript of the poem, Garland emphasizes his transformation from bookworm to master trailer, beginning the final stanza, "I threaded the wild with the keen quick eye / Of the man who knows books not at all. / I was hunter and trailer again." Omitted concluding lines suggest he had come to see the wilderness as an interlude: "Now I return to my books / To the Forum, the concert and hall" ("Klondike Notebooks," item 51c, p. 139, USC).

51. In addition to *The Trail of the Goldseekers*, "Ho, for the Klondike!" and "In the Klondike: The Grim Realities of the Overland Trail," Garland published a follow-up account of the Ashcroft route ("The Prairie Route to the Golden River," *Independent*, January 20, 1899, 245–51); an article about those who attempt the Ashcroft route entirely on foot ("Trampers on the Trail," *Cosmopolitan*, March 1899, 515–22); an article about traveling by trail in general, which curiously never mentions the Klondike region ("Hitting the Trail," *McClure's*, January 1899, 298–304); ten poems in *McClure's* (April 1899, 505–7; May 1899, 65–67); and a juvenile novel of his adventure, which carries through the action to some actual mining (first serialized in *Youth's Companion*, December 6, 1906–February 7, 1907, before appearing in book form as *The Long Trail* [New York: Harper, 1907]).

14. THE END OF THE TRAIL

1. Diary, September 16, 1898. For years Garland was uncertain whether he was born on September 14 or 16 and varied which day he celebrated. Much later he discovered a family bible with September 14 in his mother's hand.

2. "Klondike Notebooks," 164, item 51c, USC. The notebooks contain several other manuscript poems in a similar vein, clearly suggesting his desire for marriage, as in "The Klondike Girl":

I've got my gold I want a girl
A good square honest wife
I'm sick of painted hell-cats here
I've made my stake you bet your life
I've quit—I want a home
I want a youngster on my knee. (69)

3. Diary, September 26, 1898; "Biography and Gossip," *Critic*, March 1899, 257; Talcott Williams, "With the New Books," *Book News*, November 1898, 118; "Hamlin Garland's Life of Grant," *New York Times Saturday Review of Books*, October 29, 1898, 715.

4. *Daughter*, 23, 76. Garland's diary for November 3, 1898, records their first meeting after her return.

5. In her unpublished memoir "This Loving Daughter," Isabel Garland Lord (who in adulthood dropped "Mary") describes her mother's reaction to her name. In his diary for October 5, 1899, Garland records his private pronunciation as "Zu-LEE-ma." Zulime Garland's scrapbook, item 712c,4, USC; "Sculpture at the World's Fair," *Illustrated American*, March 25, 1893, 373–74.

6. "Miss Zulimi Taft," clipping dated March 1893, Springfield, Ohio, Zulime Garland's scrapbook, item 712c,4, USC.

7. Diary, November 25, 1898.

8. Tebbel, *History of Book Publishing in the United States*, 434n.

9. Brett to Frederick Macmillan, May 16, 1899, in *Archives of the Macmillan Company, Part 2: Publishing Records*, incoming correspondence, 1897–1904 (Teaneck NJ: Chadwyk-Healey, 1982), microfilmed, reel 6, pt. 2.

10. Diary, January 19, 1899. See also Garland's Macmillan contract for *Main-Travelled Roads*, *Prairie Folks*, and *Rose of Dutcher's Coolly*, dated January 23, 1899, item 669l, USC. For dollar equivalents see Williamson, "What Is the Relative Value?"

11. Following Donald Pizer's suggestion that "Mason's proposal emphasizes personal freedom so strongly that apparently some readers believed he was proposing a trial marriage," critics generally suggest the scene was added to clarify that the two are really married and not experimenting with a common-law marriage. In 1895, however, reviewers saw no ambiguity in Rose and Mason's relationship, only the implausibility of Mason's proposal. See Pizer's introduction to *Rose of Dutcher's Coolly* (Lincoln: University of Nebraska Press, 1969), xxxii. For repetition of Pizer's speculation see Robert Bray, "Hamlin Garland's *Rose of Dutcher's Coolly*," in Silet, Welch, and Boudreau, *The Critical Reception of Hamlin Garland*, 396, 406n11; and Price, "Whitman's Influence on Garland's *Rose of Dutcher's Coolly*," 200–201.

12. Garland removed "Saturday Night on the Farm" for use in *Boy Life on the Prairie*. The four additional stories are "A Day of Grace" (as "Grace . . . A Reminiscence," syndicated October 16, 1895); "Black Ephram" (as "Our Only Black Man," syndicated April 22, 1894); "The Wapsepinnicon Tiger" (syndicated February 28, 1895); and "Aidgewise Feelings" (as "A Division in the Coulé," syndicated November 1, 1896).

13. Garland, *Boy Life on the Prairie*, vi. See B. R. McElderry Jr., "*Boy Life on the Prairie*. Hamlin Garland's Best Reminiscence," *Educational Leader* 22 (1959): 5–16; Leland Krauth, "*Boy Life on the Prairie*. Portrait of the Artist as a Young American," *Markham Review* 11 (1982): 25–29; Marcia Jacobson, *Being a Boy Again: Autobiography and the American Boy Book* (Tuscaloosa: University of Alabama Press, 1994).

14. Diary, January 28, 1899.

15. Fuller to Garland, March 16, 1902, USC.

16. Garland discusses his friendship with Zangwill in "I. Zangwill," *Conservative Review*, November 1899, 404–12; and in *Roadside Meetings*, 388–444.

17. See Harriet Monroe, "Eagle's Nest Camp: A Colony of Artists and Writers," *House Beautiful*, August 1904, 5–10. Today the former art colony is the Lorado Taft Field Campus of Northern Illinois University.

18. See Diary, May 21, 1901. Garland describes his tepee in *Daughter*, 250–51, and *Companions*, 69–70.

19. In a draft for *Roadside Meetings* (item 7a, USC), Garland writes that, after his second meeting with Zulime, "I had been warned that she was engaged"; in *A Daughter of the Middle Border* he writes that Lorado told him, "She is definitely committed to another man" (83).

20. Diary, April 19, 1899.

21. *Roadside Meetings*, 418; Diary, April 19–26.

22. Garland to Isabelle Garland, April 30, 1899, item GD 261, Huntington.

23. Diary, May 6, 1899.

24. Diary, May 8, 30, 1899. Garland also recorded his observation of prostitutes in the Klondike. See "Klondike Notebooks," 69, item 51c, USC.

25. "This Loving Daughter," 16–17. "The Hustler" was serialized as "Jim Matteson of Wagon Wheel Gap," *Century*, November 1900–April 1901, before appearing as *Her Mountain Lover* (1901). Garland's occasional diary (item 50, "Literary Notes," USC) also reveals signs of his destruction of records of his courtship. Pages 185 to 222 have been cut out, corresponding to dates of his summer courtship, bracketed by a slightly revised version of his poem about the desire for marriage (the deleted stanza of "Here the Trail Ends," here titled "The Possible One") and an entry for his birthday, September 14, 1899.

26. Diary, July 8, 1899.

27. "This Loving Daughter," 4.

28. Diary, August 6, 8, 1899. For discussion of Fuller's homosexuality see Kenneth Scambray, *A Varied Harvest: The Life and Works of Henry Blake Fuller* (Pittsburgh: University of Pittsburgh Press, 1987).

29. In his diary for October 1, 1899, Garland records that his mother is "pleased" about his interest in Zulime and "Wants me to 'hurry.'"

30. "This Loving Daughter," 4.

31. *Daughter*, 123. See also Garland to Mildred Howells, January 21, 1921, in *Selected Letters*, 282.

32. Zulime Garland, diary, January 2, 1900, item 712c,5, USC.

33. Diary, October 27, 1899.

34. Garland to Franklin Garland, October 24, 1899, in *Selected Letters*, 125.

35. Diary, October 31, November 1, 1899.

36. Diary, November 17, 18, 1899.

37. *Daughter*, 144.

38. "This Loving Daughter," 37.

39. Hamlin Garland, "The New Daughter," draft of chapter 10 of *A Daughter of the Middle Border*, item GD 62, Huntington.

40. "This Loving Daughter," 5.

41. Diary, February 11, 1900.

42. See Jesse Crisler, "Hamlin Garland's Relationship with Frank Norris," *Norris Studies* 4 (2004): 5–12.

43. Zulime Garland, diary, January 9, 1900, item 712c,5, USC.

44. *Daughter*, 169. In her diary for February 25, 1900, Zulime records Susan Bailey's death (item 712c,5, USC).

45. Diary, March 18, 1900.

46. Garland to Walter Hines Page, August 27, 1899, in *Selected Letters*, 124. Garland's first fiction set in Colorado was the three-part novella "The Spirit of Sweetwater" (*Ladies' Home Journal*, August 1897, 5–6; September 1897, 9–10; October 1897, 11–12), which was then published in book form in 1898.

47. Diary, March 12, 1900; also Zulime's diary, March 13, 1900, item 712c,5, USC. *The Eagle's Heart* was serialized in the *Saturday Evening Post* beginning on June 16 and concluding on September 29, 1900.

48. Diary, October 13, 1900.

49. "Among the New Books," *Chicago Tribune*, November 2, 1900, 10; "Mr. Hamlin Garland's New Novel," *Brooklyn Daily Eagle*, December 22, 1900, 6.

50. Diary, April 12, 1900. Garland discusses the invitation in *Daughter*, 174, and *Companions*, 20–21.

51. *Daughter*, 249.

52. "Hisses for Hamlin Garland," clipping, quoted in Garland to Victor Lawson, ca. June 6, 1900, in *Selected Letters*, 103. The letter is erroneously dated as 1896. Diary, June 10, 1900. Garland declined to reply in print. The report was copied by the *Chicago Tribune*, "Address by Hamlin Garland Offends a Pioneer Gathering," June 10, 1900, 2; and "Topics of the Times," *New York Times*, June 12, 1900, 6.

53. *Daughter*, 214.

54. Diary, November 30, 1900.

55. Garland, "The Wife of a Pioneer," 42. Garland later reprinted his tribute in a limited edition of five hundred small paper and twenty-five large paper copies as *A Pioneer Mother* (1922).

56. *Companions*, 48.

57. Diary, April 26, 1901.

58. *Daughter*, 226.

59. *Daughter*, 226.

60. Oklahoma land records, item 672d, USC.

61. Diary, May 13, 1901.

62. Garland to Katherine Herne, June 3, [1901], in *Selected Letters*, 140–41. See "His Sincerity as a Playwright," part of Hamlin Garland, John J. Enneking, and B. O. Flower, "James A. Herne: Actor, Dramatist, and Man," *Arena*, September 1901, 282–91. Garland's contribution is on pp. 282–84.

63. Diary, June 26, 1901.

64. Diary, October 4, 1901.

65. See the syndicated news item "Hamlin Garland's Father Wed," *Chicago Tribune*, November 12, 1901, 3; "Hamlin Garland to Have Stepmamma," *Brooklyn Eagle*, November 12, 1901, 17. Although the newspapers give Mary Bolles's age as sixty-two, cemetery records reveal she was born on January 26, 1841, and died on March 1, 1922. When Garland wrote his father's obituary, he omitted any mention of his father's second wife (clipping pasted in "Literary Notes," item 50, USC).

66. Garland to Lummis, December 24, 1901, in *Selected Letters*, 143.

67. For Garland's recollections of Roosevelt see *Roadside Meetings*, 326–34; "My Neighbor, Theodore Roosevelt," *Everybody's*, October 1919, 9–16, 94; "Theodore Roosevelt," *Mentor*, February 2, 1920, 1–12.

68. See Daniel F. Littlefield Jr. and Lonnie E. Underhill, "Renaming the American Indian: 1890–1913," *American Studies* 12 (1971): 33–45.

69. Quoted in Hagan, *Roosevelt and Six Friends of the Indian*, 129, 130. See also Garland to Albert Shaw, January 24, 1902, in *Selected Letters*, 145–46.

70. Hamlin Garland, "The Red Man's Present Needs," *North American Review*, April 1902, 480.

71. See R. W. Meyer, "Hamlin Garland and the American Indian," *Western American Literature* 2 (1967): 109–25; John C. McGreivey, "Art and Ideas in Garland's *The Captain of the Gray-Horse Troop*," *Markham Review* 5 (1976): 52–58.

72. Flower to Garland, March 31, 1902, USC.

73. "Among the New Books," *Chicago Tribune*, April 14, 1902, 13; "A Story of Indians," *New York Times Saturday Review of Books and Art*, April 5, 1902, 228; William Morton Payne, "Recent Fiction," *Dial*, June 1, 1902, 387.

74. *Daughter*, 243. For an example of Harper's marketing of the novel, see the extended review "White Man's Road," *Harper's Weekly*, April 5, 1902, 432, accompanied by two photographs of the author, one taken by George Bernard Shaw. Zulime's striking full-page portrait appears on p. 433.

75. Diary, October 27, 1902. Garland has slightly revised this entry. In a July 27, 1940, letter to Eldon Hill (Miami), Franklin Garland briefly describes his ill-fated Mexican venture. Garland erroneously refers to it as being in Honduras in *Daughter*, 238.

15. ADRIFT

1. "This Loving Daughter," 6. Mary Isabel bases her account on her mother's description of the event to her as well as Garland's diary, portions of which she had transcribed earlier, but she reports that the pages relating to her father's anguish had since been torn out. When he went through his diaries as he prepared to compose his memoirs, Garland removed pages for July 14, 15, 16, and 17 from the diary, redated July 13 to July 15, and described his reaction to first holding his new daughter while omitting details of the delivery. In *Daughter*, 286–87, he glosses over the event's trauma.

2. Garland to Roosevelt, July 16, 1903, in *Selected Letters*, 177–78. Roosevelt's reply of July 19, 1903, is quoted in *Selected Letters*, 179n1; Garland's reply of July 22, 1903, appears in *Selected Letters*, 178–79.

3. Diary, October 20, 1903. The operation took place in Dr. Frank Seaman's New York City apartment.

4. "This Loving Daughter," 14.

5. Diary, July 15, 1902, June 22, 1903.

6. Garland to Duneka, June 29, 1903, in *Selected Letters*, 176.

7. Garland to Reynolds, June 29, 1903, Garland's letter book, 169, USC.

8. William Morton Payne, "Recent Fiction," *Dial*, January 1, 1904, 19; *Independent*, December 24, 1903, 3072; Howells to Garland, November 30, 1903, USC.

9. Harper's royalty ledgers, from publication to October 31, 1904, G4, 580. The Harper's archives, which are held in Columbia University's Butler Library, have been microfilmed as *Archives of Harper and Brothers, 1817–1914* (Teaneck NJ: Chadwyck Healey/Somerset House, 1980). See also Christopher Feeney, *Index to the Archives of Harper and Brothers, 1817–1914* (Teaneck NJ: Chadwyck Healey/Somerset House, 1980). *The Captain of the Gray-Horse Troop* was nearly as successful, selling more than 21,400 copies during its first year (G4, 514).

10. Harper's royalty ledgers, *Heroines of Fiction*, G3, 786; *The Son of Royal Langbrith*, G4, 736; *The Kentons*, G3, 787; *Cherry*, G5, 627; *The Masquerader*, G5, 628.

11. Diary, March 3, 1926, December 21, 1903.

12. See Garland to Shaw, January 31, 1902, in *Selected Letters*, 146; Franklin Garland to Eldon Hill, July 27, 1940, Miami. In three other letters to Shaw (February 19, 20, 25, 1902, Albert Shaw Papers, NYPL), Garland briefly refers to the venture.

13. Diary, December 17, 1903.

14. Franklin Garland to Garland, January 31, 1904, USC.

15. Franklin Garland to Garland, February 14, 1904, USC.

16. Franklin Garland to Garland, March 7, 14, 1904, USC.

17. *Companions*, 228.

18. July 1, 1904, statement of expense, item 672b, USC.

19. Diary, May 27, 1904. At the end of the diary Garland listed his assets. He had $20,100 invested in land in Oklahoma, West Salem, South Dakota, and Mexico, and another $3,800 in savings.

20. Franklin Garland to Eldon Hill, July 27, 1940, Miami.

21. Hamlin Garland, *The Light of the Star* (New York: Harper and Brothers, 1904), 128.

22. Diary, October 25, 1900.

23. Garland, *The Light of the Star*, 226.

24. "Garland's Theatrical Novel," *Chicago Tribune*, June 4, 1904, 7.

25. Harper's royalty ledgers, from publication to June 30, 1905, G4, 511.

26. Diary, October 3, November 8, 1904.

27. Fuller to Garland, December 9, 1907, USC.

28. See Diary, December 2, 1904. Robert Underwood Johnson, who was secretary of the academy from its founding until his death in 1937, describes the founding in *Remembered Yesteryears* (Boston: Little, Brown, 1923), 439–52. For a history of the institute and academy, see John Updike, ed., *A Century of Arts and Letters* (New York: Columbia University Press, 1998).

29. Program and letters in the Henry George Jr. Papers, NYPL.

30. "Hamlin Garland in Cell," *New York Times*, July 31, 1905, 1. The quotation is from the *Los Angeles Times* account "Got His 'Local Color,'" July 31, 1905, 11.

31. "Stole for 'Local Color,'" *New York Times*, December 21, 1905, 1.

32. *Forty Years*, 137.

33. Harper's royalty ledgers, from publication to June 30, 1906, G6, 629. Garland quotes from the letters in *Forty Years*, 140–48.

34. Diary, April 5, November 6, 1905.

35. Jack Beeson, "Da Ponte, MacDowell, Moore, and Lang: Four Biographical Essays," in *Living Legacies* [part of the Columbia University alumni magazine], summer 2000, 30. See also Garland's explanation to the press, "MacDowell's Career Ended by Overwork," *New York Times*, November 28, 1905, 7.

36. Garland to Gilder, November 12, 1905, in *Selected Letters*, 190–91.

37. "Certificate of Incorporation, The MacDowell Club of New York City"; for the club's accomplishments, see "President's Annual Report, April 1911," both from a microfilm at NYPL. See also Neil Leonard, "Edward MacDowell and the Realists," *American Quarterly* 18 (1966): 175–82. In *Companions*, 376–81, Garland describes his work with the MacDowell Club.

38. *Companions*, 292.

39. Garland to Zulime Garland, [n.d., prior to May 24, 1906], USC. Garland also explained that the doctor "found nothing organically wrong but the stomach inflamed and on a strike." Given his history of illness brought on by stress, squabbles with Zulime may have inflamed his stomach.

40. "This Loving Daughter," 5–6. Mary Isabel dates the affair as having occurred "five or six years after their marriage."

41. Diary, May 28, 31, 1906.

42. Garland to Zulime Garland, July 20, 1906, USC.

43. Diary, October 8, 1906. A partly revised manuscript of 374 typed leaves of "Jim's Paseur Abroad" is extant, item 122, USC. In *Companions*, 303, Garland comments on the work.

44. *The Long Trail* appeared as a serial in the *Youth's Companion* from December 1906 to February 1907. At a reduced royalty of 10 percent on a $1.25 book, by June 30, 1908, Garland earned $726.33 for the first year's sales—a sale of about 5,808 copies (Harper's royalty ledgers, G6, 706).

45. Diary, October 30, November 19, 1906. Quotations are of Garland's revised passages.

46. In writing *Money Magic*, Garland recycled "Mart Haney's Mate" (*Saturday Evening Post*, November 18, 1905, 1–3, 28–32), which formed the first three chapters of the novel, taking the story to Bertha's acceptance of Haney's pro-

posal. The remainder of the novel, concerning the love triangle and its effects, is new material.

47. "Hamlin Garland in a New Vein," *New York Times*, December 6, 1907, Holiday Book Number, pt. 1, 785; A. Schade van Westrum, "Mr. Garland's 'Money Magic,'" *Bookman*, December 1907, 418. Garland's royalties on the first year's sales, from publication to August 31, 1908, amounted to $1,883.73—slightly more than those for *The Light of the Star* (Harper's royalty ledgers, G6, 705).

16. "A BORN PROMOTER"

1. Fuller to Constance Garland, August 23, 1927, USC.
2. Diary, July 13, 1907.
3. "This Loving Daughter," 7.
4. *Daughter*, 327; Victoria Doyle-Jones to author, June 22, 1998, and interview, May 27, 2004.
5. Quoted in *Companions*, 324.
6. Diary, May 27, 1925.
7. "This Loving Daughter," 13.
8. Diary, June 6, 1907; *The Cliff Dweller's Yearbook* (Chicago: Chicago Historical Society, 1910), 6.
9. Names of prospective members were to be presented to the membership without the prospective inductee's knowledge; election needed to be unanimous. Garland took issue with the unanimity rule, according to which only "one black ball" was sufficient to turn down a candidate, and wanted to prevent "personal feeling" from ruling against a candidate. See "New Club of Bohemian Spirits," *Chicago Tribune* February 17, 1895, 12; Hamlin Garland to Herbert S. Stone, February 11, 1895, Stone and Kimball Papers, Midwest Manuscript Collection, Newberry Library, Chicago.
10. "Social Gossip," *Washington Post*, September 28, 1907, 7. See also Edward Thomas Hill, "The Cliff Dwellers of Chicago" (master's thesis, De Paul University, 1953), 6.
11. Diary, September 18, 1907; "Cliff Dwellers in Chicago," *Chicago Tribune*, November 7, 1907, 8.
12. See "Chicago's New Club of the Arts," *Harper's Weekly*, May 15, 1909, 30; "Giving the O. O. to Our Very Esteemed Highbrows, the Cliff Dwellers; They Starve Not, Neither Do They Sin," *Chicago Sunday Herald*, sec. 6, September 10, 1916, 2. The earliest reference to Fuller's novel is "The Cliff Dwellers," *Chicago Evening Post*, January 28, 1908 (clipping, USC).
13. See "Cliff Dwellers in Chicago," 8. Garland discusses the founding of the club—and Fuller's lack of participation—in *Daughter*, 326–27, and *Companions*,

370–72. For speculation about Fuller's refusal to join, see Ann Massa, "Henry Blake Fuller and the Cliff Dwellers: Appropriations and Misappropriations," *Journal of American Studies* 36 (2002): 69–84. Those who claim the club was named after Fuller's novel usually quote a letter to Garland in which Fuller writes, "Your club memo, I noticed the other day, contained a reference or so to me. Try to organize without me. In fact, I'm not sure that I shall join at all. Of course I'm interested in any enterprise *of yours*, but I am not naturally club-bable, and have always kept out. Most of all, I dislike 'running' things" (USC). But the letter was written on June 23, 1907, when the club was called the Attic Club and before Garland changed its name.

14. Garland himself employed the variant spelling "McDowell" when he presented an inscribed copy of *Crumbling Idols* to the composer on February 22, 1896 (copy owned by Gary Culbert). In his diary, March 10, 12, 1908, Garland records the sittings and reports the psychic to be one "Mrs. Herbein"—the Mrs. Hartley of his published accounts. In succeeding years he published many accounts of the MacDowell sitting, the fullest of which are in *The Shadow World*, 242–95, and *Forty Years*, 194–256. See also M. H. Dunlop, "Unfinished Business: Hamlin Garland and Edward MacDowell," *Old Northwest* 19 (1985): 175–85.

15. Hamlin Garland, "The 'Shadow World' Prize Winners," *Everybody's*, November 1908, 665.

16. "Garland's Trip to Shadow Land," *New York Times*, October 23, 1908, literary section, 586; Olivia Howard Dunbar, "The Shadow World," *North American Review*, March 1909, 455.

17. James L. Highlander, "Robertson Players," in *American Theatre Companies, 1888–1930*, ed. Weldon B. Durham (New York: Greenwood, 1987), 402–4; Lucy France Pierce, "An Art Theatre in Successful Operation," *Theatre*, August 1908, 214–17.

18. *Miller of Boscobel* was never published but is extant in a complete typed manuscript (item 209, USC). Jane Frances Earley established a "reading text" of the play with full editorial apparatus in her 1969 dissertation, "An Edition of Hamlin Garland's 'Miller of Boscobel'" (Northwestern University, 1969), which is the source of my discussion. Garland refers to the play under various titles in his diaries, notebooks, and letters, a reflection of his changing perception of the play's emphasis. The most frequent variant title is "Business," but others include "The Sorceress," "A Business Woman," "The Labor Leader," and "The Peace-Maker." Finally, reviewers of the play and Garland himself were inconsistent in the spelling of "Boscobel"; subsequent quotations retain the writer's spelling.

19. Diary, January 24, 1909.

20. "Theatre: 'Miller of Boscobel,'" *Wisconsin State Journal*, January 30, 1909, 2.

21. Diary, January 30, 1909.

22. "At the Playhouses," *Wisconsin State Journal*, February 1, 1909, 3.

23. Diary, February 3, 1909.

24. Burns Mantle, "News of the Theatres," *Chicago Tribune*, February 4, 1909, 8.

25. Diary, February 26, 1909; Fuller to Garland, March 12, 1909, USC.

26. From *Prairie Folks* Garland selected "William Bacon's Man," "Elder Pill, Preacher," "A Day of Grace," "Lucretia Burns," "Daddy Deering," and "Aidgwise Feelings" (restoring its original title, "A Division in the Coolly"), as well as the introductory and closing verse. From *Wayside Courtships* he chose "A Stop-Over at Tyre," "A Fair Exile," "An Alien in the Pines," "Before the Low Green Door," and "A Preacher's Love Story."

27. "Hamlin Garland Reprints" [letter], *New York Times Saturday Review of Books*, November 6, 1909, 695.

28. See Garland to Roosevelt, August 6, 1905, in *Selected Letters*, 188–89.

29. See *Daughter*, 347; and Garland to Duneka, February 17, [1910], in *Selected Letters*, 198–99.

30. Howells to Garland, March 27, 1912, in *Selected Letters of W. D. Howells*, 5:313. From the date of publication to June 31, 1911, Garland received royalties of $4,048.94—a sale of about 13,493 copies at his now increased royalty of 20 percent (Harper's royalty ledgers, G8, 668).

31. Garland to Howells, March 29, 1910, in *Selected Letters*, 199–200.

32. Robert Morss Lovett, "The Season of the Chicago Theatre Society," *The Drama*, May 1912, 241–42.

33. *Companions*, 471.

34. "The Drama Players in Chicago," *Dial*, April 16, 1912, 302.

35. Diary, July 12, 1911.

36. Diary, July 18, 1911.

37. Garland to Logan, July 24, 1911, USC.

38. Hamlin Garland, "'Starring' the Play," *Nation*, July 20, 1911, 54. The letter is dated July 14, 1911; it appeared in the *Chicago Record-Herald* on July 23.

39. "The Chicago Theatre Society," *Dial*, August 1, 1911, 65.

40. Frederick Hatton, "The Theatres," *Chicago Evening Post*, July 22, 1911, 7.

41. For the letter by Eaton (which is his public response to Garland's request for play suggestions), see *Chicago Record-Herald*, July 27, 1911: 8; for the letters from Skinner and Clark, see "The Repertory Argument" [letters column], *Chicago Record-Herald*, n.d. (Garland's clipping file, item 725c, USC).

42. "Chicago Theater Society's Repertory Announced," *Chicago Tribune*, August 18, 1911, 8, 9.

43. "Chicago Theater Society's Repertory Announced."

44. Diary, September 22, 1911.

45. Lovett, "The Season of the Chicago Theatre Society," 250.

46. Diary, February 5, 1912.

47. Diary, February 7, March 13, 1912.

48. Lovett, "The Season of the Chicago Theatre Society," 246.

49. "The Drama Players in Chicago," 302.

50. "The Drama Players in Chicago," 303; Lovett, "The Season of the Chicago Theatre Society," 258. Garland was in the audience for three performances of *The Playboy of the Western World*, and his rather snide evaluation reveals his disappointment as he compared the Abbey Players to the Drama Players' performance of *The Thunderbolt*, which was playing at the same time: "I went again to see the Irish Players but I found them very lacking on the acting side. They read well but their acting was very small and insincere. At all the strong points of the play they failed to my mind. . . . Our own company gave a wonderful performance of "The Thunderbolt" but there was nobody there to see it" (Diary, February 29, 1912). "I got still more definitely their limitations. They all read alike the same cadence and the same tempo, but read their lines as if they realized that they were literature" (Diary, March 1, 1912). For Garland's much-edited version, in which he praises the Abbey Players' performances, see *Companions*, 476–78.

51. "The Drama Players in Chicago," 303.

52. Martyn Johnson, "The Chicago Theatre Society: A Step toward the Future," *The Drama*, November 1913, 198–99.

53. Sources for this account of the 1912–13 and 1913–14 seasons include Hamlin Garland, "The New Chicago," *Craftsman*, September 1913, 55–65; Hamlin Garland, "The Wisconsin Dramatic Society in Chicago," *Play-Book*, June 1913, 20–23; Johnson, "The Chicago Theatre Society: A Step Toward the Future," 194–99; and Thomas H. Dickinson, *The Insurgent Theatre* (New York: Huebsch, 1917), 34–5.

54. "For a 'Theatre Libre': Prof. Hamlin Garland's Plans," *Chicago Daily News*, January 30, 1892 [morning edition], 1.

55. "Hamlin Garland's Tract," *New York Times Review of Books*, October 15, 1911, 617. From publication in September 1911 to June 30, 1912, Garland received royalties of $704.27—the sale of 2,708 copies at a royalty of 20 percent on a $1.30 book (Harper's royalty ledgers, G8, 678).

56. Harper's royalty ledgers show that Garland had received $13,208.50 in royalties by that date (G8, 676; G10, 628; G10, 698). All bibliographies erroneously list the Sunset Edition as having been published in 1909. For the edition, Harper's simply printed from the original plates, including the copyright page,

added a new title page and illustration for each volume, and bound the books in red cloth. The dating error likely originated in the only descriptive bibliography attempted of Garland's work, Lloyd Arvidson's "A Bibliography of the Published Writings of Hamlin Garland" (master's thesis, University of Southern California, 1952). Arvidson lists ten volumes for the edition but relied on an ad in *Publishers Weekly* for July 3, 1909, as his authority, as well as Garland's contract, which is dated February 15, 1909 (item 66gj, USC). Two of the books, however, were first published in 1910, so he should have delved deeper. In a diary entry for December 9, 1911, Garland records receiving a set, and the Harper's royalty records also date from December 1911.

57. W. D. Howells, "Mr. Garland's Books," *North American Review*, October 1912, 526, 527. Oddly enough, while the eight books are listed in an asterisked note, Howells nowhere mentions the name "Sunset Edition." Garland describes his arrangement with Howells in a diary entry for December 9, 1911, and in *Companions*, 494.

58. Diary, March 6, 1912.

59. Garland to Howells, June 29, 1912, in *Selected Letters*, 212–13.

60. See "Hamlin Garland in Fire," *New York Times*, October 8, 1912, 1; "Hamlin Garland in Peril When His Residence Burns," *Chicago Tribune*, October 8, 1912, 1. For Garland's account of the fire, see *Daughter*, 355–68.

61. Garland to Johnson, November 13, [1912], Century Company Records, NYPL.

62. Bok to Garland, December 12, 1912, USC.

63. Garland, "Half Lights," 5.

64. *Companions*, 519.

65. Duneka to Garland, April 4, 1913, USC; Diary, April 7, 1913.

66. Hamlin Garland, discarded preface to *A Son of the Middle Border*, item GD 88, Huntington.

67. Garland to Yard, August 14, 1913, in *Selected Letters*, 229.

68. "General Purpose of the Authors' League," *Bulletin of the Authors' League of America*, April 1913, 6.

69. Garland to Roosevelt, March 4, 1913, in *Selected Letters*, 220–21.

70. Garland to Johnson, May 8, 1913, Academy.

71. "American Genius to Forge Ahead, 'Immortals' Say," *Chicago Tribune*, November 15, 1913, 13; *Companions*, 523, 524.

72. Diary, January 14, 1914. The notation is Garland's later addition when he revised his diaries for his memoirs.

73. Diary, January 17, 1914.

74. Diary, February 7, 1914. The entry is Garland's later addition. In a let-

ter of August 14, 1914 (USC), Sullivan agreed to pay thirty-one hundred dollars for the serial.

75. Garland quotes Sullivan's letter in *Companions*, 537; see also *Daughter*, 378–79, and Garland's diary for February 5, 1914, where he summarizes the sales. The story was published as "Partners for a Day," *Collier's*, March 14, 1914, 5–6. "On the Road with James A. Herne" appeared in the *Century*, August 1914, 574–81.

17. A SON OF THE MIDDLE BORDER

1. "Harpers Books" [display advertisement], *New York Times*, February 7, 1914, 6.

2. Ann Barton Brown, *Alice Barber Stephens: A Pioneer Woman Illustrator* (Chadds Ford PA: Brandywine River Museum, 1984), 29.

3. Garland, "Half Lights," 5.

4. *Daughter*, 379.

5. Diary, October 21, 1914; *Daughter*, 398.

6. Quit claim deeds to West Salem property, item GD 1161, 1162, Huntington; and probate records of estate of Richard Garland, item 676a, USC. Richard Garland's will is dated December 5, 1901, a month after his remarriage.

7. "This Loving Daughter," 41.

8. Hobart Chatfield-Taylor, "Historical Sketch," in a "Society of Midland Authors" pamphlet [1917] (Society of Midland Authors Archives, Special Collections, University of Illinois at Chicago). As with the Cliff Dwellers, controversy developed over the origin of its name. The society's minutes show Garland moving that the organization be named "The Society of Midland Authors," but Chatfield-Taylor recalls that Garland wanted the name to be "The Society of Middle West Authors," with he, Chatfield-Taylor, suggesting "the word 'Midland' between flights of Mr. Garland's eloquence." But Stahl claims that he, not Garland, first referred to "The Society of Midland Authors" in a letter to Howells in November, when he initially proposed the society. See John M. Stahl, *Growing with the West: The Story of a Busy, Quiet Life* (London: Longmans, Green, 1930), 424.

9. Ralph Fletcher Seymour, *Some Went This Way: A Forty Year Pilgrimage among Artists, Bookmen, and Printers* (Chicago: Ralph Fletcher Seymour, 1945), 161.

10. Diary, December 21, 1914.

11. Henry Regnery, *The Cliff Dwellers: The History of a Chicago Cultural Institution* (Chicago: Chicago Historical Bookworks, 1990), 26–27.

12. Quoted in Karelton Hackett to Charles L. Hutchinson, February 28, 1915, Charles L. Hutchinson Papers, Midwest Manuscript Collection, Newberry Library, Chicago.

13. Seymour, *Some Went This Way*, 162.

14. Hamlin Garland, "Note on Mr. Garland's Speech at the Cliff Dwellers in Chicago on Tuesday, May 4th," item 625, USC.

15. Diary, December 18, 1915.

16. J. Stuart Blackton, "Literature and the Motion-Picture: A Message," *Bulletin of the Authors' League of America*, February 1914, 5. Garland also helped draft the Authors' League's "plan for taking care of moving picture rights" (Diary, January 6, 1916).

17. Garland to Brady, April 6, [1916], USC. For the background of Vitagraph, see Anthony Slide, *The Big V: A History of the Vitagraph Company* (Metuchen NJ: Scarecrow Press, 1976).

18. Diary, March 22, 1916.

19. Diary, March 24, 1916; "This Loving Daughter," 41.

20. Diary, June 28, 1916; Garland to Blackton, June 29, [1916], in *Selected Letters*, 236.

21. *Contemporaries*, 119.

22. For Garland's film royalties see Garland to Jasper Brady, March 31, [1920], in *Selected Letters*, 276. Garland's Vitagraph contract dated June 21, 1916, called for a five hundred dollar advance on each accepted photoplay, with a royalty of 5 percent of sales to fifty thousand dollars and 10 percent thereafter. His name was to be displayed on the film and on all advertising (item 669p, USC). *Hesper* was released as *Hesper of the Mountains* on July 31, 1916, directed by Wilfred North. William Wolbert directed the other three films: *Money Magic* (February 5, 1917); *The Captain of the Gray-Horse Troop* (May 7, 1917); and *Cavanaugh of the Forest Rangers* (1918), remade in 1925 as *Ranger of the Big Pines*, directed by W. S. Van Dyke.

23. Garland to Duneka, July 11, [1915], USC.

24. The original publication of the nine stories of *They of the High Trails* follows: "The Grub-Staker" ("The Steadfast Widow Delaney," *Saturday Evening Post*, June 14, 28, 1902); "The Cow-Boss" ("A Night Raid on Eagle River," *Century*, September 1908, 725–34); "The Remittance Man" ("The Noose: A Story of Love and the Alien," *Saturday Evening Post*, June 1906, 3–5, 18); "The Lonesome Man" ("The Man at the Gate of the Mountains," *Ladies' Home Journal*, August 1899, 9–10); "The Trail Tramp" (pt. 1, "Kelley Afoot," *Sunset*, November 1912, 919–26; pt. 2, "Kelley as Marshall" as "Kelley of Brimstone Basin," *National Sunday Magazine*, March 28, 1915, 387–88, 392–94; pt. 3, "Partners for a Day," *Collier's*, March 14, 1914, 5–6, 33); "The Prospector" ("Through the Spirit of Iapi," *Success*, February 1910, 80–82, 125–26); "The Outlaw" ("The Outlaw and the Girl," *Ladies' Home Journal*, May–July 1908); "The Leaser" (source unlocat-

ed); "The Forest Ranger" ("The Ranger and the Woman," *Collier's*, July 24, 31, August 7, 14, 21, 28, 1915).

25. W. D. Howells, "Editor's Easy Chair," *Harper's Monthly*, September 1916, 629.

26. Garland to Mary Isabel and Constance Garland, October 8, [1916], item GD 759, Huntington.

27. *Back-Trailers*, 39.

28. "This Loving Daughter," 43.

29. Diary, February 28, 1917.

30. Garland to Agar, April 17, May 31, [1916], USC.

31. "American Authors' Club Is Now Being Planned," *New York Sun*, clipping, item 65, USC.

32. See Garland to Roosevelt, December 20, [1916], in *Selected Letters*, 241; "Other Americas," clipping, item 65, USC.

33. Garland to Howells, [before March 21, 1917], in *Selected Letters*, 246. For Howells's reply of April 7, 1917, see *Selected Letters*, 246n1.

34. Hagedorn to Garland, March 1, [1917], USC. Garland, "The Volunteer Soldier," syndicated March 31, [1917], item 424, USC.

35. Roosevelt, blurb accompanying "A Son of the Middle Border. Part One. Golden Days at Cedar Valley Seminary," *Collier's*, March 31, 1917, 9. The blurb also appeared as "An Appreciation" in the 1917 edition of *They of the High Trails*.

36. Quoted in *Back-Trailers*, 18.

37. Doubleday to Garland, May 22, 1916, USC.

38. Garland to Marsh, January 10, [1917], USC.

39. Diary, March 26, 1917. Garland records that he signed the Macmillan contract for *A Son of the Middle Border* on March 11 and delivered it to Edward Marsh on March 14. Throughout the negotiations, Garland was largely indebted to Mark Sullivan, who acted as his principal confidant.

40. Diary, May 19, July 16, 1915.

41. *Contemporaries*, 65; "This Loving Daughter," 47–48.

42. Diary, October 10, 13, 15, 1915. Garland describes his experience in *Contemporaries*, 72–73.

43. Diary, February 20, 1917.

44. Burroughs to Garland, March 20, 1917, USC.

45. John H. Kellogg, *The Battle Creek Sanitarium: An Institution of Health Reconstruction—Origins, Purposes, Methods* (Battle Creek MI: Battle Creek Sanitarium, 1923), 17.

46. Hamlin Garland, "The Good Ship Sanitas," 6, item 385, USC; Diary, May 8, 1917.

47. Garland, "The Good Ship Sanitas," 24. Garland used some of the material from "The Good Ship Sanitas" in *Back-Trailers*, 57–58, and *Contemporaries*, 151–56.

48. Diary, July 7, 1917.

49. Garland to Marsh, June 24, 1917, USC. In his memoirs, Garland states that Marsh had sent the advance sheets without his knowledge—a dodge to cover up his "shameless" solicitation of his friends (*Back-Trailers*, 67; *Contemporaries*, 161).

50. "This Loving Daughter," 56. Garland describes Camp Neshonoc in *Back-Trailers*, 59–65, and in a diary entry for August 2, 1917.

51. Howells to Garland, July 20, 1917, USC.

52. Howells to Garland, July 22, 1917, in *Selected Letters of W. D. Howells*, 6:118–19.

53. Howells to Garland, August 4, 1917, USC.

54. W. D. Howells, "A Son of the Middle Border, by Hamlin Garland: An Appreciation," *New York Times Review of Books*, August 26, 1917, 309, 317.

55. Diary, August 26, 1917.

56. *Son*, 467.

57. Diary, November 21, 1917.

58. Diary, January 11, 1918. In a subsequent phone call, Matthews told Garland that he "had the largest number of votes of any candidate and that I went in with a cheer." But what Matthews didn't tell him is that Garland was elected on a second ballot. During the meeting of November 21, 1917, at which three vacancies were to be filled, of the six candidates considered, with thirty-seven ballots received, Elihu Root came in first with twenty-eight votes (and was declared duly elected); the others pooled in the teens (Garland came in fifth, with fifteen). Because the election procedures were unclear about how to resolve the close voting, the meeting adjourned until January 11, at which time "the first and second choices were added together, with the result that Mr. Brand Whitlock and Mr. Hamlin Garland were shown to have received the highest votes and those of a majority of the membership of the Academy and they were declared duly elected" (Academy minutes, January 11, 1918, Academy).

18. OUT OF STEP WITH THE MODERNS

1. In 1947 Eldon Hill wrote to Macmillan for a list of sales of Garland's books. In his reply, Harold Latham, vice-president of the company, enclosed a list of total sales to April 30, 1947, of Garland's Macmillan books. The six editions of *A Son of the Middle Border* and the number of copies sold as identified on that list are Trade (82,1787), Royal Edition (16,127), Old Edition (10,190), School

Edition (60,271), Special Autograph Edition (323), New Cheap Edition (3,876), and combined volume with *A Daughter of the Middle Border* (4,236). See Harold Latham to Eldon Hill, September 9, 1947, Miami. Additionally, Latham told Garland that the "probable first printing" of the Grosset and Dunlap "will be 250,000 copies"—a number that is likely much higher than actually occurred (Latham to Garland, August 17, 1927, USC).

2. *Back-Trailers*, 68, 69, 70.

3. Diary, December 21, 1918. The quotation incorporates Garland's later minor revisions.

4. Diary, March 31, 1918.

5. Joyce Kilmer, "Says New York Makes Writers Tradesmen," *New York Times Magazine*, May 28, 1916, 13.

6. Garland to Fred B. Millet, March 1, 1937, in *Selected Letters*, 387–88.

7. Floyd Logan, "A Memoir: Hamlin Garland," March 4, 1968, item 707, USC.

8. For the date of the contract for *A Daughter of the Middle Border*, see Diary, February 2, 1918; for his failing memory, Diary, April 16, 1919.

9. Diary, August 2, 1918.

10. Diary, August 26, 1918. Garland discusses his pain and quotes the pen-dipping entry in *Back-Trailers*, 75, 91.

11. *National Cyclopedia of American Biography*, vol. 25 (Ann Arbor: University Microfilms, 1967), 175–76.

12. Diary, September 1, 1918. See also "The Cytosts," *Bulletin of the Turck Foundation for Biologic Research* 1 [1927]: 4–8, item 705b, USC. Garland describes Turck's treatment in *Back-Trailers*, 98–101.

13. Diary, September 28, 1918. For the injection of chloroform, see Diary, October 9, 1918. Garland records a number of periodic injections of "serum" during this initial treatment, with the last, his seventh, occurring on September 11, 1919. Later, whenever he was ill, Garland visited Turck for injections of cytost until Turck's death in 1932.

14. "Pulitzer Plan of Awards," USC; Garland to Fackenthal, March 22, [1919], in *Selected Letters*, 269.

15. Garland to Eaton, February 2, [1920], in *Selected Letters*, 273; Garland to Fackenthal, February 9, [1920], Pulitzer Archives, Columbia University.

16. Butler to Garland, January 23, 1920, USC.

17. Hamilton to Garland, March 7, 1920, USC.

18. Garland to Butler, May 11, [1920], in *Selected Letters*, 278.

19. Garland to Fackenthal, May 6, [1920], Pulitzer Archives, Columbia University.

20. Garland to Phelps, April 28, [1922], in *Selected Letters*, 299.

21. Hamlin Garland, "An Un-American Art," *New York Times*, March 3, 1925, 22.

22. Garland to Sherman, February 8, [1922], in *Selected Letters*, 260.

23. Diary, January 31, 1921; Garland to Sherman, March 10, [1921], in *Selected Letters*, 286.

24. Sherman to Garland, February 18, April 16, 1921, USC.

25. Lewis to Garland, September 23, 1915, USC.

26. Garland to Fackenthal, May 11, [1921], in *Selected Letters*, 289–90. As chair of the drama jury for 1921, Garland was equally divided about the merits of the current crop of plays. Among the contenders was Zona Gale's dramatic adaptation of her novel, and with a divided jury, Garland, in similar language and motive, influenced the award of the 1921 Pulitzer Prize for drama to *Miss Lulu Bett*. "Feeling it would be a handsome thing to give the prize to a woman," he wrote Fackenthal, "Burton will join Phelps and me in giving the award to LULU BETT" (Garland to Fackenthal, May 22, [1921], in *Selected Letters*, 290–91).

27. Fackenthal to Garland, June 20, 1921, USC.

28. Lovett to Garland, June 28, 1921, USC; Lovett, "The Pulitzer Prize," *New Republic*, June 22, 1921, 114. See also Fritz H. Oehlschlaeger, "Hamlin Garland and the Pulitzer Prize Controversy of 1921," *American Literature* 51 (1979): 409–14.

29. Garland to Fackenthal, March 9, [1925], in *Selected Letters*, 320; Garland to Fackenthal, March 12, 14, [1925], Pulitzer Archives, Columbia University.

30. Quoted in Cynthia Ozick, "1918–1927: Against Modernity—Annals of the Temple," in Updike, *A Century of Arts and Letters*, 78, 51.

31. Hamlin Garland, "The Mission of the American Academy," item 399, USC.

32. Academy Board of Directors minutes, October 7, 1920, Academy.

33. Academy Board of Directors minutes, June 10, 1921, Academy.

34. Academy Board of Directors minutes, March 21, 1921, appendix, Academy.

35. Hamlin Garland, "Suggestions Concerning the Academy's Opportunities," November 18, 1921, Academy.

36. Garland to Sloane, September 15, [1921], and Sloane to Garland, September 17, 1921, Academy.

37. Garland to Sloane, November 1, 1921, Academy.

38. Hamlin Garland, "Acting Secretary Garland's Final Report," [1921], Academy.

39. "Should Women Be Elected to the Institute? A Record Drawn from the Minutes of the Institute and Council Meetings," Academy.

40. Garland to Huntington, November 14, [1926], in *Selected Letters*, 332.

41. Diary, December 31, 1922. Sales figures are from Frederick Lewis Allen, *Only Yesterday* (1931; repr., New York: Harper and Row, 1964), 137.

42. Hamlin Garland, "The Value of Melodious Speech," *Emerson Quarterly* 9 (November 1929): 6.

43. Hamlin Garland, "Announcement of Award of the Medal of the Academy for Good Diction on the Radio to Mr. Milton J. Cross by Mr. Hamlin Garland," *Proceedings in Commemoration of the Twenty-fifth Anniversary of the Founding of the American Academy of Arts and Letters*, no. 72 (New York: American Academy, 1930), 51. Cross had a long and distinguished career: from 1931 to 1975 he was the announcer for broadcasts of the Metropolitan Opera on Saturday afternoons.

44. Garland to Matthews, September 22, [1921], in *Selected Letters*, 292.

45. Garland to Matthews, [ca. October 7, 1921], in *Selected Letters*, 294.

46. Johnson to Sloane, November 21, 1921, Academy.

47. Garland to Sloane, November 26, [1921], Academy.

48. Garland to Sloane, December 6, [1921], Academy.

49. Hamlin Garland, Appendix A, Minutes of the Board of Directors, November 10, 1922, Academy.

50. Hamlin Garland, "Notes Concerning Membership," [ca. 1921], Academy.

51. Diary, January 21, 1913.

52. Johnson to Garland, June 16, 1913, USC.

53. Garland to Johnson, June 28, [1913], in *Selected Letters*, 227.

54. For discussion of the Garland-Dreiser relationship, see Lars Ahnebrink, "Garland and Dreiser: An Abortive Friendship," *Midwest Journal* 7 (1955–56): 285–92.

55. Mencken to Garland, December 8, 1916, USC.

56. Dreiser to Masters, March 7, 1940, in *Letters of Theodore Dreiser: A Selection*, ed. Robert H. Elias, vol. 3 (Philadelphia: University of Pennsylvania Press, 1959), 874.

57. Johnson to Garland, October 1, 1926, USC.

58. Garland to Grace Vanamee, July 23, [1931], Academy.

59. Garland to Matthews, May 2, [1924], Brander Matthews Papers, Rare Book and Manuscript Library, Columbia University.

60. Garland to Johnson, September 8, [1926], Academy.

61. Hamlin Garland, "Current Fiction Heroes," *New York Times Book Review*, sec. 3, December 23, 1923, 2.

62. Pattee to Garland, December 1, 1923, USC.

63. Fred Lewis Pattee, "Those Fiery Radicals of Yesteryear," *New York Times Book Review*, February 24, 1924, sec. 3, 12, 26.

64. Garland to Brigham, January 26, 1894, in *Selected Letters*, 90.

1. Diary, January 4, 1919.

2. Sullivan to Garland, December 18, 1918, USC.

3. Diary, January 6, 1919.

4. See Hamlin Garland, "My Neighbor, Theodore Roosevelt," *Everybody's*, October 1919, 9–16, 94; "Theodore Roosevelt," *Mentor*, February 2, 1920, 1–12; "Roosevelt House," *Landmark*, May 1925, 273–77. Garland also wrote the preface ("Roosevelt as Historian") to his favorite Roosevelt work, *The Winning of the West*, vol. 8 of *The Works of Theodore Roosevelt*, National Edition (New York: Scribner's, 1926), xxvii–xxxiv.

5. Garland's "story" appeared as "Recollections of Roosevelt." See Garland's letter, "Wants Roosevelt Stories," *New York Times*, February 6, 1919, 10.

6. "This Loving Daughter," 50–52; Diary, May 27, 1919.

7. Garland to Johnson, October 17, [1919], Academy.

8. Garland to Fuller, November 6, [1919], in *Selected Letters*, 259. The published letter is misdated 1918. Admission procedures are from *Reports, Constitution, By-laws, and List of Members of the Century Association* (New York: Century Association, 1920).

9. Diary, November 15, 1919.

10. "This Loving Daughter," 49.

11. "This Loving Daughter," 57; Diary, July 29, 1920. Garland discusses his experiences with the car in *Back-Trailers*, 151–54. For his psychic article, see "The Spirit World on Trial," *McClure's*, March 1920, 33–34, 92; and also "The Coming of Sir Oliver Lodge," *Touchstone*, January 1920, 217.

12. Moffat confirmed the deal in a January 13, 1920, letter to Garland (USC). The article appeared as "General Grant," *Mentor*, July 1, 1920, 1–11. See also Hamlin Garland, "Irving Bacheller: Interpreter of the Old America to the New," *Red Cross Magazine*, March 1920, 11–12.

13. Diary, January 21, 1920.

14. Diary, October 21, 1920.

15. Diary, June 21, 1921.

16. Diary, August 14, 1921.

17. Diary, September 12, 1921.

18. Garland to Hoyns, July 8, [1921], USC.

19. Garland to Latham, November 28, [1921], USC.

20. Diary, June 13, October 2, 1921.

21. Latham to Garland, October 4, 1921, USC.

22. Garland to Latham, December 18, 1921, in *Selected Letters*, 296. The reviews were by Henry B. Fuller, "Three Generations," *Freeman*, November 9, 1921,

210–11; Carl Van Doren, "The Garland-McClintock Saga," *Nation,* November 23, 1921, 601–2; and Joseph E. Chamberlin, "A Daughter of the Middle Border," *Boston Evening Transcript,* sec. 4, December 10, 1921, 7.

23. See, for example, the display ads for Macmillan books: *New York Times,* October 16, 1921, 46, and December 4, 1921, 44. Macmillan did single out *A Daughter of the Middle Border* for more distinctive display in a small (1¾" x ¾") illustrated ad in the *New York Times,* December 11, 1921, 53.

24. Diary, December 19, 1921.

25. Diary, January 4, 1922.

26. Garland to Brett, January 23, [1922], Macmillan Company Records, NYPL. Year-by-year records of sales for Garland's Macmillan books during the 1920s are not extant, but the total sales as of 1947 are. As of 1947, the trade edition of *A Daughter of the Middle Border* had sold 27,404 copies; in comparison, *A Son of the Middle Border* had sold 82,178 copies (Latham to Eldon Hill, September 9, 1947, Miami).

27. Brett to Garland, January 23, 1922, Macmillan Company Records, NYPL.

28. Garland describes his meeting with his publishers, which occurred on January 3 and 12, 1922, and the selection of the volumes, in diary entries for January 3, 12, 1922, and in *Contemporaries,* 394–96. The initial printing of the Border Edition was 2,500 sets, sold at $1.50 per volume or $15.00 per set, with a royalty of 10 percent (Henry Hoyns to Garland, February 3, 1922, USC).

29. *Back-Trailers,* 173.

30. Diary, March 6, 1922.

31. Diary, April 6, May 23, 1922.

32. White to Garland, March 20, 1922, USC. For Garland's public discussion of his Pulitzer, see *Back-Trailers,* 177–79, and *Contemporaries,* 405, 414–15.

33. Diary, April 17, 1922. The thesis was by Katherine Wickham, but Garland does not record which university the student attended, and the thesis apparently was never published.

34. Diary, August 30, 1922.

35. Marsh to Garland, August 14, 1922, USC.

36. Marsh to Garland, September 6, 1922, USC.

37. *Contemporaries,* 409–10.

38. *Contemporaries,* 410.

39. Peter Philip, "Plain Tales from the Plains," *New York Times Book Review,* October 14, 1923, 5.

40. Review of *The Book of the American Indian, Literary Review of the* New York Evening Post, December 29, 1923, 412; Henry B. Fuller, "Hamlin Garland's Book on the Indian," *New York Herald,* September 30, 1923, 6.

41. "The Redman as Material," *Booklovers' Magazine*, August 1903, 197.

42. Isabel Garland Lord to Miriam Weiss, December 21, 1963, quoted in Miriam Weiss, "Hamlin Garland's Lecture Tours: A Study of Their Context, Extent, and Purpose" (master's thesis, Memphis State University, 1964), 93. Garland describes the tour in *Back-Trailers*, 273–77.

43. "This Loving Daughter," 84.

44. See Garland to Hampden, March 18, [1923], Miami; and Diary, September 25, 1923. Mary Isabel describes her acting experience in "This Loving Daughter," 91–93.

45. Lecture circular, 1923–24 season, item 670, USC.

46. Diary, September 4, 1923.

47. Diary, February 28, October 8, 1923.

48. Garland to Latham, November 25, [1923], in *Selected Letters*, 310.

49. Garland to Latham, October 7, [1924], Miami; Diary, November 13, 1924.

50. Diary, May 27, 1925.

51. Diary, August 12, 1925. For the pirated film, *The Ranger of the Big Pines*, see *Afternoon*, 275.

52. Diary, October 18, 1925. Garland describes his householding in *Back-Trailers*, 344–52. The Garlands occupied Grey Ledge on August 14 (but the deed of sale is dated July 10, 1926 [item 672e, USC]) and the Cathedral Parkway flat on October 19.

53. "This Loving Daughter," 93–97.

54. "This Loving Daughter," 99.

55. Diary, July 1, 1926; Garland to Latham, January 15, [1926], USC.

56. Diary, April 13, 1926.

57. Diary, April 14, 1926.

58. Garland to Brett, September 11, [1926], Macmillan Company Records, NYPL.

59. Brett to Garland, September 13, 1926, Macmillan Company Records, NYPL.

60. Diary, October 18, 1926.

61. Diary, October 19, 1926. Garland discusses the publication of *Trail-Makers of the Middle Border* in *Afternoon*, 347–48.

62. Revision to *Trail-Makers of the Middle Border* contract, October 20, 1926, item 669l, USC; Diary, October 19, 1926.

63. *Hamlin Garland: Memories of the Middle Border* (New York: Macmillan, [1926]), 3. The university had offered to confer the degree in 1923, but Garland's trip to England caused a postponement. Garland was tremendously

gratified at the honor, writing, "Perhaps my mother—if she were living would say
. . . 'Why so belated?'—but it is an honor which I value even in the tendering"
(Diary, May 17, 1923). His other honorary doctorates are from Beloit College
(June 16, 1930), Northwestern University (June 3, 1933), and the University
of Southern California (November 23, 1935).

64. Diary, November 8, 18, 1926. Garland's royalty records for his Macmillan
books are incomplete, but Macmillan's advertising confirms the large sale of the
book. A display ad in the *New York Times* for December 3, 1926, announces the
"third large printing" of *Trail-Makers of the Middle Border* (12). By 1947 it had sold
34,340 copies (Latham to Eldon Hill, September 9, 1947, Miami), cumulative
sales of more than any other Macmillan title save *A Son of the Middle Border* (at
177,201 copies in its various editions). By way of comparison, *A Daughter of the
Middle Border* had sales of 27,404 copies in the trade edition and 12,854 copies in the "New Illustrated Edition"; sales of *Back-Trailers from the Middle Border*
reached 11,714 copies.

65. Diary, July 28, 1927.

66. Diary, May 1, 1928.

67. *Back-Trailers*, 376.

68. "Hamlin Garland's Reminiscences," *Los Angeles Times*, February 3, 1929,
c6; "Hamlin Garland Completes 'Middle Border' Quadrilogy," *Milwaukee Journal*,
November 17, 1928; Lester Sharaf, "Hamlin Garland Ends His Saga," *Brooklyn
Daily Eagle*, book sec., December 12, 1928, 4B; Joseph Edgar Chamberlin,
"Receders from the Middle Border," *Boston Evening Transcript*, book sec.,
November 24, 1928, 4.

69. "This Loving Daughter," 102; Diary, February 16, March 14, 1929.

20. FORTUNATE EXILE

1. *Afternoon*, 531.

2. Diary, March 5, 1929; see also *Afternoon*, 545.

3. Diary, July 29, 1929; Hamlin Garland, "The Late Henry Fuller," *New York
Times*, August 1, 1929, 26.

4. Diary, September 19, 1929.

5. Diary, May 23, 1930.

6. Garland to Ulizio, July 5, [1930], Rare Books and Manuscripts Library of
the Ohio State University Libraries; Diary, June 2, 1930. Franklin's inscribed
copy of *Maggie* is now in the Berg Collection of the New York Public Library;
Garland's copy is at the Lilly Library, Indiana University, Bloomington.

7. Diary, June 28, 1930.

8. Diary, August 27, September 24, 1930.

9. Brett to Garland, August 14, 1931, USC.

10. "Lewis Refuses Pulitzer Prize," *New York Times*, May 6, 1926, 17.

11. "Nobel Prize to Lewis Is an 'Insult' to America, Says Van Dyke, Hitting Scoffers," *New York Times*, November 29, 1930, 1.

12. "Text of Sinclair Lewis's Nobel Prize Address at Stockholm," *New York Times*, December 13, 1930: 12.

13. As told to Eldon Hill, Hill's unpublished journal, July 23, 1936, Miami.

14. "Iowans Make Plans for Annual Banquet," *Los Angeles Times*, December 20, 1930, A8; "Willa Cather Wins Medal," *Chicago Tribune*," November 15, 1930, 15; Lee Shippey, "Lee Side o' L.A.," *Los Angeles Times*, March 25, 1931, A4.

15. "Roosevelt Medals Awarded to Three," *New York Times*, June 24, 1931, 7; Garland to Mary Isabel Garland Johnson and Constance Garland Harper, October 27, 1931, in *Selected Letters*, 361.

16. Diary, August 12, September 24, 1931.

17. "This Loving Daughter," 110.

18. "This Loving Daughter," 101.

19. "This Loving Daughter," 111.

20. Latham to Garland, April 4, 1932, and Garland to Latham, April 11, 1932, USC.

21. Latham to Garland, April 14, 1932, USC.

22. Latham to Garland, April 4, 1932, USC.

23. Garland to Nicholas Murray Butler, October 1, 1932, Academy.

24. Diary, January 22, 1932.

25. Diary, July 18, August 19, 1936.

26. Garland Greever in "Centennial Tributes and a Checklist of the Hamlin Garland Papers in the University of Southern California Library," in *University of Southern California Library Bulletin 9*, ed. and comp. Lloyd Arvidson (Los Angeles: University of Southern California, 1962), 21.

27. Latham to Garland, May 19, 1933, USC. By April 30, 1947, copies sold of Garland's four volumes of memoirs were as follows: *Roadside Meetings*, 7,977; *Companions on the Trail*, 6,941; *My Friendly Contemporaries*, 3,602; *Afternoon Neighbors*, 2,456 (Latham to Hill, September 9, 1947 [Miami]).

28. Diary, June 26, 1933.

29. *Forty Years*, 386.

30. Diary, October 19, 1933. Garland discusses this episode in *Forty Years*, 357–58; see also pp. 331–61 for discussion of his séances with Dora Drane, called Delia Drake in the narrative.

31. "This Loving Daughter," 113.

32. *Forty Years*, 393.

33. Latham to Garland, June 12, 1935, USC. Macmillan sold 2,067 copies of *Forty Years of Psychic Research* by April 30, 1937, and at some point reprinted the volume. By April 30, 1947, Macmillan sold a total of 2,311 copies in the original edition and 647 in the reprint (Macmillan royalty statement, item 669l, USC; Harold Latham to Eldon Hill, September 9, 1947, Miami).

34. Diary, November 2, 1934.

35. "This Loving Daughter," 170.

36. Quoted in "This Loving Daughter," 171.

37. Diary, November 9, 11, 1936.

38. Diary, April 12, 1938.

39. Latham to Garland, May 25, 1936, USC. John Ahouse has prepared a reading text of "The Fortunate Exiles" (item 5, USC), together with an introduction and expanded table of contents, all of which are now part of the Hamlin Garland Papers at the University of Southern California.

40. Diary, October 18, 1936.

41. Garland to Zulime, Mary Isabel, and Constance Garland, July 6, [1924], item GD 432, Huntington; Diary, October 3, 1935 (copies of the Haselton film can be found in USC, Huntington, Miami, and Academy). Later, after Haselton acquired a sound-on-film camera, he arranged to reshoot some of the scenes, but Garland died before he could do so.

42. Diary, December 17, 1937.

43. Brochure and film continuity, item 707d, USC. Garland to Vanamee, September 29, 1936, Academy. The film was to have one more revival, for a time reacquainting another generation of Garland's former eminence. In 1964 Haselton arranged for a professional film editor to shorten the film from eighteen to eight and a half minutes, reedit the sequence of its scenes, and provide sound-on-film narration. Retitled "Hamlin Garland, Historian of the Midwest," the sixteen-millimeter film was marketed to the public by Bailey Films and tends to lionize Garland for his importance as a witness of westward expansion, of U.S. manifest destiny (Haselton to Isabel Garland Lord, September 6, 1964 [courtesy Victoria Doyle-Jones; copy of film in possession of author]).

44. *Crosses*, 22.

45. Hodge to Garland, October 21, 1936, Miami; H. W. Krieger to Garland (shipping invoice), March 26, 1937, USC. In *Crosses* Garland reprints a favorable report from the National Museum of Mexico in an appendix but mentions only that "the Smithsonian, the Heye Museum, the Museum of Natural History and the Southwest Museum [were] all against me" (45).

46. *Crosses*, 45.

47. Garland to Isabel Garland Lord, n.d. [marked "Friday"], item GD 566, Huntington.

48. Diary, April 25, 1937.

49. Garland to Constance Garland Harper and Isabel Garland Lord, [August 6, 1937], in *Selected Letters*, 392.

50. Diary, October 20, 1937. For Garland's letters to Latham, Putnam, and Mary Isabel regarding the Earhart séances, see *Selected Letters*, 390–96. Other diary entries and letters to Mary Isabel record the progress of the Putnam-Constance romance; Constance apparently was less serious than Putnam, for at the time nine suitors were vying for her attention.

51. Latham to Garland, August 6, 1937, USC.

52. Garland to Constance Garland Harper, [August 11, 1937], in *Selected Letters*, 396.

53. Diary, September 17, 18, 1937.

54. Constance Garland Harper to Isabel Garland Lord, n.d. [marked "Saturday"], USC.

55. Quoted in "This Loving Daughter," 222.

56. Latham to Garland, April 4, 1938, USC; Harold Latham, *My Life in Publishing* (New York: Dutton, 1965), 41.

57. Macrae to Garland, May 13, 1938, USC.

58. Mauskopf and McVaugh, *The Elusive Science*, 160–61.

59. Thomas Sughrue, "Dreams, Mystery or Facts," *New York Herald Tribune Books*, August 6, 1939, 9; Edward Wagenknecht, "Hamlin Garland's Psychic Quest," clipping, item 724c, USC.

60. See Garland to Harold Latham, September 7, 1939, Huntington; a clipping concerning the radio program (item 723, USC); and Garland to Alexander Gaylord Beaman, May 10, 1939, USC. Garland died before the film could be made.

61. Diary, June 23, 1939.

62. Royalty statement from E. P. Dutton, October 31, 1939, item 669, USC.

63. Garland to Vanamee, September 1, 1938, Academy; Garland to Vanamee, July 22, 1938, in *Selected Letters*, 408.

64. Garland's address was reported in "Academy Elects Benet and Cather," *New York Times*, November 11, 1938, 26; it was published as "Literary Fashions Old and New," *Think*, March 1939, 14, 24, 27.

65. Diary, November 10, 1938.

66. Diary, July 18, 1939.

67. "This Loving Daughter," 225, 233. Mindret Lord published a number of stories in the pulp magazines before going on to write for the movies. Under the name "Garland Lord," Mary Isabel and Mindret published four mystery novels after Garland's death: *Murder's Little Helper* (1941), *She Never Grew Old*

(1942), *Murder with Love* (1943), and *Murder, Plain and Fancy* (1943). Under her own name, Mary Isabel published *Abandon Hope* (also titled *Death Comes Courting*) in 1941.

68. Diary, February 25, 1940.

69. Garland to Eldon Hill, [ca. March 1940], in *Selected Letters*, 434. Garland died before he was able to mail the letter.

70. Diary, February 28, 1940.

71. Beaman described Garland's final moments in a letter to Eldon Hill, March 5, 1940, Miami.

INDEX

Abbey Players, 297

Abraham Lincoln (Drinkwater), 334

Across the Unknown (White), 399

The Action of the Living Cell (Turck),
332

Ade, George, 310, 318

Adventures of Buffalo Bill (Cody), 361

Adventures of Huckleberry Finn
(Twain), 130

Adventures of Tom Sawyer (Twain),
243

Afterwhiles (Riley), 93, 98

Agar, John, 316, 317

The Age of Innocence (Wharton), 335,
336

Aherne, George P., 224

Aldrich, Thomas Bailey, 62

"Alice," 45–46, 73, 143–44, 426n25

America, 100, 101

American, 129

American Academy of Arts and
Letters, 4, 357, 391; Chicago
meeting of, 304–5; formation
of, 271; Gold Medal for Good
Diction on the Radio from, 342,
380; Hamlin Garland's election
to, 326, 457n58; Hamlin
Garland's final address to, 402;
Hamlin Garland's involvement

with, 337–43; Hamlin Garland's
resignation from, 383–84; and
Sinclair Lewis, 379

American Horse (Sioux), 225

American Psychical Society, 158–59,
161, 185, 193

American Society for Psychical
Research, 157

Ames, Winthrop, 297

Anna Christie (O'Neill), 335

Annie Kilburn (Howells), 106–7

Antelope (Cheyenne), 245

April Hopes (Howells), 105

Arena, 138, 139, 140, 141, 162, 182,
204, 212, 222, 258

Arena Publishing Company,
141–42, 146, 162, 165, 172, 177

Arizona (Thomas), 292

Arrowsmith (Lewis), 379

Arts for America, 202

Atherton, Gertrude, 318

Atlantic, 217, 348

Attic Club, 282

Author's Club, 317

Authors' League of America, 4,
303–4, 313, 317, 345

Authors' Readings (Young), 70

The Awakening of the Flowers (Taft),
201

Babcock, Burton, 21, 23, 24, 39; boarding of, with Hamlin Garland, 35, 37; and the Klondike, 226, 233, 234, 235; visit to Boston by, 81

Babcock, Charles, 52

Bach, Alwyn, 380

Bacheller, Irving, 186, 192, 219, 276, 318, 328, 345, 352; *Eben Holden*, 327; investment of, with Hamlin Garland, 267, 268

Bacheller Syndicate, 173, 186, 204, 205, 219, 242

Bailey, Susan. *See* Garland, Susan

Balfour, Arthur, 157

Banks, Maud, 126

Baright, Anna, 67

Barrie, James M., 2, 246, 359

Barrymore, John, 390

Bartol, Cyrus, 64

Bashford, James Whitford, 60, 63, 74

Battle Creek Sanitarium, 321–23

Baxter, Sylvester, 150

Beach, Rex: *The Spoilers*, 327

Beadle, W. H. H., 40

Beaman, A. Gaylord, 404

Beecher, Henry Ward, 64–65

Belford's, 117, 142

Bell, Alexander Graham, 67

Bennett, James O'Donnell, 292

Benrimo, J. H.: *The Yellow Jacket*, 297

The Betty Book (White), 399

Beyond the Horizon (O'Neill), 333–34

"A Biographical Study of Hamlin Garland from 1860 to 1895" (Hill), 385

Bissell, Arthur, 292

Black Hawk (Sauk), 255

Black Riders and Other Lines (Crane), 193, 377

Blackton, J. Stuart, 313, 314

Bok, Edward, 252, 301

Bolles, Mary M., 258, 309

Bookman, 378

The Book of Susan (Dodd), 335

Booth, Edwin, 50, 85, 153, 373; influence of, on Hamlin Garland, 70–71, 78–79, 86–87; and Players Club, 228

Booth, John Wilkes, 71–72

Boston Anti-Poverty Society, 102, 104, 119, 127

Boston Evening Transcript, 82, 87, 94

The Bostonians (James), 130

Boston Public Library, 63, 77

Boston School of Oratory, 65–66, 73–74, 76, 141, 165, 192, 417n20; Hamlin Garland's resignation from, 162

Boston Single Tax League, 118

Boston University, 62–63, 67

Boucicault, Dion, 284

Boys Town (Howells), 243

Brady, Jasper, 313

Brett, George Platt, 241, 319, 355–56, 369, 370–71, 378, 383

Bridges, John, 9

Briggs, William, 306, 320, 348

Brigham, Johnson, 188–89, 191, 347

British Society for Psychical Research, 157

Brooks, Van Wyck, 4

Brown, Archer, 268

Brown, Moses True, 67, 68, 75, 151, 192; sketch of, 65–66; *Synthetic Philosophy of Expression*, 66, 68, 69, 71–72

Browne, Charles Francis, 203, 205, 240, 244, 250, 281
Browne, Francis F., 183
Bryan, William Jennings, 272
Bryant, William Cullen, 350
Bull Thigh (Cheyenne), 224
Burkhart, Stella Esther, 222
Burroughs, John, 2, 321, 323, 324, 351, 355
Burton, Richard, 333
Bush, Alva, 30, 45, 74
Butler, Nicholas Murray, 274, 334, 338, 339, 344, 379

Cable, George Washington, 65, 78, 111, 130, 178, 318
Calvin, Cecilia DeMille, 389
Calvin, Francis, 389
Carpenter, Horace T., 188, 189
Cather, Willa, 4, 265, 379
Catherwood, Mary Hartwell, 178–79, 180
A Cavalcade of the Supernatural (Cross), 399
Cedar Valley Seminarian, 38
Cedar Valley Seminary, 26, 29, 30–31, 63, 319
Central Art Association of America, 202–3, 205, 240, 250
Century, 129–30, 137, 138, 142, 165, 172, 217, 306; Hamlin Garland's submissions to, 129, 130–31, 136, 173, 348
Century Association, 350–51, 384
Chamberlin, Joseph Edgar, 119, 126, 373
Chambers, Robert: *Cyclopedia of English Literature*, 54
Chandler, Harry, 2
Chap-Book, 204, 228, 289

Chatfield-Taylor, Hobart, 310
Chemist's Club, 339
Cherry (Tarkington), 266
Chicago Single Tax Club, 164
Chicago Theater Society, 290–98, 333, 452n50
Children of the Ghetto (Zangwill), 244
Churchill, Winston: *The Crisis*, 327
Clark, Barrett H., 141, 294
Clarkson, Ralph, 202, 244, 281
Claxton, Kate, 284
Clemens, Samuel. *See* Twain, Mark
Clement, Edward, 83, 126
Cliff Dwellers (Fuller), 202, 282–83
Cliff Dwellers' Club, 4, 182, 289, 290, 304, 310, 342, 344; founding of, 281–83, 449n13; Hamlin Garland's resignation from, 311–12
Coburn Players, 297
Cody, William: *Adventures of Buffalo Bill*, 361
Collier's, 306, 307, 319
Columbian Exposition, 174–75, 178–79, 201, 240
A Connecticut Yankee in King Arthur's Court (Twain), 122, 246
Conrad, Joseph, 2, 359
Cooper, Ben, 12
Cosgrave, Jessica, 316
Cosgrave, John O'Hara, 283, 284, 316
Cosmopolitan, 170
Crane, Stephen, 191–94, 195–96, 265; *Black Riders and Other Lines*, 193, 377; *Maggie, A Girl of the Streets*, 192, 196, 377; "The Men in the Storm," 192; "An Omnibus Baby," 192; *The Red Badge of Courage*, 193, 194, 196

Garland, Franklin McClintock, 18, 21, 37, 61, 70, 137, 172, 173, 175, 309, 377, 391; as actor, 123–24, 185; birth of, 13; in "A Branch Road," 145; in Dakota, 52–53; death of wife of, 222; on Hamlin Garland, 22, 24, 34, 35, 49, 55–56; investment of, in mine, 267–69; and quitting stage, 262; and trip with Hamlin Garland, 223, 224; visit to Boston by, 81

Garland, Hamlin: as actor, 36–37; and American Academy of Arts and Letters, 337–43; arrival of, in Boston, 62; birth of, 7, 12; and Central Art Association of America, 201–4; on daughters' divorces, 388–89; as Dean of American Letters, 380–81; death of, 1, 404; and dialect, 89; dramatization of novels of, 312–14, 455n22; early jobs of, 47, 49–50; early loves of, 45–47; early writing of, 38–39; education of, 15, 20–21, 24, 30–32, 34–36, 37–39, 62–63; and evolution, 63–64, 66, 69, 77; exhibit of work of, 390–91; and farm work, 15, 20, 21, 22, 23, 25, 35, 44; first automobile of, 351–52; and First Independent Theater Association, 154–56; and Grange elevator, 30; and Homestead fire, 300; honorary degrees of, 369, 463n63; illnesses of, 226, 229, 238, 245, 250, 276, 320–23, 328, 331–32, 402–3; on immigrants, 316, 328; and impressionism, 194, 195, 201; and Indians, 206–10, 219–20, 223–26, 254–55, 259–60; investment of, in mine, 267–69; in jail, 272; and the Klondike, 226, 230–37; land investments of, 257, 267, 269, 272; lectures by, 74–75, 94, 102–3, 109, 120–21, 203, 330, 339, 364–65, 402; literary principles of, 77–78, 79, 92, 111, 131–33, 171, 180; and *Margaret Fleming*, 151, 152–54; marital difficulties of, 276–77; marriage of, 250–51; on meaning of "middle border," 7; on methods of work, 129; and modernism, 328–30; move of, to Hollywood, 375–76, 382; on need for clubs, 281, 317; and oratory, 32, 35, 50, 57, 64, 66–67, 69–70; and Ordway (Dakota Territory), 47–48, 91, 107–8; as playwright, 85, 95, 126, 136, 148–50, 285–88; as poet, 98, 190–91; and Progress and Poverty dinner, 272; psychic interests of, 156, 159–62, 185, 193, 273, 283–84, 298, 351, 386–87, 393–401; as Pulitzer juror, 332–37; on radio, 342; reading of, 24, 54–55, 56–57, 63; and realism war, 170–72, 178–80, 181–84; and receiving of Pulitzer Prize, 357–58; and receiving of Roosevelt Medal, 381; relationship of, with mother, 16, 222, 247, 248, 252–53, 255–56; relations of, with publishers, 218,

220–21, 222, 241, 261, 265, 289, 299, 301–3, 305–6, 315, 319–20, 327, 348, 352, 354–56, 365–66, 370–72, 398–99; and religion, 33; on reputation, 2, 5, 384, 403–4; response of, to criticism, 146–47, 168–69, 191, 197, 200; return of, to Osage, 89–90, 109; reviews by, 82–83, 94, 105–7, 112–13, 192; satirizing of, by Sinclair Lewis, 380; as school teacher, 51; and selling of inscribed books, 377; and selling of work, 129, 138, 139, 172, 189, 219, 254, 257, 266, 270, 273, 278, 279, 299, 315; and sex, 16; and single tax, 102–3, 118, 135–36, 170; and smallpox scare, 18; and Stephen Crane, 191–94; stillborn son of, 258; as storekeeper, 53; trip of, with Franklin Garland, 50–51; trips of, to England, 245–46, 276, 357, 358–59, 365; and veritism, 194; western trips of, 205–6, 208–10, 219, 223–26, 250–51, 254–55, 257–58, 262, 272

Garland, Hamlin, residences of: Boston, 62, 74, 137; Camp Neshonoc, 324, 351, 366; Chicago, 202, 277, 279; Dakota, 52–53, 57–60, 413n8, 414n32; Grey Ledge, 366, 370; Hollywood, 376–77; Homestead, 175–76, 262, 301, 309; Iowa, 7–8, 18, 19–20, 22, 23, 33, 408n2, 408n7, 408n17, 410n21, 412n74; New York, 185, 314, 316, 366–67, 381; Osage, 28–29

Garland, Harriet, 8

Garland, Harriet Edith, 7, 12, 21; birth of, 11; death of, 26

Garland, Isabelle McClintock, 2, 7, 12, 61, 81, 107, 252–53; death of, 255–56; description of, 15–16; and Hamlin Garland, 25, 91, 172–73; and Hamlin Garland's marriage, 251–52; marriage of, 10–11; suffering of stroke by, 108

Garland, Jessie Viola, 37, 61, 81, 91, 108, 109; birth of, 18; death of, 134, 158; marriage of, 134

Garland, Mary Isabel, 247, 249, 276, 277; as actress, 356–57, 364; birth of, 263; contracting of diphtheria by, 278; dating of, 349–50, 367; as distraction, 266–67; education of, 316; as favorite daughter, 280–81; on Hamlin Garland, 310, 321, 364, 382, 387; and Hamlin Garland's psychic interests, 398; house built for, 376; marital difficulties of, 388–89; marriage of, to Hardesty Johnson, 367–68; marriage of, to Mindret Lord, 389; in "Memories of the Middle Border," 364; move of, to Hollywood, 374; reconciliation of, with Hamlin Garland, 403; writing career of, 358

Garland, Richard, 8–9, 48

Garland, Richard Hayes, 2, 7, 13, 176, 252; Civil War service of, 13; death of, 309; description of, 14; and discipline, 14–15, 26, 28; early life of, 8–9; as farmer,

305–6, 307; and Border Edition, 356; and Sunset Edition, 299; and *Trail-Makers of the Middle Border*, 365

Harper's Monthly, 170, 192, 217

Harper's Weekly, 64, 136, 137, 142

Harris, Joel Chandler, 130

Harte, Bret, 78, 130, 246, 315

Harvard University, 63

Haselton, Guy D., 391

Hawthorne, Julian, 128

Hawthorne, Nathaniel, 62, 72, 392; *Mosses from an Old Manse*, 36

Hay, John, 271

Hayes, Rutherford B., 40

Hazelton, George: *The Yellow Jacket*, 297

Head, Franklin, 201, 203

Hearts of Oak (Herne), 124, 125

Heckman, Wallace, 244, 248

Helmholtz, Hermann von, 63

Hemingway, Ernest, 329

Herne, Chrystal, 124

Herne, Dorothy, 124

Herne, James A., 2, 122, 123, 127, 140, 145, 151, 173, 244, 252, 306, 373; collaboration of, with Hamlin Garland, 136; death of, 257–58; *Drifting Apart*, 122–23, 125, 126, 131, 136; on Hamlin Garland's psychic interests, 161; *Hearts of Oak*, 124, 125; *Margaret Fleming*, 150–51, 152–54, 155–56, 205; *Shore Acres*, 185, 186, 292; sketch of, 124

Herne, Julie, 124, 125–26, 127, 161

Herne, Katherine, 123, 131, 151, 153, 161, 252, 258; collaboration of, with Hamlin Garland, 136; sketch of, 124–25

Heroines of Fiction (Howells), 266

Herrick, Robert: *The Maternal Instinct*, 295

Hill, Eldon, 33, 384–85, 392, 403; "A Biographical Study of Hamlin Garland from 1860 to 1895," 385

Hindle Wakes (Houghton), 297

History of English Literature (Taine), 54

History of the English People (Green), 54

Hitchcock, Ethan Allen, 260

Hodge, Frederick W., 394; *Handbook of the American Indian*, 209

Holmes, Oliver Wendell, 62

Homestead Act, 23, 42–43, 48–49

The Hoosier Schoolmaster (Eggleston), 24

Horniman Players, 297

Houdini, Harry, 399

Houghton, Stanley: *Hindle Wakes*, 297

Houghton Mifflin & Co., 99

Howard, Sidney: *They Knew What They Wanted*, 337

Howe, E. W., 79, 80, 95, 373; *The Story of a Country Town*, 79, 80

Howe, Julia Ward, 341

Howells, William Dean, 2, 62, 106, 111, 115, 126, 130, 132–33, 142, 150, 151, 152, 173, 175, 252, 271, 316, 323, 347, 355, 373, 384; on *Cavanagh, Forest Ranger*, 290; on *Crumbling Idols*, 199, 200; eightieth birthday celebration of, 317–18; on Hamlin Garland, 4, 84, 85; on Hamlin Garland's marriage,

Howells, William Dean (*cont.*)
249; on Hamlin Garland's trip
to the Klondike, 229–30; on
Hesper, 266; influence of, on
Hamlin Garland, 82–85, 192;
on *Main-Travelled Roads*, 147,
186; memorial to, 339–40; and
realism war, 170; on *Rose of
Dutcher's Coolly*, 216; satirizing
of, by Sinclair Lewis, 379–80; on
A Son of the Middle Border, 300,
324–25; on *A Spoil of Office*, 167;
on Sunset Edition, 299; on *They
of the High Trails*, 315; on *Ulysses
S. Grant*, 220–21; on *Under the
Wheel*, 140–41
—Works: *Annie Kilburn*, 106–7;
April Hopes, 105; *Boys Town*, 243;
Criticism and Fiction, 170; *Heroines
of Fiction*, 266; *The Kentons*, 266;
The Minister's Charge, 82, 130;
A Modern Instance, 130; *The
Rise of Silas Lapham*, 130; *The
Son of Royal Langbrith*, 266; *The
Undiscovered Country*, 82, 418n15
Hoyns, Henry, 354
Hugo, Victor: *Les Misérables*, 74
Hull House Players, 297
Hunter, Ancella: *Gold*, 295
Huntington, Archer, 341
Hurd, Charles E., 82, 93, 122, 126,
150, 151
Hutchinson, Charles, 311

Ibsen, Henrick, 82, 329; *A Doll's
House*, 136, 154
Ingersoll, Robert, 33, 65
Irish Players, 296
Irving, Henry, 71

Is This Your Son, My Lord?
(Gardener), 141
Ivanhoe (Scott), 74

Jackson, Helen Hunt, 130
Jacobs, Frank, 39
James, Henry, 4, 130, 347, 373,
387; *The Bostonians*, 130
James, William, 157
Jean de Reszke Singers, 367
Jefferson, Joseph, 203
John Lane Co., 327
Johnson, Hardesty, 367–68, 374,
376, 388
Johnson, Robert Underwood, 301,
305, 337, 338, 341, 342–45, 350
Joint Committee of the Literary
Arts, 317
Jones, William A., 260
Journal of Parapsychology, 400
Judah, Mary, 283
June Madness (Webster), 295, 296

Keedick Lecture Bureau, 357
Kellogg, John, 321, 323
Kemeys, Edward, 204
The Kentons (Howells), 266
Kilmer, Joyce, 318, 329, 333
Kimball, Hannibal Ingalls, 177, 228
Kipling, Rudyard, 2, 218, 359
Kirkland, Joseph, 97, 111, 115,
142, 178, 373; influence of, on
Hamlin Garland, 87–89, 91–92,
94–95, 99–101; *The McVeys*, 99;
*Zury, the Meanest Man in Spring
County*, 87
KleinSmid, Rufus von, 2
Knapp, Bert S., 134